P9-DME-414

VALUATION

MEASURING AND MANAGING THE VALUE OF COMPANIES

Founded in 1807, John Wiley & Sons is the oldest independent publishing company in the United States. With offices in North America, Europe, Australia, and Asia, Wiley is globally committed to developing and marketing print and electronic products and services for our customers' professional and personal knowledge and understanding.

The Wiley Finance series contains books written specifically for finance and investment professionals as well as sophisticated individual investors and their financial advisors. Book topics range from portfolio management to e-commerce, risk management, financial engineering, valuation, and financial instrument analysis, as well as much more.

For a list of available titles, please visit our Web site at www.WileyFinance.com.

VALUATION

MEASURING AND MANAGING THE VALUE OF COMPANIES

FIFTH EDITION

McKinsey & Company

Tim Koller

Marc Goedhart

David Wessels

WILEY

JOHN WILEY & SONS, INC.

Copyright © 1990, 1994, 2000, 2005, 2010 by McKinsey & Company. All rights reserved.

Published by John Wiley & Sons, Inc., Hoboken, New Jersey.
Published simultaneously in Canada.

No part of this publication may be reproduced, stored in a retrieval system, or transmitted in any form or by any means, electronic, mechanical, photocopying, recording, scanning, or otherwise, except as permitted under Section 107 or 108 of the 1976 United States Copyright Act, without either the prior written permission of the Publisher, or authorization through payment of the appropriate per-copy fee to the Copyright Clearance Center, Inc., 222 Rosewood Drive, Danvers, MA 01923, (978) 750-8400, fax (978) 646-8600, or on the Web at www.copyright.com. Requests to the Publisher for permission should be addressed to the Permissions Department, John Wiley & Sons, Inc., 111 River Street, Hoboken, NJ 07030, (201) 748-6011, fax (201) 748-6008, or online at http://www.wiley.com/go/permissions.

Limit of Liability/Disclaimer of Warranty: While the publisher and author have used their best efforts in preparing this book, they make no representations or warranties with respect to the accuracy or completeness of the contents of this book and specifically disclaim any implied warranties of merchantability or fitness for a particular purpose. No warranty may be created or extended by sales representatives or written sales materials. The advice and strategies contained herein may not be suitable for your situation. You should consult with a professional where appropriate. Neither the publisher nor author shall be liable for any loss of profit or any other commercial damages, including but not limited to special, incidental, consequential, or other damages.

For general information on our other products and services or for technical support, please contact our Customer Care Department within the United States at (800) 762-2974, outside the United States at (317) 572-3993 or fax (317) 572-4002.

Wiley also publishes its books in a variety of electronic formats. Some content that appears in print may not be available in electronic books. For more information about Wiley products, visit our web site at www.wiley.com.

Cloth edition: ISBN 978-0-470-42465-0

Cloth edition with DCF Model Download: ISBN 978-0-470-42469-8

University edition: ISBN 978-0-470-42470-4

Workbook: ISBN 978-0-470-42464-3

DCF Model CD-ROM: ISBN 978-0-470-42457-5

DCF Model Download: ISBN 978-0-470-89455-2

Instructor's Manual: ISBN 978-0-470-42472-8

Printed in the United States of America

10 9 8 7 6 5 4 3 2

Contents

About the Authors

The authors are all current or former consultants of McKinsey & Company's corporate finance practice. Collectively they have more than 50 years of experience in consulting and financial education.

McKinsey & Company is a management-consulting firm that helps leading corporations and organizations make distinctive, lasting, and substantial improvements in their performance. Over the past seven decades, the firm's primary objective has remained constant: to serve as an organization's most trusted external advisor on critical issues facing senior management. With consultants deployed from over 80 offices in more than 40 countries, McKinsey advises companies on strategic, operational, organizational, financial, and technological issues. The firm has extensive experience in all major industry sectors and primary functional areas, as well as in-depth expertise in high-priority areas for today's business leaders.

Tim Koller is a partner in McKinsey's New York office. He leads the firm's Corporate Performance Center and is a member of the leadership group of the firm's global corporate finance practice. In his 25 years in consulting Tim has served clients globally on corporate strategy and capital markets, mergers and acquisitions (M&A) transactions, and value-based management. He leads the firm's research activities in valuation and capital markets. He was formerly with Stern Stewart & Company and with Mobil Corporation. He received his MBA from the University of Chicago.

Marc Goedhart is a senior expert in McKinsey's Amsterdam office and leads the firm's Corporate Performance Center in Europe. Over the past 15 years, Marc has served clients across Europe on portfolio restructuring, capital markets, and M&A transactions. He taught finance as an assistant professor at Erasmus University in Rotterdam, where he also earned a PhD in finance.

David Wessels is an adjunct professor of finance at the Wharton School of the University of Pennsylvania. Named by *BusinessWeek* as one of America's top business school instructors, he teaches courses on corporate valuation and private equity at the MBA and executive MBA levels. David is also a director in Wharton's executive education group, serving on the executive development faculties of several Fortune 500 companies. A former consultant with McKinsey, he received his PhD from the University of California at Los Angeles.

Preface

The first edition of this book appeared in 1990, and we are encouraged that it continues to attract readers around the world. We believe the book appeals to readers everywhere because the approach it advocates is grounded in universal economic principles. While we continue to improve, update, and expand the text as our experience grows and as business and finance continue to evolve, those universal principles do not change.

The 20 years since that first edition have been a remarkable period in business history, and managers and investors continue to face opportunities and challenges emerging from it. The events of the economic crisis that began in 2007, as well as the Internet boom and its fallout almost a decade earlier, have strengthened our conviction that the core principles of value creation are general economic rules that continue to apply in all market circumstances. Thus, the extraordinarily high anticipated profits represented by stock prices during the Internet bubble never materialized, because there was no "new economy." Similarly, the extraordinarily high profits seen in the financial sector for the two years preceding the start of the 2007 financial crisis were overstated, as subsequent losses demonstrated. The laws of competition should have alerted investors that those extraordinary profits couldn't last and might not be real.

Over the past 20 years, we have also seen confirmed that for some companies, some of the time, the stock market may not be a reliable indicator of value. Knowing that value signals from the stock market may occasionally be unreliable makes us even more certain that managers need at all times to understand the underlying, intrinsic value of their company and how it can create more value. In our view, clear thinking about valuation and skill in using valuation to guide business decisions are prerequisites for company success.

WHY THIS BOOK

Not all CEOs, business managers, and financial managers *do* understand value in great depth, although they need to understand it fully if they are to do their jobs well and fulfill their responsibilities. This book offers them the necessary understanding, its practical intent reflecting its origin as a handbook for McKinsey consultants. We publish it for the benefit of current and future managers who want their companies to create value, and also for their investors. It aims to demystify the field of valuation and to clarify the linkages between strategy and finance. So while it draws on leading-edge academic thinking, it is primarily a how-to book and one we hope that you will use again and again. This is no coffee-table tome: If we have done our job well, it will soon be full of underlinings, margin notations, and highlightings.

The book's messages are simple: Companies thrive when they create real economic value for their shareholders. Companies create value by investing capital at rates of return that exceed their cost of capital. And these two truths apply across time and geography. The book explains why these core principles of value creation are true and how companies can increase value by applying the principles to decisions, and demonstrates practical ways to implement the principles in their decision-making.

The technical chapters of the book aim to explain step-by-step how to do valuation well. We spell out valuation frameworks that we use in our consulting work, and we illustrate them with detailed case studies that highlight the practical judgments involved in developing and using valuations. Just as important, the management chapters discuss how to use valuation to make good decisions about courses of action for a company. Specifically, they will help business managers understand how to:

- Decide among alternative business strategies by estimating the value of each strategic choice.
- Develop a corporate portfolio strategy, based on understanding which business units a corporate parent is best positioned to own, and which might perform better under someone else's ownership.
- Assess major transactions, including acquisitions, divestitures, and restructurings.
- Improve a company's performance management systems to align an organization's various parts to create value.
- Communicate effectively with investors, including both who to talk and listen to and how.
- Design an effective capital structure to support the corporation's strategy and minimize the risk of financial distress.

STRUCTURE OF THE BOOK

In this fifth edition, we continue to expand the practical application of finance to real business problems, reflecting the economic events of the past decade, new developments in academic finance, and the authors' own experiences. The edition is organized in six parts, each with a distinct focus.

Part One, **Foundations of Value**, provides an overview of value creation. We make the case that managers should focus on long-term value creation despite the capital market turmoil of the past several years. We explain the two core principles of value creation: first, the idea that return on capital and growth drive cash flow, which in turn drives value, and second, the conservation of value principle, that anything that doesn't increase cash flow doesn't create value (unless it reduces risk). We devote a chapter each to return on invested capital and to growth, including strategic principles and empirical insights.

Part Two, **Core Valuation Techniques**, is a self-contained handbook for using discounted cash flow (DCF) to value a company. A reader will learn how to analyze historical performance, forecast free cash flows, estimate the appropriate opportunity cost of capital, identify sources of value, and interpret results. We also show how to use multiples of comparable companies to supplement DCF valuations.

Part Three, **Intrinsic Value and the Stock Market**, presents the empirical evidence that share prices reflect the core principles of value creation and are not influenced by earnings management, accounting results, or institutional trading factors such as cross-listings. It also describes the rare circumstances under which share prices for individual companies or, very occasionally, the market in general may temporarily violate the core principles. The final chapter explains what makes stock markets efficient, which type of investors ultimately determine the trading range of a company's share price, and the implications of their influence for managers.

Part Four, **Managing for Value**, applies the value creation principles to practical decisions that managers face. It explains how to design a portfolio of businesses; how to create value through mergers, acquisitions, and divestitures; how to construct an appropriate capital structure; and how companies can improve their communications with the financial markets.

Part Five, **Advanced Valuation Issues**, explains how to analyze and incorporate in your valuation such complex issues as taxes, pensions, reserves, inflation, and foreign currency. Part Five also includes a comprehensive case valuing Heineken N.V., the Dutch brewer, illustrating how to apply both the core and advanced valuation techniques.

Part Six, **Special Situations**, is devoted to valuation in more complex contexts. We explore the challenges of valuing high-growth companies, companies in emerging markets, cyclical companies, and banks. In addition, we show how uncertainty and flexibility affect value, and how to apply option pricing theory and decision trees in valuations.

WHAT'S NEW ABOUT THE FIFTH EDITION

Most of the case examples and empirical analyses have been updated, and we have reflected changes in accounting rules. We have enhanced the global perspective in the book with extensive examples and data from both the United States and Europe.

To make the book easier to navigate, we have broken up long chapters from the previous edition into several shorter chapters, so that each is a more manageable size and the reader can find important topics faster. In addition, we have created a new part on advanced valuation issues, removing these topics from the section dedicated to core techniques. This makes the core techniques section shorter and easier to read and also allows us more space to devote to advanced topics.

An important addition to the book is the expanded discussion of return on invested capital (ROIC) and growth in two new chapters in Part One. The new ROIC chapter shows the linkages between different levels of ROIC and different business strategies, to help executives assess whether their strategies can lead to high and sustained returns on capital. In the new growth chapter, we show the different effects on value of different types of growth, to help companies prioritize growth initiatives.

Finally, Part Three is an entirely new section that deals with the stock market. As in past editions, we show that stock market values generally reflect companies' fundamental economic performance: markets are not fooled by accounting gimmicks used to embellish results. For the fifth edition, however, we have expanded our discussion of those market inefficiencies that do occur from time to time. We also present new insights on how to segment investors into different types, how the different types of investors affect the market, and the implications of this segmentation for executives.

VALUATION SPREADSHEET

An Excel spreadsheet valuation model is available on a CD-ROM or via Web download. This valuation model is similar to the model we use in practice. Practitioners will find the model easy to use in a variety of situations: mergers and acquisitions, valuing business units for restructuring or value-based management, or testing the implications of major strategic decisions on the value of your company. We accept no responsibility for any decisions based on your inputs to the model. If you would like to purchase the model on CD-ROM (ISBN 978-0-470-42457-5), please call (800) 225-5945, or visit www.wileyvaluation .com to purchase the model via Web download (ISBN 978-0-470-89455-2).

Acknowledgments

No book is solely the effort of its authors. This book is certainly no exception, especially since it grew out of the collective work of McKinsey's corporate finance practice and the experiences of its consultants throughout the world.

Most important, we would like to thank Tom Copeland and Jack Murrin, two of the co-authors on the first three editions of this book. We are deeply indebted to them for establishing the early success of this book, for mentoring the current authors, and for their hard work in providing the foundations on which this edition builds.

Ennius Bergsma deserves our special thanks. Ennius initiated the development of McKinsey's corporate finance practice in the mid-1980s. He inspired the original internal McKinsey valuation handbook and mustered the support and sponsorship to turn that handbook into a real book for an external audience.

Concurrent with this fifth edition, McKinsey is publishing a shorter book, entitled *Value: The Four Cornerstones of Corporate Finance*, which explains the principles of value and their implications for managers and investors without going into the technical detail of this how-to guide to valuation. We've greatly benefited from the ideas of that book's co-authors, Richard Dobbs and Bill Huyett, as well as the lead editor, Neil DeCarlo.

Of course, we could not have devoted the time and energy to this book without the support and encouragement of McKinsey's corporate finance practice leadership, in particular Christian Caspar, Richard Dobbs, Bernie Ferrari, Bill Huyett, Rob Latoff, Thomas Luedi, Nick Leung, Pedro Rodeia, Michael Silber, and Vincenzo Tortoricci.

Tim and Marc lead McKinsey's Corporate Performance Center (CPC), a group of dedicated corporate finance experts that influences our thinking every day. A special thank-you to Bernie Ferrari, who initiated the group and nurtured its development. The CPC's leaders include: Ankur Agrawal, André

Annema, Andres Cottin, Bas Deelder, Susan Nolen Foushee, Regis Huc, Mimi James, Mauricio Jaramillo, Bin Jiang, Marc Metakis, Jean-Hugues Monier, Rishi Raj, Werner Rehm, Ram Sekar, and Zane Williams.

We've made extensive use of McKinsey's Corporate Performance Analytical Tool (CPAT), which provides a great database and deep analytical capability. Thank you to Bin Jiang, who developed and oversees CPAT, and to Bing Cao, who analyzed the data for us. Dick Foster, a former McKinsey colleague and mentor, inspired the development of CPAT.

Gina Campbell, our lead editor, ensured that our ideas were expressed clearly and concisely. She also had to cope with our difficult schedules, which she handled gracefully. Thank you, Gina. Karen Schenkenfelder provided careful editing and feedback throughout the process. We are indebted to her excellent eye for detail. Kim Bartko oversaw the production of the more than 300 exhibits in this book, a Herculean task given the variety of formats and technologies employed. We are also grateful to Joseph Mandel for his painstaking help with final fact-checking.

Bill Javetski and Rik Kirkland ensured that we received superior editorial support from McKinsey's external publishing team.

The intellectual origins of this book lie in the present value method of capital budgeting and in the valuation approach developed by Professors Merton Miller and Franco Modigliani (both Nobel laureates) in their 1961 *Journal of Business* article entitled "Dividend Policy, Growth and the Valuation of Shares." Others have gone far to popularize their approach. In particular, Professor Alfred Rappaport (Northwestern University) and Joel Stern (Stern Stewart & Co.) were among the first to extend the Miller-Modigliani enterprise valuation formula to real-world applications. In addition to these founders of the discipline, we would also like to acknowledge those who have personally shaped our knowledge of valuation, corporate finance, and strategy. For their support and teachings, we thank Tony Bernardo, Dick Foster, Bob Holthausen, Rob Kazanjian, Ofer Nemirovsky, Eduardo Schwartz, Chandan Sengupta, Jaap Spronk, Joel Stern, Bennett Stewart, Sunil Wahal, and Ivo Welch.

A number of colleagues worked closely with us on the fifth edition, providing support that was essential to its completion. Jonathan Reef reviewed the text and double-checked all the numbers in Part Two, Core Valuation Techniques, and Part Five, Advanced Valuation Issues. In Part One, Foundations of Value, Bin Jiang and Bing Cao provided most of the data analysis and insights, which involved crunching large amounts of data. Bas Deelder, Ankur Agrawal, and Mauricio Jaramillo drove much of our thinking about total returns to shareholders (TRS) decomposition. In Part Three, Intrinsic Value and the Stock Market, Richard Gerards supported the work showing that the markets value substance over form. Bin Jiang, Bing Cao, Werner Rehm, and Zane Williams were our thought partners on how the market behaves in aggregate. In Part Four, Managing for Value, André Annema co-wrote the divestitures chapter, while Werner Rehm contributed to the capital structure chapter. Rob

Palter and Werner Rehm contributed to the investor communications chapters. In Part Five, Advanced Valuation Issues, Martijn Olthof prepared the analysis for the Heineken case study. In Part Six, *Special Situations*, André Annema contributed to the emerging markets chapter, Bas Deelder contributed to the chapter on valuing banks, and Marco de Heer's dissertation formed the basis for the chapter on valuing cyclical companies. Michael Kuritzky, Vijen Patel, Abishek Saxena, and Ram Sekar helped write the questions at the end of the chapters in the University edition. We thank them all for their insights and hard work.

We would like to thank again all those who contributed to the first four editions. We owe a special debt to Dave Furer for help and late nights developing the original drafts of this book more than 20 years ago. The first four editions and this edition drew upon work, ideas, and analyses from Carlos Abad, Paul Adam, Buford Alexander, Petri Allas, Alexandre Amson, André Annema, the late Pat Anslinger, Vladimir Antikarov, Ali Asghar, Bill Barnett, Dan Bergman, Olivier Berlage, Peter Bisson, the late Joel Bleeke, Nidhi Chadda, Carrie Chen, Steve Coley, Kevin Coyne, Johan Depraetere, Mikel Dodd, Lee Dranikoff, Will Draper, Christian von Drathen, David Ernst, Bill Fallon, George Fenn, Susan Nolen Foushee, Russ Fradin, Gabriel Garcia, Alo Ghosh, Irina Grigorenko, Fredrik Gustavsson, Marco de Heer, Keiko Honda, Alice Hu, Régis Huc, Mimi James, Bin Jiang, Chris Jones, William Jones, Phil Keenan, Phil Kholos, David Krieger, Shyanjaw Kuo, Bill Lewis, Kurt Losert, Harry Markl, Yuri Maslov, Perry Moilinoff, Fabienne Moimaux, Jean-Hugues Monier, Mike Murray, Terence Nahar, Juan Ocampo, Martijn Olthof, Neha Patel, John Patience, Bill Pursche, S. R. Rajan, Werner Rehm, Frank Richter, David Rothschild, Michael Rudolf, Yasser Salem, Antoon Schneider, Meg Smoot, Silvia Stefini, Konrad Stiglbrunner, Ahmed Taha, Bill Trent, David Twiddy, Valerie Udale, Sandeep Vaswani, Kim Vogel, Jon Weiner, Jack Welch, Gustavo Wigman, David Willensky, Marijn de Wit, Pieter de Wit, Jonathan Witter, David Wright, and Yan Yang.

For help in preparing the manuscript and coordinating the flow of paper, e-mails, and phone calls, we owe our thanks to our assistants, Jennifer Fagundes and Denise de Jong.

We also extend thanks to the team at John Wiley & Sons, including Mary Daniello, Bill Falloon, Meg Freeborn, Pamela van Giessen, and Emilie Herman, and to the staff at Cape Cod Compositors.

Finally, thank you to Melissa Koller, Monique Donders, Jennifer Wessels, and our children. Our wives and families are our true inspirations. This book would not have been possible without their encouragement, support, and sacrifice.

VALUATION

MEASURING AND MANAGING THE VALUE OF COMPANIES

Part One

Foundations of Value

1

Why Value Value?

Value is the defining dimension of measurement in a market economy. People invest in the expectation that when they sell, the value of each investment will have grown by a sufficient amount above its cost to compensate them for the risk they took. This is true for all types of investments, be they bonds, derivatives, bank accounts, or company shares. Indeed, in a market economy, a company's ability to create value for its shareholders and the amount of value it creates are the chief measures by which it is judged.

Value is a particularly helpful measure of performance because it takes into account the long-term interests of all the stakeholders in a company, not just the shareholders. Alternative measures are neither as long-term nor as broad. For instance, accounting earnings assess only short-term performance from the viewpoint of shareholders; measures of employee satisfaction measure just that. Value, in contrast, is relevant to all stakeholders, because according to a growing body of research, companies that maximize value for their shareholders in the long term also create more employment, treat their current and former employees better, give their customers more satisfaction, and shoulder a greater burden of corporate responsibility than more shortsighted rivals. Competition among value-focused companies also helps to ensure that capital, human capital, and natural resources are used efficiently across the economy, leading to higher living standards for everyone. For these reasons, knowledge of how companies create value and how to measure value—the subjects of this book—is vital intellectual equipment in a market economy.

In response to the economic crisis unfolding since 2007, when the U.S. housing bubble burst, several serious thinkers have argued that our ideas about market economies must change fundamentally if we are to avoid similar crises in the future. The changes they propose include more explicit regulation governing what companies and investors do, as well as new economic theories. Our view, however, is that neither regulation nor new theory will prevent future bubbles or crises. The reason is that past ones have occurred largely when companies, investors, and governments have forgotten how investments create value, how to measure value properly, or both. The result has been confusion about which investments are creating real value—confusion that persists until value-destroying investments have triggered a crisis.

Accordingly, we believe that relearning how to create and measure value in the tried-and-true fashion is an essential step toward creating more secure economies and defending ourselves against future crises. That is why this fifth edition of *Valuation* rests on exactly the same core principles as the first.

The guiding principle of value creation is that companies create value by investing capital they raise from investors to generate future cash flows at rates of return exceeding the cost of capital (the rate investors require to be paid for the use of their capital). The faster companies can increase their revenues and deploy more capital at attractive rates of return, the more value they create. The combination of growth and return on invested capital (ROIC) relative to its cost is what drives value. Companies can sustain strong growth and high returns on invested capital only if they have a well-defined competitive advantage. This is how competitive advantage, the core concept of business strategy, links to the guiding principle of value creation.

The corollary of this guiding principle, known as the conservation of value, says anything that doesn't increase cash flows doesn't create value.[1] For example, when a company substitutes debt for equity or issues debt to repurchase shares, it changes the ownership of claims to its cash flows. However, it doesn't change the total available cash flows,[2] so in this case value is conserved, not created. Similarly, changing accounting techniques will change the appearance of cash flows without actually changing the cash flows, so it won't change the value of a company.

To the core principles, we add the empirical observation that creating sustainable value is a long-term endeavor. Competition tends to erode competitive advantages and, with them, returns on invested capital. Therefore, companies must continually seek and exploit new sources of competitive advantage if they are to create long-term value. To that end, managers must resist short-term pressure to take actions that create illusory value quickly at the expense of the real thing in the long term. Creating value for shareholders is not the same as, for example, meeting the analysts' consensus earnings forecast for the next quarter. It means balancing near-term financial performance against what it takes to develop a healthy company that can create value for decades ahead—a demanding challenge.

This book explains both the economics of value creation (for instance, how competitive advantage enables some companies to earn higher returns on invested capital than others) and the process of measuring value (for example, how to calculate return on invested capital from a company's accounting

---

[1] Assuming there are no changes in the company's risk profile.
[2] In Chapter 23 we show that the tax savings from debt may increase the company's cash flows.

statements). With this knowledge, companies can make wiser strategic and operating decisions, such as what businesses to own and how to make trade-offs between growth and returns on invested capital. Equally, this knowledge will enable investors to calculate the risks and returns of their investments with greater confidence.

CONSEQUENCES OF FORGETTING TO VALUE VALUE

The guiding principle of value creation—the fact that return on invested capital and growth generate value—and its corollary, the conservation of value, have stood the test of time. Alfred Marshall spoke about the return on capital relative to the cost of capital in 1890.[3] When managers, boards of directors, and investors have forgotten these simple truths, the consequences have been disastrous. The rise and fall of business conglomerates in the 1970s, hostile takeovers in the United States in the 1980s, the collapse of Japan's bubble economy in the 1990s, the Southeast Asian crisis in 1998, the Internet bubble, and the economic crisis starting in 2007 can all, to some extent, be traced to a misunderstanding or misapplication of these principles.

Market Bubbles

During the Internet bubble, managers and investors lost sight of what drove return on invested capital; indeed, many forgot the importance of this ratio entirely. When Netscape Communications went public in 1995, the company saw its market capitalization soar to $6 billion on an annual revenue base of just $85 million, an astonishing valuation. This phenomenon convinced the financial world that the Internet could change the way business was done and value created in every sector, setting off a race to create Internet-related companies and take them public. Between 1995 and 2000, more than 4,700 companies went public in the United States and Europe, many with billion-dollar-plus market capitalizations.

Many of the companies born in this era, including Amazon.com, eBay, and Yahoo!, have created and are likely to continue creating substantial profits and value. But for every solid, innovative new business idea, there were dozens of companies (including Netscape) that turned out to have nothing like the same ability to generate revenue or value in either the short or the long term. The initial stock market success of these flimsy companies represented a triumph of hype over experience.

Many executives and investors either forgot or threw out fundamental rules of economics in the rarefied air of the Internet revolution. Consider the concept of *increasing returns to scale*, also known as "network effects" or

---

[3] A. Marshall, *Principles of Economics*, vol. 1 (New York: Macmillan, 1890), 142.

"demand-side economies of scale." The idea enjoyed great popularity during the 1990s after Carl Shapiro and Hal Varian, professors at the University of California–Berkeley, described it in a book titled *Information Rules: A Strategic Guide to the Network Economy*.[4]

The basic idea is this: In certain situations, as companies get bigger, they can earn higher margins and return on capital because their product becomes more valuable with each new customer. In most industries, competition forces returns back to reasonable levels. But in increasing-returns industries, competition is kept at bay by the low and decreasing unit costs of the market leader (hence the tag "winner takes all" for this kind of industry).

Take Microsoft's Office software, a product that provides word processing, spreadsheets, and graphics. As the installed base of Office users expands, it becomes ever more attractive for new customers to use Office for these tasks, because they can share their documents, calculations, and images with so many others. Potential customers become increasingly unwilling to purchase and use competing products. Because of this advantage, Microsoft made profit margins of more than 60 percent and earned operating profits of approximately $12 billion on Office software in 2009, making it one of the most profitable products of all time.

As Microsoft's experience illustrates, the concept of increasing returns to scale is sound economics. What was unsound during the Internet era was its misapplication to almost every product and service related to the Internet. At that time, the concept was misinterpreted to mean that merely getting big faster than your competitors in a given market would result in enormous profits. To illustrate, some analysts applied the idea to mobile-phone service providers, even though mobile customers can and do easily switch providers, forcing the providers to compete largely on price. With no sustainable competitive advantage, mobile-phone service providers were unlikely ever to earn the 45 percent returns on invested capital that were projected for them. Increasing-returns logic was also applied to Internet grocery delivery services, even though these firms had to invest (unsustainably, eventually) in more drivers, trucks, warehouses, and inventory when their customer base grew.

The history of innovation shows how difficult it is to earn monopoly-sized returns on capital for any length of time except in very special circumstances. That did not matter to commentators who ignored history in their indiscriminate recommendation of Internet stocks. The Internet bubble left a sorry trail of intellectual shortcuts taken to justify absurd prices for technology company shares. Those who questioned the new economics were branded as people who simply "didn't get it"—the new-economy equivalents of defenders of Ptolemaic astronomy.

---

[4] C. Shapiro and H. Varian, *Information Rules: A Strategic Guide to the Network Economy* (Boston: Harvard Business School Press, 1999).

When the laws of economics prevailed, as they always do, it was clear that many Internet businesses, including online pet food sales and grocery delivery companies, did not have the unassailable competitive advantages required to earn even modest returns on invested capital. The Internet has revolutionized the economy, as have other innovations, but it did not and could not render obsolete the rules of economics, competition, and value creation.

Financial Crises

Behind the more recent financial and economic crises beginning in 2007 lies the fact that banks and investors forgot the principle of the conservation of value. Let's see how. First, individuals and speculators bought homes—illiquid assets, meaning they take a while to sell. They took out mortgages on which the interest was set at artificially low teaser rates for the first few years but rose substantially when the teaser rates expired and the required principal payments kicked in. In these transactions, the lender and buyer knew the buyer couldn't afford the mortgage payments after the teaser period ended. But both assumed either that the buyer's income would grow by enough to make the new payments or that the house value would increase enough to induce a new lender to refinance the mortgage at similar, low teaser rates.

Banks packaged these high-risk debts into long-term securities and sold them to investors. The securities, too, were not very liquid, but the investors who bought them—typically other banks and hedge funds—used short-term debt to finance the purchase, thus creating a long-term risk for whoever lent them the money.

When the interest rate on the home buyers' adjustable-rate debt increased, many could no longer afford the payments. Reflecting their distress, the real estate market crashed, pushing the values of many homes below the values of loans taken out to buy them. At that point, homeowners could neither make the required payments nor sell their houses. Seeing this, the banks that had issued short-term loans to investors in securities backed by mortgages became unwilling to roll over those loans, prompting the investors to sell all such securities at once. The value of the securities plummeted. Finally, many of the large banks themselves owned these securities, which they, of course, had also financed with short-term debt they could no longer roll over.

This story reveals two fundamental flaws in the decisions made by participants in the securitized mortgage market. They assumed that securitizing risky home loans made the loans more valuable because it reduced the risk of the assets. This violates the conservation of value rule. The aggregated cash flows of the home loans were not increased by securitization, so no value was created, and the initial risks remained. Securitizing the assets simply enabled their risks to be passed on to other owners: some investors, somewhere, had to be holding them. Yet the complexity of the chain of securities made it impossible to know who was holding precisely which risks. After the housing market turned, financial-services companies feared that any of their counter-parties could be holding massive risks and almost ceased to do business with one another. This was the start of the credit crunch that triggered a recession in the real economy.

The second flaw was to believe that using leverage to make an investment in itself creates value. It does not, because—referring once again to the conser-vation of value—it does not increase the cash flows from an investment. Many banks used large amounts of short-term debt to fund their illiquid long-term assets. This debt did not create long-term value for shareholders in those banks. On the contrary, it increased the risks of holding their equity.

Financial crises and excessive leverage   As many economic historians have described, aggressive use of leverage is the theme that links most major fi-nancial crises. The pattern is always the same: Companies, banks, or investors use short-term debt to buy long-lived, illiquid assets. Typically some event triggers unwillingness among lenders to refinance the short-term debt when it falls due. Since the borrowers don't have enough cash on hand to repay the short-term debt, they must sell some of their assets. The assets are illiquid, and other borrowers are trying to do the same, so the price each borrower can realize is too low to repay the debt. In other words, the borrower's assets and liabilities are mismatched.

In the past 30 years, the world has seen at least six financial crises that arose largely because companies and banks were financing illiquid assets with short-term debt. In the United States in the 1980s, savings and loan institutions funded an aggressive expansion with short-term debt and deposits. When it became clear that these institutions' investments (typically real estate) were worth less than their liabilities, lenders and depositors refused to lend more to them. In 1989, the U.S. government bailed out the industry.

In the mid-1990s, the fast-growing economies in East Asia, including Thailand, South Korea, and Indonesia, fueled their investments in illiquid industrial property, plant, and equipment with short-term debt, often denom-inated in U.S. dollars. When global interest rates rose and it became clear that the East Asian companies had built too much capacity, those companies were unable to repay or refinance their debt. The ensuing crisis destabilized local economies and damaged foreign investors.

Other financial crises fueled by too much short-term debt have included the Russian government default and the collapse of the U.S. hedge fund Long-Term Capital Management, both in 1998; the U.S. commercial real estate crisis in the early 1990s; and the Japanese financial crisis that began in 1990 and, according to some, continues to this day.

Market bubbles and crashes are painfully disruptive, but we don't need to rewrite the rules of competition and finance to understand and avoid them. Certainly the Internet has changed the way we shop and communicate. But it has not created a "New Economy," as the 1990s catchphrase went. On the contrary, it has made information, especially about prices, transparent in a way that intensifies old-style market competition in many real markets. Similarly, the financial crisis triggered in 2007 will wring out some of the economy's recent excesses, such as people buying houses they can't afford and uncontrolled credit card borrowing by consumers. But the key to avoiding the next crisis is to reassert the fundamental economic rules, not to revise them. If investors and lenders value their investments and loans according to the guiding principle of value creation and its corollary, prices for both kinds of assets will reflect the real risks underlying the transactions.

Financial crises and equity markets   Contrary to popular opinion, stock markets generally continue to reflect companies' intrinsic value during financial crises. For instance, after the 2007 crisis had started in the credit markets, equity markets too came in for criticism. In October 2008, a *New York Times* editorial thundered, "What's been going on in the stock market hardly fits canonical notions of rationality. In the last month or so, shares in Bank of America plunged to $26, bounced to $37, slid to $30, rebounded to $38, plummeted to $20, sprung above $26 and skidded back to almost $24. Evidently, people don't have a clue what Bank of America is worth."[5] Far from showing that the equity market was broken, however, this example points up the fundamental difference between the equity markets and the credit markets. The critical difference is that investors could easily trade shares of Bank of America on the equity markets, whereas credit markets (with the possible exception of the government bond market) are not nearly as liquid. This is why economic crises typically stem from excesses in credit rather than equity markets.

The two types of markets operate very differently. Equities are highly liquid because they trade on organized exchanges with many buyers and sellers for a relatively small number of securities. In contrast, there are many more debt securities than equities because there are often multiple debt instruments for each company and even more derivatives, many of which are not standardized. The result is a proliferation of small, illiquid credit markets. Furthermore, much debt doesn't trade at all. For example, short-term loans between banks and from banks to hedge funds are one-to-one transactions that are difficult to buy or sell. Illiquidity leads to frozen markets where no one will trade or where prices fall to levels far below a level that reflects a reasonable economic value. Simply put, illiquid markets cease to function as markets at all.

During the credit crisis beginning in 2007, prices on the equity markets became volatile, but they operated normally for the most part. The volatility reflected the uncertainty hanging over the real economy. (See Chapter 17 for more on volatility.) The S&P 500 index traded between 1,200 and 1,400 from January to September 2008. In October, upon the collapse of U.S. investment bank Lehman Brothers and the U.S. government takeover of the insurance

[5] Eduardo Porter, "The Lion, the Bull and the Bears," *New York Times*, October 17, 2008.

company American International Group (AIG), the index began its slide to a trading range of 800 to 900. But that drop of about 30 percent was not surprising given the uncertainty about the financial system, the availability of credit, and their impact on the real economy. Moreover, the 30 percent drop in the index was equivalent to an increase in the cost of equity of only about 1 percent,[6] reflecting investors' sense of the scale of increase in the risk of investing in equities generally.

There was a brief period of extreme equity market activity in March 2009, when the S&P 500 index dropped from 800 to 700 and rose back to 800 in less than one month. Many investors were apparently sitting on the market sidelines, waiting until the market hit bottom. The moment the index dropped below 700 seemed to trigger their return. From there, the market began a steady increase to about 1,100 in December 2009. Our research suggests that a long-term trend value for the S&P 500 index would have been in the 1,100 to 1,300 range at that time, a reasonable reflection of the real value of equities.

In hindsight, the behavior of the equity market has not been unreasonable. It actually functioned quite well in the sense that trading continued and price changes were not out of line with what was going on in the economy. True, the equity markets did not *predict* the economic crisis. However, a look at previous recessions shows that the equity markets rarely predict inflection points in the economy.[7]

BENEFITS OF FOCUSING ON LONG-TERM VALUE

There has long been vigorous debate on the importance of shareholder value relative to other measures of a company's success, such as its record on employment, social responsibility, and the environment. In their ideology and legal frameworks, the United States and the United Kingdom have given most weight to the idea that the objective function of the corporation is to maximize shareholder value, because shareholders are the owners of the corporation who elect the board of directors to represent their interests in managing the corporation's development. In continental Europe, an explicitly broader view of the objectives of business organizations has long been more influential. In many cases, this is embedded in the governance structures of the corporate form of organization. In the Netherlands and Germany, for example, the board of a large corporation has a duty to support the continuity of the business and to do that in the interests of all the corporation's stakeholders, including employees and the local community, not just its shareholders. Similar philosophies underpin corporate governance in other continental European countries.

---

[6] Richard Dobbs, Bin Jiang, and Timothy Koller, "Why the Crisis Hasn't Shaken the Cost of Capital," *McKinsey on Finance*, no. 30 (Winter 2009): 26–30.
[7] Richard Dobbs and Timothy Koller, "The Crisis: Timing Strategic Moves," *McKinsey on Finance*, no. 31 (Spring 2009): 1–5.

In much of Asia, company boards are more likely than in the United States and Europe to be controlled by family members, and they are the stakeholders whose interests will set the direction of those companies.

Our analysis and experience suggest that for most companies anywhere in the world, pursuing the creation of long-term shareholder value does not cause other stakeholders to suffer. We would go further and argue that companies dedicated to value creation are more robust and build stronger economies, higher living standards, and more opportunities for individuals.

Consider employee stakeholders. A company that tries to boost profits by providing a shabby work environment, underpaying employees, and skimping on benefits will have trouble attracting and retaining high-quality employees. With today's more mobile and more educated workforce, such a company would struggle in the long term against competitors offering more attractive environments. While it may feel good to treat people well, it is also good business.

Value-creating companies also create more jobs. When examining employment, we found that the U.S. and European companies that created the most shareholder value in the past 15 years have shown stronger employment growth. In Exhibit 1.1, companies with the highest total returns to shareholders (TRS) also had the largest increases in employment. We tested this link within individual sectors of the economy and found similar results.

An often-expressed concern is that companies that emphasize creating value for shareholders have a short time horizon that is overly focused on accounting earnings rather than revenue growth and return on invested capital. We disagree. We have found a strong positive correlation between long-term shareholder returns and investments in research and development

EXHIBIT 1.1 **Correlation between Total Returns to Shareholders (TRS) and Employment Growth**

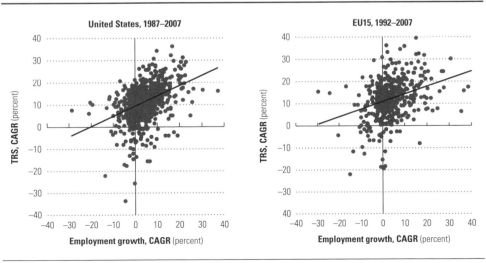

EXHIBIT 1.2 **Correlation between TRS and R&D Expenditures**

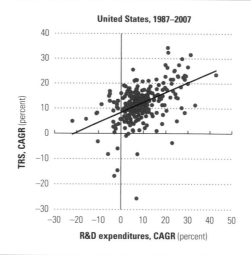

United States, 1987–2007

(R&D)—evidence of a commitment to creating value in the longer term. As shown in Exhibit 1.2, companies that earned the highest shareholder returns also invested the most in R&D. These results also hold within individual sectors in the economy.

Companies that create value also tend to show a greater commitment to meeting their social responsibilities. Our research shows that many of the corporate social responsibility initiatives that companies take can help them create shareholder value.[8] For example, IBM provides free Web-based resources on business management to small and midsize enterprises in developing economies. Helping build such businesses not only improves IBM's reputation and relationships in new markets, but also helps it develop relationships with companies that could become future customers. And Best Buy has undertaken a targeted effort to reduce employee turnover among women. The program has helped women create their own support networks and build leadership skills. As a result of the program, turnover among female employees decreased by more than 5 percent.

CHALLENGES OF FOCUSING ON LONG-TERM VALUE

Focusing on return on invested capital and revenue growth over the long term is a tough job for executives. They can't be expected to take it on unless they are sure it wins them more investor support and a stronger share price. But as later chapters will show, the evidence is overwhelming that investors

[8] Sheila Bonini, Timothy Koller, and Philip H. Mirvis, "Valuing Social Responsibility Programs," *McKinsey on Finance*, no. 32 (Summer 2009): 11–18.

do indeed value long-term cash flow, growth, and return on invested capital, and companies that perform well on those measures perform well in the stock market. The evidence also supports the corollary: companies that fail to create value over the long term do less well in the stock market.

Yet despite the evidence that shareholders value value, companies continue to listen to misguided supposed truths about what the market wants and fall for the illusion of the free lunch—hoping, for example, that one accounting treatment will lead to a higher value than another, or some fancy financial structure or improvement in earnings per share will turn a mediocre deal into a winner.

To illustrate, when analyzing a prospective acquisition, the question most frequently posed is whether the transaction will dilute earnings per share (EPS) over the first year or two. Given the popularity of EPS as a yardstick for company decisions, you would think that a predicted improvement in EPS would be an important indicator of whether the acquisition was actually likely to create value. However, there is no empirical evidence linking an increased EPS with the value created by a transaction (see Chapter 21 for the evidence). Deals that strengthen EPS and deals that dilute EPS are equally likely to create or destroy value.

If such fallacies have no impact on value, why do they prevail? We recently participated in a discussion with a company pursuing a major acquisition and its bankers about whether the earnings dilution likely to result from the deal was important. To paraphrase one of the bankers, "We know that any impact on EPS is irrelevant to value, but we use it as a simple way to communicate with boards of directors."

Yet company executives say they, too, don't believe the impact on EPS is so important. They tell us they are just using the measures the Street uses. Investors also tell us that a deal's short-term impact on EPS is not that important for them. In sum, we hear from almost everyone we talk to that a transaction's short-term impact on EPS does not matter, yet they all pay attention to it.

As a result of their focus on short-term EPS, major companies not infrequently pass up value-creating opportunities. In a survey of 400 CFOs, two Duke University professors found that fully 80 percent of the CFOs said they would reduce discretionary spending on potentially value-creating activities such as marketing and R&D in order to meet their short-term earnings targets.[9] In addition, 39 percent said they would give discounts to customers to make purchases this quarter rather than next, in order to hit quarterly EPS targets. Such biases shortchange all stakeholders.

From 1997 to 2003, a leading company consistently generated annual EPS growth of between 11 percent and 16 percent. That seems impressive until you look at measures more important to value creation, like revenue growth.

[9] John R. Graham, Cam Harvey, and Shiva Rajgopal, "The Economic Implications of Corporate Financial Reporting," *Journal of Accounting and Economics* 40 (2005): 3–73.

During the same period, the company increased revenues by only 2 percent a year. It achieved its profit growth by cutting costs, usually a good thing, and the cost cutting certainly did produce productivity improvements in the earlier years. However, as opportunities for those ran out, the company turned to reductions in marketing and product development to maintain its earnings growth. In 2003, its managers admitted they had underinvested in products and marketing and needed to go through a painful period of rebuilding, and the stock price fell.

The pressure to show strong short-term results often mounts when businesses start to mature and see their growth begin to moderate. Investors go on baying for high growth. Managers are tempted to find ways to keep profits rising in the short term while they try to stimulate longer-term growth. However, any short-term efforts to massage earnings that undercut productive investment make achieving long-term growth even more difficult, spawning a vicious circle.

Some analysts and some irrational investors will always clamor for short-term results. However, even though a company bent on growing long-term value will not be able to meet their demands all of the time, this continuous pressure has the virtue of keeping managers on their toes. Sorting out the trade-offs between short-term earnings and long-term value creation is part of a manager's job, just as having the courage to make the right call is a critical personal quality. Perhaps even more important, it is up to corporate boards to investigate and understand the economics of the businesses in their portfolio well enough to judge when managers are making the right trade-offs and, above all, to protect managers when they choose to build long-term value at the expense of short-term profits.

Applying the principles of value creation sometimes means going against the crowd. It means accepting that there are no free lunches. It means relying on data, thoughtful analysis, and a deep understanding of the competitive dynamics of your industry. We hope this book provides readers with the knowledge to help them make and defend decisions that will create value for investors and for society at large throughout their careers.

REVIEW QUESTIONS

1. What are the benefits of a long-term perspective on value creation? For companies? For the economy?
2. What is the relationship between the stock market and the real economy in terms of measures such as gross domestic product (GDP), inflation, and interest rates?
3. What are some of the common features of the 2007–2009 stock market crash and previous market crashes—for example, Japan's in the 1990s or the Internet bubble around the turn of the millennium?

4. If growth is a significant value driver, does getting bigger translate into creating value?
5. What are some of the differences between the ways the equity and credit markets operate?
6. Provide examples of businesses where network effects would or would not apply.
7. What more could be done by boards of directors and shareholders to ensure that managers pursue long-term value creation?
8. Explain the conservation of value principle. What decisions might it affect?

2

Fundamental Principles of Value Creation

In Chapter 1, we introduced the fundamental principles of corporate finance. Companies create value by investing capital to generate future cash flows at rates of return that exceed their cost of capital. The faster they can grow and deploy more capital at attractive rates of return, the more value they create. The mix of growth and return on invested capital (ROIC)[1] relative to the cost of capital is what drives the creation of value. A corollary of this principle is the conservation of value: any action that doesn't increase cash flows doesn't create value.

The principles imply that a company's primary task is to generate cash flows at rates of return on invested capital greater than the cost of capital. Following these principles helps managers decide which investments will create the most value for shareholders in the long term. The principles also help investors assess the potential value of alternative investments. Managers and investors alike need to understand in detail what relationships tie together cash flows, ROIC, and value; what consequences arise from the conservation of value; and how to factor any risks attached to future cash flows into their decision making. These are the main subjects of this chapter. The chapter concludes by setting out the relationships between cash flows, ROIC, and value in the key value driver formula—the equation underpinning discounted cash flow (DCF) valuation in both theory and practice.

GROWTH AND ROIC: DRIVERS OF VALUE

Companies create value for their owners by investing cash now to generate more cash in the future. The amount of value they create is the difference

---

[1] A simple definition of return on invested capital is after-tax operating profit divided by invested capital (working capital plus fixed assets). ROIC's calculation from a company's financial statements is explained in detail in Chapters 6 and 7.

EXHIBIT 2.1 **Growth and ROIC Drive Value**

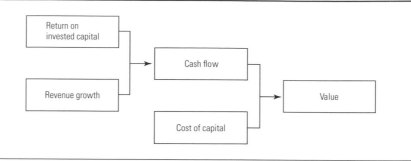

between cash inflows and the cost of the investments made, adjusted to reflect the fact that tomorrow's cash flows are worth less than today's because of the time value of money and the riskiness of future cash flows. As we will demonstrate later in this chapter, a company's return on invested capital and its revenue growth together determine how revenues are converted to cash flows. That means the amount of value a company creates is governed ultimately by its ROIC, revenue growth, and of course its ability to sustain both over time. Exhibit 2.1 illustrates this core principle of value creation.[2]

One might expect universal agreement on a notion as fundamental as value, but this isn't the case: many executives, boards, and financial media still treat accounting earnings and value as one and the same, and focus almost obsessively on improving earnings. However, while earnings and cash flow are often correlated, earnings don't tell the whole story of value creation, and focusing too much on earnings or earnings growth often leads companies to stray from a value-creating path.

For example, earnings growth alone can't explain why investors in drug-store chain Walgreens, with sales of $54 billion in 2007, and global chewing-gum maker Wm. Wrigley Jr. Company, with sales of $5 billion the same year, earned similar shareholder returns between 1968 and 2007.[3] These two successful companies had very different growth rates. During the period, the net income of Walgreens grew at 14 percent per year, while Wrigley's net income grew at 10 percent per year. Even though Walgreens was one of the fastest-growing companies in the United States during this time, its average annual shareholder returns were 16 percent, compared with 17 percent for the significantly slower-growing Wrigley. The reason Wrigley could create slightly more value than Walgreens despite 40 percent slower growth was that it earned

---

[2] In its purest form, *value* is the sum of the present values of future expected cash flows—a point-in-time measure. *Value creation* is the change in value due to company performance. Sometimes we refer to value and value creation based on explicit projections of future growth, ROIC, and cash flows. At other times, we use the market price of a company's shares as a proxy for value, and total returns to shareholders (share price appreciation plus dividends) as a proxy for value creation.

[3] Shareholder returns equal dividends plus appreciation in the share price.

a 28 percent ROIC, while the ROIC for Walgreens was 14 percent (a good rate for a retailer).

To be fair, if all companies in an industry earned the same ROIC, then earnings growth *would* be the differentiating metric. For reasons of simplicity, analysts and academics have sometimes made this assumption, but as Chapter 4 will demonstrate, returns on invested capital can vary considerably, even between companies within the same industry.

Relationship of Growth, ROIC, and Cash Flow

Disaggregating cash flow into revenue growth and ROIC helps illuminate the underlying drivers of a company's performance. Say a company's cash flow was $100 last year and will be $150 next year. This doesn't tell us much about its economic performance, since the $50 increase in cash flow could come from many sources, including revenue growth, a reduction in capital spending, or a reduction in marketing expenditures. But if we told you that the company was generating revenue growth of 7 percent per year and would earn a return on invested capital of 15 percent, then you would be able to evaluate its performance. You could, for instance, compare the company's growth rate with the growth rate of its industry or the economy, and you could analyze its ROIC relative to peers, its cost of capital, and its own historical performance.

Growth, ROIC, and cash flow are tightly linked. To see how, consider two companies, Value Inc. and Volume Inc., whose projected earnings and cash flows are displayed in Exhibit 2.2. Both companies earned $100 million in year 1 and increased their revenues and earnings at 5 percent per year, so their projected earnings are identical. If the popular view that value depends only on earnings were true, the two companies' values also would be the same. But this simple example illustrates how wrong that view can be.

Value Inc. generates higher cash flows with the same earnings because it invests only 25 percent of its profits (making its investment rate 25 percent) to achieve the same profit growth as Volume Inc., which invests 50 percent of its profits. Value Inc.'s lower investment rate results in 50 percent higher cash flows than Volume Inc. obtains from the same level of profits.

EXHIBIT 2.2 **Tale of Two Companies: Same Earnings, Different Cash Flows**

$ million

	Value Inc.					Volume Inc.				
	Year 1	Year 2	Year 3	Year 4	Year 5	Year 1	Year 2	Year 3	Year 4	Year 5
Revenue	1,000	1,050	1,102	1,158	1,216	1,000	1,050	1,102	1,158	1,216
Earnings	100	105	110	116	122	100	105	110	116	122
Investment	(25)	(26)	(28)	(29)	(31)	(50)	(53)	(55)	(58)	(61)
Cash flow	75	79	82	87	91	50	52	55	58	61

EXHIBIT 2.3 **Value Inc.: DCF Valuation**

$ millions

| | Value Inc. | | | | | | |
	Year 1	Year 2	Year 3	Year 4	Year 5	Year X	Sum
Earnings	100	105	110	116	122	...	–
Investment	(25)	(26)	(28)	(29)	(31)	...	–
Cash flow	75	79	82	87	91	...	–
Value today	68	65	62	59	56	...	1,500

Present value of 75 discounted at 10% for one year

Present value of 87 discounted at 10% for four years

We can value the two companies by discounting their future cash flows at a discount rate that reflects what investors expect to earn from investing in the company—that is, their cost of capital. For both companies, we discounted each year's cash flow to the present at a 10 percent cost of capital and summed the results to derive a total present value of all future cash flows: $1,500 million for Value Inc. (shown in Exhibit 2.3) and $1,000 million for Volume Inc.

The companies' values can also be expressed as price-to-earnings ratios (P/Es). To do this, divide each company's value by its first-year earnings of $100 million. Value Inc.'s P/E is 15, while Volume Inc.'s is only 10. Despite identical earnings and growth rates, the companies have different earnings multiples because their cash flows are so different.

Value Inc. generates higher cash flows because it doesn't have to invest as much as Volume Inc., thanks to its higher rate of ROIC. In this case, Value Inc. invested $25 million (out of $100 million earned) in year 1 to increase its revenues and profits by $5 million in year 2. Its return on new capital is 20 percent ($5 million of additional profits divided by $25 million of investment).[4] In contrast, Volume Inc.'s return on invested capital is 10 percent ($5 million in additional profits in year 2 divided by an investment of $50 million).

Growth, ROIC, and cash flow (as represented by the investment rate) are tied together mathematically in the following relationship:

$$\text{Investment Rate} = \text{Growth} \div \text{Return on Invested Capital}$$

Applying that formula to Value Inc.,

$$25\% = 5\% \div 20\%$$

---

[4] We assumed that all of the increase in profits is due to the new investment, with the return on Value Inc.'s existing capital remaining unchanged.

EXHIBIT 2.4   **Translating Growth and ROIC into Value**

Value,[1] dollars

Growth		7%	9%	13%	25%
	3%	800	1,100	1,400	1,600
	6%	600	1,100	1,600	2,100
	9%	400	1,100	1,900	2,700

ROIC

[1] Present value of future cash flows, assuming year 1 earnings of $100 and a 9% cost of capital. After 15 years all scenarios grow at 3%.

Applying it to Volume Inc.,

$$50\% = 5\% \div 10\%$$

Since the three variables are tied together, you only need two to know the third, so you can describe a company's performance with any two of the variables.

Balancing ROIC and Growth to Create Value

Exhibit 2.4 shows how different combinations of growth and ROIC translate into value. Each cell in the matrix represents the present value of future cash flows under each of the assumptions of growth and ROIC, discounted at the company's cost of capital. In this case, we're assuming a 9 percent cost of capital and a company that earns $100 in the first year.[5]

Using this simple approach, we get real-world results. Take the typical large company, which grows at about 5 to 6 percent per year (nominal), earns about a 13 percent return on equity, and has a 9 percent cost of capital. Finding the intersection of the typical company's return leads you to a value of $1,500 to $1,600. Dividing this value by earnings of $100 results in a price-to-earnings ratio of 15 to 16 times—and 15 times is the median P/E for large U.S. companies outside of a recession.

[5] We made explicit cash flow forecasts for the first 15 years and assumed that growth after that point converges on 4.5 percent in all scenarios. If a company grew faster than the economy forever, it would eventually overtake the entire world economy.

Observe that for any level of growth, value increases with improvements in ROIC. In other words, when all else is equal, a higher ROIC is always good. The same can't be said of growth. When ROIC is high, faster growth increases value, but when ROIC is lower than the company's cost of capital, faster growth necessarily destroys value, making the point where ROIC equals the cost of capital the dividing line between creating and destroying value through growth. On the line, value is neither created nor destroyed, regardless of how fast the company grows.

We sometimes hear the argument that even low-ROIC companies should strive for growth, because if a company grows, its ROIC will naturally increase. However, we find this is true only for young, start-up businesses. Most often in mature companies, a low ROIC indicates a flawed business model or unattractive industry structure.

Real-World Evidence

The logic laid out in this section is reflected in the way companies perform in the stock market. Recall the earlier explanation of why shareholder returns for Walgreens and Wrigley were the same even though earnings for Walgreens grew much faster. General Electric (GE) provides another example of the relative impact of growth and ROIC on value. GE's share price increased from about $5 in 1991 to about $40 in 2001, earning investors $519 billion from the increase in share value and distributions during the final 10 years of Jack Welch's tenure as CEO. A similar amount invested in the S&P 500 index would have returned only $212 billion.

How did GE do it? Its industrial and finance businesses both contributed significantly to its overall creation of value, but in different ways. Over the 10-year period, the industrial businesses increased revenues by only 4 percent a year (less than the growth of the economy), but their ROIC increased from about 13 percent to 31 percent. The finance businesses performed in a more balanced way, demonstrating growth of 18 percent per year and increasing ROIC from 14 percent to 21 percent. In the industrial businesses, ROIC was the key driver of value, while in the financial businesses, improvements in both growth and ROIC contributed significantly to value creation.

Clearly, the core valuation principle applies at the company level. We have found that it applies at the sector level, too. Consider companies as a whole in the consumer packaged-goods sector. Even though well-known names in the sector such as Procter & Gamble and Colgate-Palmolive aren't high-growth companies, the market values them at high earnings multiples because of their high returns on invested capital.

The typical large packaged-goods company increased its revenues only 6 percent a year from 1998 to 2007, slower than the average of about 8 percent for all large U.S. companies. Yet at the end of 2007 (before the market crash), the median P/E of consumer packaged-goods companies was about 20, compared with 17 for the median large company. The high valuation of companies in this sector rested on their high ROICs—typically above 20 percent, compared with ROICs averaging 13 percent for the median large company between 1998 and 2007.

Another example that underlines the point is a comparison of Campbell Soup Company ($8 billion in 2008 revenues) with fast-growing discount retailer Kohl's (revenues of $16 billion in 2008). In the middle years of the decade, revenues for Kohl's grew 15 percent annually, while Campbell achieved only 4 percent in annual organic growth. Yet the two companies had similar P/Es. Campbell's high ROIC of 50 percent made up for its slower growth; Kohl's ROIC averaged only 15 percent.

To test whether the core valuation principle also applies at the level of countries and the aggregate economy, we asked why large U.S.-based companies typically trade at higher multiples than large companies in the more developed Asian countries of Hong Kong, South Korea, Taiwan, and Singapore.[6] Some executives assume the reason is that investors are simply willing to pay higher prices for U.S. companies (an assumption that has prompted some non-U.S. companies to consider moving their share listing to the New York Stock Exchange in an attempt to increase their value). But the real reason U.S. companies trade at higher multiples is that they typically earn higher returns on invested capital. The median large U.S. company earned a 16 percent ROIC in 2007, while the median large Asian company earned 10 percent. Of course, these broad comparisons hide the fact that some Asian sectors and companies—for example, Toyota in automobiles—outperform their U.S. counterparts. But for the most part, Asian companies historically have focused more on growth than profitability or ROIC, which explains the large difference between their average valuation and that of U.S. companies.

More evidence showing that ROIC and growth drive value is presented in Chapters 15 and 16.

Managerial Implications

We'll dive more deeply into the managerial dimensions of ROIC and growth in Chapters 4 and 5, respectively. For now, we outline several lessons managers should learn for strategic decision making.

Start by referring back to Exhibit 2.4, because it contains the most important strategic insights for managers concerning the relative impact that changes in ROIC and growth can have on a company's value. In general, companies already earning a high ROIC can generate more additional value by increasing their rate of growth, rather than their ROIC, while low-ROIC companies will generate relatively more value by focusing on increasing their ROIC.

---

[6] The median large company in the United States had a market-to-book ratio of 2.4 in 2007, while the median large company in these four Asian countries had a median market-to-book ratio of about 1.8.

EXHIBIT 2.5 **Increasing Value: Impact of Higher Growth and ROIC**

Change in value, percent

High-ROIC company
Typical packaged-goods company

Moderate-ROIC company
Typical retailer

	High-ROIC company	Moderate-ROIC company
1% higher growth	10%	5%
1% higher ROIC	6%	15%

Source: McKinsey Corporate Performance Center analysis.

For example, Exhibit 2.5 shows that a typical high-ROIC company, such as a branded consumer packaged-goods company, can increase its value by 10 percent if it increases its growth rate by one percentage point, while a typical moderate-ROIC company, such as the average retailer, will increase its value by only 5 percent for the same increase in growth. In contrast, the moderate-ROIC company gets a 15 percent bump in value from increasing its return on invested capital by one percentage point, while the high-ROIC company gets only a 6 percent bump from the same increase in return on invested capital.

The general lesson is that high-ROIC companies should focus on growth, while low-ROIC companies should focus on improving returns before growing. Of course, this analysis assumes that achieving a one percentage point increase in growth is as easy as achieving a one percentage point increase in ROIC, everything else being constant. In reality, achieving either type of increase poses different degrees of difficulty for different companies in different industries, and the impact of a change in growth and ROIC will also vary between companies. However, every company needs to make the analysis in order to set its strategic priorities.

Until now, we have assumed that all growth earns the same ROIC and therefore generates the same value, but this is clearly unrealistic: different types of growth earn different degrees of return so not all growth is equally value-creating. Each company must understand the pecking order of growth-related value creation that applies to its industry and company type.

Exhibit 2.6 shows the value created from different types of growth for a typical consumer products company. These results are based on cases with which we are familiar, not on a comprehensive analysis, but we believe they reflect the broader reality.[7] The results are expressed in terms of value created for $1.00 of incremental revenue. For example, $1.00 of additional revenue from a new product creates $1.75 to $2.00 of value. The most important implication of this chart is the rank order. New products typically create more value for shareholders, while acquisitions typically create the least. The key to

---

[7] We identified examples for each type of growth and estimated their impact on value creation. For instance, we obtained several examples of the margins and capital requirements for new products.

EXHIBIT 2.6 **Value Creation by Type of Growth**

Shareholder value created for incremental $1.00 of revenue.[1]

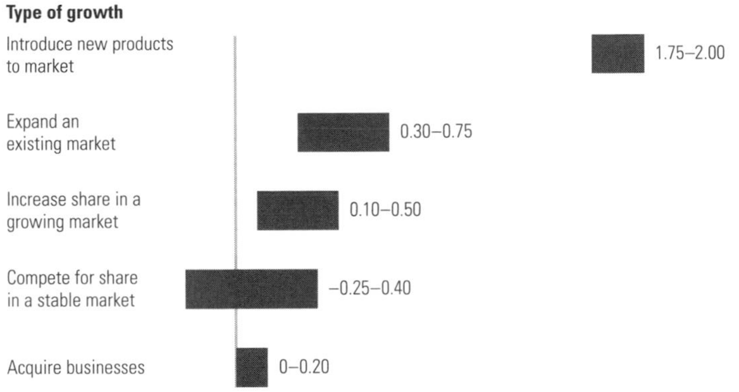

Type of growth

Type of growth	Value
Introduce new products to market	1.75–2.00
Expand an existing market	0.30–0.75
Increase share in a growing market	0.10–0.50
Compete for share in a stable market	−0.25–0.40
Acquire businesses	0–0.20

[1] Value for a typical consumer packaged-goods company.

Source: McKinsey Corporate Performance Center analysis.

the difference between these extremes is differences in ROICs for the different types of investment.

Growth strategies based on organic new product development frequently have the highest returns because they don't require much new capital; companies can add new products to their existing factory lines and distribution systems. Furthermore, the investments to produce new products are not all required at once. If preliminary results are not promising, future investments can be scaled back or canceled.

Acquisitions, by contrast, require that the entire investment be made up front. The amount of up-front payment reflects the expected cash flows from the target plus a premium to stave off other bidders. So even if the buyer can improve the target enough to generate an attractive ROIC, the rate of return is typically only a small amount higher than its cost of capital.

To be fair, this analysis doesn't reflect the risk of failure. Most product ideas fail before reaching the market, and the cost of failed ideas is not reflected in the numbers. By contrast, acquisitions typically bring existing revenues and cash flows that limit the downside risk to the acquirer. But including the risk of failure would not change the pecking order of investments from a value-creation viewpoint.

The interaction between growth and ROIC is a key factor to consider when assessing the likely impact of a particular investment on a company's overall ROIC. For example, we've found that some very successful, high-ROIC companies in the United States are reluctant to invest in growth if it will reduce their ROICs. One technology company had 30 percent operating margins and a 50+ percent ROIC, so it didn't want to invest in projects that might earn only 25 percent returns, fearing this would dilute its average returns. But as the first principle of value creation would lead you to expect, even a 25 percent return opportunity would still create value as long as the cost of capital was lower, despite the resulting decline in average ROIC.

The evidence backs this up. We examined the performance of 78 high-ROIC companies (greater than 30 percent ROIC) from 1996 to 2005.[8] Not surprisingly, the companies that created the most value (measured by total returns to shareholders over the 10 years) were those that grew fastest and maintained their high ROICs. But the second-highest value creators were those that grew fastest even though they experienced moderate declines in their ROICs. They created more value than companies that increased their ROICs but grew slowly.

We've also seen companies with low returns pursue growth on the assumption that this will also improve their profit margins and returns, reasoning that growth will increase returns by spreading fixed costs across more revenues. As we mentioned earlier in this chapter, however, except for small start-up companies, faster growth rarely fixes a company's ROIC problem. Low returns usually indicate a poor industry structure (e.g., airlines), a flawed business model, or weak execution. If a company has a problem with ROIC, the company shouldn't grow until the problem is fixed.

The evidence backs this up as well. We examined the performance of 64 low-ROIC companies from 1996 to 2005. The companies that had low growth but increased their ROICs outperformed the faster-growing companies that did not improve their ROICs.

CONSERVATION OF VALUE

A corollary of the principle that discounted cash flow drives value is the conservation of value: anything that doesn't increase cash flows doesn't create value. So value is conserved, or unchanged, when a company changes the ownership of claims to its cash flows but doesn't change the total available cash flows—for example, when it substitutes debt for equity or issues debt to repurchase shares. Similarly, changing the appearance of the cash flows without actually changing the cash flows—say, by changing accounting techniques—doesn't change the value of a company.[9] While the validity of this principle is obvious, it is worth emphasizing, because executives, investors, and pundits so often forget it—for example, when they hope that one accounting treatment will lead to a higher value than another, or that some fancy financial structure will turn a mediocre deal into a winner.

---

[8] Bin Jiang and Timothy Koller, "How to Choose between Growth and ROIC," *McKinsey on Finance* (Autumn 2007): 19–22.
[9] In some cases, a company can increase its value by reducing its cost of capital by using more debt in its capital structure. However, even in this case, the underlying change is to reduce taxes, but the overall pretax cost of capital doesn't change. See Chapter 23 for further discussion.

The battle over how companies should account for executive stock options illustrates the extent to which executives continue to believe (wrongly) that the stock market is unaware of the conservation of value. Even though there is no cash effect when executive stock options are issued, they reduce the cash flow available to existing shareholders by diluting their ownership when the options are exercised. Under accounting rules dating back to the 1970s, companies could exclude the implicit cost of executive stock options from their income statements. In the early 1990s, as options became more material, the Financial Accounting Standards Board (FASB) proposed a change to the accounting rules, requiring companies to record an expense for the value of options when they are issued. A large group of executives and venture capitalists thought investors would be spooked if options were brought onto the income statement. Some claimed that the entire venture capital industry would be decimated because young start-up companies that provide much of their compensation through options would show low or negative profits.

The FASB issued its new rules in 2004,[10] more than a decade after taking up the issue and only after the bursting of the dot-com bubble. Despite dire predictions, the stock prices of companies didn't change when the new accounting rules were implemented, because the market already reflected the cost of the options in its valuations of companies. One respected analyst said to us, "I don't care whether they are recorded as an expense or simply disclosed in the footnotes. I know what to do with the information."

In this case, the conservation of value principle explains why executives didn't need to worry about any effects that changes in stock option accounting would have on their share price. The same applies to questions such as whether an acquisition creates value simply because reported earnings increase, whether a company should return cash to shareholders through share repurchases instead of dividends, or whether financial engineering creates value. In every circumstance, executives should focus on increasing cash flows rather than finding gimmicks that merely redistribute value among investors or make reported results look better. Executives should also be wary of proposals that claim to create value unless they're clear about how their actions will materially increase the size of the pie. If you can't pinpoint the tangible source of value creation, you're probably looking at an illusion, and you can be sure that's what the market will think, too.

Foundations of the Value Conservation Principle

The value conservation principle is described in Richard Brealey and Stewart Myers's seminal textbook, *Principles of Corporate Finance*.[11] One of the earliest

---

[10] Financial Accounting Standard 123R, released in December 2004, effective for periods beginning after June 15, 2005.
[11] Richard Brealey, Stewart Myers, and Franklin Allen, *Principles of Corporate Finance*, 9th ed. (New York: McGraw-Hill/Irwin, 2007).

applications of the principle can be found in the pioneering work of Nobel Prize winners Franco Modigliani and Merton Miller, financial economists who in the late 1950s and early 1960s questioned whether managers could use changes in capital structure to increase share prices. In 1958, they showed that the value of a company shouldn't be affected by changing the structure of the debt and equity ownership unless the overall cash flows generated by the company also change.[12]

Imagine a company that has no debt and generates $100 of cash flow each year before paying shareholders. Suppose the company is valued at $1,000. Now suppose the company borrows $200 and pays it out to the shareholders. Our knowledge of the core valuation principle and the value conservation principle tells us that the company would still be worth $1,000, with $200 for the creditors and $800 for the shareholders, because its cash flow available to pay the shareholders and creditors is still $100.

In most countries, however, borrowing money does change cash flows because interest payments are tax deductible. The total taxes paid by the company are lower, thereby increasing the cash flow available to pay both shareholders and creditors. In addition, having debt may induce managers to be more diligent (because they must have cash available to repay the debt on time) and, therefore, increase the company's cash flow. On the downside, having debt could make it more difficult for managers to raise capital for attractive investment opportunities, thereby reducing cash flow. The point is that what matters isn't the substitution of debt for equity in and of itself; it only matters if the substitution changes the company's cash flows through tax reductions or if associated changes in management decisions change cash flows.

In a related vein, finance academics in the 1960s developed the idea of efficient markets. While the meaning and validity of efficient markets are subjects of continuing debate, especially after the bursting of the dot-com and real estate bubbles of the past decade, one implication of efficient market theory remains: the stock market isn't easily fooled when companies undertake actions to increase reported accounting profit without increasing cash flows. One example is the market's reaction to changes in accounting for employee stock options, just described. And when the FASB eliminated goodwill amortization effective in 2002 and the International Accounting Standards Board (IASB) did the same in 2005, many companies reported increased profits, but their underlying values and stock prices didn't change, because the accounting change didn't affect cash flows. The evidence is overwhelming that the market isn't fooled by actions that don't affect cash flow, as we will show in Chapter 16.

---

[12] F. Modigliani and M. H. Miller, "The Cost of Capital, Corporation Finance and the Theory of Investment," *American Economic Review* 48, no. 3 (1958): 261–297.

Managerial Implications

The conservation of value principle is so useful because it tells what to look for when analyzing whether some action will create value: the cash flow impact and nothing else. This principle applies across a wide range of important business decisions, such as accounting policy (Chapter 16), acquisitions (Chapter 21), corporate portfolio decisions (Chapter 19), dividend payout policy (Chapter 23), and capital structure (also Chapter 23). In this section, we provide three examples of useful applications for the conservation of value principle: share repurchases, acquisitions, and financial engineering.

Share repurchases   Share repurchases have become a popular way for companies to return cash to investors (see Chapter 23 for more detail). Until the early 1980s, more than 90 percent of the total distributions by large U.S. companies to shareholders were dividends, and fewer than 10 percent were share repurchases, but since 1998, about 50 to 60 percent of total distributions have been share repurchases.[13]

To determine whether share repurchases create value, you must compare them with some other use of the cash. For example, assume that a company borrows $100 to repurchase 10 percent of its shares. For every $100 of shares repurchased, the company will pay, say, 6 percent interest on its new debt. After tax savings of 35 percent, its total earnings would decline by $3.90. However, the number of shares has declined by 10 percent, so earnings per share (EPS) would increase by about 5 percent.

A 5 percent increase in EPS without working very hard sounds like a great deal. Assuming the company's price-to-earnings (P/E) ratio doesn't change, then its market value per share will also increase by 5 percent. In other words, you can get something for nothing: higher EPS with a constant P/E.

Unfortunately, this doesn't square with the conservation of value, because the total cash flow of the business has not increased. While EPS has increased by 5 percent, the company's debt has increased as well. With higher leverage, the company's equity cash flows will be more volatile, and investors will demand a higher return. This will bring down the company's P/E, offsetting the increase in EPS.

However, even if cash flow isn't increased by a buyback, some have rightly argued that repurchasing shares can reduce the likelihood that management will invest the cash at low returns. If this is true, and it is likely that management would otherwise have invested the money unwisely, then you have a legitimate source of value creation, because the operating cash flows of the company would increase. Said another way, when the likelihood of investing cash at low returns is high, share repurchases make sense as a tactic for avoiding value destruction. But they don't in themselves create value.

---

[13] Michael J. Mauboussin, "Clear Thinking about Share Repurchases," Legg Mason Capital Management, *Mauboussin on Strategy*, 2006.

Some argue that management should repurchase shares when its shares are undervalued. Suppose management believes that the current share price of the company doesn't reflect its underlying potential, so it buys back shares today. One year later, the market price adjusts to reflect management's expectations. Has value been created? Once again the answer is no, value has not been created; it has only been shifted from one set of shareholders (those that sold) to the shareholders that did not sell. So the holding shareholders may have benefited, but the shareholders as a whole were not affected. Buying shares when they are undervalued may be good for the shareholders who don't sell, but studies of share repurchases have shown that companies aren't very good at timing share repurchases, often buying when their share prices are high, not low.

Executives as a rule need to exercise caution when presented with transactions (like share repurchases) that appear to create value by boosting EPS. Always ask, "Where is the source of the value creation?" Some R&D–intensive companies, for example, have searched for ways to capitalize R&D spending through complex joint ventures, hoping to lower R&D expenses that reduce EPS. But does the joint venture create value by increasing short-term EPS? No, and in fact it may destroy value because the company now transfers upside potential—and risk, of course—to its partners.

Acquisitions Chapter 21 covers acquisitions in more detail, but for now we can say that acquisitions create value only when the combined cash flows of the two companies increase due to cost reductions, accelerated revenue growth, or better use of fixed and working capital.

When Johnson & Johnson purchased Pfizer's consumer health business for $16 billion in late 2006, J&J immediately announced that the combination would reduce costs by $600 million per year. These savings were successfully realized and increased the combined operating profits of J&J/Pfizer's consumer businesses by 30 percent—equal to about $5 billion to $6 billion in present value. Taking these numbers, then, the cost savings of the merger alone would recoup one-third of the purchase price, making it a likely value creator.

A revenue acceleration example also comes from Johnson & Johnson, which acquired Neutrogena (maker of skin care products) in 1994 for $924 million. With new-product development, coupled with an expansion of the brand's presence outside the United States, J&J was able to increase Neutrogena's sales from $281 million to $778 million by 2002. Exhibit 2.7 shows the extent of the new products J&J introduced under the Neutrogena brand.

The common element of both these acquisitions was radical performance improvement, not marginal change. But sometimes we have seen acquisitions justified by what could only be called magic.

Assume, for example, that Company A is worth $100 and Company B is worth $50, based on their respective expected cash flows. Company A buys Company B for $50, issuing its own shares. For simplicity, assume that the

EXHIBIT 2.7 **How Johnson & Johnson Turbocharged Neutrogena's Growth**

Product launches	Launch year		
	1994–1996	**1997–1999**	**2000–2002**
Men			• Complete men's product line
Cosmetics			• "Dermatologist Developed" line with 85+ SKUs
Hair products		• New line under "Clean" sub-brand	
Sun protection	• No-stick sunscreen • SPF hand treatment	• Transparent sunscreen	• Healthy Defense brand
Body care	• Rainbath brand (relaunch) • Norwegian Formula foot cream brand	• Body Clear brand	
Facial care			
Acne	• On-the-Spot brand acne treatment	• Multivitamin acne treatment • Oil-free acne treatment	
Moisturizers	• Healthy Skin Care brand	• Light night moisturizer products	• Visibly Firm brand
Cleansers	• Clear Pore treatment • Deep Clean, Deep Pore brands	• Extra Gentle brand • Pore Refining brand	• SkinClearing brand

Source: McKinsey Corporate Performce Center analysis.

combined cash flows are not expected to increase. What is the new Company AB worth?

Immediately after the acquisition, the two companies are the same as they were before, with the same expected cash flows, and the original shareholders of the two companies still own the shares of the combined company. So Company AB should be worth $150, and the original A shareholders' shares of AB should be worth $100, while the original B shareholders' shares of AB should be worth $50.

As simple as this seems, some executives and financial professionals will still see some extra value in the transaction. Assume that Company A is expected to earn $5 next year, so its P/E is 20 times. Company B is expected to earn $3 next year, so its P/E is 16.7 times. What then will be the P/E of Company AB? A straightforward approach suggests that the value of Company AB should remain $150. Its earnings will be $8, so its P/E will be about 18.8, between A's and B's P/Es. But here's where the magic happens. Many executives and bankers believe that once A buys B, the stock market will apply A's P/E of 20 to B's earnings. In other words, B's earnings are worth more once they are owned by A. By this thinking, the value of Company AB would be $160, a $10 increase in the combined value.

There is even a term for this: "multiple expansion" in the United States or "rerating" in the United Kingdom. The notion is that the multiple of Company B's earnings expands to the level of Company A's because the market doesn't recognize that perhaps the new earnings added to A are not as valuable. This must be so, because B's earnings will now be all mixed up with A's, and the market won't be able to tell the difference.

Another version of the multiple expansion illusion works the other way around, supposing Company B purchases Company A. We've heard the argument that since a lower–P/E company is buying a higher–P/E company, it must be getting into higher-growth businesses. Higher growth is generally good, so another theory postulates that because B is accelerating its growth, its P/E will increase.

If multiple expansion were true, all acquisitions would create value because the P/E on the lower–P/E company's earnings would rise to that of the company with the higher P/E, regardless of which was the buyer or seller. But no data exist that support this fallacy. Multiple expansion may sound great, but it is an entirely unsound way of justifying an acquisition that doesn't have tangible benefits.

Every corporate leader must know this. So why are we discussing such obvious fallacies? The answer is that companies often do justify acquisitions using this flawed logic. Our alternative approach is simple: if you can't point to specific sources of increased cash flow, the stock market won't be fooled.

Financial engineering   Another area where the value conservation principle is important is financial engineering, which unfortunately has no standard definition. Cornell University offers a concentration in financial engineering, which it calls "the design, analysis, and construction of financial contracts to meet the needs of enterprises." For our purposes, we define financial engineering a bit more broadly as the use of financial instruments or structures, other than straight debt and equity, to manage a company's capital structure and risk profile.

Financial engineering can include the use of derivatives, structured debt, securitization, and off–balance-sheet financing. While some of these activities can create real value, most don't. Even so, the motivation to engage in non–value-added financial engineering remains strong because of its short-term, illusory impact.

Consider that many of the largest hotel companies in the United States don't own most of the hotels they operate. Instead, the hotels themselves are owned by other companies, often structured as partnerships or real estate investment trusts (REITs). Unlike corporations, partnerships and REITs don't pay U.S. income taxes; taxes are paid only by their owners. Therefore, an entire layer of taxation is eliminated by placing hotels in partnerships and REITs in the United States. This method of separating ownership and operations lowers total income taxes paid to the government, so investors in the ownership and

EXHIBIT 2.8 **Cash Flows Related to Collateralized Debt Obligations**

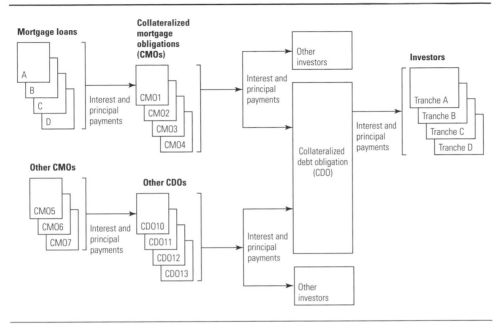

operating companies are better off as a group, because their aggregate cash flows are higher. This is an example of financial engineering that adds real value by increasing cash flows.

In contrast, as an example of questionable financial engineering, consider the collateralized debt obligations (CDOs) that contributed to the 2007–2009 financial crisis. This is the story of how a good idea taken too far almost destroyed the financial markets.

Here's how a CDO works. The sponsor of a CDO (typically a bank) creates a new legal entity called a special-purpose vehicle (SPV) that buys up a lot of loans. These loans can be corporate loans, mortgage loans, or even other CDOs. The new legal entity then issues debt securities that will be paid off by the cash flows from the loans in the SPV's portfolio.

Exhibit 2.8 illustrates the cash flows related to a CDO. Reading from left to right in the top portion of the exhibit, individual homeowners pay interest and principal to their mortgage servicer, which forwards it to an SPV that has issued collateralized mortgage obligations (CMOs). That entity pays interest and principal to its investors, which could include a CDO entity that, in turn, pays principal and interest to the various CDO investors. But the total cash flows received by the investors cannot be more than they would receive if they directly owned the loans and securities; in fact, due to fees and transaction costs, the total cash flow to the CDO holders must be lower than the cash flows from the underlying loans.

One key benefit of a CDO is that it allows banks to remove assets from their balance sheets by selling them to investors (through the CDO), thereby freeing up some of the banks' equity capital to make new loans. Making more loans, with their associated transaction fees, increases the banks' cash flows. CDOs worked well for over 20 years, doing exactly what they were intended to do. The early CDOs were pools of home mortgages that allowed banks to originate loans and then take them off their books so they could originate more loans.

But the CDOs issued in 2005 and 2006 were different and fundamentally flawed. Unlike the early CDOs, the new ones were exceptionally complex and nontransparent. For instance, new CDOs might include slices of CDOs already issued, creating nested products as interwoven as an M. C. Escher drawing (as shown in Exhibit 2.8). Even the most sophisticated investors and banks couldn't assess their risks. Instead, they relied on the rating agencies to grade the securities, because rating agencies have access to more information about credit products than investors do. The problem was that the rating agencies earned large fees from the banks (both sellers and buyers of CDOs) for their ratings, and they didn't want the banks to take their business elsewhere. With no money of their own at stake, the rating agencies pronounced many of these securities AAA or AA, the safest securities. In this elaborate process, pools of risky subprime loans came to be deemed AAA-rated securities. But that violated the conservation of value principle: the actual risks and cash flows attached to subprime loans hadn't changed at all, so the total risk of the CDOs could not have been reduced by the securitization process.

When homeowners with subprime mortgages started to miss payments in 2006 and to default, housing prices fell. Investors then realized that the CDOs and CMOs were riskier than they had thought, so they rushed to sell their stakes. The CDOs and CMOs became impossible to sell. However, investors and banks that owned these securities had often financed them with short-term debt that had to be renewed every month or quarter (or sometimes daily). Their creditors, seeing that the value of their collateral (the CDOs and CMOs) had dropped, would not refinance the short-term debt as it came due. The banks and the investors holding the CDOs had no other options but to sell the assets at fire-sale prices, go out of business, or get a government bailout.

You might ask why the banks were so exposed: wasn't the idea that they were just creating these CDOs, not actually investing in them? But they *were* investing. Indeed, when the market turned, the banks were caught with three types of risky inventory: loans they hadn't yet been able to package into CDOs and securitize; the riskiest tranches of CDOs, which they hadn't been able to sell after creating them; and long-term CDOs they had bought themselves because they believed they could finance these CDOs with cheap short-term debt and make a profit.

Banks sometimes marketed CDOs by proposing that they created additional investment opportunities for investors. However, this argument doesn't hold up to scrutiny. The claim was that investors liked CDOs because they yielded higher returns than other similarly rated securities. In other words, the yield on an AA-rated CDO was higher than an AA-rated corporate bond. But if these CDOs were rated the same as corporate bonds, why did they have higher yields? The answer, which we know from hindsight, is that they were riskier—and the market knew they were riskier, even if the rating agencies didn't. The market saw through the illusion.

RISK AND VALUE CREATION

A company's future cash flows are unknown and therefore risky, so to complete our discussion of value creation, we need to explain how risk affects value. Risk enters into valuation both through the company's cost of capital, which is the price of risk, and in the uncertainty surrounding future cash flows. Managers and investors need to pay particularly close attention to cash flow risks.

Price of Risk

The cost of capital is the price charged by investors for bearing the risk that the company's future cash flows may differ from what they anticipate when they make the investment. The cost of capital to a company equals the minimum return that investors expect to earn from investing in the company. That is why the terms *expected return to investors* and *cost of capital* are essentially the same. The cost of capital is also called the discount rate, because you discount future cash flows at this rate when calculating the present value of an investment, to reflect what you will have to pay investors.

The average cost of equity capital, or the price investors charged for their risk, in late 2009 for a large nonfinancial company was about 9 percent, and most large companies' costs of equity capital fell in the range of 8 to 10 percent. That range can seem narrow, given that it encompasses companies with predictable cash flows like Campbell Soup and highly volatile companies like Google. The range is small because investors purposely avoid putting all their eggs in one basket.

Stock market investors, especially institutional investors, typically have hundreds of different stocks in their portfolios; even the most concentrated investors have at least 50. As a result, their exposure to any single company is limited. Exhibit 2.9 shows what happens to the total risk of a portfolio of stocks as more shares are added to the portfolio. The total risk declines because companies' cash flows are not correlated. Some will increase when others decline.

One of the key insights of academic finance that has stood the test of time concerns the effect of diversification on the cost of capital. If diversification reduces risk to investors and it is not costly to diversify, then investors will not demand a return for any risks they take that they can easily eliminate through diversification. They require compensation only for risks they cannot diversify.

EXHIBIT 2.9 **Volatility of Portfolio Return: Declining with Diversification**

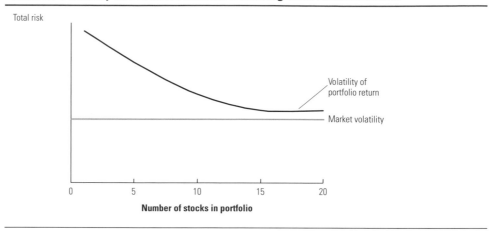

The risks they cannot diversify are those that affect all companies—for example, exposure to economic cycles. However, since most of the risks that companies face are in fact diversifiable, most risks don't affect a company's cost of capital. One way to see this in practice is to note the fairly narrow range of P/Es for large companies. Most large companies have P/Es between 12 and 20. If the cost of capital varied from 6 to 15 percent instead of 8 to 10 percent, many more companies would have P/Es below 8 and above 25.

Whether a company's cost of capital is 8 percent or 10 percent or somewhere in between is a question of great dispute (the cost of capital is discussed in more detail in Chapter 11). For decades, the standard model for measuring differences in costs of capital has been the capital asset pricing model (CAPM). The CAPM has been challenged by academics and practitioners, but so far, no practical competing model has emerged. Anyway, when returns on capital across companies vary from less than 5 percent to more than 30 percent, a one or two percentage point difference in the cost of capital seems hardly worth arguing about.

General risk affecting all companies may be priced into the cost of capital, but that does not mean executives do not need to worry about risk. The unique risks that any particular company faces of, say, running into business trouble or, even worse, bankruptcy (which clearly destroys shareholder value) are not priced into the cost of capital. Companies certainly do need to worry about the effects of such unique risk on the total cash flows from any potential investment.

Cash Flow Risk

The risk that companies must identify and manage is their cash flow risk, meaning uncertainty about their future cash flows. Finance theory is, for the most part, silent about how much cash flow risk a company should take on.

In practice, however, managers need to be aware that calculating expected cash flows can obscure material risks capable of jeopardizing their business when they are deciding how much cash flow risk to accept. They also need to manage any risks affecting cash flows that investors are unable to mitigate for themselves.

Deciding how much cash flow risk to take on   What should companies look out for? Consider an example. Project A requires an up-front investment of $2,000. If everything goes well with the project, the company earns $1,000 per year forever. If not, the company gets zero. (Such all-or-nothing projects are not unusual.) To value project A, finance theory directs you to discount the expected cash flow at the cost of capital. But what is the expected cash flow in this case? If there is a 60 percent chance of everything going well, the expected cash flows would be $600 per year. At a 10 percent cost of capital, the project would be worth $6,000 once completed. Subtracting the $2,000 investment, the net value of the project before the investment is made is $4,000.

But the project will never generate $600 per year. It will generate annual cash flows of either $1,000 or zero. That means the present value of the discounted cash flows will be either $10,000 or nothing, making the project net of the initial investment worth either $8,000 or –$2,000. The probability of it being worth the expected value of $4,000 ($6,000 less the investment) is zero. Rather than knowing the expected value, managers would be better off knowing that the project carries a 60 percent chance of being worth $8,000 and a 40 percent risk of losing $2,000. Managers can then examine the scenarios under which each outcome prevails and decide whether the upside compensates for the downside, whether the company can comfortably absorb the potential loss, and whether they can take actions to reduce the magnitude or risk of loss. The theoretical approach of focusing on expected values, while mathematically correct, hides some important information about the range and exclusivity of particular outcomes.

Moreover, some companies don't apply the expected-value approach correctly. Few companies discuss multiple scenarios, preferring a single-point forecast on which to base a yes-or-no decision. So most companies would simply represent the expected cash flows from this project as being $1,000 per year, the amount if everything goes well, and allow for uncertainty in the cash flow by arbitrarily increasing the discount rate. While you can get to the "right" answer with this approach, it has two flaws. First, there is no easy way to determine the cost of capital that gives the correct value. In this case, using a 16.7 percent cost of capital instead of 10 percent results in a project value of $6,000 before the investment and $4,000 after the investment, but the only way to know that this was the correct value would be to conduct a thorough scenario analysis. Companies sometimes arbitrarily add a risk premium to the cost of capital, but there is no way for them to know whether the amount they add is even reasonably accurate. Second, the decision makers faced with a project with cash flows of $1,000 per year and a 16.7 percent cost of capital are still not thinking through the 40 percent risk that it generates no cash at all.

How should a company think through whether to undertake the project with an upside of $8,000, a downside of –$2,000 and an expected value of $4,000? Theory says take on all projects with a positive expected value, regardless of the upside-versus-downside risk. But following the theory could be problematic.

What if the downside possibility would bankrupt the company? Consider an electric power company with the opportunity to build a nuclear power facility for $15 billion (not unrealistic in 2009 for a facility with two reactors). Suppose the company has $25 billion in existing debt and $25 billion in equity market capitalization. If the plant is successfully constructed and brought on line, it will be worth $28 billion. But there is a 20 percent chance it will fail to receive regulatory approval and be worth zero. As a single project, the expected value is $22 billion, or $7 billion net of investment. Another way to put this is that there is an 80 percent chance the project will be worth $13 billion ($28 billion less $15 billion investment) and a 20 percent chance it will be worth –$15 billion. Furthermore, failure will bankrupt the company, because the cash flow from the company's existing plants will be insufficient to cover its existing debt plus the debt on the failed plant. In this case, the economics of the nuclear plant spill over onto the value of the rest of the company. Failure will wipe out all the equity of the company, not just the $15 billion invested in the plant.

We can extend the theory to say that a company should not take on a risk that will put the rest of the company in danger. In other words, don't do anything that has large negative spillover effects on the rest of the company. This caveat would be enough to guide managers in the earlier example of deciding whether to go ahead with project A. If a $2,000 loss would endanger the company as a whole, they should forgo the project, despite its 60 percent likelihood of success. But by the same token, companies should not try to reduce risks that don't threaten the company's ability to operate normally. For example, profitable companies with modest amounts of debt should not worry about interest rate risk, because it won't be large enough to threaten to disrupt the business.

Deciding which types of risk to hedge   There are also risks that investors positively want companies to take. For example, investors in gold-mining companies and oil production companies buy those stocks to gain exposure to often-volatile gold or oil prices. If gold and oil companies attempt to hedge their revenues, that effort merely complicates life for their investors, who then have to guess how much price risk is being hedged and how and whether management will change its policy in the future. Moreover, hedging may lock in today's prices for two years, the time horizon within which it is possible to hedge those commodities, but a company's present value includes the cash flows from subsequent years at fluctuating market prices. So while hedging may reduce the short-term cash flow volatility, it will have little effect on the company's valuation based on long-term cash flows.

Some risks, like the commodity price risk in the earlier example of gold and oil companies, can be managed by shareholders themselves. Other, similar-looking risks—for example, some forms of currency risk—are harder for shareholders to generalize. The general rule is to avoid hedging the first type of risk, but hedge the second if you can.

Consider the effect of currency risk on Heineken, the global brewer. Heineken produces its flagship brand, Heineken, in the Netherlands, and ships it around the world, especially to the United States. Most other large brewers, in contrast, produce most of their beer in the same national markets in which they sell it. So for most brewers, an exchange rate change affects only the translation of their profits into their reporting currency. For example, a 1 percent change in the value of the currency of one of their non-home markets translates into a 1 percent change in revenues from those markets and a 1 percent change in profits as well. Note that the effect on revenues and profits is the same, because all the revenues and costs are in the same currency. There is no change in operating margin.

Heineken's picture is different. Consider Heineken's sales in the United States. When the exchange rate changes, Heineken's revenues in euros are affected, but not its costs. If the dollar declines by 1 percent, Heineken's euro revenues also decline by 1 percent. But since its costs are in euros, they don't change. Assuming a 10 percent margin to begin with, a 1 percent decline in the dollar will reduce Heineken's margin to 9 percent, and its profits reported in euros will decline by a whopping 10 percent.

Because Heineken's production facilities are in a different country and it is unable to pass on cost increases because it is competing with locally produced products, its foreign exchange risk is much larger than that of other global brewers. Hedging might be critical to Heineken's survival, while the other global brewers probably would not benefit from hedging, because the impact of exchange rate changes on their business is not material.

THE MATH OF VALUE CREATION

The chapters in Part Two provide a step-by-step guide for analyzing and valuing a company in practice, including how to measure and interpret the drivers of value, ROIC, and revenue growth. As a bridge between the theoretical explanation of those drivers provided earlier in this chapter and the practical guidance to come in Part Two, we introduce here the key value driver formula, a simple equation that captures the essence of valuation in practice. We first introduce some terminology that we will use throughout the book (the terms are defined in detail in Part Two):

- *Net operating profit less adjusted taxes (NOPLAT)* represents the profits generated from the company's core operations after subtracting the income taxes related to the core operations.
- *Invested capital* represents the cumulative amount the business has invested in its core operations—primarily property, plant, and equipment and working capital.
- *Net investment* is the increase in invested capital from one year to the next:

$$\text{Net Investment} = \text{Invested Capital}_{t+1} - \text{Invested Capital}_t$$

- *Free cash flow (FCF)* is the cash flow generated by the core operations of the business after deducting investments in new capital:

$$\text{FCF} = \text{NOPLAT} - \text{Net Investment}$$

- *Return on invested capital (ROIC)* is the return the company earns on each dollar invested in the business:

$$\text{ROIC} = \frac{\text{NOPLAT}}{\text{Invested Capital}}$$

(ROIC can be defined in two ways, as the return on all capital or as the return on new or incremental capital. For now, we assume that both returns are the same.)

- *Investment rate (IR)* is the portion of NOPLAT invested back into the business:

$$\text{IR} = \frac{\text{Net Investment}}{\text{NOPLAT}}$$

- *Weighted average cost of capital (WACC)* is the rate of return that investors expect to earn from investing in the company and therefore the appropriate discount rate for the free cash flow. WACC is defined in detail in Chapter 11.
- *Growth (g)* is the rate at which the company's NOPLAT and cash flow grow each year.

Assume that the company's revenues and NOPLAT grow at a constant rate and the company invests the same proportion of its NOPLAT in its business each year. Investing the same proportion of NOPLAT each year also means that the company's free cash flow will grow at a constant rate.

Since the company's cash flows are growing at a constant rate, we can begin by valuing a company using the well-known cash flow perpetuity formula:

$$\text{Value} = \frac{\text{FCF}_{t=1}}{\text{WACC} - g}$$

This formula is well established in the finance and mathematics literature.[14]

Next, define free cash flow in terms of NOPLAT and the investment rate:

$$\text{FCF} = \text{NOPLAT} - \text{Net Investment}$$
$$= \text{NOPLAT} - (\text{NOPLAT} \times \text{IR})$$
$$= \text{NOPLAT}(1 - \text{IR})$$

Earlier, we developed the relationship between the investment rate (IR), the company's projected growth in NOPLAT (g), and the return on investment (ROIC):[15]

$$g = \text{ROIC} \times \text{IR}$$

Solving for IR, rather than g, leads to

$$\text{IR} = \frac{g}{\text{ROIC}}$$

Now build this into the definition of free cash flow:

$$\text{FCF} = \text{NOPLAT} \left(1 - \frac{g}{\text{ROIC}}\right)$$

Substituting for free cash flow gives the key value driver formula:

$$\text{Value} = \frac{\text{NOPLAT}_{t=1} \left(1 - \frac{g}{\text{ROIC}}\right)}{\text{WACC} - g}$$

This formula underpins the DCF approach to valuation, and a variant of the equation lies behind the economic-profit approach. These two mathematically equivalent valuation techniques are described in detail in Chapter 6.

---

[14] For the derivation, see T. E. Copeland and J. Fred Weston, *Financial Theory and Corporate Policy*, 3rd ed. (Reading, MA: Addison Wesley, 1988), Appendix A.
[15] Technically, we should use the return on new, or incremental, capital, but for simplicity here, we assume that the ROIC and incremental ROIC are equal.

Substituting the forecast assumptions for Value Inc. and Volume Inc. in Exhibit 2.2 into the key value driver formula results in the same values we came up with when we discounted their cash flows:

Company	NOPLAT$_{t=1}$	Growth (percent)	ROIC (percent)	WACC (percent)	Value
Volume Inc.	100	5	10	10	1,000
Value Inc.	100	5	20	10	1,500

We call the key value driver formula the "Tao of corporate finance" because it relates a company's value to the fundamental drivers of economic value: growth, ROIC, and the cost of capital. You might go so far as to say that this formula represents all there is to valuation. Everything else is mere detail.

However, in most cases, we do not use this formula in practice. The reason is that in most situations, the model is overly restrictive, as it assumes a constant ROIC and growth rate going forward. For companies whose key value drivers are expected to change, we need a model that is more flexible in its forecasts. Nevertheless, while we do not use this formula in practice, it is extremely useful as a way to keep the mind focused on what drives value.

Until now, we have concentrated on how ROIC and growth drive the discounted cash flow (DCF) valuation. We can also use the key value driver formula to show that ROIC and growth determine multiples commonly used to analyze company valuation, such as price-to-earnings and market-to-book ratios. To see this, divide both sides of the key value driver formula by NOPLAT:

$$\frac{\text{Value}}{\text{NOPLAT}_{t=1}} = \frac{\left(1 - \frac{g}{\text{ROIC}}\right)}{\text{WACC} - g}$$

As the formula shows, a company's earnings multiple is driven by both its expected growth and its return on invested capital.

You can also turn the formula into a value-to-invested-capital formula. Start with the identity:

$$\text{NOPLAT} = \text{Invested Capital} \times \text{ROIC}$$

Substitute this definition of NOPLAT into the key value driver formula:

$$\text{Value} = \frac{\text{Invested Capital} \times \text{ROIC} \times \left(1 - \frac{g}{\text{ROIC}}\right)}{\text{WACC} - g}$$

Divide both sides by invested capital:[16]

$$\frac{\text{Value}}{\text{Invested Capital}} = \text{ROIC} \left(\frac{1 - \dfrac{g}{\text{ROIC}}}{\text{WACC} - g} \right)$$

Now that we have explained the logic behind the DCF approach to valuation, you may wonder why analysts' reports and investment banking pitches so often use earnings multiples, rather than valuations based on DCF analysis. The answer is partly that earnings multiples are a useful shorthand for communicating values to a wider public. A leading sell-side analyst recently told us that he uses discounted cash flow to analyze and value companies but typically communicates his findings in terms of implied multiples. For example, an analyst might say Company X deserves a higher multiple than Company Y because it is expected to grow faster, earn higher margins, or generate more cash flow. Earnings multiples are also a useful sanity check for your valuation. In practice, we always compare a company's implied multiple based on our valuation with those of its peers to see if we can explain why its multiple is higher or lower in terms of its ROIC or growth rates. See Chapter 14 for a discussion of how to analyze earnings multiples.

SUMMARY

This chapter showed that value is driven by expected cash flows discounted at a cost of capital. Cash flow, in turn, is driven by expected returns on invested capital and revenue growth. The corollary is that any management action that does not increase cash flow does not create value. These are the principal lessons of valuation and corporate finance. Although finance theory has little to say on how to approach cash flow risk, in practice managers' and investors' valuations also need to take account of any risks attached to cash flows that shareholders cannot manage for themselves. The concepts governing the theory of valuation based on discounted cash flows are expressed mathematically in the key value driver formula.

---

[16] If total ROIC and incremental ROIC are not the same, then this equation becomes

$$\frac{\text{Value}}{\text{Invested Capital}} = \text{ROIC} \left(\frac{1 - \dfrac{g}{\text{RONIC}}}{\text{WACC} - g} \right)$$

where ROIC equals the return on the company's current capital and RONIC equals the return on incremental capital.

REVIEW QUESTIONS

1. How does return on invested capital (ROIC) affect a company's cash flow? Explain the relationship between ROIC, growth, and cash flow.

2. If value is based on discounted cash flows, why should a company or investor analyze growth and ROIC?

3. Under what circumstances does growth destroy value?

4. Which type of business, a software company or an electric utility, would benefit more from improving ROIC than from increasing growth? Why?

5. Why does organic growth often create more value than growth from acquisitions? Describe how different types of organic growth might create different amounts of value.

6. What is the conservation of value principle? Provide some examples of where it might apply.

7. Under what circumstances would changing a company's capital structure affect its value?

8. What is financial engineering? When does it create value?

9. Apply the conservation of value principle to acquisitions.

10. How do diversifiable and nondiversifiable risks affect a company's cost of capital?

11. How should a company decide which risks to hold and which to hedge?

12. How much cash flow risk should a company take on? How should it manage risks with extreme outcomes that could potentially bankrupt the company but are very unlikely to occur?

3

The Expectations
Treadmill

The performance of a company and that of its management are frequently measured by total returns to shareholders (TRS). This measure combines the amount shareholders gain through any increase in the share price over a given period with the sum of dividends paid to them over the period. That sounds like a good idea: if managers focus on improving TRS to win performance bonuses, then their interests and the interests of their shareholders should be aligned. The evidence shows that this is indeed true over very long periods of more than 10 years at least. But TRS measured over periods shorter than 10 years may not reflect the actual performance of a company and its management for two main reasons.

First, improving TRS is much harder for managers leading an already successful company than for those leading a company with substantial room for improvement. The reason is that a company's progress toward performance leadership in any market will attract investors expecting more of the same, pushing up the share price. Managers then have to pull off herculean feats of real performance improvement to satisfy those expectations and continue improving TRS. We call their predicament the "expectations treadmill." Clearly, managers' capacity to influence TRS depends heavily on their business's position in the cycle of shareholder expectations, from start-up to maturity. But this position is beyond their control, making TRS in isolation an unfair measure of their performance.

Second, when TRS is analyzed in the traditional way, it doesn't show the extent to which improvements in operating performance contributed to the measure as a whole. However, improved operations constitute the only part of the measure that creates long-term value and is also within management control.

The widespread use of traditional TRS as a measure of management per-formance therefore creates perverse incentives. Managers running full tilt on the expectations treadmill may be tempted to pursue lightweight ideas that give an immediate bump to their TRS. But they will likely realize such ideas at the expense of more solid investments that would yield greater value for share-holders over the long term, despite a short-term hit to TRS. In addition, TRS may rise or fall across the board for all companies because of external factors beyond managers' control, such as changing interest rates. Strictly speaking, such factors should play no part in managers' compensation.

This chapter starts by explaining the expectations treadmill and then ex-amines the mechanics of TRS, linking them to the core principles of value creation. We propose a more fundamental approach to analyzing TRS that iso-lates the amount dependent on improvements in return on invested capital (ROIC) and revenue growth—the true drivers of value creation, as we saw in Chapters 1 and 2. Managers, boards of directors, and investors can learn much more about company performance from this more granular decomposi-tion of TRS. The chapter underlines the importance to investors and managers of understanding the expectations treadmill so they can continue to support investments that will create value for shareholders in the long term, despite their possible negative effects on TRS in the short run. The chapter ends by showing how traditional TRS *can* work as a performance measure, but only in comparison with the TRS performance of a company's peers in its sector.

WHY SHAREHOLDER EXPECTATIONS BECOME A TREADMILL

The return on capital that a company earns is not the same as the return earned by every shareholder. Suppose a company can invest $1,000 in a factory and earn $200 a year, which it pays out in dividends to its shareholders. The first investors in the company pay $1,000 in total for their shares, and if they hold the shares, they will earn 20 percent per year ($200 divided by $1,000).

Suppose that after one year, all the investors decide to sell their shares, and they find buyers who pay $2,000 for the lot. The buyers will earn only 10 percent per year on their investment ($200 divided by $2,000). The first investors will earn a 120 percent return ($200 dividends plus $1,000 gain on their shares versus their initial investment of $1,000). So the company's return on capital is 20 percent, while one group of investors earns 120 percent, and the other group earns 10 percent. All the investors collectively will earn, on a time-weighted average, the same return as the company. But individual groups of investors will earn very different returns, because they pay different prices for the shares, based on their expectations of future performance.

One way of understanding the effects of this dynamic is through the anal-ogy of a treadmill, the speed of which represents the expectations built into a company's share price. If the company beats expectations, and if the market believes the improvement is sustainable, the company's stock price goes up, in essence capitalizing the future value of this incremental improvement. This improves TRS. But it also means that managers have to run even faster just to maintain the new stock price, let alone improve it further: the speed of the treadmill quickens as performance improves. So a company with low expectations of success among shareholders at the beginning of a period may have an easier time outperforming the stock market simply because low expectations are easier to beat.

The treadmill analogy is useful because it describes the difficulty of continuing to outperform the stock market. At some point, it becomes impossible for management to deliver on accelerating expectations without faltering, just as anyone would eventually stumble on a treadmill that kept getting faster.

Consider the case of Theresa Turnaround, a fictional character based on the experience of many CEOs we know. Theresa has just been hired as the CEO of Prospectus, a company with below-average returns on capital and growth relative to competitors. Because of this past performance, the market doesn't expect much, so the value of Prospectus is low relative to competitors. Theresa hires a top-notch team and gets to work. After two years, Prospectus is gaining ground on its peers in margins and return on capital, and market share is rising. Prospectus's stock price rises twice as fast as its peers' because the market wasn't expecting the company's turnaround.

Theresa and her team continue their hard work. After two more years, Prospectus has become the industry leader in operating performance, with the highest return on capital. Because of its low starting point, the company's share price has risen at four times the rate of the industry average. Given Prospectus's new trajectory and consistent performance, the market expects continued above-average returns on capital and revenue growth.

As time goes by, Prospectus maintains its high return on capital and leading market share. But two years later, Theresa notes with frustration that her company's shares are now doing no better than those of its peers, even though the company has outperformed rivals. At this point, Theresa is trapped on the expectations treadmill: she and her team have done such a good job that the expectation of continued high performance is already incorporated into the company's share price. As long as her company delivers results in line with the market's expectations, its share price performance will be no better or worse than average.[1]

This explains why extraordinary managers may deliver only ordinary TRS: even for the extraordinary manager, it can be extremely difficult to keep beating high expectations. It also explains why managers of companies with low performance expectations might easily earn a high TRS, at least for a short time. They can create a higher TRS by delivering performance that raises shareholder expectations to the level of those of their peers in the sector.

---

[1] Theoretically, if a company's performance exactly matches expectations, its TRS will equal the cost of equity. In practice, however, with continual changes in interest rates, inflation, and economic activity, comparison to the broader market is sometimes preferable.

The danger for companies whose shareholders already have high expectations is that in their quest to achieve above-peer TRS, they may resort to misguided actions, such as pushing for unrealistic earnings growth or pursuing risky major acquisitions. Consider the electric power boom at the end of the 1990s and in the early 2000s. Deregulation led to high hopes for power-generation companies, so deregulated energy producers were spun off from their regulated parents at extremely high valuations. Mirant, for instance, was spun off from Southern Company in October 2000 with a combined equity and debt capitalization of almost $18 billion, a multiple of about 30 times earnings before interest, taxes, and amortization (EBITA)—quite extraordinary for a power-generation company. To justify its value, Mirant expanded aggressively, as did similar companies, investing in power plants in the Bahamas, Brazil, Chile, the United Kingdom, Germany, China, and the Philippines, as well as 14 U.S. states. The debt burden from these investments quickly became too much for Mirant to handle, and the company filed for bankruptcy in July 2003. The expectations treadmill pushed Mirant into taking enormous risks to justify its share price, and it paid the ultimate price.

The expectations treadmill is the dynamic behind the adage that a good company and a good investment may not be the same. In the short term, good companies may not be good investments, because future great performance might already be built into the share price. Smart investors often prefer weaker-performing companies, because they have more upside potential, as the expectations expressed in their lower share prices are easier to beat.

REAL-WORLD EFFECTS OF THE EXPECTATIONS TREADMILL

Wal-Mart and Target are two of the largest retailers in the world, with 2008 sales of $403 billion and $65 billion respectively. From 1995 through 2005, Wal-Mart outperformed Target on the key value drivers, growth and ROIC, but Target's shareholders earned higher returns. Exhibit 3.1 shows the revenue growth and return on invested capital for Wal-Mart and Target, as well as total returns to shareholders (stock price appreciation plus dividends). Wal-Mart's sales grew 13 percent per year, compared with Target's 9 percent, and Wal-Mart also earned a higher ROIC throughout the period. Yet Wal-Mart investors earned an annualized return to shareholders of only 15 percent per year, compared with Target's much higher return of 24 percent per year.

The expectations treadmill explains the mismatch between TRS and the underlying value created by the two companies. Using price-to-earnings ratios (P/Es) as a proxy for market expectations, Wal-Mart's P/E at the beginning of 1995 was 15 times, compared with only 11 for Target (see Exhibit 3.2). By the beginning of 2006, Wal-Mart's P/E had increased slightly to 16 times, while Target caught up with and overtook Wal-Mart, reaching 18 times.

EXHIBIT 3.1 **Wal-Mart vs. Target: Wal-Mart Ahead on Growth, ROIC, Not TRS**

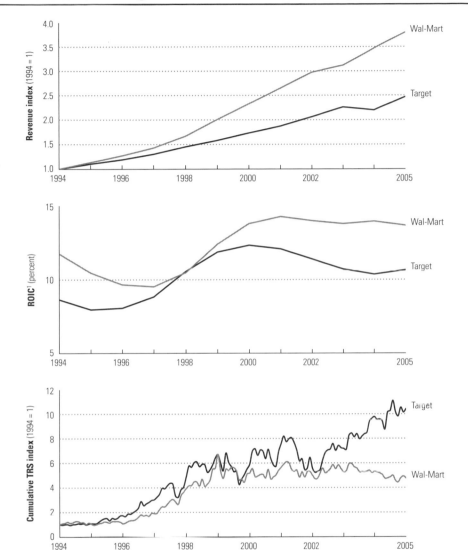

[1] 3-year rolling ROIC without goodwill, adjusted for leases.

Source: McKinsey Corporate Performance Center analysis.

Relative to Wal-Mart, Target was starting from a position of low shareholder expectations. The company's low P/E in 1995 reflected serious concerns about its Mervyn's brand, which was struggling to perform. Target eventually sold its Mervyn's and Marshall Field's brands, after which it beat expectations—thereby raising expectations of its future performance.

Which retailer did a better job? You can make arguments both ways: Target succeeded in turning its business around, and Wal-Mart succeeded in

EXHIBIT 3.2 **Wal-Mart vs. Target: P/E Increase Helps Target's TRS**

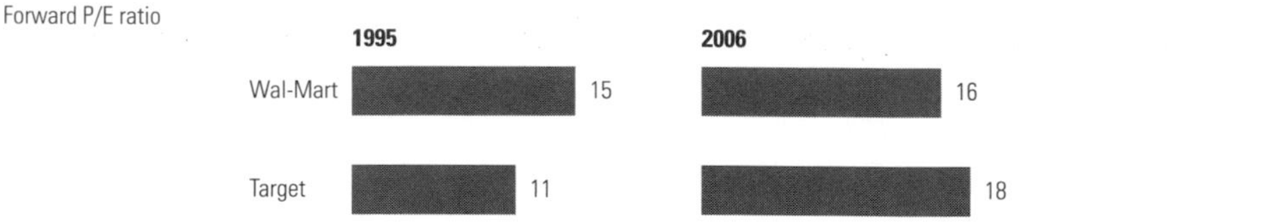

Forward P/E ratio

	1995	2006
Wal-Mart	15	16
Target	11	18

Source: McKinsey Corporate Performance Center analysis.

delivering against very high expectations. TRS might have been a fair measure of the performance of Target's managers, but it would not have reflected what a great job the Wal-Mart team did. For TRS to give deeper insight into a company's true performance, we need a more granular approach to this measure.

DECOMPOSING TRS

Decomposing TRS and quantifying its components in the manner outlined in this section serves two purposes. First, when managers, boards of directors, and investors understand the sources of changes in TRS, they are better able to evaluate management. For example, it's important to know that Wal-Mart's TRS, though lower than Target's, reflected strong underlying performance against high expectations. Second, decomposing TRS can help with setting future targets. For example, Target's managers are unlikely to repeat their high TRS, because that would probably require raising the company's P/E far above the P/Es of Wal-Mart and other strong retailers, an impossible feat.

The traditional approach to analyzing TRS treats the key components as if they were independent of each other. But while this approach is mathematically correct, it does not link TRS to the true underlying sources of value creation. The decomposition we recommend gives managers a clearer understanding of the elements of TRS they can change, those that are beyond their control, and the speed at which their particular expectations treadmill is running. This information helps managers to focus on creating lasting value and communicate to investors and other stakeholders how their plans are likely to affect TRS in the short and long terms.

The traditional approach begins with the definition of TRS as the percent change in share price plus the dividend yield:

TRS = Percent Change in Share Price + Dividend Yield

The change in share price can be expressed as a function of the change in earnings and the change in a company's P/E:[2]

TRS = Percent Increase in Earnings + Percent Change in P/E + Dividend Yield

[2] Technically, there is an additional cross-term, which reflects the interaction of the share price change and the P/E change, but it is generally small, so we ignore it here.

There are a few problems with expressing TRS this way. One is that a manager might assume that all forms of earnings growth create an equal amount of value. Yet we know from Chapter 2 that different sources of earnings growth may create different amounts of value, because each is associated with different returns on capital and therefore generates a different cash flow. For example, growth from acquisitions may reduce future dividends because of the large investments required to make acquisitions.

A second problem is that this approach suggests the dividend yield can be increased without affecting future earnings, as if dividends themselves create value. But dividends are merely a residual. For example, if a company pays a higher dividend today by taking on more debt, that simply means future dividends must be lower. Similarly, if a company manages to pay a higher dividend by forgoing attractive investment opportunities, then future dividends will suffer.

Last, the traditional expression of TRS fails to account for the impact of financial leverage: two companies that create underlying value equally well could generate very different TRS, simply because of the differences in their debt-to-equity ratios and the resulting differences in their risks, which we discuss further later in this section.

For an approach to decomposing TRS that gives clearer insight into how much of the measure derives from changes in operational performance, break up the TRS equation into four parts:

1. The value generated from revenue growth net of the capital required to grow: This figure reflects improvements in margins and capital productivity. It shows how a company's operating performance changes over a given period of time.

2. What TRS would have been without any of the growth measured in part 1: This reflects the company's stock market valuation at the beginning of the measurement period.[3]

3. Changes in shareholders' expectations about the company's performance, measured by the change in its P/E or other earnings multiple.

4. The impact of financial leverage on TRS.

Exhibit 3.3 uses the financials of a hypothetical company to compare the two TRS decomposition approaches. First, using a traditional approach, Company A has a 14.4 percent TRS, based on 7 percent earnings growth, a 3 percent change in the company's P/E (as a proxy for changed expectations), and a 4.4 percent dividend yield. Then, in the column to the right of the traditional approach, we break down the TRS of Company A into the four parts just

---

[3] TRS assuming no growth can also be called the earnings yield, as it is calculated as the inverse of a company's P/E or enterprise-value-to-EBITA ratio.

EXHIBIT 3.3 **Traditional vs. Enhanced TRS Decomposition**

Company A financials			Decomposition of TRS		
$ million	Base year	1 year later	percent	Traditional	Enhanced
Invested capital	100.0	107.0	Growth	7.0	7.0
Earnings	12.5	13.4	Required investment	–	(5.6)
			TRS from performance	7.0	1.4
P/E (multiple)	10.0	10.3			
Equity value	125.0	137.5	Zero-growth return	–	10.0
Dividends	5.0	5.5	Change in P/E	3.0	3.0
			Dividend yield	4.4	–
TRS (percent)	–	14.4	TRS (percent)	14.4	14.4

outlined. This enhanced approach shows that not much of the 14.4 percent TRS reflects the creation of new value. First, the reinvestment required to achieve 7 percent growth in earnings consumed most of the earnings growth itself, leaving TRS arising from performance at only 1.4 percent. Another 3 percent of TRS comes from a change in shareholder expectations (reflected in the P/E multiple increase), rather than performance, and the remaining 10 percent is what the TRS would have been with zero growth and if investors had not changed their expectations.

The next example shows the impact of debt financing on the TRS decomposition. Consider Company B, which is identical to Company A except for its debt financing. As detailed in Exhibit 3.4, the difference in financing means Company B generated a higher TRS of 18 percent. The traditional approach to decomposing TRS suggests that Company B's shareholders benefited from a higher dividend yield and a stronger increase in expectations. However, our more fundamental decomposition of Company B, based on zero-growth returns, growth, and changed expectations measured by the unlevered P/E (enterprise value/earnings), shows that the first three parts of the company's

EXHIBIT 3.4 **Enhancing TRS Decomposition to Uncover Effect of Leverage**

Company B financials			Decomposition of TRS		
$ million	Base year	1 year later	percent	Traditional	Enhanced
Enterprise value	125.0	137.5	Growth	7.0	7.0
Debt[1]	(25.0)	(25.0)	Required investment	–	(5.6)
Equity value	100.0	112.5	TRS from performance	7.0	1.4
P/E (multiple)	8.0	8.4	Zero-growth return	–	10.0
			Change in P/E[2]	5.5	3.0
TRS (percent)	–	18.0	Impact of financial leverage	–	3.6
			Dividend yield	5.5	–
			TRS (percent)	18.0	18.0

[1] Assumes, for illustrative purposes, that debt carries no interest.
[2] Change in P/E multiple for traditional approach vs. change in unlevered P/E multiple in enhanced approach (enterprise value/earnings).

EXHIBIT 3.5 **Wal-Mart vs. Target: TRS Decomposition**

1995–2005, percent annualized

	Target	Wal-Mart	Difference
Revenue growth	9	13	(4)
Investment for growth	(5)	(3)	(2)
Change in margin	4	–	4
TRS from performance	8	10	(2)
Zero-growth return	6	4	2
Change in P/E	5	–	5
Imapct of financial leverage	5	2	3
Other	–	(1)	1
Sum	24	15	9

decomposed TRS are in fact identical to those of Company A. The additional 3.6 percent TRS for Company B arises from the higher proportion of debt in its capital, rather than any newly created value. Adjusting for the higher financial risk associated with higher debt shows that Company B did not in fact create more value than Company A—an important fact for investors and the companies' executives.

Exhibit 3.5 returns to the comparison of Wal-Mart and Target, showing the TRS decomposition for the two retailers. While Target's 24 percent annual TRS was higher than Wal-Mart's 15 percent, Wal-Mart outperformed Target on the fraction of TRS derived from operating performance by achieving 10 percent to Target's 8 percent. Wal-Mart's revenue growth rate of 13 percent was higher than Target's rate of 9 percent, while Target's increasing margin beat Wal-Mart's relatively constant margin. Clearly, better performance in one domain by one company was offset by better performance in another domain by the other company.

Target outperformed Wal-Mart on the expectations and financial leverage components; indeed, these components accounted for 1 percent more than Target's 9 percent overall outperformance on TRS. Target's TRS assuming no future growth was higher than Wal-Mart's by two percentage points, because at the beginning of the measurement period, Target's P/E was only 11, while Wal-Mart's was 15. This would convert to a lower TRS for Wal-Mart even if neither company grew at all and their multiples remained the same. Because investors paid less for a dollar of Target's earnings in 1995, Target's existing (no-growth) earnings generate a higher yield than Wal-Mart's existing earnings.

Target's P/E increased from 11 to 18 times in 2005, generating 5 percent annual TRS, while Wal-Mart's P/E increased only slightly, generating less than 1 percent TRS (rounded to zero), indicating what a powerful boost to TRS rising shareholder expectations can provide when a company is on its way up.

Target had a further three percentage point advantage in TRS due to higher financial leverage. Target used much more debt than Wal-Mart in 1995, with a debt-to-capital ratio of 48 percent, compared with 21 percent for Wal-Mart. But Target's higher leverage in 1995 was probably not sustainable, and in fact, Target eventually reduced its debt substantially.

Leverage has a multiplier effect on TRS relative to underlying economic performance. In other words, because of Target's higher leverage, a 1 percent increase in revenues has a greater impact on Target's profits and share price than the same increase for Wal-Mart has on its share price. As we discuss in Chapter 23, however, greater leverage doesn't necessarily create value, because greater leverage equals greater risk, and greater risk can amplify weaker as well as stronger performance.

The four-part decomposition of shareholder returns can also show what options a company has for achieving higher levels of TRS in the future. For example, at the time of writing, Wal-Mart and Target had similar expectations built into their share prices (based on similar multiples), and those expectations were near the long-term averages for companies sharing their performance characteristics. Therefore, the opportunity to improve future TRS by continuing to increase expectations had already gone for Target, as had the higher-leverage option, since its capital structure had become similar to Wal-Mart's. From this, we can conclude that the TRS differentiators for the two companies over the next several years will mostly be underlying growth and returns on capital.

UNDERSTANDING EXPECTATIONS

As the examples in this chapter have shown, investors' expectations at the beginning and end of the measurement period have a big effect on TRS. A crucial issue for investors and executives to understand, however, is that a company whose TRS has consistently outperformed the market will reach a point where it will no longer be able to satisfy expectations reflected in its share price. From that point, TRS will be lower than it was in the past, even though the company may still be creating huge amounts of value. Managers need to realize and communicate to their boards and to investors that a small decline in TRS is better for shareholders in the long run at this juncture than a desperate attempt to maintain TRS through ill-advised acquisitions or new ventures.

This was arguably the point that Home Depot had reached in 1999. Earlier, we used earnings multiples to express expectations—but you can also translate those multiples into the revenue growth rate and ROIC required to satisfy current shareholder expectations by reverse engineering the share price. Such an exercise can also help managers assess their performance plans and spot any gaps between their likely outcome and the market's expectations. At the beginning of 1999, Home Depot had a market value of $132 billion, with an earnings multiple of 47. Using a discounted cash flow model that assumes constant margins and return on capital, Home Depot would have had to increase revenues by 26 percent per year over the next 15 years to maintain its 1999 share price. Home Depot's actual revenue growth through 2007 averaged 11 percent a year, an impressive number for such a large company but far below the growth required to justify its share price in 1999. It's no surprise, therefore, that Home Depot's shares underperformed the S&P 500 by 7 percent per year over the period.

What should Home Depot's board of directors have done, given its high market value in 1999? Celebrating is definitely not the answer. Some companies would try to justify their high share prices by considering all sorts of risky strategies. But given Home Depot's size, the chances of finding enough high-ROIC growth opportunities to justify its 1999 share price were virtually nil.

Realistically, there wasn't much Home Depot could have done except prepare for an inevitable sharp decline in share price: Home Depot's market value dropped from $132 billion in January 1999 to $80 billion in January 2004. Some companies can take advantage of their high share prices to make acquisitions, but that probably wasn't a good idea for Home Depot, because its organic growth was 11 percent—a large enough management challenge to maintain, even without considering that the retail industry doesn't have a track record in making large acquisitions successfully.

Home Depot's situation in 1999 was unusual. Most companies, most of the time, will not have much trouble satisfying the shareholder expectations expressed in their current share price simply by performing as well as the rest of their industry. We have reverse engineered hundreds of companies' share prices over the years using discounted cash flows. With the exception of the Internet bubble era (1999–2000), at least 80 percent of the companies have had performance expectations built into their share prices that are in line with industry growth expectations and returns on capital. TRS for a company among these 80 percent is unlikely to be much different from the industry average unless the company performs significantly better or worse than expected relative to its industry peers. The other 20 percent, however, should brace themselves for a significantly faster or slower ride on the treadmill. Managers who reverse engineer their share prices to understand expectations of their ROIC and growth can benefit from seeing on which side of this 80/20 divide they fall.

MANAGERIAL IMPLICATIONS

The expectations treadmill makes it difficult to use TRS as a performance measurement tool. As we saw in the example of Wal-Mart and Target, the sizable differences in TRS for the two companies from 1994 to 2005 masked the big difference in expectations at the beginning of the measurement period. In Home Depot's case, living up to the expectations was virtually impossible, as no company can run that fast for very long.

As a result of the expectations treadmill, many executive compensation systems tied to TRS do not reward managers for their performance as managers, since the majority of a company's short-term TRS is driven by movements in its industry and the broader market. That was the case for the many executives who became wealthy from stock options in the 1980s and 1990s, a time when share prices increased primarily because of falling interest rates, rather than anything those managers did. Conversely, many stock option gains were wiped out during the recent financial crisis. Again, the causes of these gains and losses were largely disconnected from anything managers did or didn't do (with the exception of managers in financial institutions).

Instead of focusing primarily on a company's TRS over a given period, effective compensation systems should focus on growth, ROIC, and TRS performance relative to peers. That would eliminate much of the TRS that is not driven by company-specific performance. Why hasn't such a simple solution been adopted by companies? Mostly thanks to the influence of U.S. accounting rules. Until 2004, stock options weren't reported as an expense on the income statement as long as they met certain criteria, one of which was that the exercise price had to be fixed. Any approach based on relative performance would have shown up as an expense in a company's income statement, so naturally companies adopted fixed-price options that led to higher accounting income.

A few companies have already moved to share-based compensation systems that are tied to relative performance. In 2001, General Electric granted CEO Jeffrey Immelt a performance award based on the company's TRS relative to the TRS of the S&P 500 index. We hope more companies will follow in that direction.

In addition to fixing compensation systems, executives need to become much more sophisticated in their interpretation of TRS, especially short-term TRS. If executives and boards understand what expectations are built into their own and their peers' share prices, then they can better anticipate how their actions might affect their own share prices when the market finds out about them. For example, if you're executing a great strategy that will create significant value, but the market already expects you to succeed, you can't expect to outperform on TRS. The management team and board need to know this, so the board will take a long-term view and continue to support management's value-creating priorities, even if these do not immediately strengthen the share price.

Executives also need to give up the bad habit of incessantly monitoring their stock prices. TRS is largely meaningless over short periods. In a typical three-month time frame, more than 40 percent of companies experience a share price increase or decrease of over 10 percent,[4] movements that are nothing more than random. Therefore, executives shouldn't even try to understand

---

[4] Share price movement relative to the S&P 500 index for a sample of nonfinancial companies with greater than $1 billion market capitalization, measured during 2004–2007.

daily share price changes unless prices move over 2 percent more than the peer average in a single day or 10 percent more in a quarter.

Finally, be careful what you wish for. All executives and investors like to see their company's share price increase. But once your share price rises, it's hard to keep it rising faster than the market average. The expectations treadmill is virtually impossible to escape, and we don't know any easy way to manage expectations down.

REVIEW QUESTIONS

1. What is the total returns to shareholders (TRS) figure and why is it important?

2. What is the expectations treadmill and how does it affect managers' ability to deliver above-average TRS over long periods of time?

3. What are the potential reasons why TRS over short periods of time may not reflect the actual performance of a company and its management?

4. What actions (good and bad) might managers take when investors have already-high expectations and managers desire to outperform peers on TRS?

5. Do all of the current investors in a company (e.g., Target) earn the same return on capital from their investment? Give reasons for your answer.

6. If a company performs perfectly in line with expectations, how will its TRS react in theory? How will its TRS react in practice? Why?

7. Can Company A outperform Company B on all key value drivers (e.g., growth and ROIC) but still deliver lower TRS? How?

8. Why is the old way of decomposing TRS (into changes in earnings, changes in P/E, and dividend yield) not the best way to understand a company's performance?

9. In the recommended approach to decomposing TRS, explain the theory behind the zero growth return. What is it? What drives it?

10. Given that TRS is not a clean measure of management performance and is therefore a flawed basis for management compensation, how should a company gauge management performance? What measures should it use?

Return on Invested Capital

When executives, analysts, and investors assess a business's potential to create value, they sometimes overlook the fundamental principle of value creation—namely, that the value of a business depends on its return on invested capital (ROIC) and growth. As Chapter 2 explains, the higher a company can raise its ROIC and the longer it can sustain a rate of ROIC greater than its cost of capital, the more value it will create. So being able to understand and predict what drives and sustains ROIC is critical to every strategic and investment decision.

Why do some companies develop and sustain much higher ROICs than others? Consider the difference in 2000 between eBay and Webvan, which were both newcomers at the height of the tech boom. In November 1999, eBay's market capitalization was $23 billion, while Webvan's was $8 billion. EBay continued to prosper, while Webvan soon disappeared. This is not so surprising when we look at the implications of their underlying strategies for their respective ROICs.

EBay's core business is online auctions that collect a small amount of money for each transaction between a buyer and a seller. The business needs no inventories or accounts receivable and requires little invested capital. Once started, as more buyers use eBay it attracts more sellers, in turn attracting more buyers. In addition, the marginal cost of each additional buyer or seller is close to zero. Economists say that a business in a situation like eBay's is exhibiting *increasing returns to scale*. In a business with increasing returns to scale, the first competitor to grow big can generate very high ROICs—eBay's ROIC is well over 50 percent—and will usually create the bulk of value in the market.

Webvan was an online grocery-delivery business based in California. In contrast to eBay, it had a capital-intensive business model involving substantial warehouses, trucks, and inventory. In addition, Webvan was competing with local grocery stores in selling products at very thin margins. The complexity and costs of making physical deliveries to customers within precise time frames more than offset Webvan's savings from not having physical stores. Finally, Webvan's business did not have increasing returns to scale; as demand increased, it needed more food pickers, trucks, and drivers to serve customers.

From the outset, it was clear that eBay's business model had a sound and sustainable competitive advantage that permitted high returns, while Webvan's business had no such advantage over its competitors, the grocery stores. EBay's strategy was primed for success, while Webvan's meant it was doomed.

This chapter explores how rates of return on invested capital depend on competitive advantage, itself a product of industry structure and competitive behavior; these are the relationships that explain why some companies earn only a 10 percent ROIC while others earn 50 percent. In this chapter, we demonstrate how the ROIC of any company or industry can be explained once we know enough about its sources of competitive advantage. We start by examining how strategy drives competitive advantage, which in turn drives ROIC, and what makes a rate of ROIC sustainable. In the final part of the chapter, we analyze the data, presenting 45 years of evidence on trends in ROIC. This analysis shows how ROIC varies by industry, and how rates of ROIC fluctuate or remain stable over time.

DRIVERS OF RETURN ON INVESTED CAPITAL

To understand how strategy, competitive advantage, and return on invested capital are linked, consider the following representation of ROIC:

$$\text{ROIC} = (1 - \text{Tax Rate})\frac{\text{Price per Unit} - \text{Cost per Unit}}{\text{Invested Capital per Unit}}$$

This version of ROIC has a similar meaning to the traditional definition, NOPLAT divided by invested capital. To highlight the potential sources of competitive advantage, however, we disaggregate the ratio into posttax revenue minus cost divided by invested capital per unit.[1] If a company has a competitive advantage, it earns a higher ROIC, because it either charges a price premium or produces its products more efficiently (at lower cost or lower capital per unit), or both.

The strategy model that underlies our thinking about what drives competitive advantage and ROIC is the structure-conduct-performance (SCP) framework. According to this framework, the structure of an industry influences the conduct of the competitors, which in turn drives the performance of the companies in the industry. Originally developed in the 1930s by Edward Mason,

---

[1] We introduce *units* to motivate a discussion surrounding price, cost, and volume. The formula, however, is not specific to manufacturing. Units can represent the number of hours billed, patients seen, transactions processed, and so on.

EXHIBIT 4.1 **Company Profitability: Industry Matters**

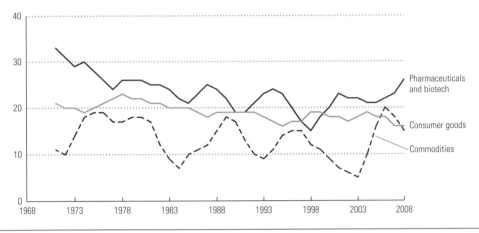

3-year rolling average of industry median pretax ROIC including goodwill, percent

Source: Compustat, McKinsey Corporate Performance Center analysis.

this framework was not widely influential in business until Michael Porter published *Competitive Strategy* in 1980, applying the model to company strategy. While there have been extensions and variations of the SCP model, such as the resource-based approach,[2] Porter's framework is probably still the most widely used for thinking about strategy. According to Porter, the intensity of competition in an industry is determined by five forces: threat of new entry, pressure from substitute products, bargaining power of buyers, bargaining power of suppliers, and the degree of rivalry among existing competitors. Companies need to choose strategies that build competitive advantages to mitigate or change the pressure of these forces and achieve superior profitability. Because the five forces differ by industry and because companies within the same industry can pursue different strategies, there can be significant variation in ROIC across and within industries.

Exhibit 4.1 underlines the importance of industry structure to ROIC. It compares the returns on invested capital over the past 38 years in three sectors: pharmaceuticals, consumer goods, and commodities. Pharmaceutical companies have outperformed both consumer goods and commodity-based companies. The returns for commodity-based companies go up and down significantly with the business cycle, but rarely reach the levels of consumer goods companies.

The reason for this difference in the industries' performances lies mainly in differences between their competitive structures. Pharmaceutical companies can develop innovative products that are subsequently protected by

---

[2] See, for example, J. Barney, "Resource-Based Theories of Competitive Advantage: A Ten-Year Retrospective on the Resource-Based View," *Journal of Management* 27 (2001): 643–650.

long-lasting patents. In the consumer goods industry, companies such as Procter & Gamble and Unilever have developed long-lasting brands that make it difficult for new competitors to gain a foothold. The companies also tend to compete for shelf space on factors other than just price. In contrast, commodity-based companies have undifferentiated products and few opportunities for innovation; for example, almost all paper mills use the same machines. This makes it difficult for any competitor to charge a price premium or build a sustainable cost advantage.

Industry structure is by no means the only determinant of ROIC, as shown by the significant variation among companies within industries. Take, for instance, the automotive industry. It has been plagued by overcapacity for years, because the industry's low returns do not deter new entrants (as shown by Korea's entry into the U.S. market) and because unionized plants are hard to close. Nevertheless, Toyota has managed to earn superior returns on invested capital because of its cost efficiencies. Its reputation for quality has also allowed Toyota to charge higher prices in the U.S. market relative to domestic manufacturers (at least until it had to make product recalls in 2009).

Finally, industry structure and competitive behavior aren't fixed; they're subject to shocks of technological innovation, changes in government regulation, and competitive entry—any or all of which can affect an entire industry or just individual companies. This is why the software industry might consistently earn high returns, but the leading companies may not be the same in 20 years, just as the leaders today were not necessarily major players 20 years ago.

COMPETITIVE ADVANTAGE

Competitive advantage derives from some combination of five sources of advantage that allow companies to charge a price premium and four sources related to cost and capital efficiency (see Exhibit 4.2). It is important to understand that competitive advantage derived from these sources is enjoyed not by

EXHIBIT 4.2 **Sources of Competitive Advantage**

Price premium	Cost and capital efficiency
Innovative products: Difficult-to-copy or patented products, services or technologies	Innovative business method: Difficult-to-copy business method that contrasts with established industry practice
Quality: Customers willing to pay a premium for a real or perceived difference in quality over and above competing products or services	Unique resources: Advantage resulting from inherent geological characteristics or unique access to raw material(s)
Brand: Customers willing to pay a premium based on brand, even if there is no clear quality difference	Economies of scale: Efficient scale or size for the relevant market
Customer lock-in: Customers unwilling or unable to replace product or service they use with a competing product or service	Scalable product/process: Ability to add customers and capacity at negligible marginal cost
Rational price discipline: Lower bound on prices established by large industry leaders through price signaling or capacity management	

entire companies but by particular business units and product lines. This is the only level of competition at which the concept of competitive advantage gives you any real traction in strategic thinking; even if a company sells soup or dog food exclusively, it may still have individual businesses and product lines with very different degrees of competitive advantage and therefore different ROICs.

On balance, price premiums offer any business the greatest scope for achieving an attractive ROIC, but they are usually more difficult to achieve than cost efficiencies. Also, the businesses or products with the most impressive returns are often those that weave together more than one advantage. Microsoft, for instance, enjoys a competitive advantage in part because of its ability to lock customers into its products, and this ability in turn allows Microsoft to charge premium prices. Microsoft also has an advantage on the cost side because it can supply products via a simple download or an inexpensive DVD, at extremely low marginal cost.

Price Premium Advantages

In commodity markets, companies are typically price takers, meaning they must sell at the market price to generate business, because the products are so hard to differentiate. To sell its products at a price premium, a company must find a way to differentiate its products from those of competitors. We distinguish five sources of price premiums.

Innovative products Innovative goods and services yield high returns on capital if they are protected by patents, difficult to copy, or both. Without either of these protections, even an innovative product won't do much to generate high returns.

Pharmaceutical companies earn high returns because they produce innovative products that, although often easy to copy, are protected by patents for up to 20 years. The business can charge a price premium during the protected period, after which generics will enter the market and drive the price down. (Even after the patent expires, there is some price stickiness for the patent holder.)

An example of an innovative product line that is not patent protected but just difficult to copy is Apple's series of iPod MP3 players. MP3 players had been on the market for several years before Apple introduced the iPod, and the core technology is the same for all competitors. The iPod is more successful, however, because of its appealing design and ease of use afforded by its user interface and integration with iTunes. Although not patent protected, good design can be difficult to copy.

Quality A term used as broadly as *quality* requires definition. In the context of competitive advantage and ROIC, quality means a real or perceived difference between one product or service and another for which consumers are willing to pay a higher price. In the car business, for example, BMW enjoys a price premium because customers perceive that its cars handle and drive better than comparable products that cost less. The cost of providing the extra quality is less than the price premium. Hence, BMW has often been able to earn higher returns than many other carmakers.

Sometimes the perception of quality lasts significantly longer than any real difference in quality, as has been the case with Honda and Toyota (at least until Toyota had to make product recalls in 2009) relative to General Motors, Ford, and Chrysler. While American and Japanese cars have been comparable in terms of quantifiable quality measures, such as the J.D. Power survey, Japanese companies have enjoyed a price premium for their products. Even when American and Japanese sticker prices on comparable vehicles were the same, American manufacturers were often forced to sell at a $2,000 to $3,000 discount, whereas Japanese cars were going for nearer the asking price.

Brand   Price premiums based on brand are sometimes hard to distinguish from price premiums based on quality, and the two are highly correlated. While the quality of a product may matter more than its established branding, sometimes the brand itself is what matters more—especially when the brand has lasted a very long time, as in the case of Coca-Cola, Perrier, Lacoste, and Mercedes-Benz.

Packaged food and durable consumer goods are good examples of sectors where brands earn price premiums for some but not all products. In some categories of packaged foods, such as breakfast cereals, customers are very loyal to brands like Cheerios, despite the availability of high-quality branded and private-label alternatives. In other categories, including meat, branding has not been successful. As a result of their strong brands, cereal companies earn returns on capital of around 30 percent, while meat processors earn returns of around 15 percent.

Customer lock-in   When replacing one company's product or service with another's is relatively costly for customers,[3] the incumbent company can charge a price premium—if not for the initial sale, then at least for additional units or for subsequent generations and iterations of the original product. Medical devices like stents, for instance, can lock in the doctors who purchase them, because doctors need time to train and become proficient in using the device for treatment. Once doctors are up to speed on a particular stent, they won't switch to a competing product unless there is a compelling reason to invest the necessary effort.

High switching costs similarly explain why Bloomberg financial terminals, although based on a relatively old technology, are still leaders in their market. Bankers and traders have invested considerable time in learning how to work with the Bloomberg terminals and are reluctant to learn another system. An installed base like Bloomberg's is a powerful driver of competitive advantage.

---

[3] Costly relative to the price of the product.

Rational price discipline In commodity industries with many competitors, the laws of supply and demand will drive down prices and ROIC. This applies not just to obvious commodities such as chemicals and paper, but also to more recently commoditized products and services, such as airline seats. It would take only a net increase of 5 to 10 percent in airline ticket prices to turn the industry's aggregate loss to an aggregate profit. But each competitor is tempted to get an edge in filling seats by keeping prices low, even when fuel prices and other costs rise for all competitors.

Occasionally, we find an industry that manages to overcome the forces of competition and set its prices at a level that earns the companies in the industry reasonable returns on capital (though rarely more than 15 percent) without breaking competition law. For example, for many years, almost all real estate agents in the United States charged a 6 percent commission on the price of each home they sold. In other cases, the government sanctions disciplined pricing in an industry through regulatory structures. For example, until the 1970s, airline fares in the United States were high because competitors were restricted from entering one another's markets. Prices collapsed when the market was deregulated in 1978.

Rational, legitimate pricing discipline typically works when one competitor acts as the leader and others quickly replicate its price moves. In addition, there must be barriers to new entrants, and each competitor must be large enough for a price war to be sure to reduce the profit on its existing volume by more than any extra profit gained from new sales. If there are smaller competitors that have more to gain from extra volume than they would lose from lower prices, then price discipline will be very difficult to maintain.

Most attempts by industry players to maintain a floor price fail. Take the paper industry, for example. Its ROICs have averaged less than 10 percent from 1965 to 2007. The industry creates this problem for itself because the companies all tend to expand at once, after demand and prices have risen. As a result, a large chunk of new capacity comes on line at the same time, upsetting the balance of supply and demand and forcing down prices and returns.

Even cartels (which are illegal in most of the world) find it difficult to maintain price levels, because each cartel member has a huge incentive to lower prices and attract more sales. This so-called free-rider issue makes it difficult to maintain price levels over long periods, even for the Organization of Petroleum Exporting Countries (OPEC), the world's largest and most prominent cartel.

Cost and Capital Efficiency Advantages

Theoretically, cost and capital efficiency are two separate competitive advantages. Cost efficiency is the ability to sell products and services at a lower cost than the competition. Capital efficiency is selling more products per dollar of invested capital than competitors. In practice, both tend to have common drivers and are hard to separate. (Is Hewlett-Packard's outsourcing of manufacturing to Asia a source of cost efficiency or capital efficiency?) Consequently, we treat the following four sources of competitive advantage as deriving from both the cost and capital efficiencies they achieve.

Innovative business method   A company's business method is the combination of its production, logistics, and pattern of interaction with customers. Most production methods can be copied, but some are difficult to copy at some times. For example, early in its life, Dell developed a new way of making and distributing personal computers. Dell sold directly to its customers, made its machines to order with almost no inventory (by assembling machines with standardized parts that could be purchased from different suppliers at different times at very low cost), and received payments from customers as soon as products shipped. In contrast, Hewlett-Packard and Compaq, its dominant competitors at that time, were producing in large batches and selling through retailers. Dell's cost and capital efficiency enabled the company initially to generate a much higher ROIC than its competitors, who couldn't switch quickly to a direct-sales model without angering their retailers and reengineering their production processes.

Interestingly, Dell's success formula eroded over time as its sales shifted from desktop to notebook computers. Notebook computers are built to much tighter part specifications, often using parts from vendors made expressly for Dell. Since everything has to fit together just right, Dell needs more support from its vendors and cannot pressure them so easily by threatening to switch to other suppliers on the basis of cost alone.

Unique resources   Sometimes a company has access to a unique resource that cannot be replicated. This gives it a significant competitive advantage. A typical example would be a mine whose ore is richer than most other ore bodies. Take two nickel-mining companies, Norilsk Nickel, which produces nickel in northern Siberia, and Vale, which produces nickel in Canada and Indonesia. The content of precious metals (e.g., palladium) in Norilsk's nickel ore is significantly higher than in Vale's. In other words, Norilsk gets not only nickel from its ore but also some high-priced palladium. As a result, Norilsk earned a pretax ROIC of 67 percent in 2007, compared with Vale's nickel division generating 25 percent. (Note that 2007 was a year of high nickel prices.)

Geography often plays a role in gaining advantage from unique resources. In general, whenever the cost of shipping a product is high relative to the value of the product—as for, say, cement or salt—producers near their customers have a unique advantage.

Economies of scale   The notion of economies of scale is often misunderstood as meaning there are automatic economies that come with size. Scale can indeed be important to value, but usually only at the regional or even local level, not in the national or global market. For example, if you're a retailer, it's much more important to be large in one city than large across the country, because costs like local warehousing and local advertising are either lumpy or fixed. Buying airtime and space in Chicago is the same whether you have one store or 10.

A key element that determines the profitability of health insurers in the United States is their ability to negotiate prices with providers (hospitals and doctors), who tend to operate locally rather than nationally. The insurer with the highest market share in a local market will be in a position to negotiate the lowest prices, regardless of its national market share. In other words, it's better to have the number one market share in 10 states than to be number one nationwide but number four in every state.

Another aspect of economies of scale is that a company gets their benefit only if the required investments in scale are large enough to deter competitors. Anyone who wants to compete with UPS or FedEx, for instance, must first pay the enormous fixed expense of installing a nationwide network, then operate at a loss for quite some time while drawing customers away from the incumbents. Even though FedEx and UPS continually have to add new costs (for planes, trucks, and drivers), these costs are variable—in contrast to the fixed cost of building the national network—and are incurred in stepwise fashion.

Size or scale can work against a business as well. In the 1980s, UPS was attacked by RPS Inc., a package delivery service that differentiated its business and pricing by offering significant discounts to commercial customers in populous areas. UPS offered only modest volume discounts, charging generally the same for each of, say, 10 packages delivered to an office building as it did for delivering one package to a residence. In essence, RPS was picking off high-margin business from UPS, and UPS's grand scale did little to prevent this. RPS's experience teaches that what matters is having the right scale in the right market.

Scalable product/process   Having products or processes that are scalable means the cost of supplying or serving additional customers is very low. Businesses with this advantage usually deliver their products and services using information technology (IT). An example is Automatic Data Processing, Inc. (ADP), which provides payroll processing and related services to small and medium-sized businesses. All customers are on the same computers and software, so adding additional customers involves negligible cost. This highly scalable business model allows margins to increase as ADP grows. Likewise, companies such as eBay and products like Microsoft Office add customers at minuscule incremental cost.

Other examples of scalable businesses include media companies that make and distribute movies or TV shows. Making the movie or show requires an initial outlay for the crew, sets, actors, and so on. But those costs are fixed regardless of how many people end up viewing and paying for the show. There may be some incremental advertising costs and very small costs associated with putting the movie on DVD or streaming it. But overall, costs do not rise as customer numbers increase.

This is not to say that all IT-based or IT-enabled businesses are scalable. Many incur costs to service each contract with clients, more like consulting firms, which are not scalable. These costs mount with the number of clients. For example, many companies that maintain data centers do so on a cost-plus basis by adding people, equipment, and facilities as they add new clients.

SUSTAINABILITY OF RETURN ON INVESTED CAPITAL

The longer a company can sustain a high ROIC, the more value the company will create. In a perfectly competitive economy, ROICs higher than the cost of capital get competed away. Whether a company can sustain a given level of ROIC depends on the length of the life cycles of its businesses and products, the length of time its competitive advantages can persist, and its potential for renewing businesses and products.

Length of Product Life Cycle

The longer the life cycle of a company's businesses and products, the better its chances of sustaining its ROIC. To illustrate, while Cheerios may not seem as exciting as an innovative, new technology, the culturally entrenched, branded cereal is likely to have a market for far longer than any new gadget. Similarly, a unique resource (like palladium-rich nickel ore) can be a durable source of advantage if it is related to a long product life cycle but will be less advantageous if it isn't. And a business model that locks customers into a product with a short life cycle is far less valuable than one that locks customers in for a long time. Once users of Microsoft's Windows have become well versed in the platform, they are unlikely to switch to a new competitor. Even Linux, a low-cost alternative to Windows, has struggled to gain market share as system administrators and end users remain wary of learning a new way of computing. Microsoft's success in extending the life cycle of Windows has been a huge source of value to the company.

Persistence of Competitive Advantage

If the company cannot prevent competition from duplicating its business, high ROIC will be short-lived, and the company's value will diminish. Consider a major cost improvement implemented by the airlines over recent years. The self-service kiosk allows passengers to purchase a ticket or print a boarding pass without waiting in line. From the airlines' perspective, fewer ground personnel can handle more people. So why has this cost improvement not translated into high ROICs for the airlines? Since every company has access to the technology, any cost improvements are passed directly to the consumer in the form of lower prices. In general, advantages that rise from brand and quality on the price side and scalability on the cost side tend to have more staying power than those arising from more temporary sources of advantage, such as an innovation, which will tend to be superseded by subsequent innovations.

Potential for Product Renewal

Few businesses or products have life cycles as long as Coca-Cola's. Most companies need to find renewal businesses and products where they can leverage existing or build new competitive advantages. This is an area where brands prove their value. Consumer goods companies excel at using their brands to launch new products: Think of Apple's success with the iPod and iPhone, Bulgari moving into fragrances, and Mars entering the ice cream business. Being good at innovating also helps companies renew products and businesses. Thus, pharmaceutical companies exist because they can discover new drugs, and a semiconductor manufacturer such as Intel relies on its technological innovation to launch new products and stay ahead of its competitors.

Some companies, such as Procter & Gamble and Johnson & Johnson, are able to protect their primary product lines while simultaneously expanding into new markets. Procter & Gamble has a strong record of continuing to introduce successful new products like Swiffer, Febreze, and Crest Whitestrips. It also anticipated the strong growth in beauty products in the early 2000s with a number of acquisitions that increased its revenues in the category from $7.3 billion to $19.5 billion from 1999 to 2008. This enabled the company to advance from owning just one billion-dollar brand (by sales) in 1999 to eight in 2008.

Johnson & Johnson similarly has earned strong returns on capital through its patented pharmaceuticals and branded consumer products lines, such as Tylenol and Johnson's Baby Shampoo. Through strong brands and capable distribution, the company has been able to maintain a price premium in the face of new entrants and alternative products. The company broadened its product portfolio to include medical devices and diagnostics in response to the strength of the health care industry and its expected growth as the baby boomers age. Exhibit 4.3 shows that Johnson & Johnson has maintained an ROIC greater than its weighted average cost of capital (WACC) over the past decades. In fact, the strength of health care in the 1990s has meant returns have risen since the 1980s. Only the Tylenol tampering scare of the 1980s and the high cost of acquisitions in the late 1990s temporarily dampened the company's strong performance.

As we will see later in this chapter, empirical studies show that over the past five decades, companies have been generally quite successful in sustaining their rates of ROIC. Apparently, when companies have found a strategy that creates competitive advantages, they are often able to sustain and renew these advantages over many years. While competition clearly plays a major role in

EXHIBIT 4.3 **Johnson & Johnson: ROIC, 1965–2008**

Rolling three-year average ROIC including goodwill, percent

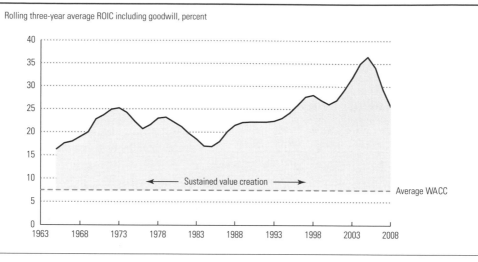

driving down ROIC, managers can sustain a high rate of return by anticipating and responding to changes in the environment better than their competitors do.

EMPIRICAL ANALYSIS OF RETURNS ON INVESTED CAPITAL

In this section, we present evidence on rates of ROIC for more than 5,000 U.S.-based nonfinancial companies since 1963. Our results come from McKinsey & Company's Corporate Performance Center database, which relies on financial data provided by Standard & Poor's Compustat. Our key findings are as follows:

- The median ROIC between 1963 and 2008 was around 10 percent and remained relatively constant throughout the period. ROIC does, however, vary dramatically across companies, with only half of the observed ROICs between 5 percent and 20 percent.

- ROICs differ by industry but not by company size. Industries that rely on sustainable competitive advantages such as patents and brands (for example, pharmaceuticals and personal products) tend to have high median ROICs (15 to 20 percent), whereas companies in basic industries, such as paper, airlines, and utilities, tend to earn low ROICs (5 to 10 percent).

- There are large variations in rates of ROIC between and within industries. Some industries earn higher median returns than others, but the spread between the best and worst performers within an industry can be significant. There are examples of companies earning attractive returns in industries where the median return is low (e.g., Wal-Mart and Intel), and vice versa.

- Rates of ROIC tend to remain fairly stable—especially compared with rates of growth, discussed in the next chapter. Industry rankings by median ROIC are stable over time, with only a few industries making a clear aggregate shift upward or downward, typically reflecting structural changes, such as the widespread consolidation in the defense industry over the past decade. Individual company ROICs gradually tend toward their industry medians over time but are fairly persistent. Two-thirds of companies that earned ROICs greater than 20 percent in 1995 were still earning at least 20 percent 10 years later.

ROIC Trends

To analyze historical corporate performance, we first measured median ROIC for each of the past 45 years. Exhibit 4.4 plots median ROIC between 1963

EXHIBIT 4.4 **U.S.-Based Nonfinancial Companies: ROIC, 1963–2008**

Annual ROIC without goodwill, percent

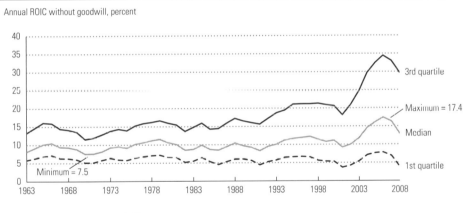

Annual ROIC with and without goodwill, percent

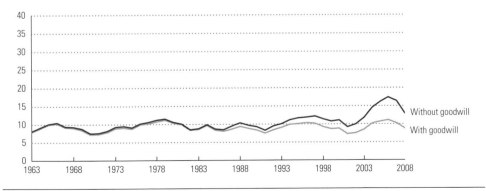

Source: Compustat, McKinsey Corporate Performance Center analysis.

and 2008 for U.S.-based nonfinancial companies.[4] ROIC is presented with and without goodwill, the difference showing the impact of mergers and acquisitions.

The average median ROIC without goodwill over these years equals about 10 percent, with annual medians oscillating in a relatively tight range between 7 and 11 percent, except during the years between 2005 and 2008. The oscillation is not random, but tied directly to the overall growth of the economy: Regressing median ROIC against gross domestic product (GDP) showed that a 100-basis-point increase in GDP growth translated into a 20-basis-point increase in median ROIC.

Stripping out the four high-inflation years, the median ROIC for the sample tends to be about two percentage points higher than the median cost of capital, which is around 8 percent. This may appear counterintuitive, given the increase in productivity over the past 45 years: The U.S. Department of Labor reports manufacturing workers were approximately 3.5 times more productive in 2003 than they were in 1963. But healthy competition has done its job of transferring the benefits from internal productivity improvements to customers and employees in the form of lower prices and higher salaries, instead of adding to corporate profits.

Until about 2004, median ROICs were stable, and a company only had to earn a return greater than 10 percent to be in the top-performing half of the sample, and toward 20 percent to be in the top quartile. In recent years, however, a company had to earn a return on capital near 20 percent to be above the median, and a return above about 25 percent to be in the top quartile.

While returns on invested capital without goodwill have been increasing, returns on invested capital with goodwill have been flat, as shown in the bottom half of Exhibit 4.4. This suggests that acquiring companies haven't been able to extract much value from their acquisitions. This is not to say they haven't improved the performance of the acquired businesses; indeed, a closer look reveals significant realized synergies driving up returns on capital without goodwill. However, these companies paid high prices for their acquisitions, so most of the value the deals created was transferred to the shareholders of the target company. (We discuss acquisitions and value creation in Chapter 21.)

The story is similar for the distribution of returns on invested capital. Exhibit 4.5 shows the distribution of returns in 1965–1967 overlaid on the returns in 1995–1997 and 2005–2007. Note that the distribution is wide for all periods, with most companies earning between 5 and 20 percent ROIC over the past 45 years. However, there has been a recent shift toward more companies earning very high returns on capital. In the 1960s, only 1 percent of companies earned returns greater than 50 percent, whereas in the early 2000s,

---

[4] The numbers in this section are based on U.S. companies because longer-term data for non-U.S. companies are not readily available. In recent years, the global distribution of returns and the U.S. distribution have been very similar.

EXHIBIT 4.5 **Distribution of ROIC: Shifting to the Right**

Percent of companies in sample, average for period

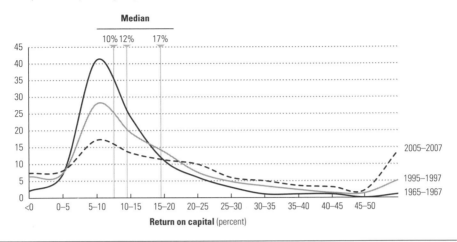

Source: Compustat, McKinsey Corporate Performance Center analysis.

14 percent of companies earned returns of that magnitude. In many cases, this improvement has occurred in industries with strong barriers to entry, such as patents or brands where gains that companies have made from decreased raw-materials prices and increased productivity have not been transferred to other stakeholders.

The distributions are much more similar when ROIC is measured with goodwill included in invested capital. This implies that top-ROIC companies are acquiring other top performers but paying full price for the acquired performance.

ROIC by Industry and Company Size

To see how differences in ROIC across industries and companies relate to likely differences in drivers of competitive advantage, we examined variations in ROIC by industry over the past 45 years. Exhibit 4.6 shows the median returns on invested capital for a range of industries, and also their upper and lower quartile ROICs. As the exhibit demonstrates, financial performance varies significantly both across and within industries. To illustrate, most apparel retailers earn high returns, but the best performers in the paper packaging industry, which has low median returns, earn higher returns than the weak performers in apparel retail. The data have limitations, because many of the companies are in multiple subindustries, making industry definitions fairly broad. Nevertheless, it is clear that both industry and company are important in explaining individual companies' ROICs. Several companies (e.g., Wal-Mart and Intel) are earning attractive returns in industries where the median return is low, and vice versa.

EXHIBIT 4.6   **ROIC Variations across and within Industries**

Industry median ROIC, without goodwill (percent)

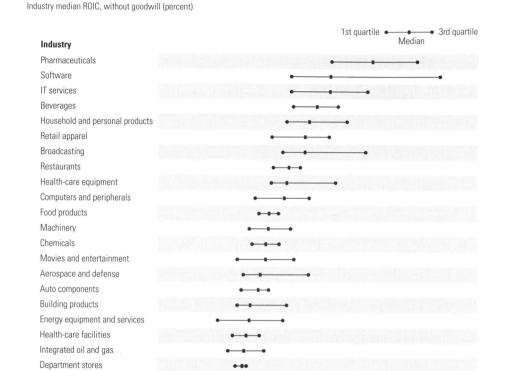

Source: Compustat, McKinsey Corporate Performance Center analysis.

Industries where companies build identifiable sustainable advantages, such as patent-protected innovations and brands, tend to generate higher returns. Pharmaceutical and biotechnology companies had a median ROIC of 23.5 percent, whereas companies in commodities and regulated industries, such as airlines and utilities, had much lower ROICs—5.8 percent and 6.3 percent, respectively. Broadcasting and software companies not only have higher median returns, but also greater variation in returns. These industries can benefit from scalability, which explains their higher returns, but compared with pharmaceutical firms, they are less protected by patents, have shorter life cycles for many products, and have lower barriers to entry. This explains their wider distribution of returns.

In contrast, department stores have a fairly narrow distribution of returns and a median ROIC of 9 percent. Unsurprisingly, this return is modest compared with industries enjoying more stable brands, patents, and scalable business models, which offer more opportunities for differentiation among individual companies.

The size of a company's revenues shows no clear relation to ROIC, suggesting that scale in terms of absolute size is rarely a source of competitive advantage, as discussed earlier in this chapter. Despite the common perception that economies of scale should continually lower unit costs, many companies reach minimum efficient scale at relatively small sizes. Beyond this point, any incremental growth comes at the same unit cost, or even at slightly higher costs as bureaucratic inefficiency and other inflexibility costs begin to grow. To grasp this point, consider Southwest Airlines, a company that had just 50 percent of the revenues of American Airlines yet three times the equity valuation at year-end 2009.

Sustaining ROIC

Although not shown in Exhibit 4.6, the industry ranking by median ROIC does not vary materially over time. Similarly, when we ranked the returns on invested capital across industries over the past 45 years into high, medium, and low groups, we found that most industries stayed in the same group over the period, as shown by Exhibit 4.7.

EXHIBIT 4.7 **Persistence of Industry ROICs**

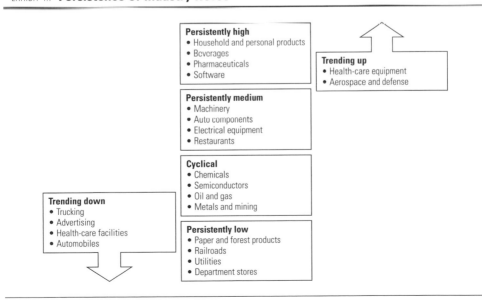

Persistently high-return industries included household and personal products, beverages, pharmaceuticals, and software. As you would expect, these industries have consistently high returns because they are scalable (software) or are protected by brands or patents. Persistently low returns characterize paper and forest products, railroads, and utilities. These are commodity industries in which price premiums are difficult to achieve because of low barriers to entry, commodity products, or regulated returns. Perhaps surprisingly, this group also includes department stores. Like commodity industries, department stores can achieve little price differentiation, so as a rule they realize persistently low returns. Some industries are cyclical, with both high and low returns at different points in the cycle, but demonstrating no clear trend up or down over time.

We did find several industries where there was a clear downward trend in returns. These included trucking, advertising, health-care facilities, and automobiles. Competition in trucking, advertising, and automobiles has increased substantially over the past five decades. Health-care facilities have had their prices squeezed by the government, insurers, and competition with nonprofits.

Industries where returns on invested capital clearly are trending up are rare. Two examples are health-care equipment and aerospace and defense. Innovation in health-care equipment has enabled the industry to produce higher-value-added, differentiated products such as stents and artificial joints, as well as more commoditized products, including syringes and forceps. Increased returns on invested capital in aerospace and defense were unexpected. However, on close examination, we found that companies in this sector have been able to reduce their capital intensity as government has effectively provided up-front funding for many more contracts. The sector's higher ROIC simply reflects a lower capital base.

We found similar evidence of sustained rates of return at the company level. We measured the sustainability of company ROICs by forming portfolios of companies earning a particular range of ROIC in each year (e.g., above 20 percent) and then tracking the median ROIC for each portfolio over the following 15 years.

Exhibit 4.8 demonstrates a pattern of reverting toward the mean. Companies earning high returns tend to see their ROIC fall gradually over the succeeding 15 years, and companies earning low returns tend to see them rise over time. Only in the portfolio containing companies generating returns between 5 and 10 percent (mostly regulated companies) do rates of return remain constant.

However, an important phenomenon shown by Exhibit 4.8 is the persistence of superior performance beyond 10 years. Although the best-performing companies cannot maintain outstanding performance over the long term, their ROIC does *not* revert all the way back to the aggregate median of around 10 percent over 15 years. Instead, the top portfolio's median ROIC drops from 29 percent to 15 percent. High-performing companies are in general

EXHIBIT 4.8 **Nonfinancial Companies: ROIC Decay Analysis**

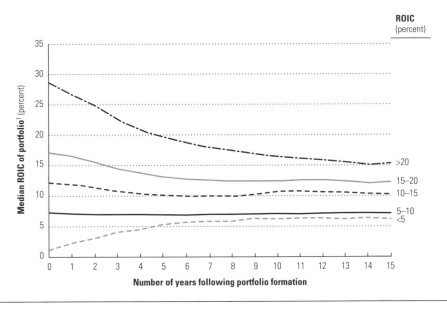

¹ At year 0, companies are grouped into one of five portfolios, based on ROIC.

Source: Compustat, McKinsey Corporate Performance Center analysis.

remarkably capable of sustaining a competitive advantage in their businesses and/or finding new business where they continue or rebuild such advantages.

Since a company's continuing value is highly dependent on long-run forecasts of ROIC and growth, this result has important implications for corporate valuation. Basing a continuing value on the economic concept that ROIC will approach WACC is overly conservative for the *typical* company generating high ROICs (continuing value is the focus of Chapter 10).

When benchmarking the historical decay of company ROICs, it is important to segment results by industry (especially if industry is a proxy for sustainability of competitive advantage). In Exhibit 4.9, we plot the ROIC decay rates for the consumer staples segment of the food and staples industry. As the exhibit demonstrates, these ROICs revert to the mean but at a much slower rate than seen in the full sample. Top performers in consumer staples have a median ROIC of 26 percent at the outset, which drops to 20 percent after 15 years, while top performers in the entire food and staples sample dropped to 15 percent. Even after 15 years, the *original* class of best performers still outperforms the worst performers by more than 13 percentage points.

Although decay rates examine the *rate* of regression toward the mean, they present only aggregate results and tell us nothing about the spread of potential future performance. Does every company generating returns greater than 20 percent eventually migrate to 15 percent, or do some companies actually generate higher returns? Conversely, do some top performers become poor

EXHIBIT 4.9 **Consumer Staples: ROIC Decay Analysis**

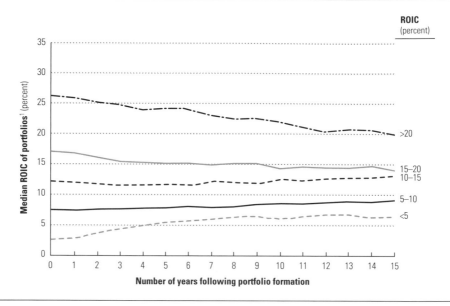

¹ At year 0, companies are grouped into one of five portfolios, based on ROIC.

Source: Compustat, McKinsey Corporate Performance Center analysis.

performers? To address this question, we measured the probability that a company will migrate from one ROIC grouping to another in 10 years. The results are presented in Exhibit 4.10. Transition probabilities read from left to right, and the rows must sum to 100 percent. Thus, for instance, a company whose ROIC was less than 10 percent in 1995 had a 57 percent chance of earning less than 10 percent in 2005.

Both high and low performers demonstrate significant stability in their performance. Companies with high or low ROICs are most likely to stay in the

EXHIBIT 4.10 **ROIC Transition Probability, 1995–2005**

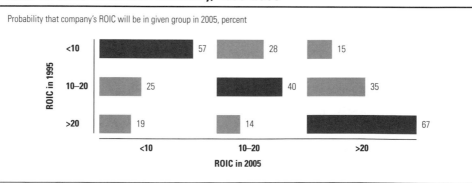

Source: Compustat, McKinsey Corporate Performance Center analysis.

same grouping (a 57 percent probability for those with ROIC below 10 percent, and a 67 percent probability for those with ROIC above 20 percent). Even among companies whose ROIC was between 10 and 20 percent, the greatest probability (40 percent) was for remaining in the same grouping 10 years later.

These results show that high-ROIC companies tend to maintain their high returns on invested capital and low-ROIC companies tend to retain their low returns. We have studied earlier time periods as well and found similar results, except that even fewer of the lower-return companies moved up into a higher group. The 1995–2005 period may be unusual in that the median company significantly increased its return on invested capital, as we discussed at the beginning of this section.

SUMMARY

There are many lessons to learn about returns on invested capital. First, these returns are driven by competitive advantages that enable companies to realize price premiums, cost and capital efficiencies, or some combination of these. Second, industry structure is an important but not exclusive determinant of ROIC. Certain industries are biased toward earning either high, medium, or low returns, but there is still significant variation in the rates of return for individual companies within each industry. Third, and most importantly, if a company finds a formula or strategy that earns an attractive ROIC, there is a good chance it can sustain that attractive return over time and through changing economic, industry, and company conditions—especially in the case of industries that enjoy relatively long product life cycles. Unfortunately, the converse is also true: If a company earns a low ROIC, that is likely to persist as well.

REVIEW QUESTIONS

1. From a value-creation perspective, is it more important for a company to know *where* to compete or *how* to compete? That is, is it more important to play in the right markets or to be the best player in your current markets?
2. Identify and discuss real examples of companies with a competitive advantage based on customer lock-in as opposed to product innovation. Which do you expect to sustain a high ROIC for a longer time?
3. Why do companies operating within the pharmaceutical and biotechnology industries typically sustain higher ROICs than firms in the technology, hardware, and equipment industries?
4. Why are competitive advantages based on brands, as in the consumer goods industry, often more important for long-term value creation than advantages based on product quality or innovation?

5. Discuss potential explanations for the widening of the distribution of ROICs across all companies over recent decades.

6. Explain the difference between ROICs excluding and ROICs including goodwill for U.S. companies: what does this difference imply and why has it increased so much over the past decade?

7. In Exhibit 4.8, the gradual decline in ROIC of the top-performing companies can be explained by gradual erosion of competitive advantages. What could be the explanation for the gradual increase in ROIC of the bottom-performing companies?

8. Discuss why, within the broader health care sector, ROIC can be declining for health-care facility companies but increasing for health-care equipment companies.

5

Growth

The business world is gripped by growth. The popular view is that a company must grow to survive and prosper, and there is certainly some truth to this. Slow-growing companies present fewer interesting opportunities for managers and so may have difficulty attracting and retaining talent. They are also much more likely to be acquired than faster-growing firms: over the past 25 years, most of the 340 companies that have disappeared from the S&P 500 index were acquired by larger companies. That explains why today's public companies are under tremendous pressure to grow.

However, growth creates value only when a company's new customers, projects, or acquisitions generate returns on invested capital (ROICs) greater than the cost of capital, as we discussed in Chapter 2. And finding good, high-value-creating projects becomes increasingly difficult as companies grow larger and their industries ever more competitive. To illustrate, in 1990, a year in which Wal-Mart added 57,000 new employees, the company's revenues grew by 26.3 percent. In 2003, the company grew physically so much bigger that it had to add another 100,000 employees, but its revenue growth that year was only 4.8 percent. To replicate 1990's revenue growth, even at 2003's improved levels of productivity, Wal-Mart would have needed to add nearly half a million people in a single year—a challenge by any standards.

Achieving the right balance between growth and return on invested capital is critically important to value creation. Our research shows that for companies with a high ROIC, shareholder returns are affected more by an increase in revenues than an increase in ROIC.[1] Indeed, we have found that if such companies let their ROIC drop a bit (though not too much) to achieve higher growth, their returns to shareholders can improve. Conversely, for companies with a low ROIC, increasing ROIC will create more value than growing will.

---

[1] See T. Koller and B. Jiang, "How to Choose between Growth and ROIC," *McKinsey on Finance*, no. 25 (Autumn 2007): 19–22.

Just as executives need to understand whether their strategies will lead to high returns on invested capital, as we discussed in the previous chapter, they also need to know which growth opportunities will create the most value. Therefore, in this chapter, we discuss the principal strategies for driving revenue growth, the ways in which growth creates value, and the challenges of sustaining growth, and then we analyze the data on corporate growth patterns over the past 45 years.

DRIVERS OF REVENUE GROWTH

Like ROIC, average industry revenue growth varies considerably across industries, and there are also big differences in growth rates among companies in the same industry. Exhibit 5.1 shows both kinds of variation for the 10 years from 1997 to 2007. In some industries, the most important contributors to the sector's overall revenue growth were price changes and mergers and acquisitions (M&A) activities. For instance, the oil and gas sector benefited from strong oil price increases to realize revenue growth of around 13 percent a year in real terms, the highest median rate for any sector. In volume terms, growth was much lower. The reverse holds for computers and peripherals, which grew at 2 percent per year in real terms. Continual downward pressure on prices for information technology (IT) hardware made the sector one of the slowest growing.

Aside from different price developments, what else explains the large differences in growth apparent among companies in the same industry? Executives need to understand the reasons for variations in growth to assess past growth and plan how to grow in the future. The first step is to disaggregate overall growth into its three main components:[2]

1. *Portfolio momentum:* This is the organic revenue growth a company enjoys because of overall expansion in the market segments represented in its portfolio.
2. *Market share performance:* This is the organic revenue growth (or reduction) a company records by gaining or losing share in any particular market. (We define market share as the company's weighted average share of the segments in which it competes.)
3. *Mergers and acquisitions (M&A):* This represents the inorganic growth a company achieves when it buys or sells revenues through acquisitions or divestments.

---

[2] This section draws on P. Viguerie, S. Smit, and M. Baghai, *The Granularity of Growth* (Hoboken, NJ: John Wiley & Sons, 2008).

EXHIBIT 5.1 **Considerable Variation in Revenue Growth**

Industry growth, inflation-adjusted, percent

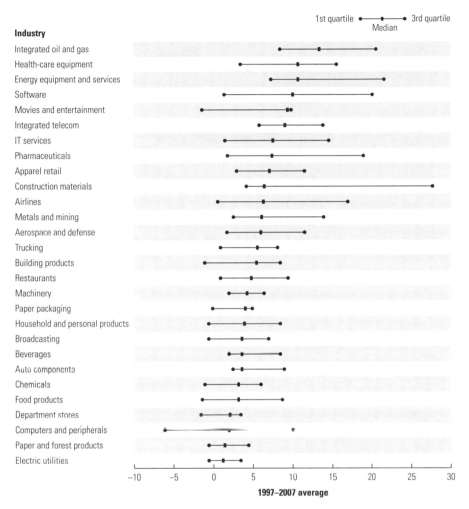

Source: Compustat, McKinsey Corporate Performance Center analysis.

Former McKinsey consultant Mehrdad Baghai and our McKinsey colleagues Sven Smit and Patrick Viguerie have analyzed the relative importance of these three components to the growth of more than 416 large companies around the world from 1999 to 2006. The results show that portfolio momentum and M&A explain far more of the differences in the growth of large companies than growth in market share does. As shown in Exhibit 5.2, Baghai, Smit, and Viguerie found that of the 10.1 percent average yearly growth achieved by the sample, 6.6 percentage points came from the growth of the market segments

EXHIBIT 5.2 **Components of Growth**

Compound annual growth rate (CAGR) of revenues for 416 large global companies, 1999–2006, percent

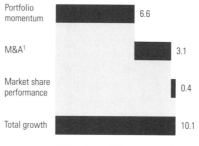

Portfolio momentum	6.6
M&A[1]	3.1
Market share performance	0.4
Total growth	10.1

Average growth by component

[1] Includes impact of changes in revenue base caused by inorganic activity and share gain/loss.

Source: P. Viguerie, S. Smit, and M. Baghai, *The Granularity of Growth* (Hoboken, NJ: Wiley, 2008).

in its portfolio, 3.1 from M&A activity, and a marginal 0.4 from market share performance.[3]

Companies can try to influence the growth rates of their portfolios in several ways. For instance, through selective acquisitions and divestments, companies can change their exposure to growing and shrinking market segments. By introducing new product categories, companies can create new markets themselves. However, managers tend to focus most attention on gaining share in their existing market segments through superior execution, often factoring market share goals into their business plans. Although this is likely to be their least significant source of growth, it remains a necessary one. To capture in full the benefits of overall market growth in any segment, a company needs to maintain its position in the segment, particularly in fast-growing segments that tend to attract innovative or low-cost entrants. Success in this endeavor hangs on the quality of its execution.

If a company's growth depends mainly on the dynamics of the sector markets in which it operates, why should there be such big differences in growth among different companies operating in the same sector? One explanation is M&A activity, which can add some three percentage points to a company's growth rate. The second and more important reason is that the average growth rate of companies competing in any sector masks big differences in growth across the sector's market segments and subsegments.

To capture this granularity of markets and understand the differences in companies' revenue growth, Baghai, Smit, and Viguerie analyzed market

[3] One might expect the average growth rate from market share gains in the sample to be close to zero. Perhaps more importantly, the entire distribution of growth rates from market share gains lies significantly below those for the other two growth components as well. See, for example, M. Baghai, S. Smit, and P. Viguerie, "The Granularity of Growth," *McKinsey on Finance*, no. 24 (Summer 2007): 25–30.

growth at the level of individual product and geographical segments with around $50 million to $200 million in sales, rather than at the company, divisional, or business unit level.[4] Their example of a large European manufacturer of personal-care products shows why analysis at this level is revealing. The company has three lines of business with apparently low prospective growth rates ranging from 1.6 percent to 7.5 percent a year. However, the range of forecast growth rates for individual product lines is much wider. For instance, the business line with the lowest expected growth rate has one of the company's best growth opportunities in one product line, at 24 percent. At the same time, the business with the highest growth rate has several product lines that are shrinking fast and may warrant divestment.

GROWTH AND VALUE CREATION

Achieving the highest revenue growth may depend on choosing the right markets and acquisitions rather than gaining market share. However, the highest growth will not necessarily create the most value, because the three drivers of growth do not all create value in equal measure. To understand why not, consider who loses under alternative revenue growth scenarios and how effectively losers can retaliate.

Increases in market share that come at the expense of established competitors rarely create much value for long, unless they push smaller competitors out of the market entirely. The reason is that established competitors can easily retaliate. Market share growth driven by price increases comes at the expense of customers, who can retaliate by reducing consumption and seeking substitute products. So new value created by price increases may not last long. Growth driven by general market expansion comes at the expense of companies in other industries, which may not even know to whom they are losing share. This category of loser is the least able to retaliate, which makes product market growth the driver likely to create the most value. The value of growth from acquisitions is harder to characterize, because it depends so much on the price of the acquisition (as discussed in Chapter 21).

Exhibit 5.3 ranks different growth tactics that fall within the three overall growth strategies according to their potential for creating value. This ranking may not be exactly the same for all industries, but it works well as a starting point. The tactics with the highest value-creating potential are all variations on entering fast-growing product markets that take revenues from distant companies, rather than from direct competitors or customers.

---

[4] See M. Baghai, S. Smit, and P. Viguerie, "Is Your Growth Strategy Flying Blind?" *Harvard Business Review* (May 2009): 86–96.

EXHIBIT 5.3 **Value of Major Types of Growth**

Value created[1]	Type of growth	Rationale
↑ Above average ↓	• Create new markets through new products	• No established competitors; diverts customer spending
	• Convince existing customers to buy more of a product	• All competitors benefit; low risk of retaliation
	• Attract new customers to the market	• All competitors benefit; low risk of retaliation
↑ Average ↓	• Gain market share in fast-growing market	• Competitors can still grow despite losing share; moderate risk of retaliation
	• Make bolt-on acquisitions to accelerate product growth	• Modest acquisition premium relative to upside potential
↑ Below average ↓	• Gain share from rivals through incremental innovation	• Competitors can replicate and take back customers
	• Gain share from rivals through product promotion and pricing	• Competitors can retaliate quickly
	• Make large acquisitions	• High premium to pay; most value diverted to selling shareholders

[1] Per dollar of revenue.

Developing *new products* or services that are so innovative as to create entirely new product categories has the highest value-creating potential. The stronger the competitive advantage a company can establish in the new product category, the higher will be its ROIC and the value created, as we discussed in the previous chapter. For example, the coronary stent commercialized in the early 1990s reduced the need for heart surgery, lowering both the risk and cost of treating cardiac problems. Owing to this innovation's overwhelming competitive advantage over traditional treatments, and also over subsequent products entering the market,[5] neither type of competitor could retaliate, so the innovators created large amounts of value. Similarly, traditional television has been unable to compete with the interactivity of the Internet and video games, as consumers have taken up these media for their home entertainment. However, competition in the new digital-entertainment category is itself fierce, so the value created per dollar of revenue in this sector is unlikely to reach the levels generated by the coronary stent.

Next in the pecking order of value-creating growth tactics comes *persuading existing customers to buy more* of a product or related products. For example, if Procter & Gamble convinces customers to wash their hands more frequently, the market for hand soap will grow faster. Direct competitors will not retaliate, because they benefit as well. The ROIC associated with the additional revenue is likely to be high because the players' manufacturing and distribution systems can typically produce the additional products at little additional cost.

[5] Products that entered the market at a later stage were less successful because of high switching costs for customers (see Chapter 4).

Clearly, the benefit will not be as large if the company has to increase costs substantially to get those sales. For example, offering bank customers insurance products requires the expense of an entirely new sales force, because the products are too complex to add to the list of products the bankers are already selling.

Attracting new customers to a market also can create substantial value. Consumer packaged-goods companies Beiersdorf and L'Oréal accelerated growth in sales of skin-care products by convincing men to use their Nivea and Biotherm products, respectively. Once again, competitors didn't retaliate because they also gained from the category expansion. Men's skin-care products aren't much different from women's, so much of the research and development (R&D), manufacturing, and distribution cost could be shared. The major incremental cost was for marketing and advertising.

The value a company can create from increasing market share depends on both the rate of growth in the market in question and the way the company goes about gaining market share. There are three main ways to grow market share (although they don't fall next to each other in the pecking order of types of growth). When a company *gains market share in a fast-growing market*, the absolute revenues of its competitors may still be growing strongly, too, so the competitors may not retaliate. However, gaining share in a mature market is more likely to provoke retaliation by competitors.

Gaining share from *incremental innovation*—for example, through incremental technology improvements that neither fundamentally change a product nor create an entirely new category and are possible to copy—won't create much value or maintain the advantage for long. From a customer's viewpoint, hybrid and electric vehicles aren't fundamentally different from gas or diesel vehicles, so they cannot command much of a price premium to offset their higher costs. The total number of vehicles sold will not increase, and if one company gains market share for a while, competitors will try to take it back, as competitors can quickly copy each other's innovations. All in all, the auto companies aren't likely to create much value from hybrid or electric vehicles.

Gaining share through *product pricing and promotion* in a mature market rarely creates much value, if any. Huggies and Pampers dominate the disposable-diaper market, are financially strong, and can easily retaliate if the other tries to gain share, so any growth arising from, say, an intense advertising campaign that hits directly at the other competitor will provoke retaliation. And as Amazon continued expanding into the U.S. consumer electronics retail market in 2009, Wal-Mart retaliated with price cuts on key products such as top-selling video games and game consoles, even though Amazon's $20 billion in sales in 2008 were a fraction of Wal-Mart's $406 billion sales in the same year.

In concentrated markets, share battles often lead to a cycle of market share give-and-take, but rarely a permanent share gain for any one competitor, unless that competitor changes the product or its delivery enough to create what is effectively a new product. The possible exception is when stronger companies gain share from smaller, weaker competitors and force the weaker players out of the market entirely.

Price increases, over and above cost increases, can create value as long as any resulting decline in sales is small. However, they tend not to be repeatable: if a company or number of competitors get away with a price increase one year, they are unlikely to have the same good fortune the next. Furthermore, the first increase could be eroded fairly quickly. Otherwise, you would see some companies increasing their profit margins year after year, while in reality, long-term increases in profit margins are rare. There was an exception among packaged-goods companies in the mid-1990s. They passed on increases in commodity costs to customers but did not lower prices when their commodity costs subsequently declined. But even they haven't been able to do the same thing since.

There are two main approaches to growing through acquisitions. Growth through *bolt-on acquisitions* can create value if the premium paid for the target is not too high. Bolt-on acquisitions make incremental changes to a business model—for example, by completing or extending a company's product offering or filling gaps in its distribution system. IBM has been very successful in bolting on smaller software companies and subsequently marketing their applications through its existing global sales and distribution system, which can absorb the additional sales without too much extra investment. Because such acquisitions are relatively small, they boost IBM's growth but add little cost and complexity.

In contrast, creating growth through *large acquisitions*—say, half the size or more of the acquiring company—tends to create less value. Large acquisitions typically occur when a market has begun to mature and the industry has excess capacity. While the acquiring company shows revenue growth, the combined revenues often do not increase, and sometimes they decrease because customers prefer to have multiple suppliers. Any new value comes primarily from cost cutting, not from growth. Furthermore, integrating the two companies requires significant investments and involves far more complexity and risk than integrating small, bolt-on acquisitions.

The logic explaining why growth from product market growth creates greater and more sustainable value than taking share is compelling. Nevertheless, the dividing line between the two types of growth can be fuzzy. For instance, some innovations prevent existing competitors from retaliating, even though the innovator's products and services may not appear to be that new. Wal-Mart's innovative approach to retailing in the 1960s and 1970s offered an entirely new shopping experience to its customers, who flocked to the company's stores. One could argue that Wal-Mart was merely taking share away from small local stores. But the fact that its competitors could not retaliate suggests that Wal-Mart's approach constituted a truly innovative product. However, if Wal-Mart were to grow by winning customers from Target, that would count as market share gain, because Target and Wal-Mart offer their retailing product in a similar fashion.

Since underlying product market growth tends to create the most value, companies should aim to be in the fastest-growing product markets so they can achieve growth that consistently creates value. If a company is in the wrong markets and can't easily get into the right ones, it may do better by sustaining growth at the same level as its competitors while finding ways to improve and sustain its ROIC. But that is easier said than done.

DIFFICULTY OF SUSTAINING GROWTH

Sustaining high growth is much more difficult than sustaining ROIC, especially for larger companies. The math is simple. Suppose your core product markets are growing at the rate of the gross domestic product (GDP) (say, 5 percent nominal growth) and you currently have $10 billion in revenues. Ten years from now, assuming you grow at 5 percent a year, your revenues will be $16.3 billion. Assume you aspire to grow organically at 8 percent a year. In 10 years, your revenues will need to be $21.6 billion. Therefore, you will need to find new sources of revenues that can grow to over $5.3 billion per year by the 10th year. Adjusting for inflation of 2 percent, you need an extra $4.3 billion per year in today's dollars. Another way to think of it is that you would need to reinvent a Fortune 500 company to find such revenues.[6] If your product markets are growing at only 5 percent, how can you possibly achieve that magnitude of growth?

Given this difficulty, some companies' growth targets are unrealistic. We know of one with sales already in excess of $5 billion that has announced growth targets of more than 20 percent a year for the next 20 years. Since annual world economic growth is typically less than 4 percent in real terms,[7] and many companies are competing for a share of that growth, company growth targets need to be more pragmatic.

Sustaining growth is difficult because most product markets have natural life cycles. The market for a product—by which we mean the market for a narrow product category sold to a specific customer segment in a specific geography—typically follows an S-curve over its life cycle until maturity, as shown on the left side of Exhibit 5.4. The right side shows the growth curves for various real products, scaled to their relative penetration of U.S. households. First, a product has to prove itself with early adopters. Growth then accelerates as more people want to buy the product, until it reaches its point of maximum penetration. After this point of maturity, and depending on the nature of the product, either sales growth falls back to the same rate of growth as the population or the economy, or sales may start to shrink. To illustrate, autos and

---

[6] The cutoff point for the Fortune 500 in terms of revenues was around $4 billion in 2009.
[7] World GDP growth was 4 percent a year between 2000 and 2007—the strongest economic growth in decades. See World Bank, "2009 World Development Indicators" (2009).

EXHIBIT 5.4 **Variation in Growth over Product Life Cycle**

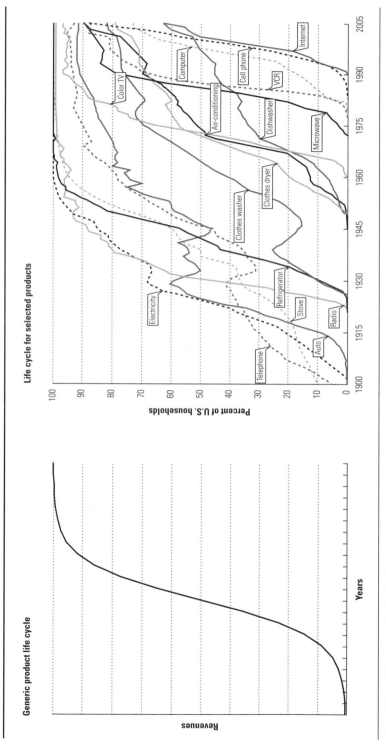

Generic product life cycle

Life cycle for selected products

Source: W. Cox and R. Alm, "You Are What You Spend," *New York Times*, February 10, 2008.

EXHIBIT 5.5 **Wal-Mart and eBay: Growth Trajectories**

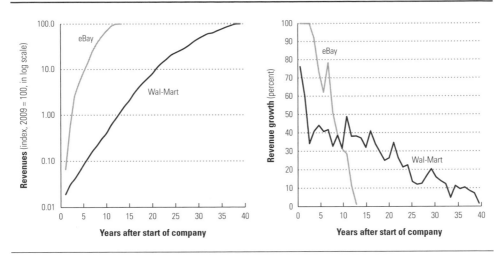

Source: McKinsey Corporate Performance Center analysis.

packaged snacks have continued to grow in line with economic growth for half a century or more, while videocassette recorders lasted less than 20 years before they declined and disappeared.

While the pattern of growth is usually the same for every product and service, the amount and pace of growth will vary for each one. Exhibit 5.5 compares Wal-Mart and eBay. While both have some activities outside their core business, they are largely one-product companies. Wal-Mart's growth did not dip below 10 percent until the end of the 1990s, some 35 years after it was founded. In contrast, eBay saw its growth fall to below 10 percent after only 12 years, having grown very rapidly to reach maturity early. Because eBay is an Internet-based auction house, it doesn't need to add many more staff members in order to grow. In contrast, Wal-Mart, as a physical retailer, has to add people as quickly as it adds stores and sales. The speed at which Wal-Mart can hire and train people limits its rate of growth relative to eBay. But Wal-Mart's core market is much larger than eBay's. In 2008, Wal-Mart generated $406 billion of revenues, mostly from its core discount and supercenter stores, whereas eBay generated only about $8.5 billion of revenues because its core addressable market is so much smaller.

Sustaining high growth presents major challenges to companies. Given the natural life cycle of products, the only way to achieve consistently high growth is to consistently find new product markets and enter them successfully in time to enjoy their more profitable high-growth phase. Exhibit 5.6 illustrates this by showing the cumulative sales for a company that introduces one new product in one market (geographic or customer segment) in each year. All products are identical in terms of sales volume and growth; their growth rates are very

EXHIBIT 5.6 **The Challenge of Sustaining High Growth**

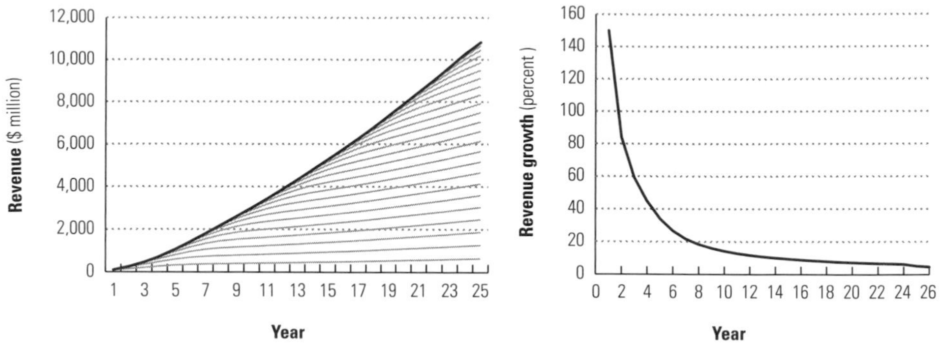

Source: McKinsey Corporate Performce Center analysis.

high in the beginning and eventually slow to 3 percent once the market is fully penetrated. Although the company continues to launch new products that are just as successful as their predecessors, aggregate sales growth slows down rapidly as the company gets bigger. In the long term, growth approaches 3 percent, equal to the long-term growth rate of the markets for the company's products. Ultimately, a company's growth and size are constrained by the growth and size of its product markets and the number of product markets in which it competes.

   To sustain high growth, companies need to overcome this "portfolio tread-mill" effect: for each product that matures and declines in revenues, the company needs to find a similar-sized replacement product to stay level in revenues—and even more to continue growing. Think of the pharmaceutical industry, which showed unprecedented growth from the mid-1990s, thanks to so-called blockbuster drugs such as Lipitor and Celebrex. When the patents for this generation of drugs expire between 2010 and 2015, revenues from them will plummet. Pharmaceutical companies need to launch similar-sized drugs just to make up the difference, let alone keep growing. But finding sizable new sources of growth requires more experimentation and a longer time horizon than many companies are willing to invest in. In another industry, General Electric's GE Capital business was a side business in 1981, when it generated about 8 percent of GE's profits. Only after 26 years of consistent investment did it reach 50 percent of GE's profits in 2005.

EMPIRICAL ANALYSIS OF CORPORATE GROWTH

In this section, we present our findings on the level and persistence of corporate growth for more than 5,000 U.S.-based nonfinancial companies over the past

45 years. Our analysis of their revenue growth follows the same procedure as our analysis of ROIC data in Chapter 4, except here we use three-year rolling averages to moderate distortions caused by currency fluctuations and M&A activity.[8] We also use real, rather than nominal, data to analyze all corporate growth results, because even mature companies saw a dramatic increase in revenues during the 1970s as inflation increased prices. (Ideally, we would report statistics on *organic* revenue growth, but current reporting standards do not require companies to disclose the effects of currencies and M&A on their revenues.) Our overall findings concerning revenue growth are as follows:

- The median rate of revenue growth between 1963 and 2007 was 5.4 percent in real terms. Real revenue growth fluctuates more than ROIC, ranging from 0.9 percent in 1992 to 9.4 percent in 1966.

- High growth rates decay very quickly. Companies growing faster than 20 percent (in real terms) typically grow at only 8 percent within five years and at 5 percent within 10 years.

- Extremely large companies struggle to grow. Excluding the first year, companies entering the Fortune 50 grow at an average of only 1 percent (above inflation) over the following 15 years.

Growth Trends

We start by examining aggregate levels and trends of corporate growth. Exhibit 5.7 presents median (real) revenue growth rates between 1963 and 2007. The average median revenue growth rate between 1963 and 2007 equals 5.4 percent per year and oscillates between roughly 1 percent and 9 percent. Median revenue growth demonstrates no trend over time.

A real revenue growth of 5.4 percent is quite high when compared with real GDP growth in the United States (3.2 percent). Why the difference? Possible explanations abound. The first is self-selection: companies with good growth opportunities need capital to grow. Since public markets are large and liquid, high-growth companies are more likely to be publicly traded than privately held ones. We measure only publicly traded companies, so our growth results are likely to be higher. Secondly, as companies become increasingly specialized and outsource more services, firms providing services will grow and develop quickly without affecting the GDP figures. Consider Electronic Data Systems (EDS), a company that provides information technology (IT) and data services. As companies outsource management of their IT to EDS, GDP will not change, since it measures aggregate output. Yet EDS's high growth will influence our sample.

---

[8] For more detail on how to define and separate organic, M&A, and currency-driven revenue growth, see Chapter 21.

EXHIBIT 5.7 **Long-Term Revenue Growth for Nonfinancial Companies**

3-year revenue growth rate,[1] adjusted for inflation, percent

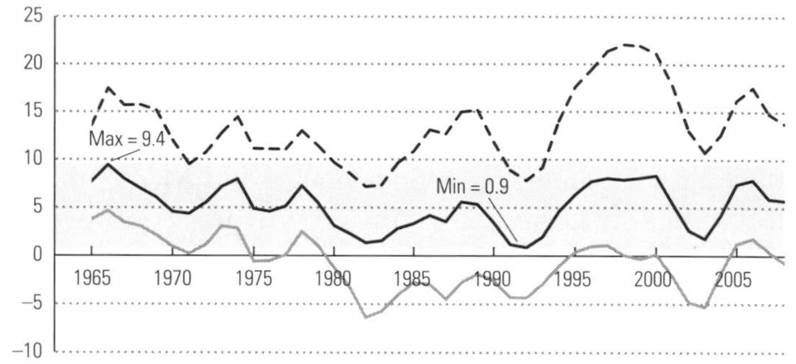

	Average	Median
3rd quartile	13.5	13.0
Median	5.2	5.4
1st quartile	−0.7	−0.4

[1] Compound annual growth rate.

Source: Compustat, McKinsey Corporate Performance Center analysis.

A third explanation is global expansion. Many of the companies in our sample create products and generate revenue outside the United States, which again will not affect U.S. GDP. Next comes our focus on median measures. A significant portion of U.S. GDP is driven by large companies, which tend to grow more slowly. But we measure the median corporate growth rates; the median company is typically small, and small public companies grow faster. Finally, although we use rolling averages and medians, these cannot eliminate but only dampen the effects of M&A and currency fluctuations, which do not reflect organic growth.

In addition to mapping median growth, Exhibit 5.7 also reveals that from 1973 to 2005, at least one-quarter of all companies shrank in real terms almost every year. Thus, although most companies publicly project healthy growth over the next five years, in reality many mature firms will shrink. This underlines the need to exercise caution before projecting strong growth for a valuation, especially in mature sectors.

Exhibit 5.8 shows the distribution of real revenue growth from 1997 to 2007. The median revenue growth rate was 5.9 percent, with about one-third of the companies increasing revenues faster than 10 percent. (This includes the effect of acquisitions, so fewer companies grew faster than 10 percent just through organic growth.)

Growth Across Industries

The spread of growth rates across industries varies dramatically, as did the spread of ROICs, described in the previous chapter. Exhibit 5.1 showed that some sectors (including health-care equipment, software, movies and entertainment, and integrated telecom) had annual growth rates in excess of

EXHIBIT 5.8 **Distribution of Growth Rates**

Inflation-adjusted 1997–2007 revenue growth rate[1] distribution, percent

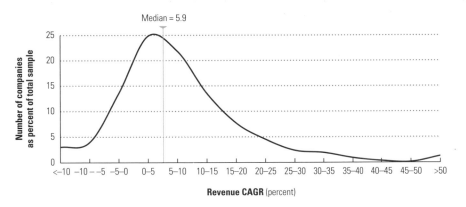

¹ Compound annual growth rate.

Source: Compustat, McKinsey Corporate Performance Center analysis.

9 percent, vastly outgrowing others (food products, department stores, paper and forest products, and electric utilities) with growth rates of 3 percent or less.

Yet, unlike the ranking of industries by ROIC, the ranking of industries by growth varies significantly over time, as shown in Exhibit 5.9. Some of the variation is explained by structural factors, such as changes in customer demand or competition from substitute products. Industries that were among the fastest growing between 1967 and 1977, with growth of 9 percent or more (for example, restaurants and beverages), dropped to mediocre growth levels as their markets matured over recent decades. Broadcasting had very strong growth between 1977 and 1997, but its growth dropped over the past 10 years to just 4 percent (its growth rate in the 1960s) as substitute Internet-based services became available. In other cases, the variation in growth derives from the business cycle, which affects some industries more than others. For example, the cycle-sensitive sectors of construction materials, trucking, airlines, and building products move up and down in the growth rankings much more than health-care equipment and household and personal products, for which demand is more stable. And the commodities price boom of the past decade has driven growth rates in integrated oil and gas, energy equipment and services, and metals and mining to their highest levels of the past 45 years.

In spite of this high degree of variation, some sectors have consistently been among the fastest growing. These include software, IT services, and health-care equipment, where demand has remained strong for four decades. Others, such as auto components, food products, and department stores, have consistently had among the lowest growth rates, as their markets had already reached maturity in the 1970s, the first decade shown in Exhibit 5.9.

EXHIBIT 5.9 **Unstable Growth for Industries**

Industry median 10-year revenue CAGR, adjusted for inflation, percent

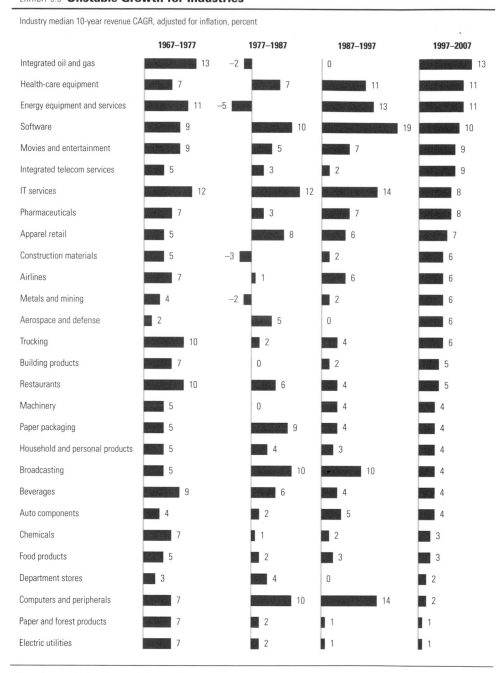

	1967–1977	1977–1987	1987–1997	1997–2007
Integrated oil and gas	13	−2	0	13
Health-care equipment	7	7	11	11
Energy equipment and services	11	−5	13	11
Software	9	10	19	10
Movies and entertainment	9	5	7	9
Integrated telecom services	5	3	2	9
IT services	12	12	14	8
Pharmaceuticals	7	3	7	8
Apparel retail	5	8	6	7
Construction materials	5	−3	2	6
Airlines	7	1	6	6
Metals and mining	4	−2	2	6
Aerospace and defense	2	5	0	6
Trucking	10	2	4	6
Building products	7	0	2	5
Restaurants	10	6	4	5
Machinery	5	0	4	4
Paper packaging	5	9	4	4
Household and personal products	5	4	3	4
Broadcasting	5	10	10	4
Beverages	9	6	4	4
Auto components	4	2	5	4
Chemicals	7	1	2	3
Food products	5	2	3	3
Department stores	3	4	0	2
Computers and peripherals	7	10	14	2
Paper and forest products	7	2	1	1
Electric utilities	7	2	1	1

Source: Compustat, McKinsey Corporate Performance Center analysis.

EXHIBIT 5.10 **Revenue Growth Decay Analysis**

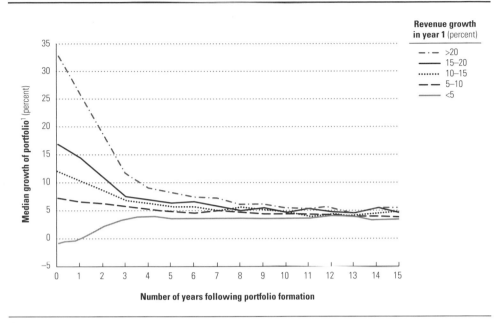

¹ At year 0, companies are grouped into one of five portfolios, based on revenue growth.

Source: Compustat, McKinsey Corporate Performance Center analysis.

Sustaining Growth

Understanding a company's potential for growing revenues in the future is critical to valuation and strategy assessment. Yet developing reasonable projections is a challenge, especially given the upward bias in growth expectations demonstrated by research analysts and the media. Research shows that analyst forecasts of one-year-out aggregate earnings growth for the S&P 500 are systematically overoptimistic, exceeding actual earnings growth by 10 percentage points or more.[9]

To put long-term corporate growth rates in their proper perspective, we present historical rates of growth decay over the past 45 years. Companies were segmented into five portfolios, depending on their growth rate in the year the portfolio was formed. Exhibit 5.10 plots how each portfolio's median company grows over time. As the exhibit shows, growth decays very quickly; high growth is not sustainable for the typical company. Within three years, the difference across portfolios reduces considerably, and by year 5, the highest-growth portfolio outperforms the lowest-growth portfolio by less than 5 percentage points. Within 10 years, this difference drops to less than 2 percentage points. Comparing the decay of growth with that of ROIC shown

[9] See, for example, M. Goedhart, B. Russell, and Z. Williams, "Prophets and Profits," *McKinsey on Finance*, no. 2 (Autumn 2001): 11–14.

EXHIBIT 5.11 **Dramatic Fall in Revenue Growth Rate for Companies Reaching Fortune 50**

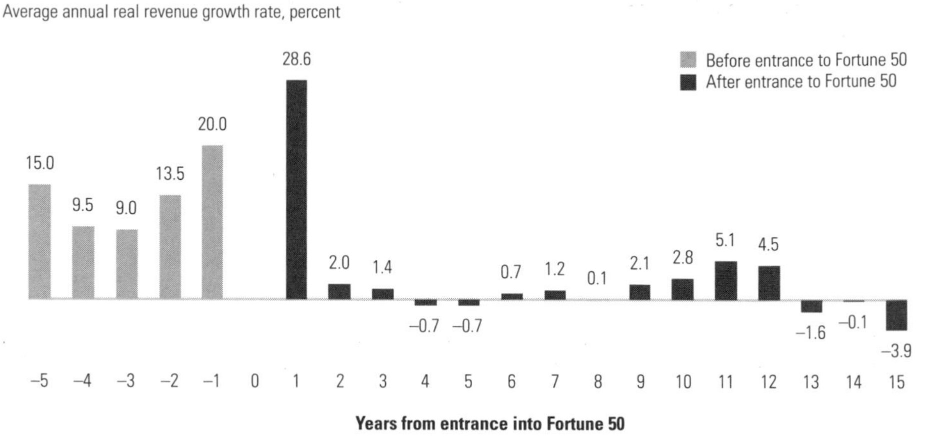

Average annual real revenue growth rate, percent

Source: Corporate Executive Board, "Stall Points: Barriers to Growth for the Large Corporate Enterprise" (1998).

in the previous chapter, we see that although companies' rates of ROIC generally remain fairly stable over time—top companies still outperform bottom companies by more than 10 percentage points after 15 years—rates of growth do not.

As we discussed earlier in this chapter, companies struggle to maintain high growth because product life cycles are finite and growth gets more difficult as companies get bigger. Exhibit 5.11 summarizes results compiled by the Corporate Executive Board to show what happens to real revenue growth when companies enter the Fortune 50.[10] Although they show strong growth before entering the Fortune 50 (often because of acquisitions), their growth drops dramatically afterward. In the five years before entering, real revenue growth varies between 9 percent and 20 percent. And although average growth is high in the year immediately following entry (28.6 percent), in every subsequent year, growth is a lot lower. In fact, in five of the 15 years after entry, the new entrants shrink in real terms.

Do any companies counter this norm? The short answer is no. Exhibit 5.12 allocates companies to groupings by their growth rates and shows the probability of a company moving between the groupings over time. Clearly, maintaining high growth is uncommon. Of the companies reporting less than 5 percent revenue growth from 1994 to 1997, 55 percent continued to report growth below 5 percent 10 years later. High-growth companies don't fare much better: of the companies growing faster than 15 percent from 1994 to 1997, 44 percent grew at real rates below 5 percent 10 years later. Only 25 percent of

[10] Corporate Executive Board, "Stall Points: Barriers to Growth for the Large Corporate Enterprise" (1998).

EXHIBIT 5.12 **Revenue Growth Transition Probability**

Probability that company's growth rate[1] will be in given group from 2004 to 2007, percent

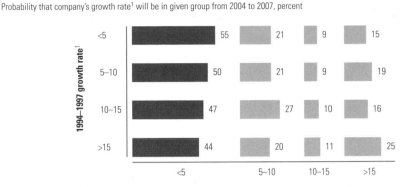

1994–1997 growth rate[1]

	<5	5–10	10–15	>15
<5	55	21	9	15
5–10	50	21	9	19
10–15	47	27	10	16
>15	44	20	11	25

2004–2007 growth rate[1]

[1] Compound annual growth rate.

Source: Compustat, McKinsey Corporate Performance Center analysis.

high-growth companies maintained better than 15 percent real growth 10 years later, most of which was probably driven by acquisitions. High growth is very difficult to sustain—much more difficult than high ROIC.

SUMMARY

To maximize value for their shareholders, companies should understand what drives growth and what makes it value-creating. Long-term revenue growth for large companies is almost exclusively driven by the growth of the markets they operate in and by the acquisitions they undertake (and the markets the acquired companies operate in). Although gains in market share contribute to revenues in the short term, these are far less important for long-term growth.

Revenue growth is not all that matters for creating value; the value created per dollar of additional revenues is the crucial point. In general, this depends on how easily competitors can respond to a company's growth strategy. The growth strategy with the highest potential in this respect is true product innovation, because entirely new product categories by definition have no established competition. Attracting new customers to an existing product or persuading existing customers to buy more of it also can create substantial value, because direct competitors in the same market tend to benefit as well. Growth through bolt-on acquisitions can add value, because such acquisitions can boost revenue growth at little additional cost and complexity. Typically much less attractive is revenue growth from market share gains, because it comes at the expense of established, direct competitors, who are likely to retaliate, especially in maturing markets.

Sustaining high growth is no less a challenge than initiating it. Because most products have natural life cycles, the only way to achieve lasting high growth is to continue introducing new products at an increasing rate—which is just about impossible. Not surprisingly, growth rates for large companies decay much faster than do returns on invested capital; growth rates for even the fastest-growing companies tend to fall back to below 5 percent within 10 years.

REVIEW QUESTIONS

1. Discuss the three generic sources of a company's growth, their relative importance for its growth, and what this means for a company's strategy.
2. For which type of company is additional growth likely to create more value: a high-ROIC company in a mature market or a low-ROIC company in a fast-growing market? Give reasons for your answer.
3. Why could growth through a series of bolt-on acquisitions create more value than growth through a single large acquisition? (Consider premium paid and synergies created for each individual transaction.)
4. Identify and discuss an example where growth in market share through a price war created long-term value for a company.
5. Why do fast-growing companies typically fail to sustain their high growth rates?
6. Why do company growth rates typically converge much more quickly toward the average rate across all companies than their rates of ROIC, given that both ultimately depend on the underlying product life cycles?
7. Discuss why the ranking of industries by growth varies more over time than their ranking by ROIC.
8. If growth from gaining market share through product promotion and pricing rarely creates much value, why do most consumer goods companies put so much effort into it?

Part Two

Core Valuation Techniques

6

Frameworks for Valuation

In Part One, we built a conceptual framework to show what drives value. In broad terms, a company's value is driven by its ability to earn a healthy return on invested capital (ROIC) and by its ability to grow. Healthy rates of return and growth result in high cash flows, the ultimate source of value.

Part Two offers a step-by-step guide for analyzing and valuing a company in practice, including technical details for properly measuring and interpreting the drivers of value. Among the many ways to value a company (see Exhibit 6.1 for an overview), we focus particularly on two: enterprise discounted cash flow (DCF) and discounted economic profit. When applied correctly, both valuation methods yield the same results; however, each model has certain benefits in practice. Enterprise DCF remains a favorite of practitioners and academics because it relies solely on the flow of cash in and out of the company, rather than on accounting-based earnings. The discounted economic-profit valuation model is gaining in popularity because of its close link to economic theory and competitive strategy. Economic profit highlights whether a company is earning its cost of capital and how its financial performance is expected to change over time. Given that the two methods yield identical results and have different but complementary benefits, we recommend creating *both* enterprise DCF and economic-profit models when valuing a company.

Both the enterprise DCF and economic-profit models discount future income streams at the weighted average cost of capital (WACC). WACC-based models work best when a company maintains a relatively stable debt-to-value ratio. If a company's debt-to-value ratio is expected to change, WACC-based models can still yield accurate results but are more difficult to apply. In such cases, we recommend an alternative to WACC-based models: adjusted present value (APV). APV specifically forecasts and values any cash flows associated with capital structure separately, rather than embedding their value in the cost of capital.

The chapter also includes a discussion of capital cash flow and equity cash flow valuation models. Because these two valuation models mix together

EXHIBIT 6.1 **Frameworks for DCF-Based Valuation**

Model	Measure	Discount factor	Assessment
Enterprise discounted cash flow	Free cash flow	Weighted average cost of capital	Works best for projects, business units, and companies that manage their capital structure to a target level.
Discounted economic profit	Economic profit	Weighted average cost of capital	Explicitly highlights when a company creates value.
Adjusted present value	Free cash flow	Unlevered cost of equity	Highlights changing capital structure more easily than WACC-based models.
Capital cash flow	Capital cash flow	Unlevered cost of equity	Compresses free cash flow and the interest tax shield in one number, making it difficult to compare operating performance among companies and over time.
Equity cash flow	Cash flow to equity	Levered cost of equity	Difficult to implement correctly because capital structure is embedded within the cash flow. Best used when valuing financial institutions.

operating performance and capital structure in cash flow, they lead more easily to mistakes. For this reason, we avoid capital cash flow and equity cash flow valuation models, except when valuing banks and other financial institutions, where capital structure is an inextricable part of operations (for how to value banks, see Chapter 36).

ENTERPRISE DISCOUNTED CASH FLOW MODEL

The enterprise DCF model discounts free cash flow, meaning the cash flow available to all investors—equity holders, debt holders, and any other nonequity investors—at the weighted average cost of capital, meaning the blended cost for all investor capital. The claims on cash flow of debt holders and other nonequity investors are subtracted from enterprise value to determine equity holders' value.[1] Equity valuation models, in contrast, value only the equity holders' claims against operating cash flows. Exhibit 6.2 demonstrates the relationship between enterprise value and equity value. For this company, equity holders' value can be calculated either directly at $227.5 million or by estimating enterprise value ($427.5 million) and subtracting debt ($200.0 million).

Although both methods lead to identical results when applied correctly, the equity method is difficult to apply, since matching equity cash flows with the correct cost of equity is particularly challenging (for more on this, see the section

---

[1] Throughout this chapter, we refer to debt and other nonequity claims. Other nonequity claims arise when stakeholders have a claim against the company's future cash flow but do not hold traditional interest-bearing debt or common equity. Nonequity claims include debt equivalents (e.g., operating leases and unfunded pension liabilities) and hybrid securities (e.g., convertible debt and employee options).

EXHIBIT 6.2 **Enterprise Valuation of a Single-Business Company**

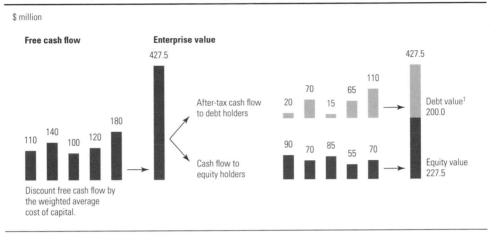

$ million

^{1} Debt value equals discounted after-tax cash flow to debt holders plus the present value of interest tax shield.

on equity valuation later in this chapter). Consequently, to value a company's equity, we recommend valuing the *enterprise* first and then subtracting the value of any nonequity financial claims.

The enterprise method is especially useful when applied to a multibusiness company. As shown in Exhibit 6.3, the enterprise value equals the summed value of the individual operating units less the present value of the corporate-center costs, plus the value of nonoperating assets.^{2} If you use enterprise discounted cash flow instead of the equity cash flow model, you can value individual projects, business units, and even the entire company with a consistent methodology.

Valuing a company's common equity using enterprise DCF is a four-part process:

1. Value the company's operations by discounting free cash flow at the weighted average cost of capital.
2. Identify and value nonoperating assets, such as excess marketable securities, nonconsolidated subsidiaries, and other equity investments. Summing the value of operations and nonoperating assets gives enterprise value.
3. Identify and value all debt and other nonequity claims against the enterprise value. Debt and other nonequity claims include (among others)

^{2} Many investment professionals define enterprise value as interest-bearing debt plus the market value of equity minus excess cash, whereas we define enterprise value as the value of operations plus nonoperating assets. The two definitions are equivalent for companies without nonoperating assets (e.g., excess cash and nonconsolidated subsidiaries) and debt equivalents (e.g., unfunded pension liabilities).

EXHIBIT 6.3 **Enterprise Valuation of a Multibusiness Company**

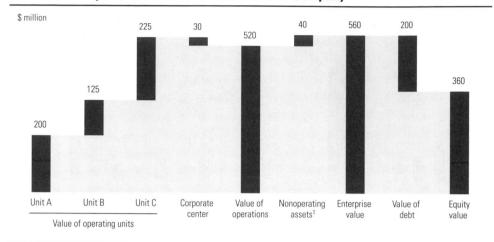

¹ Including excess cash and marketable securities.

fixed-rate and floating-rate debt, unfunded pension liabilities, employee options, and preferred stock.

4. Subtract the value of nonequity financial claims from enterprise value to determine the value of common equity. To estimate price per share, divide equity value by the number of current shares outstanding.

Exhibit 6.4 presents the results of an enterprise DCF valuation for Home Depot, the world's largest retailer of home improvement products. We use Home Depot throughout the chapter to compare valuation methods. To value Home Depot, discount each annual projected cash flow by the company's weighted average cost of capital.[3] Next, sum the present values of all the annual cash flows to determine the present value of operations. For simplicity, the first year's cash flow is discounted by one full year, the second by two full years, and so on. Since cash flows are generated throughout the year, and not as a lump sum, discounting in full-year increments understates the appropriate discount factor. Therefore, adjust the present value upward by half a year;[4] the resulting value of operations is $65.3 billion.

To this value, add nonoperating assets (e.g., excess cash and other nonoperating assets) to estimate enterprise value. For Home Depot, enterprise value ($65.8 billion) almost mirrors the value of operations ($65.3 billion) because its

---

[3] To generate identical results across valuation methods, we have not adjusted results for rounding error. Rounding errors occur in most exhibits.

[4] A half-year adjustment is made to the present value for Home Depot because we assume cash flow is generated symmetrically around the midyear point. For companies dependent on year-end holidays, cash flows will be more heavily weighted toward the latter half of the year. In this case, the adjustment should be smaller.

EXHIBIT 6.4 **Home Depot: Enterprise DCF Valuation**

Forecast year	Free cash flow ($ million)	Discount factor (@ 8.5%)	Present value of FCF ($ million)
2009	5,909	0.922	5,448
2010	2,368	0.850	2,013
2011	1,921	0.784	1,506
2012	2,261	0.723	1,634
2013	2,854	0.666	1,902
2014	3,074	0.614	1,889
2015	3,308	0.567	1,874
2016	3,544	0.522	1,852
2017	3,783	0.482	1,822
2018	4,022	0.444	1,787
Continuing value	92,239	0.444	40,966
Present value of cash flow			62,694
Midyear adjustment factor			1.041
Value of operations			65,291
Value of excess cash			–
Value of long-term investments			361
Value of tax loss carry-forwards			112
Enterprise value			65,764
Less: Value of debt			(11,434)
Less: Value of capitalized operating leases			(8,298)
Equity value			46,032
Number of shares outstanding (December 2008)			1.7
Equity value per share			27.1

nonoperating assets are negligible. From enterprise value, subtract the present value of debt and other nonequity claims. Departing from its historically conservative capital structure, the company issued a considerable amount of debt ($11.4 billion) following the acquisition of Hughes Supply in 2006. Similar to most retailers, Home Depot uses off-balance-sheet operating leases ($8.3 billion) to finance its stores. Dividing the resulting equity value by the number of shares outstanding (1.7 billion) leads to an estimate of per-share value of $27.10. During the first half of 2009, Home Depot's stock price traded in the mid-$20s.

Over the next few pages, we outline the enterprise DCF valuation process. Although we present it sequentially, valuation is an iterative process. To value operations, we reorganize the company's financial statements to separate operating items from nonoperating items and capital structure; we then analyze the company's historical performance; define and project free cash flow over the short, medium, and long run; and discount the projected free cash flows at the weighted average cost of capital.

Valuing Operations

The value of operations equals the discounted value of future free cash flow. Free cash flow equals the cash flow generated by the company's operations, less any reinvestment back into the business. As defined at the beginning of this section, free cash flow is the cash flow available to all investors—equity holders, debt holders, and any other nonequity investors—so it is independent of capital structure. Consistent with this definition, free cash flow must be discounted using the weighted average cost of capital, because the WACC represents rates of return required by the company's debt and equity holders blended together, and as such is the company's opportunity cost of funds.

Reorganizing the financial statements   A robust valuation model requires a clear account of financial performance. Although return on invested capital (ROIC) and free cash flow (FCF) are critical to the valuation process, they cannot be computed directly from a company's reported financial statements. Whereas ROIC and FCF are intended to measure the company's operating performance, financial statements mix operating performance, nonoperating performance, and capital structure. Therefore, to calculate ROIC and FCF, we must first reorganize the accountant's financial statements into new statements that separate operating items, nonoperating items, and financial structure.

This reorganization leads to two new terms: invested capital and net operating profit less adjusted taxes (NOPLAT). Invested capital represents the investor capital required to fund operations, without distinguishing how the capital is financed. NOPLAT represents the total after-tax operating income generated by the company's invested capital, available to all financial investors.

Exhibit 6.5 presents the historical NOPLAT and invested capital for Home Depot and one of its direct competitors, Lowe's. To calculate ROIC, divide NOPLAT by average invested capital. In 2008, Home Depot's return on invested capital equaled 8.0 percent (based on a two-year average of invested capital), which almost matches its 2008 weighted average cost of capital of 8.3 percent.

Next, use the reorganized financial statements to calculate free cash flow, which will be the basis for our valuation. Defined in a manner consistent with ROIC, free cash flow is derived directly from NOPLAT and the change in invested capital. Unlike the accountant's cash flow from operations (provided in the company's annual report), free cash flow is independent of nonoperating items and capital structure.

Exhibit 6.6 presents historical free cash flow for both Home Depot and Lowe's. As seen in the exhibit, Home Depot generated $3.7 billion in free cash flow in 2008, whereas the free cash flow of Lowe's is considerably smaller. This isn't necessarily a problem for Lowe's. Its free cash flow is small because the company is reinvesting most of its gross cash flow to grow its business.

Analyzing historical performance   Once the company's financial statements are reorganized, analyze the company's historical financial performance. By

EXHIBIT 6.5 **Home Depot and Lowe's: Historical ROIC Analysis**

$ million

	Home Depot			Lowe's		
	2006	**2007**	**2008**	**2006**	**2007**	**2008**
Net sales	90,837	77,349	71,288	46,927	48,283	48,230
Cost of merchandise sold	(61,054)	(51,352)	(47,298)	(30,729)	(31,556)	(31,729)
Selling, general, and administrative	(18,348)	(17,053)	(17,846)	(9,884)	(10,656)	(11,176)
Depreciation	(1,645)	(1,693)	(1,785)	(1,162)	(1,366)	(1,539)
Add: Operating lease interest	441	536	486	185	169	199
Adjusted EBITA	10,231	7,787	4,845	5,337	4,874	3,985
Operating cash taxes	(3,986)	(3,331)	(1,811)	(2,071)	(1,973)	(1,496)
NOPLAT	6,245	4,456	3,033	3,266	2,901	2,489
Invested capital						
Operating working capital	4,556	3,490	3,490	1,725	1,792	2,084
Net property and equipment	26,605	27,476	26,234	18,971	21,361	22,722
Capitalized operating leases	9,141	7,878	8,298	3,034	3,528	3,913
Other operating assets, net of operating liabilities	(1,027)	(1,635)	(2,129)	(126)	(461)	(450)
Invested capital (excluding goodwill)[1]	39,275	37,209	35,893	23,604	26,220	28,269
Goodwill and acquired intangibles	7,092	1,309	1,134	–	–	–
Cumulative amortization and unreported goodwill	177	49	49	730	730	730
Invested capital (including goodwill)[1]	46,543	38,567	37,075	24,334	26,950	29,000
Return on invested capital (percent)						
ROIC excluding goodwill (average)[1]	16.7	11.7	8.3	14.5	11.6	9.1
ROIC including goodwill (average)[1]	14.5	10.5	8.0	14.0	11.3	8.9

[1] Goodwill includes goodwill, acquired intangibles, cumulative amortization, and unreported goodwill.

thoroughly analyzing the past, we can document whether the company has created value, whether it has grown, and how it compares with its competitors. A good analysis needs to focus on the key drivers of value: return on invested capital, revenue growth, and free cash flow. Understanding how these drivers behaved in the past will help you make more reliable estimates of future cash flow.

Exhibit 6.7 presents a 10-year summary of Home Depot's pretax operating margin, a critical component of return on invested capital. Before Robert Nardelli was hired as CEO in 2002, the company spent roughly 70 percent of revenue on merchandise and 19 percent on selling expenses, leading to an operating profit near 10 percent. During his tenure, Nardelli focused the organization on reducing the cost of merchandise. This led to a 2 percent increase in operating margin. In 2007, Frank Blake replaced Nardelli as CEO and stated he would make improved customer service a core part of the future strategy.[5] As a result, profitability dropped as selling expenses increased from 20 percent

[5] "Home Depot to Scale Back Growth: Back-to-Basics Plan Projected to Cut Earnings," *Atlanta Journal Constitution*, March 1, 2007.

EXHIBIT 6.6 **Home Depot and Lowe's: Historical Free Cash Flow**

$ million

	Home Depot			Lowe's		
	2006	2007	2008	2006	2007	2008
NOPLAT	6,245	4,456	3,033	3,266	2,901	2,489
Depreciation	1,645	1,693	1,785	1,162	1,366	1,539
Gross cash flow	7,890	6,149	4,818	4,428	4,267	4,028
Change in operating working capital	(936)	(739)	–	168	(67)	(292)
Net capital expenditures	(3,349)	(3,577)	(543)	(3,779)	(3,756)	(2,900)
Decrease (increase) in capitalized operating leases	(1,214)	1,262	(419)	291	(494)	(385)
Investments in goodwill and acquired intangibles	(3,525)	–	175	–	–	–
Decrease (increase) in net other operating assets	224	457	494	52	335	(11)
Increase (decrease) in accumulated other comprehensive income	(99)	445	(832)	–	7	(14)
Gross investment	(8,899)	(2,152)	(1,125)	(3,268)	(3,975)	(3,602)
Free cash flow	(1,009)	3,998	3,693	1,160	292	426
After-tax nonoperating income	(6)	334	(72)	52	42	44
Decrease (increase) in nonoperating assets	2	8,384	283	134	(376)	311
Cash flow available to investors	(1,013)	12,716	3,904	1,346	(42)	781
Reconciliation of cash flow to investors						
After-tax interest expense	244	432	390	127	148	199
After-tax operating lease interest expense	274	333	303	114	105	124
Decrease (increase) in debt	(7,576)	(1,769)	1,996	(905)	(2,244)	620
Decrease (increase) in capitalized operating leases	(1,214)	1,262	(419)	291	(494)	(385)
Flows to debt holders	(8,272)	258	2,269	(373)	(2,485)	557
Decrease (increase) in nonoperating deferred taxes	(282)	302	270	–	–	–
Dividends	1,395	1,709	1,521	276	428	491
Repurchased and retired shares	5,889	10,336	(190)	1,400	2,007	(267)
Adjustments to retained earnings	257	111	34	43	8	–
Flows to equity holders	7,259	12,458	1,635	1,719	2,443	224
Cash flow available to investors	(1,013)	12,716	3,904	1,346	(42)	781

to 24 percent of revenue. A reliable estimate of future sales expenses is critical for an accurate assessment of enterprise value based on future cash flow.

Projecting revenue growth, ROIC, and free cash flow

The next task in building an enterprise DCF valuation is to project revenue growth, return on invested capital, and free cash flow. Exhibit 6.8 graphs historical ROIC, projected ROIC, and revenue growth for Home Depot. As the graphs demonstrate, the company's revenue growth and ROIC fell dramatically with the collapse of the U.S. housing market. Sell-side research analysts forecast a gradual recovery by 2011 but do not project growth and return on invested capital to return to their historical levels, given the maturity of the market.

EXHIBIT 6.7 **Home Depot: Operating Margin Analysis**

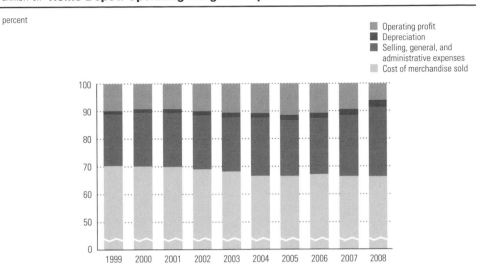

Note: SG&A and operating profit adjusted for operating leases.

EXHIBIT 6.8 **Home Depot: Projected Revenue Growth and ROIC**

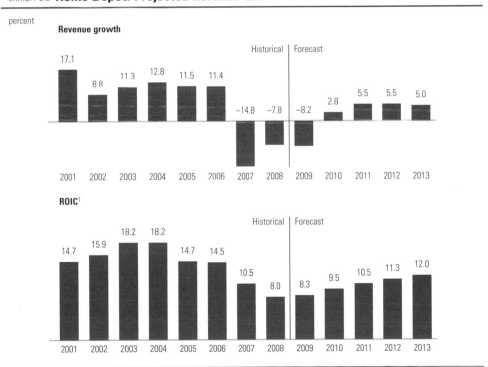

[1] ROIC measured using two-year average invested capital with goodwill and acquired intangible assets.

EXHIBIT 6.9 **Home Depot: Projected Free Cash Flow**

$ million

	Historical			Forecast		
	2006	**2007**	**2008**	**2009**	**2010**	**2011**
NOPLAT	6,245	4,456	3,033	2,971	3,269	3,780
Depreciation	1,645	1,693	1,785	1,639	1,685	1,778
Gross cash flow	7,890	6,149	4,818	4,610	4,954	5,558
Change in operating working capital	(936)	(739)	–	292	(73)	(163)
Net capital expenditures	(3,349)	(3,577)	(543)	503	(2,355)	(3,151)
Decrease (increase) in capitalized operating leases	(1,214)	1,262	(419)	678	(212)	(434)
Investments in goodwill and acquired intangibles	(3,525)	–	175	–	–	–
Decrease (increase) in net other operating assets	224	457	494	(174)	54	111
Increase (decrease) in accumulated other comprehensive income	(99)	445	(832)	–	–	–
Gross investment	(8,899)	(2,152)	(1,125)	1,299	(2,586)	(3,637)
Free cash flow	(1,009)	3,998	3,693	5,909	2,368	1,921

Free cash flow, which is driven by revenue growth and ROIC, provides the basis for an enterprise DCF valuation. Exhibit 6.9 shows a summarized free cash flow calculation for Home Depot.[6] To forecast Home Depot's free cash flow, start with forecasts of NOPLAT and invested capital. Over the short run (the first few years), forecast each financial-statement line item, such as gross margin, selling expenses, accounts receivable, and inventory (see Chapter 9 for detail on how to forecast cash flows). Moving further out, individual line items become difficult to project. Therefore, over the medium horizon (5 to 10 years), focus on the company's key value drivers, such as operating margin, the operating tax rate, and capital efficiency. At some point, though, projecting even key drivers on a year-by-year basis becomes meaningless. To value cash flows beyond this point, use a continuing-value formula, described next.

Estimating continuing value   At the point where predicting the individual key value drivers on a year-by-year basis becomes impractical, do not vary the individual drivers over time. Instead, use a perpetuity-based continuing value, such that:

$$\text{Value of Operations} = \frac{\text{Present Value of Free Cash Flow}}{\textit{during Explicit Forecast Period}} + \frac{\text{Present Value of Free Cash Flow}}{\textit{after Explicit Forecast Period}}$$

Although many continuing-value models exist, we prefer the key value driver model presented in Chapter 2. The key value driver formula is superior

---

[6] Free cash flow does not incorporate any financing-related cash flows such as interest expense or dividends. A good stress test for an enterprise valuation model is to change future interest rates or dividend payout ratios and observe free cash flow. Free cash flow forecasts should not change when you adjust the cost of debt or dividend policy.

EXHIBIT 6.10 **Home Depot: Continuing Value**

$ million

Key inputs[1]	
Projected NOPLAT in 2019	6,122
NOPLAT growth rate in perpetuity (g)	4.0%
Return on new invested capital (RONIC)	12.2%
Weighted average cost of capital (WACC)	8.5%

$$\text{Continuing value}_t = \frac{\text{NOPLAT}_{t+1}\left(1 - \dfrac{g}{\text{RONIC}}\right)}{\text{WACC} - g}$$

$$= 91,440$$

[1] Enterprise valuation based on $92,239 million; the precise calculation without rounding.

to alternative methodologies because it is based on cash flow and links cash flow directly to growth and ROIC. The key value driver formula is expressed as follows:

$$\text{Continuing Value}_t = \frac{\text{NOPLAT}_{t+1}\left(1 - \dfrac{g}{\text{RONIC}}\right)}{\text{WACC} - g}$$

The formula requires a forecast of net operating profit less adjusted taxes (NOPLAT) in the year *following* the end of the explicit forecast period, the long-run forecast for return on new capital (RONIC), the weighted average cost of capital (WACC), and long-run growth in NOPLAT (g).

Exhibit 6.10 presents an estimate for Home Depot's continuing value. Based on a final-year estimate of NOPLAT ($6.1 billion), return on new investment (12.2 percent) slightly above the cost of capital (8.5 percent), and a long-term growth rate of 4 percent, the continuing value is estimated at $92.2 billion. This value is then discounted into today's dollars and added to the value from the explicit forecast period to determine Home Depot's operating value. (Exhibit 6.4 discounts continuing value in 2018 back to 2009.)

Alternative methods and additional details for estimating continuing value are provided in Chapter 10.

Discounting free cash flow at the weighted average cost of capital   To determine the value of operations, discount each year's forecast of free cash flow for time and risk. When you discount any set of cash flows, make sure to define the cash flows and discount factor consistently. In an enterprise valuation, free cash flows are available to all investors. Consequently, the discount factor for free cash flow must represent the risk faced by all investors. The weighted average cost of capital (WACC) blends the rates of return required by debt holders (k_d) and equity holders (k_e). For a company financed solely with debt and equity, the WACC is defined as follows:

$$\text{WACC} = \frac{D}{D + E}k_d(1 - T_m) + \frac{E}{D + E}k_e$$

where debt (D) and equity (E) are measured using market values. Note how the cost of debt has been reduced by the marginal tax rate (T_m). The reason for doing this is that the interest tax shield (ITS) has been excluded from free cash flow. Since the interest tax shield has value, it must be incorporated in the valuation. Enterprise DCF values the tax shield by reducing the weighted average cost of capital.

Why move interest tax shields from free cash flow to the cost of capital? By calculating free cash flow as if the company were financed entirely with equity, we can compare operating performance across companies and over time without regard to capital structure. By focusing solely on operations, we can develop a clearer picture of historical performance, and this leads to better performance measurement and forecasting.

Although applying the weighted average cost of capital is intuitive and relatively straightforward, it has some drawbacks. If you discount all future cash flows with a constant cost of capital, as most analysts do, you are implicitly assuming the company keeps its capital structure constant at a target ratio of debt to equity. But if a company plans, say, to increase its debt-to-value ratio, the current cost of capital will understate the expected tax shields. The WACC can be adjusted to accommodate a changing capital structure. However, the process is complicated, and in these situations, we recommend an alternative method such as adjusted present value (APV).

The weighted average cost of capital for Home Depot is presented in Exhibit 6.11. Home Depot funds operations with a mix of debt and equity. Compared with earlier years, the company is using a substantial amount of debt to fund operations, making its net debt-to-value 31.5 percent. The higher debt-to-value is a result of the company's use of debt to fund acquisitions, use of excess cash to repurchase shares, and a drop in equity value resulting from the collapse of the U.S. housing market. The increase in leverage has led to a drop in the company's debt rating and an increase in equity risk. Even so, Home Depot's weighted average cost of capital remains quite low (8.5 percent), as interest rates are at historical lows.

This cost of capital is used to discount each year's forecasted cash flow, as well as the continuing value. The result is the value of operations.

EXHIBIT 6.11 **Home Depot: Weighted Average Cost of Capital**

percent

Source of capital	Proportion of total capital	Cost of capital	Marginal tax rate	After-tax cost of capital	Contribution to weighted average[1]
Debt	31.5	6.8	37.6	4.2	1.3
Equity	68.5	10.4		10.4	7.1
WACC	100.0				8.5

[1] Total does not sum due to rounding error.

Identifying and Valuing Nonoperating Assets

Many companies own assets that have value but whose cash flows are not included in accounting revenue or operating profit. As a result, the cash generated by these assets is not part of free cash flow and must be valued separately.

For example, consider equity investments, known outside the United States as nonconsolidated subsidiaries. When a company owns a small minority stake in another company, it will not record the company's revenue or costs as part of its own. Instead, the company will record only its proportion of the other company's net income as a separate line item.[7] Including net income from nonconsolidated subsidiaries as part of the parent's operating profit will distort margins, since only the subsidiaries' profit is recognized and not the corresponding revenues. Consequently, nonconsolidated subsidiaries are best analyzed and valued separately. The quality of this analysis, however, will depend on how much the other company discloses: typically, the workings of nonconsolidated subsidiaries are not clearly visible to the company's shareholders.

Other nonoperating assets include excess cash, tradable securities, and customer financing arms. A detailed process for identifying and valuing nonoperating assets can be found in Chapter 12.

Identifying and Valuing Nonequity Claims

To convert enterprise value into equity value, subtract any nonequity claims, such as short-term debt, long-term debt, unfunded retirement liabilities, capitalized operating leases, and outstanding employee options. Common equity is a residual claimant, receiving cash flows only *after* the company has fulfilled its other contractual claims. Careful analysis of all potential claims against cash flows is therefore critical.

In today's increasingly complex financial markets, nonequity claims are not always easy to spot. For example, throughout the first decade of the 2000s, numerous banks moved assets and the debt that financed them off the balance sheet into special investment vehicles (SIVs). Since SIVs are structured as separate legal entities, the originating banks are not contractually responsible for the debt. Yet to regain trust with bank clients who lent the SIV money, many banks decided to repurchase the assets and guarantee the corresponding debt. In November 2008, Citigroup repurchased $17 billion in SIV-owned assets. Its share price dropped 23 percent on the day of the announcement.[8]

---

[7] For minority stakes between 20 percent and 50 percent, the parent company will recognize its proportion of the subsidiary's income. A parent that owns less than a 20 percent stake in another company records only dividends paid as part of its own income. This makes valuation of stakes less than 20 percent extremely challenging.

[8] "Citi's Slide Deepens as Investors Bail Out: Shares Drop 23% as SIV Move, Analyst's Warning Spook Market; Pandit Points to Strengths," *Wall Street Journal*, November 20, 2008.

Although a comprehensive list of nonequity claims is impractical, here are the most common:

- *Debt:* If available, use the market value of all outstanding debt, including fixed- and floating-rate debt. If that information is unavailable, the book value of debt is a reasonable proxy, unless the probability of default is high or interest rates have changed dramatically since the debt was originally issued. Any valuation of debt, however, should be consistent with your estimates of enterprise value. (See Chapter 11 for more details.)

- *Operating leases:* These represent the most common form of off-balance-sheet debt. Under certain conditions, companies can avoid capitalizing leases as debt on their balance sheets, although required payments must be disclosed in the footnotes.

- *Unfunded retirement liabilities:* During the early 2000s, accounting bodies around the globe began requiring companies to report on the balance sheet the present value of unfunded retirement liabilities. If these liabilities are not explicitly visible (line items are often consolidated), check the company's note on pensions to determine the size of any unfunded liabilities and where they are reported on the balance sheet.

- *Preferred stock:* Although the name denotes equity, preferred stock in well-established companies more closely resembles unsecured debt.

- *Employee options:* Each year, many companies offer their employees compensation in the form of options. Since options give the employee the right to buy company stock at a potentially discounted price, they can have great value.

- *Minority interest:* When a company controls a subsidiary but does not own 100 percent, the investment must be consolidated on the parent company's balance sheet. The funding other investors provide is recognized on the parent company's balance sheet as minority interest. When valuing minority interest, it is important to realize the minority interest holder does not have a claim on the company's assets, but rather a claim on the subsidiary's assets.

The identification and valuation of nonequity financial claims are covered in detail in Chapter 12. A detailed discussion of how to analyze operating leases, unfunded pension liabilities, and employee options is presented in Chapter 27.

A common mistake made when valuing companies is to double-count claims already deducted from cash flow. Consider a company with a pension shortfall. You have been told the company will make extra payments to eliminate the liability. If you deduct the present value of the liability from enterprise value, you should not model the extra payments within free cash flow; that would mean double-counting the shortfall (once in cash flow and once as a claim), leading to an underestimate of equity value.

Valuing Equity

Once you have identified and valued all nonequity claims, subtract the claims from enterprise value to determine equity value. Home Depot has traditional debt ($11.4 billion) and capitalized operating leases ($8.3 billion). To value Home Depot's common equity, subtract each of these claims from Home Depot's enterprise value (see Exhibit 6.4).

To determine Home Depot's share price, divide the estimated common-stock value by the number of *undiluted* shares outstanding. Do not use diluted shares. We have already valued convertible debt and employee stock options separately. If we were to use diluted shares, we would be double-counting the options' value.

At the end of fiscal year 2008, Home Depot had 1.7 billion shares outstanding. Dividing the equity estimate of $46.0 billion by 1.7 billion shares generates an estimated value of $27 per share. The estimated share value assumes Home Depot can rebound from the 2008 recession, with returns slightly above its cost of capital and growth back in line with gross domestic product (GDP). During the first half of 2009, Home Depot's actual stock price traded between $20 and $25 per share.

ECONOMIC-PROFIT-BASED VALUATION MODELS

The enterprise DCF model is a favorite of academics and practitioners because it relies solely on how cash flows in and out of the company. Complex accounting can be replaced with a simple question: Does cash change hands? One shortfall of enterprise DCF, however, is that each year's cash flow provides little insight into the company's economic performance. Declining free cash flow can signal either poor performance or investment for the future. The economic-profit model highlights how and when the company creates value yet leads to a valuation that is identical to that of enterprise DCF.

Economic profit measures the value created by the company in a single period and is defined as follows:

$$\text{Economic Profit} = \text{Invested Capital} \times (\text{ROIC} - \text{WACC})$$

Since ROIC equals NOPLAT divided by invested capital, we can rewrite the equation as follows:

$$\text{Economic Profit} = \text{NOPLAT} - (\text{Invested Capital} \times \text{WACC})$$

In Exhibit 6.12, we present economic-profit calculations for Home Depot using both methods. Historically, Home Depot earned significant economic profits. But as the housing boom waned in 2007, ROIC fell below the company's cost of capital, and as a result economic profit became negative. Research

EXHIBIT 6.12 **Home Depot: Economic Profit Summary**

$ million

	Historical			Forecast		
	2006	2007	2008	2009	2010	2011
Method 1:						
Return on invested capital (percent)[1]	15.9	9.6	7.9	8.0	9.6	10.8
Weighted average cost of capital (percent)	8.4	8.2	8.3	8.5	8.5	8.5
Economic spread (percent)	7.5	1.4	−0.4	−0.4	1.1	2.3
× Invested capital (beginning of year)	39,389	46,543	38,567	37,075	34,137	35,038
= Economic profit (loss)	2,950	629	(162)	(164)	383	818
Method 2:						
Invested capital (beginning of year)	39,389	46,543	38,567	37,075	34,137	35,038
× Weighted average cost of capital (percent)	8.4	8.2	8.3	8.5	8.5	8.5
Capital charge	3,295	3,827	3,195	3,135	2,886	2,962
NOPLAT	6,245	4,456	3,033	2,971	3,269	3,780
Capital charge	(3,295)	(3,827)	(3,195)	(3,135)	(2,886)	(2,962)
Economic profit (loss)	2,950	629	(162)	(164)	383	818

[1] ROIC measured using beginning of year capital.

analysts expected economic profit to become positive again in 2009, but nowhere near its level before the housing boom.

To demonstrate how economic profit can be used to value a company—and to demonstrate its equivalence to enterprise DCF, consider a stream of growing cash flows valued using the growing-perpetuity formula:

$$\text{Value}_0 = \frac{\text{FCF}_1}{\text{WACC} - g}$$

In Chapter 2, we transformed this cash flow perpetuity into the key value driver model. The key value driver model is superior to the simple cash flow perpetuity model, because it explicitly models the relationship between growth and required investment. Using a few additional algebraic steps (see Appendix A) and the assumption that the company's ROIC on new projects equals historical ROIC, we can transform the cash flow perpetuity into a key value driver model based on economic profits:

$$\text{Value}_0 = \text{Invested Capital}_0 + \frac{\text{Invested Capital}_0 \times (\text{ROIC} - \text{WACC})}{\text{WACC} - g}$$

Finally, we substitute the definition of economic profit:

$$\text{Value}_0 = \text{Invested Capital}_0 + \frac{\text{Economic Profit}_1}{\text{WACC} - g}$$

As can be seen in the economic-profit-based key value driver model, the operating value of a company equals its book value of invested capital plus the present value of all future value created. In this case, the future economic profits are valued using a growing perpetuity, because the company's economic profits are increasing at a constant rate over time. The formula also demonstrates that when future economic profit is expected to be zero, the value of operations will equal invested capital. If a company's value of operations exceeds its invested capital, be sure to identify the sources of competitive advantage that allows the company to maintain superior financial performance.

More generally, economic profit can be valued as follows:

$$\text{Value}_0 = \text{Invested Capital}_0 + \sum_{t=1}^{\infty} \frac{\text{Invested Capital}_{t-1} \times (\text{ROIC}_t - \text{WACC})}{(1 + \text{WACC})^t}$$

Since the economic-profit valuation was derived directly from the free cash flow model (see Appendix B for a general proof of equivalence), any valuation based on discounted economic profits will be identical to enterprise DCF. To assure equivalence, however, you must use the following values:

- Beginning-of-year invested capital (i.e., last year's value).
- The same invested-capital number for both economic profit and ROIC. For example, ROIC can be measured either with or without goodwill. If you measure ROIC without goodwill, invested capital must also be measured without goodwill. All told, it doesn't matter how you define invested capital, as long as you are consistent.
- A constant cost of capital to discount projections.

Exhibit 6.13 presents the valuation results for Home Depot using economic profit. Economic profits are explicitly forecast for 10 years; the remaining years are valued using an economic-profit continuing-value formula.[9] Comparing the equity value from Exhibit 6.4 with that of Exhibit 6.13, we see that the estimate of Home Depot's intrinsic value is the same, regardless of the method.

---

[9] To calculate continuing value, you can use the economic-profit-based key value driver formula, but only if RONIC equals historical ROIC in the continuing-value year. If RONIC going forward differs from the final year's ROIC, then the equation must be separated into current and future economic profits:

$$\text{Value}_t = \text{IC}_t + \underbrace{\frac{\text{IC}_t\,(\text{ROIC}_{t+1} - \text{WACC})}{\text{WACC}}}_{\text{Current Economic Profits}} + \underbrace{\frac{\text{PV}(\text{Economic Profit}_{t+2})}{\text{WACC} - g}}_{\text{Future Economic Profits}}$$

such that

$$\text{PV}(\text{Economic Profit}_{t+2}) = \frac{\text{NOPLAT}_{t+1}\left(\frac{g}{\text{RONIC}}\right)(\text{RONIC} - \text{WACC})}{\text{WACC}}$$

EXHIBIT 6.13 **Home Depot: Economic Profit Valuation**

Year	Invested capital[1] ($ million)	ROIC[1] (percent)	WACC (percent)	Economic profit ($ million)	Discount factor (@ 8.5%)	Present value of economic profit ($ million)
2009	37,075	8.0	8.5	(164)	0.922	(151)
2010	34,137	9.6	8.5	383	0.850	325
2011	35,038	10.8	8.5	818	0.784	641
2012	36,897	11.6	8.5	1,145	0.723	827
2013	38,900	12.3	8.5	1,487	0.666	991
2014	40,821	12.3	8.5	1,550	0.614	952
2015	42,748	12.2	8.5	1,611	0.567	913
2016	44,665	12.2	8.5	1,671	0.522	873
2017	46,568	12.2	8.5	1,731	0.482	834
2018	48,453	12.1	8.5	1,789	0.444	795
Continuing value				41,922	0.444	18,619
Present value of economic profit						25,619
Invested capital in 2008						37,075
Invested capital plus present value of economic profit						62,694
Midyear adjustment factor						1.041
Value of operations						65,291
Value of excess cash						—
Value of long-term investments						361
Value of tax loss carry-forwards						112
Enterprise value						65,764
Value of debt						(11,434)
Less: Value of capitalized operating leases						(8,298)
Equity value						46,032

[1] Invested capital is measured at the beginning of the year.

The benefits of economic profit become apparent when we examine the drivers of economic profit, ROIC and WACC, on a year-by-year basis in Exhibit 6.13. The current valuation is contingent on a small and gradual improvement in ROIC from 8.0 percent to 12.1 percent, conservative by most measures. This stands in stark contrast to our assessment in 2004, when the market valuation was dependent on maintaining high returns on capital:

> The valuation depends on Home Depot's ability to maintain current levels of ROIC (17.5 percent) well above the WACC (9.3 percent). If the company's markets become saturated, growth could become elusive, and some companies might compete on price to steal market share. If this occurs, ROICs will drop, and economic profits will revert to zero.[10]

---

[10] Tim Koller, Marc Goedhart, and David Wessels, *Valuation: Measuring and Managing the Value of Companies*, 4th ed. (Hoboken, NJ: John Wiley & Sons, 2005), 119.

Explicitly modeling ROIC as a primary driver of economic profit prominently displays expectations of value creation. Conversely, the free cash flow model fails to show this dynamic. Free cash flow could continue to grow, even as ROIC falls.

ADJUSTED PRESENT VALUE MODEL

When building an enterprise DCF or economic-profit valuation, most financial analysts discount all future flows at a constant weighted average cost of capital. Using a constant WACC, however, assumes the company manages its capital structure to a target debt-to-value ratio.

In most situations, debt grows in line with company value. But suppose the company planned to change its capital structure significantly. Indeed, companies with a high proportion of debt often pay it down as cash flow improves, thus lowering their future debt-to-value ratios. In these cases, a valuation based on a constant WACC would overstate the value of the tax shields. Although the WACC can be adjusted yearly to handle a changing capital structure, the process is complex. Therefore, we turn to an alternative model: adjusted present value (APV).

The adjusted present value model separates the value of operations into two components: the value of operations as if the company were all-equity financed and the value of tax shields that arise from debt financing:[11]

$$
\begin{array}{c}\text{Adjusted}\\\text{Present Value}\end{array} = \begin{array}{c}\text{Enterprise Value as if the}\\\text{Company Was All-Equity Financed}\end{array} + \begin{array}{c}\text{Present Value of}\\\text{Tax Shields}\end{array}
$$

The APV valuation model follows directly from the teachings of economists Franco Modigliani and Merton Miller, who proposed that in a market with no taxes (among other things), a company's choice of financial structure will not affect the value of its economic assets. Only market imperfections, such as taxes and distress costs, affect enterprise value.

When building a valuation model, it is easy to forget these teachings. To see this, imagine a company (in a world with no taxes) that has a 50–50 mix of debt and equity. If the company's debt has an expected return of 5 percent and the company's equity has an expected return of 15 percent, its weighted average cost of capital would be 10 percent. Suppose the company decides to issue more debt, using the proceeds to repurchase shares. Since the cost of

[11] In this book, we focus on the tax shields generated by interest expense. On a more general basis, the APV values any incremental cash flows associated with capital structure, such as tax shields, issue costs, and distress costs. Distress costs include direct costs, such as court-related fees, and indirect costs, such as the loss of customers and suppliers.

debt is lower than the cost of equity, it would appear that issuing debt to retire equity should lower the WACC, raising the company's value.

This line of thinking is flawed, however. In a world without taxes, a change in capital structure would not change the cash flow generated by operations, nor the risk of those cash flows. Therefore, neither the company's enterprise value nor its cost of capital would change. So why did we think it would? When adding debt, we adjusted the weights, but we failed to properly increase the cost of equity. Since debt payments have priority over cash flows to equity, adding leverage increases the risk to equity holders. When leverage rises, they demand a higher return. Modigliani and Miller postulated that this increase would perfectly offset the change in weights.

In reality, taxes play a role in determining capital structure. Since interest is tax deductible, profitable companies can lower taxes by raising debt. But if the company relies too heavily on debt, the company's customers and suppliers may fear bankruptcy and walk away, restricting future cash flow (academics call this distress costs or deadweight costs). Rather than model the effect of capital-structure changes in the weighted average cost of capital, APV explicitly measures and values the cash flow effects of financing separately.

To build an APV-based valuation, value the company as if it were all-equity financed. Do this by discounting free cash flow by the unlevered cost of equity (what the cost of equity would be if the company had no debt).[12] To this value, add any value created by the company's use of debt. Exhibit 6.14 values Home Depot using adjusted present value. Since we assume (for expositional purposes) that Home Depot will manage its capital structure to a target debt-to-value level of 35 percent, the APV-based valuation leads to the same value for equity as did enterprise DCF (see Exhibit 6.4) and economic profit (see Exhibit 6.13). A simplified proof of equivalence between enterprise DCF and adjusted present value can be found in Appendix C. The following subsections explain APV in detail.

Valuing Free Cash Flow at Unlevered Cost of Equity

When valuing a company using the APV, we explicitly separate the unlevered value of operations (V_u) from any value created by financing, such as tax shields (V_{txa}). For a company with debt (D) and equity (E), this relationship is as follows:

$$V_u + V_{txa} = D + E \tag{6.1}$$

A second result of Modigliani and Miller's work is that the total risk of the company's assets, real and financial, must equal the total risk of the financial

---

[12] Free cash flow projections in the APV model are identical to those presented in Exhibit 6.4. Continuing value is computed using the key value driver formula. Only the cost of capital changes.

EXHIBIT 6.14 **Home Depot: Valuation Using Adjusted Present Value**

Year	Free cash flow ($ million)	Interest tax shield ($ million)	Discount factor (@ 9.3%)	Present value of FCF ($ million)	Present value of ITS ($ million)
2009	5,909	502	0.915	5,408	460
2010	2,368	498	0.838	1,984	417
2011	1,921	521	0.767	1,473	399
2012	2,261	549	0.702	1,587	385
2013	2,854	578	0.642	1,834	371
2014	3,074	604	0.588	1,807	355
2015	3,308	630	0.538	1,780	339
2016	3,544	657	0.493	1,746	323
2017	3,783	684	0.451	1,705	308
2018	4,022	711	0.413	1,660	293
Continuing value	78,175	14,064	0.413	32,256	5,803
Present value				53,240	9,454

Present value of FCF	53,240
Present value of interest tax shields	9,454
Present value of FCF and interest tax shields	62,694
Midyear adjustment factor	1.041
Value of operations	65,291
Value of excess cash	–
Value of long-term investments	361
Value of tax loss carry-forwards	112
Enterprise value	65,764
Less: Value of debt	(11,431)
Less: Value of capitalized operating leases	(8,298)
Equity value	46,032

claims against those assets. Thus, in equilibrium, the blended cost of capital for operating assets (k_u, which we call the unlevered cost of equity) and financial assets (k_{txa}) must equal the blended cost of capital for debt (k_d) and equity (k_e):

$$\underbrace{\frac{V_u}{V_u + V_{txa}} k_u}_{\substack{\text{Operating} \\ \text{Assets}}} + \underbrace{\frac{V_{txa}}{V_u + V_{txa}} k_{txa}}_{\text{Tax Assets}} = \underbrace{\frac{D}{D + E} k_d}_{\text{Debt}} + \underbrace{\frac{E}{D + E} k_e}_{\text{Equity}} \tag{6.2}$$

In the corporate-finance literature, academics combine Modigliani and Miller's two equations to solve for the cost of equity—to demonstrate the relationship between leverage and the cost of equity. In Appendix C, we algebraically rearrange equation 6.2 to solve for the levered cost of equity:

$$k_e = k_u + \frac{D}{E}(k_u - k_d) - \frac{V_{txa}}{E}(k_u - k_{txa}) \tag{6.3}$$

As this equation indicates, the cost of equity depends on the unlevered cost of equity plus a premium for leverage, less a reduction for the tax deductibility of debt. Note that when a company has no debt ($D = 0$) and subsequently no tax shields ($V_{txa} = 0$), k_e equals k_u. This is why k_u is referred to as the unlevered cost of equity.

Determining the unlevered cost of equity with market data   To use the APV, discount projected free cash flow at the unlevered cost of equity, k_u. Unfortunately, k_u cannot be observed directly. In fact, none of the variables on the left side of equation 6.2 can be observed directly. Only the values on the right—that is, those related to debt and equity—can be estimated using market data. Because there are so many unknowns and only one equation, we must impose additional restrictions to build an implementable relationship between k_e and k_u.

Method 1: Assume k_{txa} equals k_u   If you believe the company will manage its debt-to-value ratio to a target level (the company's debt will grow with the business), then the value of the tax shields will track the value of the operating assets. Thus, the risk of tax shields will equal the risk of operating assets ($k_{txa} = k_u$). Setting k_{txa} equal to k_u, equation 6.3 can be simplified as follows:

$$k_e = k_u + \frac{D}{E}(k_u - k_d) \tag{6.4}$$

The unlevered cost of equity can now be solved using the observed cost of equity, the cost of debt, and the market debt-to-equity ratio.

Method 2: Assume k_{txa} equals k_d   If you believe the market debt-to-equity ratio will not remain constant, then the value of interest tax shields will be more closely tied to the value of forecasted debt, rather than operating assets. In this case, the risk of tax shields is equivalent to the risk of debt. (When a company is unprofitable, it cannot use interest tax shields, the risk of default rises, and the value of debt drops.) Setting k_{txa} equal to k_d, equation 6.3 can be simplified as follows:

$$k_e = k_u + \frac{D - V_{txa}}{E}(k_u - k_d) \tag{6.5}$$

In this equation, the relationship between k_e and k_u relies on observable variables, such as the market value of debt, market value of equity, cost of debt, and cost of equity, as well as one unobservable variable: the present value of tax shields (V_{txa}). To use equation 6.5, discount expected future tax shields at the cost of debt (to remain consistent with the underlying assumption), and then solve for the unlevered cost of equity.

To avoid having to value the tax shields explicitly, many practitioners further refine the preceding equation by imposing an additional restriction: that the absolute dollar level of debt is constant. If the dollar level of debt is constant, V_{txa} simplifies to $D \times T_m$ (the market value of debt times the marginal tax rate), and equation 6.5 becomes:

$$k_e = k_u + (1 - T_m) \frac{D}{E} (k_u - k_d) \qquad (6.6)$$

Although equation 6.6 is commonly used, its usefulness is limited because the assumptions are extremely restrictive.

Choosing the appropriate formula Which formula should you use to estimate the unlevered cost of equity, k_u? It depends on how you see the company managing its capital structure going forward and whether the debt is risk free. The majority of companies have relatively stable capital structures (as a percentage of expected value), so we strongly favor the first method.

In periods of high debt, such as financial distress and leveraged buyouts, the second method is appropriate. Yet even if a company's tax shields are predetermined for a given period, eventually they will track value. For instance, successful leveraged buyouts pay down debt for a period of time, but once the debt level becomes reasonable, debt will more likely track value than remain constant. Thus, even in situations where leverage is high, we recommend the first method.

Valuing Tax Shields and Other Capital Structure Effects

To complete an APV-based valuation, forecast and discount capital structure side effects such as tax shields, security issue costs, and distress costs. Since Home Depot has only a small probability of default, we estimated the company's future interest tax shields using the company's promised yield to maturity and marginal tax rate (see Exhibit 6.15). To calculate the expected interest payment in 2009, multiply the prior year's net debt of $19.7 billion by the expected yield of 6.8 percent (net debt equals reported debt plus capitalized operating leases minus excess cash). This results in an expected interest payment of $1.3 billion. Next, multiply the expected interest payment by the marginal tax rate of 37.6 percent, for an expected interest tax shield of $502 million in 2009. To determine the continuing value of interest tax shields beyond 2018, use a growth perpetuity based on 2019 interest tax shields, the unlevered cost of capital, and growth in NOPLAT.

For companies with significant leverage, the company may not be able to fully use the tax shields (it may not have enough profits to shield). If there is a significant probability of default, you must model expected tax shields, rather

EXHIBIT 6.15 **Home Depot: Forecast of Interest Tax Shields**

Forecast year	Prior-year net debt ($ million)	Expected interest rate (percent)	Interest payment ($ million)	Marginal tax rate (percent)	Interest tax shield ($ million)
2009	19,732	6.8	1,337	37.6	502
2010	19,540	6.8	1,324	37.6	498
2011	20,447	6.8	1,386	37.6	521
2012	21,571	6.8	1,462	37.6	549
2013	22,683	6.8	1,537	37.6	578
2014	23,702	6.8	1,606	37.6	604
2015	24,739	6.8	1,676	37.6	630
2016	25,790	6.8	1,748	37.6	657
2017	26,854	6.8	1,820	37.6	684
2018	27,934	6.8	1,893	37.6	711
Continuing value	29,030	6.8	1,967	37.6	739

than the tax shields based on promised interest payments. To do this, reduce each promised tax shield by the cumulative probability of default.

CAPITAL CASH FLOW MODEL

When a company actively manages its capital structure to a target debt-to-value level, both free cash flow (FCF) and the interest tax shield (ITS) are discounted at the unlevered cost of equity, k_u:

$$V = \sum_{t=1}^{\infty} \frac{\text{FCF}_t}{(1+k_u)^t} + \sum_{t=1}^{\infty} \frac{\text{ITS}_t}{(1+k_u)^t}$$

In 2000, Richard Ruback of the Harvard Business School argued that there is no need to separate free cash flow from tax shields when both flows are discounted by the same cost of capital.[13] He combined the two flows and named the resulting cash flow (FCF plus interest tax shields) capital cash flow (CCF):

$$V = \text{PV(Capital Cash Flows)} = \sum_{t=1}^{\infty} \frac{\text{FCT}_t + \text{ITS}_t}{(1+k_u)^t}$$

Given that Ruback's assumptions match those of the weighted average cost of capital, the capital cash flow and WACC-based valuations will lead to identical results. In fact, we now have detailed three distinct but identical

---

[13] Richard S. Ruback, "Capital Cash Flows: A Simple Approach to Valuing Risky Cash Flows," Social Science Research Network (March 2000).

valuation methods created solely around how they treat tax shields: WACC (tax shield valued in the cost of capital), APV (tax shield valued separately), and CCF (tax shield valued in the cash flow).

Although FCF and CCF lead to the same result when debt is proportional to value, we believe free cash flow models are superior to capital cash flow models. Why? By keeping NOPLAT and FCF independent of leverage, we can cleanly evaluate the company's operating performance over time and across competitors. A clean measure of historical operating performance leads to better forecasts.

CASH-FLOW-TO-EQUITY VALUATION MODEL

Each of the preceding valuation models determined the value of equity indirectly by subtracting debt and other nonequity claims from enterprise value. The equity cash flow model values equity directly by discounting cash flows to equity at the cost of equity, rather than at the weighted average cost of capital.[14]

Exhibit 6.16 details the cash flow to equity for Home Depot. Cash flow to equity starts with net income. Next, add back noncash expenses, and subtract investments in working capital, fixed assets, and nonoperating assets. Finally, add any increases in debt and other nonequity claims, and subtract decreases in debt and other nonequity claims. Alternatively, you can compute cash flow to equity as dividends plus share repurchases minus new equity issues. The two methods generate identical results.[15]

To value Home Depot, discount projected equity cash flows at the cost of equity (see Exhibit 6.17). Unlike enterprise-based models, this method makes no adjustments to the DCF value for nonoperating assets, debt, or capitalized operating leases. Rather, they are embedded as part of the equity cash flow.

---

[14] The equity method can be difficult to implement correctly because capital structure is embedded in the cash flow, so forecasting is difficult. For companies whose operations are related to financing, such as financial institutions, the equity method is appropriate. We discuss valuing financial institutions in Chapter 36.

[15] When performing a stand-alone equity cash flow valuation, calculate the continuing value using an equity-based variant of the key value driver formula:

$$V_e = \frac{\text{Net Income}\left(1 - \frac{g}{\text{ROE}}\right)}{k_e - g}$$

To tie the free cash flow and equity cash flow models, you must convert free cash flow continuing-value inputs into equity cash flow inputs. We did this using the following equation:

$$\text{Net Income}\left(1 - \frac{g}{\text{ROE}}\right) = \frac{\text{NOPLAT}\left(1 - \frac{g}{\text{ROIC}}\right)}{1 + \frac{D}{E}\left(1 - \frac{k_e - (1-T)k_d}{k_e - g}\right)}$$

EXHIBIT 6.16 **Home Depot: Equity Cash Flow Summary**

$ million

	Historical			Forecast		
	2006	**2007**	**2008**	**2009**	**2010**	**2011**
Net income	5,761	4,395	2,260	2,183	2,477	2,947
Depreciation	1,645	1,693	1,785	1,639	1,685	1,778
Amortization	117	9	–	–	–	–
Gross cash flow	7,523	6,097	4,045	3,822	4,162	4,725
Change in operating working capital	(936)	1,066	–	292	(73)	(163)
Decrease (increase) in net long-term operating assets	(7,006)	4,152	(740)	329	(2,300)	(3,040)
Decrease (increase) in nonoperating assets	5	(324)	306	–	–	–
Decrease (increase) in net deferred tax liabilities	122	(715)	(284)	226	3	6
Increase (decrease) in short-term debt	(1,395)	2,029	(280)	75	107	107
Increase (decrease) in long-term debt	8,971	(260)	(1,716)	411	588	583
Cash flow to equity	7,284	12,045	1,331	5,155	2,486	2,218
Reconciliation of cash flow to equity						
Dividends	1,395	1,709	1,521	1,436	1,629	1,939
Share repurchases (net of stock issued)	5,889	10,336	(190)	3,719	856	279
Cash flow to equity	7,284	12,045	1,331	5,155	2,486	2,218

EXHIBIT 6.17 **Home Depot: Cash-Flow-to-Equity Valuation**

Forecast year	Cash flow to equity[1] ($ million)	Discount factor (@ 10.4%)	Present value of CFE ($ million)
2009	5,044	0.906	4,569
2010	2,486	0.821	2,040
2011	2,218	0.743	1,649
2012	2,498	0.673	1,682
2013	2,952	0.610	1,800
2014	3,145	0.552	1,738
2015	3,349	0.500	1,676
2016	3,556	0.453	1,612
2017	3,764	0.411	1,546
2018	3,974	0.372	1,478
Continuing value	63,569	0.372	23,646
Present value of cash flow to equity			43,436
Midyear adjustment amount			2,597
Equity value			46,032

[1] Cash flow to equity in 2009 excludes $111 million change in nonoperating deferred tax liabilities, as their value is incorporated elsewhere.

Once again, note how the valuation, derived using equity cash flows, matches each of the prior valuations. This occurs because we have modeled Home Depot's debt-to-value ratio at a constant level. If leverage is expected to change, the cost of equity must be appropriately adjusted to reflect the change in risk imposed on equity holders. Although formulas exist to adjust the cost of equity (as we did in the APV section earlier in this chapter), many of the best-known formulas are built under restrictions that may be inconsistent with the way you are implicitly forecasting the company's capital structure via the cash flows. This will cause a mismatch between cash flows and the cost of equity, resulting in an incorrect valuation.

It is quite easy to change the company's capital structure without realizing it when using the cash-flow-to-equity model—and that is what makes implementing the equity model so risky. Suppose you plan to value a company whose debt-to-value ratio is 15 percent. You believe the company will pay extra dividends, so you increase debt to raise the dividend payout ratio. Presto! Increased dividends lead to higher equity cash flows and a higher valuation. Even though operating performance has not changed, the equity value has mistakenly increased. What happened? Using new debt to pay dividends causes a rise in net debt to value. Unless you adjust the cost of equity, the valuation will rise incorrectly.

Another shortcoming of the direct equity approach emerges when valuing a company by business unit. The direct equity approach requires allocating debt and interest expense to each unit. This creates extra work yet provides few additional insights.

OTHER APPROACHES TO DISCOUNTED CASH FLOW

In this chapter, we valued Home Depot by discounting nominal cash flows at a cost of capital based on observable interest rates. An alternative is to value companies by projecting cash flow in real terms (e.g., in constant 2009 dollars) and discounting this cash flow at a real discount rate (e.g., the nominal rate less expected inflation). But most managers think in terms of nominal rather than real measures, so nominal measures are often easier to communicate. In addition, interest rates are generally quoted nominally rather than in real terms (excluding expected inflation).

A second difficulty occurs when calculating and interpreting ROIC. The historical statements are nominal, so historical returns on invested capital are nominal. But if the projections for the company use real rather than nominal forecasts, returns on new capital are also real. Projected returns on total capital (new and old) are a combination of nominal and real, so they are impossible to interpret. The only way around this is to restate historical performance on a real basis—a complex and time-consuming task. The extra insights gained rarely equal the effort, except in extremely high-inflation environments, described in Chapter 29.

A second alternative to the enterprise DCF method outlined earlier is to discount pretax cash flows by a pretax hurdle rate (the market-based cost of capital multiplied by 1 plus the marginal tax rate) to determine a pretax value. This method, however, leads to three fundamental inconsistencies. First, the government calculates taxes on profits after depreciation, not on cash flow after capital expenditures. By discounting pretax cash flow at the pretax cost of capital, you implicitly assume capital investments are tax deductible when made, not as they are depreciated. Furthermore, short-term investments, such as accounts receivable and inventory, are never tax deductible. Selling a product at a profit is what leads to incremental taxes, not holding inventory. By discounting pretax cash flow at the pretax cost of capital, you incorrectly assume investments in operating working capital are tax deductible. Finally, it can be shown that even when net investment equals depreciation, the final result will be downward biased—and the larger the cost of capital, the larger the bias. This bias occurs because the method is only an approximation, not a formal mathematical relationship. Because of these inconsistencies, we recommend against discounting pretax cash flows at a pretax hurdle rate.

ALTERNATIVES TO DISCOUNTED CASH FLOW

To this point, we have focused solely on discounted cash flow models. Two additional valuation techniques exist: multiples (comparables) and real options.

Multiples

Assume that you have been asked to value a company that is about to go public. Although you project and discount free cash flow to derive an enterprise value, you worry that your forecasts lack precision. One way to place your DCF model in the proper context is to create a set of comparables. One of the most commonly used comparables is the enterprise value (EV)–to–earnings before interest, taxes, and amortization (EBITA) multiple. To apply the EV/EBITA multiple, look for a set of comparable companies, and multiply a representative EV/EBITA multiple by the company's EBITA. For example, assume the company's EBITA equals $100 million and the typical EV/EBITA multiple in the industry is 9 times. Multiplying 9 by $100 million leads to an estimated value of $900 million. Is the enterprise DCF valuation near $900 million? If not, what enables the company to earn better (or worse) returns or to grow faster (or slower) than other companies in the industry?

Although the concept of multiples is simple, the methodology is misunderstood and often misapplied. In Chapter 14, we demonstrate how to build and interpret forward-looking comparables, independent of capital structure and other nonoperating items.

Real Options Using Replicating Portfolios

In 1997 Robert Merton and Myron Scholes won the Nobel Prize in economics for developing an ingenious method to value derivatives that avoids the need to estimate either cash flows or the cost of capital. (Fischer Black would have been named as a third recipient, but the Nobel Prize is not awarded posthumously.) Their model relies on what today's economists call a "replicating portfolio." They argued that if there exists a portfolio of traded securities whose future cash flows perfectly mimic the security you are attempting to value, the portfolio and security must have the same price. As long as we can find a suitable replicating portfolio, we need not discount future cash flows.

Given the model's power, there have been many recent attempts to translate the concepts of replicating portfolios to corporate valuation. This valuation technique is commonly known as real options. Unlike those for financial options, however, replicating portfolios for companies and their projects are difficult to create. Therefore, although options-pricing models may teach powerful lessons, today's applications are limited. We cover valuation using options-based models in Chapter 32.

SUMMARY

This chapter described the most common DCF valuation models, with particular focus on the enterprise DCF model and the economic-profit model. We explained the rationale for each model and reasons why each model has an important place in corporate valuation. The remaining chapters in Part Two describe a step-by-step approach to valuing a company. These chapters explain the technical details of valuation, including how to reorganize the financial statements, analyze return on invested capital and revenue growth, forecast free cash flow, compute the cost of capital, and estimate an appropriate terminal value.

REVIEW QUESTIONS

1. Exhibit 6.18 presents the income statement and reorganized balance sheet for BrandCo, an $800 million consumer products company. Using the methodology outlined in Exhibit 6.5, determine NOPLAT for year 1. Assume an operating tax rate of 25 percent. Using the methodology outlined in Exhibit 6.6, determine free cash flow for year 1.

EXHIBIT 6.18 **BrandCo: Income Statement and Reorganized Balance Sheet**

$ million

Income statement			Reorganized balance sheet		
	Today	Year 1		Today	Year 1
Revenues	800.0	840.0	Operating working capital[1]	70.1	73.6
Operating costs	(640.0)	(672.0)	Property and equipment	438.4	460.3
Depreciation	(40.0)	(42.0)	Invested capital	508.5	533.9
Operating profit	120.0	126.0			
			Debt	200.0	210.0
Interest expense	(16.0)	(16.0)	Shareholders' equity	308.5	323.9
Earnings before taxes	104.0	110.0	Invested capital	508.5	533.9
Taxes	(26.0)	(27.5)			
Net income	78.0	82.5			

[1] Accounts payable has been netted against inventory to determine operating working capital.

2. BrandCo currently has 50 million shares outstanding. If BrandCo's shares are trading at $19.16 per share, what is the company's market capitalization (value of equity)? Assuming the market value of debt equals today's book value of debt, what percentage of the company's enterprise value is attributable to debt, and what percentage is attributable to equity? Using these weights, compute the weighted average cost of capital. Assume the pretax cost of debt is 8 percent, the cost of equity is 12 percent, and the marginal tax rate is 25 percent.

3. Using free cash flow computed in Question 1 and the weighted average cost of capital computed in Question 2, estimate BrandCo's enterprise value using the growing-perpetuity formula. Assume free cash flow grows at 5 percent.

4. Assuming the market value of debt equals today's book value of debt, what is the intrinsic equity value for BrandCo? What is the intrinsic value per share? Does it differ from the share price used to determine the cost of capital weightings?

5. What are the three components required to calculate economic profit? Determine BrandCo's economic profit in year 1.

6. Using economic profit calculated in Question 5 and the weighted average cost of capital computed in Question 2, value BrandCo using the economic-profit-based key value driver model. Does the calculation generate enterprise value or equity value? Should discounted economic profit be greater than, equal to, or less than discounted free cash flow? Hint: remember, prior-year invested capital must be used to determine ROIC and capital charge.

7. Using the methodology outlined in Exhibit 6.16, determine equity cash flow for year 1. Use the growing-perpetuity formula (based on equity cash flow) to compute BrandCo's equity value. Assume the cost of equity is 12 percent and cash flows are growing at 5 percent.

7

Reorganizing the Financial Statements

Traditional financial statements—the income statement, balance sheet, and statement of cash flows—are not organized for robust assessments of operating performance and value. The balance sheet mixes together operating assets, nonoperating assets, and sources of financing. The income statement similarly combines operating profits with the costs of financing, such as interest expense.

To prepare the financial statements for analysis of economic performance, you need to reorganize the items on the balance sheet, income statement, and statement of cash flows into three categories of components: operating, nonoperating, and sources of financing. This will entail searching through the notes to separate accounts that aggregate operating and nonoperating items. Although this task seems mundane, it is crucial for avoiding the common traps of double-counting, omitting cash flows, or hiding leverage that artificially boosts reported performance.

Since the process of reorganizing the financial statements is complex, this chapter proceeds in three steps. In step 1, we present a simple example demonstrating how to build invested capital, net operating profit less adjusted taxes (NOPLAT), and free cash flow (FCF). In the second step, we apply this method to the financial statements for Home Depot and Lowe's, commenting on some of the intricacies of implementation. In the final step, we provide a brief summary of advanced analytical topics, including how to adjust for operating leases, pensions, capitalized expenses, and restructuring charges. An in-depth analysis of each of these topics can be found in Part Five.

REORGANIZING THE ACCOUNTING STATEMENTS: KEY CONCEPTS

To calculate return on invested capital (ROIC) and free cash flow (FCF), we need to reorganize the balance sheet to create invested capital and likewise reorganize the income statement to create net operating profit less adjusted taxes (NOPLAT). Invested capital represents the total investor capital required to fund operations, without regard to how the capital is financed. NOPLAT represents the total after-tax operating profit (generated by the company's invested capital) that is available to all financial investors.

Return on invested capital and free cash flow are both derived from NOPLAT and invested capital. ROIC is defined as:

$$ROIC = \frac{NOPLAT}{Invested\ Capital}$$

and free cash flow is defined as:

$$FCF = NOPLAT + Noncash\ Operating\ Expenses$$
$$- Investment\ in\ Invested\ Capital$$

By combining noncash operating expenses, such as depreciation, with investment in invested capital, we can also express FCF as:

$$FCF = NOPLAT - Net\ Increase\ in\ Invested\ Capital$$

Invested Capital: Key Concepts

To build an economic balance sheet that separates a company's operating assets from its nonoperating assets and financial structure, we start with the traditional balance sheet. The accountant's balance sheet is bound by the most fundamental rule of accounting:

$$Assets = Liabilities + Equity$$

Typically, assets consist primarily of operating assets (OA), such as receivables, inventory, and property, plant, and equipment. Liabilities consist of operating liabilities (OL), such as accounts payable and accrued salaries, and interest-bearing debt (D), such as notes payable and long-term debt. Equity (E) consists of common stock, possibly preferred stock, and retained earnings. Using this more explicit breakdown of assets, liabilities, and equity leads to an expanded version of the balance sheet relationship:

$$Operating\ Assets = Operating\ Liabilities + Debt + Equity$$

The traditional balance sheet equation, however, mixes operating liabilities and sources of financing on the right side of the equation. Moving operating liabilities to the left side of the equation leads to invested capital:

$$\text{Operating Assets} - \text{Operating Liabilities} = \text{Invested Capital} = \text{Debt} + \text{Equity}$$

With this new equation, we have rearranged the balance sheet to reflect more accurately capital used for operations and the financing provided by investors to fund those operations. Note how invested capital can be calculated using the operating method—that is, operating assets minus operating liabilities—or the financing method, which equals debt plus equity.

For many companies, the previous equation is too simple. Assets consist of not only core operating assets, but also nonoperating assets (NOA), such as marketable securities, prepaid pension assets, nonconsolidated subsidiaries, and other long-term investments. Liabilities consist of not only operating liabilities and interest-bearing debt, but also debt equivalents (DE), such as unfunded retirement liabilities, and equity equivalents (EE), such as deferred taxes and income-smoothing provisions (we explain equivalents in detail later in the chapter). Expanding our original balance sheet equation:

$$
\begin{array}{ccccc}
\text{OA} & \text{NOA} & \text{OL} & \text{D} + \text{DE} & \text{E} + \text{EE} \\
\text{Operating} + \text{Nonoperating} = \text{Operating} + & \text{Debt and} & + & \text{Equity and} \\
\text{Assets} & \text{Assets} & \text{Liabilities} & \text{Its Equivalents} & \text{Its Equivalents}
\end{array}
$$

Rearranging leads to total funds invested:

$$
\begin{array}{ccccc}
\text{OA} - \text{OL} & \text{NOA} & \text{Total} & \text{D} + \text{DE} & \text{E} + \text{EE} \\
\text{Invested} + \text{Nonoperating} = & \text{Funds} = & \text{Debt and} & + & \text{Equity and} \\
\text{Capital} & \text{Assets} & \text{Invested} & \text{Its Equivalents} & \text{Its Equivalents}
\end{array}
$$

From an investing perspective, total funds invested equals invested capital plus nonoperating assets. From the financing perspective, total funds invested equals debt and its equivalents, plus equity and its equivalents. Exhibit 7.1 rearranges the balance sheet into invested capital for a simple hypothetical company with only a few line items. A more sophisticated example, using real companies, is developed later in the chapter.

Net Operating Profit Less Adjusted Taxes: Key Concepts

To determine a company's after-tax operating profit, you need to compute net operating profit less adjusted taxes (NOPLAT). NOPLAT is the after-tax profit generated from core operations, excluding any gains from nonoperating assets or financing expenses, such as interest. Whereas net income is the profit available to equity holders only, NOPLAT is the profit available to *all* investors,

EXHIBIT 7.1 **An Example of Invested Capital**

$ million

Accountant's balance sheet	Prior year	Current year	Invested capital	Prior year	Current year	
Assets			**Assets**			
Inventory	200	225	Inventory	200	225	Operating liabilities
Net PP&E	300	350	Accounts payable	(125)	(150)	are netted against
Equity investments	15	25	Operating working capital	75	75	operating assets
Total assets	515	600				
			Net PP&E	300	350	
Liabilities and equity			Invested capital	375	425	
Accounts payable	125	150				
Interest-bearing debt	225	200	Equity investments	15	25	Nonoperating assets are not included in
Common stock	50	50	Total funds invested	390	450	invested capital
Retained earnings	115	200				
Total liabilities and equity	515	600	**Reconciliation of total funds invested**			
			Interest-bearing debt	225	200	
			Common stock	50	50	
			Retained earnings	115	200	
			Total funds invested	390	450	

including providers of debt, equity, and any other types of investor financing. It is critical to define NOPLAT consistently with your definition of invested capital and include only those profits generated by invested capital.

To calculate NOPLAT, we reorganize the accountant's income statement (see Exhibit 7.2) in three fundamental ways. First, interest is not subtracted from operating profit, because interest is considered a payment to the company's financial investors, not an operating expense. By reclassifying interest as a financing item, we make NOPLAT independent of the company's capital structure.

Second, when calculating after-tax operating profit, exclude any nonoperating income generated from assets that were excluded from invested capital. Mistakenly including nonoperating income in NOPLAT without including the associated assets in invested capital will lead to an inconsistent definition of ROIC (the numerator and denominator will include unrelated elements).

Finally, since reported taxes are calculated after interest and nonoperating income, they are a function of nonoperating items and capital structure. Keeping NOPLAT focused solely on operations requires that the effects of interest expense and nonoperating income also be removed from taxes. To calculate operating taxes, start with reported taxes, add back the tax shield caused by interest expense, and remove the taxes paid on nonoperating income. The resulting operating taxes should equal the hypothetical taxes that would be reported by an all-equity, pure operating company.

Since interest is tax deductible, leverage has value. But rather than factor tax shields into NOPLAT, we will account for all financing costs (including interest

EXHIBIT 7.2 **An Example of NOPLAT**

$ million

Accountant's income statement		NOPLAT	
	Current year		Current year
Revenues	1,000	Revenues	1,000
Operating costs	(700)	Operating costs	(700)
Depreciation	(20)	Depreciation	(20)
Operating profit	280	Operating profit	280
Interest	(20)	Operating taxes[1]	(70)
Nonoperating income	4	NOPLAT	210
Earnings before taxes	264		
		After-tax nonoperating income[1]	3
Taxes	(66)	Income available to investors	213
Net income	198		
		Reconciliation with net income	
		Net income	198
		After-tax interest expense[1]	15
		Income available to investors	213

Taxes are calculated on operating profits

Do not include income from any asset excluded from invested capital as part of NOPLAT

Treat interest as a financial payout to investors, not an expense

[1] Assumes a marginal tax of 25% on all income.

and its tax shield) in the cost of capital. Similarly, taxes for nonoperating income must be accounted for and should be netted directly against nonoperating income, since they are not included as part of NOPLAT.

Free Cash Flow: Key Concepts

To value a company's operations, we discount projected free cash flow at an appropriate risk-adjusted cost of capital. Free cash flow is the after-tax cash flow available to all investors: debt holders and equity holders. Unlike "cash flow from operations" reported in a company's annual report, free cash flow is independent of financing and nonoperating items. It can be thought of as the after-tax cash flow—as if the company held only core operating assets and financed the business entirely with equity. Free cash flow is defined as:

$$FCF = NOPLAT + Noncash\ Operating\ Expenses$$
$$-\ Investments\ in\ Invested\ Capital$$

As shown in Exhibit 7.3, free cash flow excludes nonoperating flows and items related to capital structure. Unlike the accountant's cash flow statement, the free cash flow statement starts with NOPLAT (instead of net income). As discussed earlier, NOPLAT excludes nonoperating income and interest expense. Instead, interest (and its tax shield) is treated as a financing cash flow.

EXHIBIT 7.3 **An Example of Free Cash Flow**

$ million

Accountant's cash flow statement	Current year	Free cash flow	Current year	
Net income	198	NOPLAT	210	
Depreciation	20	Depreciation	20	
Decrease (increase) in inventory	(25)	Gross cash flow	230	Subtract investments in operating items from gross cash flow
Increase (decrease) in accounts payable	25			
Cash flow from operations	218	Decrease (increase) in inventory	(25)	
		Increase (decrease) in accounts payable	25	
Capital expenditures	(70)	Capital expenditures	(70)	
Decrease (increase) in equality investments	(10)	Free cash flow	160	Evaluate cash flow from nonoperating assets separately from core operations
Cash flow from investing	(80)			
		After-tax nonoperating Income	3	
Increase (decrease) in debt	(25)	Decrease (increase) in equity investments	(10)	
Increase (decrease) in common stock	–	Cash flow available to investors	153	
Dividends	(113)			
Cash flow from financing	(138)	**Reconciliation of cash flow available to investors**		Treat interest as a financial payout to investors, not an expense
		After-tax interest	15	
		Increase (decrease) in interest-bearing debt	25	
		Increase (decrease) in common stock	–	
		Dividends	113	
		Cash flow available to investors	153	

Net investments in nonoperating assets and the gains, losses, and income associated with these nonoperating assets are not included in free cash flow. Instead, nonoperating cash flows should be valued separately. Combining free cash flow and nonoperating cash flow leads to cash flow available to investors. As is true with total funds invested and NOPLAT, cash flow available to investors can be calculated using two methodologies: one starts from where the cash flow is generated, and the other starts with the recipients of the cash flow. Although the two methods seem redundant, checking that both give you the same result can help you avoid line item omissions and classification pitfalls.

REORGANIZING THE ACCOUNTING STATEMENTS: IN PRACTICE

Reorganizing the statements can be difficult, even for the savviest analyst. Which items are operating assets? Which are nonoperating? Which items should be treated as debt? As equity? In the following pages, we address these questions through an examination of Home Depot, the world's largest home improvement retailer, with stores located throughout North America, and comparison with Lowe's, a direct competitor of Home Depot. Home Depot has grown rapidly over the past 10 years, generating strong returns and cash flow. But its core markets have become increasingly saturated, the real estate market has soured, and the company now faces new challenges.

Invested Capital: In Practice

This section applies the process just outlined for reorganizing financial statements to the financial statements for Home Depot and Lowe's. It demonstrates how to compute invested capital and total funds invested, and how to reconcile the two methods for computing total funds invested.

Computing Invested Capital

To compute invested capital, first reorganize the company's balance sheet. In Exhibit 7.4, we present reorganized balance sheets for Home Depot and Lowe's. The reorganized versions we present are more detailed than the balance sheets reported in each company's respective annual reports, because we have searched the footnotes for information that enables us to disaggregate any accounts that mix together operating and nonoperating items. For instance, a search of Home Depot's 2007 notes reveals that the company aggregates equity investments, intangible assets, and long-term deferred taxes within the "other assets" line item (no description of other assets was provided in 2008).[1] Since "other assets" combines operating and nonoperating items, the balance sheet in its original form would be unusable for valuation purposes.

Invested capital sums operating working capital (current operating assets minus current operating liabilities); fixed assets (e.g., net property, plant, and equipment); intangible assets (e.g., goodwill); and net other long-term operating assets (net of long-term operating liabilities). Exhibit 7.5 demonstrates this line-by-line aggregation for Home Depot and Lowe's. In the following subsections, we examine each element in detail.

Operating working capital   Operating working capital equals operating current assets minus operating current liabilities. Operating current assets comprise all current assets necessary for the operation of the business, including working cash balances, trade accounts receivable, inventory, and prepaid expenses. Specifically *excluded* are excess cash and marketable securities—that is, cash greater than the operating needs of the business. Excess cash generally

---

[1] According to Home Depot's 2007 10-K, "The Company purchased a 12.5% equity interest in the newly formed HD Supply for $325 million, which is included in Other Assets in the accompanying Consolidated Balance Sheets." Regarding acquired intangibles, "The Company's intangible assets at the end of fiscal 2007 and 2006, which are included in Other Assets in the accompanying Consolidated Balance Sheets, consisted of [$100 million in 2007] and [$778 million in 2006]."

EXHIBIT 7.4 **Home Depot and Lowe's: Historical Balance Sheets**

$ million

	Home Depot			Lowe's		
	2006	2007	2008	2006	2007	2008
Assets						
Cash and cash equivalents	614	457	525	796	530	661
Receivables, net	3,223	1,259	972	–	–	–
Merchandise inventories	12,822	11,731	10,673	7,144	7,611	8,209
Short-term deferred tax assets	561	535	491	161	247	166
Other current assets	780	692	701	213	298	215
Total current assets	18,000	14,674	13,362	8,314	8,686	9,251
Net property and equipment	26,605	27,476	26,234	18,971	21,361	22,722
Goodwill	6,314	1,209	1,134	–	–	–
Notes receivable	343	342	36	165	509	253
Other assets: Equity investments	–	325	325	–	–	–
Other assets: Acquired intangibles	778	100	–	–	–	–
Other assets: Long-term deferred tax assets	7	–	4	–	–	–
Other assets: Undisclosed	216	198	69	317	313	460
Total assets	52,263	44,324	41,164	27,767	30,869	32,686
Liabilities and equity						
Short-term debt	18	2,047	1,767	111	1,104	1,021
Accounts payable	7,356	5,732	4,822	3,524	3,713	4,109
Accrued salaries	1,295	1,094	1,129	372	424	434
Deferred revenue	1,634	1,474	1,165	731	717	674
Short-term deferred tax liabilities	30	10	5	–	–	–
Other accrued expenses	2,598	2,349	2,265	1,801	1,793	1,784
Total current liabilities	12,931	12,706	11,153	6,539	7,751	8,022
Long-term debt	11,643	11,383	9,667	4,325	5,576	5,039
Deferred income taxes	1,416	688	369	735	670	660
Other long-term liabilities	1,243	1,833	2,198	443	774	910
Common stock and paid-in capital	8,051	5,885	6,133	864	745	1,012
Retained earnings	33,052	11,388	12,093	14,860	15,345	17,049
Accumulated other comprehensive income	310	755	(77)	1	8	(6)
Treasury stock	(16,383)	(314)	(372)	–	–	–
Total liabilities and shareholders' equity	52,263	44,324	41,164	27,767	30,869	32,686

represents temporary imbalances in the company's cash position and is discussed later in this section.[2]

Operating current liabilities include those liabilities that are related to the ongoing operations of the firm. The most common operating liabilities are those related to suppliers (accounts payable), employees (accrued salaries),

---

[2] In a company's financial statements, accountants often distinguish between cash and marketable securities, but not between working cash and excess cash. We provide guidance on distinguishing working cash from excess cash later in this chapter.

EXHIBIT 7.5 **Home Depot and Lowe's: Invested Capital Calculations**

$ million

	Home Depot			Lowe's		
	2006	2007	2008	2006	2007	2008
Total funds invested: Uses						
Operating cash	614	457	525	796	530	661
Receivables, net	3,223	1,259	972	–	–	–
Merchandise inventories	12,822	11,731	10,673	7,144	7,611	8,209
Other current assets	780	692	701	213	298	215
Operating current assets	17,439	14,139	12,871	8,153	8,439	9,085
Accounts payable	(7,356)	(5,732)	(4,822)	(3,524)	(3,713)	(4,109)
Accrued salaries	(1,295)	(1,094)	(1,129)	(372)	(424)	(434)
Deferred revenue	(1,634)	(1,474)	(1,165)	(731)	(717)	(674)
Other accrued expenses	(2,598)	(2,349)	(2,265)	(1,801)	(1,793)	(1,784)
Operating current liabilities	(12,883)	(10,649)	(9,381)	(6,428)	(6,647)	(7,001)
Operating working capital	4,556	3,490	3,490	1,725	1,792	2,084
Net property and equipment	26,605	27,476	26,234	18,971	21,361	22,722
Capitalized operating leases[1]	9,141	7,878	8,298	3,034	3,528	3,913
Other long-term assets, net of liabilities	(1,027)	(1,635)	(2,129)	(126)	(461)	(450)
Invested capital (excluding goodwill and acquired intangibles)	39,275	37,209	35,893	23,604	26,220	28,269
Goodwill and acquired intangibles	7,092	1,309	1,134	–	–	–
Cumulative amortization and unrecorded goodwill[2]	177	49	49	730	730	730
Invested capital	46,543	38,567	37,075	24,334	26,950	29,000
Excess cash	–	–	–	–	–	–
Nonconsolidated investments	343	667	361	165	509	253
Tax loss carry-forwards[3]	66	101	124	(33)	(1)	(56)
Total funds invested	46,952	39,335	37,560	24,466	27,458	29,197
Total funds invested: Sources						
Short-term debt	18	2,047	1,767	111	1,104	1,021
Long-term debt	11,643	11,383	9,667	4,325	5,576	5,039
Capitalized operating leases[1]	9,141	7,878	8,298	3,034	3,528	3,913
Debt and debt equivalents	20,802	21,308	19,732	7,470	10,208	9,973
Deferred income taxes: operating[3]	480	105	114	541	422	438
Deferred income taxes: nonoperating[3]	164	159	(111)	–	–	–
Cumulative amortization and unrecorded goodwill[2]	177	49	49	730	730	730
Common stock and paid-in capital	8,051	5,885	6,133	864	745	1,012
Retained earnings	33,052	11,388	12,093	14,860	15,345	17,049
Accumulated other comprehensive income	310	755	(77)	1	8	(6)
Treasury stock	(16,383)	(314)	(372)	–	–	–
Equity and equity equivalents	26,151	18,027	17,829	16,996	17,250	19,223
Total funds invested	46,952	39,335	37,560	24,466	27,458	29,197

[1] Capitalized operating lease adjustments are detailed in Exhibit 7.14.
[2] Goodwill and cumulative amortization adjustments are detailed in Exhibit 7.6.
[3] Deferred tax adjustments are detailed in Exhibit 7.8.

customers (deferred revenue), and the government (income taxes payable).[3] If a liability is deemed operating rather than financial, it should be netted from operating assets to determine invested capital. Interest-bearing liabilities are nonoperating and should *not* be netted from operating assets.

Some argue that operating liabilities, such as accounts payable, are a form of financing and should be treated no differently than debt. However, this would lead to an inconsistent definition of NOPLAT and invested capital. NOPLAT is the income available to both debt and equity holders, so when you are determining ROIC, you should divide NOPLAT by debt plus equity. Although a supplier may charge customers implicit interest for the right to pay in 30 days, the charge is an indistinguishable part of the price, and hence an indistinguishable part of the cost of goods sold. Since cost of goods sold is subtracted from revenue to determine NOPLAT, operating liabilities must be subtracted from operating assets to determine invested capital.[4]

Net property, plant, and equipment The book value of net property, plant, and equipment (e.g., production equipment and facilities) is always included in operating assets. Situations that require using the market value or replacement cost are discussed in Chapter 8.

Net other operating assets If other long-term assets and liabilities are small—and not detailed by the company—we can assume they are operating. To determine net other long-term operating assets, subtract other long-term liabilities from other long-term assets. This figure should be included as part of invested capital. If, however, other long-term assets and liabilities are relatively large, you will need to disaggregate each account into its operating and non-operating components before you can calculate net other long-term operating assets.

For instance, a relatively large other long-term assets account might include nonoperating items such as deferred tax assets, prepaid pension assets, intangible assets related to pensions, nonconsolidated subsidiaries, and other equity investments. Nonoperating items should not be included in invested capital. Long-term liabilities might similarly include operating and nonoperating items. Operating liabilities are liabilities that result directly from an ongoing operating activity. For instance, Home Depot warranties some products beyond one year, collecting customer funds today but recognizing the revenue (and resulting income) only gradually over the warranty period. However, most long-term liabilities are not operating liabilities, but rather what we

---

[3] Retailers, such as Home Depot and Lowe's, receive customer prepayments from gift cards, prepaid product installations, and anticipated customer returns (for which funds are received but revenue is not recognized).

[4] Alternatively, we could compute return on operating assets by adding back to NOPLAT the estimated financing cost associated with any operating liabilities. This approach, however, is unnecessarily complex, requires information not readily available, and fails to provide additional insight.

deem debt and equity equivalents. These include unfunded pension liabilities, unfunded postretirement medical costs, restructuring reserves, and deferred taxes.

Where can you find the breakdown of other assets and other liabilities? In some cases, companies provide a table in the footnotes. Most of the time, however, you must work through the footnotes, note by note, searching for items aggregated within other assets and liabilities. For instance, in 2007, Home Depot aggregated a nonoperating equity investment (HD Supply) within other assets. This was reported solely in the 2007 footnote titled, "Disposition and Acquisitions."

Goodwill and acquired intangibles   In Chapter 8, return on invested capital is analyzed both with and without goodwill and acquired intangibles. ROIC with goodwill and acquired intangibles measures a company's ability to create value after paying acquisition premiums. ROIC without goodwill and acquired intangibles measures the competitiveness of the underlying business. For instance, Belgian brewer InBev has a lower ROIC with goodwill and acquired intangibles than Dutch brewer Heineken, but this difference is attributable to premiums InBev paid to acquire breweries, not poor operating performance. When ROIC is computed without goodwill and acquired intangibles, InBev's operating performance is best in class. To prepare for both analyses, compute invested capital with and without goodwill and acquired intangibles.

To evaluate goodwill and acquired intangibles properly, you need to make two adjustments. Unlike other fixed assets, goodwill and acquired intangibles do not wear out, nor are they replaceable. Therefore, you need to adjust reported goodwill and acquired intangibles upward to recapture historical amortization and impairments.[5] (To maintain consistency, amortization and impairments will not be deducted from revenues to determine NOPLAT.) In Exhibit 7.6, amortization and impairments dating back to 1999 are added back to Home Depot's recorded goodwill and acquired intangibles. For instance, Home Depot reported $117 million in amortization in 2006. This amount was added to the 2005 cumulative amortization of $60 million to give a total of $177 million in cumulative amortization for 2006.[6] In 2007, Home Depot sold a subsidiary, HD Supply, to a consortium of investors. Subsequently, goodwill, acquired intangibles, and cumulative amortization all dropped. In 2008,

---

[5] The implementation of new accounting standards (in 2001 for the United States and 2005 for Europe) radically changed the way companies account for acquisitions. Today, whether paid in cash or in stock, acquisitions must be recorded on the balance sheet using the purchase methodology. Second, goodwill is not amortized. Instead, the company periodically tests the level of goodwill to determine whether the acquired business has lost value. If it has, goodwill is impaired (written down). Intangible assets (which differ from goodwill in that they are separable and identifiable) are amortized over the perceived life of the asset.

[6] The calculation of cumulative amortization and impairments will not always match cumulative amortization reported in the company's financial statements, since reported cumulative amortization does not include impairments.

EXHIBIT 7.6 **Home Depot and Lowe's: Adjustments to Goodwill and Acquired Intangibles**

$ million

	2004	2005	2006	2007	2008
Home Depot					
Goodwill	1,394	3,286	6,314	1,209	1,134
Acquired intangibles	–	398	778	100	–
Unrecorded goodwill related to pooling	–	–	–	–	–
Cumulative amortization and impairments	31	60	177	49	49
Adjusted goodwill and acquired intangibles	1,425	3,744	7,269	1,358	1,183
Lowe's					
Goodwill	–	–	–	–	–
Acquired intangibles	–	–	–	–	–
Unrecorded goodwill related to pooling	730	730	730	730	730
Cumulative amortization and impairments	–	–	–	–	–
Adjusted goodwill and acquired intangibles	730	730	730	730	730

Home Depot did not provide details on acquired intangibles or amortization, so cumulative amortization was left constant.

The second adjustment required is to add to recorded goodwill any unrecorded goodwill (due to the old pooling of interest/merger accounting). Consider Lowe's acquisition of Eagle Garden & Hardware in 1998. Since the acquisition was recorded using pooling, no goodwill was recognized. Had Lowe's used purchase accounting, the company would have recorded $730 million in goodwill.[7] To include pooling transactions, estimate and record the incremental goodwill while simultaneously adjusting equity to represent the value of shares given away. Exhibit 7.6 shows Lowe's recapitalized goodwill from the Eagle Garden & Hardware acquisition.

Not all intangible assets are generated through corporate acquisitions. Consider purchased customer contracts, for example. Companies sometimes purchase customer contracts from distributors or competitors. In these cases, the purchase cost is recognized as an intangible asset and amortized over the life of the contract.

Computing Total Funds Invested

Invested capital represents the capital necessary to operate a company's core business. In addition to invested capital, companies can also own nonoperating assets. Nonoperating assets include excess cash and marketable securities, certain financing receivables (e.g., credit card receivables), nonconsolidated

---

[7] On the final day of trading, Eagle had 29.1 million shares outstanding at a price of $37.75. Thus, Lowe's paid approximately $1.1 billion. According to its last 10-Q, Eagle had only $370 million in total equity. Pooled goodwill equals $1.1 billion less $370 million, or $730 million.

subsidiaries, and excess pension assets. Summing invested capital and nonoperating assets leads to total funds invested.

We next evaluate various types of nonoperating assets, beginning with excess cash and marketable securities.

Excess cash and marketable securities   Do not include excess cash in invested capital. By its definition, excess cash is unnecessary for core operations. Rather than mix excess cash with core operations, analyze and value excess cash separately. Given its liquidity and low risk, excess cash will earn very small returns. Failing to separate excess cash from core operations will incorrectly depress the company's apparent ROIC.

Companies do not disclose how much cash they deem necessary for operations. Nor does the accountant's definition of cash versus marketable securities distinguish working cash from excess cash. To estimate the size of working cash, we examined the cash holdings of the S&P 500 nonfinancial companies. Between 1993 and 2000, the companies with the smallest cash balances held cash just below 2 percent of sales. If this is a good proxy for working cash, any cash above 2 percent should be considered excess.[8] Neither Home Depot nor Lowe's carried excess cash in 2007, although they each held as much as $1.5 billion in the early 2000s.

Financial subsidiaries   Some companies, including IBM, Siemens, and Caterpillar, have financing subsidiaries that finance customer purchases. Because these subsidiaries charge interest on financing for purchases, they resemble banks. Since bank economics are quite different from those of manufacturing companies, you should separate line items related to the financial subsidiary from the line items for the manufacturing business. Then evaluate the return on capital for each type of business separately. Otherwise, significant distortions of performance will make comparison with other companies impossible.

Nonconsolidated subsidiaries and equity investments   Nonconsolidated subsidiaries and equity investments should be measured and valued separately from invested capital. When a company owns a minority stake in another company, it will record the investment as a single line item on the balance sheet and will not record the individual assets owned by the subsidiary. On the income statement, only income from the subsidiary will be recorded on the parent's income statement, not the subsidiary's revenues or costs. Since only income

---

[8] This aggregate figure, however, is not a rule. Required cash holdings vary by industry. For instance, one study found that companies in industries with higher cash flow volatility hold higher cash balances. To assess the minimum cash needed to support operations, look for a minimum clustering of cash to revenue across the industry. For more on predictive cash balances, see T. Opler, L. Pinkowitz, R. Stulz, and R. Williamson, "The Determinants and Implications of Corporate Cash Holdings," *Journal of Financial Economics* 52, no. 1 (1999): 3–46. For more on why companies hold excess cash, see F. Foley, J. Hartzell, S. Titman, and G. Twite, "Why Do Firms Hold So Much Cash? A Tax-Based Explanation," *Journal of Financial Economics* 86, no. 3 (December 2007): 579–607.

and not revenue is recorded, including nonconsolidated subsidiaries as part of operations will distort margins and capital turnover. Therefore, we recommend separating nonconsolidated subsidiaries from invested capital and analyzing and valuing nonconsolidated subsidiaries separately from core operations.

Prepaid and intangible pension assets   If a company runs a defined-benefit pension plan for its employees, it must fund the plan each year. And if a company funds its plan faster than its pension expenses dictate, under U.S. Generally Accepted Accounting Principles (GAAP) and International Accounting/ Financial Reporting Standards (IAS/IFRS), the company can recognize a portion of the excess assets on the balance sheet. Pension assets are considered a nonoperating asset and not part of invested capital. Their value is important to the equity holder, so they will be valued later, but separately from core operations. We examine pension assets in detail in Chapter 27.

Tax loss carry-forwards   Treat tax loss carry-forwards—also known as net operating losses (NOLs)—as a nonoperating asset. The treatment of deferred taxes is discussed in more detail in a subsequent subsection.

Other nonoperating assets   Other nonoperating assets, such as excess real estate and discontinued operations, also should be excluded from invested capital.

Reconciling total funds invested   Total funds invested can be calculated as invested capital plus nonoperating assets, as in the previous section, or as the sum of net debt, equity, and their equivalents. The totals produced by the two approaches should reconcile. A summary of sources of financing is presented in Exhibit 7.7. We next examine each of these sources of capital contributing to total funds invested.

EXHIBIT 7.7 **Sources of Financing**

Source of capital	Description
Debt	Interest-bearing debt from banks and public capital markets
Debt equivalents	Off-balance-sheet debt and one-time debts owed to others that are not part of ongoing operations (e.g., severance payments as part of a restructuring, an unfunded pension liability, or expected environmental remediation following a plant closure)
Hybrid securities	Claims that have equity characteristics but are not yet part of owner's equity (e.g., convertible debt and employee options)
Minority interest	External shareholder that owns a minority position in one of the company's consolidated subsidiaries
Equity	Common stock, additional paid-in capital, retained earnings, and accumulated other comprehensive income
Equity equivalents	Balance sheet accounts that arise because of noncash adjustments to retained earnings; similar to debt equivalents but not deducted from enterprise value to determine equity value (e.g., most deferred-tax accounts and income-smoothing provisions)

Debt Debt includes any short-term or long-term interest-bearing liability. Short-term debt includes commercial paper, notes payable, and the current portion of long-term debt. Long-term debt includes fixed debt, floating debt, and convertible debt with maturities of more than a year.

Debt equivalents such as retirement liabilities and restructuring reserves If a company's defined-benefit plan is underfunded, it must recognize the underfunding as a liability. The amount of underfunding is not an operating liability. Rather, we treat unfunded pension liabilities and unfunded postretirement medical liabilities as a debt equivalent (and treat the net interest expense associated with these liabilities as nonoperating). It is as if the company must borrow money to fund the plan. Treating unfunded retirement expenses as debt might seem hypothetical, but for some companies, the issue has become real. In June 2003, General Motors issued $17 billion in debt, using the proceeds to reduce its pension shortfall, not to fund operations.[9]

Other debt equivalents, such as reserves for plant decommissioning and restructuring, are discussed in Chapter 26.

Hybrid securities Hybrid securities are claims against enterprise value that have characteristics similar to equity but are not part of current equity. The three most common hybrid securities are convertible debt, preferred stock, and employee options.

Minority interest A minority interest occurs when a third party owns some percentage of one of the company's consolidated subsidiaries. If a minority interest exists, treat the balance sheet amount as an equity equivalent. Treat the earnings attributable to any minority interest as a financing cash flow similar to dividends.

Equity Equity includes original investor funds, such as common stock and additional paid-in capital, as well as investor funds reinvested into the company, such as retained earnings and accumulated other comprehensive income (OCI). In the United States, accumulated OCI consists primarily of currency adjustments and aggregate unrealized gains and losses from liquid assets whose value has changed but that have not yet been sold. IFRS also includes accumulated OCI within shareholders' equity but reports each reserve separately. Any stock repurchased and held in the treasury should be deducted from total equity.

Equity equivalents such as deferred taxes Equity equivalents are balance sheet accounts that arise because of noncash adjustments to retained

---

[9] R. Barley and C. Evans, "GM Plans Record Bond Sale Thursday to Plug Pension Gap," Reuters News, June 26, 2003.

earnings. Equity equivalents are similar to debt equivalents; they differ only in that they are not deducted from enterprise value to determine equity value.

The most common equity equivalent, deferred taxes, arises from differences in how investors and the government account for taxes. For instance, the government typically uses accelerated depreciation to determine a company's tax burden, whereas the accounting statements are prepared using straight-line depreciation. This leads to cash taxes that are lower than reported taxes during the early years of an asset's life. For growing companies, this difference will cause reported taxes consistently to overstate the company's actual tax burden. To avoid this bias, use cash taxes to determine NOPLAT. Since reported taxes will now match cash taxes, the deferred tax account is no longer necessary. This is why the original deferred tax account is referred to as an equity equivalent. It represents the adjustment to retained earnings that would be made if the company reported cash taxes to investors.

Not every deferred tax account should be incorporated into cash taxes, but only deferred tax assets (DTAs) and liabilities (DTLs) *associated with on-going operations.*[10] Nonoperating tax liabilities, such as deferred taxes related to pensions, should instead be valued as part of the corresponding liability. To compute operating cash taxes accurately, separate deferred taxes into the following three categories, and treat them as recommended:

1. *Tax loss carry-forwards:* Nonoperating tax assets such as tax loss carry-forwards should be treated as nonoperating assets.

2. *Operating deferred tax assets and liabilities:* Deferred tax liabilities (net of deferred tax assets) related to the ongoing operation of the business should be treated as equity equivalents. They will be used to compute operating cash taxes in the next section.

3. *Nonoperating deferred tax assets and liabilities:* Treat deferred tax liabilities (net of deferred tax assets) related to accounting conventions (such as acquired intangibles), nonoperating assets (such as pensions), or financial liabilities (such as convertible debt) as equity equivalents, but do *not* include them in cash taxes.

Exhibit 7.8 uses Home Depot's deferred tax footnote to disaggregate deferred taxes into tax loss carry-forwards, operating DTLs, and nonoperating DTLs. Tax loss carry-forwards totaled $124 million in 2008. Tax loss carry-forwards are a nonoperating asset and are treated as such when reorganizing the balance sheet in Exhibit 7.5. Operating deferred tax liabilities totaled $114 million in 2008. These liabilities include accounts related to accelerated

---

[10] Separating deferred taxes into operating and nonoperating items is a complex task and requires advanced knowledge of accounting conventions. For an in-depth discussion of deferred taxes, see Chapter 25.

EXHIBIT 7.8 **Home Depot: Deferred-Tax Assets and Liabilities**

$ million

Reported in Home Depot 10-K notes	2006	2007	2008	Reorganized financials	2006	2007	2008
Assets				**Tax loss carry-forwards**			
Accrued self-insurance liabilities	419	440	460	Net operating losses	66	108	136
State income taxes	–	105	118	Valuation allowance	–	(7)	(12)
Other accrued liabilities	603	601	490	Tax loss carry-forwards	66	101	124
Net operating losses	66	108	136				
Other deferred-tax assets	–	54	307	**Operating deferred taxes**			
Deferred-tax assets	1,088	1,308	1,511	Accelerated depreciation	(1,365)	(1,133)	(1,068)
				Accelerated inventory deduction	(137)	(118)	(114)
Valuation allowance	–	(7)	(12)	Accrued self-insurance liabilities	419	440	460
Net deferred-tax assets	1,088	1,301	1,499	State income taxes	–	105	118
				Other accrued liabilities	603	601	490
Liabilities				Operating deferred-tax assets (liabilities)	(480)	(105)	(114)
Accelerated depreciation	(1,365)	(1,133)	(1,068)				
Accelerated inventory deduction	(137)	(118)	(114)	**Nonoperating deferred taxes**			
Goodwill and other intangibles	(361)	(69)	(78)	Goodwill and other intangibles	(361)	(69)	(78)
Other deferred-tax liabilities	(103)	(144)	(118)	Other deferred-tax liabilities	(103)	(144)	(118)
Deferred-tax liabilities	(1,966)	(1,464)	(1,378)	Other deferred-tax assets	–	54	307
				Nonoperating deferred-tax assets (liabilities)	(464)	(159)	111
Deferred-tax assets (liabilities)	(878)	(163)	121	Deferred-tax assets (liabilities)	(878)	(163)	121

Source: Home Depot 10-K notes, 2006–2008.

depreciation, inventory valuation, and self-insurance. Operating DTLs are treated as an equity equivalent in Exhibit 7.5, and the change in operating DTLs will be the basis for computing cash taxes later in this chapter. The remaining items are classified as nonoperating deferred tax liabilities.

NOPLAT: In Practice

This section details how to calculate net operating profits less adjusted taxes (NOPLAT) and how to reconcile this figure with net income. NOPLAT represents total income generated from operations available to all investors.

Calculating NOPLAT

To determine NOPLAT for Home Depot and Lowe's, we turn to their respective income statements (see Exhibit 7.9) and convert the income statement into NOPLAT (see Exhibit 7.10).

Net operating profit (NOP or EBITA)   NOPLAT starts with earnings before interest, taxes, and amortization of acquired intangibles (EBITA), which equals

EXHIBIT 7.9 **Home Depot and Lowe's: Historical Income Statement**

$ million

	Home Depot			Lowe's		
	2006	2007	2008	2006	2007	2008
Net sales	90,837	77,349	71,288	46,927	48,283	48,230
Cost of merchandise sold	(61,054)	(51,352)	(47,298)	(30,729)	(31,556)	(31,729)
Selling, general, and administrative	(18,348)	(17,053)	(17,846)	(9,884)	(10,656)	(11,176)
Depreciation	(1,645)	(1,693)	(1,785)	(1,162)	(1,366)	(1,539)
Amortization	(117)	(9)	–	–	–	–
EBIT	9,673	7,242	4,359	5,152	4,705	3,786
Interest and investment income	27	74	18	52	45	40
Interest expense	(392)	(696)	(624)	(206)	(239)	(320)
Nonrecurring charge	–	–	(163)	–	–	–
Earnings before taxes	9,308	6,620	3,590	4,998	4,511	3,506
Income taxes	(3,547)	(2,410)	(1,278)	(1,893)	(1,702)	(1,311)
Earnings from continuing operations	5,761	4,210	2,312	3,105	2,809	2,195
Discontinued operations	–	185	(52)	–	–	–
Net income	5,761	4,395	2,260	3,105	2,809	2,195

revenue less operating expenses (e.g., cost of goods sold, selling costs, general and administrative costs, depreciation).

Why use EBITA and not EBITDA? When a company purchases a physical asset such as equipment, it capitalizes the asset on the balance sheet and depreciates the asset over its lifetime. Since the asset loses economic value over time, depreciation must be included as an operating expense when determining NOPLAT.

Why use EBITA and not EBIT? After all, the same argument could be made for the amortization of acquired intangibles: They, too, have fixed lives and lose value over time. But the accounting for intangibles differs from the accounting for physical assets. Unlike capital expenditures, organic investment in intangibles such as brands are *expensed* and not capitalized. Thus, when the acquired intangible loses value and is replaced through further investment, the reinvestment is expensed, and the company is penalized twice: once through amortization and a second time through reinvestment. Using EBITA avoids double-counting amortization expense in this way.

Adjustments to EBITA   In some companies, nonoperating gains and expenses are embedded within EBITA. To ensure that EBITA arises solely from operations, dig through the notes to weed out nonoperating items. The most common nonoperating items are gains (or losses) related to pensions, embedded interest expenses from operating leases, and restructuring charges hidden in the cost of sales. Each of these is briefly addressed at the end of this chapter and in detail in the chapters in Part Five covering advanced valuation issues.

EXHIBIT 7.10 **Home Depot and Lowe's: NOPLAT Calculation**

$ million

	Home Depot			Lowe's		
	2006	**2007**	**2008**	**2006**	**2007**	**2008**
Income statement						
Net sales	90,837	77,349	71,288	46,927	48,283	48,230
Cost of merchandise sold	(61,054)	(51,352)	(47,298)	(30,729)	(31,556)	(31,729)
Selling, general, and administrative	(18,348)	(17,053)	(17,846)	(9,884)	(10,656)	(11,176)
Depreciation	(1,645)	(1,693)	(1,785)	(1,162)	(1,366)	(1,539)
EBITA	9,790	7,251	4,359	5,152	4,705	3,786
Add: Operating lease interest[3]	441	536	486	185	169	199
Adjusted EBITA	10,231	7,787	4,845	5,337	4,874	3,985
Operating cash taxes	(3,986)	(3,331)	(1,811)	(2,071)	(1,973)	(1,496)
NOPLAT	6,245	4,456	3,033	3,266	2,901	2,489
Operating cash taxes						
Operating taxes[1]	3,873	2,956	1,820	2,043	1,854	1,512
Increase (decrease) in operating deferred taxes[2]	113	375	(9)	28	119	(16)
Operating cash taxes	3,986	3,331	1,811	2,071	1,973	1,496
Reconciliation with net income						
Net income	5,761	4,395	2,260	3,105	2,809	2,195
Decrease (increase) in operating deferred taxes[2]	(113)	(375)	9	(28)	(119)	16
Adjusted net income	5,648	4,020	2,269	3,077	2,690	2,211
After-tax interest expense	244	432	390	127	148	199
After-tax operating lease interest expense[3]	274	333	303	114	105	124
Total income available to investors	6,166	4,784	2,962	3,318	2,943	2,533
Nonoperating taxes	23	(103)	(71)	(20)	(14)	(19)
Loss (gain) from discontinued operations	–	(185)	52	–	–	–
After-tax nonrecurring charges	–	–	102	–	–	–
After-tax amortization of intangibles	73	6	–	–	–	–
After-tax interest income	(17)	(46)	(11)	(32)	(28)	(25)
NOPLAT	6,245	4,456	3,033	3,266	2,901	2,489

[1] Operating taxes calculation detailed in Exhibit 7.12.
[2] Operating deferred tax liabilities, net of operating deferred tax assets.
[3] Operating lease interest detailed in Exhibit 7.14.

Operating cash taxes   Since nonoperating items also affect reported taxes, they must be *adjusted* to an all-equity, operating level. Since interest expense is deductible before taxes, highly leveraged companies will have smaller tax burdens. Although a smaller tax burden will lead to a higher valuation, we recommend valuing financing effects in the weighted average cost of capital (WACC) or valuing them separately using adjusted present value (APV)—but not as part of after-tax operating profit.

The reasons for adjusting taxes are quite complex. In Chapter 25, we provide an in-depth explanation of the process we recommend for computing operating cash taxes. In this chapter, we focus on the simplest method. To estimate operating taxes, proceed in three steps:

1. Search the footnotes for the tax reconciliation table. For tables presented in dollars, build a second reconciliation table in percent, and vice versa. Data from both tables are necessary to complete the remaining steps.
2. Using the percent-based tax reconciliation table, determine the marginal tax rate. Multiply the marginal tax rate by adjusted EBITA to determine marginal taxes on EBITA.
3. Using the dollar-based tax reconciliation table, adjust operating taxes by other operating items not included in the marginal tax rate. The most common adjustment is related to differences in foreign tax rates.

To demonstrate the three-step process, let's examine the operating tax rate for Home Depot. Start by converting the reported tax reconciliation table to percentages. The results of this conversion are presented in the right-hand half of Exhibit 7.11. To convert a line item from dollars to percent, divide the line item by *earnings before taxes* ($3,590 million in 2008). Earnings before taxes are reported on the income statement.

Next, use the percentage-based tax reconciliation table to determine the marginal tax rate. You can use the company's statutory rate plus state or local taxes to calculate a proxy for the marginal rate. In 2008, Home Depot paid 37.6 percent in federal (35.0 percent) and state (2.6 percent) taxes. Use this marginal rate to compute taxes on adjusted EBITA. Exhibit 7.12 presents the calculation of marginal taxes on adjusted EBITA for Home Depot. In 2008, taxes on adjusted EBITA equaled $1,820 million (37.6 percent times $4,845 million in EBITA).

After computing taxes on adjusted EBITA, search the dollar-based reconciliation table for other operating taxes. For Home Depot, the only operating taxes

EXHIBIT 7.11 **Home Depot: Tax Reconciliation Tables**

$ million	2006	2007	2008		percent	2006	2007	2008
Tax reconciliation				**Step 1:**	**Reformatted tax reconciliation**			
Income taxes at statutory rate	3,258	2,317	1,257		Income taxes at statutory rate	35.0	35.0	35.0
State income taxes, net of federal	261	196	92		State income taxes, net of federal	2.8	3.0	2.6
Foreign rate differences	5	–	–		Foreign rate differences	0.1	–	–
Other, net	23	(103)	(71)		Other, net	0.2	(1.6)	(2.0)
Reported taxes	3,547	2,410	1,278		Reported taxes	38.1	36.4	35.6
Earnings before taxes	9,308	6,620	3,590					

Source: Home Depot 2008 10-K, note 6.

EXHIBIT 7.12 **Home Depot: Operating Taxes and Operating Cash Taxes**

$ million

		2004	2005	2006	2007	2008
Operating taxes						
Step 2:	Marginal tax rate (percent)	37.7	38.0	37.8	38.0	37.6
	× Adjusted EBITA	8,214	9,731	10,231	7,787	4,845
	= Marginal taxes on EBITA	3,098	3,698	3,868	2,956	1,820
Step 3:	Other operating taxes	(17)	(10)	5	–	–
	Operating taxes	3,081	3,688	3,873	2,956	1,820
Operating cash taxes						
	Operating taxes	3,081	3,688	3,873	2,956	1,820
	Increase in operating deferred taxes[1]	(548)	668	113	375	(9)
	Operating cash taxes	2,533	4,356	3,986	3,331	1,811

[1] Increase in operating deferred tax liabilities, net of operating deferred tax assets, as reported in Exhibit 7.8.

paid beyond marginal taxes were foreign rate differences.[11] In 2006, foreign rate differences resulted in $5 million of additional operating taxes. Therefore, increase taxes on adjusted EBITA by $5 million to determine operating taxes in 2006.

The tax reconciliation table for Home Depot is quite simple and requires few adjustments. For large multinationals, however, the tax footnote can be complex and may require multiple adjustments.

Adjusting for cash taxes   We recommend using operating cash taxes actually paid, if possible, rather than accrual-based taxes reported.[12] The simplest way to calculate cash taxes is to subtract the increase in *net operating deferred tax liabilities* (DTLs) from operating taxes. Exhibit 7.8 separates Home Depot's net operating DTLs from its nonoperating DTLs. Home Depot's net operating DTLs have been falling over the past few years, so reported taxes understate actual cash taxes. Subtracting (or adding) the annual increase (or decrease) in deferred taxes gives cash taxes. In 2008, operating taxes were decreased by $9 million because *operating* deferred tax liabilities rose from $105 million to $114 million, as reported in Exhibit 7.8.

Using changes in deferred taxes to compute cash taxes requires special care. As discussed in the section on invested capital, only changes in *operating-based* deferred taxes are included in cash taxes. Otherwise, changes in deferred

[11] Countries have different statutory tax rates on income. Thus, when a company's foreign income is taxed at a rate lower than its domestic income, a deduction appears on the tax reconciliation table. When foreign income is repatriated, a company's home country typically requires it to pay the difference between the two rates.

[12] Not every company discloses enough information to separate operating deferred taxes, such as accelerated depreciation, from nonoperating deferred taxes, such as those related to prepaid pension assets. When this information is unavailable, we recommend using operating taxes without a cash adjustment.

taxes might be double-counted: once in NOPLAT and potentially again as part of the corresponding item.[13] Also, deferred tax accounts rise and fall as a result of acquisitions and divestitures. However, only organic increases in deferred taxes should be included in cash taxes, not increases resulting from consolidation. For companies involved in multiple mergers and acquisitions, a clean measure of cash taxes may be impossible to calculate. When this is the case, use operating taxes rather than cash taxes.

Reconciliation to Net Income

To ensure that the reorganization is complete, we recommend reconciling net income to NOPLAT (see the lower half of Exhibit 7.10). To reconcile NOPLAT, start with net income, and add back (or subtract) the increase (or decrease) in operating deferred tax liabilities. Next, add back after-tax interest expense from both debt and capitalized operating leases. This determines the income available to all investors. To calculate NOPLAT, add back nonoperating expenses (such as nonoperating taxes, after-tax nonrecurring charges, and the after-tax amortization of intangibles), and subtract after-tax gains and income from nonoperating assets. We do this for Home Depot and Lowe's in Exhibit 7.10.

Nonoperating income, gains, and losses   To remain consistent with the calculation of invested capital, calculate NOPLAT without interest income and without gains or losses from the corresponding assets that have been excluded. Historical returns on excess cash and other nonoperating assets should be calculated and evaluated separately.

Free Cash Flow: In Practice

This subsection details how we build free cash flow from Home Depot and Lowe's reorganized financial statements. It shows how to add in cash flow from nonoperating assets to arrive at cash flow available to investors and how to reconcile that sum with the total flow of financing.

Calculating Free Cash Flow

Free cash flow is defined as:

$$FCF = NOPLAT + Noncash\ Operating\ Expenses$$
$$- Investments\ in\ Invested\ Capital$$

---

[13] For instance, cash flow related to future taxes on pension shortfalls should be computed using projected contributions, not on the historical deferred tax account.

EXHIBIT 7.13 **Home Depot and Lowe's: Free Cash Flow Calculation**

$ million

	Home Depot			Lowe's		
	2006	2007	2008	2006	2007	2008
NOPLAT	6,245	4,456	3,033	3,266	2,901	2,489
Depreciation	1,645	1,693	1,785	1,162	1,366	1,539
Gross cash flow	7,890	6,149	4,818	4,428	4,267	4,028
Change in operating working capital	(936)	(739)	–	168	(67)	(292)
Net capital expenditures	(3,349)	(3,577)	(543)	(3,779)	(3,756)	(2,900)
Decrease (increase) in capitalized operating leases	(1,214)	1,262	(419)	291	(494)	(385)
Investments in goodwill and acquired intangibles	(3,525)	–	175	–	–	–
Decrease (increase) in net long-term operating assets	224	457	494	52	335	(11)
Increase (decrease) in accumulated other comprehensive income	(99)	445	(832)	–	7	(14)
Gross investment	(8,899)	(2,152)	(1,125)	(3,268)	(3,975)	(3,602)
Free cash flow	(1,009)	3,998	3,693	1,160	292	426
After-tax interest income	17	46	11	32	28	25
After-tax nonrecurring charge	–	–	(102)	–	–	–
Loss (gain) from discontinued operations	–	185	(52)	–	–	–
Nonoperating taxes	(23)	103	71	20	14	19
Decrease (increase) in excess cash	–	–	–	11	–	–
Decrease (increase) in long-term investments	5	(324)	306	129	(344)	256
Decrease (increase) in net loss carry-forwards	(3)	(35)	(23)	(6)	(32)	55
Sale of HD Supply	–	8,743	–	–	–	–
Nonoperating cash flow	(4)	8,718	211	186	(334)	355
Cash flow available to investors	(1,013)	12,716	3,904	1,346	(42)	781
After-tax interest expense	244	132	390	127	148	199
After-tax operating lease interest expense	274	333	303	114	105	124
Decrease (increase) in short-term debt	1,395	(2,029)	280	(79)	(993)	83
Decrease (increase) in long-term debt	(8,971)	260	1,716	(826)	(1,251)	537
Decrease (increase) in capitalized operating leases	(1,214)	1,262	(419)	291	(494)	(385)
Flows to debt holders	(8,272)	258	2,269	(373)	(2,485)	557
Decrease (increase) in nonoperating deferred taxes	(282)	302	270	–	–	–
Dividends	1,395	1,709	1,521	276	428	491
Repurchased and retired shares	5,889	10,336	(190)	1,400	2,007	(267)
Adjustments to retained earnings	257	111	34	43	8	–
Flows to equity holders	7,259	12,458	1,635	1,719	2,443	224
Cash flow available to investors	(1,013)	12,716	3,904	1,346	(42)	781

[1] Increase in nonoperating deferred tax liabilities, net of nonoperating deferred tax assets.

Exhibit 7.13 builds the free cash flow calculation and reconciles free cash flow to cash flow available to investors for both Home Depot and Lowe's. The components of free cash flow are gross cash flow, investments in invested capital, and effects of acquisitions and divestitures.

Gross cash flow Gross cash flow represents the cash flow generated by the company's operations. It represents the cash available for investment and investor payout without the company having to sell nonoperating assets (e.g., excess cash) or raise additional capital. Gross cash flow has two components:

1. *NOPLAT:* As previously defined, net operating profits less adjusted taxes are the after-tax operating profits available to all investors.

2. *Noncash operating expenses:* Some expenses deducted from revenue to generate NOPLAT are noncash expenses. To convert NOPLAT into cash flow, add back noncash expenses. The two most common noncash expenses are depreciation and noncash employee compensation. Do not add back intangibles amortization and impairments to NOPLAT; they were not subtracted in calculating NOPLAT.

Investments in invested capital   To maintain and grow their operations, companies must reinvest a portion of their gross cash flow back into the business. To determine free cash flow, subtract gross investment from gross cash flow. We segment gross investment into five primary areas:

1. *Change in operating working capital:* Growing a business requires investment in operating cash, inventory, and other components of working capital. Operating working capital excludes nonoperating assets, such as excess cash, and financing items, such as short-term debt and dividends payable.

2. *Net capital expenditures:* Net capital expenditures equals investments in property, plant, and equipment (PP&E), less the book value of any PP&E sold. Net capital expenditures are estimated by adding the increase in net PP&E to depreciation. Do not estimate capital expenditures by taking the change in gross PP&E. Since gross PP&E drops when companies retire assets (which has no cash implications), the change in gross PP&E will often understate the actual amount of capital expenditures.

3. *Change in capitalized operating leases:* To keep the definitions of NOPLAT, invested capital, and free cash flow consistent, include investments in capitalized operating leases in gross investment.

4. *Investment in goodwill and acquired intangibles:* For acquired intangible assets, where cumulative amortization has been added back, we can estimate investment by computing the change in net goodwill and acquired intangibles. For intangible assets that are being amortized, use the same method as for determining net capital expenditures (by adding the increase in net intangibles to amortization).

5. *Change in other long-term operating assets, net of long-term liabilities:* Subtract investments in other net operating assets. As with invested capital, do not confuse other long-term operating assets with other long-term nonoperating assets, such as equity investments and excess pension

assets. Changes in equity investments need to be evaluated—but should be measured separately.

Since companies translate foreign balance sheets into their home currencies, changes in accounts will capture both true investments (which involve cash) and currency-based restatements (which are merely accounting adjustments and not the flow of cash in or out of the company). Removing the currency effects line item by line item is impossible. But we can partially undo their effect by subtracting the increase in the equity item titled "foreign currency translation effect," which under U.S. GAAP and IFRS is found within the "accumulated other comprehensive income" (OCI) account.[14] By subtracting the increase, we undo the effect of changing exchange rates.

Effect of acquisitions and divestitures   Another effect that contributes to the change in balance sheet accounts is restatements due to acquisitions and divestitures. For instance, Home Depot divested its HD Supply business in 2007 for approximately $8 billion. This caused an artificial drop in many accounts on the balance sheet, such as inventory, even though the company continued to invest in these accounts. As an example, consider merchandise inventories reported in Exhibit 7.4. The account decreased by $1.1 billion from $12,822 million in 2006 to $11,731 million in 2007. From a cash perspective, however, the company reported (in their 2007 cash flow from operating activities) an investment of $491 million in inventory. To reconcile the change in accounts with the actual cash expenditures, the difference of $1,582 million was reallocated to "sale of HD Supply" and recorded as a nonoperating cash flow.[15] Although not shown, adjustments related to the sale of HD Supply in 2007 are made to a number of accounts, including receivables, inventories, accounts payable, deferred revenues, PP&E, goodwill, and acquired intangibles.

Cash Flow Available to Investors

Although not included in free cash flow, cash flows related to nonoperating assets are valuable in their own right. They must be evaluated and valued separately and then added to free cash flow to give the total cash flow available to investors:

$$\begin{matrix} \text{Present Value} & & \text{Value of} & & \text{Total Value} \\ \text{of Company's} & + & \text{Nonoperating} & = & \text{of} \\ \text{Free Cash Flow} & & \text{Assets} & & \text{Enterprise} \end{matrix}$$

---

[14] In the 2008 annual report, Home Depot reported that "Accumulated Other Comprehensive Income consists primarily of foreign currency translation adjustments." Therefore, the change in accumulated other comprehensive income is included in gross investment in Exhibit 7.13.

[15] Adjusting for acquisitions and divestitures is a time-consuming process. Therefore, adjust cash flow to allow for the effects of both only when the resulting adjustments will be substantial.

To reconcile free cash flow with total cash flow available to investors, include the following nonoperating cash flows:

- *Cash flow related to excess cash and marketable securities:* Excess cash and marketable securities generate cash flow through interest income and asset sales. When you add investment income to cash flow, it must be added back on an after-tax basis, using the marginal tax rate.

- *Cash flow from other nonoperating assets:* Add other nonoperating income and gains (or subtract losses) less increases in other nonoperating assets (or plus decreases). It is best to combine nonoperating income and changes in nonoperating assets; otherwise, a distorted picture could emerge. Consider a company that impaired a $100 million equity investment. If we examine the change in equity investments alone, it appears that the company sold $100 million in nonoperating assets. But this assessment is misleading because no cash actually changed hands; the asset was merely marked down. If we combine the $100 million change (positive cash flow) with the $100 million reported loss (negative cash flow) from the income statement, we see the true impact is zero.

Reconciling Cash Flow Available to Investors

Cash flow available to investors should be identical to total financing flow. By modeling cash flow to and from investors, you will catch mistakes otherwise missed. Financial flows include flows related to debt, debt equivalents, and equity:

- *After-tax interest expenses:* After-tax interest should be treated as a financing flow. When computing after-tax interest, use the same marginal tax rate used for NOPLAT.

- *Debt issues and repurchases:* The change in debt represents the net borrowing or repayment on all the company's interest-bearing debt, including short-term debt, long-term debt, and capitalized operating leases.

- *Dividends:* Dividends include all cash dividends on common and preferred shares. Dividends paid in stock have no cash effects and should be ignored.

- *Share issues and repurchases:* When new equity is issued or shares are repurchased, four accounts will be affected: common stock, additional paid-in capital, treasury shares, and retained earnings (for shares that are retired). Although different transactions will have varying effects on the individual accounts, we focus on the aggregate change of the four accounts combined. In Exhibit 7.13, we refer to the aggregate change as "repurchased and retired shares."

- *Change in debt equivalents:* Since accrued pension liabilities and accrued postretirement medical liabilities are considered debt equivalents (see Chapter 27 for more on issues related to pensions and other postretirement benefits), their changes should be treated as a financing flow. Equity equivalents such as operating deferred taxes should not be included in the financing flow, because they are already included as part of NOPLAT.

ADVANCED ANALYTICAL ISSUES

Until now, we have focused on the issues you will typically encounter when analyzing a company. Depending on the company, you may come across difficult (and technical) accounting issues that can affect the estimation of NOPLAT, invested capital, and free cash flow. In this section, we summarize a set of advanced analytical topics, including operating leases, pensions, capitalized research and development (R&D), restructuring charges, and restructuring reserves. Although we provide a brief summary of these topics here, each one is discussed in depth in the chapters of Part Five, "Advanced Valuation Issues." Note, however, that not every issue will lead to material differences in ROIC, growth, and free cash flow. Before collecting extra data and estimating required unknowns, decide whether the adjustment will further your understanding of a company and its industry.

Operating Leases

When a company leases an asset under certain conditions, it need not record either an asset or a liability. Instead, it records the asset's rental charge as an expense and reports future commitments in the notes. To compare asset intensity meaningfully across companies with different leasing policies, include the value of the lease as an operating asset, with a corresponding debt recorded as a financing item. Otherwise, companies that lease assets will appear "capital light" relative to identical companies that purchase the assets.

Companies typically do not disclose the value of their leased assets. Chapter 27 evaluates alternatives for estimating value. We focus on one in particular: multiplying rental expense by an appropriate capitalization factor, based on the cost of debt (k_d) and average asset life.[16] As shown in Chapter 27, the asset value can be estimated as:

$$\text{Asset Value}_{t-1} = \left(\frac{\text{Rental Expense}_t}{k_d + \frac{1}{\text{Asset Life}}} \right)$$

[16] Chapter 27 derives an appropriate capitalization factor based on the cost of secured debt and average asset life.

EXHIBIT 7.14 **Home Depot and Lowe's: Capitalizing Operating Leases**

$ million

	Home Depot			Lowe's		
	2006	2007	2008	2006	2007	2008
EBITA						
EBITA	9,790	7,251	4,359	5,152	4,705	3,786
Implied interest[1]	441	536	486	185	169	199
Adjusted EBITA	10,231	7,787	4,845	5,337	4,874	3,985
Operating cash taxes						
Operating cash taxes	3,819	3,128	1,629	2,000	1,909	1,420
Tax shield on operating lease interest expense	167	204	182	71	64	76
Adjusted operating cash taxes	3,986	3,331	1,811	2,071	1,973	1,496
NOPLAT						
NOPLAT (using rental expense)	5,971	4,123	2,730	3,152	2,796	2,366
NOPLAT (capitalizing operating leases)	6,245	4,456	3,033	3,266	2,901	2,489
Invested capital						
Invested capital	37,403	30,689	28,778	21,300	23,422	25,086
Capitalized operating leases	9,141	7,878	8,298	3,034	3,528	3,913
Invested capital (with operating leases)	46,543	38,567	37,075	24,334	26,950	29,000
Return on average capital (percent)						
ROIC (using rental expenses)	17.3	12.1	9.2	14.3	12.5	9.8
ROIC (capitalizing operating leases)	14.5	10.5	8.0	14.0	11.3	8.9

[1] Implied interest equals each company's cost of debt times the prior year's value of operating leases. We normally prefer to use the secured cost of debt to compute an embedded interest expense, but instead use the company's cost of debt in order to tie enterprise DCF to equity cash flow valuation in Chapter 6.

For Home Depot, if we apply the 5.2 percent cost of secured debt (AA-rated debt) current at the time of writing and assume an asset life of 20 years, we can convert $846 million in rental expense to $8.3 billion in operating leases.[17] Exhibit 7.14 presents the resulting adjustment for operating leases for Home Depot and Lowe's. If operating leases are capitalized on the balance sheet, eliminate the interest cost embedded in rental expense from operating profits. In Exhibit 7.14, $486 million in embedded interest is added back to reported EBITA to compute adjusted EBITA. Also, operating taxes are adjusted to remove the associated tax shield. This raises both the numerator (NOPLAT) and the denominator (invested capital) of ROIC, but making these adjustments typically lowers a company's ROIC. For Home Depot, return on average invested capital drops from 9.2 percent to 8.0 percent upon the capitalization of leases.

The choice of accounting treatment for leases will not affect intrinsic value as long as it is incorporated correctly in free cash flow, the cost of capital,

[17] We use AA-rated debt in May 2009 to estimate lease interest cost because, unlike Home Depot's general obligation debt, leases are typically collateralized by physical assets. Rental expense is not typically disclosed in the financial statements. For Home Depot, rental expense of $846 million is reported in Note 9, Leases, in the company's 2008 annual report.

and debt equivalents. Chapter 27 describes the process for valuing leases in depth, and includes adjustments to free cash flow, cost of capital, and enterprise value.

Pensions and Other Postretirement Benefits

Following the passage of FASB Statement 158 under U.S. GAAP in 2006, companies now report the present value of pension shortfalls (and excess pension assets) directly on the balance sheet.[18] Since excess pension assets do not generate operating profits, nor do pension shortfalls fund operations, pension accounts should not be included in invested capital. Instead, pension assets should be treated as nonoperating, and pension shortfalls as a debt equivalent (and both should be valued separately from operations).[19] Reporting rules under IFRS (IAS 19) differ slightly in that companies can postpone recognition of their unfunded pension obligations resulting from changes in actuarial assumptions, but only as long as the cumulative unrecognized gain or loss does not exceed 10 percent of the obligations. This difference in accounting standards will not affect the treatment of excess pension assets or shortfalls when you are reorganizing the balance sheet, but will affect the valuation. For companies reporting under IFRS, search the notes for the current value of obligations.

FASB Statement 158 addressed deficiencies concerning pension obligations on U.S. balance sheets, but not on income statements. Pension expense, often embedded in cost of sales, aggregates the benefits given to employees for current work (known as the service cost) and the interest cost associated with pension liabilities, less the expected return on plan assets. The difference between expected return and interest cost will distort operating profit. Thus, to reflect the true economic expenses of pension benefits given to employees during the current period, remove the accounting pension expense from cost of sales, and replace it with service cost and amortization of prior service costs reported in the notes. For companies that use IFRS, extra care is required. The components of net pension cost can be included in different line items in the income statement (e.g., interest costs as part of interest expenses). Companies typically disclose the amounts for each component and the line on the income statement where the amount is included. Chapter 27 details how to use the pension note to create a clean measure of operating profit. The chapter also discusses how to analyze and value pensions.

---

[18] From December 2006, FASB Statement 158 eliminated pension smoothing on the balance sheet. Companies are now required to report excess pension assets and unfunded pension obligations on the balance sheet at their current values, not smoothed value as in the past.

[19] If pension accounts are not explicitly detailed on the company's balance sheet, search the pension footnote to determine where they are embedded. Often excess pension assets are embedded in other assets, and unfunded pension liabilities in other liabilities.

Capitalized Research and Development

In line with the conservative principles of accounting, accountants expense research and development (R&D), advertising, and certain other expenses in their entirety in the period they are incurred, even when economic benefits resulting from such expenses continue beyond the current reporting period. For companies that rely significantly on intangible assets, this practice will dramatically understate invested capital and overstate return on capital. If possible, therefore, R&D and other quasi investments should be capitalized and amortized in a manner similar to that used for capital expenditures. Equity should be adjusted correspondingly to balance the invested-capital equation.

If you decide to capitalize R&D, the R&D expense must *not* be deducted from revenue to calculate operating profit. Instead, deduct the amortization associated with past R&D investments, using a reasonable amortization schedule. Since amortization is based on past investments (versus expense, which is based on current outlays), this will prevent cuts in R&D from driving short-term improvements in ROIC.

Similar to the choice of accounting treatment for leasing, the choice of whether to capitalize certain expenses will not affect computed value; it will affect only perceptions of value creation. Chapter 28 analyzes the complete valuation process, including adjustments to free cash flow, and final value.

Nonoperating Charges and Restructuring Reserves

Provisions are noncash expenses that reflect future costs or expected losses. Companies record provisions by reducing current income and setting up a corresponding reserve as a liability (or deducting the amount from the relevant asset).

For the purpose of analyzing and valuing a company, we categorize provisions into one of four types: ongoing operating provisions, long-term operating provisions, nonoperating restructuring provisions, or provisions created for the purpose of smoothing income (transferring income from one period to another). Based on the characteristics of each provision, adjust the financial statements to reflect the company's true operating performance:

- *Ongoing operating provisions:* Operating provisions such as product warranties are part of operations. Therefore, deduct the provision from revenue to determine NOPLAT, and deduct the corresponding reserve from net operating assets to determine invested capital.

- *Long-term operating provisions:* For certain liabilities, such as expected plant decommissioning costs, deduct the operating portion from revenue to determine NOPLAT, and treat the interest portion as nonoperating. Treat the corresponding reserve as a debt equivalent.

- *Nonoperating provisions:* Restructuring charges, such as expected severance during a layoff, are nonoperating. Treat the expense as nonoperating and the corresponding reserve as a debt equivalent.

- *Income-smoothing provisions:* Provisions for the sole purpose of income smoothing should be treated as nonoperating, and their corresponding reserve as an equity equivalent. Since income-smoothing provisions are noncash, they do not affect value.

The process for classifying and properly adjusting for provisions and reserves is complex. Chapter 26 provides examples.

REVIEW QUESTIONS

1. Exhibit 7.15 presents the income statement and balance sheet for Companies A, B, and C. Compute each company's return on assets, return on equity, and return on invested capital. Based on the three ratios, which company has the best operating performance?

2. Why does the return on assets differ between Company A and Company B? Why do companies with equity investments tend to have a lower return on assets than companies with only core operations?

3. Why does the return on equity differ between Company A and Company C? Is this difference attributable to operating performance? Does return on assets best reflect operating performance? If not, which ratio does and why?

EXHIBIT 7.15 **Ratio Analysis: Consolidated Financial Statements**

$ million

	Company A	Company B	Company C
Operating profit	100	100	100
Interest	–	–	(20)
Earnings before taxes	100	100	80
Taxes	(25)	(25)	(20)
Net income	75	75	60
Balance sheet			
Inventory	125	125	125
Property and equipment	400	400	400
Equity investments	–	50	–
Total assets	525	575	525
Accounts payable	50	50	50
Debt	–	–	200
Equity	475	525	275
Liabilities and equity	525	575	525

EXHIBIT 7.16 **HealthCo: Income Statement and Balance Sheet**

$ million

Income statement			Balance sheet		
	Prior year	Current year		Prior year	Current year
Revenues	605	665	Working cash	5	5
Cost of sales	(200)	(210)	Accounts receivable	45	55
Selling costs	(300)	(320)	Inventories	15	20
Depreciation	(40)	(45)	Current assets	65	80
Operating profit	65	90			
			Property, plant, and equipment	250	260
Interest expense	(5)	(15)	Prepaid pension assets	10	50
Gain on sale	–	25	Total assets	325	390
Earnings before taxes	60	100			
			Accounts payable	10	15
Taxes	(16)	(40)	Short-term debt	20	40
Net income	44	60	Restructuring reserves	20	–
			Current liabilities	50	55
			Long-term debt	70	70
			Shareholders' equity	205	265
			Liabilities and equity	325	390

4. Exhibit 7.16 presents the income statement and balance sheet for HealthCo, a $665 million health care company. Compute NOPLAT, average invested capital, and ROIC. Assume an operating tax rate of 25 percent and a marginal tax rate of 35 percent.[20] If the weighted average cost of capital is 9 percent, is the company creating value?

5. Using the reorganized financial statements created in Question 4, what is the free cash flow for HealthCo in the current year?

6. You decide to look closer at HealthCo's current-year tax reconciliation footnote. The table reports $35 million in statutory taxes, a $5 million credit for manufacturing investments, and a one-time tax expense of $10 million related to a past-year audit. Reported taxes are therefore $40 million. What is HealthCo's statutory tax rate, operating tax rate, and effective rate? Why does computing the operating tax rate require judgment?

7. Many companies hold significant amounts of excess cash, that is, cash above the amount required for day-to-day operations. Does including excess cash as part of invested capital distort the ROIC upward or downward? Why?

---

[20] If you choose to reconcile NOPLAT with net income, nonoperating taxes are $1.5 million and $14.0 million in the prior and current year respectively. This will not match the in-depth tax analysis in Question 6.

8

Analyzing Performance
and Competitive Position

Understanding a company's past is essential to forecasting its future. For that reason, a critical component of valuation is the robust analysis of historical performance. Always start with the key drivers of value: return on invested capital (ROIC) and revenue growth. Examine trends in the company's long-run performance and its performance relative to that of its peers, so you can base your forecasts of future cash flows on reasonable assumptions about the company's key value drivers.

Start by analyzing ROIC, both with and without goodwill. ROIC with goodwill measures the company's ability to create value over and above premiums paid for acquisitions. ROIC without goodwill is a better measure of the company's performance compared with that of its peers. Then drill down into the components of ROIC to build an integrated view of the company's operating performance, and understand which aspects of the business are responsible for its overall performance. Next, examine the drivers of revenue growth. Is revenue growth driven, for instance, more by organic growth (critical to value creation, as discussed in Chapter 5) or by currency effects, which are largely beyond management control and probably not sustainable? Finally, assess the company's financial health to determine whether it has the financial resources to conduct business and make short- and long-term investments.

The first three sections of this chapter go through the steps involved in analyzing ROIC, revenue growth, and financial health, respectively. The final section of this chapter covers an alternative measure of financial performance: cash flow return on investment (CFROI).

ANALYZING RETURNS ON INVESTED CAPITAL

In Chapter 7, we reorganized the income statement into net operating profit less adjusted taxes (NOPLAT) and the balance sheet into invested capital. ROIC measures the ratio of NOPLAT to invested capital:

$$\text{ROIC} = \frac{\text{NOPLAT}}{\text{Invested Capital}}$$

Since profit is measured over an entire year, whereas capital is measured only at one point in time, we recommend that you average starting and ending invested capital. Companies that report ROIC in their annual reports often use starting capital. If new assets acquired during the year generate additional income, however, using starting capital alone will overestimate ROIC.

ROIC is a better analytical tool for understanding the company's performance than return on equity (ROE) or return on assets (ROA) because it focuses solely on a company's operations. Return on equity mixes operating performance with capital structure, making peer group analysis and trend analysis less meaningful. Return on assets (even when calculated on a preinterest basis) is an inadequate measure of performance because it not only includes nonoperating assets but also ignores the benefits of accounts payable and other operating liabilities that together reduce the amount of capital required from investors.

Exhibit 8.1 plots ROIC for Home Depot and Lowe's from 2000 to 2008 based on invested capital and NOPLAT calculations (presented in Exhibits 7.5 and 7.10). The ROIC at Home Depot outpaced Lowe's by approximately five percentage points during the early 2000s. This gap disappeared in 2005, when Home Depot began acquiring other companies.[1] Although core operating profit improved in 2005, the premiums paid for acquisitions lowered ROIC. In 2007, the U.S. housing market collapsed, and ROIC fell dramatically for both companies. By 2008, Home Depot's ROIC trailed Lowe's by approximately one percentage point, with both companies earning roughly their cost of capital.

Analyzing ROIC with and without Goodwill and Acquired Intangibles

ROIC should be computed both with and without goodwill and acquired intangibles,[2] because each ratio analyzes different things. For instance, a company

---

[1] In 2005, Home Depot completed 21 acquisitions, including National Waterworks and Williams Bros. Lumber Company. According to the company's 2005 10-K, the total cash paid for businesses acquired in fiscal 2005 was $2.5 billion.

[2] Goodwill and acquired intangibles are intangible assets purchased in an acquisition. To be classified as an acquired intangible, the asset must be separable and identifiable, such as patents. Goodwill describes assets that are not separable or identifiable. In our analysis, we treat goodwill identically to acquired intangibles. Therefore, we will often shorten the expression *goodwill and acquired intangibles* to *goodwill.*

EXHIBIT 8.1 **Home Depot and Lowe's: Return on Invested Capital**[1]

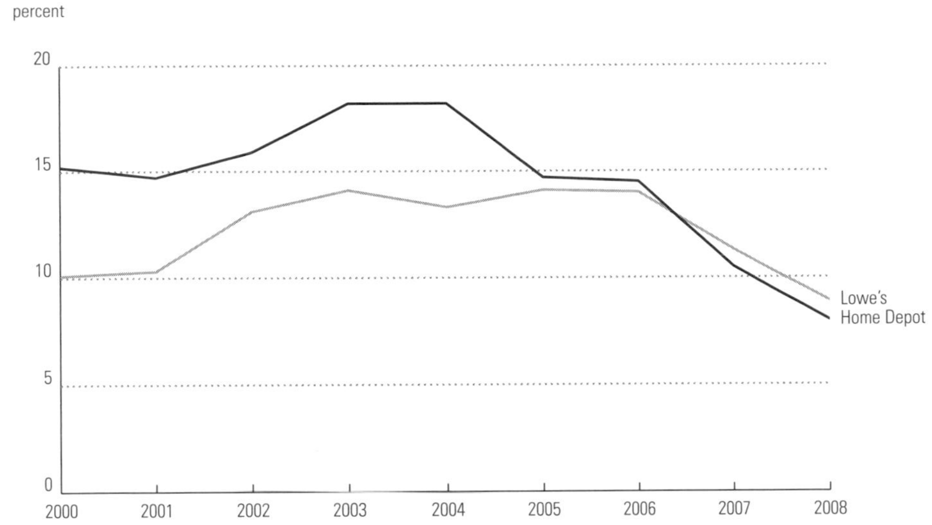

percent

[1] ROIC measured with goodwill and acquired intangibles. Goodwill and acquired intangibles do not meaningfully affect ROIC for either company.

that purchases another at a premium to book must spend real resources to acquire valuable economic assets. If the company does not properly compensate investors for the funds spent (or shares given away), it will destroy value. Thus, when you measure aggregate value creation for the company's shareholders, measure ROIC with goodwill. Conversely, ROIC excluding goodwill measures the underlying operating performance of the company and its businesses and is used to compare performance against peers and to analyze trends. It is not distorted by the price premiums paid for acquisitions.

For both Home Depot and Lowe's, goodwill is a relatively small part of invested capital, but for companies that make significant acquisitions, the difference between ROIC with and without goodwill can be large. Exhibit 8.2 presents ROIC with and without goodwill for the U.S. pharmacy CVS Caremark and a leading competitor. In 2006, CVS, as it was then known, earned an 18.4 percent ROIC without goodwill, compared with 17.9 percent for its leading competitor. In 2007, CVS purchased Caremark, a pharmaceutical benefits manager (PBM). PBMs have little working capital or fixed assets, so they have high ROICs. Consequently, CVS's aggregate ROIC without goodwill rose to 33.6 percent by 2008, reflecting the addition of a high-ROIC business. This aggregate ROIC cannot be used for benchmarking against peers, however. To understand the company's future value-creating potential, you need to examine the company's performance at the business unit level, because its two major businesses have such different underlying economics.

EXHIBIT 8.2 **CVS Caremark: Return on Invested Capital**

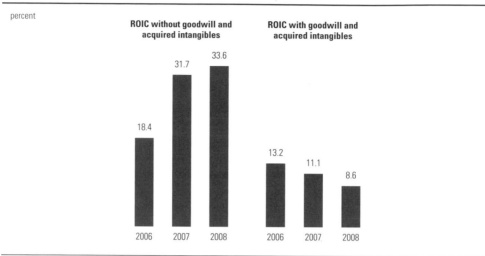

percent

Whereas CVS Caremark's ROIC without goodwill exceeds that of its competitor, the converse is true when ROIC is measured with goodwill. The premiums paid for acquisitions drop CVS Caremark's ROIC from 18.4 percent to 13.2 percent in 2006, below that of its leading competitor. Since the 2007 Caremark acquisition required a premium as well, the combined company's ROIC with goodwill fell to just 8.6 percent by 2008. Does the significant difference in ROIC when measured with and without goodwill imply the acquisition destroys value? It is too early to judge: since cost savings and cross selling opportunities take time to realize, it may take several years for the acquisition's return on capital to exceed its cost of capital.

Analyzing ROIC Using Market versus Book Invested Capital

The traditional measure of ROIC divides NOPLAT by invested capital stated at book value. Thus, ROIC represents the rate of return on capital at its original cost (less depreciation). Although this provides a good ex post measure of financial performance, it should not be used to make entry and exit decisions. Consider a company that built a facility for $1 billion five years ago. The facility is currently generating just $10 million in NOPLAT. Because the facility's 1 percent ROIC is well below its 10 percent cost of capital, the CEO recommends selling the facility. But what if the facility can be sold for only $50 million because the facility has little value to another owner? In this case, the rate of return (based on market-based opportunity costs, not book value) is 20 percent. At $50 million, the CEO would be better off keeping the facility than selling it, assuming current profits can be maintained.

Decomposing ROIC to Build an Integrated Perspective of Company Economics

Between 2006 and 2008, ROICs at both Home Depot and Lowe's fell dramatically. But what is causing this drop in performance? To understand which elements of a company's business are driving the company's ROIC, split apart the ratio as follows:

$$\text{ROIC} = (1 - \text{Operating Cash Tax Rate}) \times \frac{\text{EBITA}}{\text{Revenues}} \times \frac{\text{Revenues}}{\text{Invested Capital}}$$

The preceding equation is one of the most powerful equations in financial analysis. It demonstrates the extent to which a company's ROIC is driven by its ability to maximize profitability (EBITA divided by revenues, or the operating margin), optimize capital turnover (measured by revenues over invested capital), or minimize operating taxes.

Each of these components can be further disaggregated, so that each expense and capital item can be analyzed, line item by line item. Exhibit 8.3 shows how the components can be organized into a tree. On the right side of the tree are operational financial ratios, the drivers of value over which the manager has control. As we read from right to left, each subsequent box is a function

EXHIBIT 8.3 **Home Depot and Lowe's: ROIC Tree, 2008**

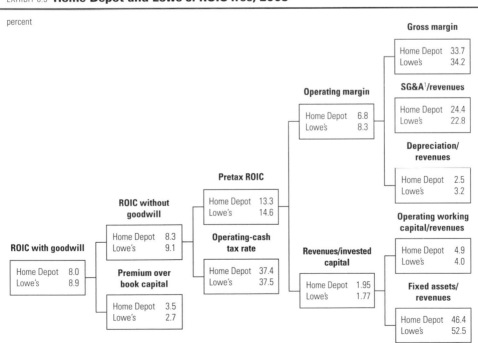

[1] Implicit interest expense related to capitalized operating leases has been removed from selling, general, and administrative (SG&A) expense.

of the boxes to its right. For example, operating margin equals gross margin less SG&A/revenues less depreciation/revenues, and pretax ROIC equals operating margin times capital turnover. (SG&A refers to selling, general, and administrative expense.)

Once you have calculated the historical drivers of ROIC, compare them with the ROIC drivers of other companies in the same industry. You can then weigh this perspective against your analysis of the industry structure (opportunities for differentiation, barriers to entry or exit, etc.) and a qualitative assessment of the company's strengths and weaknesses.

To illustrate, in 2008 Home Depot's ROIC (8.0 percent) lagged Lowe's ROIC (8.9 percent) by approximately one percentage point. Using the ROIC tree in Exhibit 8.3, we can examine which drivers were responsible for the difference. From a margin perspective, Home Depot's operating margin was 6.8 percent versus 8.3 percent for Lowe's. The lower operating margin is primarily attributable to higher SG&A expense. According to press reports, the rise in SG&A reflects the cost of additional floor personnel to improve the customer experience. Whether this translates to higher sales through better service in the future is a key to the company's valuation.

Analyzing capital efficiency, we see that Home Depot averages 1.95 times revenue to average invested capital, compared with only 1.77 times for Lowe's. For these two companies, capital efficiency derives primarily from the efficiency of fixed assets, which in turn results from more revenues per dollar of store investment. So are Home Depot's stores more efficient or operating at higher-traffic locations? Perhaps, but after further investigation, it appears that a typical Lowe's store is newer and thus more expensive than Home Depot's average store. Newer stores may be a burden today (from a capital turnover perspective) but could lead to an advantage in customer retention going forward.

Line item analysis A comprehensive valuation model will convert every line item in the company's financial statements into some type of ratio. For the income statement, most items are taken as a percentage of sales. (Exceptions exist; operating cash taxes, for instance, should be calculated as a percentage of pretax operating profits, not as a percentage of sales.)

For the balance sheet, each line item can also be taken as a percentage of revenues (or for inventories and payables, to avoid distortion caused by changing prices, as a percentage of cost of goods sold). For operating current assets and liabilities, you can also convert each line item into days, using the following formula:[3]

$$\text{Days} = 365 \times \frac{\text{Balance Sheet Item}}{\text{Revenues}}$$

---

[3] If the business is seasonal, operating ratios such as inventories should be calculated using quarterly data.

EXHIBIT 8.4 **Home Depot and Lowe's: Operating Current Assets in Days**

Number of days in revenues

	Home Depot			Lowe's		
	2006	2007	2008	2006	2007	2008
Operating cash	2.5	2.2	2.7	6.2	4.0	5.0
Receivables, net	13.0	5.9	5.0	–	–	–
Merchandise inventories[1]	76.7	83.4	82.4	84.9	88.0	94.4
Other current assets	3.1	3.3	3.6	1.7	2.3	1.6
Operating current assets	95.2	94.7	93.6	92.7	94.3	101.1

[1] Merchandise inventories computed using cost of merchandise sold, rather than revenues.

The use of days lends itself to a simple operational interpretation. As can be seen in Exhibit 8.4, Home Depot's average inventory holding time (using cost of merchandise sold as a base) has risen from 77 to 82 days. For Lowe's, the inventory time is slightly higher, rising from 85 days to 94 days. The increase in inventory holding periods is not surprising, given the sharp decline in revenues for both companies.

Nonfinancial analysis   In an external analysis, ratios are often confined to financial performance. If you are working from inside a company, however, or if the company releases operating data, link operating drivers directly to return on invested capital. By evaluating the operating drivers, you can better assess whether any differences in financial performance between competitors are sustainable.

Consider airlines, which are required for safety reasons to release a tremendous amount of operating data. Exhibit 8.5 details financial and operating data from three U.S. network carriers and three U.S. discount carriers for 2008.[4] Financial data include revenues, fuel costs, salaries, and other operating expenses. Operating data include the number of employees, measured using full-time equivalents, and available seat-miles (ASMs), the common measurement of capacity for U.S. airlines.

Exhibit 8.6 transforms the data presented in Exhibit 8.5 into a branch on the ROIC tree. Each box in the tree compares the average statistics for the three network carriers versus the three discount carriers. Because of losses at United and JetBlue, both types of carriers have negative operating margins (operating loss divided by total revenues, averaged across three carriers).

For airlines, operating margin is driven by three accounts: aircraft fuel, labor expenses, and other expenses. At first glance, it appears that the three network carriers match the three discount carriers in labor costs. Labor expenses as a percentage of revenues average 23.5 percent for the three network

[4] Network carriers have extensive networks, relying primarily on the hub-and-spoke system. Discount carriers typically fly point to point. In return for a lower price, they fly to fewer locations, use less-traveled airports, and offer fewer services.

EXHIBIT 8.5 **Financial and Operating Statistics across U.S. Airlines, 2008**

$ million

	Network carriers			Discount carriers		
	American	**Delta[1]**	**United**	**AirTran**	**JetBlue**	**Southwest**
Revenues	23,766	22,697	20,194	2,552	3,388	11,023
Aircraft fuel and related taxes	9,014	7,346	7,722	1,195	1,352	3,713
Salaries and related costs	6,655	4,802	4,311	475	694	3,340
Other operating expenses	8,773	10,436	9,983	969	1,656	3,521
Operating profit (loss)	(676)	113	(1,822)	(87)	(314)	449
Operating statistics						
Full-time equivalents	84,100	57,706	50,000	7,600	9,895	35,499
Available seat-miles (millions)	163,532	165,639	135,861	23,809	32,442	103,271

[1] Delta numbers adjusted for the acquisition of Northwest Airlines on October 29, 2008.

carriers and 23.1 percent for the network carriers. But this statistic is misleading. To see why, disaggregate the ratio of labor expenses to revenue using available seat-miles (ASMs):

$$\frac{\text{Labor Expenses}}{\text{Revenues}} = \left(\frac{\text{Labor Expenses}}{\text{ASMs}}\right) \Big/ \left(\frac{\text{Revenues}}{\text{ASMs}}\right)$$

The ratio of labor expenses to revenues is a function of labor expenses per ASM and revenues per ASM. Labor expenses per ASM are the labor costs required to fly one mile, and revenues per ASM represent average price per mile. Although labor expenses to revenues are similar for both carrier types, how they get there differs greatly. The discount carriers have a 38 percent advantage in labor cost per mile (2.5 cents per mile versus 3.4 cents for the

EXHIBIT 8.6 **Operational Drivers of Labor Expenses to Revenues**

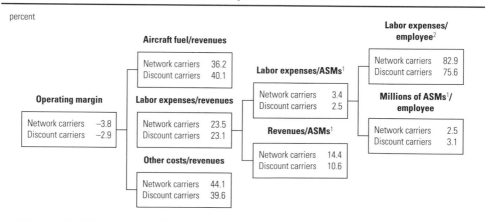

[1] Available seat-miles (ASMs) are the standard unit of capacity for the U.S. airline industry. Labor expense and revenue ratios measured in cents per mile.
[2] Labor expenses per employee measured in $ thousands.

network carrier). But what the network carriers lose in labor costs, they recover with higher prices. Because of their locations and reach, network carriers can charge an average price 35 percent higher than the discount carriers (14.4 cents per mile versus 10.6 cents per mile).

But what is driving this differential in labor expenses per ASM? Are the discounter's employees more productive? Or are they paid less? To answer these questions, disaggregate labor expenses to ASMs, using the following equation:

$$\frac{\text{Labor Expenses}}{\text{ASM}} = \left(\frac{\text{Labor Expenses}}{\text{Employees}}\right) \Big/ \left(\frac{\text{ASMs}}{\text{Employees}}\right)$$

There are two drivers of labor expenses per ASM: the first term represents the average salary per full-time employee; the second measures the productivity of each full-time employee (millions of ASMs flown per employee). The boxes on the right side of Exhibit 8.6 report the calculations for this equation. The average salary is 9 percent higher for the three network carriers, and productivity per mile is 19.2 percent lower. Although the salary differential appears significant, it is quite small compared with earlier in the decade, when average salaries differed by a factor of almost two.

Analyzing performance using operating drivers gives additional insight into the competitive differences among airlines. But the analysis is far from done. In fact, a thoughtful analysis will often raise more questions than answers. For instance, can the salary difference between network and discount carriers be explained by the mix of employees (pilots are more expensive than gate personnel), the location of the employees (New York is more expensive than Texas), or poor contract negotiations? Each of these analyses will provide additional insight into the each carrier type's ability to survive and prosper.

ANALYZING REVENUE GROWTH

In Chapter 2, we determined that the value of a company is driven by ROIC, cost of capital, and growth in cash flows. But what drives long-term growth in cash flows? Assuming profits and reinvestment stabilize at steady rates over the long term, any long-term growth in cash flows will be directly tied to long-term growth in revenues. And by analyzing historical revenue growth, you can assess the potential for growth in the future.

The calculation of year-to-year revenue growth is straightforward, but the results can be misleading. The three prime culprits distorting revenue growth are the effects of changes in currency values, mergers and acquisitions, and changes in accounting policies. Strip out from revenues any distortions created by these effects in order to base forecast revenues for valuation on sustainable precedents.

EXHIBIT 8.7 **Compass and Sodexo: Revenue Growth Analysis**

percent

	Compass			Sodexo		
	2006	2007	2008	2006	2007	2008
Organic revenue growth	7.0	5.0	5.9	6.4	8.4	7.7
Currency effects	1.0	(5.1)	5.1	2.8	(3.7)	(6.7)
Portfolio changes	(22.9)	(5.0)	0.4	0.4	(0.1)	0.7
Reported revenue growth	(14.9)	(5.1)	11.4	9.6	4.6	1.7

Exhibit 8.7 demonstrates how misleading raw year-to-year revenue growth figures can be. Compass (based in the United Kingdom) and Sodexo (based in France) are global providers of canteen services in businesses, schools, and sporting venues. In 2008, total revenues at Compass grew by 11.4 percent, and revenues at Sodexo grew by 1.7 percent. The difference in growth rates appears dramatic but is driven primarily by changes in currency values (pounds sterling versus euros), not by organic revenue growth. Stripping out currency effects, acquisitions, and divestitures, organic revenue growth at Sodexo (7.7 percent) actually outpaced that of Compass (5.9 percent) by nearly two percentage points.

Given recent swings in currency values and large portfolio changes effected through restructurings by many companies, historical revenue growth for large multinationals can be extremely volatile, making benchmarking difficult. For Compass, revenue growth varied between negative 14.9 percent in 2006 and positive 11.4 percent in 2008. Sodexo exhibited similar volatility. In contrast, organic growth is more stable. Compass's organic revenue growth averaged 6.0 percent, and Sodexho's averaged 7.6 percent over the same period, but neither varied more than one percentage point from their average value.

In the next three sections, we examine drivers of revenue growth and discuss their effect on performance measurement, forecasting, and ultimately valuation.

Currency Effects

Multinational companies conduct business in many currencies. At the end of each reporting period, these revenues are converted to the currency of the reporting company. If foreign currencies are rising in value relative to the company's home currency, this translation, at better rates, will lead to higher revenue numbers. Thus, a rise in revenue may not reflect increased pricing power or greater quantities sold, but simply depreciation in the company's home currency.

Exhibit 8.8 reports revenue by geography for Compass and Sodexo. The companies have similar geographic mixes, with roughly 40 percent of

EXHIBIT 8.8 **Compass and Sodexo: Effect of Currencies on Revenue Growth**

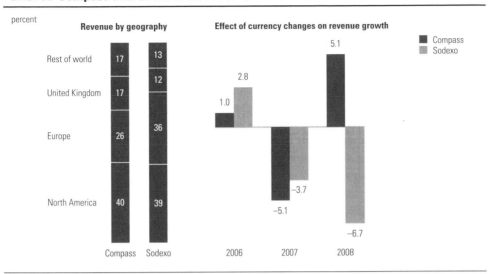

revenues coming from North America. Since each company translates U.S. dollars into a different currency, exchange rates will affect each company quite differently.

Compass translates U.S. dollars from its North American business into British pounds. Given the weakening of the pound against the U.S. dollar ($2.04 per pound in 2007 versus $1.78 per pound in 2008), Compass reported an increase in revenues of 5.1 percent attributable to the weakening pound. For Sodexo, exchange rates had the opposite effect. As the euro strengthened against the dollar, Sodexho translated revenue from North America into fewer euros, leading to a 6.7 percent drop in euro-denominated revenue.

The right side of Exhibit 8.8 demonstrates the dramatic effects of volatility in exchange rates. Movements that hurt Compass in 2007 reversed themselves in 2008. Failing to acknowledge these currency movements can lead to a critical misunderstanding of a global company's ability to grow organically.

Mergers and Acquisitions

Growth through acquisition may have very different effects on ROIC from internal growth because of the sizable premiums a company must pay to acquire another company. Therefore, it is important to understand how companies have been generating historical revenue growth: through acquisition or internally.

Stripping the effect of acquisitions from reported revenues is difficult. Unless an acquisition is deemed material by the company's accountants, company filings do not need to detail or even report the acquisition. For larger acquisitions, a company will report pro forma statements that recast historical

EXHIBIT 8.9 **Effect of Acquisitions on Revenue Growth**

$ million

	Year 1	Year 2	Year 3	Year 4	Year 5
Revenue by company					
Parent company	100.0	110.0	121.0	133.1	146.4
Target company	20.0	22.0	24.2	26.6	29.3
Consolidated revenues					
Revenue from parent	100.0	110.0	121.0	133.1	146.4
Revenue from target	–	–	14.1	26.6	29.3
Consolidated revenues[1]	100.0	110.0	135.1	159.7	175.7
Growth rates (percent)					
Consolidated revenue growth	–	10.0	22.8	18.2	10.0
Organic growth	–	10.0	10.0	10.0	10.0

[1] Only consolidated revenues are reported in a company's annual report.

financials as though the acquisition were completed at the beginning of the fiscal year. Revenue growth, then, should be calculated using the pro forma revenue numbers.[5] If the target company publicly reports its own financial data, you can construct pro forma statements manually by combining revenue of the acquirer and target for the prior year. But beware: The bidder will include partial-year revenues from the target for the period after the acquisition is completed. To remain consistent year to year, reconstructed prior years also must include only partial-year revenue.

Exhibit 8.9 presents the hypothetical purchase of a target company in the seventh month of year 3. Both the parent company and the target are growing organically at 10 percent per year. Consolidated revenues, however, spike during the two years surrounding the acquisition. Whereas the individual companies are growing at 10 percent each and every year, consolidated revenue growth is reported at 22.8 percent in year 3 and 18.2 percent in year 4.

To create an internally consistent comparison for years 3 and 4, adjust the prior year's consolidated revenues to match the current year's composition. To do this, add seven months of the target's year 2 revenue (7/12 × $22 million = $12.8 million) to the parent's year 2 revenue ($110.0 million). This leads to adjusted year 2 revenues of $122.8 million, which matches the composition of year 3. To compute an organic growth rate, compare year 3 revenues ($135.1 million) to adjusted year 2 revenues ($122.8 million). The resulting organic revenue growth rate equals 10 percent, which matches the underlying organic revenue growth of the individual companies.

[5] For example, Cablevision Systems purchased *Newsday* in July 2008. Consolidated revenue for Cablevision Systems in 2008 includes revenue generated by *Newsday*, but only subsequent to July 29, 2008. Since 2008 includes five months of *Newsday* revenue and 2007 does not, the company's consolidated revenue cannot be compared with the prior year's revenue without adjustment.

Even though the acquisition occurs in year 3, the revenue growth rate for year 4 also will be affected by the acquisition. Year 4 contains a full year of revenues from the target. Therefore, year 3 revenue must also contain a full year of target revenue. Consequently, year 3 should be increased by five months of target revenue ($5/12 \times \$24.2$ million $= \$10.1$ million).

Accounting Changes and Irregularities

Each year, the Financial Accounting Standards Board (FASB) in the United States and the International Accounting Standards Board (IASB) make recommendations concerning the financial treatment of certain business transactions. Most changes in revenue recognition policies do not come as formal pronouncements from the boards themselves, but from task forces that issue topic notes. Companies then have a set amount of time to implement the required changes. Changes in a company's revenue recognition policy can significantly affect revenues during the year of adoption, distorting the one-year growth rate.[6] You therefore need to eliminate their effects in order to understand real historical revenue trends.

Consider Emerging Issues Task Force (EITF) 09-3 from the FASB, which changes the way revenue is recognized for companies that package computer hardware and software. Before 2010, companies were required to follow Statement of Position (SOP) 97-2, which states that revenue should be recognized using "contract accounting." For example, Apple recognizes the revenue from the sale of an iPhone over 24 months because the company provides free software upgrades for two years. Under EITF 09-3, companies will be able to recognize hardware revenue and profit at the point of sale. When Apple adjusts to the new rule, it will recognize the majority of iPhone revenue immediately versus gradually over two years. This will cause an artificial rise in Apple's revenue during the year of the accounting change.

If an accounting change is material, a company will document the change in its section on management discussion and analysis (MD&A). The company will also recast its historical financial statements. Some companies do not fully document changes in accounting policy, and this can lead to distorted views of performance.

Decomposing Revenue Growth to Build an Integrated Perspective of Company Economics

Once the effects of mergers and acquisitions, currency translations, and accounting changes have been removed from the year-to-year revenue growth

---

[6] Revenue recognition changes can also affect margins and capital turnover ratios. They will not, however, affect free cash flow.

numbers, analyze organic revenue growth from an operational perspective. The most standard breakdown is:

$$\text{Revenues} = \frac{\text{Revenues}}{\text{Units}} \times \text{Units}$$

Using this formula, determine whether prices or quantities are driving growth. Do not, however, confuse revenue per unit with price; they can be different. If revenue per unit is rising, the change could be due to rising prices, or the company could be shifting its product mix from low-priced to high-priced items.

The operating statistics that companies choose to report (if any) depend on the norms of the industry and the practices of competitors. For instance, most retailers provide information on the number of stores they operate, the number of square feet in those stores, and the number of transactions they conduct annually. By relating different operating statistics to total revenues, we can build a deeper understanding of the business. Consider this retailing standard:

$$\text{Revenues} = \frac{\text{Revenues}}{\text{Stores}} \times \text{Stores}$$

Using the operating statistics reported in Exhibit 8.10, we discover that Home Depot not only has more stores than Lowe's, but also generates more revenue per store ($31.1 million per store for Home Depot versus $29.2 million for Lowe's). Using the three operating statistics, we can build ratios on revenues per store, transactions per store, square feet per store, dollars per transaction, and number of transactions per square foot.

Although operating ratios are powerful in their own right, what can really change one's thinking about performance is how the ratios are changing over time. Exhibit 8.11 organizes each ratio into a tree. Rather than report a calculated ratio, such as revenues per store, however, we report the growth in the ratio and relate this back to the growth in revenue. At Home Depot, store-based revenues declined by 7.9 percent in 2008, while Lowe's held revenues flat in the same year. How did Lowe's avoid the growth problems of Home Depot? Actually, it did not. Lowe's kept aggregate revenues flat by opening 115 stores,

EXHIBIT 8.10 **Home Depot and Lowe's: Operating Data**

	Home Depot			Lowe's		
	2006	**2007**	**2008**	**2006**	**2007**	**2008**
Store revenues[1] ($ million)	78,337	76,793	70,736	46,906	48,276	48,211
Number of stores	2,147	2,234	2,274	1,385	1,534	1,649
Number of transactions (million)	1,330	1,336	1,272	680	720	740
Square footage at fiscal year-end (million)	224	235	238	157	174	187

[1] Store revenues are revenues generated by customer transactions. They do not include other revenues.

EXHIBIT 8.11 **Home Depot and Lowe's: Revenue Growth Analysis, 2008**

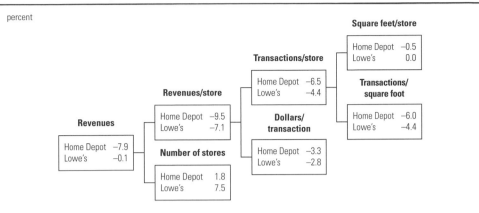

but same-store sales fell by 7.1 percent. Since Home Depot opened just 40 new stores, its decline in aggregate revenue was more dramatic. But remember: growth is a powerful valuation driver, but only when combined with an ROIC greater than the cost of capital. If Lowe's cannot earn its cost of capital on the new stores, the growth will destroy value, and the company's stock price will suffer as a result.

Stripping out the growth in stores, we can focus on the within-store growth. The implications of this analysis are extremely important, to the point that financial analysts have a special name for growth in revenue per store: *comps*, shorthand for comparables, or year-to-year same-store sales. Why is this revenue growth important? First, how many stores to open is an investment choice, whereas same-store sales growth reflects each store's ability to compete effectively in its local market. Second, new stores require large capital investments, whereas comps growth requires little incremental capital. Higher revenues and less capital lead to higher capital turnover, which leads to higher ROIC.

CREDIT HEALTH AND CAPITAL STRUCTURE

To this point, we have focused on the operating performance of the company and its ability to create value. We have examined the primary drivers of value: a company's return on invested capital and organic revenue growth. In the final step of historical analysis, we focus on how the company has financed its operations. What proportion of invested capital comes from creditors instead of from equity investors? Is this capital structure sustainable? Can the company survive an industry downturn? (See Chapter 23 for a detailed explanation of capital structure choices.)

To determine how robust a company's capital structure is, we examine two related but distinct concepts: liquidity (via the interest coverage ratio) and leverage. Liquidity measures the company's ability to meet short-term obligations, such as interest expenses, rental payments, and required principal payments. Leverage measures the company's ability to meet obligations over the long term. Since this book's focus is not credit analysis, we detail only a few ratios that credit analysts use to evaluate a company's capital structure and credit health.

Coverage

The company's ability to meet short-term obligations is measured with ratios that incorporate three measures of earnings:

1. Earnings before interest, taxes, and amortization (EBITA).
2. Earnings before interest, taxes, depreciation, and amortization (EBITDA).
3. Earnings before interest, taxes, depreciation, amortization, and rental expense (EBITDAR).

The ratios used to measure ability to meet short-term obligations are the traditional interest coverage ratio and a more advanced measure, the ratio of EBITDAR to the sum of interest expense and rental expense.

Interest coverage is calculated by dividing either EBITA or EBITDA by interest. The first coverage ratio, EBITA to interest, measures the company's ability to pay interest using profits without cutting capital expenditures intended to replace depreciating equipment. The second ratio, EBITDA to interest, measures the company's ability to meet short-term financial commitments using both current profits and the depreciation dollars earmarked for replacement capital. Although EBITDA provides a good measure of the short-term ability to meet interest payments, most companies cannot compete effectively without replacing worn assets.

Like the interest coverage ratio, the ratio of EBITDAR to interest expense plus rental expense measures the company's ability to meet its known future obligations, including the effect of operating leases. For many companies, especially retailers, including rental expenses is a critical part of understanding the financial health of the business.

Exhibit 8.12 presents financial data and coverage ratios for Home Depot and Lowe's. For 2008, Home Depot's EBITA/interest coverage ratio equals 7.0 times, whereas Lowe's has an interest coverage ratio of 11.8 times. Using regression results from Exhibit 23.5, we can translate each company's interest coverage ratio into a credit rating. Home Depot's Standard & Poor's credit rating as of May 2009 was BBB+. Lowe's was rated A+. These ratings match the model's prediction based on each company's interest coverage ratio.

EXHIBIT 8.12 **Home Depot and Lowe's: Measuring Coverage**

$ million

	Home Depot			Lowe's		
	2006	**2007**	**2008**	**2006**	**2007**	**2008**
EBITA	9,790	7,251	4,359	5,152	4,705	3,786
EBITDA	11,435	8,944	6,144	6,314	6,071	5,325
EBITDAR[1]	12,393	9,768	6,990	6,632	6,440	5,724
Interest	392	696	624	206	239	320
Rental expense	958	824	846	318	369	399
Interest plus rental expense	1,350	1,520	1,470	524	608	719
Coverage ratios						
EBITA/interest	25.0	10.4	7.0	25.0	19.7	11.8
EBITDA/interest	29.2	12.9	9.8	30.7	25.4	16.6
EBITDAR/interest plus rental expense	9.2	6.4	4.8	12.7	10.6	8.0

[1] Earnings before interest, taxes, depreciation, amortization, and rental expense.

Since both companies maintain investment-grade ratings, the likelihood of default is quite small.

Leverage

To better understand the power (and danger) of leverage, consider the relationship between return on equity (ROE) and return on invested capital (ROIC):

$$\text{ROE} = \text{ROIC} + [\text{ROIC} - (1 - T)\,k_d]\,\frac{D}{E}$$

As the formula demonstrates, a company's ROE is a direct function of its ROIC, its spread of ROIC over its after-tax cost of debt (k_d), and its book-based debt-to-equity ratio (D/E). Consider a company that is earning an ROIC of 10 percent and has an after-tax cost of debt of 5 percent. To raise its ROE, the company can either increase its ROIC (through operating improvements) or increase its debt-to-equity ratio (by swapping debt for equity). Although each strategy can lead to an identical change in ROE, increasing the debt-to-equity ratio makes the company's ROE more sensitive to changes in operating performance (ROIC). Thus, while increasing the debt-to-equity ratio can increase ROE, it does so by increasing the risks faced by shareholders.

To assess leverage, measure the company's (market) debt-to-equity ratio over time and against peers. Does the leverage ratio compare favorably with the industry? How much risk is the company taking? We answer these and other questions related to leverage in depth in Chapter 23.

Payout Ratio

The dividend payout ratio equals total common dividends divided by net income available to common shareholders. We can better understand the company's financial situation by analyzing the payout ratio in relation to its cash flow reinvestment ratio (examined earlier):

- If the company has a high dividend payout ratio and a reinvestment ratio greater than 1, then it must be borrowing money to fund negative free cash flow, to pay interest, or to pay dividends. But is this sustainable?

- A company with positive free cash flow and low dividend payout is probably paying down debt (or aggregating excess cash). In this situation, is the company passing up the valuable tax benefits of debt or hoarding cash unnecessarily?

Valuation Metrics

To conclude your assessment of capital structure, measure the shareholders' perception of future performance by calculating a market multiple. To build a market multiple, divide core operating value[7] by a normalizing factor, such as revenue, EBITA, or the book value of invested capital. By comparing the multiple of one company versus another, you can examine how the market perceives the company's future relative to other companies.

Exhibit 8.13 presents the core-operating-value-to-EBITA multiple for Home Depot and Lowe's between 2000 and 2009. In the early 2000s, both companies traded at extremely high multiples. By 2004, both companies stabilized at roughly 10 times EBITA. In Chapter 14, we describe how to build and analyze a robust set of market comparables.

ALTERNATIVES TO ROIC

For companies with large, uneven capital expenditures, ROIC may vary significantly over the asset's life, and this can give a distorted picture of when value is created. In this case, it may be helpful to convert ROIC into a measure similar to internal rate of return (IRR). One common measure based on the principles of IRR is cash flow return on investment (CFROI).[8]

Consider a livery company that plans to purchase a luxury sedan for $40,000. The vehicle will operate for four years. Since revenues are independent of the sedan's age, the vehicle will earn relatively constant profits over the four

---

[7] In Chapter 6, core operating value is defined as enterprise value less the market value of nonoperating assets, such as excess cash and nonconsolidated subsidiaries.

[8] For more information, see B. Madden, *CFROI Valuation: A Total System Approach to Valuing the Firm* (Oxford, UK: Butterworth-Heinemann, 1999).

EXHIBIT 8.13 **Home Depot and Lowe's: Core Operating Value[1] to EBITA**

Multiple of EBITA

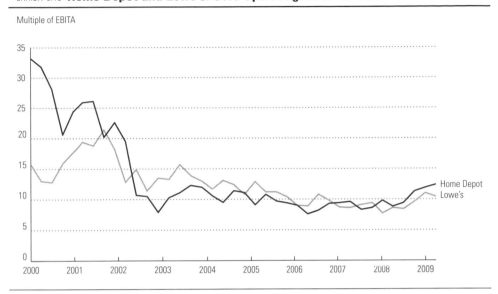

[1] Core operating values equals enterprise values less the market value of nonoperating assets.

years. In Exhibit 8.14, we present the NOPLAT, invested capital, and return on invested capital for the livery company. Note how the vehicle's ROIC rises from 8.9 percent to 26.7 percent over its life. If the company's cost of capital is 15 percent, it appears that the investment destroys value during its first two years but creates value during the last two years.

Alternatively, you could calculate the internal rate of return for each sedan. Using the classic IRR formula, you would find that the sedan earns an IRR of 12.7 percent over its life. Calculating IRR, however, requires

EXHIBIT 8.14 **Project-Based Return on Invested Capital**

$ thousand

	Year 0	Year 1	Year 2	Year 3	Year 4
Revenues	–	100	100	100	100
Operating costs	–	(86)	(86)	(86)	(86)
Depreciation	–	(10)	(10)	(10)	(10)
NOPLAT	–	4	4	4	4
Working capital	5	5	5	5	–
Fixed assets	40	30	20	10	–
Invested capital	45	35	25	15	–
ROIC[1] (percent)	–	8.9	11.4	16.0	26.7

[1] ROIC measured on beginning-of-year capital.

EXHIBIT 8.15 **Home Depot: CFROI, 2008**

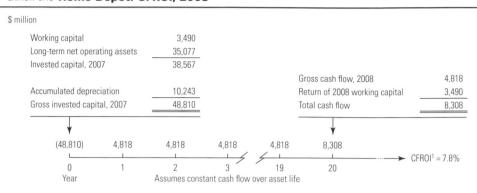

$ million

Working capital	3,490
Long-term net operating assets	35,077
Invested capital, 2007	38,567
Accumulated depreciation	10,243
Gross invested capital, 2007	48,810

Gross cash flow, 2008	4,818
Return of 2008 working capital	3,490
Total cash flow	8,308

[1] Results of internal rate of return (IRR) calculation on the cash flow stream.

making subjective forecasts, so it does not offer a consistent measure of historical performance.

Cash flow return on investment (CFROI) removes the subjectivity of year-by-year forecasting yet provides a smoothed measure. To calculate CFROI in a given year, use the traditional IRR methodology of setting the net present value to 0 and then solving for the discount rate. To avoid the subjectivity of forecasting, CFROI assumes a fixed cash flow for a fixed number of periods (the company's estimated asset life). To calculate CFROI, we need three components: the initial investment, the annual cash flow, and residual value. The initial investment equals the gross invested capital measured in the prior period (gross invested capital equals invested capital plus accumulated depreciation). The annual cash flow equals NOPLAT plus depreciation. The residual value equals NOPLAT plus depreciation, plus the return of the original working capital.

Exhibit 8.15 calculates the CFROI in 2008 for Home Depot. To measure initial investment, we add 2007's invested capital ($38,567 million) to 2007's accumulated depreciation ($10,243 million).[9] The annual gross cash flow over 20 years is $4,818 million (as measured by 2008 gross cash flow), and the return of working capital equals $3,490 million in year 20. Using a spreadsheet IRR function, we arrive at a CFROI of 7.8 percent.

CFROI captures the lumpiness of an investment better than ROIC. But it is complex to calculate and requires assumptions about the investment's estimated asset life. Weighing the simplicity of ROIC versus the smoothness

[9] Operating working capital, invested capital, and gross cash flow are defined in Chapter 7. Accumulated depreciation is found between gross property, plant, and equipment (PP&E) and net PP&E on the balance sheet. If only net PP&E appears on the balance sheet, check the notes for accumulated depreciation.

of CFROI, we suggest using CFROI only when companies have the following characteristics:

- Lumpy capital expenditure patterns.
- Fixed assets with long lives (over 15 years).
- Large ratio of fixed assets to working capital.

GENERAL CONSIDERATIONS

Although it is impossible to provide a comprehensive checklist for analyzing a company's historical financial performance, here are some guidelines to keep in mind:

- Look back as far as possible (at least 10 years). Long time horizons will allow you to determine whether the company and industry tend to revert to some normal level of performance, and whether short-term trends are likely to be permanent.
- Disaggregate value drivers—both ROIC and revenue growth—as far as possible. If possible, link operational performance measures with each key value driver.
- If there are any radical changes in performance, identify the source. Determine whether the change is temporary or permanent, or merely an accounting effect.

REVIEW QUESTIONS

1. JetCo is a manufacturer of high-speed aircraft. The company generates $100 million in operating profit on $600 million of revenue and $800 million of invested capital. JetCo's primary competitor, Gulf Aviation, generates $100 million in NOPLAT on $800 million in revenue. Gulf Aviation has $600 million in invested capital. Based on the preceding data, which company is creating more value? Assume an operating tax rate of 25 percent and cost of capital of 8 percent.

2. Using the data presented in Question 1, decompose ROIC into operating margin and capital turnover for each company. Which ratio is the key determinant of ROIC: operating margin or capital turnover?

3. DefenseCo announces a purchase of Gulf Aviation for $1.1 billion in cash. Consequently, Gulf Aviation's invested capital with goodwill and acquired intangibles rises from $600 million to $1.1 billion. The following year, while conducting its annual review of Gulf Aviation, senior management at

DefenseCo asks you the following questions: Based on the profitability figures presented in Question 1, is Gulf Aviation creating value for DefenseCo? Which company, JetCo or Gulf Aviation, has the best financial performance in the industry?

4. Gulf Aviation generates $800 million in revenue per year, with no material growth. The consolidated revenues for DefenseCo are $1.5 billion in year 1, $1.8 billion in year 2 (the year of the acquisition), and $2.5 billion in year 3. If DefenseCo closed the acquisition of Gulf Aviation on October 1 of year 2, what is the apples-to-apples organic growth for DefenseCo in year 2 and year 3? How does organic growth differ from the growth in reported revenues? Assume Gulf Aviation revenues are consolidated into DefenseCo only after the acquisition close date and that the fiscal year closes for both companies on December 31 of each year.

5. Using an Internet search tool, locate Procter & Gamble's investor relations web site. Under "Financial Reporting," you will find the company's 2009 annual report. In the annual report's section titled "Management's Discussion and Analysis," you will find a discussion on revenue growth. How fast did the company grow (or shrink) revenues in 2009? How much growth is attributable to price, number of units sold, foreign exchange impacts, and shifts in the mix of products sold? How does this compare to 2008 (which can also be found in the 2009 annual report)? What would the growth have been on a constant currency basis? Is the difference with and without foreign exchange impacts meaningful?

6. Which interest coverage ratio, EBITDA to interest or EBITA to interest, will lead to a higher number? When is the EBITDA interest ratio more appropriate than the EBITA ratio? When is the EBITA interest coverage ratio more appropriate than the EBITDA ratio?

9

Forecasting Performance

In Part One, "Foundations of Value," we focused on how to forecast long-run value drivers that are consistent with economic theory and historical evidence. In this chapter, we focus on the *mechanics* of forecasting—specifically, how to develop an integrated set of financial forecasts that reflect the company's expected performance.

Although the future is unknowable, careful analysis can yield insights into how a company may develop. This chapter shows how to build a well-structured spreadsheet model: one that separates raw inputs from computations, flows from one worksheet to the next, and is flexible enough to handle multiple scenarios. Next we discuss the process of forecasting. To arrive at future cash flow, we forecast the income statement, balance sheet, and statement of retained earnings. The forecasted financial statements provide the information necessary to compute net operating profit less adjusted taxes (NOPLAT), invested capital, return on invested capital (ROIC), and ultimately free cash flow (FCF).

While you are building a forecast, it is easy to become engrossed in the details of individual line items. But we stress, once again, that you must place your aggregate results in the proper context. You can do much more to improve your valuation through a careful analysis of whether your forecast of future ROIC is consistent with the company's ability to compete than by precisely (but perhaps inaccurately) forecasting accounts receivable 10 years out. For this reason, we start by discussing the proper length and detail of a forecast.

DETERMINE LENGTH AND DETAIL OF THE FORECAST

Before you begin forecasting individual line items, you must determine how many years to forecast and how detailed your forecast should be. The typical solution, described in Chapter 6, is to develop an explicit forecast for a number of years and then to value the remaining years by using a perpetuity formula, such as the key value driver formula introduced in Chapter 2. Whatever perpetuity formula you choose, all the continuing-value approaches assume steady-state performance. Thus, the explicit forecast period must be long enough for the company to reach a steady state, defined by the following characteristics:

- The company grows at a constant rate by reinvesting a constant proportion of its operating profits into the business each year.
- The company earns a constant rate of return on both existing capital and new capital invested.

As a result, free cash flow for a steady-state company will grow at a constant rate and can be valued using a growth perpetuity. The explicit forecast period should be long enough that the company's growth rate is less than or equal to that of the economy. Higher growth rates would eventually make companies unrealistically large relative to the aggregate economy.

In general, we recommend using an explicit forecast period of 10 to 15 years—perhaps longer for cyclical companies or those experiencing very rapid growth. Using a short explicit forecast period, such as five years, typically results in a significant undervaluation of a company or requires heroic long-term growth assumptions in the continuing value. Even so, a long forecast period raises its own issues—namely, the difficulty of forecasting individual line items 10 to 15 years into the future. To simplify the model and avoid the error of false precision, we often split the explicit forecast into two periods:

1. A detailed five-year to seven-year forecast, which develops complete balance sheets and income statements with as many links to real variables (e.g., unit volumes, cost per unit) as possible.
2. A simplified forecast for the remaining years, focusing on a few important variables, such as revenue growth, margins, and capital turnover.

This approach not only simplifies the forecast, but it also forces you to focus on the business's long-term economics, rather than the individual line items of the forecast. The Heineken case presented in Chapter 31 demonstrates how a two-stage explicit forecast period works.

COMPONENTS OF A GOOD MODEL

If you combine 15 years of financial forecasts with 10 years of historical analysis, any valuation spreadsheet becomes complex. Therefore, you need to design

EXHIBIT 9.1 **Sample Spreadsheet**

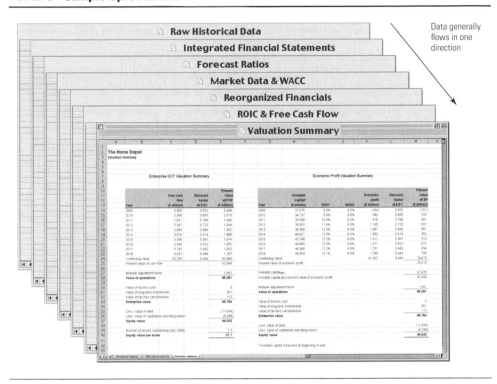

and structure your model before starting to forecast. Many designs are possible. In our example (see Exhibit 9.1), the spreadsheet contains seven worksheets:

1. *Raw historical data:* Collect raw data from the company's financial statements, footnotes, and external reports in one place. Report the raw data in their original form.

2. *Integrated financial statements:* Using figures from the raw-data worksheet, create a set of historical financials that find the right level of detail. The income statement should be linked with the balance sheet through retained earnings. This worksheet will contain historical and forecasted financial statements.

3. *Historical analysis and forecast ratios:* For each line item in the financial statements, build historical ratios, as well as forecasts of future ratios. These ratios will generate the forecasted financial statements contained on the previous sheet.

4. *Market data and weighted average cost of capital (WACC):* Collect all financial market data on one worksheet. This worksheet will contain estimates of beta, the cost of equity, the cost of debt, and the weighted average cost of capital, as well as historical market values and valuation/trading multiples for the company.

5. *Reorganized financial statements:* Once you have built a complete set of financial statements (both historical and forecast), reorganize the financial statements to calculate NOPLAT, its reconciliation to net income, invested capital, and its reconciliation to total funds invested.

6. *ROIC and FCF:* Use the reorganized financials to build return on invested capital, economic profit, and free cash flow. Future free cash flow will be the basis of your valuation.

7. *Valuation summary:* This worksheet presents discounted cash flows, discounted economic profits, and final results. The valuation summary includes the value of operations, value of nonoperating assets, value of nonequity claims, and the resulting equity value.

Well-built valuation models have certain characteristics. First, original data and user input are collected in only a few places. For instance, we limit original data and user input to just three worksheets: raw data (worksheet 1), forecasts (worksheet 3), and market data (worksheet 4). To provide additional clarity, denote raw data and user input in a different color from calculations. Second, whenever possible, a given worksheet should feed into the next worksheet. Formulas should not bounce from sheet to sheet without clear direction. Raw data should feed into integrated financials, which, in turn, should feed into ROIC and FCF. Third, unless specified as data input, numbers should never be hard-coded into a formula. Hard-coded numbers are easily lost as the spreadsheet grows in complexity. Finally, avoid using formulas that come built into the spreadsheet software, such as the net present value (NPV) formula. Built-in formulas can obscure the model's logic and make auditing results difficult.

MECHANICS OF FORECASTING

The enterprise discounted cash flow (DCF) valuation model relies on forecasted free cash flow (FCF). But as noted at the beginning of this chapter, FCF forecasts should be created indirectly by first forecasting the income statement, balance sheet, and statement of retained earnings. Compute forecasts of free cash flow in the same way as when analyzing historical performance. (A well-built spreadsheet will use the same formulas for historical and forecasted ROIC and FCF without any modification.)

We break the forecasting process into six steps:

1. *Prepare and analyze historical financials.* Before forecasting future financials, you must build and analyze historical financials.

2. *Build the revenue forecast.* Almost every line item will rely directly or indirectly on revenues. Estimate future revenues by using either a top-down (market-based) or bottom-up (customer-based) approach. Forecasts should be consistent with historical economy-wide evidence on growth.

3. *Forecast the income statement.* Use the appropriate economic drivers to forecast operating expenses, depreciation, interest income, interest expense, and reported taxes.

4. *Forecast the balance sheet: invested capital and nonoperating assets.* On the balance sheet, forecast operating working capital; net property, plant, and equipment; goodwill; and nonoperating assets.

5. *Forecast the balance sheet*: *investor funds.* Complete the balance sheet by computing retained earnings and forecasting other equity accounts. Use excess cash and/or new debt to balance the balance sheet.

6. *Calculate ROIC and FCF.* Calculate ROIC to assure forecasts are consistent with economic principles, industry dynamics, and the company's ability to compete. To complete the forecast, calculate free cash flow as the basis for valuation. Future FCF should be calculated the same way as historical FCF.

Give extra emphasis to forecasting revenues. Almost every line item in the spreadsheet will be either directly or indirectly driven by revenues, so you should devote enough time to arrive at a good revenue forecast, especially for rapidly growing businesses.

Step 1: Prepare and Analyze Historical Financials

Before you start building a forecast, you must input the company's historical financials into a spreadsheet program. To do this, you can rely on data from a professional service, such as Capital IQ Compustat or Thomson ONE Banker, or you can use financial statements directly from the company's filings. Professional services offer the benefit of standardized data (i.e., financial data formatted into a set number of categories). Since data items do not change across companies, a single model can analyze any company. However, using a standardized data set carries a cost. Many of the specified categories aggregate important items, hiding critical information. For instance, Compustat groups "advances to sales staff" (an operating asset) and "pension and other special funds" (a nonoperating asset) into a single category titled "other assets." Because of this, models based solely on preformatted data can lead to significant errors in the estimation of value drivers, and hence to poor valuations.

Alternatively, you can build a model using financials from the company's annual report. To use raw data, however, you must dig. Often, companies aggregate critical information to simplify their financial statements. Consider, for instance, the financial data for Boeing presented in Exhibit 9.2. On Boeing's reported balance sheet, the company consolidates many items into the account titled "accounts payable and other liabilities." In the notes to the balance sheet, note 11 details this line item. Some of the components (such as accounts payable) are operating liabilities, and others are nonoperating (for

EXHIBIT 9.2 **Boeing Company: Current Liabilities in Balance Sheet**

$ million

	2007	2008
Balance sheet		
Accounts payable and other liabilities	16,676	17,587
Advances in excess of related costs	13,847	12,737
Income taxes payable	253	41
Short-term debt and current portion of long-term debt	762	560
Current liabilities	31,538	30,925
From note 11: Liabilities, commitments, and contingencies		
Accounts payable	5,714	5,871
Accrued compensation and employee benefit costs	4,996	4,479
Product warranty liabilities	962	959
Environmental remediation	679	731
Forward loss recognition	607	1,458
Other liabilities	3,718	4,089
Accounts payable and other liabilities	16,676	17,587

Source: Boeing Company annual report, 2008.

instance, environmental remediation, which is a debt equivalent, and forward loss recognition, which is an equity equivalent).

We prefer to collect raw data on a separate worksheet. On the raw-data sheet, record financial data as originally reported, and never combine multiple data into a single cell. Once you have collected raw data from the reported financials and notes, use the data to build a set of financial statements: the income statement, balance sheet, and statement of retained earnings. Although the statement of retained earnings appears redundant, it will be critical for error checking during the forecasting process, because it connects the income statement to the balance sheet.

As you build the integrated financials, you must decide whether to aggregate immaterial line items. Analyzing and forecasting numerous immaterial items can lead to confusion, introduce mistakes, and cause the model to become unwieldy. Returning to the Boeing example presented in Exhibit 9.2, product warranty liabilities amount to less than 2 percent of Boeing's revenues. Therefore, the valuation model can be simplified (if so desired) by combining these relatively immaterial operating liabilities with other operating liabilities. When aggregating, however, make sure never to combine operating and nonoperating accounts into a single category. If operating and nonoperating accounts are combined, you cannot calculate ROIC and FCF properly.

Step 2: Build the Revenue Forecast

To build a revenue forecast, you can use a *top-down* forecast, in which you estimate revenues by sizing the total market, determining market share, and forecasting prices. Alternatively, with the *bottom-up* approach you can use the company's own forecasts of demand from existing customers, customer turnover, and the potential for new customers. When possible, use both methods to establish bounds for the forecast.

The top-down approach can be applied to any company. For companies in mature industries, the aggregate market grows slowly and is closely tied to economic growth and other long-term trends, such as changing consumer preferences. In these situations, you can rely on professional forecasts of the aggregate market, and focus your own efforts on forecasting market share by competitor.[1] To do this, you must determine which companies have the capabilities and resources to compete effectively and capture share. A good place to start, of course, is with historical financial analysis. But more importantly, make sure to address how the company is positioned for the future. Does it have the required products and services to capture share? Do other competitors have products and services that will displace the company's market position? A good forecast will address each of these issues.

Over the short term, top-down forecasts should build on the company's announced intentions and capabilities for growth. For instance, retailers like Wal-Mart Stores have well-mapped plans for new store openings, which are their primary driver of revenue growth. Oil companies like British Petroleum (BP) have proven reserves and relatively fixed amounts of refining capacity. And pharmaceutical companies like Merck & Company have a fixed set of drugs under patent and in clinical trials.

In emerging-product markets, the top-down approach is especially helpful but often requires more work than for established markets. For instance, consider the fairly recent launch of 3G (third-generation) smart phones, such as the BlackBerry Storm or the Apple iPhone. Given the smart phone's lack of history, how do you estimate the potential size and speed of penetration for companies in the smart phone market? You could start by sizing the current cellular phone market. Analyze whether smart phones, given their greater functionality, will be adopted by even more users than traditional cell phones, or perhaps by fewer because of their high price. Next, forecast how quickly smart phones will penetrate the market. To do this, look at the speed of penetration for other handheld electronics, such as the pager, the PDA, or the last-generation cell phone. It is necessary to determine the characteristics that drive penetration speeds in each of these markets and to compare the smart phone with these characteristics. Finally, what price (and margin) do you expect from the smart phone? How many companies are developing the product, and how competitive will the market be? As you can see, there are more questions than

---

[1] For the European clothing industry, for instance, Datamonitor publishes the report "Value Clothing in European Retail." This report includes a forecast of store numbers, sales densities, and per capita expenditure for each of the 27 countries of the European Union.

answers. The key is structuring the analysis and applying historical evidence from comparable markets whenever possible.

Whereas a top-down approach starts with the aggregate market and predicts penetration rates, price changes, and market shares, a bottom-up approach relies on projections of customer demand. In some industries, a company's customers will have projected their own revenue forecasts and can give their suppliers a rough estimate of their own purchase projections. By aggregating across customers, you can determine short-term forecasts of revenues from the current customer base. Next, estimate the rate of customer turnover. If customer turnover is significant, you have to eliminate a portion of estimated revenues. As a final step, project how many new customers the company will attract and how much revenue those customers will contribute. The resulting bottom-up forecast combines new customers with revenues from existing customers.

Regardless of the method, forecasting revenues over long time periods is imprecise. Customer preferences, technologies, and corporate strategies change. These often unpredictable changes can profoundly influence the winners and losers in the marketplace. Therefore, you must constantly reevaluate whether the current forecast is consistent with industry dynamics, competitive positioning, and the historical evidence on corporate growth. If you lack confidence in your revenue forecast, use multiple scenarios to model uncertainty. Doing this not only will bound the forecast, but also will help company management make better decisions. A discussion of scenario analysis can be found in Chapter 13.

Step 3: Forecast the Income Statement

With a revenue forecast in place, forecast individual line items related to the income statement. To forecast a line item, use a three-step process:

1. *Decide what economic relationships drive the line item.* For most line items, forecasts will be tied directly to revenues. Some line items will be economically tied to a specific asset (or liability). For instance, interest income is usually generated by cash and marketable securities; if this is the case, forecasts of interest income should be tied to cash and marketable securities.

2. *Estimate the forecast ratio.* For each line item on the income statement, compute historical values for each ratio, followed by estimates for each of the forecast periods. To get the model working properly, initially set the forecast ratio equal to the previous year's value. Once the entire model is complete, return to the forecast page, and input your best estimates.

EXHIBIT 9.3 **Partial Forecast of the Income Statement**

Forecast worksheet

percent	2009	Forecast 2010
Revenue growth	20.0	20.0
Cost of goods sold/revenues	37.5	37.5
Selling and general expenses/revenues	18.8	
Depreciation$_t$/net PP&E$_{t-1}$[1]	7.9	

Step 1: Choose a forecast driver, and compute historical ratios.

Step 2: Estimate the forecast ratio.

Income statement

$ million	2009	Forecast 2010
Revenues	240.0	288.0
Cost of goods sold	(90.0)	(108.0)
Selling and general expenses	(45.0)	
Depreciation	(19.0)	
EBITA	86.0	
Interest expense	(23.0)	
Interest income	5.0	
Nonoperating income	4.0	
Earnings before taxes	72.0	
Provision for income taxes	(24.0)	
Net income	48.0	

Step 3: Multiply the forecast ratio by next year's estimate of revenues (or appropriate forecast driver).

[1] Net PP&E = net property, plant, and equipment.

3. *Multiply the forecast ratio by an estimate of its driver.* Since most line items are driven by revenues, most forecast ratios, such as cost of goods sold (COGS) to revenues, should be applied to estimates of future revenues. This is why a good revenue forecast is critical. Any error in the revenue forecast will be carried through the entire model. Ratios dependent on other drivers should be multiplied by their respective drivers.

Exhibit 9.3 presents the historical income statement and partially completed forecast for a hypothetical company. To demonstrate the three-step process, we forecast cost of goods sold. In the first step, we calculate historical COGS as a function of revenues, which equals 37.5 percent. For simplicity, we initially set next year's ratio equal to 37.5 percent as well. Finally, we multiply the forecast ratio by an estimate of next year's revenues: 37.5 percent × $288 million = $108 million.

Note that we did not forecast COGS by increasing the account by 20 percent (the same growth rate as revenues). Although this process leads to the same *initial* answer, it dramatically reduces flexibility. By using a forecast ratio rather than a growth rate, we can either vary estimates of revenues (and COGS will change in step) or vary the forecast ratio (for instance, to value a potential improvement). If we had increased the COGS directly, however, we could only vary the COGS growth rate.

EXHIBIT 9.4 **Typical Forecast Drivers for the Income Statement**

	Line item	Typical forecast driver	Typical forecast ratio
Operating	Cost of goods sold (COGS)	Revenue	COGS/revenue
	Selling, general, and administrative (SG&A)	Revenue	SG&A/revenue
	Depreciation	Prior-year net PP&E	$\text{Depreciation}_t/\text{net PP\&E}_{t-1}$
Nonoperating	Nonoperating income	Appropriate nonoperating asset, if any	Nonoperating income/nonoperating asset or growth in nonoperating income
	Interest expense	Prior-year total debt	$\text{Interest expense}_t/\text{total debt}_{t-1}$
	Interest income	Prior-year excess cash	$\text{Interest income}_t/\text{excess cash}_{t-1}$

Exhibit 9.4 presents typical forecast drivers and forecast ratios for the most common line items on financial statements. The appropriate choice for a forecast driver, however, depends on the company and the industry in which it competes.

Operating expenses For each operating expense on the income statement—such as cost of goods sold; selling, general, and administrative; and research and development—we recommend generating forecasts based on revenues. In most cases, the process for operating expenses is straightforward. However, as we outlined in Chapter 7, the income statement sometimes embeds certain nonoperating items in operating expenses. As you would in proper historical analysis, estimate forecast ratios excluding nonoperating items. For instance, companies with pension plans will include expected returns from pension assets as part of COGS. In extreme cases, changes in pension accounts can significantly distort historical COGS-to-revenue ratios. When this occurs, recalculate the historical COGS-to-revenue ratios excluding the effects of pensions.

Depreciation To forecast depreciation, you have three options. You can forecast depreciation as either a percentage of revenues or a percentage of property, plant, and equipment (PP&E); or—if you are working inside the company—you can also generate depreciation forecasts based on equipment purchases and depreciation schedules.

If capital expenditures are smooth, the choice between the first two methods won't matter. But if capital expenditures are lumpy, you will get better forecasts if you use PP&E as the forecast driver. To see this, consider a company that makes a large capital expenditure every few years. Since depreciation is directly tied to a particular asset, it should increase only following an expenditure. If

EXHIBIT 9.5 **Completed Forecast of the Income Statement**

Forecast worksheet

percent	2009	Forecast 2010
Revenue growth	20.0	20.0
Cost of goods sold/revenues	37.5	37.5
Selling and general expenses/revenues	18.8	18.8
Depreciation$_t$/net PP&E$_{t-1}$	9.5	9.5
EBITA/revenues	35.8	35.8
Interest rates		
Interest expense	7.6	7.6
Interest income	5.0	5.0
Nonoperating items		
Nonoperating income growth	33.3	33.3
Taxes		
Operating tax rate	34.4	34.4
Statutory tax rate	40.0	40.0
Average tax rate	33.3	33.6

Income statement

$ million	2009	Forecast 2010
Revenues	240.0	288.0
Cost of goods sold	(90.0)	(108.0)
Selling and general expenses	(45.0)	(54.0)
Depreciation	(19.0)	(23.8)
EBITA	86.0	102.3
Interest expense	(23.0)	(22.2)
Interest income	5.0	3.0
Nonoperating income	4.0	5.3
Earnings before taxes	72.0	88.4
Provision for income taxes	(24.0)	(29.7)
Net income	48.0	58.8

you tie depreciation to sales, it will incorrectly grow as revenues grow, even when capital expenditures haven't been made.

When using PP&E as the forecast driver, tie depreciation to net PP&E, rather than gross PP&E. Ideally, depreciation would be tied to gross PP&E. Otherwise, a company that purchases only one asset would see an unrealistic drop in depreciation as the asset value depreciates (the ratio of depreciation to net PP&E is fixed, not the dollar amount). But tying depreciation to gross PP&E requires modeling asset retirements, which can be tricky. Specifically, when assets are fully depreciated, they must be removed from gross PP&E, or else you will overestimate depreciation (and consequently its tax shield) in the later years.

If you have access to detailed, internal information about the company's assets, you can build formal depreciation tables. For each asset, project depreciation using an appropriate depreciation schedule, asset life, and salvage value. To determine company-wide depreciation, combine the annual depreciation of each asset.

In Exhibit 9.5, we present a forecast of depreciation, as well as the remaining line items on the income statement. In this example, we assume capital expenditures are smooth. Therefore, we forecast depreciation as a percentage of sales.

Nonoperating income   Nonoperating income is generated by nonoperating assets, such as customer financing, nonconsolidated subsidiaries, and other equity investments. For nonconsolidated subsidiaries and other equity investments, the forecast methodology depends on how much information is reported. For investments in which the parent company owns less than 20 percent, the company records only dividends received and asset sales. The nonoperating asset is recorded at cost, which remains unchanged until sold. For these investments, you cannot use traditional drivers to forecast cash flows; instead, estimate future nonoperating income by examining historical growth in nonoperating income or by examining the revenue and profit forecasts of publicly traded comparables that are comparable to the equity investment.

For nonconsolidated subsidiaries with greater than 20 percent ownership, the parent company records income even when it is not paid out. Also, the recorded asset grows as the investment's retained earnings grow. Thus, you can estimate future income from the nonconsolidated investment either by forecasting a nonoperating income growth rate or by forecasting return on equity (nonoperating income as a percentage of the appropriate nonoperating asset) based on industry dynamics and the competitive position of the subsidiary.

Since nonoperating income is typically excluded from free cash flow and the corresponding nonoperating asset is valued separately from core operations, you do not need a robust forecast of nonoperating income for an accurate valuation. The forecast is required only to build a complete income statement and balance sheet or for cash flow planning.

Interest expense and interest income   Interest expense (or income) should be tied directly to the liability (or asset) that generates the expense (or income). The appropriate driver for interest expense is total debt. Total debt, however, is a function of interest expense, and this circularity leads to implementation problems. To see this, consider a rise in operating costs. If the company uses debt to fund short-term needs, total debt will rise to cover the financing gap caused by lower profits. This increased debt load will cause interest expense to rise, dropping profits even further. The reduced level of profits, once again, requires more debt. To avoid the complexity of this feedback effect, compute interest expense as a function of the *prior year's* total debt. This shortcut will simplify the model and minimize implementation error.[2]

To forecast *interest expense* for our hypothetical company using the prior year's debt, we need the company's historical income statement (presented in Exhibit 9.5) and balance sheet (presented in Exhibit 9.6). To estimate future interest expense, start with the 2009 interest expense of $23 million, and divide by 2008's total debt of $304 million (the sum of $224 million in short-term debt plus $80 million in long-term debt). This ratio equals 7.6 percent. To estimate the 2010 interest expense, multiply the estimated forecast ratio (7.6 percent) by 2009's total debt ($293 million), which leads to a forecast of $22.2 million. In this example, interest expense is falling, even while revenues rise, because

---

[2] If you are using last year's debt multiplied by current interest rates to forecast interest expense, the forecast error will be greatest when year-to-year changes in debt are significant.

EXHIBIT 9.6 **Historical Balance Sheet**

$ million

	2008	2009		2008	2009
Assets			**Liabilities and equity**		
Operating cash	5.0	5.0	Accounts payable	15.0	20.0
Excess cash	100.0	60.0	Short-term debt	224.0	213.0
Inventory	35.0	45.0	Current liabilities	239.0	233.0
Current assets	140.0	110.0			
			Long-term debt	80.0	80.0
Net PP&E	200.0	250.0	Common stock	65.0	65.0
Equity investments	100.0	100.0	Retained earnings	56.0	82.0
Total assets	440.0	460.0	Total liabilities and equity	440.0	460.0

total debt is shrinking. Thus, net income can change as a percentage of revenues even when forecast ratios are constant.

Using historical interest rates to forecast interest expense is a simple, straightforward estimation method. And since interest expense is not part of free cash flow, the choice of how to forecast interest expense will not affect the company's valuation (the cost of debt is modeled as part of the weighted average cost of capital). When a company's financial structure is a critical part of the forecast, however, split debt into two categories: existing debt and new debt. Until repaid, existing debt should generate interest expense consistent with contractual rates. Interest expense based on new debt, in contrast, should be paid at current market rates. Unless management specifically projects particular maturities, assume the company will maintain the average duration of its current debt. Projected interest expense should be calculated using a yield to maturity for comparably rated debt at a similar duration.

Estimate *interest income* the same way, with forecasts based on the asset generating the income. Be careful: Interest income can be generated by a number of different investments, including excess cash, short-term investments, customer financing, and other long-term investments. If a footnote details the historical relationship between interest income and the assets that generate the income (and the relationship is material), develop a separate calculation for each asset.

Provision for income taxes   Do not forecast the provision for income taxes as a percentage of earnings before taxes. If you do, ROIC and FCF in forecast years will inadvertently change as leverage and nonoperating income change. Instead, start with a forecast of operating taxes, and adjust for nonoperating taxes.

Exhibit 9.7 presents the forecast process for income taxes. To determine operating taxes in 2010, multiply the *operating* tax rate (34.4 percent) by earnings

EXHIBIT 9.7 **Forecast of Reported Taxes**

$ million

	2009	Forecast 2010
Operating taxes		
EBITA	86.0	102.3
× Operating tax rate (percent)	34.4	34.4
1 = Operating taxes	29.6	35.2
Nonoperating taxes		
Interest expense	(23.0)	(22.2)
Interest income	5.0	3.0
Nonoperating income	4.0	5.3
Nonoperating income (expenses), net	(14.0)	(13.8)
× Marginal tax rate (percent)	40.0	40.0
2 = Nonoperating taxes	(5.6)	(5.5)
1 + **2** Provision for income taxes	24.0	29.7

before interest, taxes, and amortization (EBITA).[3] Earlier, we estimated EBITA equal to $103.2 million for 2010. Do not use the statutory tax rate to forecast operating taxes. Many companies pay taxes at rates below their local statutory rate because of low foreign rates and operating tax credits. Failing to recognize operating credits can cause errors in forecasts of free cash flow. Also, if you use historical tax rates to forecast future tax rates, you implicitly assume that these special incentives will grow in line with EBITA. If this is not the case, EBITA should be taxed at the marginal rate, and tax credits should be forecast one by one.

Next, forecast nonoperating taxes. Although such taxes are not part of free cash flow, a robust forecast of them will provide insights about earnings and cash needs. For each line item between EBITA and earnings before taxes, compute the marginal taxes related to that item. If the company does not report each item's marginal tax rate, use the statutory rate. In Exhibit 9.7, we multiply the cumulative net nonoperating expense ($13.8 million in 2010) by the statutory tax rate of 40 percent. We can do this because each item's marginal income tax rate is the same. When marginal tax rates differ across nonoperating items, forecast nonoperating taxes line by line.

To determine the 2010 provision for income taxes, sum operating taxes ($35.2 million) and nonoperating taxes (–$5.5 million). You now have a forecast

---

[3] In Chapter 7, we estimated the operating tax rate using a three-step process. First, we convert the tax reconciliation table to percent (or dollars, if reported in percent). Second, to estimate marginal taxes on EBITA, we multiply the statutory tax rate found in the tax reconciliation table by EBITA. Third, we add other operating taxes to marginal taxes on EBITA. Other operating taxes are found in the dollar-reported tax reconciliation table. To determine the operating tax rate, divide operating taxes by EBITA.

EXHIBIT 9.8 **Stock versus Flow Example**

	Year 1	Year 2	Year 3	Year 4
Revenues (dollars)	1,000	1,100	1,200	1,300
Accounts receivable (dollars)	100	105	117	135
Stock method				
Accounts receivable as a percentage of revenues (percent)	10.0	9.5	9.8	10.4
Flow method				
Change in accounts receivable as a percentage of the change in revenues (percent)	–	5.0	12.0	18.0

of $29.7 million for reported taxes, calculated such that future values of FCF and ROIC will not change with leverage.

Step 4: Forecast the Balance Sheet: Invested Capital and Nonoperating Assets

To forecast the balance sheet, first forecast invested capital and nonoperating assets. Do not, however, forecast excess cash or sources of financing (such as debt and equity). Excess cash and sources of financing require special treatment and will be handled in step 5.

When you forecast the balance sheet, one of the first issues you face is whether to forecast the line items in the balance sheet directly (in stocks) or indirectly by forecasting changes (in flows). For example, the stock approach forecasts end-of-year receivables as a function of revenues, and the flow approach forecasts the *change* in receivables as a function of the growth in revenues. We favor the stock approach. The relationship between the balance sheet accounts and revenues (or other volume measures) is more stable than that between balance sheet changes and changes in revenues. Consider the example presented in Exhibit 9.8. The ratio of accounts receivable to revenues remains within a tight band between 9.5 percent and 10.4 percent, while the ratio of changes in accounts receivable to changes in revenues ranges from 5 percent to 18 percent.

To forecast the balance sheet, start with items related to invested capital and nonoperating assets. Exhibit 9.9 summarizes forecast drivers and forecast ratios for the most common line items.

Operating working capital   To start the balance sheet, forecast items within operating working capital, such as accounts receivable, inventories, accounts payable, and accrued expenses. Remember, operating working capital excludes any nonoperating items, such as excess cash (cash not needed to operate the business), short-term debt, and dividends payable.

EXHIBIT 9.9 **Typical Forecast Drivers for the Balance Sheet**

	Line item	Typical forecast driver	Typical forecast ratio
Operating line items	Accounts receivable	Revenues	Accounts receivable/revenues
	Inventories	Cost of goods sold	Inventories/COGS
	Accounts payable	Cost of goods sold	Accounts payable/COGS
	Accrued expenses	Revenues	Accrued expenses/revenue
	Net PP&E	Revenues	Net PP&E/revenue
	Goodwill and acquired intangibles	Acquired revenues	Goodwill and acquired intangibles/ acquired revenue
Nonoperating line items	Nonoperating assets	None	Growth in nonoperating assets
	Pension assets or liabilities	None	Trend toward zero
	Deferred taxes	Operating taxes or corresponding balance sheet item	Change in operating deferred taxes/ operating taxes, or deferred taxes/ corresponding balance sheet item

When forecasting operating working capital, estimate most line items as a percentage of revenues or in days' sales.[4] Possible exceptions are inventories and accounts payable. Since these two accounts are tied to input prices, estimate them instead as a percentage of cost of goods sold (which is also tied to input prices). As a practical matter, we usually simplify the forecast model by projecting each working-capital item using revenues. The distinction is material only when price is expected to deviate significantly away from cost per unit.

Exhibit 9.10 presents a forecast of operating working capital, long-term operating assets, and nonoperating assets (investor funds will be detailed later). All working-capital items are forecast in days, most of which are computed using revenues. Working cash is estimated at 7.6 days sales, inventory at 182.5 days COGS, and accounts payable at 81.1 days COGS. We forecast in days for the added benefit of tying forecasts more closely to operations. For instance, if management announces its intention to reduce its inventory holding period from 180 days to 120 days, we can compute changes in value by adjusting the forecast directly.

Property, plant, and equipment   Consistent with our earlier argument concerning stocks and flows, net PP&E should be forecast as a percentage of revenues. A common alternative is to forecast capital expenditures as a percentage of revenues. However, this method too easily leads to unintended increases or

---

[4] To compute a ratio in days sales, multiply the percent-of-revenue ratio by 365. For instance, if accounts receivable equal 10 percent of revenues, this translates to accounts receivable at 36.5 days sales. On average, the company collects its receivables in 36.5 days.

EXHIBIT 9.10 **Partial Forecast of the Balance Sheet**

Forecast worksheet

Forecast ratio	2009	Forecast 2010
Working capital		
Operating cash (days sales)	7.6	7.6
Inventory (days COGS)	182.5	182.5
Accounts payable (days COGS)	81.1	81.1
Fixed assets		
Net PP&E/revenues (percent)	104.2	104.2
Nonoperating assets		
Growth in equity investments (percent)	–	–

Balance sheet

$ million	2009	Forecast 2010
Assets		
Operating cash	5.0	6.0
Excess cash	60.0	–
Inventory	45.0	54.0
Current assets	110.0	–
Net PP&E	250.0	300.0
Equity investments	100.0	100.0
Total assets	460.0	–
Liabilities and equity		
Accounts payable	20.0	24.0
Short-term debt	213.0	–
Current liabilities	233.0	–
Long-term debt	80.0	–
Common stock	65.0	–
Retained earnings	82.0	–
Total liabilities and equity	460.0	–

decreases in capital turnover (the ratio of PP&E to revenues). Over long periods, companies' ratios of net PP&E to revenues tend to be quite stable, so we favor the following three-step approach for PP&E:

1. Forecast net PP&E as a percentage of revenues.
2. Forecast depreciation, typically as a percentage of gross or net PP&E.
3. Calculate capital expenditures by summing the increase in net PP&E plus depreciation.

To continue our example, we use the forecasts presented in Exhibit 9.10 to estimate expected capital expenditures. In 2009, net PP&E equaled 104.2 percent of revenues. If this ratio is held constant for 2010, the forecast of net PP&E equals $300 million. To estimate capital expenditures, compute the increase in net PP&E from 2009 to 2010 and add 2010 depreciation from Exhibit 9.5:

$$\text{Capital Expenditures} = \text{Net PP\&E}_{2010} - \text{Net PP\&E}_{2009} + \text{Depreciation}_{2010}$$
$$= \$300.0 \text{ million} - \$250.0 \text{ million} + \$23.8 \text{ million}$$
$$= \$73.8 \text{ million}$$

If you forecast net PP&E as a percentage of sales, always calculate and analyze implied capital expenditures. For companies with low growth rates and improvements in capital efficiency, the resulting projections of capital expenditures may be negative (implying asset sales). Although positive cash flows generated by asset sales are possible, they are unlikely.

Goodwill and acquired intangibles   A company records goodwill and acquired intangibles when the price it paid for an acquisition exceeds the target's book value. For most companies, we choose not to model potential acquisitions explicitly, so we set revenue growth from acquisitions equal to zero and hold goodwill constant at its current level. We prefer this approach because of the empirical literature documenting how the typical acquisition fails to create value (any synergies are transferred to the target through high premiums). Since adding a zero-NPV investment will not increase the company's value, forecasting acquisitions is unnecessary. In fact, by forecasting acquired growth in combination with the company's current financial results, you make implicit (and often hidden) assumptions about the present value of acquisitions. For instance, if the forecast ratio of goodwill to acquired revenues implies positive NPV for acquired growth, increasing the growth rate from acquired revenues can dramatically increase the resulting valuation, even when good deals are hard to find.

If you decide to forecast acquisitions, first assess what proportion of future revenue growth they are likely to provide. For example, consider a company that generates $100 million in revenues and has announced an intention to grow by 10 percent annually—5 percent organically and 5 percent through acquisitions. In this case, measure historical ratios of goodwill and acquired intangibles to acquired revenues, and apply those ratios to acquired revenues. For instance, assume the company historically adds $3 in goodwill for every $1 of acquired revenues. Multiplying the expected $5 million of acquired growth by 3, we obtain an expected increase of $15 million in goodwill. Make sure, however, to perform a reality check on your results by varying acquired growth and observing the resulting changes in company value. Confirm that your results are consistent with the company's historical performance concerning recent acquisitions and market-wide empirical evidence.

Nonoperating assets, debt and equity equivalents   Next, forecast nonoperating assets (such as nonconsolidated subsidiaries and equity investments) and debt and equity equivalents (such as pension liabilities and deferred taxes). Because many nonoperating items are valued using methods other than discounted cash flow (see Chapter 12), we usually create forecasts of these items solely for the purpose of financial planning and cash management. For instance, consider unfunded pension liabilities. Assume management announces its intention to reduce unfunded pensions by 50 percent over the next five years. To value unfunded pensions, do not discount the projected outflows over the next five years. Instead, use the current actuarial assessments of the shortfall, which appear in the note on pensions. The rate of reduction will have no valuation implications but will affect the ability to pay dividends or may require additional debt at particular times. To this end, model a reasonable time frame for eliminating pension shortfalls.

We are extremely cautious about forecasting (and valuing) nonconsolidated subsidiaries and other equity investments. Valuations should be based on assessing the investments currently owned, not on discounting the forecast changes in their book values and/or their corresponding income. If a forecast is necessary for planning, keep in mind that income from associates is often noncash, and nonoperating assets often grow in a lumpy fashion unrelated to a company's revenues. To forecast equity investments, rely on historical precedent to determine the appropriate level of growth.

Regarding deferred tax assets and liabilities, those *used to* occur primarily through differences in depreciation schedules (investor and tax authorities use different depreciation schedules to determine taxable income). Today, deferred taxes arise for many reasons, including tax adjustments for pensions, stock-based compensation, acquired-intangibles amortization, and deferred revenues. For sophisticated valuations that require extremely detailed forecasts, forecast deferred taxes line by line, tying each tax to its appropriate driver (see Chapter 25 for an in-depth discussion of deferred taxes). In most situations, forecasting operating deferred taxes by computing the proportion of taxes likely to be deferred will lead to reasonable results. For instance, if operating taxes are estimated at 34.4 percent of EBITA and the company historically could incrementally defer one-fifth of operating taxes paid, we assume it can defer one-fifth of 34.4 percent going forward. Operating-related deferred tax liabilities will then increase by the amount deferred.

Step 5: Forecast the Balance Sheet: Investor Funds

To complete the balance sheet, forecast the company's sources of financing. To do this, rely on the rules of accounting. First, use the principle of clean surplus accounting:

$$\text{Retained Earnings}_{2010} = \text{Retained Earnings}_{2009} + \text{Net Income}_{2010} - \text{Dividends}_{2010}$$

Returning to our earlier example, Exhibit 9.11 presents the statement of retained earnings. To estimate retained earnings in 2010, start with 2009 retained earnings of $82.0 million (see Exhibit 9.10). To this value, add the 2010 forecast of net income (from the income statement) of $58.8 million (see Exhibit 9.5). Next, estimate the dividend payout. In 2009, the company paid out 45.8 percent of net income in the form of dividends. Applying a 45.8 percent payout ratio to estimated net income leads to $26.9 million in expected dividends. Using the clean surplus relationship, we estimate 2010 retained earnings at $113.8 million.

At this point, five line items remain: excess cash, short-term debt, long-term debt, a new account titled "newly issued debt," and common stock. Some

EXHIBIT 9.11 **Statement of Retained Earnings**

$ million

	2008	2009	Forecast 2010
Starting retained earnings	36.0	56.0	82.0
Net income	36.0	48.0	58.8
Dividends declared	(16.0)	(22.0)	(26.9)
Ending retained earnings	56.0	82.0	113.8
Dividends/net income (percent)	44.4	45.8	45.8

combination of these line items must make the balance sheet balance. For this reason, these items are often referred to as "the plug." In simple models, assume common stock remains constant and existing debt either remains constant or is retired on schedule, according to contractual terms. To complete the balance sheet, set one of the remaining two items (excess cash or newly issued debt) equal to zero. Then use the primary accounting identity—assets equal liabilities plus shareholders' equity—to determine the remaining item.

Exhibit 9.12 presents the elements of this process for our example. First, hold short-term debt, long-term debt, and common stock constant. Next, sum total assets, excluding excess cash: cash ($6 million), inventory ($54 million), net

EXHIBIT 9.12 **Forecast Balance Sheet: Sources of Financing**

$ million

	2008	2009	2010	Completed 2010	
Assets					**Step 1:** Determine retained earnings using the clean surplus relationship, forecast existing debt using contractual terms, and keep common stock constant.
Operating cash	5.0	5.0	6.0	6.0	
Excess cash	100.0	60.0	–	35.8	
Inventory	35.0	45.0	54.0	54.0	
Current assets	140.0	110.0	–	95.8	
Net PP&E	200.0	250.0	300.0	300.0	
Equity investments	100.0	100.0	100.0	100.0	**Step 2:** Test which is higher, assets excluding excess cash, or liabilities and equity excluding newly issued debt.
Total assets	440.0	460.0	–	495.8	
Liabilities and equity					
Accounts payable	15.0	20.0	24.0	24.0	
Short-term debt	224.0	213.0	213.0	213.0	**Step 3:** If assets excluding excess cash are higher, set excess cash equal to zero, and plug the difference with the newly issued debt. Otherwise, plug with excess cash.
Current liabilities	239.0	233.0	237.0	237.0	
Long-term debt	80.0	80.0	80.0	80.0	
Newly issued debt	–	–	–	–	
Common stock	65.0	65.0	65.0	65.0	
Retained earnings	56.0	82.0	113.8	113.8	
Total liabilities and equity	440.0	460.0	–	495.8	

PP&E ($300 million), and equity investments ($100 million) total $460 million. Then sum total liabilities and equity, excluding newly issued debt: accounts payable ($24 million), short-term debt ($213 million), long-term debt ($80 million), common stock ($65 million), and retained earnings ($113.8 million) total $496.2 million. Because residual liabilities and equity (excluding newly issued debt) are greater than residual assets (excluding excess cash), newly issued debt is set to zero. Now total liabilities and equity equal $495.8 million. To assure that the balance sheet balances, we set the only remaining item, excess cash, equal to $35.8 million. This increases total assets to $495.8 million, and the balance sheet is complete.

To implement this procedure in a spreadsheet, use the spreadsheet's pre-built "IF" function. Use the function to set excess cash to zero when assets (excluding excess cash) exceed liabilities and equity (excluding newly issued debt). Conversely, if assets are less than liabilities and equity, use the function to set short-term debt equal to zero and excess cash equal to the difference.

How capital structure affects valuation   When using excess cash and newly issued debt to complete the balance sheet, you will likely encounter one common side effect: As growth drops, newly issued debt will drop to zero, and excess cash will become very large. But what if a drop in leverage is inconsistent with your long-term assessments concerning capital structure? From a valuation perspective, this side effect does not matter. Excess cash and debt are not included as part of free cash flow, so they do not affect the enterprise valuation. Capital structure affects enterprise DCF only through the weighted average cost of capital. Thus, only an adjustment to WACC will lead to a change in valuation.

To bring capital structure in the balance sheet in line with capital structure implied by WACC, adjust the dividend payout ratio or amount of net share repurchases. For instance, as the dividend payout is increased, retained earnings will drop, and this should cause excess cash to drop as well. By varying the payout ratio, you can also test the robustness of your free cash flow model. Specifically, ROIC and FCF, and hence value, should not change when the dividend rate is adjusted.

How you choose to model the payout ratio depends on the requirements of the model. In most situations, you can adjust the dividend payout ratio by hand when needed (remember, the ratio does not affect value but rather brings excess cash and newly issued debt closer to reality). For more complex models, determine net debt (total debt less excess cash) by applying the target net-debt-to-value ratio modeled in the WACC at each point in time. Next, using the target debt-to-value ratio, solve for the required dividend payout. To do this, however, a valuation must be performed in each forecast year and iterated backward—a time-consuming process for a feature that will not affect the final valuation.

Step 6: Calculate ROIC and FCF

Once you have completed your income statement and balance sheet forecasts, calculate ROIC and FCF for each forecast year. This process should be straightforward if you have already computed ROIC and FCF historically. Since a full set of forecast financials is available, merely copy the two calculations across from historical financials to projected financials.

The resulting ROIC projections should be consistent with the empirical evidence provided in Part One, "Foundations of Value." For companies that are creating value, future ROICs should fit one of three general patterns: ROIC should either remain near current levels (when the company has a distinguishable sustainable advantage), trend toward an industry or economic median, or trend to the cost of capital. Think through the economics of the business to decide what is appropriate.

ADDITIONAL ISSUES

The preceding sections detailed the process for creating a comprehensive set of financial forecasts. When forecasting, you are likely to come across three additional issues: forecasting using nonfinancial operating drivers, forecasting using fixed and variable costs, and handling the impact of inflation.

Nonfinancial Operating Drivers

Until now, we have created forecasts that rely solely on financial drivers. In industries where prices are changing or technology is advancing, forecasts should incorporate nonfinancial ratios, such as volume and productivity.

Consider the turmoil in the airline industry during the early 2000s. Fares requiring Saturday-night stays and advance purchases disappeared as competition intensified. Network carriers could no longer distinguish business travelers, their primary source of profit, from leisure travelers. As the average price dropped, costs rose as a percentage of sales. But were airlines truly becoming higher-cost? And how would this trend continue? To forecast changes more accurately, we need to separate price from volume (as measured by seat-miles). Then, instead of forecasting costs as a percentage of revenues, forecast costs as a function of expected quantity, in this case seat-miles. For instance, rather than forecast fuel cost as a percentage of revenues, project it using gallons of fuel per seat-mile, combined with a market forecast for the price of oil.

The same concept applies to advances in technology. For instance, rather than estimate labor as a percentage of revenues, one could forecast units per employee and average salary per employee. By separating these two drivers of labor costs, you can model a direct relationship between productivity improvements from new technology and estimated changes in units per employee.

Fixed versus Variable Costs

When you are valuing a small project, it is important to distinguish fixed costs (incurred once to create a basic infrastructure) from variable costs (correlated with volume). When you are valuing an individual project, only variable costs should be increased as revenues grow.

At the scale of most publicly traded companies, however, the distinction between fixed and variable costs is often immaterial, because nearly every cost is variable. For instance, consider a mobile-phone company that transmits calls using radio-frequency towers. In spite of the common perception that the tower is a fixed cost, this is true for only a given number of subscribers. As subscribers increase beyond a certain limit, new towers must be added, even in an area with preexisting coverage. The same holds true for technology purchases (such as servers) and support functions (such as human resources). What is a fixed cost in the short run for small increases in activity becomes variable over the long run even at reasonable growth rates (10 percent annual growth doubles the size of a company in about seven years). Since corporate valuation is about long-run profitability and growth, nearly every cost should be treated as variable.

When an asset, such as computer software, is truly scalable, it should be treated as a fixed cost. Be careful, however. Many technologies, such as computer software, quickly become obsolete, requiring new incremental expenditures for the company to remain competitive. In this case, a cost deemed fixed actually requires repeated cash outflows.

Inflation

In Chapter 6, we recommended that financial statement forecasts and the cost of capital be estimated in nominal currency units (with price inflation), rather than real currency units (without price inflation). To remain consistent, the nominally based financial forecast and the nominally based cost of capital must reflect the same expected general inflation rate. This means the inflation rate built into the forecast must be derived from an inflation rate implicit in the cost of capital.[5]

When possible, derive the expected inflation rate from the term structure of government bond rates. The nominal interest rate on government bonds

---

[5] Individual line items may have specific inflation rates that are higher or lower than the general rate, but they should still derive from the general rate. For example, the revenue forecast should reflect the growth in units sold and the expected increase in unit prices. The increase in unit prices, in turn, should reflect the generally expected level of inflation in the economy plus or minus an inflation rate differential for that specific product. Suppose general inflation is expected to be 4 percent and unit prices for the company's products are expected to increase at one percentage point less than general inflation. Overall, the company's prices would be expected to increase at 3 percent per year. If we assume a 3 percent annual increase in units sold, we would forecast 6.1 percent annual revenue growth $(1.03 \times 1.03 - 1)$.

EXHIBIT 9.13 **Expected Inflation versus Growth in the Consumer Price Index**

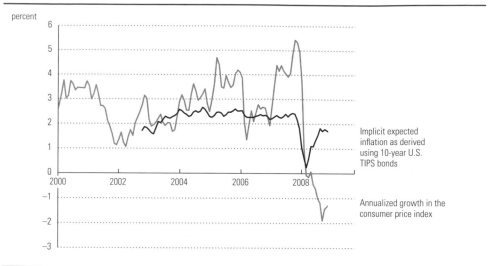

Source: Bloomberg and Federal Reserve Bank of St. Louis.

reflects investor demand for a real return plus a premium for expected inflation. Estimate expected inflation as the nominal rate of interest less an estimate of the real rate of interest, using the following formula:

$$\text{Expected Inflation} = \frac{(1 + \text{Nominal Rate})}{(1 + \text{Real Rate})} - 1$$

To estimate expected inflation, start by calculating the nominal yield to maturity on a 10-year government bond. But how do you find the real rate? Starting in 1981, the British government began issuing *linkers*. A linker is a bond that protects against inflation by growing the bond's coupons and principal at the consumer price index (CPI). Consequently, the yield to maturity on a linker is the market's expectation of the real interest rate for the life of the bond. Since the British first introduced inflation-indexed bonds, more than 20 countries have followed suit, including Brazil, the European Central Bank, Israel, South Africa, and the United States. In October 2009, the yield on a 10-year U.S. Treasury bond equaled 3.2 percent, and the yield on a U.S. Treasury inflation-protected security (TIPS) bond equaled 1.5 percent.[6] To determine expected inflation, apply the previous formula:

$$\text{Expected Inflation} = \frac{1.032}{1.015} - 1 = 0.017$$

---

[6] Daily Treasury Real Yield Curve Rates, October 1, 2009.

Expected inflation, as measured by the difference in nominal and real bonds, thus equaled 1.7 percent annually over the next 10 years.

Exhibit 9.13 presents annualized growth in the U.S. consumer price index (CPI) versus expected 10-year inflation implied by traditional U.S. Treasury bonds and U.S. TIPS. In the exhibit, expected inflation (as measured by the formula) precedes changes in the actual consumer price index, which is a measure of historical inflation. Since the 10-year TIPS bond is based on long-term inflation, the implied inflation rate is much more stable than the one-year change in CPI (in mid-2008, CPI grew at more than 5 percent when crude oil spiked). The credit crisis of 2008 broke new ground for the 10-year TIPS. Implied inflation dropped to zero, and immediately after, consumer prices began to fall. In early 2009, implied inflation began to rise, followed by an increase in CPI later in the year.

Inflation can also distort historical analysis, especially when it exceeds 5 percent annually. In these situations, historical financials should be adjusted to reflect operating performance independent of inflation. We discuss the impact of high inflation rates in Chapter 29.

REVIEW QUESTIONS

1. Using an Internet search tool, locate Procter & Gamble's investor relations web site. Under "Financial Reporting," you will find the company's 2009 annual report. In 2009, the company reported $8.6 billion in "accrued and other liabilities" and $79.0 billion in revenue, such that accrued and other liabilities equaled 10.9 percent of revenue. Using data provided in Note 3 of the annual report, discuss why a forecast ratio of 10.9 percent going forward would distort your forecast of free cash flow. How should the balance sheet be expanded to prevent this?

2. Exhibit 9.14 presents the income statement and balance sheet for PartsCo, a $900 million supplier of machinery parts. Next year, the company is expected to grow revenues by 15 percent to $1,035 million. Using the methodology outlined in Exhibit 9.3, forecast next year's income statement for PartsCo. Assume next year's forecast ratios are identical to this year's ratios. Forecast depreciation as a percentage of last year's property and equipment. Forecast interest as a percentage of last year's total debt.

3. Using the methodology outlined in Exhibit 9.10, forecast the operating items on next year's balance sheet for PartsCo. Forecast each balance sheet item as a function of revenue, except inventory and accounts payable, which should be forecast as a function of cost of sales. Your forecast should be consistent with the revenue and cost of sales forecast in Question 2.

4. Using the methodology outlined in Exhibit 9.12, forecast the financing items on next year's balance sheet for PartsCo. Assume long-term debt remains

EXHIBIT 9.14 **PartsCo: Consolidated Financial Statements**

$ million

Income statement

	Prior year	Current year
Revenues	782.6	900.0
Cost of sales	(508.7)	(612.0)
Selling costs	(156.5)	(171.0)
Depreciation	(27.0)	(31.3)
Operating profit	90.4	85.7
Interest	(5.0)	(7.5)
Earnings before taxes	85.4	78.2
Taxes	(31.1)	(30.8)
Net Income	54.3	47.4

Balance sheet

	Prior year	Current year
Working cash	15.0	12.3
Accounts receivable	85.8	111.0
Inventory	69.7	75.5
Current assets	170.5	198.8
Property and equipment	626.1	720.0
Total assets	796.6	918.8
Liabilities and equity		
Accounts payable	33.7	44.1
Short-term debt	–	19.4
Current liabilities	33.7	63.5
Long-term debt	170.0	215.0
Shareholders' equity	592.9	640.3
Liabilities and equity	796.6	918.8

at $215 million, no external equity is raised, and no dividends are paid. If necessary, use short-term debt to finance cash shortfalls. Your forecast should be consistent with forecasts in Questions 2 and 3.

5. The chief financial officer of PartsCo has asked you to rerun the forecast of the company's income statement and balance sheet at a growth rate of 5 percent. If the company generates more cash than it needs, how can the balance sheet be adjusted to handle this? What alternatives exist to handle new cash?

6. The Federal Reserve Bank of St. Louis provides extensive interest rate and economic data. Using an Internet search tool, find the web site: "St. Louis Fed: Economic Data—FRED." In the FRED database's search box, type "FII10." This number is the Series ID for the 10-year Treasury inflation-indexed security. Using FRED data, determine the security's yield to maturity as of January 1, 2010. Next, type "GS10" in the database search box, which is the Series ID for a comparable 10-year Treasury. What is the yield to maturity for the 10-year Treasury bond as of January 1, 2010? What is the inflation rate implied by the two bonds?

10

Estimating
Continuing Value

As described in Chapter 6, continuing value (CV) provides a useful method for simplifying company valuations. To estimate a company's value, separate a company's expected cash flow into two periods, and define the company's value as follows:

$$\text{Value} = \frac{\text{Present Value of Cash Flow}}{during \text{ Explicit Forecast Period}} + \frac{\text{Present Value of Cash Flow}}{after \text{ Explicit Forecast Period}}$$

The second term is the continuing value: the value of the company's expected cash flow beyond the explicit forecast period. Making simplifying assumptions about the company's performance during this period (e.g., assuming a constant rate of growth and return on capital) allows you to estimate continuing value by using formulas instead of explicitly forecasting and discounting cash flows over an extended period.

A thoughtful estimate of continuing value is essential to any valuation, because continuing value often accounts for a large percentage of a company's total value. Exhibit 10.1 shows continuing value as a percentage of total value for companies in four industries, given an eight-year explicit forecast. In these examples, continuing value accounts for 56 percent to 125 percent of total value. These large percentages do not necessarily mean that most of a company's value will be created in the continuing-value period. Often continuing value is large because profits and other inflows in the early years are offset by outflows for capital spending and working-capital investment—investments that should generate higher cash flow in later years. We discuss the interpretation of continuing value in more detail later in this chapter.

This chapter begins with the recommended continuing-value formulas for discounted cash flow (DCF) and economic-profit valuation. We then discuss

EXHIBIT 10.1 **Continuing Value as a Percentage of Total Value**

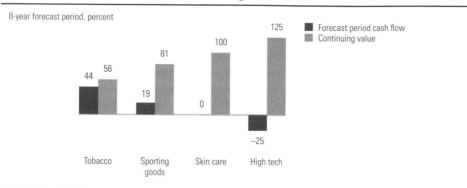

8-year forecast period, percent

■ Forecast period cash flow
▨ Continuing value

issues commonly raised about how to interpret continuing value and suggest some best practices in estimating continuing-value parameters such as growth and return on invested capital. Finally, we compare the recommended formulas with other continuing-value techniques and discuss more advanced formulas.

The continuing-value formulas developed over the next few pages are consistent with the DCF and economic profit. This is important because continuing value is sometimes treated as though it differs from the DCF of the explicit forecast period. For example, some acquirers estimate continuing value for a target company by applying the same price-to-earnings multiple five years in the future as the multiple they are currently paying for the target. By doing this, they are assuming that someone would be willing to pay the same multiple for the target company five years from now, regardless of changes in growth and return prospects over that period. This type of circular reasoning leads to inaccurate (and often overly optimistic) valuations. Instead, acquirers should try to estimate what the multiple should be at the end of the forecast period, given the industry conditions at that time.

RECOMMENDED FORMULA FOR DCF VALUATION

If you are using the enterprise DCF model, you should estimate continuing value by using the value driver formula derived in Chapter 2:

$$\text{Continuing Value}_t = \frac{\text{NOPLAT}_{t+1}\left(1 - \frac{g}{\text{RONIC}}\right)}{\text{WACC} - g}$$

where NOPLAT_{t+1} = net operating profit less adjusted taxes in the first year after the explicit forecast period
g = expected growth rate in NOPLAT in perpetuity
RONIC = expected rate of return on new invested capital
WACC = weighted average cost of capital

A simple example demonstrates that the value driver formula does, in fact, replicate the process of projecting the cash flows and discounting them to the present. Begin with the following cash flow projections:

	YEAR				
	1	2	3	4	5
NOPLAT	$100	$106	$112	$119	$126
Net investment	50	53	56	60	63
Free cash flow	$ 50	$ 53	$ 56	$ 60	$ 63

The same pattern continues after the first five years presented. In this example, the growth rate in net operating profit less adjusted taxes (NOPLAT) and free cash flow each period is 6 percent. The rate of return on net new investment is 12 percent, calculated as the increase in NOPLAT from one year to the next, divided by the net investment in the prior year. The weighted average cost of capital (WACC) is assumed to be 11 percent.

To compare the methods of computing continuing value, first discount a long forecast—say, 150 years:

$$CV = \frac{50}{1.11} + \frac{53}{(1.11)^2} + \frac{56}{(1.11)^3} + \cdots + \frac{50(1.06)^{149}}{(1.11)^{150}}$$
$$CV = 999$$

Next, use the growing free cash flow (FCF) perpetuity formula:

$$CV = \frac{50}{11\% - 6\%}$$
$$CV = 1,000$$

Finally, use the value driver formula:

$$CV = \frac{100 \left(1 - \frac{6\%}{12\%} \right)}{11\% - 6\%}$$
$$CV = 1,000$$

All three approaches yield virtually the same result. (If we had carried out the discounted cash flow beyond 150 years, the result would have been the same.)

Although the value driver formula and the growing FCF perpetuity formula are technically equivalent, applying the FCF perpetuity is tricky, and it is easy to make a common conceptual error. The typical error is to estimate incorrectly the level of free cash flow that is consistent with the growth rate being forecast. If growth in the continuing-value period is forecast to be less than the growth in the explicit forecast period (as is normally the case), then the proportion of NOPLAT that must be invested to generate growth also is likely to be less. In the continuing-value period, more of each dollar of NOPLAT becomes free cash flow available for the investors. If this transition is not explicitly taken into consideration, the continuing value could be significantly underestimated. Later in this chapter, we provide an example that illustrates what can go wrong when using the cash flow perpetuity formula.

Because perpetuity-based formulas rely on parameters that never change, use a continuing-value formula only when the company has reached a steady state, with low revenue growth and stable operating margins. Chapters 4 and 5 provide guidance for thinking about return on capital and long-term growth. In addition, when estimating the continuing-value parameters, keep in mind the following technical considerations:

- *NOPLAT:* The level of NOPLAT should be based on a normalized level of revenues and sustainable margin and return on invested capital (ROIC). The normalized level of revenues should reflect the midpoint of the company's business cycle and cycle average profit margins.

- *RONIC:* The expected rate of return on new invested capital (RONIC) should be consistent with expected competitive conditions. Economic theory suggests that competition will eventually eliminate abnormal returns, so for many companies, set RONIC equal to WACC. However, for companies with sustainable competitive advantages (e.g., brands and patents), you might set RONIC equal to the return the company is forecast to earn during later years of the explicit forecast period. Chapter 4 contains data on the long-term returns on capital for companies in different industries.

- *Growth rate:* Few companies can be expected to grow faster than the economy for long periods. The best estimate is probably the expected long-term rate of consumption growth for the industry's products, plus inflation. Sensitivity analyses also are useful for understanding how the growth rate affects continuing-value estimates. Chapter 5 provides empirical evidence on historical corporate growth rates.

- *WACC:* The weighted average cost of capital should incorporate a sustainable capital structure and an underlying estimate of business risk consistent with expected industry conditions.

The key value driver formula is highly sensitive to the formula's parameters. Exhibit 10.2 shows how continuing value, calculated using the value driver formula, is affected by various combinations of growth rate and RONIC. The example assumes a $100 million base level of NOPLAT and a 10 percent WACC. At an expected RONIC of 14 percent, changing the growth rate from

EXHIBIT 10.2 **Impact of Continuing-Value Assumptions**

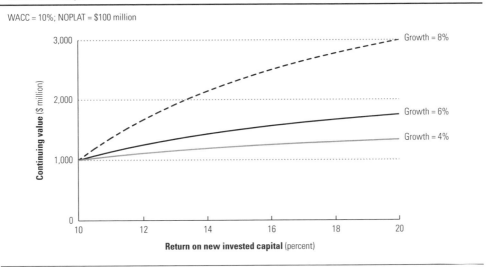

WACC = 10%; NOPLAT = $100 million

6 percent to 8 percent increases the continuing value by 50 percent, from about $1.4 billion to about $2.1 billion.

RECOMMENDED FORMULA FOR ECONOMIC-PROFIT VALUATION

With the economic-profit approach, the continuing value does not equal the value of the company following the explicit forecast period, as it does for discounted free cash flow. Instead, it is the incremental value over the company's invested capital at the end of the explicit forecast period. The total value of the company is as follows:

$$\text{Value} = \begin{array}{c}\text{Invested Capital}\\\text{at Beginning}\\\text{of Forecast}\end{array} + \begin{array}{c}\text{Present Value of Forecast}\\\text{Economic Profit during}\\\text{Explicit Forecast Period}\end{array} + \begin{array}{c}\text{Present Value of Forecast}\\\text{Economic Profit after}\\\text{Explicit Forecast Period}\end{array}$$

The economic-profit continuing value is the last term in the preceding equation. Although this continuing value differs from the DCF continuing value, today's value of the company will be the same, given the same projected financial performance.

The economic-profit formula for continuing value is:

$$CV_t = \text{Economic Profits in Year } t+1 + \text{Economic Profits beyond Year } t+1$$
$$= \frac{IC_t(ROIC_t - WACC)}{WACC} + \frac{PV(\text{Economic Profit}_{t+2})}{WACC - g}$$

such that

$$PV(\text{Economic Profit}_{t+2}) = \frac{NOPLAT_{t+1}\left(\frac{g}{RONIC}\right)(RONIC - WACC)}{WACC}$$

where IC_t = invested capital at the end of the explicit forecast period
$ROIC_t$ = ROIC on existing capital after the explicit forecast period
WACC = weighted average cost of capital
g = expected growth rate in NOPLAT in perpetuity
RONIC = expected rate of return on new invested capital after the explicit forecast period

According to the formula, total economic profit following the explicit forecast equals the present value of economic profit in the first year after the explicit forecast in perpetuity, plus any incremental economic profit after that year. Incremental economic profit is created by additional growth at returns exceeding the cost of capital. If expected RONIC equals WACC, the third term (economic profits beyond year 1) equals zero, and the continuing economic-profit value is the value of the first year's economic profit in perpetuity.

DCF-based and economic-profit-based continuing values are directly related but not identical. The continuing value using a DCF will equal the sum of the economic-profit continuing value plus the amount of invested capital in place at the end of the explicit forecast period.

SUBTLETIES OF CONTINUING VALUE

Three misunderstandings about continuing value are common. First is the misperception that the length of the explicit forecast affects the company's value. Second, people confuse return on new invested capital (RONIC) with return on invested capital (ROIC). Setting RONIC equal to WACC in the continuing-value formula does not imply the company will not create value beyond the explicit forecast period. Since return on capital from existing capital will remain at original levels, ROIC will only gradually approach the cost of capital. Finally, some analysts incorrectly infer that a large continuing value relative to the company's total value means value creation occurs primarily after the explicit forecast period.

Does Length of Forecast Affect a Company's Value?

While the length of the explicit forecast period you choose is important, it does not affect the value of the company; it only affects the distribution of the company's value between the explicit forecast period and the years that follow.

EXHIBIT 10.3 **Comparison of Total-Value Estimates Using Different Forecast Horizons**

Modeling assumptions

	Years 1–5	Years 6+
Growth	9	6
RONIC	16	12
WACC	–12	–12
Spread	4	0

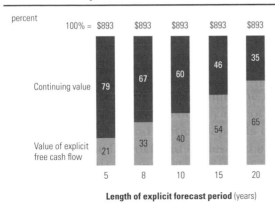

In Exhibit 10.3, value is $893, regardless of how long the forecast period is. With a forecast horizon of five years, the continuing value accounts for 79 percent of total value. With an eight-year horizon, the continuing value accounts for only 67 percent of total value. As the explicit forecast horizon grows longer, value shifts from the continuing value to the explicit forecast period, but the total value always remains the same. To see how the value shift works, compare Exhibits 10.4 and 10.5. Exhibit 10.4 details the calculations for the valuation model using a five-year explicit forecast period, whereas Exhibit 10.5 repeats the analysis with an eight-year period.

EXHIBIT 10.4 **Valuation Using Five-Year Explicit Forecast Period**

$ million

	Year 1	Year 2	Year 3	Year 4	Year 5	Base for CV
NOPLAT	100.0	109.0	118.8	129.5	141.2	149.6
Depreciation	20.0	21.8	23.8	25.9	28.2	
Gross cash flow	120.0	130.8	142.6	155.4	169.4	
Gross investment	(76.3)	(83.1)	(90.6)	(98.7)	(107.6)	
Free cash flow (FCF)	43.8	47.7	52.0	56.7	61.8	
Discount factor	0.893	0.797	0.712	0.636	0.567	
Present value of FCF	39.1	38.0	37.0	36.0	35.0	

Present value of FCF_{1-5}	185.1
Continuing value	707.5
Total value	892.6

Calculation of continuing value (CV)

$$CV_5 = \frac{NOPLAT_{CV}\left(1-\frac{g}{RONIC}\right)}{WACC - g} = \frac{149.6\left(1-\frac{6\%}{12\%}\right)}{12\% - 6\%} = \$1{,}246.9$$

$$CV_0 = \frac{CV_5}{(1+WACC)^5} = \frac{1{,}246.9}{(1.12)^5} = \$707.5$$

EXHIBIT 10.5 **Valuation Using Eight-Year Explicit Forecast Period**

$ million

	Year 1	Year 2	Year 3	Year 4	Year 5	Year 6	Year 7	Year 8	Base for CV
NOPLAT	100.0	109.0	118.8	129.5	141.2	149.6	158.6	168.1	178.2
Depreciation	20.0	21.8	23.8	25.9	28.2	29.9	31.7	33.6	
Gross cash flow	120.0	130.8	142.6	155.4	169.4	179.6	190.3	201.7	
Gross investment	(76.3)	(83.1)	(90.6)	(98.7)	(107.6)	(104.7)	(111.0)	(117.7)	
Free cash flow (FCF)	43.8	47.7	52.0	56.7	61.8	74.8	79.3	84.1	
Discount factor	0.893	0.797	0.712	0.636	0.567	0.507	0.452	0.404	
Present value of FCF	39.1	38.0	37.0	36.0	35.0	37.9	35.9	34.0	

Present value of FCF$_{1-8}$	292.9	**Calculation of continuing value (CV)**
Continuing value	599.8	
Total value	892.6	

$$CV_8 = \frac{NOPLAT_{CV}\left(1 - \frac{g}{RONIC}\right)}{WACC - g} = \frac{178.2\left(1 - \frac{6\%}{12\%}\right)}{12\% - 6\%} = \$1,485.1$$

$$CV_0 = \frac{CV_8}{(1 + WACC)^8} = \frac{1,485.1}{(1.12)^8} = \$599.8$$

In Exhibit 10.4, NOPLAT starts at $100 million. During the first five years, NOPLAT grows at 9 percent per year. Following year 5, NOPLAT growth slows to 6 percent. To compute gross cash flow, add depreciation to NOPLAT. Free cash flow equals gross cash flow minus gross investment. To compute the company's gross investment, multiply NOPLAT by the reinvestment rate, where the reinvestment rate equals the ratio of growth to ROIC (9 percent divided by 16 percent), plus depreciation. To determine the present value of the company, sum the present value of the explicit forecast period cash flows plus the present value of continuing value. (Since the continuing value is measured as of year 5, the continuing value of $1,246.9 million is discounted by five years, not by six, a common mistake.) The total value equals $892.6 million.

Exhibit 10.5 details the calculations for a valuation model that uses an eight-year explicit forecast period and a continuing value that starts in year 9. The structure and forecast inputs of the model are identical to those of Exhibit 10.4. In the first five years, growth is 9 percent, and ROIC equals 16 percent. After five years, growth drops to 6 percent, and ROIC drops to 12 percent. As can be seen by comparing Exhibits 10.4 and 10.5, total value under each valuation method is identical. Since the underlying value drivers are the same in both valuations, the results will be the same. The length of your forecast horizon should affect only the proportion of total value allocated between the explicit forecast period and continuing value, not the total value.

The choice of forecast horizon will indirectly affect value if it is associated with changes in the economic assumptions underlying the continuing-value estimate. You can unknowingly change your performance forecasts when you change your forecast horizon. Many forecasters assume that the rate of return on new invested capital will equal the cost of capital in the continuing-value period but that the company will earn returns exceeding the cost of capital during the explicit forecast period. By extending the explicit forecast period, you also implicitly extend the time period during which returns on new capital are expected to exceed the cost of capital. Therefore, extending the forecast period indirectly raises the value.

So how do you choose the appropriate length of the explicit forecast period? The explicit forecast should be long enough that the business will have reached a steady state by the end of the period. Suppose you expect the company's margins to decline as its customers consolidate. Margins are currently 12 percent, and you forecast they will fall to 9 percent over the next seven years. In this case, the explicit forecast period must be at least seven years, because continuing-value approaches cannot account for the declining margin (at least not without complex computations). The business must be operating at an equilibrium level for the continuing-value approaches to be useful. If the explicit forecast is more than seven years, there will be no effect on the total value of the company.

Confusion about Competitive-Advantage Period

A related issue is the concept of a company's competitive-advantage period, or period of supernormal returns. This is the notion that companies will earn returns above the cost of capital for a period of time, followed by a decline to the cost of capital. While this concept is useful, linking it to the length of the forecast is dangerous. One reason is simply that, as we just showed, there is no direct connection between the length of the forecast and the value of a company.

More important is that the length of competitive advantage is sometimes inappropriately linked to the explicit forecast period. Remember, the key value driver formula is based on incremental returns on capital, not company-wide average returns. If you set incremental returns on new invested capital (RONIC) in the continuing-value period equal to the cost of capital, you are *not* assuming that the return on total capital (old and new) will equal the cost of capital. The original capital (prior to the continuing-value period) will continue to earn the returns projected in the last forecast period. In other words, the company's competitive-advantage period has not come to an end once the continuing-value period is reached. For example, imagine a retailer whose early stores are located in high-traffic, high-growth areas. The company's early stores earn a superior rate of return and fund ongoing expansion. But as the company grows, new locations become difficult to find, and the ROIC related to expansion starts to drop. Eventually, the ROIC on the newest store will approach the cost of capital. But does this imply ROIC on early stores will

EXHIBIT 10.6 **Gradual Decline in Average ROIC According to Continuing-Value Formula**

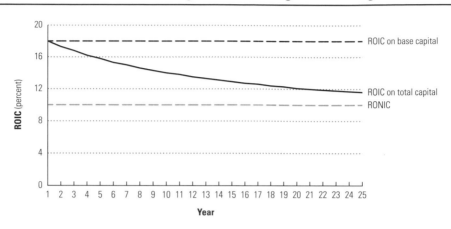

drop to the cost of capital as well? Probably not. A great location is hard to beat.

Exhibit 10.6 shows the implied average ROIC, assuming that projected continuing-value growth is 4.5 percent, the return on base capital is 18 percent, RONIC is 10 percent, and WACC is 10 percent. The average return on all capital declines only gradually. From its starting point at 18 percent, it declines to 14 percent (the halfway point to RONIC) after 10 years in the continuing-value period. It reaches 12 percent after 21 years, and 11 percent after 37 years.

When Is Value Created?

Executives often state uncomfortably that "all the value is in the continuing value." Exhibit 10.7 illustrates the problem for a hypothetical company, Innovation, Inc. Based on discounted free cash flow, it appears that 85 percent of Innovation's value comes from the continuing value. But there are other interesting ways to interpret the source of value.

Exhibit 10.8 suggests an alternative: a business components approach. Innovation, Inc. has a base business that earns a steady 12 percent return on capital and is growing at 4 percent per year. It also has developed a new product line that will require several years of negative cash flow for development of a new sales channel, which management hopes will lead to organic growth. As shown in Exhibit 10.8, the base business has a value of $877 million, or 71 percent of Innovation's total value. So 71 percent of the company's value comes from operations that are currently generating strong, stable cash flow. Only 29 percent of total value is attributable to the unpredictable growth business. When the situation is viewed this way, uncertainty plays only a small role in the total value.

EXHIBIT 10.7 **Innovation, Inc.: Free Cash Flow Forecast and Valuation**

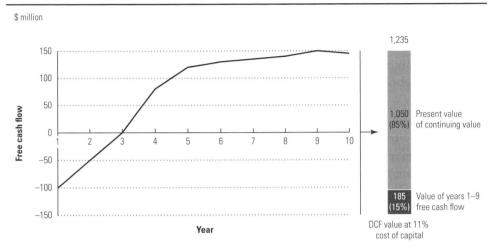

We can use the economic-profit model to generate another interpretation of continuing value. Exhibit 10.9 compares the components of value for Innovation, Inc., using the discounted free cash flow approach, the business components approach, and an economic-profit model. Under the economic-profit model, 62 percent of Innovation's value is simply the book value of invested capital. The rest of the value, $468 million, is the present value of projected economic profit, and of that, only 30 percent of total value is generated during the continuing-value period—a much smaller share than under the discounted FCF model.

EXHIBIT 10.8 **Innovation, Inc.: Valuation by Components**

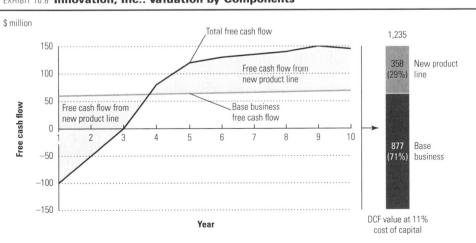

EXHIBIT 10.9 **Innovation, Inc.: Comparison of Continuing-Value Approaches**

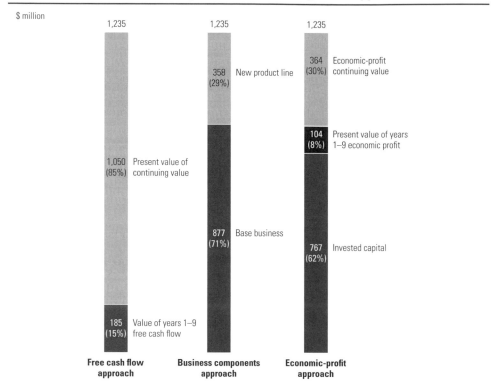

$ million

Free cash flow approach: 1,235 total; 1,050 (85%) Present value of continuing value; 185 (15%) Value of years 1–9 free cash flow.

Business components approach: 1,235 total; 358 (29%) New product line; 877 (71%) Base business.

Economic-profit approach: 1,235 total; 364 (30%) Economic-profit continuing value; 104 (8%) Present value of years 1–9 economic profit; 767 (62%) Invested capital.

COMMON PITFALLS

Estimating a company's performance 10 to 15 years out is not a precise process. Common mistakes in estimating continuing value include naive base year extrapolation and both naive and purposeful overconservatism.

Naive Base Year Extrapolation

Exhibit 10.10 illustrates a common error in forecasting the base level of free cash flow: assuming that the investment rate is constant, so NOPLAT, investment, and FCF all grow at the same rate. From year 9 to year 10 (the last forecast year), the company's earnings and cash flow grow by 10 percent. You believe revenue growth in the continuing-value period will be 5 percent per year. A common, yet incorrect, forecast for year 11 (the continuing-value base year) simply increases every line item from year 10 by 5 percent, as shown in the third column. This forecast is wrong because the increase in working capital is far too large, given the projected increase in sales. Since revenues are growing more slowly, the proportion of gross cash flow devoted to increasing working capital should decline significantly, as shown in the last column. In the final column, the increase in working capital should be the amount necessary to

EXHIBIT 10.10 **Correct and Incorrect Methods of Forecasting Base FCF**

$ million

	Year 9	Year 10	Year 11 (5% growth) Incorrect	Year 11 (5% growth) Correct
Revenues	1,000	1,100	1,155	1,155
Operating expenses	(850)	(935)	(982)	(982)
EBITA	150	165	173	173
Operating taxes	(60)	(66)	(69)	(69)
NOPLAT	90	99	104	104
Depreciation	27	30	32	32
Gross cash flow	117	129	136	136
Capital expenditures	(30)	(33)	(35)	(35)
Increase in working capital	(27)	(30)	(32)	(17)
Gross investment	(57)	(63)	(67)	(52)
Free cash flow	60	66	69	84
Supplemental calculations				
Working capital, year-end	300	330	362	347
Working capital/revenues (percent)	30.0	30.0	31.3	30.0

maintain the year-end working capital at a constant percentage of revenues. The naive approach continually increases working capital as a percentage of revenues and will significantly understate the value of the company. Note that in the third column, free cash flow is 18 percent lower than it should be. The same problem applies to capital expenditures, though we limited the example to working capital to keep it simple. Using the value driver formula, instead of a cash flow perpetuity, automatically avoids the problem of naive base year extrapolation.

Naive Overconservatism

Many financial analysts routinely assume that the incremental return on capital during the continuing-value period will equal the cost of capital. This practice relieves them of having to forecast a growth rate, since growth in this case neither adds nor destroys value. For some businesses, this assumption is too conservative. For example, both Coca-Cola's and PepsiCo's soft-drink businesses earn high returns on invested capital, and their returns are unlikely to fall substantially as they continue to grow, due to the strength of their brands. An assumption that RONIC equals WACC for these businesses would understate their values. Even when RONIC remains high, growth will eventually drop as the market matures. Therefore, any assumption that RONIC is greater than WACC should be coupled with an economically reasonable growth rate.

EXHIBIT 10.11 **Continuing-Value Estimates for a Sporting Goods Company**

Technique	Assumptions	Continuing value ($ million)
Book value	Per accounting records	268
Liquidation value	80% of working capital	186
	70% of net fixed assets	
Price-to-earnings ratio	Industry average of 15 ×	624
Market-to-book ratio	Industry average of 1.4 ×	375
Replacement cost	Book value adjusted for inflation	275
Perpetuity based on final year's cash flow	Normalized FCF growing at inflation rate	428

This problem applies equally to almost any business selling a product or service that is unlikely to be duplicated, including many pharmaceutical companies, numerous consumer products companies, and some software companies.

Purposeful Overconservatism

Analysts sometimes are overly conservative because of the uncertainty and size of the continuing value. But if continuing value is to be estimated properly, the uncertainty should cut both ways: The results are just as likely to be higher than an unbiased estimate as they are to be lower. So conservatism overcompensates for uncertainty. Uncertainty matters, but it should be modeled using scenarios, not through conservatism.

EVALUATING OTHER APPROACHES TO CONTINUING VALUE

Several alternative approaches to continuing value are used in practice, often with misleading results. A few approaches are acceptable if used carefully, but we prefer the methods recommended earlier because they explicitly rely on the underlying economic assumptions embodied in the company analysis. Other approaches tend to obscure the underlying economic assumptions. Exhibit 10.11 illustrates, for a sporting goods company, the wide dispersion of continuing-value estimates arrived at by different techniques. This section explains why we prefer the recommended approaches. We classify the most common techniques into two categories: (1) other DCF approaches, and (2) non-cash-flow approaches.

Other DCF Approaches

The recommended DCF formulas can be modified to derive additional continuing-value formulas with more restrictive (and sometimes unreasonable) assumptions.

One variation is the *convergence* formula. For many companies in competitive industries, we expect that the return on net new investment will eventually converge to the cost of capital as all the excess profits are competed away. This assumption allows a simpler version of the value driver formula, as follows:

$$CV = \frac{NOPLAT_{t+1}}{WACC}$$

The derivation begins with the value driver formula:

$$CV = \frac{NOPLAT_{t+1}\left(1 - \frac{g}{RONIC}\right)}{WACC - g}$$

Assume that RONIC = WACC (that is, the return on incremental invested capital equals the cost of capital):

$$CV = \frac{NOPLAT_{t+1}\left(1 - \frac{g}{WACC}\right)}{WACC - g}$$

$$= \frac{NOPLAT_{t+1}\left(\frac{WACC - g}{WACC}\right)}{WACC - g}$$

Canceling the term WACC − g leaves a simple formula:

$$CV = \frac{NOPLAT_{t+1}}{WACC}$$

The fact that the growth term has disappeared from the equation does *not* mean that the nominal growth in NOPLAT will be zero. The growth term drops out because new growth adds nothing to value, as the return associated with growth equals the cost of capital. This formula is sometimes interpreted as implying zero growth (not even with inflation), but this is not the case.

Misinterpretation of the convergence formula has led to another variant: the *aggressive-growth* formula. This formula assumes that earnings in the continuing-value period will grow at some rate, most often the inflation rate. The conclusion is then drawn that earnings should be discounted at the real WACC rather than the nominal WACC. The resulting formula is:

$$CV = \frac{NOPLAT_{t+1}}{WACC - g}$$

Here, g is the inflation rate. This formula can substantially overstate continuing value because it assumes that NOPLAT can grow without any incremental capital investment. This is unlikely (or impossible), because any growth will probably require additional working capital and fixed assets.

EXHIBIT 10.12 **Rates of Return Implied by Alternative Continuing-Value Formulas**

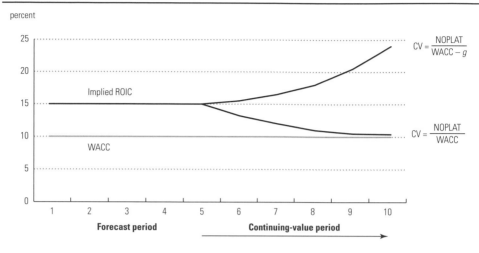

To see the critical assumption hidden in the preceding formula, we analyze the key value driver formula as RONIC approaches infinity:

$$CV = \frac{NOPLAT_{t+1}\left(1 - \frac{g}{RONIC}\right)}{WACC - g}$$

$$RONIC \rightarrow \infty, \text{ therefore } \frac{g}{RONIC} \rightarrow 0$$

$$CV = \frac{NOPLAT_{t+1}(1 - 0)}{WACC - g}$$

$$= \frac{NOPLAT_{t+1}}{WACC - g}$$

Exhibit 10.12 compares the two variations of the key value driver formula, showing how the average return on invested capital (both existing and new investment) behaves under the two assumptions. In the aggressive-growth case, NOPLAT grows without any new investment, so the return on invested capital eventually approaches infinity. In the convergence case, the average return on invested capital moves toward the weighted average cost of capital as new capital becomes a larger portion of the total capital base.

Non-Cash-Flow Approaches

In addition to DCF techniques, non-cash-flow approaches to continuing value are sometimes used. Three common approaches are multiples, liquidation value, and replacement cost.

Multiples   Multiples approaches assume that a company will be worth some multiple of future earnings or book value in the continuing period. But how do you estimate an appropriate future multiple?

A common approach is to assume that the company will be worth a multiple of earnings or book value based on the multiple for the company today. Suppose we choose today's current industry average price-to-earnings (P/E) ratio. This ratio reflects the economic prospects of the industry during the explicit forecast period as well as the continuing-value period. In maturing industries, however, prospects at the end of the explicit forecast period are likely to be very different from today's. Therefore, we need a different P/E that reflects the company's prospects at the end of the forecast period. What factors will determine that ratio? As discussed in Chapter 3, the primary determinants are the company's expected growth, the rate of return on new capital, and the cost of capital. The same factors are in the key value driver formula. Unless you are comfortable using an arbitrary P/E, you are much better off with the value driver formula.

When valuing an acquisition, companies sometimes fall into the circular reasoning that the P/E for the continuing value should equal the P/E paid for the acquisition. In other words, if I pay 18 times earnings today, I should be able to sell the business for 18 times earnings at the end of the explicit forecast period. In most cases, the reason a company is willing to pay a particular P/E for an acquisition is that it plans to improve the target's earnings. So the effective P/E it is paying on the improved level of earnings will be much less than 18. Once the improvements are in place and earnings are higher, buyers will not be willing to pay the same P/E unless they can make additional improvements. Chapter 14 describes other common mistakes made when using multiples.

Liquidation value   The liquidation value approach sets the continuing value equal to the estimated proceeds from the sale of the assets, after paying off liabilities at the end of the explicit forecast period. Liquidation value is often far different from the value of the company as a going concern. In a growing, profitable industry, a company's liquidation value is probably well below the going-concern value. In a dying industry, liquidation value may exceed going-concern value. Do not use this approach unless liquidation is likely at the end of the forecast period.

Replacement cost   The replacement cost approach sets the continuing value equal to the expected cost to replace the company's assets. This approach has at least two drawbacks. First, not all tangible assets are replaceable. The company's organizational capital can be valued only on the basis of the cash flow the company generates. The replacement cost of just the company's tangible assets may greatly understate the value of the company.

Second, not all the company's assets will ever be replaced. Consider a machine used only by this particular industry. As long as it generates a positive cash flow, the asset is valuable to the ongoing business of the company. But the replacement cost of the asset may be so high that replacing it is not economical. Here, the replacement cost may exceed the value of the business as an ongoing entity.

ADVANCED FORMULAS FOR CONTINUING VALUE

In certain situations, you may want to break up the continuing-value (CV) period into two periods with different growth and ROIC assumptions. You might assume that during the first eight years after the explicit forecast period, the company will grow at 8 percent per year and earn an incremental ROIC of 15 percent. After those eight years, the company's growth rate will slow to 5 percent, and incremental ROIC will drop to 11 percent. In a situation such as this, you can use a two-stage variation of the value driver formula for DCF valuations:

$$
CV = \left[\frac{NOPLAT_{t+1}\left(1 - \frac{g_A}{RONIC_A}\right)}{WACC - g_A} \right] \left[1 - \left(\frac{1 + g_A}{1 + WACC}\right)^N \right]
$$

$$
+ \left[\frac{NOPLAT_{t+1}(1 + g_A)^N \left(1 - \frac{g_B}{RONIC_B}\right)}{(WACC - g_B)(1 + WACC)^N} \right]
$$

where
N = number of years in the first stage of the CV period
g_A = expected growth rate in the first stage of the CV period
g_B = expected growth rate in the second stage of the CV period
$RONIC_A$ = expected incremental ROIC during the first stage of the CV period
$RONIC_B$ = expected incremental ROIC during the second stage of the CV period

Note that g_A can take any value; it does not have to be less than the weighted average cost of capital. Conversely, g_B must be less than WACC for this formula to be valid. (Otherwise the formula goes to infinity, and the company takes over the entire world economy.)

A two-stage variation can also be used for the economic-profit continuing-value formula:[1]

$$CV = \frac{\text{Economic Profit}_{t+1}}{\text{WACC}}$$

$$+ \left[\frac{\text{NOPLAT}_{t+1} \left(\dfrac{g_A}{\text{RONIC}_A} \right) (\text{RONIC}_A - \text{WACC})}{\text{WACC}(\text{WACC} - g_A)} \right] \left[1 - \left(\frac{1 + g_A}{1 + \text{WACC}} \right)^N \right]$$

$$+ \frac{\text{NOPLAT}(1 + g_A)^N \left(\dfrac{g_B}{\text{RONIC}_B} \right) (\text{RONIC}_B - \text{WACC})}{\text{WACC}(\text{WACC} - g_B)(1 + \text{WACC})^N}$$

These formulas always assume that the return on the base level of capital remains constant at the level of the last year of the explicit forecast.

If you want to model a decline in ROIC for all capital, including the base level of capital, it is best to model this into the explicit forecast. It is difficult to model changes in average ROIC with formulas, because the growth rate in revenues and NOPLAT will not equal the growth rate in FCF, and there are multiple ways for the ROIC to decline. You could model declining ROIC by setting the growth rate for capital and reducing NOPLAT over time (in which case NOPLAT will grow much slower than capital). Or you could set the growth rate for NOPLAT and adjust FCF each period (so FCF growth again will be slower than NOPLAT growth). The dynamics of these relationships are complex, and we do not recommend embedding the dynamics in continuing-value formulas, especially when the key value drivers become less transparent.

REVIEW QUESTIONS

1. Exhibit 10.13 presents free cash flow and economic profit forecasts for ApparelCo, a $250 million company that produces men's clothing. ApparelCo is expected to grow revenues, operating profits, and free cash flow at 6 percent per year indefinitely. The company earns a return on new capital of 15 percent. The company's cost of capital is 10 percent. Using the key value driver formula, what is the continuing value as of year 5? Using discounted cash flow, what is the value of operations for ApparelCo? What percentage of ApparelCo's total value is attributable to the continuing value?

2. Since growth is stable for ApparelCo, you decide to start the continuing value with year 3 cash flows (i.e., cash flows in year 3 and beyond are

---

[1] Thanks to Peter de Wit and David Krieger for deriving this formula.

EXHIBIT 10.13 **ApparelCo: Free Cash Flow and Economic Profit Forecasts**

$ million

	Today	Year 1	Year 2	Year 3	Year 4	Year 5	Continuing value[1]
Revenues	250.0	265.0	280.9	297.8	315.6	334.6	354.6
Operating costs	(225.0)	(238.5)	(252.8)	(268.0)	(284.1)	(301.1)	(319.2)
Operating profit	25.0	26.5	28.1	29.8	31.6	33.5	35.5
Operating taxes	(6.3)	(6.6)	(7.0)	(7.4)	(7.9)	(8.4)	(8.9)
NOPLAT	18.8	19.9	21.1	22.3	23.7	25.1	26.6
Net investment	–	(8.0)	(8.4)	(8.9)	(9.5)	(10.0)	–
Free cash flow	–	11.9	12.6	13.4	14.2	15.1	–
Economic profit							
NOPLAT	–	19.9	21.1	22.3	23.7	25.1	26.6
Invested capital $_{t-1}$	–	132.5	140.5	148.9	157.8	167.3	177.3
× Cost of capital (percent)	–	10.0	10.0	10.0	10.0	10.0	10.0
Capital charge	–	13.3	14.0	14.9	15.8	16.7	17.7
Economic profit	–	6.6	7.0	7.4	7.9	8.4	8.9

[1] Rounding error will cause small distortions in valuation.

part of the continuing value). Using the key value driver formula (and data provided in Question 1), what is the continuing value as of year 2? Using discounted cash flow, what is the value of operations for ApparelCo? What percentage of ApparelCo's total value is attributable to the continuing value? How do these percentages compare to Question 1?

3. Using the economic profit formula, what is the continuing value for ApparelCo as of year 5? Using discounted economic profit, what is the value of operations for ApparelCo? What percentage of ApparelCo's total value is attributable to current invested capital, to interim economic profits, and to economic profits in the continuing value period?

4. Since growth is stable for ApparelCo, you decide to start the continuing value with year 3 economic profits (i.e., economic profits in year 3 and beyond are part of the continuing value). Using the economic profit formula (and data provided in Question 1), what is the continuing value as of year 2? Using discounted economic profit, what is the value of operations for ApparelCo? What percentage of ApparelCo's total value is attributable to the continuing value? How do these compare to Question 3?

5. A colleague suggests that a 6 percent growth rate is too low for revenue, profit, and cash flow growth beyond year 5. He suggests raising growth to 12 percent in the continuing value. If NOPLAT equals $26.6 million, return on new capital equals 15 percent, and the cost of capital equals 10 percent, what is the continuing value as of year 5? Is there an alternative model that is more appropriate?

6. SuperiorCo earns a return on invested capital of 20 percent on its existing stores. Given intense competition for new stores sites, you believe new stores will only earn their cost of capital. Consequently, you set return on new capital (8 percent) equal to the cost of capital (8 percent) in the continuing value formula. A colleague argues that this is too conservative, as SuperiorCo will create value well beyond the forecast period. What is the flaw in your colleague's argument?

11

Estimating the Cost of Capital

To value a company using enterprise discounted cash flow (DCF), discount your forecast of free cash flow (FCF) by the weighted average cost of capital (WACC). The WACC represents the opportunity cost that investors face for investing their funds in one particular business instead of others with similar risk.

The most important principle underlying successful implementation of the cost of capital is consistency between the components of the WACC and free cash flow. Since free cash flow is the cash flow available to all financial investors, the company's WACC must also include the required return for each investor. To assure consistency among these elements, the cost of capital must meet the following criteria:

- It must include the opportunity costs of all investors—debt, equity, and so on—since free cash flow is available to all investors, who expect compensation for the risks they take.

- It must weight each security's required return by its target market-based weight, not by its historical book value.

- Any financing-related benefits or costs, such as interest tax shields, not included in free cash flow must be incorporated into the cost of capital or valued separately using adjusted present value.[1]

---

[1] For most companies, discounting forecast free cash flow at a constant WACC is a simple, accurate, and robust method of arriving at a corporate valuation. If, however, the company's target capital structure is expected to change significantly—for instance, in a leveraged buyout, WACC can overstate (or understate) the impact of interest tax shields. In this situation, you should discount free cash flow at the unlevered cost of equity and value tax shields and other financing effects separately (as described in Chapter 6).

- It must be computed after corporate taxes (since free cash flow is calculated in after-tax terms).

- It must be based on the same expectations of inflation as those embedded in forecasts of free cash flow.

- The duration of the securities used to estimate the cost of capital must match the duration of the cash flows.

Bearing these criteria in mind, to determine the weighted average cost of capital for a particular enterprise, you need to estimate the WACC's three components: the cost of equity, the after-tax cost of debt, and the company's target capital structure. Since *none* of the variables are directly observable, we employ various models, assumptions, and approximations to estimate each component. These models estimate the expected return on alternative investments with similar risk using market prices. This is why the term *expected return* is used interchangeably with cost of capital. Since the cost of capital is also used for allocating capital within the firm, it can also be referred to as a required return or hurdle rate.

In this chapter, we begin by defining the components of WACC and introducing the assumptions underlying their estimation. The next three sections detail how to estimate the cost of equity, cost of debt, and target capital structure, respectively. The chapter concludes with a discussion of WACC estimation when the company employs a complex capital structure.

WEIGHTED AVERAGE COST OF CAPITAL

In its simplest form, the weighted average cost of capital equals the weighted average of the after-tax cost of debt and cost of equity:

$$\text{WACC} = \frac{D}{V}k_d(1 - T_m) + \frac{E}{V}k_e$$

where D/V = target level of debt to enterprise value using market-based (not book) values

E/V = target level of equity to enterprise value using market-based values

k_d = cost of debt

k_e = cost of equity

T_m = company's marginal income tax rate

The equation shows the three critical components of the WACC: the cost of equity, the after-tax cost of debt, and the target mix between the two securities.[2]

---

[2] For companies with other securities, such as preferred stock, additional terms must be added to the cost of capital, representing each security's expected rate of return and percentage of total enterprise value.

EXHIBIT 11.1 **Weighted Average Cost of Capital**

Component	Methodology	Data requirements	Considerations
Cost of equity	Capital asset pricing model (CAPM)	• Risk-free rate	Use a long-term government rate denominated in same currency as cash flows.
		• Market risk premium	The market risk premium is difficult to measure. Various models point to a risk premium between 4.5% and 5.5%.
		• Company beta	To estimate beta, lever the company's industry beta to company's target debt-to-equity ratio.
After-tax cost of debt	Expected return proxied by yield to maturity on long-term debt	• Risk-free rate	Use a long-term government rate denominated in same currency as cash flows.
		• Default spread	Default spread is determined by company's bond rating and amount of physical collateral.
		• Marginal tax rate	In most situations, use company's statutory tax rate. The marginal tax rate should match marginal tax rate used to forecast net operating profit less adjusted taxes (NOPLAT).
Capital structure	Proportion of debt and equity to enterprise value		Measure debt and equity on a market, not book, basis. Use a forward-looking target capital structure.

Exhibit 11.1 identifies the methodology and data required for estimating each component.

The cost of equity is determined by three factors: the risk-free rate of return, the market-wide risk premium (the expected return of the market portfolio less the return of risk-free bonds), and a risk adjustment that reflects each company's riskiness relative to the average company. In this book, we use the capital asset pricing model (CAPM) to estimate a company's risk adjustment factor. The CAPM adjusts for company-specific risk through the use of beta, which measures a stock's co-movement with the market and represents the extent to which a stock may diversify the investor's portfolio. Stocks with high betas must have excess returns that exceed the market risk premium; the converse is true for low-beta stocks.

To approximate the after-tax cost of debt for an investment-grade firm, use the company's after-tax yield to maturity (YTM) on its long-term debt. For companies with publicly traded debt, calculate yield to maturity directly from the bond's price and promised cash flows. For companies whose debt trades infrequently, use the company's debt rating to estimate the yield to maturity. Since free cash flow is measured without interest tax shields, measure the cost of debt on an after-tax basis using the company's marginal tax rate.

Finally, the after-tax cost of debt and cost of equity should be weighted using target levels of debt to value and equity to value. For mature companies,

The cost of capital does not include expected returns of operating liabilities, such as accounts payable. Required compensation for capital provided by customers, suppliers, and employees is included in operating expenses, so it is already incorporated in free cash flow. Including operating liabilities in the WACC would incorrectly double-count their cost of financing.

EXHIBIT 11.2 **Home Depot: Weighted Average Cost of Capital**

percent

Source of capital	Proportion of total capital	Cost of capital	Marginal tax rate	After-tax opportunity cost	Contribution to weighted average[1]
Debt	31.5	6.8	37.6	4.2	1.3
Equity	68.5	10.4		10.4	7.1
WACC	100.0				8.5

[1] Total does not sum due to rounding error.

the target capital structure is often approximated by the company's current debt-to-value ratio, using market values of debt and equity. As will be explained later in this chapter, you should not use book values.

In Exhibit 11.2, we present the WACC calculation for Home Depot. The company's cost of equity was estimated using the CAPM, which led to a cost of equity of 10.4 percent. To apply the CAPM, we used the May 2009 10-year U.S. government zero-coupon STRIPS[3] rate of 3.9 percent, a market risk premium of 5.4 percent, and an industry beta of 1.21. To estimate Home Depot's pretax cost of debt, we used the May 2009 yield to maturity on BBB+ rated debt, which led to a cost of debt of 6.8 percent. In Chapter 7, we estimated Home Depot's marginal tax rate at 37.6 percent,[4] so its after-tax cost of debt equals 4.2 percent. Finally, we assume Home Depot will maintain a current debt-to-value ratio of 31.5 percent going forward.[5] Adding the weighted contributions from debt and equity, we arrive at a WACC equal to 8.5 percent.

We discuss each component of the weighted average cost of capital in the following sections.

ESTIMATING THE COST OF EQUITY

The cost of equity is built on the three factors: the risk-free rate, the market risk premium, and a company-specific risk adjustment. The most commonly used model to estimate the cost of equity is the capital asset pricing model (CAPM). Other models include the Fama-French three-factor model and the arbitrage pricing theory model (APT). The three models differ primarily in

[3] Introduced by the U.S. Treasury in 1985, STRIPS stands for "separate trading of registered interest and principal of securities." The STRIPS program enables investors to hold and trade the individual components of Treasury notes and bonds as separate securities.

[4] The marginal tax rate used to determine the after-tax cost of debt must match the marginal tax rate used to determine free cash flow. For Home Depot, the marginal tax rate equals the summation of federal (35 percent) and state (2.6 percent) income taxes, presented in Exhibit 7.11.

[5] Net debt equals reported debt plus the present value of operating leases, less excess cash. Since we last examined Home Depot in 2004, the debt-to-value ratio has risen substantially, from 8.3 percent to 31.5 percent, following the acquisition of Hughes Supply in 2006. Given the company's recent focus on core operations and the challenging economy, the company will probably reduce its debt-to-value ratio. For simplicity, we assume the company will maintain its current capital structure.

how they define risk. The CAPM defines a stock's risk as its sensitivity to the stock market,[6] whereas the Fama-French three-factor model defines risk as a stock's sensitivity to three portfolios: the stock market, a portfolio based on firm size, and a portfolio based on book-to-market ratios.

Despite recent criticism, we believe that the CAPM remains the best model for estimating the cost of equity if you are developing a WACC to use in a company valuation. We analyze these three models next, starting with a detailed examination of the CAPM.

Capital Asset Pricing Model

Because the CAPM is discussed at length in modern finance textbooks,[7] we will not delve into the theory here. Instead, we focus on best practices for implementation.

The CAPM postulates that the expected rate of return on any security equals the risk-free rate plus the security's beta times the market risk premium:

$$E\left(R_i\right) = r_f + \beta_i \left[E\left(R_m\right) - r_f\right]$$

where $E(R_i)$ = expected return of security i
r_f = risk-free rate
β_i = stock's sensitivity to the market
$E(R_m)$ = expected return of the market

In the CAPM, the risk-free rate and market risk premium, defined as the difference between $E(R_m)$ and r_f, are common to all companies; only beta varies across companies. Beta represents a stock's incremental risk to a diversified investor, where risk is defined as the extent to which the stock covaries with the aggregate stock market.

Consider HJ Heinz, a manufacturer of ketchup and frozen foods, and Motorola, a maker of cellular phones and set-top boxes. Basic consumer foods purchases are relatively independent of the stock market's value, so the beta for Heinz is low; we estimated it at 0.60. Based on a risk-free rate of 3.9 percent and a market risk premium of 5.4 percent, the cost of equity for Heinz is estimated at 7.1 percent (see Exhibit 11.3). In contrast, technology companies tend to have high betas. When the economy struggles, the stock market drops, and companies stop purchasing new technology. Thus, Motorola's value is highly correlated with the market's value, and its beta is high. Based on a beta of 1.5, Motorola's expected rate of return is 12.0 percent. Since Heinz offers greater

---

[6] In theory, the market portfolio represents the value-weighted portfolio of all assets, both traded (such as stocks) and untraded (such as a person's skill set). Throughout this chapter, we use a well-diversified stock portfolio, such as the Morgan Stanley Capital International (MSCI) World Index, as a proxy for the market portfolio.

[7] For example, Richard Brealey, Stewart Myers, and Franklin Allen, *Principles of Corporate Finance*, 9th ed. (New York: McGraw-Hill, 2008); and Thomas Copeland, Fred Weston, and Kuldeep Shastri, *Financial Theory and Corporate Policy* (Boston: Addison-Wesley, 2005).

EXHIBIT 11.3 **Capital Asset Pricing Model (CAPM)**

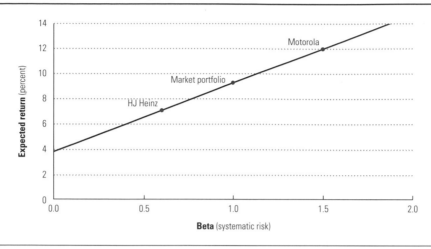

protection against market downturns than Motorola does, investors are will-ing to pay a premium for the stock, driving down the stock's expected return. Conversely, since Motorola offers little diversification in relation to the market portfolio, the company must earn a higher return to entice investors.

Although the CAPM is based on solid theory (the 1990 Nobel Prize in economics was awarded to the model's primary author, William Sharpe), the model provides little guidance for its use in valuation. For instance, when valuing a company, which risk-free rate should you use? How do you estimate the market risk premium and beta? In the following section, we address these issues. Our general conclusions are the following:

- To estimate the risk-free rate in developed economies, use highly liq-uid, long-term government securities, such as the 10-year zero-coupon STRIPS.
- Based on historical averages and forward-looking estimates, the appro-priate market risk premium is between 4.5 and 5.5 percent.
- To estimate a company's beta, use an industry-derived unlevered beta relevered to the company's target capital structure. Company-specific betas vary too widely over time to be used reliably.

Estimating the risk-free rate   To estimate the risk-free rate, we look to gov-ernment default-free bonds.[8] Government bonds come in many maturities.

---

[8] In its most general form, the risk-free rate is defined as the return on a portfolio (or security) that has no covariance with the market (represented by a CAPM beta of 0). Hypothetically, one could construct a zero-beta portfolio, but given the cost and complexity of designing such a portfolio, we recommend focusing on long-term government *default-free* bonds. Although not necessarily *risk free,* long-term government bonds in the United States and Western Europe have extremely low betas.

EXHIBIT 11.4 **Government Zero-Coupon Yields, May 2009**

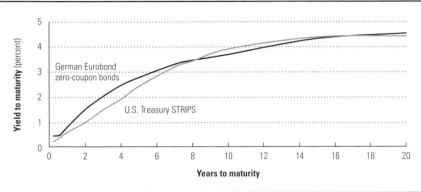

Source: Bloomberg.

For instance, the U.S. Treasury issues bonds with maturities ranging from one month to 30 years. However, different maturities can generate different yields to maturity. Which maturity should you use?

Ideally, each cash flow should be discounted using a government bond with the same maturity. For instance, a cash flow generated 10 years from today should be discounted by a cost of capital derived from a 10-year zero-coupon government bond (known as STRIPS). We prefer government STRIPS because long-term government bonds make interim interest payments, causing their effective maturity to be shorter than their stated maturity.

In reality, few practitioners discount each cash flow using a matched maturity. For simplicity, most choose a single yield to maturity from the government STRIPS that best matches the entire cash flow stream being valued. For U.S.-based corporate valuation, the most common proxy is 10-year government STRIPS (longer-dated bonds such as the 30-year Treasury bond might match the cash flow stream better, but their illiquidity means their prices and yield premiums may not reflect their current value). When valuing European companies, we prefer the 10-year German Eurobond. German bonds have higher liquidity and lower credit risk than bonds of other European countries. Always use government bond yields denominated in the same currency as the company's cash flow to estimate the risk-free rate. This way inflation will be modeled consistently between cash flow and the discount rate.

In Exhibit 11.4, we plot the yield to maturity for various U.S. and German zero-coupon STRIPS versus their years to maturity (a relationship commonly known as the yield curve or term structure of interest rates). As of May 2009, 10-year U.S. Treasury STRIPS were trading at 3.9 percent, and German zero-coupon bonds were trading at 3.7 percent.

If you are valuing a company or long-term project, do *not* use a short-term Treasury bill to determine the risk-free rate. When introductory finance textbooks calculate the CAPM, they typically use a short-term Treasury rate because they are estimating expected returns for the next *month*. As can be seen in Exhibit 11.4, short-term Treasury bills (near the *y*-axis) traded well below 10-year bonds in May 2009. Investors typically demand higher interest rates from long-term bonds when they believe short-term interest rates will rise over time. Using the yield from a short-term bond as the risk-free rate in a valuation fails to recognize that a bondholder can probably reinvest at higher rates when the short-term bond matures. Thus, the short-term bond rate misestimates the opportunity cost of investment for longer-term projects.

Estimating the market risk premium   Sizing the market risk premium—the difference between the market's expected return and the risk-free rate—is arguably the most debated issue in finance. The ability of stocks to outperform bonds over the long run has implications for corporate valuation, portfolio composition, and retirement savings. But similar to a stock's expected return, the expected return on the market is unobservable. And since no single model for estimating the market risk premium has gained universal acceptance, we present the results of various models.

Methods to estimate the market risk premium fall into three general categories:

1. Estimating the future risk premium by measuring and extrapolating historical returns.
2. Using regression analysis to link current market variables, such as the aggregate dividend-to-price ratio, to project the expected market risk premium.
3. Using DCF valuation, along with estimates of return on investment and growth, to reverse engineer the market's cost of capital.

None of today's models precisely estimate the market risk premium. Still, based on evidence from each of these models, we believe the market risk premium varies continually between 4.5 and 5.5 percent and as of May 2009 equaled 5.4 percent. We step through the three models next.

Historical market risk premium   Investors, being risk averse, demand a premium for holding stocks rather than bonds. If the level of risk aversion hasn't changed over the past 100 years, then historical excess returns should be a reasonable proxy for future premiums. For the best measurement of the risk premium using historical data, follow these guidelines:

- *Calculate the premium relative to long-term government bonds.* When calculating the market risk premium, compare historical market returns with the return on 10-year government bonds. As discussed in the previous section, long-term government bonds better match the duration of a company's cash flows than do short-term bonds.

- *Use the longest period possible.* When using historical observations to predict future results, how far back should you look? If the market risk premium is stable, a longer history will reduce estimation error. Alternatively, if the premium changes and estimation error is small, a shorter period is better. To determine the appropriate historical period, consider any trends in the market risk premium compared with the noise associated with short-term estimates.

   To test for the presence of a long-term trend, we regress the U.S. market risk premium against time. Over the past 108 years, no statistically significant trend is observable.[9] Based on regression results, the average excess return has fallen by 4.2 basis points a year, but this result cannot be statistically distinguished from zero. In addition, premiums calculated over shorter periods are extremely noisy. For instance, U.S. stocks outperformed bonds by 18 percent in the 1950s but offered no premium in the 1970s. Given the lack of any discernible trend and the significant volatility of shorter periods, you should use the longest time series possible.

- *Use an arithmetic average of longer-dated intervals (such as 10 years).* When reporting market risk premiums, most data providers report an annual number, such as 6.1 percent per year. But how do they convert a century of data into an annual number? And is the annualized number even relevant?

Annual returns can be calculated using either an arithmetic average or a geometric average. An arithmetic (simple) average sums each year's observed premium and divides by the number of observations (T):

$$\text{Arithmetic Average} = \frac{1}{T} \sum_{t=1}^{T} \frac{1 + R_m(t)}{1 + r_f(t)} - 1$$

A geometric average compounds each year's excess return and takes the root of the resulting product:

$$\text{Geometric Average} = \left(\prod_{t=1}^{T} \frac{1 + R_m(t)}{1 + r_f(t)} \right)^{1/T} - 1$$

---

[9] Some authors, such as Jonathan Lewellen, argue that the market risk premium does change over time—and can be measured using financial ratios, such as the dividend yield. We address these models separately. J. Lewellen, "Predicting Returns with Financial Ratios," *Journal of Financial Economics* 74, no. 2 (2004): 209–235.

The choice of averaging methodology will affect the results. For instance, between 1900 and 2009, U.S. stocks outperformed long-term government bonds by 6.1 percent per year when averaged arithmetically. Using a geometric average, the number drops to 4.0 percent. This difference is not random; arithmetic averages always exceed geometric averages when returns are volatile.

So which averaging method on historical data best estimates the *expected* future rate of return? To estimate the mean (expectation) for any random variable, well-accepted statistical principles dictate that the arithmetic average is the best unbiased estimator. Therefore, to determine a security's expected return for *one period*, the best unbiased predictor is the arithmetic average of many one-period returns. A one-period risk premium, however, can't value a company with many years of cash flow. Instead, long-dated cash flows must be discounted using a compounded rate of return. But when compounded, the arithmetic average will generate a discount factor that is biased upward (too high). The cause of the bias is quite technical, so we provide only a summary here.

There are two reasons why compounding the historical arithmetic average leads to a biased discount factor. First, the arithmetic average is measured with error. Although this estimation error will not affect a one-period forecast (the error has an expectation of zero), squaring the estimate (as you do in compounding) in effect squares the measurement error, causing the error to be positive. This positive error leads to a multiyear expected return that is too high. Second, a number of researchers have argued that stock market returns are negatively autocorrelated over time. If positive returns are typically followed by negative returns (and vice versa), then squaring the average will lead to a discount factor that overestimates the actual two-period return, again causing an upward bias.

To correct for the bias caused by estimation error and negative autocorrelation in returns, we have two choices. First, we can calculate multiyear returns directly from the data, rather than compound single-year averages. Using this method, a cash flow received in 10 years will be discounted by the average 10-year market risk premium, not by the annual market risk premium compounded 10 times.[10] In Exhibit 11.5, we present arithmetic averages for holding periods of 1, 2, 4, 5, and 10 years.[11] From 1900 through 2009, the average one-year excess return equaled 6.1 percent. The average 10-year cumulative excess

---

[10] Jay Ritter writes, "There is no theoretical reason why one year is the appropriate holding period. People are used to thinking of interest rates as a rate per year, so reporting annualized numbers makes it easy for people to focus on the numbers. But I can think of no reason other than convenience for the use of annual returns." J. Ritter, "The Biggest Mistakes We Teach," *Journal of Financial Research* 25 (2002): 159–168.

[11] To compute the average 10-year cumulative return, we use overlapping 10-year periods. To avoid underweighting early and late observations (for instance, the first observation would be included only once, whereas a middle observation would be included in 10 separate samples), we create a synthetic 10-year period by combining the most recent observations with the oldest observations. Nonoverlapping windows lead to similar results but are highly dependent on the starting year.

EXHIBIT 11.5 **Cumulative Returns for Various Intervals, 1900–2009**

percent

		Average cumulative returns			Annualized returns	
Arithmetic mean of	**U.S. stocks**	**U.S. government bonds**	**U.S. excess returns**	**U.S. excess returns**	**Blume estimator**
1-year holding periods	11.2	5.4	6.1	6.1	6.1
2-year holding periods	23.7	11.1	12.3	6.0	6.1
4-year holding periods	50.8	23.7	24.4	5.6	6.0
5-year holding periods	66.5	30.7	31.0	5.5	6.0
10-year holding periods	170.7	73.7	69.1	5.4	5.9

Source: Morningstar SBBI data, Morningstar Dimson, Marsh, Staunton Global Returns data.

return equaled 69.1 percent. This translates to an annual rate of 5.4 percent. The range of excess returns falls between 5.4 percent and 6.1 percent.

Alternatively, researchers have used simulation to show that an estimator proposed by Marshall Blume best adjusts for problems caused by estimation error and autocorrelation of returns:[12]

$$R = \left(\frac{T - N}{T - 1} \right) R_A + \left(\frac{N - 1}{T - 1} \right) R_G$$

where T = number of historical observations in the sample

N = forecast period being discounted

R_A — arithmetic average of the historical sample

R_G = geometric average of the historical sample

Blume's estimator depends on the length of time for which you plan to discount. The first year's cash flow should be discounted using the arithmetic average ($T = 110, N = 1$), whereas the 10th year's cash flow should discounted based on a return constructed with a 91.7 percent weighting on the arithmetic average and an 8.3 percent weighting on the long-term geometric average ($T = 110, N = 10$). In the last column of Exhibit 11.5, we report Blume's estimate for the market risk premium by the length of the forecast window.

The bottom line? No matter how we annualize excess returns, group the aggregation windows, or simulate estimators, the excess return on U.S. stocks over government bonds generally falls between 5 and 6 percent.

Adjust the result for econometric issues, such as survivorship bias   Other statistical difficulties exist with historical risk premiums. According to one argument,[13]

---

[12] D. C. Indro and W. Y. Lee, "Biases in Arithmetic and Geometric Averages Premia," *Financial Management* 26, no. 4 (Winter 1997); and M. E. Blume, "Unbiased Estimators of Long Run Expected Rates of Return," *Journal of the American Statistical Association* 69, no. 347 (September 1974).

[13] S. Brown, W. Goetzmann, and S. Ross, "Survivorship Bias," *Journal of Finance* (July 1995): 853–873.

even properly measured historical premiums can't predict future premiums, because the observable sample includes only countries with strong historical returns. Statisticians refer to this phenomenon as survivorship bias. Zvi Bodie writes, "There were 36 active stock markets in 1900, so why do we only look at two, [the UK and U.S. markets]? I can tell you—because many of the others don't have a 100-year history, for a variety of reasons."[14]

Since it is unlikely that the U.S. stock market will replicate its performance over the next century, we adjust downward the historical market risk premium. Elroy Dimson, Paul Marsh, and Mike Staunton find that between 1900 and 2005, the U.S. arithmetic annual return exceeded a 17-country composite return by 0.8 percent in real terms.[15] If we subtract a 0.8 percent survivorship premium from the U.S. excess returns reported in Exhibit 11.5, the difference implies that the U.S. market risk premium falls between 4.6 and 5.3 percent.

Estimating the market risk premium with current financial ratios   Although we find no long-term trend in the historical risk premium, many argue that the market risk premium is predictable using observable variables, such as current financial ratios, or forward-looking estimation models. Different forms of measurement converge on an appropriate range of market risk premium of 4.5 to 5.5 percent, which has held even during the financial crisis of 2008.

The use of current financial ratios, such as the aggregate dividend-to-price ratio, the aggregate book-to-market ratio, or the aggregate ratio of earnings to price, to estimate the expected return on stocks is well documented and dates back to Charles Dow in the 1920s. The concept has been tested by many authors.[16] To predict the market risk premium using financial ratios, regress excess market returns against a financial ratio, such as the market's aggregate dividend-to-price ratio:

$$R_m - r_f = \alpha + \beta \ln \left(\frac{\text{Dividend}}{\text{Price}} \right) + \varepsilon$$

where α = the regression intercept, β = the regression slope, and ε represents noise in the regression.

Using advanced regression techniques unavailable to earlier authors, Jonathan Lewellen found that dividend yields *do* predict future market returns. However, the model has a major drawback: the risk premium prediction

---

[14] Z. Bodie, "Longer Time Horizon 'Does Not Reduce Risk,'" *Financial Times*, January 26, 2002.

[15] E. Dimson, P. Marsh, and M. Staunton, "The Worldwide Equity Premium: A Smaller Puzzle," in *Handbook of Investments: Equity Risk Premium*, ed. R. Mehra (Amsterdam: Elsevier Science, 2007).

[16] E. Fama and K. French, "Dividend Yields and Expected Stock Returns," *Journal of Financial Economics* 22, no. 1 (1988): 3–25; R. F. Stambaugh, "Predictive Regressions," *Journal of Financial Economics* 54, no. 3 (1999): 375–421; and J. Lewellen, "Predicting Returns with Financial Ratios," *Journal of Financial Economics* 74, no. 2 (2004): 209–235.

can be negative (as it was in the late 1990s). A negative risk premium is inconsistent with risk-averse investors who demand a premium for holding volatile securities. Other authors question the explanatory power of financial ratios, arguing that a financial analyst relying solely on data available at the time would have done better using unconditional historical averages (as we did in the last section) in place of more sophisticated regression techniques.[17]

Estimating the market risk premium with forward-looking models A stock's price equals the present value of its dividends. Assuming dividends are expected to grow at a constant rate, we can rearrange the growing perpetuity to solve for the market's expected return:

$$\text{Price} = \frac{\text{Dividend}}{k_e - g} \quad \text{converts to} \quad k_e = \frac{\text{Dividend}}{\text{Price}} + g$$

where k_e = cost of equity
g = expected growth in dividends

In the previous section, Lewellen and others regressed market returns on the dividend-to-price ratio. Using a simple regression, however, ignores valuable information and oversimplifies a few market realities. First, the dividend-to-price yield itself depends on the expected growth in dividends, which simple regressions ignore (the regression's intercept is determined by the data). Second, dividends are only one form of corporate payout. Companies can use free cash flow to repurchase shares or hold excess cash for significant periods of time; consider Microsoft, which accumulated more than $50 billion in liquid securities before paying its first dividend.

Using the principles of discounted cash flow and estimates of growth, various authors have attempted to reverse engineer the market risk premium. Two studies used analyst forecasts to estimate growth,[18] but many argue that analyst forecasts focus on the short term and are severely upward-biased. In a 2001 working paper, Fama and French use long-term dividend growth rates as a proxy for future growth, but they focus on dividend yields, not on available cash flow.[19] Alternatively, our own research has focused on *all* cash

---

[17] A. Goyal and I. Welch, "Predicting the Equity Premium with Dividend Ratios," *Management Science* 49, no. 5 (2003): 639–654.

[18] J. Claus and J. Thomas, "Equity Premia as Low as Three Percent? Evidence from Analysts' Earnings Forecasts for Domestic and International Stocks," *Journal of Finance* 56, no. 5 (October 2001): 1629–1666; and W. R. Gebhardt, C. M. C. Lee, and B. Swaminathan, "Toward an Implied Cost of Capital," *Journal of Accounting Research* 39, no. 1 (2001): 135–176.

[19] Eugene F. Fama and Kenneth R. French, "The Equity Premium," Center for Research in Security Prices Working Paper 522 (April 2001).

EXHIBIT 11.6 **Real and Nominal Expected Market Returns**

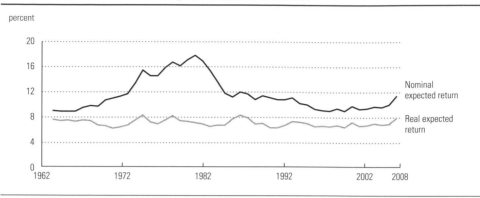

flow available to equity holders, as measured by a modified version of the key value driver formula (detailed in Chapter 2):[20]

$$k_e = \frac{\text{Earnings}\left(1 - \dfrac{g}{\text{ROE}}\right)}{\text{Price}} + g \quad \text{because} \quad CF_e = \text{Earnings}\left(1 - \frac{g}{\text{ROE}}\right)$$

where ROE = return on equity
CF_e = cash flow to equity holders

Based on this formula, we used the long-run return on equity (13.5 percent) and the long-run growth in real gross domestic product (GDP) (3.5 percent) to convert a given year's S&P 500 median earnings-to-price ratio into the cost of equity.[21]

Exhibit 11.6 plots the nominal and real expected market returns between 1962 and 2008. The results are striking. After inflation is stripped out, the expected market return (*not* excess return) is remarkably constant, averaging 7 percent. For the United Kingdom, the real market return is slightly more volatile, averaging 6 percent. Based on these results, we estimate the current market risk premium by subtracting the current real long-term risk-free rate from the real equity return of 7 percent (for U.S. markets). In May 2009, the yield on a U.S. Treasury inflation-protected securities (TIPS) equaled 1.6 percent. Subtracting 1.6 percent from 7.0 percent gives an estimate of the risk premium at 5.4 percent.

Appropriate range of market risk premium Although many in the finance profession disagree about how to measure the market risk premium, we believe

---

[20] Marc H. Goedhart, Timothy M. Koller, and Zane D. Williams, "The Real Cost of Equity," *McKinsey on Finance*, no. 5 (Autumn 2002): 11–15.

[21] Using a two-stage model (i.e., short-term ROE and growth rate projections, followed by long-term estimates) did not change the results in a meaningful way. Estimated reinvestment rates (g/ROE) were capped at 70 percent of earnings.

4.5 to 5.5 percent is an appropriate range. Historical estimates found in most textbooks (and locked in the minds of many), which often report numbers near 8 percent, are too high for valuation purposes because they compare the market risk premium versus short-term bonds, use only 75 years of data, and are biased by the historical strength of the U.S. market.

Even the recent severe financial crisis has not caused a dramatic rise in the market risk premium. Between October 2007 and March 2009, the S&P 500 index dropped by more than 50 percent as the global financial crisis dominated the news. Many of our clients questioned whether a lower appetite for risk among investors caused the drop in value, implying a dramatic rise in the market risk premium and consequently the cost of capital. The data say no. Using the key value driver formula and the parameters outlined earlier, the real cost of equity rose only one percentage point during the crisis, from 6.8 percent in 2007 to 7.8 percent in 2008. This rise matches the increase in the risk premium reported by chief financial officers (CFOs) to the Duke CFO survey.[22] So why the large drop in equity prices? The global financial crisis leaked into the real economy, and corporate earnings suffered as a result. Based on these results, we do not believe companies should increase the risk premium embedded in their internal hurdle rates.

Estimating beta   According to the CAPM, a stock's expected return is driven by beta, which measures how much the stock and entire market move together. Since beta cannot be observed directly, you must *estimate* its value. To do this, begin by measuring a raw beta using regression, and then improve the estimate by using industry comparables and smoothing techniques. Even with a robust estimation process, judgment is still required. When necessary, consider how the industry is likely to move with the economy, in order to bound your results.

Start with the empirical estimation of beta. The most common regression used to estimate a company's raw beta is the market model:

$$R_i = \alpha + \beta R_m + \varepsilon$$

In the market model, the stock's return (R_i), not price, is regressed against the market's return.

In Exhibit 11.7, we plot 60 months of Home Depot stock returns versus Morgan Stanley Capital International (MSCI) World Index returns between 2001 and 2006.[23] The solid line represents the "best fit" relationship between

---

[22] John Graham and Campbell Harvey, "The Equity Risk Premium amid a Global Financial Crisis," SSRN working paper (May 14, 2009).

[23] Even though Home Depot matched the market in aggregate losses during 2007 and 2008 (37 percent for Home Depot versus 35 percent for the MSCI World Index), a slight difference in timing caused the two measures to be uncorrelated. Prior to 2007, Home Depot's market beta was relatively stable. For this reason, we measure unlevered beta as of 2006.

EXHIBIT 11.7 **Home Depot: Stock Returns, 2001–2006**

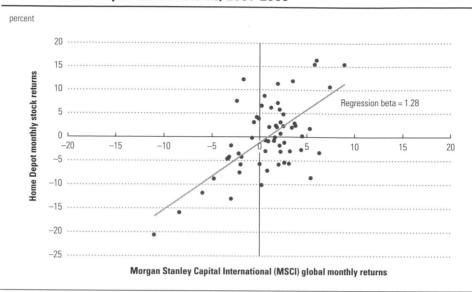

percent

Home Depot monthly stock returns

Morgan Stanley Capital International (MSCI) global monthly returns

Home Depot's stock returns and the stock market. The slope of this line is commonly denoted as beta. For Home Depot, the company's raw beta (slope) is 1.28. Since typical betas range between 0 and 2, with the value-weighted average beta equaling 1, this raw result implies Home Depot is riskier than the typical stock.

But why did we choose to measure Home Depot's returns in months? Why did we use five years of data? And how precise is this measurement? The CAPM is a one-period model and provides little guidance on how to use it for valuation. Yet following certain market characteristics and the results of a variety of empirical tests leads to several guiding conclusions:

- The measurement period for raw regressions should include at least 60 data points (e.g., five years of monthly returns). Rolling betas should be graphed to search for any patterns or systematic changes in a stock's risk.

- Raw regressions should be based on monthly returns. Using more frequent return periods, such as daily and weekly returns, leads to systematic biases.

- Company stock returns should be regressed against a value-weighted, well-diversified market portfolio, such as the MSCI World Index, bearing in mind that this portfolio's value may be distorted if measured during a market bubble.

Next, recalling that raw regressions provide only estimates of a company's true beta, improve the results from the regression by deriving an unlevered

EXHIBIT 11.8 **IBM: Market Beta, 1985–2008**

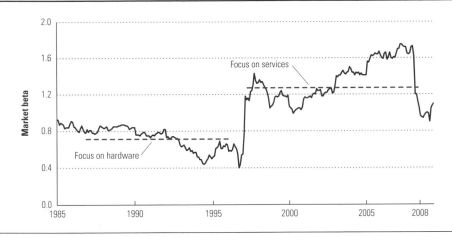

industry beta and then relevering the industry beta to the company's target capital structure. If no direct competitors exist, you should adjust raw company betas by using a smoothing technique. We describe the basis for our conclusions next.

Measurement period   Although there is no common standard for the appropriate measurement period, we follow the practice of data providers such as Morningstar Ibbotson, which use five years of monthly data to determine beta. Using five years of monthly data originated as a rule of thumb during early tests of the CAPM.[24] In subsequent tests of optimal measurement periods, researchers confirmed five years as appropriate.[25] Not every data provider uses five years. The data service Bloomberg, for instance, creates raw betas using two years of weekly data.

Because estimates of beta are imprecise, plot the company's rolling 60-month beta to *visually inspect* for structural changes or short-term deviations. For instance, changes in corporate strategy or capital structure often lead to changes in risk for stockholders. In this case, a long estimation period would place too much weight on irrelevant data.

In Exhibit 11.8, we graph IBM's raw beta between 1985 and 2008. As the exhibit shows, IBM's beta hovered near 0.7 in the 1980s and most of the 1990s but rose dramatically in the late 1990s to a peak above 1.6 in 2007. This rise in beta occurred during a period of great change for IBM, as the company

---

[24] F. Black, M. Jensen, and M. Scholes, "The Capital Asset Pricing Model: Some Empirical Tests," in *Studies in Theory of Capital Markets*, ed. M. Jensen (New York: Praeger, 1972).

[25] Alexander and Chervany tested the accuracy of estimation periods from one to nine years. They found four-year and six-year estimation periods performed best but were statistically indistinguishable. G. Alexander and N. Chervany, "On the Estimation and Stability of Beta," *Journal of Financial and Quantitative Analysis* 15 (1980): 123–137.

moved from hardware (such as mainframes) to services (such as consulting). Subsequently, using a long estimation period (for instance, 10 years) would underestimate the risk of the company's new business model.

Frequency of measurement   In 1980, Nobel laureate Robert Merton argued that estimates of covariance, and subsequently beta, improve as returns are measured more frequently.[26] Implementing Merton's theory, however, has proven elusive. Empirical problems make high-frequency beta estimation unreliable. Therefore, we recommend using monthly data.

Using daily or even weekly returns is especially problematic when the stock is rarely traded. An illiquid stock will have many reported returns equal to zero, not because the stock's value is constant but because it hasn't traded (only the last trade is recorded). Consequently, estimates of beta on illiquid stocks are biased downward. Using longer-dated returns, such as monthly returns, lessens this effect. One proposal for stocks that trade infrequently even on a monthly basis is to sum lagged betas.[27] In lagged-beta models, a stock's return is simultaneously regressed on concurrent market returns and market returns from the prior period. The two betas from the regression are then summed.

A second problem with using high-frequency data is the bid-ask bounce. Periodic stock prices are recorded at the last trade, and the recorded price depends on whether the last trade was a purchase (using the ask price) or a sale (using the bid price). A stock whose intrinsic value remains unchanged will therefore bounce between the bid and ask prices, causing distortions in beta estimation. Using longer-period returns dampens this distortion.

Over the past few years, promising research on high-frequency beta estimation has emerged, spawned by improvements in computing power and data collection. One study applied a filter to daily data to extract information about beta while avoiding the microstructure issues just described.[28] Another used five-minute returns to measure beta, and the estimation method produced more accurate measurements than the standard 60-month rolling window.[29] Since that research was limited to highly liquid stocks, however, we continue to focus on longer-dated intervals in practice.

Market portfolio   In the CAPM, the market portfolio equals the value-weighted portfolio of all assets, both traded (such as stocks and bonds) and

---

[26] R. Merton, "On Estimating the Expected Return on the Market," *Journal of Financial Economics* 8 (1980): 323–361.

[27] M. Scholes and J. T. Williams, "Estimating Betas from Nonsynchronous Data," *Journal of Financial Economics* 5 (1977): 309–327. See also E. Dimson, "Risk Measurement When Shares Are Subject to Infrequent Trading," *Journal of Financial Economics* 7 (1979): 197–226.

[28] B. Chen and J. Reeves, "Dynamic Asset Beta Measurement," University of New South Wales, School of Banking and Finance (May 31, 2009).

[29] T. Bollerslev and B. Y. B. Zhang, "Measuring and Modeling Systematic Risk in Factor Pricing Models Using High-Frequency Data," *Journal of Empirical Finance* 10 (2003): 533–558.

untraded (such as private companies and human capital). Since the true market portfolio is unobservable, a proxy is necessary. For U.S. stocks, the most common proxy is the S&P 500, a value-weighted index of large U.S. companies. Outside the United States, financial analysts rely on either a regional index like the MSCI Europe Index or the MSCI World Index, a value-weighted index comprising large stocks from 23 developed countries (including the United States).

Most well-diversified indexes, such as the S&P 500 and MSCI World Index, are highly correlated (the two indexes had a 95.8 percent correlation between 2000 and 2009). Thus, the choice of index will have only a small effect on beta. For instance, Home Depot's regression beta with respect to the MSCI World Index is 1.28, whereas the company's beta with respect to the S&P 500 is slightly higher at 1.41. Do *not*, however, use a local market index. Most countries are heavily weighted in only a few industries and, in some cases, a few companies. Consequently, when measuring beta versus a local index, you are not measuring market-wide systematic risk, but rather a company's sensitivity to a particular industry.

In the late 1990s, equity markets rose dramatically, but this increase was confined primarily to extremely large capitalization stocks and stocks in the telecommunications, media, and technology sectors (commonly known as TMT). Historically, TMT stocks contribute approximately 15 percent of the market value of the S&P 500. Between 1998 and 2000, this percentage rose to 40 percent. And as the market portfolio changed, so too did industry betas. Exhibit 11.9 presents the median beta over time for stocks outside TMT, such as food companies, airlines, and pharmaceuticals.[30] The median beta drops from 1.0 to 0.6 as TMT becomes a dominant part of the overall market portfolio.

With the collapse of the TMT sector in 2001, TMT stocks returned to their original proportion of the overall market. Since beta is computed using historical data, however, the median non-TMT beta still reflected the TMT-heavy market composition. Instead of using the 2001 beta to evaluate future cash flows as of 2001, a more appropriate beta would be from 1997, when the market composition last matched the 2001 composition. Remember, the end goal is not to measure beta historically, but rather to use the historical estimate as a predictor of future value. In this case, recent history isn't very useful and should not be overweighted.

Although it is too early to tell, we suspect a similar phenomenon occurred during 2007 and 2008 with financial institutions. During the late 2000s, financial institutions became a greater proportion of the market portfolio as interest rates dropped and lending was quite profitable. With their collapse in late 2008, betas

---

[30] André Annema and Marc Goedhart, "Better Betas," *McKinsey on Finance*, no. 6 (Winter 2003): 10–13; and André Annema and Marc Goedhart, "Betas: Back to Normal," *McKinsey on Finance*, no. 20 (Summer 2006): 14–16.

EXHIBIT 11.9 **Effect of the Dot-Com Bubble on Beta**

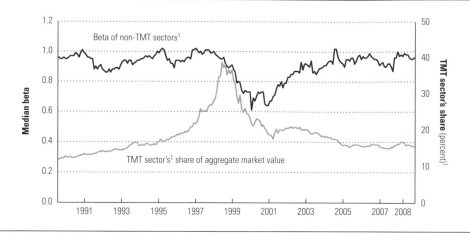

[1] TMT = telecommunications, media, and technology.

measured using 2008 data probably do not reflect future betas as well as betas measured prior to 2007.

Improving estimates of beta: Industry betas   Estimating beta is an imprecise process. Earlier, we used historical regression to estimate Home Depot's raw beta at 1.28. But the regression's R-squared was only 37 percent, and the standard error of the beta estimate was 0.216. Using two standard errors as a guide, we feel confident Home Depot's true beta lies between 0.85 and 1.71—hardly a tight range.

To improve the precision of beta estimation, use industry, rather than company-specific, betas.[31] Companies in the same industry face similar *operating* risks, so they should have similar operating betas. As long as estimation errors across companies are uncorrelated, overestimates and underestimates of individual betas will tend to cancel, and an industry median (or average) beta will produce a superior estimate.[32]

Simply using the median of an industry's raw regression betas, however, overlooks an important factor: leverage. A company's beta is a function of not only its operating risk, but also the financial risk it takes. Shareholders of a company with more debt face greater risks, and this increase is reflected in

---

[31] Consider two companies in the same industry competing for a large customer contract. Depending on which company wins the contract, one company's stock price will rise; the other company's stock price will fall. If the market rises during this period, the winning company will have a higher measured beta, and the losing company will have a lower measured beta, even though the decision had nothing to do with market performance. Using an industry beta to proxy for company risk lessens the effect of idiosyncratic shocks.

[32] Statistically speaking, the sample average will have the lowest mean squared error. However, because sample averages are heavily influenced by outliers, we recommend examining both the mean and median betas.

beta. Therefore, to compare companies with similar operating risks, you must first strip out the effect of leverage. Only then can you compare betas across an industry.

To undo the effect of leverage (and its tax shield), we rely on the theories of Franco Modigliani and Merton Miller, introduced in Chapter 6. According to Modigliani and Miller, the weighted average risk of a company's financial claims equals the weighted average risk of a company's economic assets. Using beta to represent risk, this relationship is as follows:

$$\underbrace{\frac{V_u}{V_u + V_{txa}}\beta_u}_{\text{Operating Assets}} + \underbrace{\frac{V_{txa}}{V_u + V_{txa}}\beta_{txa}}_{\text{Tax Assets}} = \underbrace{\frac{D}{D+E}\beta_d}_{\text{Debt}} + \underbrace{\frac{E}{D+E}\beta_e}_{\text{Equity}}$$

where V_u = value of the company's operating assets
V_{txa} = value of the company's interest tax shields
D = market value of the company's debt
E = market value of the company's equity

In Appendix D, we rearrange the equation to solve for the beta of equity (β_e). This leads to:

$$\beta_e = \beta_u + \frac{D}{E}(\beta_u - \beta_d) - \frac{V_{txa}}{E}(\beta_u - \beta_{txa})$$

To simplify the formula further, most practitioners impose two additional restrictions.[33] First, because debt claims have first priority, the beta of debt tends to be low. Thus, for simplicity, many assume the beta of debt is 0. Second, if the company maintains a constant capital structure, the value of tax shields will fluctuate with the value of operating assets, and beta of the tax shields (β_{txa}) will equal the beta of the unlevered company (β_u). Setting β_{txa} equal to β_u eliminates the final term:

$$\beta_e = \beta_u \left(1 + \frac{D}{E}\right) \tag{11.1}$$

Thus, a company's equity beta equals the company's operating beta (commonly known as the unlevered beta) times a leverage factor. As leverage rises, so will the company's equity beta. Using this relationship, we can convert

---

[33] In Chapter 6, we detail alternative restrictions that can be imposed to simplify the general equation regarding risk. Rather than repeat the analysis, we focus on the least restrictive assumption for mature companies: that debt remains proportional to value. For a full discussion of which restrictions to impose and how they affect the cost of capital, see the section on adjusted present value in Chapter 6.

EXHIBIT 11.10 **Determining Industry Beta**[1]

	Home Depot	Lowe's
Unlevering calculation		
Regression beta (step 1)	1.28	0.69
Debt-to-equity in 2006	0.26	0.16
Unlevered beta (step 2)	1.01	0.59
Relevering calculation		
Industry-average unlevered beta (step 3)	0.80	0.80
Debt-to-equity in 2008	0.51	0.32
Relevered beta (step 4)	1.21	1.06
Debt-to-equity ratio, 2006 ($ million)		
Short-term debt	18	111
Long-term debt	11,643	4,325
Operating leases	9,141	3,034
Less: Excess cash	0	0
Total net debt	20,802	7,470
Share price ($)	40	31
Shares outstanding (millions)	1,970	1,525
Market value of equity	79,115	47,504
Debt-to-equity ratio, 2006	0.26	0.16

[1] Even though Home Depot matched the market in aggregate losses during 2007 and 2008, a slight difference in timing caused the two measures to be uncorrelated. Prior to 2007, Home Depot's market beta was relatively stable. For this reason, we measure unlevered beta as of 2006. To determine the current cost of capital, we relever the 2006 industry beta at 2008 debt-to-equity levels.

equity betas into unlevered betas. Since unlevered betas focus solely on operating risk, they can be averaged across an industry (assuming industry competitors have similar operating characteristics).

To estimate an industry-adjusted company beta, use the following four-step process. First, regress each company's stock returns against the MSCI World Index to determine raw beta. In Exhibit 11.10, we report regression betas for Home Depot (1.28) and Lowe's (0.69). Second, to unlever each beta, calculate each company's market-debt-to-equity ratio, which equals 0.26 for Home Depot and 0.16 for Lowe's. Applying equation 11.1 leads to an unlevered beta of 1.01 for Home Depot and 0.59 for Lowe's. In step 3, determine the industry unlevered beta by calculating the median (in this case, the median and average betas are the same).[34] In the final step, relever the industry unlevered beta to each company's *target* debt-to-equity ratio (using current market values as proxies). Home Depot's relevered industry beta equals 1.21, which we use in Exhibit 11.2 to estimate the cost of capital. Note how the relevered beta differs across companies even though unlevered beta is the same for all companies within the industry.

---

[34] In most industries, more than two company betas are available. For Home Depot, Lowe's is the only publicly traded competitor. As a general rule, use as many direct comparables as possible.

Unlevered cost of equity   As just demonstrated, we can unlever an equity beta in order to improve beta estimation for use in the CAPM and WACC. We also can use unlevered industry betas to estimate a company's unlevered cost of equity for use in an adjusted present value (APV) valuation. To compute the unlevered cost of equity, simply apply the CAPM to the industry unlevered beta.

Improving estimates of beta: Smoothing   For well-defined industries, an industry beta will suffice. But if few direct comparables exist, an alternative is beta smoothing. Smoothing dampens extreme observations toward the overall average. Consider the simple smoothing process used by Bloomberg:

$$\text{Adjusted Beta} = 0.33 + 0.67(\text{Raw Beta})$$

Using this formula smooths raw regression estimates toward 1. For instance, a raw beta of 0.5 leads to an adjusted beta of 0.67, while a raw beta of 1.5 leads to an adjusted beta of 1.34.

Bloomberg's smoothing mechanism dates back to Marshall Blume's observation that betas revert to the mean.[35] Today, more advanced smoothing techniques exist.[36] Although the proof is beyond the scope of this book, the following adjustment will reduce beta estimation error:

$$\beta_{\text{adj}} = \frac{\sigma_\varepsilon^2}{\sigma_\varepsilon^2 + \sigma_b^2}(1) + \left(1 - \frac{\sigma_\varepsilon^2}{\sigma_\varepsilon^2 + \sigma_b^2}\right)\beta_{\text{raw}}$$

where σ_ε = standard error of the regression beta
σ_b = cross-sectional standard deviation of all betas

The raw regression beta receives the most weight when the standard error of beta from the regression (σ_ε) is smallest. In fact, when beta is measured perfectly ($\sigma_\varepsilon = 0$), the raw beta receives all the weight. Conversely, if the regression provides no meaningful results (σ_ε is very large), you should set beta equal to 1.

Alternatives to the CAPM: Fama-French Three-Factor Model

In 1992, Eugene Fama and Kenneth French published a paper in the *Journal of Finance* that received a great deal of attention because they concluded: "In short, our tests do not support the most basic prediction of the SLB [Sharpe-Lintner-Black] Capital Asset Pricing Model that average stock returns are positively

[35] M. Blume, "Betas and Their Regression Tendencies," *Journal of Finance* 30 (1975): 1–10.
[36] For instance, see P. Jorion, "Bayes-Stein Estimation for Portfolio Analysis," *Journal of Financial and Quantitative Analysis* 21 (1986): 279–292.

related to market betas."[37] At the time, theirs was the most recent in a series of empirical studies that questioned the usefulness of estimated betas in explaining the risk premium on equities. Among the factors negatively or positively associated with equity returns were the size of the company, a seasonal (January) effect, the degree of financial leverage, and the firm's book-to-market ratio.[38] Based on prior research and their own comprehensive regressions, Fama and French concluded that equity returns are inversely related to the size of a company (as measured by market capitalization) and positively related to the ratio of a company's book value to its market value of equity.

Given the strength of Fama and French's empirical results, the academic community now measures risk with a model commonly known as the Fama-French three-factor model. With this model, a stock's excess returns are regressed on excess market returns (similar to the CAPM), the excess returns of small stocks over big stocks (SMB), and the excess returns of high book-to-market stocks over low book-to-market stocks (HML).[39] Because the risk premium is determined by a regression on the SMB and HML stock portfolios, a company does not receive a premium for being small. Instead, the company receives a risk premium if its stock returns are correlated with those of small stocks or high book-to-market companies. The SMB and HML portfolios are meant to replicate unobservable risk factors, factors that cause small companies with high book-to-market values to outperform their CAPM expected returns.

To run a Fama-French regression, regress the company's monthly stock returns on the returns for three portfolios: the market portfolio, the SMB portfolio, and the HML portfolio. Given the model's popularity, Fama-French portfolio returns are now available from professional data providers.

We use the Fama-French three-factor model to estimate Home Depot's cost of equity in Exhibit 11.11. To determine the company's three betas, regress Home Depot stock returns against the excess market portfolio, SMB, and HML. The regression in Exhibit 11.11 used monthly returns and was specified as follows:

$$R_i - r_f = \alpha + \beta_1(R_m - r_f) + \beta_2(R_s - R_b) + \beta_3(R_h - R_l) + \varepsilon$$

---

[37] E. Fama and K. French, "The Cross-Section of Expected Stock Returns," *Journal of Finance* (June 1992): 427–465.

[38] R. Blanz, "The Relationship between Return and the Market Value of Common Stocks," *Journal of Financial Economics* (March 1981): 3–18; M. Reinganum, "Misspecification of Capital Asset Pricing: Empirical Anomalies Based on Earnings Yields and Market Values," *Journal of Financial Economics* (March 1981): 19–46; S. Basu, "The Relationship between Earnings Yield, Market Value and Return for NYSE Common Stocks: Further Evidence," *Journal of Financial Economics* (June 1983): 129–156; L. Bhandari, "Debt/Equity Ratio and Expected Common Stock Returns: Empirical Evidence," *Journal of Finance* (April 1988): 507–528; D. Stattman, "Book Values and Stock Returns," *Chicago MBA: A Journal of Selected Papers* (1980): 25–45; and B. Rosenberg, K. Reid, and R. Lanstein, "Persuasive Evidence of Market Inefficiency," *Journal of Portfolio Management* (1985): 9–17.

[39] For a complete description of the factor returns, see E. Fama and K. French, "Common Risk Factors in the Returns on Stocks and Bonds," *Journal of Financial Economics* 33 (1993): 3–56.

EXHIBIT 11.11 **Home Depot's Fama-French Cost of Equity, 2006**

Factor	Average monthly premium[1] (percent)	Average annual premium (percent)	Regression coefficient[2]	Contribution to expected return (percent)
Market portfolio		5.4	1.39	7.5
SMB portfolio	0.23	2.8	(0.09)	(0.3)
HML portfolio	0.40	5.0	(0.14)	(0.7)
Premium over risk-free rate[3]				6.6
			Risk-free rate	3.9
			Cost of equity	10.5

[1] SMB and HML premiums based on average monthly returns data, 1926–2009.
[2] Based on monthly returns data, 2002–2006.
[3] Summation rounded to one decimal point.

As the exhibit indicates, Home Depot's market portfolio beta is slightly higher in the Fama-French regression than when measured in Exhibit 11.7, but its raw cost of equity is lower because Home Depot is negatively correlated with small companies (small companies outperform big companies) and companies with a high book-to-market ratio (high book-to-market companies outperform low book-to-market companies). Based on the historical annualized premiums for SMB (2.8 percent) and HML (5.0 percent), Home Depot's cost of equity equals 10.5 percent, versus 10.8 percent from the CAPM using a regression beta. (These values are not comparable to the cost of equity presented in Exhibit 11.2, which used relevered industry betas.)

The Fama-French model suffers from the same implementation issues as the CAPM. For instance, how much data should you use to determine each factor's risk premium? Since 1926, small companies have outperformed large companies, but since the premium's discovery in 1982, they have not.[40] Should returns be regressed using monthly data? Should regressions use five years of data? Given the model's recent development, many of these questions are still under investigation.

Alternatives to the CAPM: Arbitrage Pricing Theory

Another alternative to the CAPM, the arbitrage pricing theory (APT), resembles a generalized version of the Fama-French three-factor model. In the APT, a security's actual returns are generated by k factors and random noise:

$$R_i = \alpha + \beta_1 F_1 + \beta_2 F_2 + \cdots + \beta_k F_k + \varepsilon$$

where F_i = return on factor i

[40] Small stocks outperformed large stocks from 1926 to 2009, with significant separation occurring between 1975 and 1984. However, from 1963 to 1973 and from 1984 to 2000, large stocks outperformed small stocks.

By creating well-diversified factor portfolios, a security's expected return must equal the risk-free rate plus the cumulative sum of its exposure to each factor times the factor's risk premium (λ):[41]

$$E(R_t) = r_f + \beta_1\lambda + \beta_2\lambda + \cdots + \beta_k\lambda_k$$

Otherwise, arbitrage (positive return with zero risk) is possible.

On paper, the theory is extremely powerful. Any deviations from the model result in unlimited returns with no risk. In practice, implementation of the model has been tricky, as there is little agreement about how many factors there are, what the factors represent, or how to measure the factors. For this reason, use of the APT resides primarily in the classroom.

In Defense of Beta

Fama and French significantly damaged the credibility of the CAPM and beta. Today, most academics rely on three-factor models to measure *historical* risk. Even so, the three-factor model has its critics. To start, the CAPM is based on solid theory about risk and return (albeit with strong assumptions), whereas the Fama-French model is based purely on empirical evidence. Although the latter model has been loosely tied to risk factors such as illiquidity (size premium) and default risk (book-to-market premium), no theory has gained universal acceptance.

In addition, S. P. Kothari, Jay Shanken, and Richard Sloan argue that beta may work better than portrayed in Fama and French. They point out that Fama and French's statistical tests were of low enough power that the tests could not reject a nontrivial (beta-related) risk premium of 6 percent over the post-1940 period.[42] Second, when they used annual returns rather than monthly returns to estimate beta (to avoid seasonality in returns), they found a significant linear relationship between beta and returns. Finally, they argue that the economic magnitude of the size factor is quite small, and book-to-market premiums could be a result of survivorship bias.

Other research argues that the Fama-French three-factor model historically outperforms the CAPM because either beta or the market portfolio has been improperly measured. In a recent study, a one-factor model based on time-varying betas eliminated the book-to-market effect.[43] Betas conditioned on observable information, such as labor income, also perform better than

---

[41] For a thorough discussion of the arbitrage pricing theory, see Mark Grinblatt and Sheridan Titman, *Financial Markets & Corporate Strategy*, 2nd ed. (New York: McGraw-Hill, 2001).

[42] S. Kothari, J. Shanken, and R. Sloan, "Another Look at the Cross-Section of Expected Returns," *Journal of Finance* (December 1995).

[43] A. Ang and J. Chen, "CAPM over the Long Run: 1926–2001" (working paper, University of Southern California, 2004); C. Armstrong, S. Banerjee, and C. Corona, "Uncertainty about Betas and Expected Returns," McCombs Research Paper Series ACC-07-09 (August 6, 2009).

older models.[44] Another article argues that regressions based on equity-only portfolios, such as the S&P 500, lead to the incorrect measurement of beta.[45] This faulty measurement is correlated with leverage, which in turn is correlated with size and book-to-market ratio. When the researchers controlled for leverage, excess returns associated with HML and SMB disappeared.

The bottom line? It takes a better theory to kill an existing theory, and we have yet to see the better theory. Therefore, we continue to use the CAPM while keeping a watchful eye on new research in the area.

ESTIMATING THE AFTER-TAX COST OF DEBT

The weighted average cost of capital blends the cost of equity with the after-tax cost of debt. To estimate the cost of debt for investment-grade companies, use the yield to maturity of the company's long-term, option-free bonds. Multiply your estimate of the cost of debt by 1 minus the marginal tax rate to determine the cost of debt on an after-tax basis.

Technically speaking, yield to maturity is only a proxy for expected return, because the yield is actually a *promised* rate of return on a company's debt (it assumes all coupon payments are made on time and the debt is paid in full). An enterprise valuation based on the yield to maturity is therefore theoretically inconsistent, as expected free cash flows should be discounted by an expected return, not a promised yield. For companies with investment-grade debt, the probability of default is so low that this inconsistency is immaterial, especially when compared with the estimation error surrounding beta and the market risk premium. Thus, for estimating the cost of debt for a company with investment-grade debt (debt rated at BBB or better), yield to maturity is a suitable proxy. For companies with below-investment-grade debt, we recommend using adjusted present value (APV) based on the unlevered cost of equity rather than the WACC to value the company.

Bond Ratings and Yield to Maturity

To solve for yield to maturity (YTM), reverse engineer the discount rate required to set the present value of the bond's promised cash flows equal to its price:

$$\text{Price} = \frac{\text{Coupon}}{(1 + \text{YTM})} + \frac{\text{Coupon}}{(1 + \text{YTM})^2} + \cdots + \frac{\text{Face} + \text{Coupon}}{(1 + \text{YTM})^N}$$

[44] T. Santos and P. Veronesi, "Labor Income and Predictable Stock Returns," *Review of Financial Studies* 19 (2006): 1–44.
[45] M. Ferguson and R. Shockley, "Equilibrium 'Anomalies,'" *Journal of Finance* 58, no. 6 (2003): 2549–2580.

EXHIBIT 11.12 **Home Depot: Trading Data on Corporate Debt**

Bond: 5.875% due December 2036

Trade time	Trade volume ($ thousand)	Bond price (dollars)	Yield (percent)
16:15:51	29	78.75	7.75
16:15:51	29	78.75	7.75
14:48:00	5	78.00	7.83
14:03:19	110	81.85	7.43
12:08:43	2,000	80.06	7.62
12:08:00	2,000	80.06	7.62
12:08:00	2,000	80.00	7.62
12:08:00	2,000	80.06	7.62
12:06:22	2,000	80.25	7.60
	Home Depot bond yield		7.62
	30-year U.S. Treasury yield		(4.39)
	Home Depot default premium		3.23

Source: Financial Industry Regulatory Authority (FINRA) TRACE system, May 28, 2009.

Ideally, yield to maturity should be calculated on liquid, option-free, long-term debt. As discussed earlier in this chapter, short-term bonds do not match the duration of the company's free cash flow. If the bond is rarely traded, the bond price will be stale. Using stale prices will lead to an outdated yield to maturity. Yield to maturity will also be distorted when corporate bonds have attached options, such as callability or convertibility, as their value will affect the bond's price but not its promised cash flows.

In the United States, you can download the yield to maturity for corporate debt free of charge using the TRACE pricing database.[46] Exhibit 11.12 displays TRACE data for Home Depot's 5.875 percent bonds due in December 2036. TRACE reports four data items: when the trade occurred, the size of the trade, the bond price, and the implied yield to maturity. As can be seen in the exhibit, the 2036 bond trades infrequently—only nine times in four hours. Home Depot's short-maturity debt trades more frequently, but at only five years to maturity, its duration is a poor match for the company's long-term cash flows. When measuring the yield to maturity, use trades greater than $1 million, as smaller trades are unreliable. Large trades for Home Depot's 2036 bond were completed at 7.62 percent (3.23 percent above the 30-year U.S. Treasury bond).

For companies with only short-term bonds or bonds that rarely trade, determine yield to maturity by using an indirect method. First, determine the company's credit rating on unsecured long-term debt. Next, examine the average yield to maturity on a portfolio of long-term bonds with the same

---

[46] The Financial Industry Regulatory Authority (FINRA) introduced TRACE (Trade Reporting and Compliance Engine) in July 2002. The system captures and disseminates transactions in investment-grade, high-yield, and convertible corporate debt, representing all over-the-counter market activity in these bonds.

EXHIBIT 11.13 **Yield Spread over U.S. Treasuries by Bond Rating, May 2009**

Basis points

Rating	Maturity (years)						
	1	2	3	5	7	10	30
Aaa/AAA	36	59	55	69	82	58	139
Aa2/AA	154	140	150	160	168	139	179
A1/A+	159	153	166	169	168	139	182
A2/A	183	178	192	193	189	152	190
A3/A−	195	194	213	210	210	177	199
Baa1/BBB+	324	310	336	333	324	288	320
Baa2/BBB	332	315	340	338	328	292	324
Baa3/BBB−	402	408	425	433	421	380	416
Ba2/BB	559	583	586	590	578	545	577
B2/B	870	916	913	925	909	878	904

Source: Bloomberg.

credit rating. Use this yield as a proxy for the company's implied yield on long-term debt.

Since the probability of default is critical to bond pricing, professional rating agencies, such as Standard & Poor's (S&P) and Moody's, will rate a company's debt. To determine a company's bond rating, a rating agency will examine the company's most recent financial ratios, analyze the company's competitive environment, and interview senior management. Corporate bond ratings are freely available to the public and can be downloaded from rating agency web sites. For example, consider Home Depot. On July 5, 2007, S&P downgraded Home Depot long-term debt from A+ to BBB+. Moody's quickly followed, downgrading Home Depot to Baa1 on July 27, 2007. For a short period, the two agencies' ratings were different, but such splits in ratings occur relatively infrequently (if they do, use the most recent rating).

Once you have a rating, convert the rating into a yield to maturity. Exhibit 11.13 presents U.S. corporate yield spreads over U.S. government bonds. All quotes are presented in basis points, where 100 basis points equals 1 percent. Since Home Depot is rated BBB+ by S&P and Baa1 by Moody's, we estimate that the 10-year yield to maturity is 288 basis points over the 10-year U.S. Treasury bond. Adding 2.9 percent to the risk-free rate of 3.9 percent equals 6.8 percent.[47]

Using the company's bond ratings to determine the yield to maturity is a good alternative to calculating the yield to maturity directly. Never, however, approximate the yield to maturity using a bond's coupon rate. Coupon rates are set by the company at time of issuance and only approximate the yield if the

---

[47] In May 2009, the 30-year default spread for BBB+-rated corporate bonds equaled 3.2 percent. This matches the default spread for Home Depot's 2036 bonds. Individual bonds can trade at rates different from the average for a variety of reasons, including anticipation of a ratings change and different levels of recoverable collateral.

bond trades near its par value. When valuing a company, you must estimate expected returns relative to *today's* alternative investments. Thus, when you measure the cost of debt, estimate what a comparable investment would earn if bought or sold today.

Below-Investment-Grade Debt

In practice, few financial analysts distinguish between expected and promised returns. But for debt below investment grade, using the yield to maturity as a proxy for the cost of debt can cause significant error.

To understand the difference between expected returns and yield to maturity, consider the following example. You have been asked to value a one-year zero-coupon bond whose face value is $100. The bond is risky; there is a 25 percent chance the bond will default and you will recover only half the final payment. Finally, the cost of debt (not yield to maturity), estimated using the CAPM, equals 6 percent. Based on this information, you estimate the bond's price by discounting *expected* cash flows by the cost of debt:

$$\text{Price} = \frac{E\,(\text{CF})}{1 + k_d} = \frac{(.75)(\$100) + (.25)(\$50)}{1.06} = \$82.55$$

Next, to determine the bond's yield to maturity, place promised cash flows, rather than expected cash flows, into the numerator. Then solve for the yield to maturity:

$$\text{Price} = \frac{\text{Promised CF}}{1 + \text{YTM}} = \frac{\$100}{1 + \text{YTM}} = \$82.55$$

Solving for YTM, the $82.55 price leads to a 21.1 percent yield to maturity.

This yield to maturity is *much* higher than the cost of debt. So what drives the yield to maturity? Three factors: the cost of debt, the probability of default, and the recovery rate after default. When the probability of default is high and the recovery rate is low, the yield to maturity will deviate significantly from the cost of debt. Thus, for companies with high default risk and low ratings, the yield to maturity is a poor proxy for the cost of debt.

When a company is rated BB (non-investment-grade) or below, we do not recommend using the weighted average cost of capital to value the company. Instead, use adjusted present value (APV). The APV model discounts projected free cash flow at the company's industry-based unlevered cost of equity (see Exhibit 11.10) and adds the present value of tax shields. For more on APV valuation, see Chapter 6.

Incorporating the Interest Tax Shield

To calculate free cash flow (using techniques detailed in Chapter 7), we compute taxes as if the company were entirely financed by equity. By using all-equity taxes, we can make comparisons across companies and over time, without regard to capital structure. Yet since the tax shield has value, it must be accounted for. In an enterprise DCF using the WACC, the tax shield is valued as part of the cost of capital. To value the tax shield, reduce the cost of debt by the marginal tax rate:

$$\text{After-Tax Cost of Debt} = \text{Cost of Debt} \times (1 - T_m)$$

Chapter 7 details how to calculate the marginal tax rate for historical analysis. For use in the cost of capital, you should calculate the marginal tax rate in a consistent manner, with one potential modification to account for the timing of future tax payments. According to research by John Graham, the statutory marginal tax rate overstates the *future* marginal tax rate because of rules related to tax loss carry-forwards, tax loss carry-backs, investment tax credits, and alternative minimum taxes.[48] For instance, when a company loses money, it will receive a cash credit only if it has been profitable in the past three years; otherwise, it must carry the loss forward until it is once again profitable.

Graham uses simulation to estimate the realizable marginal tax rate on a company-by-company basis. For investment grade companies, use the statutory rate. For instance, because Home Depot is highly profitable, Graham's model estimates the company's future marginal statutory tax rate at the full 35 percent. The typical company, however, does not always fully use its tax shields. Graham estimates that the marginal tax rate is on average 5 percentage points below the statutory rate.

USING TARGET WEIGHTS TO DETERMINE THE COST OF CAPITAL

With our estimates of the cost of equity and after-tax cost of debt, we can now blend the two expected returns into a single number. To do this, use the target weights of debt and equity to enterprise value, on a market (not book) basis:

$$\text{WACC} = \frac{D}{V}k_d(1 - T_m) + \frac{E}{V}k_e$$

[48] J. Graham and L. Mills, "Using Tax Return Data to Simulate Corporate Marginal Tax Rates," *Journal of Accounting and Economics* 46 (2009): 366–388; and J. Graham, "Proxies for the Corporate Marginal Tax Rate," *Journal of Financial Economics* 42 (1996): 187–221.

Using market values to weight expected returns in the cost of capital follows directly from the formula's derivation (see Appendix C for a derivation of free cash flow and WACC). But consider a more intuitive explanation: the WACC represents the expected return on an *alternative* investment with identical risk. Rather than reinvest in the company, management could return capital to investors, who could reinvest elsewhere. To return capital without changing the capital structure, management can repay debt and repurchase shares, but must do so at their *market* value. Conversely, book value represents a sunk cost, so it is no longer relevant.

The cost of capital should rely on target weights, rather than current weights, because at any point, a company's current capital structure may not reflect the level expected to prevail over the life of the business. The current capital structure may merely reflect a short-term swing in the company's stock price, a swing that has yet to be rebalanced by management. Thus, using today's capital structure may cause you to overestimate (or underestimate) the value of tax shields for companies whose leverage is expected to drop (or rise).

Many companies are already near their target capital structure. If the company you are valuing is not, decide how quickly the company will achieve the target. In the simplest scenario, the company will rebalance immediately and maintain the new capital structure. In this case, using the target weights and a constant WACC (for all future years) will lead to a reasonable valuation. If you expect the rebalancing to happen over a significant period of time, then use a different cost of capital each year, reflecting the capital structure at the time. In practice, this procedure is complex; you must correctly model the weights, as well as the changes in the cost of debt and equity (because of increased default risk and higher betas). For extreme changes in capital structure, modeling enterprise DCF using a constant WACC can lead to significant error. In this case, value the company with adjusted present value (APV).

To estimate the target capital structure for a company you are valuing from an external perspective, use a combination of three approaches:

1. Estimate the company's current market-value-based capital structure.
2. Review the capital structure of comparable companies.
3. Review management's implicit or explicit approach to financing the business and its implications for the target capital structure.

Estimating Current Capital Structure

To determine the company's current capital structure, measure the market value of all claims against enterprise value. For most companies, the claims will consist primarily of debt and equity (we address more complex securities in this chapter's final section). If a company's debt and equity are publicly traded, simply multiply the quantity of each security by its most recent price.

Most difficulties arise when securities are not traded such that prices can be readily observed.

Debt   In the United States, the current market value of a company's debt can be determined using the TRACE pricing database. Exhibit 11.12 shows that Home Depot's 2036 bond traded at $80.06, or 80.06 percent of par value at 12:08 on May 28, 2009. To determine the market value of the bond, multiply 80.06 percent by the bond's book value of $2,959 million, which equals $2,369 million.[49] Since a bond's price depends on its coupon rate versus its yield, not every Home Depot bond trades at the same price. The Home Depot bond maturing in 2016 recently closed at 98.53 percent of par over the same time period. Consequently, value each debt separately.

If an observable market value is not readily available, value debt securities at book value, or use discounted cash flow. In most cases, book value reasonably approximates the current market value. This will not be the case, however, if interest rates have changed since the time of issuance or the company is in financial distress. In these two situations, the current price will differ from book value because either expected cash flows have changed (increased probability of default lowers expected cash flow) or the discount rate has changed from its original level (interest rates drive discount rates).[50]

In these situations, value each bond separately by discounting promised cash flows at the appropriate yield to maturity. The size and timing of coupons will be disclosed in the notes of a company's annual report. Determine the appropriate yield to maturity by examining the yields from comparably rated debt with similar maturities.

Debt-equivalent claims   Next, value off-balance-sheet debt, such as operating leases and pension liabilities. As detailed in Chapter 27, operating leases can be valued using the following formula:

$$\text{Lease Value}_{t-1} = \frac{\text{Rental Expense}_t}{k_d + \dfrac{1}{\text{Asset Life}}}$$

Include operating leases in debt only if you plan to adjust free cash flow for operating leases as well. Consistency between free cash flow and the cost of capital is paramount.

Any pension adjustments made to free cash flow must be properly represented in the debt portion of the cost of capital. Specifically, if you add back any pension-related tax shields during adjustments to net operating profit less

---

[49] Home Depot reports the book value for each of its bonds in note 6 of its 2008 annual report.
[50] For floating-rate bonds, changes in Treasury rates won't affect value, since coupons float with Treasury yields. Changes in market-based default premiums, however, will affect the market value of floating-rate bonds, since bonds are priced at a fixed spread above Treasury yields.

adjusted taxes (NOPLAT), you must account for the tax shields in the present value of pension liabilities and the cost of debt.

Equity   If common stock is publicly traded, multiply the market price by the number of shares *outstanding*. The market value of equity should be based on shares outstanding in the capital market. Therefore, do not use shares issued, as they may include shares repurchased by the company.

At this point, you may be wondering why you are valuing the company if you are going to rely on the market's value of equity in the cost of capital. Shouldn't you be using the estimated equity value? The answer is no. Remember, you are only estimating today's market value to frame management's philosophy concerning capital structure. To value the company, use *target* weights.

For privately held companies, no market-based values are available. In this case, you must determine equity value (for the cost of capital) either using a multiples approach or through DCF iteratively. To perform an iterative valuation, assume a reasonable capital structure, and value the enterprise using DCF. Using the estimate of debt to enterprise value, repeat the valuation. Continue this process until the valuation no longer materially changes.

Reviewing Capital Structure of Comparable Companies

To place the company's current capital structure in the proper context, compare its capital structure with those of similar companies. Exhibit 11.14 presents the median debt-to-value levels for 10 industries. As the exhibit shows,

EXHIBIT 11.14 **Median Debt to Value by Industry**[1]

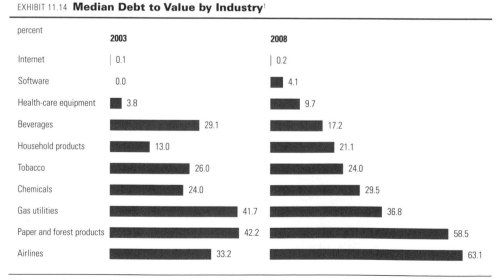

[1] S&P 1500 classified by Global Industry Classification System (GICS) industry. Debt to value measured using market values.

high-growth industries like software and health-care equipment, especially those with intangible investments, tend to use very little debt. Industries with heavy fixed investment in tangible assets, like utilities and airlines, tend to have higher debt levels. Economy-wide, the median debt-to-value ratio for S&P 1500 nonfinancials is 22.5 percent, and the median debt-to-equity ratio is 28.9 percent.

As Exhibit 11.14 demonstrates, industry debt-to-value ratios change over time. As share prices dropped during the financial crisis of 2008, the debt-to-value ratio rose for most industries, but by unequal proportions. Industries prone to the economic downturn, such as airlines, saw the largest rise in leverage, whereas staples like gas utilities experienced a decline in their relative leverage. Given the turmoil of 2008, a one-year view is probably misleading. For a proper perspective, examine the long-term trend for your company's particular industry.

For a company to have a different capital structure from that of its industry is perfectly acceptable, but you should understand why. For instance, is the company by philosophy more aggressive or innovative in the use of debt financing, or is the capital structure only a temporary deviation from a more conservative target? Often, companies finance acquisitions with debt they plan to retire quickly or refinance with a stock offering. Alternatively, is there anything different about the company's cash flow or asset intensity that can explain the difference? Always use comparables to help you assess the reasonableness of estimated debt-to-equity levels.

Reviewing Management's Financing Philosophy

As a final step, review management's historical financing philosophy (or question management outright). Has the current team been actively managing the company's capital structure? Is the management team aggressive in its use of debt? Or is it overly conservative? Consider Nike, the athletic shoe company. Although cash flow is strong and stable, the company rarely issues debt. From a financing perspective, it doesn't need to issue additional securities; investments can be funded with current profits.

Over the long run, one would expect most companies to aim toward a target capital structure that minimizes cost of capital. We address the choice of capital structure in Chapter 23.

COMPLEX CAPITAL STRUCTURES

The weighted average cost of capital is determined by weighting each security's expected return by its proportional contribution to total value. For a complex security, such as convertible debt, measuring expected return is challenging. Is a convertible bond like straight debt, enabling us to use the yield to maturity?

Is it like equity, enabling us to use the CAPM? In actuality, it is neither, so we recommend an alternative method.

If the treatment of hybrid securities will make a material difference in valuation results,[51] we recommend using adjusted present value (APV). In the APV, enterprise value is determined by discounting free cash flow at the industry-based unlevered cost of equity. The value of incremental cash flows related to financing, such as interest tax shields, is then computed separately. To determine the company's unlevered cost of equity, use the unlevered industry beta. This avoids the need to compute company-specific components, such as the debt-to-equity ratio, a required input in the unlevering equation.

In some situations, you may still desire an accurate representation of the cost of capital. In these cases, split hybrid securities into their individual components. For instance, you can replicate a convertible bond by combining a traditional bond with a call option on the company's stock. You can further disaggregate a call option into a portfolio consisting of a risk-free bond and the company's stock. By converting a complex security into a portfolio of debt and equity, you once again have the components required for the traditional cost of capital. The process of creating replicating portfolios to value options is discussed in Chapter 32.

REVIEW QUESTIONS

1. São Paolo Foods is a Brazilian producer of breads and other baked goods. Over the past year, profitability has been strong and the share price has risen from R$15 per share to R$25 per share. The company has 20 million shares outstanding. The company's borrowing is conservative; the company has only R$100 million in debt. The debt trades at a yield to maturity 50 basis points above Brazilian risk-free bonds. São Paolo Foods has a market beta of 0.7. If the Brazilian risk-free rate is 7 percent, the market risk premium is 5 percent, and the marginal tax rate is 30 percent, what is São Paolo's cost of capital?

2. São Paolo Foods (introduced in Question 1) is considering a leveraged recapitalization of the company. Upon announcement, management expects the share price to rise by 10 percent. If the company raises R$200 million in new debt to repurchase shares, how many shares can the company repurchase? Assuming management will actively manage to the new capital structure, estimate the company's new market beta. If the company's cost of

---

[51] If the hybrid security is unlikely to be converted, it can be treated as traditional debt. Conversely, if the hybrid security is well in the money, it should be treated as traditional equity. In these situations, errors are likely to be small, and a WACC-based valuation remains appropriate.

debt rises to 100 basis points above the Brazilian risk-free rate, what will its new cost of capital equal?

3. Your company, EuropeCo (a conglomerate of food, beverages, and consumer products), has announced its intention to purchase São Paolo Foods (introduced in Question 1). If the German risk-free rate is 5 percent and the beta of EuropeCo is 0.9, what is the cost of capital for São Paolo Foods once under EuropeCo control?

4. In 2009, the median price-to-earnings ratio for the S&P 500 was 11.1. If the long-run return on equity is 13.5 percent and the long-run growth in GDP is expected to be 6.7 percent (3.5 percent real growth and 3.2 percent inflation), what is the real cost of equity implied by the equity-denominated key value driver formula?

5. Market betas are typically computed with five years of monthly data or two weeks of yearly data. For computational simplicity, we present only 12 data points. Using a spreadsheet regression package or other software tool, compute a regression beta for the following data:

Returns, in percent

	1	2	3	4	5	6	7	8	9	10	11	12
Company	1.3	2.0	5.0	−1.0	−1.4	2.2	6.1	0.3	−4.0	3.8	−1.2	0.0
Market	1.0	1.2	3.4	0.3	−0.6	3.7	4.8	−2.3	−4.5	3.9	−1.3	1.8

6. You are analyzing a distressed bond with one year to maturity. The bond has a face value of $100 and pays a coupon rate of 5 percent per year. The bond is currently trading at $80. What is the yield to maturity on the bond? If the probability of default is 35 percent, what is the cost of debt? Assume that upon default only 50 percent of face value will be recovered and that remaining coupons will not be paid.

12

Moving from Enterprise Value to Value per Share

When you have completed the valuation of core operations, as described in Chapter 6, you are ready to estimate enterprise value, equity value, and value per share. Enterprise value represents the value of the entire company, while equity value represents the portion owned by shareholders. To determine enterprise value, add to the value of core operations the value of non-operating assets, such as excess cash and nonconsolidated subsidiaries. To convert enterprise value to equity value, subtract short-term and long-term debt, debt equivalents (such as unfunded pension liabilities), and hybrid securities (such as employee stock options). Finally, to estimate value per share, divide the resulting equity value by the most recent number of undiluted shares outstanding.[1]

When converting core operations to enterprise value, be sure to follow these two guiding principles: (1) avoid double-counting, and (2) evaluate interdependencies between the value of core operations and the value of nonoperating assets. To avoid double-counting, take care not to value separately any asset or liability embedded in free cash flow. For instance, nonconsolidated subsidiaries are typically treated as nonoperating because any income generated by nonconsolidated subsidiaries appears in the parent company's nonoperating income, not in earnings before interest, taxes, and amortization (EBITA). That income must therefore be valued separately from EBITA. Conversely, if you choose to include nonoperating income as part of EBITA, do not value the nonconsolidated subsidiary separately.

Double-counting can also occur when moving from enterprise value to equity value. Any financing expense included in EBITA, such as rental expense

---

[1] Estimating the value per share completes the technical aspect of the valuation, yet the job is not complete. It is time to revisit the valuation with a comprehensive look at its implications. We examine this process in Chapter 13.

EXHIBIT 12.1 **Sample Comprehensive Valuation Buildup**

$ million

DCF value of operations	5,000
Excess cash and marketable securities	50
Excess real estate	5
Nonconsolidated subsidiaries	270
Financial subsidiary	300
Tax loss carry-forwards	10
Discontinued operations	30
Enterprise value	5,665

→ Nonoperating assets

Interest-bearing debt	
Bank loans	(250)
Bonds	(550)
Debt equivalents	
Operating leases	(250)
Securitized receivables	(50)
Unfunded pension liabilities	(150)
Long-term operating provisions	(50)
Nonoperating provisions	(75)
Contingent liabilities	(40)
Debt and debt equivalents	(1,415)

→ Debt and debt equivalents

Hybrid claims	
Convertible debt	(200)
Preferred stock	(100)
Employee stock options	(50)
Minority interests	(150)
Equity value	3,750

→ Hybrid claims and minority interest

from operating leases, should not be deducted again to determine equity value. Also, watch out for any interdependencies between enterprise value and financial claims against the company. For example, the value of debt for a company in financial distress will typically vary with enterprise value. Changes in operating performance will affect not just the value of the company, but also the likelihood of default. For that reason, and contrary to what is often assumed, the value of debt will not remain constant as enterprise value changes.

This chapter lays out the process for converting core operating value (via discounted cash flow) into enterprise value and subsequently into equity value. Exhibit 12.1 details the valuation buildup for a complex hypothetical company to demonstrate a comprehensive analysis of nonoperating items. For many companies, nonoperating assets comprise only excess cash, and financial claims comprise only traditional debt.

As noted already in this chapter, converting core operating value into enterprise value entails adding to the value of operations the value of nonoperating assets whose income is not included in EBITA and consequently excluded from free cash flow. The most common nonoperating assets are excess cash, nonconsolidated subsidiaries (also known as equity investments), and financial subsidiaries. To complete enterprise value, add the value of other nonoperating assets such as tax loss carry-forwards, excess pension assets, excess real estate, and discontinued operations. The resulting enterprise value represents the total value of the company that can be allocated among the various claim holders.

Converting enterprise value to equity value entails deducting nonequity claims. Similar to nonoperating assets, nonequity claims are financial claims against enterprise value whose expenses are not included in EBITA and consequently excluded from free cash flow. Double-counting an expense and its associated liability would bias your valuation downward. The most typical nonequity claims—bank loans and corporate bonds—are reported on the balance sheet; but off-balance-sheet debt, such as operating leases, securitized receivables, and contingent claims, are not and must be estimated separately. Hybrid securities, such as preferred stock, convertible debt, and employee options, have characteristics of both debt and equity. Such hybrids require special care, as their valuations are highly dependent on enterprise value, so you should value them using option-pricing models rather than book value. Finally, if minority shareholders have claims against certain consolidated subsidiaries, deduct the value of minority interest.

Using the valuation buildup as our framework, we will go step-by-step through how to value nonoperating assets, debt and debt equivalents, hybrid securities, and minority interests, ending with the final step in valuation, estimating the intrinsic value per share.

VALUING NONOPERATING ASSETS

Although not included in operations, nonoperating assets still represent value to the shareholder. Thus, you must estimate the market value of each nonoperating asset separately and add the resulting value to the DCF value of operations to arrive at enterprise value. If necessary, adjust for circumstances that could affect shareholders' ability to capture the full value of these assets. For example, if the company has announced it will sell off a nonoperating asset in the near term, deduct the estimated capital gains taxes (if any) on the asset from its market value. If ownership of the asset is shared with another company, include only your company's portion of the value.

In this section, we identify the most common nonoperating assets and describe how to handle these in the valuation.

Excess Cash and Marketable Securities

Nonoperating assets that can be converted into cash on short notice and at low cost are classified as excess cash and marketable securities. Under U.S.

Generally Accepted Accounting Principles (GAAP) and International Financial Reporting Standards (IFRS), companies must report such assets at their fair market value on the balance sheet. You can use the most recent book values as a proxy for the market value of these assets unless you have reason to believe they have significantly changed in value since the reporting date (as in the case of volatile equity holdings).

In general, we do not recommend valuing liquid nonoperating assets yourself if the market values are available. If you decide to perform a DCF valuation of liquid securities, estimate meaningful cash flow projections, and discount these at the appropriate cost of capital. In general, this will not equal the company's weighted average cost of capital (WACC). For example, discounting interest income from U.S. government bonds owned by the company at the company's WACC would lead to an undervaluation, because the appropriate opportunity cost of capital for U.S. government securities is the risk-free rate.

Nonconsolidated Subsidiaries and Equity Investments

Nonconsolidated subsidiaries and equity investments are companies in which the parent company holds a noncontrolling equity stake. Because the parent company does not have formal control over these subsidiaries, their financials are not consolidated, so these investments must be valued separately from operations. Under U.S. GAAP and IFRS, there are two ways in which nonconsolidated subsidiaries can appear in the parent company's accounts:

1. For equity stakes between 20 percent and 50 percent, the parent company is assumed to have influence but not control over the subsidiary. The equity holding in the subsidiary is reported in the parent balance sheet at the investment's historical cost plus any reinvested income. The parent company's portion of the subsidiary's profits is shown below operating profit on the parent company's income statement.

2. For equity stakes below 20 percent, the parent company is assumed to have no influence. The equity holdings are shown at historical cost on the parent's balance sheet. The parent's portion of the subsidiary's *dividends* is included below operating profit on the income statement.

Publicly traded subsidiaries   If the subsidiary is publicly listed, use the market value for the company's equity stake. Verify that the market value is indeed a good indicator of intrinsic value. In some cases, these listed subsidiaries have very limited free float and/or very low liquidity, so the share price may not properly reflect current information.

Exhibit 12.2 presents a partial enterprise valuation of Philips, a Dutch consumer products, health care, and lighting company. As of October 2008, Philips

EXHIBIT 12.2   **Philips Enterprise Value, October 2008**

€ millions

	Holding (percent)				
Core operating value		21,630	**Valuation of LG Display stake**		
			Market capitalization (millions of won)		10,433,000
Associates					
LG Display	19.9	1,236 ◄——	÷ Currency conversion (wons/euro)		1,680
TPV Technologies	13.4	95	Market capitalization (millions of euros)		6,211
NXP Semiconductors	19.9	598	× Percent ownership		19.9
Pace Micro Technologies	23.0	76	Ownership stake (millions of euros)		1,236
Excess cash		8,233			
Enterprise value		31,868			

Source: UBS Analyst Report, October 2008, Thomson First Call.

owned stakes in a few unconsolidated subsidiaries.[2] One significant investment was LG Display, a South Korean manufacturer of TFT-LCD panels for use in televisions, notebook computers, and other applications. Although LG Display is publicly traded, Philips used subsidiary accounting for LG Display because the company was "represented on the board of directors and continues to exercise influence." Under this accounting classification, the book value reported on the balance sheet will not represent the investment's current value.

To estimate Philips's stake in LG Display, start with LG Display's market capitalization (10,433 billion won), and divide by the exchange rate of South Korean won to euros (1,680). This converts LG Display's local market capitalization into euros. To determine the value of Philips's partial ownership, multiply the resulting market capitalization in euros by Philips's ownership stake (19.9 percent).

Repeat this process for each of Philips's holdings to find each subsidiary's contribution to Philips's enterprise value.

Privately held subsidiaries   If the subsidiary is not listed but you have access to its financial statements, perform a separate DCF valuation of the equity stake. Discount the cash flows at the appropriate cost of capital (which, as before, is not necessarily the parent company's WACC). Also, when completing the parent valuation, include only the value of the parent's equity stake and not the subsidiary's entire enterprise value or equity value.

If the parent company's accounts are the only source of financial information for the subsidiary, we suggest the following alternatives to DCF:

- *Simplified cash-flow-to-equity valuation:* This is a feasible approach when the parent has a 20 to 50 percent equity stake, because the subsidiary's net income and book equity are disclosed in the parent's

---

[2] On March 11, 2009, Philips announced the sale of its remaining stake in LG Display.

accounts.[3] Build forecasts for how the equity-based key value drivers (net income growth and return on equity) will develop, so you can project cash flows to equity. Discount these cash flows at the *cost of equity* for the subsidiary in question and not at the parent company's cost of capital.

- *Multiples valuation:* As a second alternative, estimate the partial stake using a price-to-earnings and/or market-to-book multiple. If the company owns 20 to 50 percent of the subsidiary, apply an appropriate multiple to reported income.

- *Tracking portfolio:* For parent equity stakes below 20 percent, you may have no information beyond the investment's original cost—that is, the book value shown in the parent's balance sheet. Even applying a multiple is difficult because neither net income nor the current book value of equity is reported. If you know when the stake was acquired, you can approximate its current market value by applying the relative price change for a portfolio of comparable stocks over the same holding period.

You should triangulate your results as much as possible, given the lack of precision for these valuation approaches.

Loans to Other Companies

For loans to nonconsolidated subsidiaries and other companies, use the reported book value. This is a reasonable approximation of market value if the loans were given at fair market terms and if the borrower's credit risk and general interest rates have not changed significantly since issuance. If this is not the case, you should perform a separate DCF valuation of the promised interest and principal payments at the yield to maturity for corporate bonds with similar risk and maturity.

Finance Subsidiaries

To make their products more accessible, some companies operate customer financing businesses.[4] Because financial subsidiaries differ greatly from manufacturing and services businesses, it is critical to separate revenues, expenses, and balance sheet accounts associated with the subsidiary from core operations. Failing to do so will distort return on invested capital, free cash flow, and ultimately your perspective on the company's valuation.

To demonstrate the proper analysis of a company with a customer financing subsidiary—and analytical pitfalls—we have constructed a hypothetical

---

[3] The book value of the subsidiary equals the historical acquisition cost plus retained profits, which is a reasonable approximation of book equity. If any goodwill is included in the book value of the subsidiary, this should be deducted.

[4] Companies that sell expensive products typically offer financing of purchases. Significant customer financing subsidiaries exist at Caterpillar, IBM, and Textron, among others.

EXHIBIT 12.3 **FinanceCo: Income Statement and Balance Sheet**

$ million

Income statement		Balance sheet	
Sales of machinery	1,100	Operating assets	3,000
Revenues of financial products	300	Financial receivables	3,500
Total revenues	1,400	Total assets	6,500
Cost of goods sold	(800)		
Interest expense of financial products	(250)	Operating liabilities	500
Total operating costs	(1,050)	General obligation debt	700
		Debt related to financial products	3,200
Operating profit	350	Stockholders' equity	2,100
Interest expense, general obligation	(50)	Total liabilities and equity	6,500
Net income	300		

company, FinanceCo. Exhibit 12.3 presents FinanceCo's income statement and balance sheet. Last year, the company sold $1,100 million of machinery at a cost of $800 million. The company finances a significant percentage of its products for its customers, generating $300 million per year in lease revenue. The company currently holds $3,500 million in financial receivables. To finance its leasing business, FinanceCo raises securitized debt, collateralized by the financial receivables. The company also has general obligation debt to fund everyday operations.

To analyze FinanceCo, start by constructing separate income statements and balance sheets for the manufacturing and customer financing subsidiaries. Most companies will denote which line items are related to each group. For line items that consolidate expenses across both groups (such as selling and administrative expenses), search in the company's notes for financial statements by business segment.

Exhibit 12.4 presents the reorganized financial statements for the manufacturing group and the customer financing subsidiary. The manufacturing group's operating profit equals $300 million ($1,100 million in revenue less $800 million in cost of goods sold). Invested capital equals $2,500 million ($3,000 million in operating assets less $500 million in operating liabilities). Return on invested capital (ROIC) for the manufacturing group is 12.0 percent. For the customer financing subsidiary, return on equity is a better measure than ROIC, because capital structure is an integral part of a financial institution's operations. To compute return on equity, divide net income ($50 million) by allocated equity ($300 million).[5] This leads to a return on allocated equity of 16.7 percent.

---

[5] An allocation of equity is required because equity is not available by business segment. The simplest method to allocate equity is to net the group's liabilities against the group's assets. This can be misleading, however, because one group can borrow against the collective assets of the company, lowering the amount of allocated equity beyond what a stand-alone company can hold. As an alternative, use an industry benchmark for the debt-to-equity of stand-alone financing companies.

EXHIBIT 12.4 **FinanceCo: Reorganized Financial Statements**

$ million

Manufacturing subsidiary		Customer financing subsidiary	
Operating profit		**Net income**	
Sales of machinery	1,100	Revenues of financial products	300
Cost of goods sold	(800)	Interest expense of financial products	(250)
Operating profit	300	Net income	50
Reorganized balance sheet		**Reorganized balance sheet**	
Operating assets	3,000	Financial receivables	3,500
Operating liabilities	(500)		
Invested capital	2,500	Debt related to financial products	3,200
		Allocated equity	300
General obligation debt	700	Liabilities and allocated equity	3,500
Allocated equity	1,800		
Invested capital	2,500		
Return on invested capital (percent)	12.0	Return on allocated equity (percent)	16.7

Using the returns calculated in Exhibit 12.4, we can benchmark each of FinanceCo's subsidiaries against its peers. We cannot, however, aggregate the ratios to determine a combined return for FinanceCo as a whole. For instance, the ratio of FinanceCo's operating profit ($350 million) to FinanceCo's net assets ($2,500 million in net operating assets plus $3,500 in financial receivables) equals 5.8 percent, which is well below the 12.0 percent return on invested capital for the manufacturing group. This downward bias is caused by the small spread banks typically earn on loaned assets. A common alternative is to sum the manufacturing subsidiary's operating profit with the finance subsidiary's net income, divided by the invested capital of manufacturing plus the allocated equity from the financing business. This ratio blends the ROIC of manufacturing with the ROE of the financing business into a single ratio. Since blending different ratio types can cause systematic distortions, we recommend benchmarking each business separately.

To value a customer financing subsidiary, use the process and tools for valuing financial institutions (detailed in Chapter 36).

Discontinued Operations

Discontinued operations are businesses being sold or closed down. The earnings from discontinued operations are explicitly shown in the income statement, and the associated net asset position is disclosed on the balance sheet. Because discontinued operations are no longer part of a company's operations, their value should not be modeled as part of free cash flow or included in the DCF value of operations. Under U.S. GAAP and IFRS, the assets and liabilities associated with the discontinued operations are written down to their fair value and disclosed as a net asset on the balance sheet, so the most recent book value is usually a reasonable approximation.[6]

Excess Real Estate

Excess real estate and other unutilized assets are assets no longer required for the company's operations. As a result, any cash flows that the assets could generate are excluded from the free cash flow projection, and the assets are not included in the DCF value of operations. Identifying these assets in an outside-in valuation is nearly impossible unless they are specifically disclosed in the company's footnotes. For that reason, only internal valuations are likely to include their value separately as a nonoperating asset. For excess real estate, use the most recent appraisal value when it is available. Alternatively, estimate the real estate value either by using a multiple, such as value per square meter, or by discounting expected future cash flows from rentals at the appropriate cost of capital. Of course, be careful to exclude any operating real estate from these figures, because that value is implicitly included in the free cash flow projections and value of operations.

We do not recommend a separate valuation for unutilized operating assets unless they are expected to be sold in the near term. If the financial projections for the company reflect growth, the value of any underutilized assets should instead be captured in lower future capital expenditures.

Tax Loss Carry-Forwards

As detailed in Chapter 25, there are three types of deferred tax assets (DTAs): operating DTAs, nonoperating DTAs, and tax loss carry-forwards. Only tax loss carry-forwards should be valued separately.[7] Tax loss carry-forwards—or net operating losses (NOLs), as they are called in the United States—are the tax credits generated by past losses. They can be used to lower future taxes. To value tax loss carry-forwards, create a separate account for the accumulated tax loss carry-forwards, and forecast the development of this account by adding any future losses and subtracting any future taxable profits on a year-by-year basis. For each year in which the account is used to offset taxable profits,

[6] Any upward adjustment to the current book value of assets and liabilities is limited to the cumulative historical impairments on the assets. Thus, the fair market value of discontinued operations could be higher than the net asset value disclosed in the balance sheet.

[7] Operating deferred tax assets (DTAs), such as those corresponding to ongoing inventory write-downs, are incorporated directly into net operating profit less adjusted taxes (NOPLAT) and subsequently free cash flow. Therefore, operating DTAs should not be valued separately. Nonoperating DTAs, such as pension-related DTAs, should be ignored. Instead, value the future tax burden (or relief) associated with the nonoperating asset as part of the nonoperating asset. For instance, pension DTAs represent taxes that were paid when historical contributions exceeded recognized expenses. Since past taxes paid are unrelated to future cash savings, they are irrelevant to valuation. Future cash savings are based on the current level of pension underfunding.

discount the tax savings at the cost of debt. Some practitioners simply set the carry-forwards' value at the tax rate times the accumulated tax losses.

Excess Pension Assets

Surpluses in a company's pension funds show up as net pension assets on the balance sheet. (Small amounts are typically embedded within other assets.) Following recent changes to U.S. accounting standards, excess pension assets are typically reported at market value.[8] On an after-tax basis, the pension's value depends on management's plans going forward. If pensions are expected to be dissolved soon, subtract liquidation taxes (typically set higher than the marginal tax rate) from the market value of excess pension assets. Otherwise, subtract taxes at the marginal rate (which reflects lower future contributions). For details on pension accounting and valuation, see Chapter 27.

VALUING DEBT AND DEBT EQUIVALENTS

With enterprise value in hand, you are ready to determine equity value. You do this by subtracting from enterprise value the value of nonequity financial claims, which are typically found in the liabilities section of the balance sheet. Remember, deduct only those financial claims that are not incorporated as part of free cash flow. Also, be aware that not all financial claims have to be reported on the balance sheet, so make sure to search the footnotes carefully for undisclosed liabilities.

In this section, we go though the most typical financial claims and how to determine their value.

Debt

Corporate debt comes in many forms: commercial paper, notes payable, fixed and floating bank loans, corporate bonds, and capitalized leases. If the debt is relatively secure and actively traded, use its market value.[9] If the debt instrument is not traded, estimate current value by discounting the promised interest payments and the principal repayment at the yield to maturity. The book value of debt is a reasonable approximation for fixed-rate debt if interest rates and default risk have not significantly changed since the debt issuance. For floating-rate debt, market value is not sensitive to interest rates, and book

---

[8] Under IFRS, companies can still report excess pension assets at book value. If pensions are not marked to market, search the company's pension footnote for the value of excess pension assets.

[9] When a bond's yield is below its coupon rate, the bond will trade above its face value. Intuition dictates that, at most, the bond's face value should be deducted from enterprise value. Yet since enterprise value is computed using the cost of debt (via the weighted average of cost of capital), subtracting face value is inconsistent with how enterprise value is computed. In cases where bonds are callable at face value, market prices will rarely exceed face value.

EXHIBIT 12.5 **Valuation of Equity Using Scenario Analysis**

$ million

	Enterprise value	Face value of debt	Equity value[1]	Probability (percent)	Weighted equity value
Scenario A					
New owner successfully implements value improvements.	1,500	1,200	300	50	150
Scenario B					
Company maintains current performance.	900	1,200	–	50	–
				Equity value	150

[1] Equity value equals enterprise value less the face value of debt or zero, whichever is greater.

value is a reasonable approximation if the company's default risk has been fairly stable.

If you are using your valuation model to test changes in operating performance (for instance, a new initiative that will improve operating margins), the value of debt may differ from its current market value. Always check interest coverage ratios to test whether the company's bond rating will change under the new forecasts—often they will not. A change in bond rating can be translated into a new yield to maturity for debt, which in turn will allow you to revalue the debt. For more on debt ratings and interest rates, see Chapter 23.

Highly levered companies   For companies with significant debt or companies in financial distress, valuing debt requires careful analysis. For distressed companies, the value of the debt will be at a significant discount to its book value and will fluctuate with the value of the enterprise. Essentially, the debt has become similar to equity: its value will depend directly on your estimate for the enterprise value, and you should not simply deduct the current market value of the debt.

For distressed companies, apply an integrated-scenario approach to value operations as well as equity. Exhibit 12.5 presents a simple two-scenario example of equity valuation with significant debt. In scenario A, the company's new owner is able to implement improvements in operating margin, inventory turns, and so on. In scenario B, changes are unsuccessful, and performance remains at its current level. For each scenario, estimate the enterprise value conditional on your financial forecasts, deduct the *full value* of the debt[10] and other nonequity claims,[11] and calculate the equity value as the residual (which should be zero for any scenario where the conditional enterprise value is less than the value of debt plus other nonequity claims). Next, weight each

[10] That is, the market value of debt for a nondistressed company—typically close to book value.
[11] All nonequity claims need to be included in the scenario approach for distressed companies. The order in which nonequity claims are paid upon liquidation will make a difference for the value of nonequity claims, but not for the equity value.

scenario's conditional value of equity by its probability of occurrence to obtain an estimate for the value of equity. For the company in Exhibit 12.5, scenario A leads to an equity valuation of $300 million, whereas the equity value in scenario B is zero. If the probability of each scenario is 50 percent, the weighted average value of equity is $150 million.

The scenario valuation approach treats equity like a call option on enterprise value. A more comprehensive model would estimate the entire distribution of potential enterprise values and use an option-pricing model, such as the Black-Scholes model, to value equity.[12] Using an option-pricing model to value equity, however, has serious practical drawbacks. First, to model the distribution of enterprise values, you must forecast the expected change and volatility for each source of uncertainty, such as revenue growth and gross margin. This too easily becomes a mechanical exercise that replaces a thoughtful analysis of the underlying economics of potential scenarios. Second, most options models treat each source of uncertainty as independent of the others. This can lead to outcomes that are economically unrealistic. For these reasons, we believe a thoughtful scenario analysis will lead to a more accurate valuation than an options model will.

Operating Leases

Under certain restrictions, companies can avoid capitalizing leased assets on their balance sheets. Instead, they treat rental charges for so-called operating leases as an expense. In Chapter 6, we outlined a method for capitalizing leased assets. If NOPLAT, invested capital, and consequently free cash flow are adjusted for operating leases, you must deduct the present value of operating leases from enterprise value to determine equity value. Do *not* subtract the value of operating leases, however, if no adjustments are made. Chapter 27 details the valuation of leases.

Securitized Receivables

When companies sell accounts receivable to a third party, the discount on the sale is typically embedded in either selling, general, and administrative (SG&A) expense or interest expense. Deduct the value of securitized receivables from enterprise value when discounts are incorporated in interest expense *or* if you adjust SG&A to remove embedded discounts. Chapter 27 discusses the valuation of securitized receivables in detail.

Unfunded Pension and Other Postretirement Liabilities

Unfunded retirement liabilities should be treated as debt equivalents and deducted from enterprise value to determine equity value. Following recent

---

[12] Option-pricing models are described in Chapter 32.

changes to accounting standards, unfunded pension and other retirement liabilities are typically reported at market value. If pensions are not marked to market, search the company's pension footnote for the value of unfunded pension liabilities. Since the future contributions to fill unfunded liabilities are tax deductible at the marginal tax rate, multiply unfunded pension liabilities by 1 minus the marginal tax rate. For details on pension accounting and valuation, please see Chapter 27.

Provisions

Certain provisions other than retirement-related liabilities need to be deducted as nonequity financial claims. Following the guidelines in Chapter 7, we distinguish four types of provisions and value them as follows:

1. Ongoing operating provisions (e.g., for warranties and product returns) are already accounted for in the free cash flows and should therefore *not be deducted* from enterprise value.

2. Long-term operating provisions (e.g., for plant-decommissioning costs) *should be deducted* from enterprise value as debt equivalents. Because these provisions cover cash expenses that are payable in the long term, they are typically recorded at the discounted value in the balance sheet. In this case, there is no need to perform a separate DCF analysis, and you can *use the book value of the liability* in your valuation.

3. Nonoperating provisions (e.g., for restructuring charges resulting from layoffs) *should be deducted* from enterprise value as a debt equivalent. Although a discounted value would be ideal, the book value from the balance sheet is often a reasonable approximation. These provisions are recorded on the financial statements at a nondiscounted value, because outlays are usually in the near term.

4. Income-smoothing provisions do not represent actual future cash outlays, so they should *not be deducted* from enterprise value. These provisions are difficult to find and will disappear as companies around the world adopt IFRS.

For specifics on how to identify, analyze, and value provisions, see Chapter 26.

Contingent Liabilities

Certain liabilities are not disclosed in the balance sheet but are separately discussed in the notes to the balance sheet. Examples are possible liabilities from pending litigation and loan guarantees. When possible, estimate the associated expected after-tax cash flows (if the costs are tax deductible), and discount these at the cost of debt. Unfortunately, assessing the probability of such cash flows materializing is difficult, so the valuation should be interpreted with caution. To provide some boundaries on your final valuation, estimate the value of contingent liabilities for a range of probabilities.

VALUING HYBRID SECURITIES AND MINORITY INTERESTS

For stable companies, the current values of debt and debt equivalents are typically independent of enterprise value. For hybrid securities and minority interests, this is not the case. Each must be valued in conjunction with estimates of enterprise value. The most common hybrid securities are convertible debt, convertible preferred stock, and employee stock options.

Convertible Debt and Convertible Preferred Stock

Convertible bonds are corporate bonds that can be exchanged for common equity at a predetermined conversion ratio. A convertible bond is essentially a package of a straight corporate bond plus a call option on equity (the conversion option).[13] Because the conversion option can have significant value, this form of debt requires treatment different from that of regular corporate debt.

The value of convertibles depends on the enterprise value. In contrast to straight debt, neither the book value nor the simple DCF value of bond cash flows is a good proxy for the value of convertibles. Depending on the information available, there are three potential methods:

1. *Market value:* If your estimate of value per share is near the market price and the convertible bond is actively traded, use its market value. If you plan to modify enterprise value (via operating changes), the market value is no longer appropriate, as convertible debt value will change with enterprise value.

2. *Black-Scholes value:* When the market value is inappropriate, we recommend using an option-based valuation for convertible debt. In contrast to the treatment of employee stock options, annual reports do not provide any information on the value of convertible debt. Accurate valuation of convertible bonds with option-based models is not straightforward, but following methods outlined by John Ingersoll, you can apply an adjusted Black-Scholes option-pricing model for a reasonable approximation.[14]

---

[13] See R. Brealey, S. Myers, and F. Allen, *Principles of Corporate Finance*, 8th ed. (New York: McGraw-Hill, 2006), chap. 23. If you are doing a discounted-cash-flow-to-equity valuation, you subtract only the value of the conversion option from your DCF valuation. The straight-debt component of the convertible debt has already been included in the equity cash flows.

[14] For more on the valuation of employee stock options, see, for example, J. Hull and A. White, "How to Value Employee Stock Options," *Financial Analysts Journal* 60, no. 1 (January/February 2004): 114–119.

EXHIBIT 12.6 **Hasbro Convertible Debt, November 2008**

$ million

Capital structure	Market value	Black-Scholes value	Conversion value	Book value
Enterprise value	5,050.0	5,050.0	5,050.0	
Traditional debt	(556.3)	(556.3)	(556.3)	(605.2)
→ Convertible debt at 2.75% due 2021	(334.3)	(326.4)	–	(249.8)
Unfunded pensions	(38.3)	(38.3)	(38.3)	(38.3)
Employee options	(134.0)	(134.0)	(134.0)	
Equity value	3,987.1	3,994.9	4,321.4	
Number of shares (million)				
Number of nondiluted shares	142.6	142.6	142.6	
→ New shares issued	–	–	11.6	
Number of diluted shares	142.6	142.6	154.2	
Value per share (dollars)	28.0	28.0	28.0	

Source: Hasbro 2007 10-K, NASD TRACE system, Black Scholes option pricing model.

3. *Conversion value:* The conversion value approach assumes that all convertible bonds are immediately exchanged for equity and ignores the time value of the conversion option. It leads to reasonable results when the conversion option is deep in the money, meaning the bond is more valuable when converted into equity than held for future coupon and principal payments.

In Exhibit 12.6, we illustrate all three valuation methods for the toy manufacturer Hasbro. The first column values Hasbro's equity using the market price of each bond. Market prices for U.S. corporate debt are reported on the Financial Industry Regulatory Authority (FINRA) TRACE system. In November 2008, Hasbro's traditional debt traded at a small discount to its book value. Conversely, the company's convertible debt traded at a significant premium ($334.3 million versus $249.8 million in book value) because the bonds are convertible into equity at a discount. According to the debt contract, the bonds are convertible at $21.60 per share.[15] At this conversion price, $249.8 million in bonds are convertible into 11.56 million shares. With Hasbro's stock trading at $28, the bonds can be converted into the equivalent of $323.7 million (known as intrinsic value). The convertible bond's market price ($334.3 million) trades slightly higher than the bond's intrinsic value given the unlimited upside and downside protection the bonds offer.

To model the value of Hasbro's convertible debt, disaggregate the value of convertible debt into underlying straight debt and the option value to convert. The value of straight debt equals the net present value of a 2.75 percent coupon

[15] Reported in Hasbro's 2007 annual report, note 7.

bond yielding 7.81 percent (the yield on comparable bonds without conversion features), maturing in 12 years (the remaining life). Without conversion, Hasbro's debt is valued at 61.5 percent of face value, or $153.6 million.[16]

To determine an option's value, you need six inputs: the underlying asset value, the strike price, the dividend rate on the underlying asset, the volatility of the underlying asset, the risk-free rate, and the time to maturity. For the option embedded in Hasbro's convertible bond, the underlying asset is 11.56 million shares of Hasbro stock, whose current value equals $323.7 million (11.56 million shares times $28 per share). The strike price equals $153.6 million (the current value of straight debt). The expected dividend rate (1.97 percent) and volatility of Hasbro's shares (22.0 percent) are reported in the company's 10-K. The bond's time to maturity is 12 years, and the current risk-free rate is 4.79 percent.[17] Inputting the data into a Black-Scholes estimator leads to an option value of $172.8 million. Thus, the Black-Scholes value of the convertible debt equals $326.4 million ($153.6 in straight debt plus $172.8 in option value).

A simple alternative to option pricing is the conversion value approach. Under the conversion value approach, convertible bonds are converted immediately into equity. Since Hasbro's bonds are convertible into 11.6 million shares, nondiluted shares are increased from 142.6 million to 154.2 million. The third column of Exhibit 12.6 zeros out convertible debt and divides by diluted shares. In this case, each approach leads to a similar value because the value of conversion is much higher than the value of traditional debt (known as being in the money). For bonds out of the money, the conversion approach will lead to an underestimation of the bonds' value. Therefore, we recommend using an option valuation model, such as Black-Scholes.

Employee Stock Options

Many companies offer their employees stock options as part of their compensation. Options give the holder the right, but not the obligation, to buy company stock at a specified price, known as the exercise price. Since employee stock options have long maturities and the company's stock price could eventually rise above the exercise price, options can have great value.

Employee stock options affect a company valuation in two ways. First, the value of options that will be *granted in the future* needs to be captured in the free cash flow projections or in a separate DCF valuation, following the guidelines in Chapter 7. If captured in the free cash flow projections, the value of future options grants is included in the value of operations and should not be treated as a nonequity claim. Second, the value of options *currently outstanding* must

---

[16] Without the conversion feature, the bond would trade at a significant discount to face value, because the bond's coupon is well below its yield to maturity.

[17] Hasbro issued convertible debt that is callable when the stock price is above $27. Since Hasbro is likely to recall the bond soon, the effective time to maturity on the bond is much less than 12 years. When we tested various times to maturity, however, the changes in bond price were small.

be subtracted from enterprise value as a nonequity claim. Note, however, that the value of the options will depend on your estimate of enterprise value, and your option valuation should reflect this.

The following approaches can be used for valuing employee options:

- We recommend using the *estimated market value from option valuation models*, such as Black-Scholes or more advanced binomial (lattice) models. Under U.S. GAAP and IFRS, the notes to the balance sheet report the total value of all employee stock options outstanding, as estimated by such option-pricing models. Note that this value is a good approximation only if your estimate of share price is close to the one underlying the option values in the annual report. Otherwise, you need to create a new valuation using an option-pricing model. The notes disclose the information required for valuation.[18]

- The *exercise value approach* provides only a lower bound for the value of employee options. It assumes that all options are exercised immediately and thereby ignores the time value of the options. The resulting valuation error increases as options have longer time to maturity, the company's stock has higher volatility, and the company's share price is closer to the exercise price. Given that a more accurate valuation is already disclosed in the annual report, we do not recommend this method. However, it is still quite common among practitioners.

Exhibit 12.7 provides an example of the two valuation methods. The first method uses Black-Scholes to value both outstanding and currently exercisable options. The value of outstanding options will be less than that of exercisable options, because outstanding options include some options that will be lost if the employee leaves the company.

To estimate the value of employee stock options, you need six inputs: the current stock price, the average strike price, the stock's dividend rate, the stock's volatility, the risk-free rate, and the time to maturity. Hasbro's current share price equals $28. The other inputs are disclosed in Hasbro's 10-K for both outstanding and exercisable options. For outstanding options, the weighted average strike price equals $22, the expected dividend rate equals 1.97 percent, the volatility of Hasbro's shares equals 22.0 percent, and the average time to maturity is reported at 4.83 years. The current risk-free rate is 4.79 percent. The Black-Scholes estimator prices the average option at $9.24.[19] With 14.5 million options outstanding, the aggregate value of options is valued at $134.0 million.

---

[18] For more on the valuation of employee stock options, see, for example, Hull and White, "How to Value Employee Stock Options."

[19] Using Black-Scholes to determine the value of a single option on an average strike price will undervalue a portfolio of options with a spread of strike prices. Unless you know the spread of strike prices, you cannot measure the bias.

EXHIBIT 12.7 **Hasbro Employee Options, November 2008**

$ million

Company financial structure	Black-Scholes		Exercise value approach
	Value of outstanding options	Value of exercisable options	
Enterprise value	5,050.0	5,050.0	5,050.0
Traditional debt	(556.3)	(556.3)	(556.3)
Convertible debt at 2.75% due 2021	(334.3)	(334.3)	(334.3)
Unfunded pensions	(38.3)	(38.3)	(38.3)
→ Employee options: value	(134.0)	(98.6)	–
→ Employee options: exercise proceeds	–	–	199.3
Equity value	3,987.1	4,022.5	4,320.3
Number of shares (million)			
Number of nondiluted shares	142.6	142.6	142.6
→ New shares issued	–	–	9.7
Number of diluted shares	142.6	142.6	152.3
Value per share (dollars)	28.0	28.2	28.4

Source: Hasbro 2007 10-K, NASD TRACE system, Black-Scholes option-pricing model.

To estimate share price, deduct the aggregate value from enterprise value, and divide by the number of undiluted shares.

Under the exercise value approach, employee options are assumed to be exercised immediately. According to Hasbro's 10-K, 9.73 million shares are immediately exercisable at an average strike price of $20.50, for total proceeds of $199.3 million. Exercise of employee options generates cash for the company and increases shares outstanding from 142.6 million to 152.3 million. Dividing equity value by diluted shares leads to a value of $28.4, slightly higher than the value under the Black-Scholes method.

Minority Interests

When a company controls, but does not fully own a subsidiary, the subsidiary's financial statements must be fully consolidated in the group accounts. Without any further adjustment, the full value of the subsidiary would be improperly included in the parent company valuation. Therefore, you need to deduct the value of the third-party minority stake in the subsidiary as a nonequity financial claim.

Because minority stakes are to a certain extent the mirror image of non-consolidated subsidiaries, the recommended valuation for minority interests is similar to that of nonconsolidated subsidiaries; see the corresponding section for more details. If the minority stake is publicly listed, as in the case of minority carve-outs (see Chapter 22), use the proportional market value owned by outsiders to deduct from enterprise value. Alternatively, you can perform a separate valuation using a DCF approach, multiples, or a tracking portfolio, depending on the amount of information available. Remember, however, that a minority interest is a claim on a subsidiary, not the entire company. Thus, any valuation should be directly related to the subsidiary and not the company as a whole.

ESTIMATING VALUE PER SHARE

The final step in a valuation is to calculate the value per share. Assuming that you have used an option-based valuation approach for convertible bonds and employee options, divide the total equity value by the number of *undiluted* shares outstanding. Use the undiluted (rather than diluted) number of shares because the full values of convertible debt and stock options have already been deducted from the enterprise value as nonequity claims. Also, use the most recent number of undiluted shares outstanding. Do not use the weighted average of shares outstanding; they are reported in the financial statements to determine average earnings per share.

The number of shares outstanding is the gross number of shares issued, less the number of shares held in treasury. Most U.S. and European companies report the number of shares issued and those held in treasury under shareholders' equity. However, some companies show treasury shares as an investment asset, which is incorrect from an economic perspective. Treat them, instead, as a reduction in the number of shares outstanding.

If you used the conversion and exercise value method to account for employee options and convertible debt and stock options, divide by the diluted number of shares.

REVIEW QUESTIONS

1. MarineCo manufactures, markets, and distributes recreational motor boats. Using discounted free cash flow, you value the company's operations at $2,500 million. The company has a 20 percent stake in a nonconsolidated subsidiary. The subsidiary is valued at $500 million. The investment is recorded on MarineCo's balance sheet as an equity investment of $50 million. MarineCo is looking to increase its ownership. The company's marginal tax rate is 30 percent. Based on this information, what is MarineCo's enterprise value? If new management announced its plan to sell the company's stake in the subsidiary at its current value, how would that change your valuation?

2. MarineCo has unfunded pension liabilities valued at $200 million, recorded as a long-term liability. MarineCo has detailed a potential legal judgment of $100 million for defective engines in its annual report. Since management estimates a 90 percent likelihood the judgment will be enforced against the engine maker and not MarineCo, they did not report a liability on the balance sheet. The company's marginal tax rate is 30 percent. If MarineCo's enterprise value is $2,600 million, what is MarineCo's equity value?

3. To finance customer purchases, MarineCo recently started a customer financing unit. MarineCo's income statement and balance sheet are provided in Exhibit 12.8. Separate MarineCo's income statement and balance sheet into the two segments: manufacturing and the customer financing unit. Assume equity in the financing subsidiary is the difference between finance receivables and debt related to those receivables. What is the return on invested capital for the manufacturing segment? What is the return on equity for the customer financing subsidiary?

4. In Question 3, we computed ROE based on an equity calculation equal to the difference between finance receivables and debt related to those receivables. Why might this ROE measurement lead to a result that is too high?

5. You are valuing a company using probability-weighted scenario analysis. You carefully model three scenarios, such that the resulting enterprise value equals $300 million in Scenario 1, $200 million in Scenario 2, and $100 million in Scenario 3. The probability of each scenario is 25 percent, 50 percent, and 25 percent respectively. What is the expected enterprise value? What is the expected equity value? Management announces a new plan that eliminates the downside scenario, making Scenario 2 that much more likely. What happens to enterprise value and equity value? Why does enterprise value rise more than equity value?

EXHIBIT 12.8 **MarineCo: Income Statement and Balance Sheet**

$ million

Income statement		Balance sheet	
Sales of machinery	1,500	Operating assets	2,200
Revenues of financial products	400	Financial receivables	4,000
Total revenues	1,900	Total assets	6,200
Cost of goods sold	(1,000)	Operating liabilities	400
Interest expense of financial products	(350)	General obligation debt	–
Total operating costs	(1,350)	Debt related to customer financing	3,600
		Stockholders' equity	2,200
Operating profit	550	Total liabilities and equity	6,200
Interest expense, general obligation	(80)		
Net income	470		

6. You are valuing a technology company whose enterprise value is $800 million. The company has no debt, but considerable employee options (10 million in total). Based on option pricing models, you value the options at $6.67 per option. If the company has 40 million shares outstanding, what is the company's equity value and value per share? What is the value per share using the exercise value approach? Assume the average strike price equals $15.

13

Calculating and Interpreting Results

Now that the valuation model is complete, we are ready to put it to work. Start by testing the validity of the model. Even a carefully planned model can have mechanical errors or errors in economic logic. To help you avoid this, we present a set of systematic checks and other tricks of the trade that test the robustness of the model. During this verification, also ensure that key ratios are consistent with the economics of the industry.

Once you are comfortable that the model works, learn the ins and outs of your valuation by changing each forecast input one at a time. Examine how each part of your model changes, and determine which inputs have the largest effect on the company's valuation and which have little or no impact. Since forecast inputs are likely to change in concert, build a sensitivity analysis that tests multiple changes at a time. Use this analysis to prioritize strategic actions.

Next, to deepen the understanding offered by your valuation, use scenario analysis. Start by determining the key uncertainties that affect the company's future, and use these uncertainties to construct multiple forecasts. Uncertainty can be as simple as whether a particular product launch will be successful, or as complex as which technology will dominate the market. Construct a comprehensive forecast consistent with each scenario, and weight the resulting equity valuations by their probability of occurring. Scenario analysis will not only guide your valuation range, but also inform your thinking about strategic actions and resource allocation under alternative situations.

Finally, we offer a major caveat: for a multibusiness company, a sum-of-the-parts valuation is often the only way to estimate a company's value accurately. By this we mean valuing the business units separately and aggregating their value to arrive at the company's value. The reason for using this method is that business units often have different financial prospects. Averaging across the units is not meaningful and will not provide useful comparisons. We close this chapter with a discussion on how to value a company by parts.

VERIFYING VALUATION RESULTS

Once you have a workable valuation model, you should perform several checks to test the logic of your results, minimize the possibility of errors, and ensure that you understand the forces driving the valuation. Start by making sure that the model is technically robust—for example, by checking that the balance sheet balances in each forecast year. Second, test whether results are consistent with industry economics. For instance, do key value drivers, such as return on invested capital (ROIC), change in a way that is consistent with the intensity of competition? Next, compare the model's output with the current share price. Can differences be explained by economics, or is an error possible? We address each of these tasks next.

Is the Model Technically Robust?

Ensure that all checks and balances in your model are in place. Your model should reflect the following fundamental equilibrium relationships:

- In the unadjusted financial statements, the balance sheet should balance every year, both historically and in forecast years. Check that net income flows correctly into dividends paid and retained earnings.
- In the rearranged financial statements, check that the sum of invested capital plus nonoperating assets equals the cumulative sources of financing. Is net operating profit less adjusted taxes (NOPLAT) identical when calculated top down from sales and bottom up from net income? Does net income correctly link to dividends and retained earnings in adjusted equity?
- Does the change in excess cash and debt line up with the cash flow statement?

A good model will automatically compute each check as part of the model. A technical change to the model that breaks a check can then be clearly signified. To stress-test the model, change a few key inputs in an extreme manner. For instance, if gross margin is increased to 99 percent or lowered to 1 percent, do the statements still balance?

As a final consistency check, adjust the dividend payout ratio. Since payout will change funding requirements, the company's capital structure will change. Because NOPLAT, invested capital, and free cash flow are independent of capital structure, these values should not change with changes in the payout ratio. If they do, the model has a mechanical flaw.

Is the Model Economically Consistent?

The next step is to check that your results reflect appropriate value driver economics. If the projected returns on invested capital are above the weighted average cost of capital (WACC), the value of operations should be above the book value of invested capital. If, in addition, growth is high, the value of operations should be considerably above book value. If not, a computational error has probably been made. Compare your valuation results with a back-of-the-envelope value estimate based on the key value driver formula, taking long-term average growth and return on invested capital as key inputs.

Make sure that patterns of key financial and operating ratios are consistent with economic logic:

- *Are the patterns intended?* For example, does invested-capital turnover increase over time for sound economic reasons (economies of scale) or simply because you modeled future capital expenditures as a fixed percentage of revenues? Are future cash tax rates changing dramatically because you forecast deferred tax assets as a percentage of revenues or operating profit?

- *Are the patterns reasonable?* Avoid large step changes in key assumptions from one year to the next, because these will distort key ratios and could lead to false interpretations. For example, a large single-year improvement in capital efficiency could make capital expenditures in that year negative, leading to an unrealistically high cash flow.

- *Are the patterns consistent with industry dynamics?* In certain cases, reasonable changes in key inputs can lead to unintended consequences. Exhibit 13.1 presents price and cost data for a hypothetical company that competes in a competitive industry. To keep pace with inflation, you forecast the company's prices to increase by 3 percent per year. Because of cost efficiencies, operating costs are expected to drop to by 2 percent per year. In isolation, each rate appears innocuous. Computing ROIC reveals a significant trend. Between year 1 and year 10, ROIC grows from 9.3 to 39.2 percent—unlikely in a competitive industry. Since cost advantages are difficult to protect, competition is likely to mimic production and lower prices to capture share. A good model will highlight this economic inconsistency.

- Is a steady state reached for the company's economics by the end of the explicit forecasting period (that is, when you apply a continuing-value formula)? A company achieves a steady state only when its free cash flows are growing at a constant rate. If this is not the case, extend the explicit forecast period while keeping the key performance ratios constant.

EXHIBIT 13.1 **ROIC Impact of Small Changes: Sample Price and Cost Trends**

dollars

	Year 1	Year 2	Year 3	Year 4	Year 5	...	Year 10	Growth (percent)
Price	50.0	51.5	53.0	54.6	56.3	...	65.2	3.0
Number of units	100.0	103.0	106.1	109.3	112.6	...	130.5	
Revenue	5,000.0	5,304.5	5,627.5	5,970.3	6,333.9	...	8,512.2	
Cost per unit	43.0	42.1	41.3	40.5	39.7	...	35.9	−2.0
Number of units	100.0	103.0	106.1	109.3	112.6	...	130.5	
Cost	4,300.0	4,340.4	4,381.2	4,422.4	4,464.0	...	4,677.8	
Profit	700.0	964.1	1,246.3	1,547.9	1,869.9	...	3,834.4	
Invested capital	7,500.0	7,725.0	7,956.8	8,195.5	8,441.3	...	9,785.8	
ROIC (percent)	9.3	12.5	15.7	18.9	22.2	...	39.2	

Are the Results Plausible?

Once you believe the model is technically sound and economically consistent, you should test whether its valuation results are plausible.

If the company is listed, compare your results with the market value. If your estimate is far from the market value, do not jump to the conclusion that the market is wrong. Your default assumption should be that the market is right, unless you have specific indications that not all relevant information has been incorporated in the share price—for example, due to a small free float or low liquidity of the stock.

Also perform a sound multiples analysis. Calculate the implied forward-looking valuation multiples of the operating value over, for example, earnings before interest, taxes, and amortization (EBITA), and compare these with equivalently defined multiples of traded peer-group companies. Chapter 14 describes how to do a proper multiples analysis. Make sure you can explain any significant differences with peer-group companies in terms of the companies' value drivers and underlying business characteristics or strategies.

SENSITIVITY ANALYSIS

With a robust model in hand, test how the company's value responds to changes in key inputs. Senior management can use sensitivity analysis to prioritize the actions most likely to affect value materially. From the investor's perspective, sensitivity analysis can focus on which inputs to investigate further and monitor more closely. Sensitivity analysis also helps bound the valuation range when there is uncertainty about the inputs.

EXHIBIT 13.2 **Sample Sensitivity Analysis**

Driver	Change	Valuation impact ($ million)
Margin	1 percentage point reduction in selling expense	29
Growth	1 percentage point increase in price each year for the next five years	26
Growth	1 percentage point increase in output each year for the next five years	14
Margin	1 percentage point reduction in the operating tax rate	11
Capital	5-day reduction in inventory	8

Assessing the Impact of Individual Drivers

Start by testing each input one at a time to see which has the largest impact on the company's valuation. In Exhibit 13.2, we present a sample sensitivity analysis. Among the alternatives presented, a permanent one percentage point reduction in selling expenses has the greatest effect on the company's valuation.[1] The analysis will also show which drivers have the least impact on value. Too often, we find our clients focusing on actions that are easy to measure but fail to affect value very much.

Although an input-by-input sensitivity analysis will increase your knowledge about which inputs drive the valuation, its use is limited. First, inputs rarely change in isolation. For instance, an increase in selling expenses is likely to accompany an increase in revenue growth. Second, when two inputs are changed simultaneously, interactions can cause the combined effect to differ from the sum of the individual effects. Therefore, you cannot compare a one percentage point increase in selling expenses with a one percentage point increase in growth. If there are interactions in the movements of inputs, the one-by-one analysis would miss them. To capture possible interactions, you need to analyze trade-offs.

Analyzing Trade-Offs

Strategic choices typically involve trade-offs between inputs into your valuation model. For instance, raising prices leads to fewer purchases, lowering inventory results in more missed sales, and entering new markets often affects both growth and margin. Exhibit 13.3 presents an analysis that measures the impact on a valuation when two inputs are changed simultaneously. Based on an EBITA margin of 14 percent and revenue growth of 3 percent (among other forecasts), a hypothetical company is currently valued at $365 million.

---

[1] Some analysts test the impact of both positive and negative changes to each driver and then plot the results from largest to smallest variation. Given its shape, the resulting chart is commonly known as a "tornado" chart.

EXHIBIT 13.3 **Valuation Isocurves by Growth and Margin**

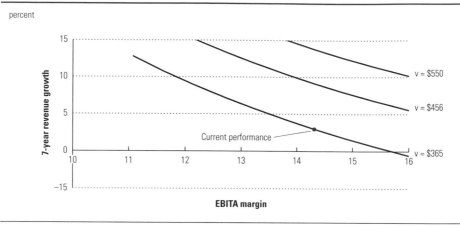

The curve drawn through this point represents all the possible combinations of EBITA margin and revenue growth that lead to the same valuation. (Economists call this an isocurve.) To increase the valuation by 25 percent (from $365 million to $456 million), the organization needs to move northeast to the next isocurve. Using this information, management can set performance targets that are consistent with the company's valuation aspirations and competitive environment.

When performing sensitivity analysis, do not limit yourself to changes in financial variables. Check how changes in sector-specific nonfinancial value drivers affect the final valuation. For example, if you increase customer churn rates for a telecommunications company, does company value decrease? Can you explain with back-of-the-envelope estimates why the change is so large (or so small)?

CREATING SCENARIOS

Valuation requires a forecast, but the future can take many paths. A government might pass legislation affecting the entire industry. A new discovery could revolutionize a competitor's product portfolio. Since the future is never truly knowable, consider making financial projections under multiple scenarios. The scenarios should reflect different assumptions regarding future macroeconomic, industry, or business developments, as well as the corresponding strategic responses by industry players. Collectively, the scenarios should capture the future states of the world that would have the most impact on future value creation and a reasonable chance of occurrence. Assess how likely it is that the key assumptions underlying each scenario will change, and assign to each scenario a probability of occurrence.

When analyzing the scenarios, critically review your assumptions concerning the following variables:

- *Broad economic conditions:* How critical are these forecasts to the results? Some industries are more dependent on basic economic conditions than others are. Home building, for example, is highly correlated with the overall health of the economy. Branded food processing, in contrast, is less so.

- *Competitive structure of the industry:* A scenario that assumes substantial increases in market share is less likely in a highly competitive and concentrated market than in an industry with fragmented and inefficient competition.

- *Internal capabilities of the company* that are necessary to achieve the business results predicted in the scenario: Can the company develop its products on time and manufacture them within the expected range of costs?

- *Financing capabilities of the company* (which are often implicit in the valuation): If debt or excess marketable securities are excessive relative to the company's targets, how will the company resolve the imbalance? Should the company raise equity if too much debt is projected? Should the company be willing to raise equity at its current market price?

Complete the alternative scenarios suggested by the preceding analyses. The process of examining initial results may well uncover unanticipated questions that are best resolved by creating additional scenarios. In this way, the valuation process is inherently circular. Performing a valuation often provides insights that lead to additional scenarios and analyses.

In Exhibits 13.4 and 13.5, we provide a simplified example of a scenario approach to discounted cash flow (DCF) valuation. The company being valued faces great uncertainty because of a new-product launch for which it has spent considerable time and money on research and development (think of cellular phone makers moving from traditional cell phones to smart phones, such as Apple's iPhone). If the new product is a top seller, revenue growth will more than double over the next few years. Returns on invested capital will peak at above 20 percent and remain above 12 percent in perpetuity. If the product launch fails, however, growth will continue to erode as the company's current products become obsolete. Lower average selling prices will cause operating margins to fall. The company's returns on invested capital will decline to levels below the cost of capital, and the company will struggle to earn its cost of capital in the long term. Exhibit 13.4 presents forecasts on growth, operating margin, and capital efficiency that are consistent with each of these two scenarios.

Next, build a separate free cash flow model for each set of forecasts. Although not presented here, the resulting cash flow models are based on the

EXHIBIT 13.4 **Key Value Drivers by Scenario**

percent

		Financial forecasts							Scenario assessment
	2009A	2010	2011	2012	2013	2014	2015	C.V.	
Scenario 1									
Revenue growth	5.0	12.0	15.0	14.0	12.0	10.0	5.0	3.5	The new product introduction leads to a spike in revenue growth.
After-tax operating margin	7.5	9.0	11.0	14.0	14.0	12.0	10.0	8.0	Margins improve to best in class, as consumers pay a price premium for the product.
× Capital turnover (times)	1.5	1.4	1.3	1.4	1.5	1.6	1.6	1.6	Capital turnover drops slighly during the product launch as the company builds inventory to meet expected demand.
Return on invested capital	11.3	12.6	14.3	19.6	21.0	19.2	16.0	12.8	
Scenario 2									
Revenue growth	5.0	3.0	(1.0)	(1.0)	1.5	1.5	1.5	1.5	Revenue growth drops as competitors steal share.
Operating margins	7.5	7.0	6.5	6.0	5.5	5.5	6.5	6.5	Lower prices put pressure on margins; cost reductions cannot keep pace.
× Capital turnover (times)	1.5	1.4	1.4	1.4	1.3	1.3	1.3	1.3	Capital efficiency falls as price pressure reduces revenue. Inventory reductions mitigate fall.
Return on invested capital	11.3	9.8	9.1	8.4	7.2	7.2	8.5	8.5	

EXHIBIT 13.5 **Example of a Scenario Approach to DCF Valuation**

$ million

		Description
Scenario 1		
Value of operations	5,044	
Nonoperating assets	672	The company's new product launch reinvigorates
Enterprise value	5,716	revenue growth. Higher average selling prices lead to increased operating margins and consequently higher ROICs. ROICs decay as the new product matures, but
Interest-bearing debt	(2,800)	future offerings keep ROIC above the cost of capital.
Equity value	2,916	
Scenario 2		
Value of operations	1,993	The company launches a new product, but the product
Nonoperating assets	276	is seen as inferior to other offerings. Revenue growth
Enterprise value	2,269	remains stagnant and even declines as prices erode and the company loses share. Returns on capital eventually
Interest-bearing debt	(2,269)	rise to the cost of capital as management refocuses on
Equity value	–	cost reduction.

67% probability

Probability-weighted equity value: 1,954

33% probability

DCF methodology outlined in Chapter 6. Exhibit 13.5 presents the valuation results. In the case of a successful product launch, the DCF value of operations equals $5,044 million. The nonoperating assets consist primarily of nonconsolidated subsidiaries, and given their own reliance on the product launch, they are valued at the implied NOPLAT multiple for the parent company, $672 million. A comprehensive scenario will examine all items, including nonoperating items, to make sure they are consistent with the scenario's underlying premise. We next deduct the face value of the debt outstanding at $2,800 million (we assume interest rates have not changed, so the market value of debt equals the face value). The resulting equity value is $2,916 million.

If the product launch fails, the DCF value of operations is only $1,993 million. In this scenario, the value of the subsidiaries is much lower ($276 million), as their business outlook has deteriorated due to the failure of the new product. The value of the debt is no longer $2,800 million in this scenario. Instead, the debt holders would end up with $2,269 million by seizing the enterprise. In scenario 2, the common equity would have no value.

Given the approximately two-thirds probability of success for the product, the probability-weighted equity value across both scenarios amounts to $1,954 million. Since estimates of scenario probabilities are likely to be rough at best, determine the range of probabilities that point to a particular strategic action. For instance, if this company were an acquisition target available for $1.5 billion, any probability of a successful launch above 50 percent would lead to value creation. Whether the probability is 67 percent or 72 percent does not affect the decision outcome.

When using the scenario approach, make sure to generate a complete valuation buildup from value of operations to equity value. Do not shortcut the process by deducting the face value of debt from the scenario-weighted value of operations. Doing this would seriously underestimate the equity value because the value of debt is different in each scenario. In this case, the equity value would be undervalued by $175 million ($2,800 million face value minus $2,625 million probability-weighted value of debt).[2] A similar argument holds for nonoperating assets.

Creating scenarios also helps you understand the company's key priorities. In our example, reducing costs or cutting capital expenditures in the downside scenario will not meaningfully affect value. Any improvements in the downside scenario whose value is less than $531 million ($2,800 million in face value less $2,269 million in market value) will accrue primarily to the debt holders. In contrast, increasing the odds of a successful launch has a much greater impact on shareholder value. Increasing the success probability from two-thirds to three-fourths would boost shareholder value by more than 10 percent.

VALUATION BY PARTS

Our analysis up to this point has focused on single-business companies. Many companies have multiple business units, each competing in segments with different economic characteristics. For instance, Dutch-based Philips competes in health care, consumer products, and lighting. U.S.-based Sunoco competes in gasoline refining, chemicals, and high-quality coke used to make steel. Since the economics for each company's segments are different, you must determine the company's aggregate operating value one business unit at time. By valuing the entire company with a single forecast, you risk missing critical trends and consequently distorting the valuation.

Exhibit 13.6 presents ROIC and growth by segment for ConsumerCo. This is a $425 million company with three business units: branded consumer products (the company sells well-known brands in personal care); private-label production (for large discount chains selling products under their own names); and organic products (premium products made with natural materials). The size of each bubble represents last year's revenue for the segment.

ConsumerCo has characteristics similar to many of the world's large companies. The company's primary business unit, branded consumer products, has returns well above its 9 percent cost of capital, but the business is mired in slow-growth mature markets. The closest adjacent market, private label, is growing quickly but does not match the returns of branded products. In fact,

---

[2] This also explains why using the market price of bonds or debt in your valuation can lead to errors if the bonds trade at a significant discount to their face value due to default risk (see Chapter 12's discussion of the treatment of debt as a nonequity claim). Deducting the market price of such bonds from the probability-weighted value of operations would be correct only if your assumptions on default scenarios and probabilities were to reflect precisely those of bond investors in the capital market.

EXHIBIT 13.6 **ConsumerCo: Revenue Growth and ROIC by Segment**

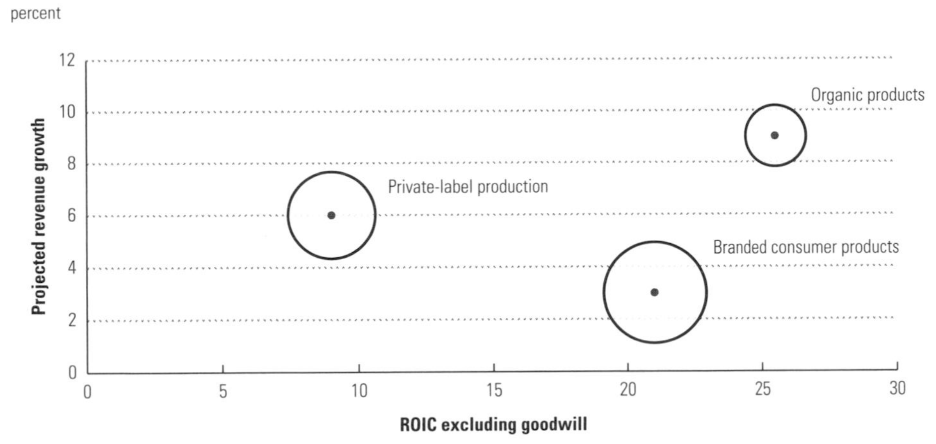

percent

Note: The size of each bubble represents last year's revenue for the segment.

private label's ROIC hovers around the cost of capital. The star, organic products, has both higher returns and high growth, but is it big enough to affect the company's valuation?

Exhibit 13.7 presents the operating value by segment for ConsumerCo. Not surprisingly, the high returns and large scale in branded products lead to the largest valuation ($364.9 million) of the three segments. Because the organic products segment combines high growth with high returns, organic products are a close second ($219.2 million), even though current revenues are only one-third those of branded products. Private label is only a small portion of value, contributing just 10 percent of the company's overall value. As a result, the segments have extremely different enterprise-value-to-EBITA multiples. Private label is valued at just 5.9 times EBITA, whereas the organic products segment is valued at 11.2 times. Note how the aggregate multiple (8.8 times) matches none of the businesses. Compare the valuation split with the revenue split presented at the right side of Exhibit 13.7. As in the case of the enterprise value multiples, the mismatch between revenue and value is dramatic.

The fact that the private-label business unit creates such a small proportion of ConsumerCo's aggregate valuation can have competitive implications. Imagine you manage a small, cost-efficient private-label company. Every day, it feels as if ConsumerCo competes against your business more and more. You fear ConsumerCo will use its large size to drive prices even lower. But can it? ConsumerCo's managers will likely face pressure to do just the opposite: to bring returns on invested capital in line with the ROICs of other divisions. Senior executives typically benchmark performance not just against competing companies, but also against other business units within their own company, even if they are in different industries from each other.

EXHIBIT 13.7 **ConsumerCo: Valuation by Segment**

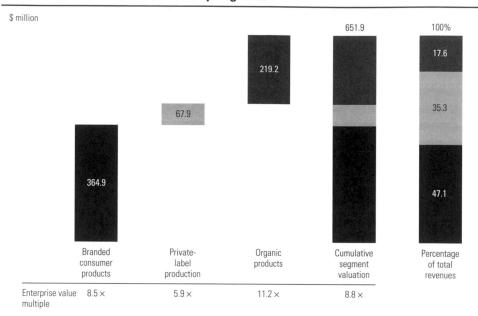

Over the next few pages, we highlight the complexities related to valuing a multibusiness company. Similar to valuing a single-business company, start by building a complete set of financial statements. Next, reorganize the financial statements to create NOPLAT, invested capital, ROIC, and free cash flow. Finally, discount each cash flow at a weighted average cost of capital that matches the risk of the business, rather than the aggregate cost of capital for the company.

Creating Business Unit Financial Statements

To value a company's individual business units, you need income statements, balance sheets, and cash flow statements. Ideally, these financial statements should approximate what the business units would look like if they were stand-alone companies. Creating the financial statements for business units requires consideration of three issues: allocating corporate overhead costs, dealing with intercompany transactions, and dealing with incomplete information when using public information.

Corporate costs Most multibusiness companies have shared services and corporate overhead, so you need to decide which costs should be allocated and which retained at the corporate level. For services that the corporate center provides, such as payroll, human resources, and accounting, allocate the costs by cost drivers. For example, the aggregate cost of human resource services

EXHIBIT 13.8 **Income Statement: Intercompany Eliminations**

$ millions

	Unit A	Unit B	Eliminations	Consolidated
External revenues	600	400	–	1,000
Internal revenues	200	–	(200)	–
Reported revenues	800	400	(200)	1,000
Cost of sales	(600)	(300)	200	(700)
Gross profit	200	100	–	300

provided by the corporate parent can be allocated by the number of employees in each business unit. When costs are incurred because the units are part of a larger company (for example, the CEO's compensation or the corporate art collection), do not allocate the costs. They should be retained as a corporate cost center and valued separately for two reasons: First, allocating corporate costs to business units reduces the comparability with pure-play business unit peers that don't incur such costs (most business units already have their own chief executives, CFOs, and controllers who are comparable to pure-play competitors). Second, keeping the corporate center as a separate unit reveals how much of a drag it creates on the company's value.

Intercompany sales   Sometimes business units provide goods and services to one another. To arrive at consolidated corporate results, accountants eliminate the internal revenues, costs, and profits to prevent double counting. Only revenues and costs from external sources remain at the consolidated level.

Exhibit 13.8 demonstrates how transactions between business units are accounted for. Unit A sells raw materials to the open market. It also provides Unit B with $200 million in materials. Unit B uses these raw materials, as well as others, to generate $400 million in external revenue. To consolidate the income statement, the company's accountants will eliminate Unit A's internally generated revenue of $200 million and $200 million in Unit B's cost of goods sold. Since one unit's revenues are another unit's costs, the cash flow benefits derived by one unit are offset by the cash outflows faced by the other. Consequently, the DCF value of Unit A (including internal revenues and profit) plus the DCF value of Unit B will equal the overall entity.[3]

Although aggregate cash flow and consequently enterprise DCF valuation will be unaffected by intersegment revenues, applying industry revenue multiples to each business unit in order to triangulate an aggregate company

---

[3] The cumulative value of business units will equal the aggregate value, but the value split depends on the level of transfer pricing between the two units. The higher the transfer price, the more aggregate value is transferred to Unit A. To accurately value each business unit, record intercompany transfers at the value that would be transacted with third parties. Otherwise, the relative value of the business units will be distorted.

EXHIBIT 13.9 **ConsumerCo: Publicly Available Business Unit Data**

$ million

	Branded consumer products	Private-label production	Organic products	Corporate	Consolidated
Revenues	200.0	150.0	75.0	–	425.0
Intersegment revenues	15.0	50.0	–	–	65.0
Operating profit	43.1	11.5	19.6	(5.0)	69.2
Depreciation[1]	20.0	11.3	7.5	1.0	39.8
Capital expenditures	22.0	16.9	22.5	(1.0)	60.4
Assets	177.8	111.1	66.7	10.0	365.6

[1] Included in operating profit.

valuation can lead to overestimation of company value. Since Unit A reports $800 million in revenue and Unit B reports $400 million in revenue, the aggregate unit revenues are $1.2 billion, which is $200 million higher than the actual amount. Applying a 2× revenue multiple (for example) to each business leads to an aggregate value of $2.4 billion, which is $400 million higher than what is appropriate. A similar distortion occurs with operating profit multiples.[4] To use multiples, you must eliminate intercompany revenues and profits.

Reorganizing the financial statements with incomplete information   If you are valuing a multibusiness company from the outside in, you will not have complete financial statements by business unit. Exhibit 13.9 uses ConsumerCo to show the disclosure typical of U.S. listed companies. (Disclosures under International Financial Reporting Standards [IFRS] are similar.) Under U.S. Generally Accepted Accounting Principles (GAAP), companies disclose revenues, operating profit (or something similar such as EBITA), depreciation, capital expenditures, and assets by segment. You need to convert these items to NOPLAT and invested capital.

NOPLAT   To estimate NOPLAT, start with reported EBITA by business unit. Next, allocate operating taxes, the pension adjustment (to eliminate pension accounting), and the operating lease adjustment (eliminating interest expense embedded in rental expense) to each of the business units. (For more information on these adjustments, see Chapter 7.) Use the effective overall corporate tax rate for all business units unless you have information to estimate each unit's tax rate. After estimating NOPLAT, reconcile the sum of all

---

[4] If Unit B orders raw materials from Unit A but holds the raw materials in inventory, cumulative business unit profits will overstate aggregate profits. This occurs because Unit A books the profit from the transaction, but Unit B does not book the cost (i.e., the transaction does not appear on Unit B's income statement). Applying a profit multiple to business unit earnings will therefore overstate the company's value.

business unit NOPLATs to consolidated net income in order to ensure that all adjustments have been properly made.

Invested capital   To estimate invested capital, start with total assets by business unit, and subtract estimates for nonoperating assets and non-interest-bearing operating liabilities. (Note that many companies will hold nonoperating assets at the corporate level, not the unit level. In this case, no adjustment is necessary.) Nonoperating assets include excess cash, investments in nonconsolidated subsidiaries, pension assets, and deferred tax assets. To measure invested capital excluding goodwill, subtract allocated goodwill by business unit.

Non-interest-bearing operating liabilities include accounts payable, taxes payable, and accrued expenses. They can be allocated to the business units by either revenue or total assets. Do not treat intercompany payables as an operating liability.[5] Once you have estimated invested capital for the business units and corporate center, reconcile these estimates with the total invested capital derived from the consolidated statements.

Cost of Capital

Each business unit should be valued at its own cost of capital, because the systematic risk (beta) of operating cash flows and their ability to support debt—that is, the implied capital structure—will differ by business unit. To determine a business unit's cost of capital, you need the unit's target capital structure, its cost of equity (as determined by its beta), and its cost of borrowing. (For details on estimating the weighted average cost of capital, see Chapter 11.)

First, estimate each business unit's target capital structure. We recommend using the median capital structure of publicly traded peers, especially if most peers have similar capital structures. Next, using the debt levels based on industry medians, aggregate the business unit debt to see how the total compares with the company's total target debt level (not necessarily its current level).[6] If the sum of business unit debt differs from the consolidated company's target debt, we typically record the difference as a corporate item, valuing its

---

[5] Multibusiness companies typically manage cash and debt centrally for all business units. Business units with positive cash flow typically forward all cash generated to the corporate center, sometimes setting up an intercompany receivable from the corporate parent. Units with negative cash flow receive cash from the parent to pay their bills, setting up an intercompany payable to the parent. These intercompany receivables and payables are *not* like third-party receivables and payables, so they should not be treated as part of operating working capital. They should be treated like intercompany equity in the calculation of invested capital.

[6] The allocation of debt among business units for legal or internal corporate purposes is generally irrelevant to the economic analysis of the business units. The legal or internal debt is generally driven by tax purposes or is an accident of history (cash-consuming units have lots of debt). These allocations rarely are economically meaningful and should be ignored.

tax shield separately (or tax cost when the company is more conservatively financed). We do this to minimize differences between the cost of capital and the valuation of the business units relative to their peers.

Next, determine the levered beta and cost of equity for each business unit. To determine a business unit's beta, first estimate an unlevered sector median beta, as detailed in Chapter 10. Relever the beta using the same business unit capital structure derived previously. For corporate-center cash flows, use a weighted average of the business unit costs of capital.

When you value a company by summing the business unit values, there is no need to estimate a corporate-wide cost of capital or to reconcile the business unit betas with the corporate beta. The individual business unit betas are more relevant than the corporate beta, which is subject to significant estimation error, especially when the company is widely diversified.

THE ART OF VALUATION

Valuation can be highly sensitive to small changes in assumptions about the future. Take a look at the sensitivity of a typical company with a forward-looking price-to-earnings ratio of 15 to 16. Increasing the cost of capital for this company by half a percentage point will decrease the value by approximately 10 percent. Changing the growth rate for the next 15 years by one percentage point annually will change the value by about 6 percent. For high-growth companies, the sensitivity is even greater. The sensitivity is highest when interest rates are low, as they have been since the late 1990s.

In light of this sensitivity, it should be no surprise that the market value of a company fluctuates over time. Historical volatilities for a typical stock over the past several years have been around 25 percent per annum. Taking this as an estimate for future volatility, the market value of a typical company could well fluctuate around its expected value by 15 percent over the next month.[7]

We typically aim for a valuation range of plus or minus 15 percent, which is similar to the range used by many investment bankers. Even valuation professionals cannot always generate exact estimates. In other words, keep your aspirations for precision in check.

REVIEW QUESTIONS

1. You are valuing DistressCo, a company struggling to hold market share. The company currently generates $120 million in revenue, but its revenue is expected to shrink to $100 million next year. Cost of sales currently equals

---

[7] Based on a 95 percent confidence interval for the end-of-month price of a stock with an expected return of 9 percent per year.

$90 million and depreciation equals $18 million. Working capital equals $36 million and equipment equals $120 million. Using this data, construct operating profit and invested capital for the current year. You decide to build an as-is valuation of DistressCo. To do this, you forecast each ratio (such as cost of sales to revenues) at its current level. Based on this forecast method, what are operating profits and invested capital expected to be next year? What are two critical operating assumptions (identify one for profits, and one for capital) embedded in this forecast method?

2. You decide to value a steady-state company using probability-weighted scenario analysis. In Scenario 1, NOPLAT is expected to grow at 6 percent and ROIC equals 16 percent. In Scenario 2, NOPLAT is expected to grow at 2 percent and ROIC equals 8 percent. Next year's NOPLAT is expected to equal $100 million and the weighted average cost of capital is 10 percent. Using the key value driver formula introduced in Chapter 2, what is the enterprise value in each scenario? If each scenario is equally likely, what is the enterprise value for the company?

3. A colleague recommends a shortcut to value the company in Question 2. Rather than compute each scenario separately, he recommends averaging each input, such that growth equals 4 percent and ROIC equals 12 percent. Will this lead to the same enterprise value found in Question 2? Which method is correct? Why?

4. Using an Internet search tool, locate Procter & Gamble's investor relations web site. Under "Financial Reporting," you will find the company's 2009 annual report. In the annual report's section titled "Management's Discussion and Analysis," you will find growth by segment. How many segments does Procter & Gamble report? Using 2009 as a proxy, does each segment have the same organic growth characteristics? Set organic growth equal to sum of volume excluding acquisitions, price, and mix/other. Based on growth by segment, should Procter & Gamble be valued as a whole, or should individual segments be valued separately?

5. Using an Internet search tool, locate Procter & Gamble's investor relations web site. Under "Financial Reporting," you will find the company's 2009 annual report. In Note 11 of the 2009 annual report, you will find financials by segment. What are the operating margins by segment? Based on operating margins by segment, should Procter & Gamble be valued as a whole, or should individual segments be valued separately?

14

Using Multiples to Triangulate Results

Discounted cash flow (DCF) analysis is the most accurate and flexible method for valuing projects, divisions, and companies. Any analysis, however, is only as accurate as the forecasts it relies on. A careful multiples analysis—comparing a company's multiples with those of similar companies—can be useful in making such forecasts and the DCF valuations they generate more accurate. Such an analysis can help test the plausibility of cash flow forecasts, explain mismatches between a company's performance and those of its competitors, and support useful discussions about which companies the market believes are strategically positioned to create more value than other industry players.

Exhibit 14.1 presents the trading multiples for eight large specialty retailers, including Home Depot, as of December 2009. (Comparing Home Depot with only home improvement competitors would have been more revealing, but other large-scale home improvement retailers, such as Menards, are not publicly traded.) The left side of the exhibit presents four types of market data: the value of equity (referred to as market capitalization), the value of debt, gross enterprise value (the combined value of debt and equity), and net enterprise value (gross enterprise value less nonoperating assets).[1] The right side of the exhibit presents three multiples: net enterprise value divided first by next year's projection of revenue, then by earnings before interest, taxes, depreciation, and amortization (EBITDA), and finally by earnings before interest, taxes, and amortization of acquired intangibles (EBITA). For example, to compute Home Depot's enterprise-value-to-EBITA multiple, divide net enterprise

---

[1] When defining multiples, many practitioners refer to enterprise value as debt plus the market value of equity minus cash. We refine this definition to debt plus equity minus the value of all nonoperating assets, and name the resulting value *net enterprise value*. In Chapter 6, we defined debt plus equity minus nonoperating assets as *core operating value*.

EXHIBIT 14.1   **Specialty Retail: Trading Multiples, December 2009**

$ million

Ticker	Company	Market capitalization	Debt and debt equivalents	Gross enterprise value	Net enterprise value	1-year forward multiples (times)		
						Revenue	EBITDA	EBITA
AZO	AutoZone	7,915	2,783	10,698	10,535	1.5	7.5	8.5
BBBY	Bed Bath & Beyond	10,368	–	10,368	9,477	1.3	9.5	11.3
BBY	Best Buy	16,953	2,476	19,429	18,525	0.4	6.0	7.4
HD	Home Depot	49,601	11,434	61,035	60,510	0.9	9.2	13.0
LOW	Lowe's	34,814	6,060	40,874	39,960	0.8	8.3	12.2
PETM	PetSmart	3,386	634	4,019	3,867	0.7	6.5	10.4
SHW	Sherwin-Williams	7,029	1,099	8,128	8,044	1.1	9.5	11.4
SPLS	Staples	18,054	3,518	21,572	20,938	0.9	10.1	13.2
				Mean		1.0	8.3	10.9
				Median		0.9	8.8	11.4
				Deviation (percent)[1]		38.1	17.3	18.2

[1] Deviation = standard deviation/median.

value ($60,510 million) by next year's projection of EBITA ($4,645 million);[2] the result equals 13.0. Because the multiple uses a projection, rather than the last year's reported figure, it is called a forward multiple.

For large specialty retailers, multiples range from 7.4 times to 13.2 times EBITA. Most tables show the mean and median, but as you'll see later in this chapter, those statistics are irrelevant unless the companies in the sample have similar prospects for growth and return on invested capital (ROIC). Home Depot and Lowe's trade at the high end of this range, at 13.0 times and 12.2 times respectively. Does a high multiple mean Home Depot is overvalued? No—as we discuss later in this chapter, their higher multiples are due to unusually low current earnings relative to expected long-term performance.[3]

To carry out a useful analysis of comparable multiples, keep in mind three requirements:

1. *Use the right multiple.* For most analyses, enterprise value to EBITA is the best multiple for comparing valuations across companies. Although the price-to-earnings (P/E) ratio is widely used, it is distorted by capital structure and nonoperating gains and losses.

[2] The one-year forward projection of Home Depot's EBITA equals the consensus analyst projection reported by Thomson One Banker.

[3] Home Depot margins fell dramatically during the financial crisis of 2008. Homeowners who were actively renovating before 2008 stopped purchasing home improvement supplies once the housing market collapsed. Analysts predict an improvement in Home Depot's margins and cash flow, but current earnings do not reflect this.

2. *Calculate the multiple in a consistent manner.* Base the numerator (value) and denominator (earnings) on the same underlying assets. For instance, if you exclude excess cash from value, exclude interest income from the earnings.

3. *Use the right peer group.* A set of industry peers is a good place to start. Refine the sample to peers that have similar outlooks for long-term growth and return on invested capital (ROIC).

Once you have created an appropriate peer group and properly measured the multiples, you'll often find that differences in multiples can be explained by differences in companies' performances or an earnings estimate that is based on unrepresentative performance. For this reason, avoid using an average or median multiple to describe an industry. An average multiple ignores critical differences in ROIC and growth potential across companies.

In this chapter, we demonstrate the requirements for carrying out a robust analysis of comparable multiples. We examine a range of alternative multiples, including, for instance, the enterprise-value-to-revenue multiple and the price-to-earnings-growth (PEG) ratio. We conclude the chapter with a discussion of nonfinancial multiples.

USING THE RIGHT MULTIPLE

When computing and comparing industry multiples, always start with enterprise value to EBITA. It tells more about a company's value than any other multiple. To show why, we return to the key value driver formula created in Chapter 2. The key value driver is a cash-flow-based valuation formula that has been rearranged to focus on the drivers of value: next year's net operating profit less adjusted taxes (NOPLAT), return on invested capital (ROIC), growth (g), and the weighted average cost of capital (WACC):

$$\text{Value} = \frac{\text{NOPLAT}_{t=1}\left(1 - \frac{g}{\text{ROIC}}\right)}{\text{WACC} - g}$$

To build a pretax enterprise value multiple, disaggregate NOPLAT into EBITA and the company's operating tax rate (T):

$$\text{Value} = \frac{\text{EBITA}\,(1 - T)\left(1 - \frac{g}{\text{ROIC}}\right)}{\text{WACC} - g}$$

and divide both sides by EBITA:

$$\frac{\text{Value}}{\text{EBITA}} = \frac{(1 - T)\left(1 - \frac{g}{\text{ROIC}}\right)}{\text{WACC} - g}$$

The resulting equation is an algebraic representation of the commonly used multiple enterprise value (EV) to EBITA. The multiple is similar to the price-to-earnings (P/E) ratio but focuses on enterprise value, rather than share price. From the equation, we can see that four factors drive the EV-to-EBITA multiple: the company's growth rate, its return on invested capital, the operating tax rate, and the cost of capital. If you limit your analysis to domestic companies in the same industry, the tax rate and cost of capital will be similar across peers, improving comparability. Conversely, growth and ROIC often differ across companies, so you should not expect multiples to be identical across an industry.

Exhibit 14.2 presents the distribution of EV-to-EBITA multiples for all non-financial companies in the S&P 500. The majority fall between 7 times and 11 times EBITA. If the company or industry you are examining falls outside this range, make sure to identify the reason. In the case of Home Depot, which trades at 13.0 times one-year forward EBITA, operating profits are well below the company's historical average. With the denominator lower than usual, the resulting multiple is higher than usual. Computing the enterprise value multiple at 2005 margin levels, the multiple is 8.0, well within the standard range (more on this later in the chapter).

EXHIBIT 14.2   **S&P 500:**[1] **Distribution of Enterprise Value to EBITA, December 2009**

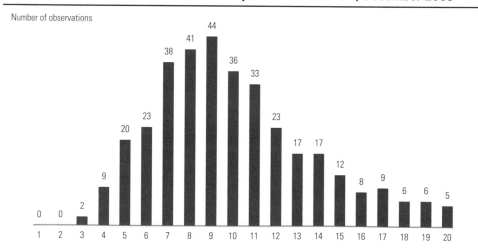

[1] Excluding financial institutions, real estate companies, and companies with extremely small or negative EBITA.

Why EV to EBITA, Not Price to Earnings?

Although widely reported, the price-to-earnings multiple has two major flaws. First, the P/E is affected by a company's capital structure, not just its operating performance. Second, unlike EBITA, net income is calculated after nonoperating items such as amortization of intangible assets and one-time gains and losses. Thus, a nonoperating loss, such as a noncash write-off, can significantly lower earnings, causing the P/E to be artificially high.

Throughout this book, we have focused on the drivers of operating performance—ROIC, growth, and free cash flow—because the traditional metrics, such as return on assets and return on equity, mix the effects of operations and capital structure. The same logic holds for multiples. Since P/Es mix capital structure and nonoperating items with expectations of operating performance, a comparison of P/Es is a less reliable guide to companies' relative value than a comparison of EV to EBITA.

To show how capital structure distorts the P/E, Exhibit 14.3 presents financial data for four companies, named A through D. Companies A and B trade at 10 times enterprise value to EBITA, and Companies C and D trade at 25 times enterprise value to EBITA. In each pair, the companies have different P/Es. Companies A and B differ only in how their business is financed, not in their operating performance. The same is true for Companies C and D.

Since Companies A and B trade at typical enterprise value multiples, the price-to-earnings ratio drops for the company with higher leverage. This is because the enterprise-value-to-EBITA ratio ($1,000 million/$100 million = 10 times) is lower than the ratio of debt value to interest expense ($400 million/ $20 million = 20 times). Since the blend of debt (at 20 times) and pretax equity

EXHIBIT 14.3   **P/E Multiple Distorted by Capital Structure**

$ million

	Company A	Company B	Company C	Company D
Income statement				
EBITA	100	100	100	100
Interest expense	–	(20)	–	(25)
Earnings before taxes	100	80	100	75
Taxes	(40)	(32)	(40)	(30)
Net income	60	48	60	45
Market values				
Debt	–	400	–	500
Equity	1,000	600	2,500	2,000
Enterprise value (EV)	1,000	1,000	2,500	2,500
Multiples (times)				
EV to EBITA	10.0	10.0	25.0	25.0
Price to earnings	16.7	12.5	41.7	44.4

must equal the enterprise value (at 10 times), the pretax equity multiple (10 times for Company A and 7.5 times for Company B) must drop below 10 times to offset the greater weight placed on high multiple debt.[4] The opposite is true when enterprise value to EBITA exceeds the ratio of debt to interest expense (less common, given today's low interest rates). Company D has a higher P/E than Company C because Company D uses more leverage than Company C. In this case, a high pretax P/E (greater than 25 times) must be blended with the debt multiple (20 times) to generate an enterprise-value-to-EBITA multiple of 25 times.

A second problem with the P/E is that earnings include many nonoperating items, such as restructuring charges and write-offs. Since many nonoperating items are one-time events, multiples based on P/Es can be misleading. In 2002, AOL–Time Warner wrote off nearly $100 billion in goodwill and other intangibles. Even though EBITA equaled $6.4 billion, the company recorded a $98 billion net loss. Since earnings were negative, the company's 2002 P/E was meaningless.

Why EV to EBITA, Not EV to EBIT?

For nearly all peer groups, EBITA leads to a better enterprise value multiple than EBIT does. Amortization is an accounting artifact that arises from past acquisitions. Since it is not tied to future cash flows, amortization will distort an enterprise value multiple.[5] To analyze the distortion caused by acquisition-based amortization, Exhibit 14.4 presents financial data for three companies, named A, B, and C. Each company generates the same level of underlying operating profitability; they differ only in size. Company A is three-quarters the size of Company C, and Company B is one-quarter the size of Company C.

Concerned that its smaller size may lead to a competitive disadvantage, Company A purchases Company B. Assuming no synergies, the combined financial statements of Companies A and B are identical to Company C with

---

[4] In Appendix E, we derive the explicit relationship between a company's actual P/E and its unlevered P/E (PE_u)—the P/E as if the company were entirely financed with equity. Assuming no taxes, a company's P/E can be expressed as follows:

$$\frac{P}{E} = \bar{K} + \frac{\bar{K} - PE_u}{\left(\dfrac{D}{V}\right)(k_a)(PE_u) - 1} \quad \text{such that } \bar{K} = \frac{1}{k_d}$$

where k_d is the cost of debt and D/V is the ratio of debt to value. For companies with large unlevered P/Es (i.e., companies with significant opportunities for future value creation), P/E systematically increases with leverage. Conversely, companies with small unlevered P/Es would exhibit a drop in P/E as leverage rises.

[5] Depreciation and amortization are both noncash expenses. Unlike amortization, however, depreciation of physical assets must be replaced to maintain ongoing operations. Since the level of depreciation is a good predictor of future cash outlays, it should be included in the enterprise value multiple.

EXHIBIT 14.4   **Enterprise-Value-to-EBIT Multiple Distorted by Acquisition Accounting**

$ million

	Before acquisition			After A acquires B	
	Company A	**Company B**	**Company C**	**Company A + B**	**Company C**
EBIT					
Revenues	375	125	500	500	500
Cost of sales	(150)	(50)	(200)	(200)	(200)
Depreciation	(75)	(25)	(100)	(100)	(100)
Amortization	–	–	–	(25)	–
EBIT	150	50	200	175	200
Invested capital					
Organic capital	750	250	1,000	1,000	1,000
Acquired intangibles	–	–	–	125	–
Invested capital	750	250	1,000	1,125	1,000
Enterprise value	1,125	375	1,500	1,500	1,500
Multiples (times)					
EV to EBITA	5.0	5.0	5.0	5.0	5.0
EV to EBIT	7.5	7.5	7.5	8.6	7.5

two exceptions: acquired intangibles and amortization. Acquired intangibles are recognized when a company is purchased for more than its book value. In this case, Company B was purchased for $375 million, which is $125 million greater than its book value. If these acquired intangibles are separable and identifiable, such as patents, they must be amortized over the estimated life of the asset. Assuming an asset life of five years, $25 million in amortization will be recorded each year.

At the bottom of Exhibit 14.4, we report enterprise value multiples using EBITA and EBIT, both before and after the acquisition. Since all three companies generate the same level of operating performance, they trade at identical multiples before the acquisition. Following the acquisition, however, amortization expense causes EBIT to drop for the combined company and the enterprise value-to-EBIT multiple to rise. This rise in the multiple does not reflect a premium, however: remember, no synergies were created. It is merely an accounting artifact. Companies that acquire other companies must recognize amortization, whereas companies that grow organically have none to recognize. To avoid forming a distorted picture of their relative operating performance, use enterprise value-to-EBITA multiples.

In certain industries, such as software, amortization is recorded because of capitalized investments rather than acquisitions. In these cases, separate software amortization from acquisition amortization and subtract the software amortization from EBITDA to compute EBITA. Do not subtract acquisition-related amortization.

Why EV to EBITA, Not EV to EBITDA?

A common alternative to the EBITA multiple is the EBITDA multiple. Many practitioners use EBITDA multiples because depreciation is, strictly speaking, a noncash expense, reflecting sunk costs, not future investment. This logic, however, does not apply uniformly. For many industries, depreciation of existing assets is the accounting equivalent of setting aside the future capital expenditure that will be required to replace the assets. Subtracting depreciation from the earnings of such companies therefore is necessary to understand their true value.

To see this, consider two companies that differ in only one aspect: in-house versus outsourced production. Company A manufactures its products using its own equipment, whereas Company B outsources manufacturing to a supplier. Exhibit 14.5 provides financial data for each company. Since Company A owns its equipment, it recognizes significant annual depreciation—in this case, $200 million. Company B has less equipment, so its depreciation is only $50 million. However, Company B's supplier will include its own depreciation costs in its price, and Company B will consequently pay more for its raw materials. Because of this difference, Company B generates EBITDA of only $350 million, versus $500 million for Company A. This difference in EBITDA will lead to differing multiples: 6.0 times for Company A versus 8.6 times for Company B. Does this mean Company B trades at a valuation premium? No, when Company A's depreciation is deducted from its earnings, both companies trade at 10.0 times EBITA.

When computing the EV-to-EBITDA multiple in the previous example, we failed to recognize that Company A (the company that owns its equipment) will

EXHIBIT 14.5 **Enterprise-Value-to-EBITDA Multiple Distorted by Capital Investment**

$ million

	Company A	Company B		Company A	Company B
Income statement			**Free cash flow**		
Revenues	1,000	1,000	NOPLAT	210	210
Raw materials	(100)	(250)	Depreciation	200	50
Operating costs	(400)	(400)	Gross cash flow	410	260
EBITDA	500	350			
			Investment in working capital	(60)	(60)
Depreciation	(200)	(50)	Capital expenditures	(200)	(50)
EBITA	300	300	Free cash flow	150	150
Operating taxes	(90)	(90)	Enterprise value	3,000	3,000
NOPLAT	210	210			
Multiples (times)					
EV to EBITA	10.0	10.0			
EV to EBITDA	6.0	8.6			

have to expend cash to replace aging equipment ($200 million for Company A versus $50 million for Company B). Since capital expenditures are recorded in free cash flow and not NOPLAT, the EBITDA multiple is distorted.

In certain situations, EBITDA scales a company's valuation better than EBITA. These occur when current depreciation is not an accurate predictor of future capital expenditures. For instance, consider two companies, each of which owns a machine that produces identical products. Both machines have the same cash-based operating costs, and each company's products sell for the same price. If one company paid more for its equipment (for whatever reason—perhaps poor negotiation), it will have higher depreciation and, thus, lower EBITA. Valuation, however, is based on future discounted cash flow, not past profits. And since both companies have identical cash flow, they should have identical values.[6] We would therefore expect the two companies to have identical multiples. Yet, because EBITA differs across the two companies, their multiples will differ as well.

Use Forward-Looking Multiples

When building multiples, the denominator should use a forecast of profits, rather than historical profits. Unlike backward-looking multiples, forward-looking multiples are consistent with the principles of valuation—in particular, that a company's value equals the present value of future cash flow, not sunk costs. Second, forward-looking earnings are typically normalized, meaning they better reflect long-term cash flows by avoiding one-time past charges.

Empirical evidence shows that forward-looking multiples are indeed more accurate predictors of value than historical multiples are. One empirical study examined the characteristics and performance of historical multiples versus forward industry multiples for a large sample of companies trading on U.S. exchanges.[7] When multiples for individual companies were compared with their industry multiples, their historical earnings-to-price (E/P) ratios had 1.6 times the standard deviation of one-year forward E/P ratios (6.0 percent versus 3.7 percent). Other research, which used multiples to predict the prices of 142 initial public offerings, also found that multiples based on forecast earnings outperformed those based on historical earnings.[8] As the analysis moved from multiples based on historical earnings to multiples based on one- and two-year forecasts, the average pricing error fell from 55.0 percent to 43.7 percent to

---

[6] Since depreciation is tax deductible, a company with higher depreciation will have a smaller tax burden. Lower taxes lead to higher cash flows and a higher valuation. Therefore, even companies with identical EBITDAs will have different EBITDA multiples. The distortion, however, is less pronounced.

[7] J. Liu, D. Nissim, and J. Thomas, "Equity Valuation Using Multiples," *Journal of Accounting Research* 40 (2002): 135–172.

[8] M. Kim and J. R. Ritter, "Valuing IPOs," *Journal of Financial Economics* 53, no. 3 (1999): 409–437.

EXHIBIT 14.6   **Pharmaceuticals: Backward- and Forward-Looking Multiples, December 2007**

	Price/earnings	Enterprise value/EBITA	
	2007 net income	Estimated 2008 EBITA[1]	Estimated 2012 EBITA[1]
Merck	38	16	12
Bristol-Myers Squibb	27	17	12
Abbott	24	16	12
Eli Lilly	20	13	12
Novartis	20	17	13
Pfizer	19	13	13
Johnson & Johnson	18	15	12
Sanofi-Aventis	16	13	12
GlaxoSmithKline	14	15	12
Wyeth	13	12	12
AstraZeneca	12	15	12
Schering-Plough[2]	n/a	16	11

[1] Consensus analyst forecast.
[2] Schering-Plough recorded loss in 2007, so no multiple is reported.

28.5 percent, respectively, and the percentage of firms valued within 15 percent of their actual trading multiple increased from 15.4 percent to 18.9 percent to 36.4 percent.

To build a forward-looking multiple, choose a forecast year for EBITA that best represents the long-term prospects of the business. In periods of stable growth and profitability, next year's estimate will suffice. For companies generating extraordinary earnings (either too high or too low) or for companies whose performance is expected to change, use projections further out.

Exhibit 14.6 compares backward-looking P/Es with forward-looking EV-to-EBITA multiples for a set of large pharmaceutical companies. The backward-looking P/Es range from 12 to 38 times. One company, Schering-Plough, does not have a meaningful P/E, since its earnings were negative.[9] The ratio of enterprise value to the next year's projected EBITA also shows significant variation, as each company's current performance does not represent its long-term value well. When we extend the forecast window to five years, the variation across companies all but disappears.

[9] On November 19, 2007, Schering-Plough purchased Organon BioSciences and expensed $3.7 billion of in-process research and development related to the acquisition. This one-time charge caused net income to be negative.

CALCULATING THE MULTIPLE IN A CONSISTENT MANNER

In a recent presentation to a group of professional investors, we provided the audience with financial data on two companies. We then asked the audience which company traded at a higher enterprise value multiple. The results were surprising. Upon polling the group, we discovered there was no common agreement on how to compute the enterprise value multiple. A group of 100 professionals generated nearly a dozen different comparisons. Further investigation revealed that inconsistencies in how enterprise value was defined were the primary cause of this divergence.

There is only one approach to building an enterprise-value-to-EBITA multiple that is theoretically consistent. Enterprise value must include all investor capital but *only* the portion of value attributable to assets that generate EBITA. Including value in the numerator without including its corresponding income in the denominator will systematically distort the multiple upward. Conversely, failing to recognize a source of investor capital, such as minority interest, will understate the numerator, biasing the multiple downward. If the company holds nonoperating assets or has claims on enterprise value other than debt and equity, these must be accounted for.

Exhibit 14.7 presents three companies, A through C, each with identical enterprise-value-to-EBITA multiples. Company A holds only core operating assets and is financed by traditional debt and equity. Its combined market value of debt and equity equals $900 million. Dividing $900 million by $100 million in EBITA leads to an enterprise value multiple of 9 times.

Company B operates a similar business to Company A, but it also owns $100 million in excess cash and a minority stake in a nonconsolidated subsidiary, valued at $200 million. Since excess cash and nonconsolidated subsidiaries do not contribute to EBITA, they should not be included in the numerator of an EV-to-EBITA multiple. To compute an enterprise value that is consistent with EBITA, sum the market value of debt and equity ($1,200 million), and subtract the market value of nonoperating assets ($300 million).[10] Divide the resulting net enterprise value ($900 million) by EBITA ($100 million). The result is an EV-to-EBITA multiple of 9, which matches that of Company A. Failing to subtract the market value of nonoperating assets will lead to a multiple that is too high. For instance, when debt plus equity is divided by EBITA for Company B, the resulting multiple is 12 times, three points higher than the correct value of 9.

Similar adjustments must be made for financial claims other than debt and equity. To calculate enterprise value consistently with EBITA, you must include

---

[10] Alternatively, we could adjust the denominator rather than the numerator by adding interest income to EBITA. This definition of EV to EBITA is consistent but is biased upward. This is because the multiple for excess cash typically exceeds that of core operations. The greater the proportion of cash to overall value, the higher the resulting multiple.

EXHIBIT 14.7 **Enterprise Value Multiples and Complex Ownership**

$ million

	Company A	Company B	Company C
Partial income statement			
EBITA	100	100	100
Interest income	–	4	–
Interest expense	(18)	(18)	(18)
Earnings before taxes	82	86	82
Gross enterprise value			
Value of core operations	900	900	900
Excess cash	–	100	–
Nonconsolidated subsidiaries	–	200	–
Gross enterprise value	900	1,200	900
Debt	300	300	300
Minority interest	–	–	100
Market value of equity	600	900	500
Gross enterprise value	900	1,200	900
Multiples (times)			
Net enterprise value to EBITA	9.0	9.0	9.0
Debt plus equity minus cash to EBITA	9.0	11.0	9.0
Debt plus equity to EBITA	9.0	12.0	8.0

the market value of all financial claims, not just debt and equity. For Company C, outside investors hold a minority stake in a consolidated subsidiary. Since the minority stake's value is supported by EBITA, it must be included in the enterprise value calculation. Otherwise, the EV-to-EBITA multiple will be biased downward. For instance, when only debt plus equity is divided by EBITA for Company C, the resulting multiple is only 8 times.

As a general rule, any nonoperating asset that does not contribute to EBITA should be removed from enterprise value. This includes not only the market value of excess cash and nonconsolidated subsidiaries, as just mentioned, but also excess real estate, other investments, and the market value of prepaid pension assets. Financial claims include debt and equity, but also minority interest, the value of unfunded pension liabilities, and the value of employee grants outstanding. A detailed discussion of nonoperating assets and financial claims is presented in Chapter 12.

Advanced Adjustments

In Chapter 7, we described how EBITA can be distorted by operating leases and pension expense. Since a robust enterprise value multiple relies on a clean measure of EBITA, you must adjust EBITA for pension expense and operating leases before evaluating industry multiples.

Operating leases   Companies with significant operating leases will have an artificially low enterprise value (because we are ignoring the value of lease-based debt) and an artificially low EBITA (because rental expense includes interest costs). To compare companies with significantly different leasing policies, increase enterprise value by the value of operating leases and increase EBITA by the embedded interest. Because the values of operating leases and embedded interest are not reported and must be estimated, compute each company's multiple with and without the adjustment. The valuation of operating leases is discussed in Chapter 27.

Pension expense   Among other things, pension expense nets the expected return from plan assets from service costs. Since a company's management team chooses the level of expected return, two companies with identical pension plans could recognize different pension expenses. For instance, if Company A chooses a higher expected return than Company B, it will recognize a lower pension expense, and consequently a higher EBITA. This will distort Company A's enterprise value multiple downward. Chapter 27 describes how to adjust EBITA for pension expense.

USING THE RIGHT PEER GROUP

To analyze a company using comparable multiples, you must first select a peer group. Sometimes, a company lists its competitors in its annual report. If the company doesn't disclose its competition, you can use an industry classification system such as Standard Industrial Classification (SIC) codes.[11] Home Depot's SIC code, however, contains more than 20 companies, many of which are not directly comparable because they sell very different products or rely on different business models. A slightly better but proprietary system is the Global Industry Classification Standard (GICS) system, recently developed by Standard & Poor's and Morgan Stanley. A recent study found that GICS classifications do a significantly better job of explaining cross-sectional variations in valuation multiples, forecast and realized growth rates, research and development (R&D) expenditures, and key financial ratios.[12]

---

[11] Beginning in 1997, SIC codes were replaced by a major revision called the North American Industry Classification System (NAICS). The NAICS six-digit code not only provides for newer industries, but also reorganizes the categories on a production/process-oriented basis. The Securities and Exchange Commission (SEC), however, still lists companies by SIC code.

[12] S. Bhojraj, C. M. C. Lee, and D. Oler, "What's My Line? A Comparison of Industry Classification Schemes for Capital Market Research" (working paper, Ithaca, NY: Cornell University, May 2003), http://ssrn.com/abstract=356840.

EXHIBIT 14.8   **Factors for Choosing a Peer Group**

	Valuation multiples		Consensus projected financial performance			Performance characteristics
	Enterprise value/ EBITA		Sales growth, 2010–13 (percent)	EBITA margin, 2010 (percent)		
Company A	7		5	12		Low growth, low margin
Company B	7		3	6		
Company C	9		4	21		Low growth, high margin
Company D	9		3	24		
Company E	11		7	18		High growth, high margin
Company F	13		8	24		

Peers from the same industry typically trade at similar multiples but will still show variation. To see why, reexamine the enterprise value multiple presented earlier in the chapter:

$$\frac{\text{Value}}{\text{EBITA}} = \frac{(1 - T)\left(1 - \frac{g}{\text{ROIC}}\right)}{\text{WACC} - g}$$

This multiple is driven by growth, ROIC, the operating tax rate, and the weighted average cost of capital. Peers in the same industry will have similar risk profiles and consequently similar costs of capital. Peers from the same country will face similar tax rates. Growth and ROIC, however, can and often do vary within an industry.

The most common flaw is to compare a particular company's multiple with an average multiple of other companies in the same industry, regardless of differences in their performance. Once you narrow the peer group appropriately to those with comparable performance characteristics, multiples that otherwise seem far off base often become perfectly sensible. Exhibit 14.8 shows the multiples of six disguised technology companies and their projected financial performances. Our client, Company C, had simply looked at the left side of the exhibit and expressed discontent that its multiple was lower than the multiples of some of its peers. When you factor in all the companies' performances, however, the multiples make sense.

The companies fall into three performance buckets that align with different multiples. The companies with the lowest margins and low growth expectations had multiples of 7 times. The companies with low growth but high margins had multiples of 9 times. Finally, the companies with high growth and high margins had multiples of 11 to 13 times. Company C may disagree with its expected growth versus peers, but the multiple itself appears to be where it should be.

To choose a peer group, only use companies whose underlying characteristics, such as production methodology (capital intensive versus capital light), distribution channels (online versus bricks and mortar), and research and development (internal versus acquired), lead to similar growth and ROIC characteristics.

Once you have collected a list of peers and measured their multiples properly, the digging begins. You must answer a series of questions: Why are the multiples different across the peer group? Do certain companies in the group have superior products, better access to customers, recurring revenues, or economies of scale? If these strategic advantages translate to superior ROIC and growth rates, better-positioned companies should trade at higher multiples. You must understand what products they sell, how they generate revenue and profits, and how they grow.

ALTERNATIVE MULTIPLES

Although we have so far focused on enterprise value multiples based on EBITA, other multiples can prove helpful in certain situations. The enterprise-value-to-sales multiple can be useful in bounding valuations with volatile EBITA. The price-to-earnings-growth (PEG) ratio somewhat controls for different growth rates across companies. Nonfinancial multiples can be useful for young companies where current financial information is not relevant. We discuss each of these alternative multiples in this section.

Enterprise Value to Revenues

Generally speaking, price-to-sales multiples are not particularly useful for explaining company valuations. As shown earlier, an enterprise-value-to-EBITA multiple assumes similar growth rates and returns on incremental capital. An enterprise-value-to-sales multiple imposes an additional important restriction: similar operating margins on the company's existing business. For most industries, this restriction does not hold. Therefore, limit your analysis of the enterprise-to-sales multiple to companies with volatile earnings or other situations when earnings fail to represent long-term operating potential.

The relationship between enterprise value to sales and enterprise value to EBITA can be analyzed using the following disaggregation:[13]

$$\frac{\text{Value}}{\text{Revenue}} = \frac{\text{Value}}{\text{EBITA}} \times \frac{\text{EBITA}}{\text{Revenue}}$$

---

[13] The two sides are equivalent because EBITA cancels in the numerator and the denominator.

EXHIBIT 14.9   **S&P 500:[1] Revenue Multiple versus EBITA Margin, December 2009**

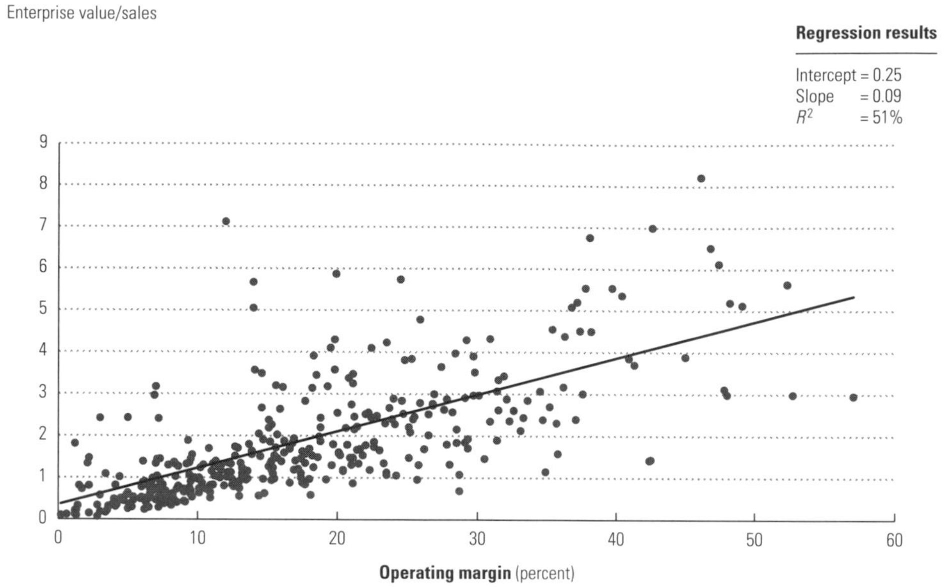

Enterprise value/sales

Regression results

Intercept = 0.25
Slope   = 0.09
R^2 = 51%

Operating margin (percent)

[1] Excluding financial institutions, real estate companies, and companies with negative EBITA margin.

Based on the equation, the EV-to-sales multiple equals the EV-to-EBITA multiple times operating margin. Thus, the EV-to-sales multiple is a function of ROIC and growth (discussed earlier in the chapter) as well as EBITA margin.

Exhibit 14.9 presents the relationship between enterprise value multiples and EBITA margins for nonfinancial companies in the S&P 500 in December 2009. According to this regression analysis, a company with zero EBITA margin would trade at 0.25 times revenue. Every one-percentage-point increase in EBITA margin translates to a 0.09 increase in the EV-to-sales multiple. For instance, the typical company with a 10 percent EBITA margin should trade near 1.15 times revenue (0.25 + 0.09 × 10).

The relationship between EV-to-sales multiples and margin holds for the specialty retailers presented in Exhibit 14.1. AutoZone trades at 1.5 times revenues, the highest of the peer set. Best Buy trades at just 0.4 times revenues. These multiples reflect the difference in EBITA margins between the two retailers. Between 2004 and 2008, AutoZone averaged 17 percent EBITA margins, whereas Best Buy averaged just 5 percent.

PEG Ratios

The enterprise-value-to-EBITA multiple will differ across companies when projections of ROIC and growth differ. To control for the variation in growth, analysts sometimes report a price-to-earnings-growth (PEG) ratio. The traditional way to calculate PEG ratios is to divide the P/E by expected growth in

EXHIBIT 14.10   **Specialty Retail: Enterprise-Value-Based PEG Ratios, December 2009**

Ticker	Company	Enterprise value/EBITA	Projected EBITA growth[1] (percent)	Enterprise PEG ratio
AZO	AutoZone	8.5	5.3	1.6
BBBY	Bed Bath & Beyond	11.3	9.3	1.2
BBY	Best Buy	7.4	8.6	0.9
HD	Home Depot	13.0	8.9	1.5
LOW	Lowe's	12.2	7.7	1.6
PETM	PetSmart	10.4	3.3	3.2
SHW	Sherwin-Williams	11.4	6.0	1.9
SPLS	Staples	13.2	7.7	1.7

[1] Consensus analyst projections of compounded annual EBITA growth between 2010 and 2014.

earnings per share, but our modified version is based on the enterprise value multiple:

$$\text{Adjusted PEG Ratio} = \frac{\text{Enterprise Value Multiple}}{100 \times \text{Expected EBITA Growth Rate}}$$

Exhibit 14.10 calculates the adjusted PEG ratios for the specialty retailers listed in Exhibit 14.1. To calculate Home Depot's adjusted PEG ratio (1.5 times), divide the company's forward-looking enterprise value multiple (13.0 times) by its expected EBITA growth rate (8.9 percent). Based on the adjusted PEG ratio, Home Depot trades at a slight premium to Lowe's. Using the key value driver formula as our guide, this is not surprising. Since the PEG ratio controls only for growth, companies with higher ROICs should trade at higher levels. According to analyst estimates, Home Depot's ROIC is expected to exceed that of Lowe's as the two companies recover from the 2008 financial crisis.

The PEG ratio's ability to control for variation in growth rates appears to give it a leg up on the standard enterprise value multiple. Yet the PEG ratio has its own drawbacks that can lead to valuation errors. First, the PEG ratio controls only for growth, not for ROIC. Therefore, differences will still exist across companies within an industry. Second, there is no standard time frame for measuring expected growth. You may find yourself wondering whether to use one-year, two-year, or long-term growth. Exhibit 14.10 uses analyst projections for four-year expected EBITA growth (the longest window available).

Finally, PEG ratios assume a linear relationship between multiples and growth, such that no growth implies zero value. Exhibit 14.11 uses the average PEG ratio to value a hypothetical industry with five companies. Each company has a long-term expected ROIC of 15 percent and a WACC equal to 9 percent, and each pays cash taxes at 30 percent. The five hypothetical companies differ only in their growth rates, which vary from 2 percent to 6 percent. Using the key value driver formula, we estimate each company's enterprise value multiple. Note how the line that plots enterprise value versus growth is curved and has a positive intercept (even zero-growth firms have positive values). The PEG

EXHIBIT 14.11 **PEG Ratio Estimation Error**

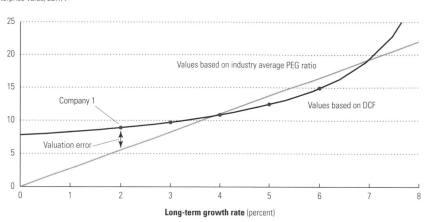

ratio, by contrast, is linear and has a zero intercept. If the industry average PEG ratio is multiplied by firm growth to approximate firm value, a company with constant profits would have an implied value of zero. As a result, the typical application of industry PEG ratios will systematically undervalue companies with low growth rates.

To avoid undervaluing low-growth companies, some financial analysts (and most academics) use a regression analysis to determine a representative multiple. The regression is based on the following equation:

$$\frac{EV}{EBITA_i} = a + b \left(\text{Expected Growth}_i\right)$$

This regression analysis, however, does not adjust for the nonlinear relationship between growth and value. More advanced regression techniques can be employed, but unless the sample is large, the regression often fails to provide useful insight.

Multiples Based on Nonfinancial (Operational) Data

In the late 1990s, numerous Internet companies went public with meager sales and negative profits. For many financial analysts, valuing the young companies was a struggle because of the great uncertainty surrounding potential market size, profitability, and required investments. Financial multiples that normally provide a benchmark for valuation were rendered useless because profitability (measured in any form) was often negative.

To overcome this shortcoming, academics and practitioners alike relied on nonfinancial multiples, which compare enterprise value with one or more non-operating financial statistics, such as web site hits, unique visitors, or number of subscribers. In 2000, *Fortune* reported market-value-to-customer multiples for a series of Internet companies.[14] *Fortune* determined that Yahoo! was trading at $2,038 per customer, Amazon.com was trading at $1,400 per customer, and NetZero at $1,140 per customer. The article suggested, "Placing a value on a Website's customers may be the best way to judge an [Internet] stock."

To use a nonfinancial multiple effectively, you must follow the same guidelines outlined earlier in this chapter. The nonfinancial metric must be a reasonable predictor of future value creation, and thus somehow tied to ROIC and growth. In the example cited previously, Yahoo! traded at a higher multiple than Amazon.com because Yahoo!'s incremental costs per user are much smaller, an advantage that can reasonably be expected to translate into higher profits per user.

Nonfinancial measures did play an important role in the early valuation of Internet stocks. The first academic study about Internet valuations examined a sample of 63 publicly traded Internet firms in the late 1990s.[15] The study found that the number of unique visitors to a web site or the number of pages on a site viewed per visit was directly correlated to a company's stock price, even after controlling for the company's current financial performance. The power of a given nonfinancial metric, however, depended on the company. For portal and content companies such as Yahoo!, page views and unique visitors were both correlated to a company's market value. For e-tailers such as Amazon.com, only the page views per visit were correlated with value. Evidently, the market believed that merely stopping by would not translate to future cash flow for e-tailers.

For Internet companies in the late 1990s, investors focused on nonfinancial metrics because early financial results were unrelated to long-term value creation. As the industry matured, however, financial metrics became increasingly important. Later research found that gross profit and R&D spending became increasingly predictive, whereas nonfinancial data lost power.[16] This research indicates a return to traditional valuation metrics even for the so-called new economy stocks, as the relevance of nonfinancial metrics diminished over the 24-month testing period.

Two cautionary notes about using nonfinancial multiples to analyze and value companies: First, nonfinancial multiples should be used only when they provide incremental explanatory power above financial multiples. If a company cannot translate visitors, page views, or subscribers into profits and cash flow, the nonfinancial metric is meaningless, and a multiple based on financial forecasts is better. Second, nonfinancial multiples, like all multiples, are *relative*

---

[14] E. Schonfeld, "How Much Are Your Eyeballs Worth?" *Fortune,* February 21, 2000, 197–200.

[15] B. Trueman, M. H. F. Wong, and X. J. Zhang, "The Eyeballs Have It: Searching for the Value in Internet Stocks," *Journal of Accounting Research* 38 (2000): 137–162.

[16] P. Jorion and E. Talmor, "Value Relevance of Financial and Non Financial Information in Emerging Industries: The Changing Role of Web Traffic Data" (working paper no. 021, London Business School Accounting Subject Area, 2001).

valuation tools. They measure one company's valuation relative to another, normalized by some measure of size. They do not measure absolute valuation levels. At the height of the Internet bubble, the valuations of many Web-based companies parted company with the core principles of value creation altogether (see Chapter 1). To value a company correctly, you must always remember to ask: Is a value of $2,038 per customer too much?

SUMMARY

Of the available valuation tools, discounted cash flow continues to deliver the best results. However, a thoughtful comparison of selected multiples for the company you are valuing with multiples from a carefully selected group of peers merits a place in your tool kit as well. When that comparative analysis is careful and well reasoned, it not only provides a useful check of your DCF forecasts but also provides critical insights into what drives value in a given industry. Just be sure that you analyze the underlying reasons that multiples differ from company to company, and never view multiples as a shortcut to valuation. Instead, approach your multiples analysis with as much care as you bring to your DCF analysis.

REVIEW QUESTIONS

1. Exhibit 14.12 presents market and profit data for three companies. Using this data, compute enterprise-value-to-EBITDA and enterprise-value-to-EBITA for Companies 1 and 2. Is the net difference between Company 1 and Company 2 the same for both ratios? If not, why might this be?

2. Exhibit 14.12 presents market and profit data for three companies. If Company 3 has nonoperating assets valued at $50 million, what are the

EXHIBIT 14.12 **Multiples Analysis: Market and Profit Data**

$ million

	Company 1	Company 2	Company 3
Market data			
Share price (dollars)	25	16	30
Shares outstanding (millions)	5	8	15
Short-term debt	25	15	30
Long-term debt	50	70	40
Operating profit			
EBITDA	25	30	59
EBITA	22	23	51

company's appropriate enterprise-value-to-EBITDA and enterprise-value-to-EBITA multiples?

3. You are valuing multiple steady-state companies in the same industry. Company A is projected to earn $160 in EBITA, grow at 2 percent per year, and generate ROICs equal to 15 percent. Company B is projected to earn $100 in EBITA, grow at 6 percent per year, and generate ROICs equal to 10 percent. Both companies have an operating tax rate of 25 percent and a cost of capital of 10 percent. What are the enterprise-value-to-EBITA multiples for both companies? Does higher growth lead to a higher multiple in this case?

4. You are valuing multiple steady-state companies in the same industry. Company A is projected to earn $160 in EBITA, grow at 2 percent per year, and generate ROICs equal to 15 percent. Company C is projected to earn $120 in EBITA, grow at 5 percent per year, and generate ROICs equal to 12 percent. Both companies have an operating tax rate of 25 percent and a cost of capital of 10 percent. What are the enterprise-value-to-EBITA multiples for both companies? Does higher growth lead to a higher multiple in this case? Why do the results differ between Questions 3 and 4?

5. Two companies have the same long-term prospects concerning growth and ROIC. One of the companies temporarily stumbles during a new product launch, and profits drop considerably as the company scrambles to fix the error. Will this company trade at a higher or lower enterprise value multiple than its stable peer? Why?

6. LeverCo is financed entirely by equity. The company generates operating profit equal to $80 million. LeverCo currently trades at an equity value of $900 million. At a tax rate of 25 percent, what is the price-to-earnings multiple for LeverCo? New management decides to increase leverage through a share repurchase. The company issues a $400 million bond to repurchase $400 million in equity. If the bond pays interest at 5 percent and share price remains unchanged, what is the company's new price-to-earnings ratio? How can you predict the direction the P/E ratio will move without performing the calculation?

Part Three

Intrinsic Value and the Stock Market

15

Market Value Tracks Return on Invested Capital and Growth

Over the past 15 years, investing in the stock market has been a roller-coaster ride. In the second half of the 1990s, the Standard & Poor's (S&P) 500 index more than tripled in value to an all-time high of almost 1,500. Previous unknowns, such as Amazon and America Online (AOL), became stock market superstars along with a galaxy of other new economy and dot-com entrants. Then the market crashed, and many lesser stars flickered out. After 2003, stocks recovered at a stunning pace, and by 2007, the S&P 500 had regained its all-time high. However, the market crashed again in 2008 as a result of the credit crisis, losing around 50 percent of its value in the course of a few months.

People are questioning whether long-held valuation theories can explain such dramatic swings in share prices. Some even assert that stock markets lead lives of their own, detached from the realities of economic growth and business profitability. But have market values and the discounted cash flow (DCF) valuations described in Chapter 6 really separated? Does it make sense to view the stock market as an arena where emotions rule supreme?

We think not. Certainly, prices for some stocks in some sectors can be driven in the short term by irrational behavior, as we discuss in Chapter 17. For shorter periods of time, the market as a whole can lose touch with fundamental laws grounded in economic growth and returns on investment. And clearly not all market players follow investment strategies based on those rules, as we explore in Chapter 18. But in the long term, market data show that individual stocks and the market as a whole do follow these fundamental laws. Indeed, the extent to which company valuations based on the fundamental approach have matched stock market values over the past four decades is remarkable.

This chapter presents the research findings on which we base our conclusion that, as in the real economy, return on capital and growth are the main drivers of company values in the capital markets:

- Valuation levels for the stock market as a whole clearly reflect the underlying fundamental performance of companies in the real economy.

- At any point in time, companies with higher return on invested capital (ROIC) and those with higher growth—as long as their ROIC is above the cost of capital—are valued more highly in the stock market.

- Over the long term (10 years and more), higher ROIC and growth also lead to higher total returns to shareholders (TRS) in the stock market. However, over shorter periods (three years and less), TRS can be strongly influenced by changes in investor expectations.

- For any individual company, whether increasing revenue growth or return on capital will create more value depends on the company's performance. A company with a higher ROIC at the outset will gain more value from growing revenue; one with a lower ROIC will gain more from improving its ROIC. Market valuations reflect the effects of this relationship between rates of ROIC and growth on fundamental valuations.

Our studies indicate that, in most cases and nearly all of the time, managers can safely assume that share prices reflect the markets' best estimate of intrinsic value. Therefore managers should continue to make decisions based on discounted cash flow and economic profit. When the market undergoes a period of irrational behavior, as we explain in Chapter 17, smart managers can detect and perhaps exploit the resulting market deviations. But even decisions taken in moments of market irrationality should be governed by fundamental valuation principles.

STOCK MARKETS TRACK ECONOMIC FUNDAMENTALS

The behavior of the world's key stock markets since the mid-1990s has confused and frustrated investors and managers. It has led many to question whether the stock market is anything more than a giant roulette table essentially unconnected to the real economy shaped by inflation rates, interest rates, growth in gross domestic product (GDP), and corporate profits. However, close scrutiny of real economic activity and stock market movements over time shows that the former does indeed directly explain the latter. In fact, the stock market's real surprise lies not in its occasional spectacular price bubbles but, rather, in how closely the market has mirrored economic fundamentals through two centuries of technological revolutions, monetary changes, political and economic crises, and wars. And this is true not just for the U.S. stock market. We believe stock markets in Europe and Asia also correctly reflect these regions' different underlying economic circumstances and prospects.

Explaining Market Returns over Two Centuries

U.S. equities over the past 200 years have on average achieved total returns to shareholders of about $6\frac{1}{2}$ percent annually, adjusted for inflation. Breathtaking market bubbles, crashes, or scandals tend to capture public attention, as during the financial crisis triggered in 2008, the high-tech market frenzy around the turn of the millennium, the Black Monday crash of October 1987, the leveraged buyout (LBO) craze of the 1980s, and, of course, the Wall Street crash of 1929. But the effect of any of these relatively short-lived events pales into insignificance against the backdrop of decade after decade of stock returns at a consistent premium over government bonds and bills (Exhibit 15.1). In the long term, as Exhibit 15.1 shows, stock markets are far from chaotic.

That $6\frac{1}{2}$ percent long-term real return on common stocks is no random number, either. Its origins lie in the fundamental performance of companies

EXHIBIT 15.1 **Stock Performance against Bonds in the Long Run, 1801–2010**

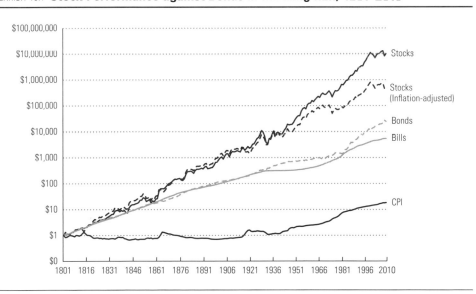

Source: Jeremy J. Siegel, *Stocks for the Long Run: The Definitive Guide to Financial Market Returns and Long-Term Investment Strategies* (New York: McGraw-Hill; 2002); Ibbotson Associates; Morningstar EnCorr SBBI Index Data.

and the returns investors have expected for taking on the risk of investing in them. One way to understand this linkage is to examine the real economy's underlying performance and its relationship to stocks. The median price-earnings (P/E) ratio in the U.S. stock market tends to hover around a level of about 15 over the long term. Assuming that the typical investor's risk preferences are stable, we can easily connect shareholders' long-term returns with the fundamental performance of companies. The P/E for a company with constant growth and return on capital is defined as:

$$P/E = \frac{1 - \frac{g}{ROE}}{k - g}$$

where g = growth, ROE = return on equity, and k = cost of equity.

If markets are pricing the company's stock correctly, the expected return on the stock should equal the cost of equity, so that:

$$\text{Expected Return} = k = \frac{E \times \left(1 - \frac{g}{ROE}\right)}{P} + g$$

We can interpret this as the sum of the cash flow yield on the stock plus the earnings growth rate.

Over the past 70 years, real corporate profits have grown about 3 to $3\frac{1}{2}$ percent per year. If P/Es revert to a normal level over time, stock prices should therefore also increase about 3 to $3\frac{1}{2}$ percent per year. In addition, corporate America, as a whole, typically reinvests about 50 percent of its profits every year to achieve this profit growth, leaving the other half to be paid to shareholders as dividends and share repurchases. Following the formula, this translates to a cash yield to shareholders of about 3 to $3\frac{1}{2}$ percent at the long-term average P/E of 15.[1] Adding the annual 3 to $3\frac{1}{2}$ percent increase in share prices to the cash yield of 3 to $3\frac{1}{2}$ percent results in total real shareholder returns of about $6\frac{1}{2}$ percent per year.

Understanding Recent Market Movements

We have seen how long-term average stock market returns are consistent with long-term average economic fundamentals over the past 200 years. To understand how changes in economic fundamentals drive changes in stock market valuation levels, we begin by identifying five more recent eras, each

---

[1] The payout ratio is driven by a company's growth and its return on capital. The 50 percent payout ratio is based on a typical company earning a 12 to 13 percent return on equity and growing at 3.5 percent in real terms, or 5 to 6 percent including inflation. The cash yield of 3.5 percent equals the inverse of the price-to-earnings ratio times the payout ratio.

EXHIBIT 15.2 **Fundamentals Drive Stock Performance over Five Eras**

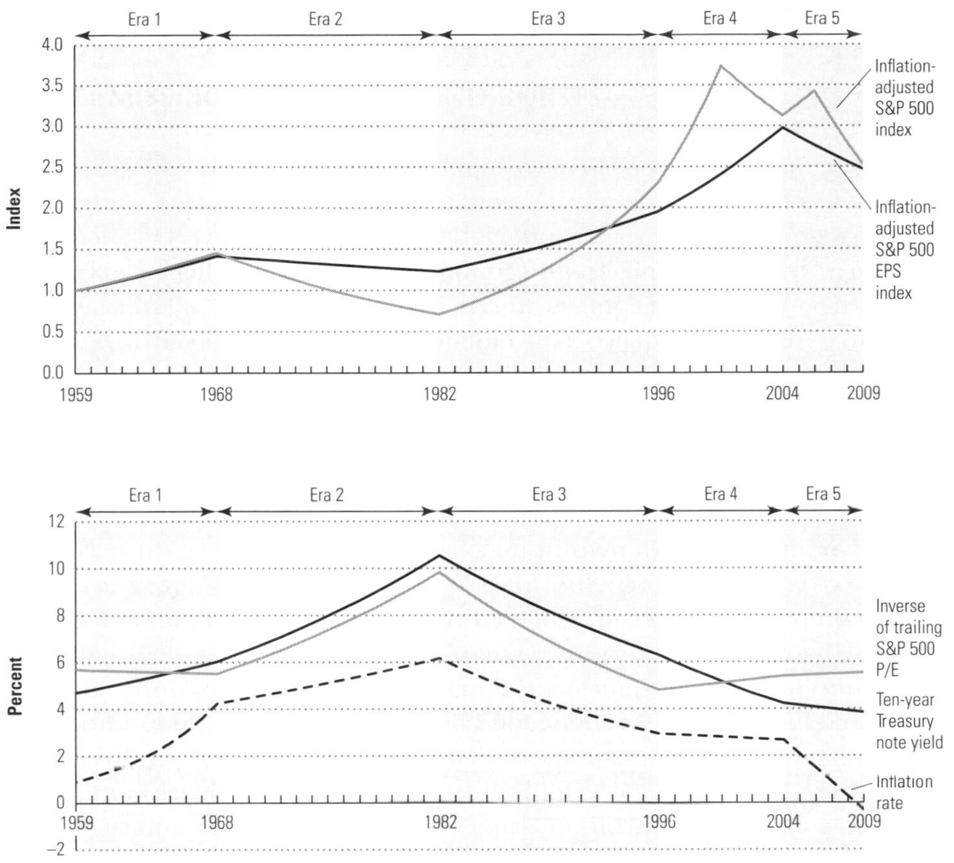

Source: Bloomberg, McKinsey Corporate Performance Center analysis, Institutional Brokers' Estimate System, Bureau of Economic Analysis.

distinguished by different fundamental forces shaping the U.S. economy and stock market. Exhibit 15.2 shows the level of the S&P 500 over the 50 years from the end of 1959 to early 2009 across these five distinct eras. Note that we smoothed out most of the short-term volatility in the stock market so we can compare the underlying movement of the market with similar stylized trends in earnings, P/Es, and interest and inflation rates. (We use the inverse of the P/E so it can more easily be compared with inflation and interest rates.)

With these charts in mind, we can now examine each of the five economic eras more closely, observing how the behavior of the stock market during each era has reflected events in the underlying real economy.

The carefree sixties: 1960 to 1968   During the carefree 1960s, real GDP grew at a healthy and stable 2.7 percent per year. Inflation remained between 1 and 1.5 percent per year until 1966, when it began to creep up, reaching 4.2 percent in 1968. Corporate profits grew a bit faster than the economy at 3.9 percent, and the P/E stayed within a narrow band of 15 to 18 times. As a result, the S&P 500 index increased about 5 percent per year. Adding dividends, shareholders earned an average real return of about 9 percent per year, slightly above the long-term average.

The great inflation: 1968 to 1982   During the next 14 years, inflation was the driving force in the economy and the markets. The inflation rate was 4.2 percent in 1968, then gradually increased to 11.0 percent in 1974, peaked at 13.5 percent in 1980, and returned to 6.1 percent in 1982. Although the 1973 and 1981 oil crises played an important role, what made inflation spiral out of control was flawed government policy. As a result, this was an era of volatile economic growth with four official recessions (1969–1970, 1973–1975, 1980, and 1981–1982). The U.S. government finally managed to bring inflation under control in the early 1980s.

The double impact of inflation and recession kept corporate profits flat in real terms over the 14 years. The P/E declined from about 18 in 1968 to about 10 in 1982 as the cost of capital and reinvestment requirements were driven up by higher inflation. The combination of no growth in profits and a decline in the price-to-earnings ratio led to real TRS of minus 1 percent per year.

Return to normalcy: 1982 to 1996   Between 1982 and 1996, interest rates and inflation fell dramatically. Ten-year U.S. government bond yields were above 10 percent in 1982 and then fell, more or less steadily, to 6 percent in 1996. Over this period, real profits for the S&P 500 increased at about 3 percent per year, close to the long-term average growth. The decline in inflation and interest rates drove price-to-earnings ratios back up to more typical levels in the mid- to high teens by 1996.

As P/Es recovered, the S&P 500 index generated exceptional annual TRS of 16 percent in nominal terms and 12 percent in real terms, more than double the 6½ percent stock market return over the past 200 years.

The long period of strong performance from 1982 to 1996 created much confusion. Many investors and managers did not understand that the market's strong performance was largely one-off, driven by inflation and interest rates returning to normal levels. Without this effect, the real return to shareholders would have been about 7 percent per year, more in line with the long-term average.[2]

---

[2] See T. Koller and Z. Williams, "What Happened to the Bull Market?," *McKinsey on Finance*, no. 1 (Summer 2001): 6–9.

The technology bubble and burst: 1996 to 2004   Between 1996 and 2004, the S&P 500 index produced total returns to shareholders of about 5 percent per year, falling about 1.5 percentage points short of the long-term average. What everyone remembers, though, is what happened in the middle. The S&P 500 went from 741 in 1996 to 1,527 in 2000 before falling back to 1,112 in 2003. As we explain in Chapter 17, this movement was caused by a bubble in the technology and megacap stocks. For example, from 1996 to 2000 the technology and megacap stocks increased by a median of 62 percent (total, not annual), while the rest of the companies in the S&P 500 increased by a median of 21 percent. In the decline that followed, this pattern reversed.

Leveraging and credit crisis: 2004 to 2008   The S&P 500 briefly hit another peak of 1,565 in mid-2007 before dropping to 667 in March 2009. Unlike the 2000 peak, which was underpinned by extraordinary P/Es, the 2007 peak was a result of unusually high corporate profits. The ratio of total profits for the S&P 500 companies to GDP soared in 2006 to an unprecedented 5.7 percent—much higher than the historical average of about 2.3 percent.[3] But in mid-2007, a financial crisis started to unfold that would drive the world's economy into its steepest downturn since the 1930s. As corporate profits dived, stock markets across the world lost more than half of their value from their peak levels in 2007. Over the 2004–2008 period, real returns to shareholders were no more than –5 percent per year.

In August 2009, the S&P 500 traded at over 1,000, translating into a P/E of 14.5 for 2009 consensus earnings. While there was great uncertainty about earnings at that time, the market appeared to be returning to typical valuation levels.

Modeling the Market over One-Year Periods

The fundamental performance of companies and of the economy also explains the level of the stock market over shorter periods of time. We estimated a fundamental P/E for the U.S. stock market for each year from 1962 to 2008, using a simple equity DCF valuation model following the value driver formula first presented in Chapter 2.[4] The results show that the overall market closely tracks our expected fundamental P/E ratio.

For this DCF model, we forecast each aggregate key value driver for the market, such as return on equity (ROE) and growth using economic fundamentals of the entire U.S. economy. In each year, we used long-term fundamental values as estimates for future rates of ROE and growth and the cost of equity. Long-term rates of ROE and growth in the U.S. economy have been

---

[3] We also used the corporate profit measures published by the U.S. Bureau of Economic Analysis (BEA) and found a pattern similar to that of the S&P 500.

[4] We used a two-stage version of the standard value driver formula, and we replaced ROIC with return on equity and replaced weighted average cost of capital (WACC) with cost of equity to obtain the market-to-book ratio of equity instead of invested capital (see also Chapter 10).

EXHIBIT 15.3 **Estimating Fundamental Market Valuation Levels**

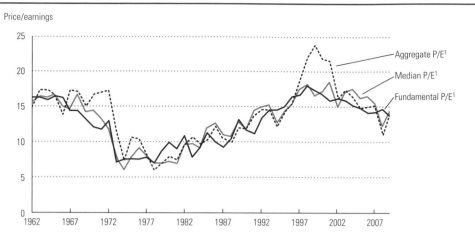

[1] P/E is 12-month forward-looking price-to-earnings ratio.

Source: McKinsey Corporate Performace Center analysis.

remarkably stable for the past 45 years, despite some deep recessions and periods of strong economic growth. The median ROE for all U.S. companies has been more or less stable at 12 to 15 percent. Long-term growth in GDP for the U.S. economy has been about 3 percent a year in real terms since 1945,[5] and its rolling average has not deviated significantly from that level in any five- to seven-year subperiod. In a separate analysis, we estimated that the inflation-adjusted cost of equity since 1962 has also been fairly stable at about 6½ to 7 percent.[6]

Using the DCF valuation model, we estimated what the price-to-earnings and market-to-book ratios would have been for the U.S. stock market for each year between 1962 and 2008, had they been based on these fundamental economic factors.[7] Exhibit 15.3 compares our resulting fundamental values with actual P/Es for the median company. We did a similar analysis for the European stock markets and obtained similar results.

We were surprised by how well this simple, fundamental valuation model fits the stock market's actual price-earnings levels over the past four and a half decades, despite periods of extremely high economic growth in the 1960s and 1990s, as well as periods of low growth and high inflation in the 1970s and

[5] For the U.S. economy, corporate earnings as a percentage of GDP have been remarkably constant over the past 40 years at around 6 percent.

[6] For estimates of the inflation-adjusted cost of equity for the stock market as a whole, see Chapter 11 and M. Goedhart, T. Koller, and Z. Williams, "The Real Cost of Equity," *McKinsey on Finance*, no. 5 (Autumn 2002): 11–15.

[7] See M. Goedhart, T. Koller, and Z. Williams, "Living with Lower Market Expectations," *McKinsey on Finance*, no. 8 (Summer 2004): 7–11.

1980s. Over the long term, the stock market as a whole does indeed follow the simple, fundamental economic principles discussed in Chapter 2: value is driven by returns on capital, growth, and—via the cost of capital—interest rates. By and large, the U.S. stock market has been fairly priced and in general has oscillated around its fundamental price-to-earnings ratios.

As we discuss in Chapter 17, the stock market has been through some significant deviations from intrinsic value, most recently in the late 1990s and the years leading up to 2007, when P/Es in the stock market were too high compared with our fundamental estimates. But in the first case, as in earlier notable deviations, the market corrected itself within a few years to its intrinsic valuation level, and the same seems to be true of the deviation working itself out at the time of writing, fall 2009.

COMPANY VALUATION LEVELS TRACK RETURN ON INVESTED CAPITAL AND GROWTH

What holds for the stock market as a whole also holds for individual companies. In examining how the market value of particular companies tracks ROIC and growth, we first must distinguish between what drives *market valuation levels* at any one moment and what drives *total returns to shareholders* (TRS) over time. Market valuation levels are determined by the company's absolute level of long-term expected growth and performance—that is, expected revenue and earnings growth and expected ROIC. Total returns to shareholders are measured by changes in the market valuation of a company over some specific time period, and are driven by changes in investor expectations for long-term future returns on capital and growth. The drivers of TRS are discussed in the next section. Here we focus on the drivers of market valuation levels.

Value, Return on Invested Capital, and Growth: Theoretical Relationship

On the left side of Exhibit 15.4, we show that the relative market value of a company, as measured by the ratio of market value to capital, is determined by the company's growth and its spread of ROIC over the weighted average cost of capital (WACC). The higher a company's ROIC, the higher its relative market value (shown on the vertical axis) for the same rate of revenue growth (shown on the horizontal axis). Moreover, the bigger the positive spread between a company's ROIC and the WACC (7.5 percent in this example), the more it will gain in relative market value from growth. When rates of ROIC fall below the cost of capital, higher growth leads to *lower* valuations.

These results, introduced in Chapter 2, are based on a two-stage variant of the key value driver formula. (See Chapter 10 on continuing value for details of the two-stage version underlying Exhibit 15.4.) Following this model, a typical

EXHIBIT 15.4 **Market Value, ROIC, and Growth: Theoretical Relationship**

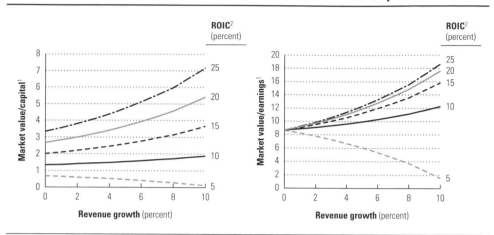

[1] Market value is enterprise value, capital is invested capital, and earnings is earnings before interest and taxes (EBITA).
[2] Valuation assumes a competitive advantage period of 15 years, after which ROIC equals WACC at 7.5 percent and growth equals 3 percent in continuing value.

company in the S&P 500 with an expected growth rate of 4 percent and a ROIC of 15 percent should be valued at 2.5 times invested capital.

In practice, analysts and investors often express valuation levels in terms of an earnings multiple, such as the P/E or the ratio of enterprise value to earnings before interest, taxes, and amortization (EBITA), shown on the right side of Exhibit 15.4, rather than a multiple of capital. Using this measure, the value of the typical S&P 500 company mentioned earlier translates to 10.6 times its earnings.

Of course, the same fundamental relationship between ROIC and growth holds for both valuation multiples. However, note that the relationship is less pronounced for the earnings multiple, because it is equal to the capital multiple scaled by return on capital:

$$\frac{\text{Value}}{\text{Earnings}} = \frac{\text{Value}}{\text{Capital}} \left(\frac{\text{Capital}}{\text{Earnings}} \right) = \frac{\text{Value}}{\text{Capital}} \left(\frac{1}{\text{Return on Capital}} \right)$$

The difference between two companies' intrinsic value creation is hard to derive from their earnings multiples alone, especially when both have low growth. In fact, two companies with very different ROICs could have almost identical earnings multiples if they have low expected future growth. However, their value-to-capital ratios would clearly show the differences in their underlying value creation potential.

To illustrate, take a second company with growth identical to the first (at 4 percent) but a significantly lower ROIC of 10 percent. Using the same model, this second company would be valued at a market-value-to-capital multiple of

1.5. This represents a 40 percent discount to the higher-performing company, as the second company extracts far less value from its capital base. But its earnings multiple would be at 9.6, only 9 percent lower than the first company's 10.6, mainly because the earnings base of the second already reflects its lower ROIC. Obviously, it needs to invest more capital to grow its revenue by the same amount as the first company. But given that expected growth for both is only 4 percent, the differences in their ROICs have limited effect on their required investments and the earnings multiples. As this example shows, much clearer evidence of how ROIC and growth drive intrinsic company valuations can be derived from capital multiples than from earnings multiples.

Value, Return on Invested Capital, and Growth: Evidence of Actual Relationship

As shown in Exhibit 15.5, there is evidence that these principles are at work in the stock market. For a sample of some 1,700 of the largest listed companies in the world grouped by industry,[8] we took their average ROIC for the previous three years as a proxy for expected future returns, and the analysts' consensus estimate of their three-year growth outlook as the proxy for long-term expected growth. Note that the median ratio of market value to capital for the full sample is 2.7, based on a median ROIC of 14.2 percent and median expected growth of 5.4 percent. That ratio comes quite close to the 2.5 multiple we derived from the theoretical model of Exhibit 15.4.

Furthermore, note that industries with higher ratios of market value to capital also have higher growth and/or higher ROIC driven by better sales margins and capital turnover. Health care and technology companies have the highest valuation levels, thanks to having the highest ROIC combined with superior growth. Utilities are typically valued at low market-value-to-capital multiples because of their regulated low return on capital and low expected growth. As discussed earlier, these patterns are fundamentally the same for market-value-to-earnings ratios but somewhat less marked.

In some cases, the three-year consensus growth estimates shown are not a good proxy for long-term growth. For example, the oil and gas industry had relatively low valuation multiples in spite of high consensus growth prospects for the next three years. The stock market in 2006 expected the sector's short-term growth to be high, as oil prices were soaring at the time, but apparently factored into its valuation that these prices would come down again and depress long-term growth.

Within industries, we see a similar pattern. For example, in an analysis of 130 European and U.S. publicly traded chemical companies between 1963 and

---

[8] This sample comprises the 1,700 largest listed companies (excluding financials) by market capitalization at the end of 2006 from the United States, Europe, Australia, New Zealand, and Japan.

EXHIBIT 15.5 **Market Value versus ROIC and Growth across Key Industry Sectors**

Largest global companies by market capitalization (excluding financial institutions), 2006 median

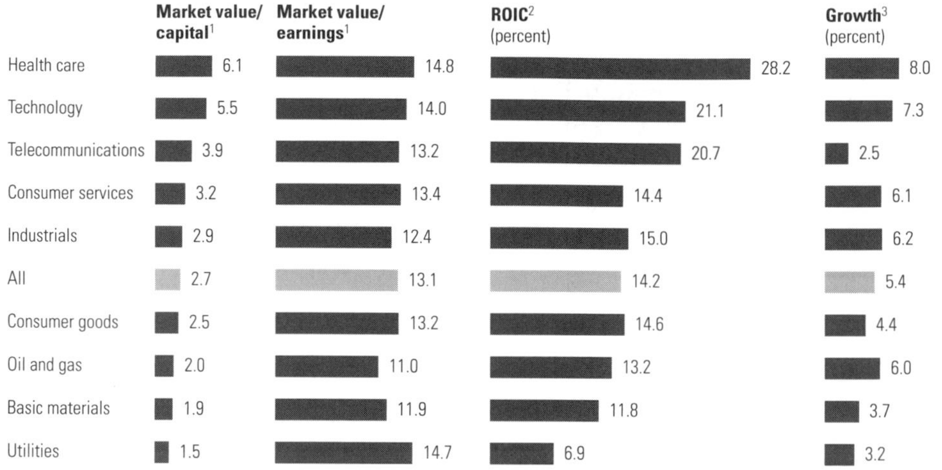

	Market value/ capital[1]	Market value/ earnings[1]	ROIC[2] (percent)	Growth[3] (percent)
Health care	6.1	14.8	28.2	8.0
Technology	5.5	14.0	21.1	7.3
Telecommunications	3.9	13.2	20.7	2.5
Consumer services	3.2	13.4	14.4	6.1
Industrials	2.9	12.4	15.0	6.2
All	2.7	13.1	14.2	5.4
Consumer goods	2.5	13.2	14.6	4.4
Oil and gas	2.0	11.0	13.2	6.0
Basic materials	1.9	11.9	11.8	3.7
Utilities	1.5	14.7	6.9	3.2

[1] Market value is enterprise value, capital is invested capital excluding goodwill, and earnings is earnings before interest, taxes, depreciation, and amortization (EBITDA).
[2] Average return on invested capital excluding goodwill over 2004–2006.
[3] Analyst consensus forecast of annual revenue growth for 2007–2009.

Source: McKinsey Corporate Performance Center analysis, Institutional Brokers' Estimate System.

2001,[9] those with higher sales growth achieved a higher market valuation only if they could generate returns above their cost of capital, which is close to the average ROIC in this industry. As shown by the market value/capital ratios in the following table, the market penalized companies that attempted growth but earned returns below their cost of capital:

Market value/Capital, 2002		Sales growth	
		Below average	Above average
ROIC	Above average	1.5	1.6
	Below average	1.3	0.5

The same principles hold for individual companies. We compared the ratios of market value to capital of the previous sample of the world's 1,700 largest listed companies versus their expected ROIC and growth. Much as we did in the previous test, we took each company's previous three-year average ROIC as a proxy for expected future returns and the analyst consensus forecast of its earnings growth in the three years to come as the proxy for expected future growth. We grouped the companies by growth

[9] T. Augat, E. Bartels, and F. Budde, "Multiple Choice for the Chemicals Industry," *McKinsey on Finance*, no. 8 (Summer 2003): 1–7.

EXHIBIT 15.6 **Market Value, ROIC, and Growth: Empirical Relationship**

Largest global companies by market capitalization (excluding financial institutions)

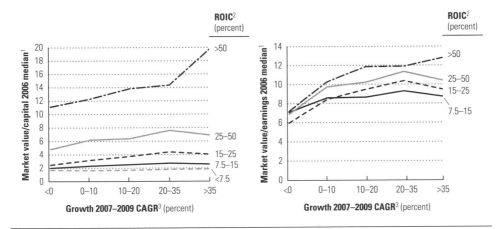

[1] Market value equals enterprise value, capital is invested capital excluding goodwill, and earnings is earnings
  before interest, taxes, depreciation, and amortization (EBITDA).
[2] Average return on invested capital excluding goodwill over 2004–2006.
[3] Analyst consensus forecast of annual earnings growth for 2007–2009.

Source: McKinsey Corporate Performance Center analysis, Institutional Brokers' Estimate System.

and ROIC into quintiles and estimated the median market-value-to-capital ratio for each of the five groups. Exhibit 15.6 shows the results of this analysis. (On the right side, we left out the lowest ROIC cohort from the market-value-to-earnings chart, because very small or even negative earnings tend to generate distorted market-value-to-earnings ratios.) Although these empirical results do not fit the theoretical model perfectly, they demonstrate that for any level of growth, higher rates of ROIC lead to higher market values, and above a given level of ROIC, higher growth also leads to higher value. Thus, the market does indeed appear to value companies based on growth and ROIC.

We also tested these results by regressing the market-value-to-capital ratios against growth and ROIC. The results, shown in Exhibit 15.7, are compelling: variations in their ROIC and growth account for more than 35 percent of the variation between the companies' market-value-to-capital ratios. We then divided the full sample into the five ROIC cohorts from Exhibit 15.6. Within each cohort, we regressed the market-value-to-capital ratios against growth and found, as theory would predict, that as ROIC increases, the impact of growth on value is stronger. For the lowest-ROIC subgroup (ROIC less than 7.5 percent), growth has a much greater positive effect on value than we would expect. However, the results in this subgroup are mainly driven by highly valued health care and technology companies with low or negative current earnings but very strong long-term performance and growth prospects in 2006.

EXHIBIT 15.7 **Market Value, ROIC, and Growth: Regression Analysis**

Largest global companies by market capitalization (excluding financial institutions)

| Dependent variable | Independent variable (t-statistics in parentheses) | | | R^2 (percent) | Sample size |
	Constant	ROIC[2]	Growth[3]		
Market value/earnings[1]	8.03	1.24	35.60	26	2,016
	(48.149)	(3.749)	(25.661)		
Market value/capital[1]	1.12	10.61	25.45	36	2,054
	(6.129)	(28.487)	(18.156)		
Market value/capital[1]					
ROIC ≤ 7.5%	1.79		21.79	14	386
	(4.419)		(7.900)		
7.5% < ROIC ≤ 15.0%	2.24		4.68	7	568
	(31.00)		(6.340)		
15.0% < ROIC ≤ 25.0%	3.06		12.54	8	469
	(16.537)		(6.480)		
25.0% < ROIC ≤ 50.0%	6.18		14.43	7	401
	(21.360)		(5.570)		
ROIC > 50.0%	10.36		56.44	22	230
	(11.145)		(8.080)		

[1] Market value is enterprise value, capital is invested capital excluding goodwill, and earnings is earnings before interest, taxes, depreciation, and amortization (EBITDA).
[2] Average return on capital excluding goodwill for 2004–2006.
[3] Analyst consensus forecast of annual revenue growth for 2007–2009.

Source: McKinsey Corporate Performance Center analysis, Institutional Brokers' Estimate System.

Differences in fundamental economic performance also explain variations in market valuation levels from country to country. Between 1993 and 2003, for example, average P/E and market-to-book ratios were significantly higher for the U.S. market than in European and key Asian markets.[10] U.S. market-to-book ratios were between 2.5 and 3.0, compared with ratios around 2.0 to 2.5 in European markets and between 1.5 and 2.0 in most Asian markets. Although accounting rules, monetary conditions, and corporate governance have differed in these regions over time, differences in company performance can explain most of the differences in their stock market valuations, particularly in the case of return on capital. To illustrate, U.S. companies consistently earned higher returns on capital over the period (around 13 to 15 percent) than companies in Europe (10 to 13 percent) and Asia (5 to 10 percent).

Since expected future growth and returns for companies are not directly measurable, we cannot assert that these tests give scientific proof for our claims. But they do provide evidence that the combined impact of growth and return on capital on cash flow drives both the intrinsic and the market value of companies.

[10] See M. Goedhart, T. Koller, and N. Leung, "The Scrutable East," *McKinsey on Finance*, no. 13 (Autumn 2003): 14–16.

TOTAL RETURNS TO SHAREHOLDERS TRACK PERFORMANCE AGAINST EXPECTATIONS

As discussed in Chapter 3, total returns to shareholders (TRS) are determined by performance against expectations, not absolute levels of performance. As a result, TRS is not always a good measure of intrinsic value creation. Companies that deliver high returns on capital and growth over a given period can still show disappointing TRS if investors had expected even better performance at the beginning of the period or had lowered their expectations at the end. For example, on July 13, 2004, Intel reported a second-quarter net income of $1.76 billion, almost double the amount it had reported for that period a year earlier. Nevertheless, Intel's share price declined by 11 percent on the day of the announcement. The reason for the decline was that Intel's simultaneously reported sales and margins, considered important indicators for long-term profitability in the sector, were below the market's expectations, prompting investors to anticipate lower returns in future.

Total Returns to Shareholders, Expectations, Return on Invested Capital, and Growth: Theoretical Relationship

It is important to make a distinction between expected and realized TRS. By definition, the expected TRS always equals the company's cost of capital, as shown in Chapter 3. A company's realized TRS, in contrast, can differ significantly from the cost of capital because it depends on both performance and expectations. As discussed in more detail in Chapter 3, realized TRS has the following key drivers:

- *Initial expectations.* Given two companies with identical performance in terms of return on capital and growth, the company with the highest initial earnings multiple will show the lowest realized rate of TRS over a given period.

- *Realized return on capital and growth.* Keeping all other drivers of realized TRS constant, a higher realized return on invested capital will always lead to higher TRS. Higher growth leads to higher shareholder returns only if return on capital exceeds the cost of capital.

- *Changes in expectations.* Keeping all other value drivers constant, an increase in investors' expectations of future cash flows, as measured by an increase in the earnings multiple (reflecting a rise in the share price), leads to higher returns to shareholders.

Given these relationships, changes in expectations can have a much bigger impact on realized TRS than actual performance, especially over short periods of time—say, up to three years. Over longer periods—say, of at least 10 years—TRS is not as strongly influenced by changes in expectations and

EXHIBIT 15.8 **TRS, Expectations, ROIC, and Growth across Key Industry Sectors**

Largest global companies by market capitalization (excluding financial institutions), 1996–2006, median percent

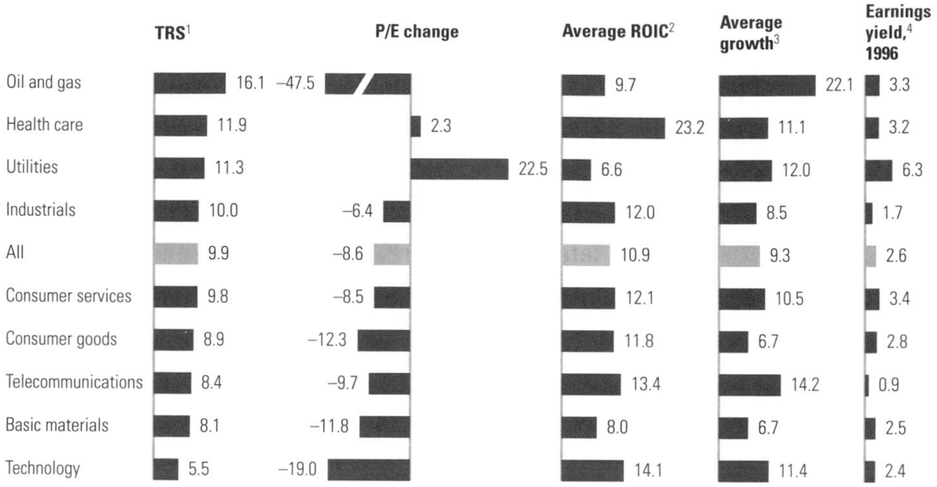

	TRS[1]		P/E change		Average ROIC[2]	Average growth[3]	Earnings yield,[4] 1996
Oil and gas	16.1	−47.5			9.7	22.1	3.3
Health care	11.9		2.3		23.2	11.1	3.2
Utilities	11.3			22.5	6.6	12.0	6.3
Industrials	10.0	−6.4			12.0	8.5	1.7
All	9.9	−8.6			10.9	9.3	2.6
Consumer services	9.8	−8.5			12.1	10.5	3.4
Consumer goods	8.9	−12.3			11.8	6.7	2.8
Telecommunications	8.4	−9.7			13.4	14.2	0.9
Basic materials	8.1	−11.8			8.0	6.7	2.5
Technology	5.5	−19.0			14.1	11.4	2.4

[1] Annualized total return to shareholders for 1996–2006.
[2] Average return on invested capital including goodwill for 1996–2006.
[3] Average annual revenue growth for 1996–2006.
[4] Inverse of P/E ratio.

Source: McKinsey Corporate Performance Center analysis.

more clearly linked to realized return on invested capital and growth relative to expectations at the start of the 10-year period. Changes in expectations tend to matter less as the period increases over which TRS is measured because, as our empirical analyses show, earnings multiples have a strong tendency to revert to their mean over the longer term (see, e.g., Exhibit 15.3).

Total Returns to Shareholders, Expectations, Return on Invested Capital, and Growth: Evidence of Actual Relationship

Because of the interaction of performance and expectations, the fit between patterns of ROIC, growth, and TRS for different industries is not as close as the fit between those key value drivers and the ratios of market value to capital or market value to earnings. Exhibit 15.8 compares levels of TRS for the world's largest companies sector by sector from 1996 to 2006 with each sector's score in the four main drivers of realized TRS: change in the P/E, ROIC, growth, and initial earnings yield. Clearly, stronger scores in all the drivers are more frequent in sectors that deliver higher TRS. A strong improvement in investor expectations, as measured by the relative change in P/E, has a particularly beneficial impact. But it is the combination of all drivers that ultimately determines the TRS ranking: strong scores on the intrinsic value drivers may counteract declining investor expectations, and vice versa.

For example, from 1996 to 2006, the oil and gas industry delivered the highest sector TRS, more than 16 percent a year, even though investor expectations of the sector's performance dropped sharply over the period, as shown by a 47.5 percent decline in its P/E. The key to the sector's strong shareholder returns was spectacular revenue growth of 22.1 percent a year. In contrast, the utilities sector had on average neither strong growth nor a high ROIC. Nevertheless, its annualized TRS over the period was a creditable 11.3 percent, mostly explained by a turnaround in investor expectations. Initial expectations for the industry were low, reflected in a high initial earnings yield. But expectations improved strongly over the 10-year period, leading to a TRS for utilities well above those of industries with stronger rates of ROIC and growth, such as consumer goods, telecoms, and basic materials.

TRS is also increasingly correlated with growth as ROIC rises—just as we would expect from the theoretical model. We grouped the companies into quintiles by their 10-year sales growth and ROIC levels. For each quintile, we calculated the median TRS from 1996 to 2006 (see Exhibit 15.9). TRS was clearly higher for companies with higher rates of ROIC, and the higher the rate of ROIC, the higher the rate of revenue growth. However, shareholder returns varied a lot within each cohort, reflecting the influence of investor expectations on this measure, just as we saw in the sector overview.

EXHIBIT 15.9 **Long-Term TRS, ROIC, and Growth: Empirical Evidence**

Largest global companies by market capitalization (excluding financial institutions), percent

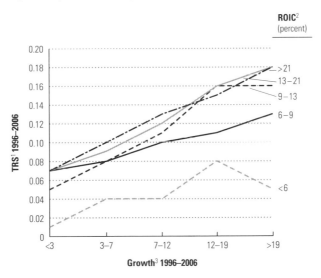

¹ Annualized total return to shareholders.
² Average return on invested capital excluding goodwill 1996–2006.
³ Average annual revenue growth.

Source: McKinsey Corporate Performance Center analysis.

EXHIBIT 15.10 **TRS, Expectations, ROIC, and Growth: Regression Analysis**

Largest global companies by market capitalization (excluding financial institutions)

Dependent variable	Constant	ROIC[1]	Growth[2]	P/E change[3]	Initial earnings yield[4]	R^2 (percent)	Sample size
TRS 1996–2006	0.03	0.08	0.28	−0.01	0.90	27	1,466
	(6.335)	(6.492)	(15.665)	(−1.825)	(11.873)		
TRS 2003–2006	0.09	0.09	0.37	0.03	1.39	17	1,799
	(8.512)	(2.774)	(13.587)	(4.188)	(8.731)		

[1] Average return on invested capital including goodwill for 1996–2006, 2003–2006.
[2] Average annual revenue growth for 1996–2006, 2003–2006.
[3] Relative change in P/E ratio from 1996–2006, 2003–2006.
[4] Inverse of 1996, 2003 P/E ratio.

Source: McKinsey Corporate Performance Center analysis.

To test the difference in degree to which expectations and performance drive returns to shareholders, we also conducted a formal statistical analysis. We regressed long-term and short-term realized TRS against all the key factors determining TRS—change in expectations as measured by the change in P/E, ROIC, growth, and initial expectations as measured by the initial earnings yield—following the model used in this chapter. As the model would suggest, there is a strong relationship between the long-term, 10-year TRS and all of the key drivers (see Exhibit 15.10). More than 25 percent of the TRS variation across the sample is explained by the differences in return on capital, growth, and expectations.[11] For each additional percentage point of growth, a company's annualized TRS would be higher by 0.28 percentage point. An additional percentage point of ROIC over the period would contribute 0.08 percentage point of TRS. Regardless of subsequent ROIC and growth, the initial expectations would add 0.90 percentage point of TRS for each percentage point difference in starting earnings yield. Changes in expectations, as measured by the change in the earnings multiple over the 10-year period, had no significant impact on TRS.

Expectations had a stronger influence on TRS over the short term. Between 2003 and 2006, the coefficients for change in P/E and initial earnings yield are bigger than for the 10-year period, illustrating that, over the short term, a company's TRS depends strongly on changes in market expectations. We should therefore be cautious in using short-term TRS as a measure of corporate performance, especially as changes in investor expectations do not always reflect underlying fundamentals (see Chapter 17).

The empirical evidence confirms what the models predict: TRS is driven by ROIC and growth and by investors' expectations. Over the long term, companies with higher ROIC and growth do tend to deliver stronger returns to shareholders, although the role of investor expectations should not be

[11] As measured by the R^2 of the regression.

underestimated. Over the short term, the influence of expectations on shareholder returns is even greater and more likely to dominate ROIC and growth in influencing TRS for specific companies or sectors.

SUMMARY

In spite of the recent turmoil in European and U.S. stock markets, there is overwhelming evidence that markets are reflecting economic fundamentals. Valuation levels for those markets as a whole over the past 45 years and equity returns over the past 200 years are generally consistent with long-term performance in the real economy in terms of economic growth, inflation, and corporate returns on capital.

The market also gets it right at the level of individual companies: those with higher ROIC and higher growth (at returns above their cost of capital) are valued more highly in the stock market, as measured by their price-to-earnings ratios or market-value-to-capital ratios, and generate higher long-term returns for shareholders. In line with what theory predicts, companies with higher returns on capital benefit more from growth, and those with lower returns on capital gain more from improving their returns.

REVIEW QUESTIONS

1. Explain how long-term price-to-earnings ratios in the U.S. stock market of around 15 times are consistent with long-term expected stock returns of around 6 to 7 percent a year in real terms.

2. Analysis of stock market eras over the past 50 years shows that inflation was the single most important driver of total returns to shareholders (TRS) for the market as a whole. Discuss why inflation has such a strong impact on share prices. (Use the value driver model.)

3. Why are differences in companies' value creation more apparent from comparing their market-value-to-capital multiples than their market-value-to-earnings multiples?

4. Discuss what pattern you would expect over time for market-value-to-capital and market-value-to-earnings multiples in an industry where earnings show little long-term growth but high cyclicality.

5. Assume a company's price-to-earnings ratio varies randomly in the band of values between 12 and 18 over time. For simplicity, assume its earnings are stable for the next 10 years and no dividends are paid. What is the bandwidth for the company's future annualized TRS over a horizon of 1 year and 10 years?

6. In many companies executive compensation is linked to the company's annual TRS (or margin of TRS above its peers). Discuss pros and cons of using TRS as a basis for executive compensation.

7. Exhibit 15.1 shows how (cumulative) returns on investments in the equity market index have consistently exceeded returns on investments in government bonds over the past 200 years. This being the case, would you recommend that investors consider not investing in government bonds at all? What would a chart of annual returns on investment in equity and bonds look like—and does its shape influence your recommendation?

8. Fundamentals explain less of the variation in TRS than in market-value-to-book-value or market-value-to-earnings ratios (as measured by the R^2 shown in Exhibits 15.7 and 15.10). This holds true even when TRS is measured over 10-year periods. Why is TRS less clearly linked to fundamentals?

16

Markets Value Substance,
Not Form

As shown in the previous chapter, stock market valuations reflect companies' long-term return on invested capital (ROIC) and revenue growth, the economic fundamentals that drive their long-term cash flows. Yet many managers remain obsessed by the representation of cash flows rather than their quality, an obsession demonstrated by managers' efforts to meet earnings per share (EPS) targets, to remain included in a major stock index, or to obtain a cross-listing. Such managers believe these efforts are critical to maintaining or improving their share price. But as evidence presented in this chapter demonstrates, capital markets are not moved by such efforts in the long term. Ultimately, the measures of real value creation—ROIC and growth—are the only drivers of market value.

- Managers can go to great lengths to achieve analysts' expectations of EPS or to smooth earnings from quarter to quarter. But the evidence shows clearly that stock markets reward neither predictable nor smooth earnings. A company's share price is driven by its long-term economic fundamentals.

- Stock markets are perfectly capable of seeing the economic reality behind different forms of accounting information. Therefore, managers should not be overly concerned with how their share price might be affected by new accounting rules (for instance, changes in the treatment of options or goodwill), since these do not affect their underlying economics.

- Since investors value substance over form, managers need not worry about whether their shares are split into smaller shares, traded in one or many developed stock markets, or included in a large stock market index. None of these measures will make any material difference to the share price, as they too leave the underlying economics of the company unchanged.

Our findings confirm that there is indeed "no free lunch": what is easy to achieve generally does not create value. As we already demonstrated in Chapter 15, in most cases and at almost all times, managers can safely assume that share prices reflect the markets' best estimate of intrinsic value. They should therefore continue to base their business decisions on discounted cash flow (DCF) and economic profit. This is our advice even when the market is gripped by one of its occasional episodes of irrational behavior. As we explain in the following two chapters, fundamental valuation principles may also help smart managers exploit opportunities from such market deviations.

MANAGING EARNINGS: NOT WORTH THE EFFORT

On July 17, 2008, Google Inc. announced second-quarter earnings of $4.63 per share, just 2 percent short of the $4.72 consensus analyst expectation. Its share price subsequently fell by more than 12 percent on the same day, the largest single-day loss for the stock since Google went public in 2004. Witnessing such events, many managers have concluded that stock markets are increasingly sensitive to short-term earnings that undershoot analysts' expectations, or to volatility in earnings generally. Academic research suggests that managers significantly stepped up their efforts to hit analysts' targets for corporate earnings during the 1990s,[1] and in a 2004 survey, more than three-quarters of the financial executives questioned said they would forgo measures creating economic value to avoid missing earnings targets and suffering the associated market reactions.[2]

Companies endeavor to avoid earnings surprises in three ways. Sometimes they sensibly try to lead analysts to adjust their earnings forecasts over time and in a controlled manner by gradually providing new information. Sometimes they manage the earnings number toward the analysts' target, but in a manner that has no impact on value. For example, companies may have some freedom to decide when they recognize sales and earnings, depending on whether long-term contractual sales are booked in full when the contract is closed or spread out over its lifetime. Or they can choose to capitalize customer acquisition costs or research and development (R&D) expenses—both means of

---

[1] L. Brown, "A Temporal Analysis of Earnings Surprises: Profits versus Losses," *Journal of Accounting Research*, 39, no. 2 (September 2001): 221–241; and F. Degeorge, J. Patel, and R. Zeckhauser, "Earnings Management to Exceed Thresholds," *Journal of Business* 72, no. 1 (1999): 1–33.

[2] J. Graham, C. Harvey, and S. Rajgopal, "The Economic Implications of Corporate Financial Reporting," *Journal of Accounting and Economics* 40, nos. 1–3 (December 2005): 3–73.

boosting reported earnings used by fast-growing companies in telecommunications and software.[3] Such moves to shift earnings or costs from one period to the next cause no actual damage to a company's prospects, because they do not directly affect cash flow or value. But they might mislead some investors and executives about the economic fundamentals of the company.

The last and more detrimental forms of earnings management involve changes to a company's business. These *do* directly affect current or future cash flows, and possibly shareholder value. Examples include reducing marketing expenses, providing customer incentives, or deferring divestments to meet a profit target.[4] Some companies are reported to have timed the sale of real estate, other assets, or entire businesses to meet analysts' profit expectations or targets.

The evidence, however, shows that the stock market is not much concerned by earnings volatility and offers no rewards for predictable earnings. More importantly, the market sees through most attempts by management to game corporate earnings in order to meet analysts' expectations. It maintains its focus—correctly—on fundamental drivers of long-term cash flows.

The Market Does Not Care about Earnings Volatility

Some managers believe investors will pay a premium for steady earnings growth. Indeed, executives regularly cite stabilizing earnings growth as a reason for strategic actions. For example, the CEO of Conoco justified a pending merger with Phillips Petroleum in part by asserting that the merger would offer greater earnings stability over the commodity price cycle.[5]

Of course, investors consider both the return and risk profiles of a company in setting its share price. But rational investors focus on the company's return and risk in terms of cash flows, not earnings. So why would the market value steady and predictable profit growth? The academic literature is not completely conclusive on this point, but most authors find that earnings variability has either limited or no impact on market value and shareholder returns.

Recent research by Rountree, Weston, and Allayannis[6] shows that ratios of market value to capital certainly are diminished by cash flow volatility, but not by earnings volatility; investors see through any earnings smoothing that is unconnected to cash flow. In a recent publication reviewing 30 years of U.S. profit data,[7] McInnis finds no correlation between variability in EPS and a

---

[3] See also D. Aboody and B. Lev, "The Value Relevance of Intangibles: The Case of Software Capitalization," *Journal of Accounting Research* 36 (1998): 161–191.

[4] We discuss in Chapter 22 that companies sometimes refrain from value-creating divestments because of the associated earnings dilution.

[5] Analyst teleconference, November 19, 2001.

[6] See B. Rountree, J. Weston, and G. Allayannis, "Do Investors Value Smooth Performance?," *Journal of Financial Economics* 90, no. 3 (December 2008): 237–251.

[7] J. McInnis, "Earnings Smoothness, Average Returns, and Implied Cost of Equity Capital," *Accounting Review* (January 2010).

company's market value. Although Barnes does find a statistically significant relationship between the two,[8] he demonstrates that the impact of earnings variability on market value is limited: between the 1 percent of companies with the lowest earnings volatility and the 1 percent with the highest lies a difference in market-to-book ratios of less than 10 percent.[9] Similarly, Koller and Rajan find that variability of earnings growth rates has a weak statistical relationship to shareholder returns and value, but the role of variability is insignificant relative to the part played by earnings growth and return on capital in driving shareholder returns and value.[10]

To test the relationship between earnings variability and value, we followed the approach taken by Koller and Rajan, but with a larger and more recent sample representing the largest 1,500 European companies between 2000 and 2007.[11] Our results confirmed their earlier results: variability in earnings growth rates had no meaningful effect on shareholder returns or value (see Exhibit 16.1). We compared each company's annual earnings growth rate with its average earnings growth rate over the entire period and estimated each company's growth variability. There was no relationship between earnings variability and the market performance measures of total returns to shareholders (TRS) and ratio of market value to capital, after controlling for differences in underlying performance (that is, earnings growth and ROIC) and industry sector. Long-term earnings growth, ROIC, and industry sector together explained 34 percent of TRS for the entire sample over a five-year period, while earnings variability did not explain market performance measures to any significant degree at all. We likewise found no statistically significant relationship of earnings variability to the market-to-capital ratio.

Part of the explanation for the results is that smooth earnings growth is a myth. Almost no companies have smooth earnings growth. Exhibit 16.2 shows five firms among the 10 percent of 500 large companies[12] that had the least volatile earnings growth from 1998 to 2007. Of the companies we examined, Walgreens was the only one with seven years of steady earnings growth, and only a handful had earnings growth that was steady for four or more years. Most companies with relatively stable earnings growth follow a pattern similar to the four companies other than Walgreens in Exhibit 16.2: several years of steady growth interrupted by a sudden decline in earnings. For 460 of the companies, earnings fell in at least one year of the period studied.

---

[8] R. Barnes, "Earnings Volatility and Market Valuation: An Empirical Investigation," LBS Accounting Subject Area Working Paper ACCT 019 (2003).

[9] The difference was 0.2, and the average market-to-book ratio for the entire sample was around 2.

[10] T. Koller and S. Rajan, "Who's Afraid of Variable Earnings?," *McKinsey on Finance*, no. 4 (Summer 2002): 13–17.

[11] The sample consists of 1,503 European (excluding Russia) and U.K. companies with a 2007 market capitalization in excess of €200 million.

[12] These were the 500 largest nonfinancial U.S. companies by revenue.

EXHIBIT 16.1 **No Relationship between Shareholder Value and Earnings Variability**

Independent variable (t-statistics in parentheses)

Dependent variable	Constant	ROIC	EPS growth	EPS volatility	Utilities	Telecom	Technology	Oil and gas	Health care	Financials	Consumer services	Consumer goods	Basic materials	R^2 (percent)
TRS 2000–2007[1]	0.071	0.082	0.378		0.026	−0.125	−0.134	0.057	−0.019	−0.035	−0.079	−0.000	0.014	31
	(8.537)	(2.615)	(15.376)		(1.549)	(−4.259)	(−6.356)	(3.128)	(−1.155)	(−3.863)	(−6.583)	(−0.020)	(0.979)	
TRS 2000–2007[1]	0.089	0.032	0.396	−0.002	0.014	−0.120	−0.156	0.032	−0.026	−0.034	−0.073	−0.010	0.005	34
	(7.604)	(0.741)	(11.805)	(−0.310)	(0.636)	(−2.316)	(−4.911)	(1.476)	(−1.324)	(−3.167)	(−4.729)	(−0.730)	(0.268)	
Market value/capital[2]	1.750	11.137	0.156		−0.832	−0.221	0.309	−0.492	0.452	−1.274	−0.173	−0.519	−0.795	45
	(12.663)	(19.692)	(0.406)		(−3.238)	(−6.511)	(0.821)	(−1.739)	(1.625)	(−8.853)	(−0.902)	(−2.900)	(−3.624)	
Market value/capital[2]	1.114	13.014	0.445	−0.145	−0.406	−0.320	−0.457	−0.323	0.357	−1.008	0.273	−0.106	−0.425	52
	(5.844)	(18.025)	(0.869)	(−1.775)	(−1.245)	(−6.397)	(−0.942)	(−1.019)	(1.150)	(−6.060)	(1.128)	(−0.516)	(−1.609)	

[1] Annualized excess return over market return.
[2] Enterprise value/invested capital excluding goodwill. For financial institutions: market value of equity/book value of equity.

Source: Bloomberg, McKinsey Corporate Performance Center analysis.

EXHIBIT 16.2 **Earnings Growth of Least Volatile Companies: Not So Smooth**

Earnings growth,[1] percent

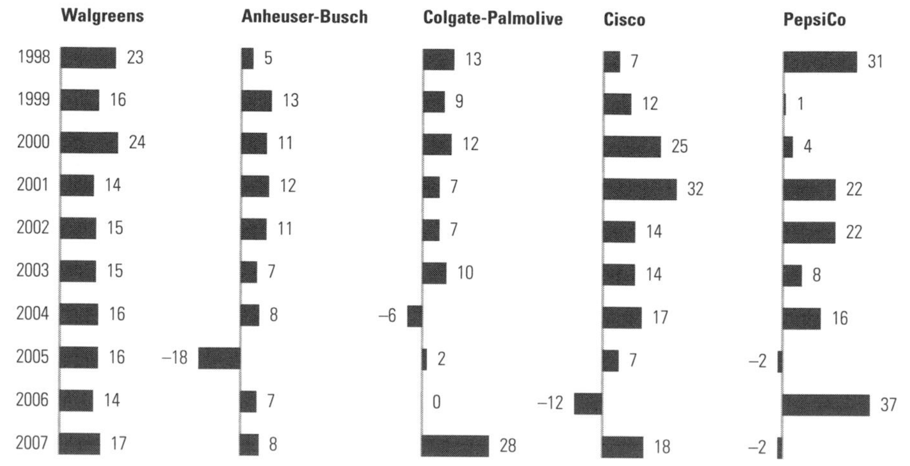

	Walgreens	Anheuser-Busch	Colgate-Palmolive	Cisco	PepsiCo
1998	23	5	13	7	31
1999	16	13	9	12	1
2000	24	11	12	25	4
2001	14	12	7	32	22
2002	15	11	7	14	22
2003	15	7	10	14	8
2004	16	8	−6	17	16
2005	16	−18	2	7	−2
2006	14	7	0	−12	37
2007	17	8	28	18	−2

[1] Earnings is defined as net income before extraordinary items, adjusted for goodwill impairment.

Source: McKinsey Corporate Performance Center analysis.

Markets Dig beneath Earnings Announcements

When a high-profile company misses an earnings target, it certainly makes headlines, but the impact of short-term earnings on share prices should not be overstated. Research undertaken on a large sample of quarterly earnings announcements by U.S. companies between 1992 and 1997 showed that earnings surprises explained less than 2 percent of share price volatility in the four weeks surrounding the announcements.[13] In fact, more than 40 percent of companies delivering a positive earnings surprise actually had a negative return, or vice versa.

There is a good reason why missing or meeting short-term EPS targets explains so little of share price volatility: investors place far more importance on a company's economic fundamentals than on reported earnings. Sometimes, however, short-term earnings are the only data investors have on which to base their judgment of fundamental corporate performance. In these cases, investors may interpret a missed EPS target as an omen of a decline in long-term performance and management credibility, so they lower the company's share price accordingly. If management can convince the market that poor short-term earnings will not affect long-term profitability or growth or might even herald an improvement, then the share price need not fall.

[13] W. Kinney, D. Burgstahler, and R. Martin, "Earnings Surprise 'Materiality' as Measured by Stock Returns," *Journal of Accounting Research* 40, no. 5 (December 2002): 1297–1329.

EXHIBIT 16.3 **Long-Term Performance Expectations Drive Share Price**

Median abnormal return[1] on 595 announcements of fiscal-year earnings for 2007 by European companies, percent

		Lower	Higher
Change in long-term expectations (change in expected EPS for 2009)	Positive	1.5 ($n = 127$)	2.4 ($n = 203$)
	Negative	−0.5 ($n = 118$)	−0.6 ($n = 142$)

Short-term surprise
(actual EPS 2007 relative to
expected EPS for 2007)

[1] Excess return over market return.

Source: Bloomberg, McKinsey Corporate Performance Center analysis.

To find evidence for the market's focus on long-term fundamentals as opposed to short-term earnings, we measured how share prices reacted in the three days following profit announcements for 2007 from the largest European companies by market capitalization.[14] As shown in Exhibit 16.3, we divided the companies into four groups along two dimensions: (1) Was the earnings announcement a positive or a negative surprise? (2) Did analysts' expectations of the company's earnings for the subsequent two years increase or decrease on the announcement?[15] Based on the median share price movement for each group (recorded in the center of each quadrant), share prices of companies announcing lower than expected earnings did not fall if the announcement did not affect the outlook for longer-term business profitability. However, when such an earnings surprise clearly signaled that long-term profit expectations were too high, the share price fell sharply.

The results shown reflect only the impact of surprises on earnings per share, but we obtained almost identical results for operating-profit surprises. This gives us further confidence that market reactions to negative surprises had nothing to do with companies failing to meet short-term earnings targets per se. Price falls occurred only when such failures stemmed from real changes in long-term fundamental prospects.

Similarly, share prices do not rise if the market believes a positive earnings surprise is simply the result of some imaginative accounting. For example, research confirms that markets do not respond favorably to earnings increases dependent on high accruals. Companies announcing such an increase find that

[14] The sample includes the 595 largest companies from Europe (excluding Russia).

[15] The analysts' expectations are based on Institutional Brokers' Estimate System consensus forecasts for 2007, 2008, and 2009.

EXHIBIT 16.4 **Market Reaction to Pharmaceutical Product Announcements**

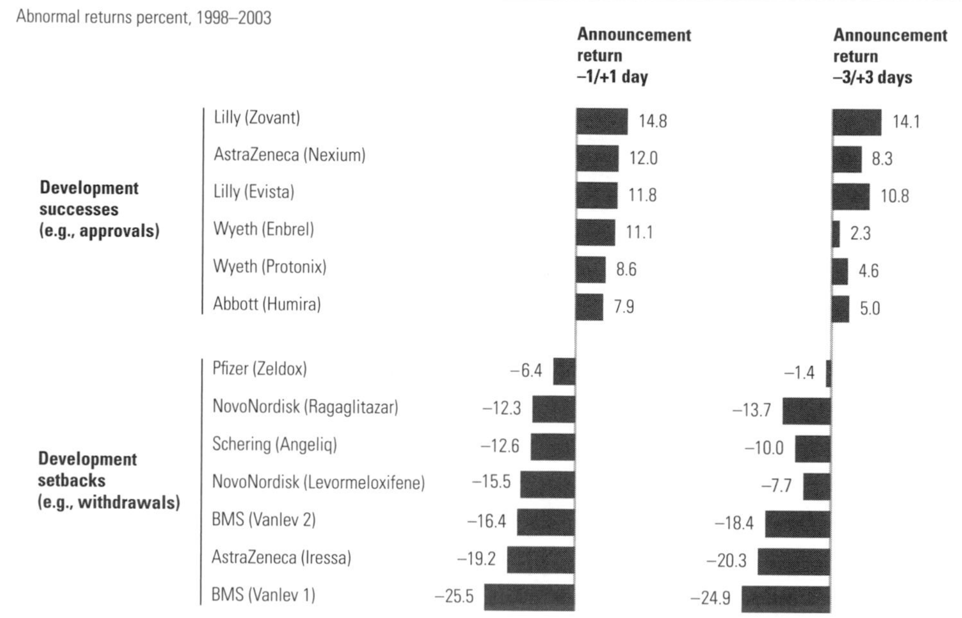

Abnormal returns percent, 1998–2003

		Announcement return −1/+1 day	Announcement return −3/+3 days
Development successes (e.g., approvals)	Lilly (Zovant)	14.8	14.1
	AstraZeneca (Nexium)	12.0	8.3
	Lilly (Evista)	11.8	10.8
	Wyeth (Enbrel)	11.1	2.3
	Wyeth (Protonix)	8.6	4.6
	Abbott (Humira)	7.9	5.0
Development setbacks (e.g., withdrawals)	Pfizer (Zeldox)	−6.4	−1.4
	NovoNordisk (Ragaglitazar)	−12.3	−13.7
	Schering (Angeliq)	−12.6	−10.0
	NovoNordisk (Levormeloxifene)	−15.5	−7.7
	BMS (Vanlev 2)	−16.4	−18.4
	AstraZeneca (Iressa)	−19.2	−20.3
	BMS (Vanlev 1)	−25.5	−24.9

Source: Datastream, Factiva, McKinsey Corporate Performance Center analysis.

subsequent shareholder returns are poor relative to peers.[16] And investors are wise to be wary when accruals contribute substantially to earnings, because this typically indicates that a company has reached a turning point and will post lower earnings in the future.

Investors' approach to pharmaceutical stocks further confirms their focus on economic fundamentals beyond earnings figures. In the pharmaceutical industry, announcements about products under development can affect share prices far more than quarterly earnings announcements. This makes sense because product and pipeline development are much better indicators of the long-term growth and profitability of pharmaceutical companies than short-term earnings. Markets understand this well, and as Exhibit 16.4 shows, prices react strongly to pipeline announcements, even though these herald no impact on current earnings.

The academic literature offers evidence that firms that consistently meet or exceed earnings expectations are more highly valued by the stock market and generate higher returns to shareholders.[17] There are even indications

---

[16] K. Chan, L. Chan, N. Jegadeesh, and J. Lakonishok, "Earnings Quality and Stock Returns," *Journal of Business* 79, no. 3 (2006): 1041–1082.

[17] For an overview, see S. Korthari, "Capital Markets Research in Accounting," *Journal of Accounting and Economics* 31, nos. 1–3 (September 2001): 105–231.

that the rewards for exceeding investors' expectations of earnings—and the penalties for missing them—have increased since the mid-1990s.[18] To a large extent, however, this market response is to be expected if markets are following fundamentals: when companies surprise investors by consistently performing better than expected, over time investors are likely to revise their outlook of underlying performance, resulting in a higher share price.[19] They do not base such an adjustment on just one earnings surprise in a single quarter. Rather, they anticipate future performance of the underlying business in line with consistent experience. Research findings indicate that the market is making the right assumption: firms that repeatedly exceed earnings expectations also show superior business performance in terms of profitability and growth in subsequent years.[20]

Some researchers suggest that the value premium for such companies is higher than justified by the analysts' earnings outlook.[21] However, managers should not take this as an argument for manufacturing earnings surprises. One reason is that such premiums are difficult to estimate, because the analysts' outlook typically concerns no more than three years of future earnings, which represent only a small portion of a company's total value. Second, as we just noted, only companies that produce positive surprises for several years in succession develop the premiums.[22] One lucky shot will not be enough. Finally, the longer a company surprises the market with its earnings, the harsher the market reaction when it breaks the pattern. Any premium in the company's valuation builds up gradually over a long string of positive earnings surprises. But this is very rapidly lost when the market loses confidence in continuing outperformance.

Overall, the evidence shows that the stock market is highly sophisticated in interpreting earnings announcements. Investors base their buy, sell, or keep decisions on a good deal more information and analysis than just a glance at the bottom-line earnings number.

---

[18] L. Brown and M. Caylor, "A Temporal Analysis of Quarterly Earnings Thresholds: Propensities and Valuation Consequences," *Accounting Review* 80, no. 2 (2005): 423–440.

[19] Research shows that investors underreact to positive earnings surprises. Analyst earnings forecasts and share prices adjust only gradually over time to the news on an improved outlook for the company. See V. Bernard and J. Thomas, "Post-Earnings-Announcement Drift: Delayed Price Response or Risk Premium," *Journal of Accounting Research* 27 (1989): 1–36. For our purposes, it is less relevant whether the market absorbs news in several days or in months; the share price eventually reflects underlying fundamentals.

[20] E. Bartov, D. Givoly, and C Hayn, "The Rewards to Meeting or Beating Earnings Expectations," *Journal of Accounting and Economics* 33, no. 2 (June 2002): 173–204.

[21] M. Barth, J. Elliott, and M. Finn, "Market Rewards Associated with Patterns of Increasing Earnings," *Journal of Accounting Research* 37, no. 2 (Autumn 1999): 387–413.

[22] R. Kasznik and M. McNichols, "Does Meeting Earnings Expectations Matter? Evidence from Analyst Forecast Revisions and Share Prices," *Journal of Accounting Research* 40, no. 3 (June 2002): 727–759.

ECONOMICS OF ACCOUNTING INFORMATION: NO MYSTERY TO THE MARKET

Indeed, stock price data suggest that the market digs deeply beneath not just reported earnings but all of a company's accounting information in order to understand the underlying economic fundamentals. Share prices will therefore move if information in the accounts reflects unexpected changes in underlying cash flows. For instance, an accounting disclosure such as goodwill impairment will lower the price if the adjustment reveals lower than expected benefits from past acquisitions. Similarly, changing from last-in first-out (LIFO) to first-in first-out (FIFO) inventory accounting can swing share prices, not because of the resulting change in reported earnings, but because of the tax implications. At the same time, changes in the accounting numbers that do not reflect any cash flow changes or reflect only changes that had already been anticipated by the market will leave share prices unchanged. Such immaterial modifications include changes in accounting standards, options expensing, and most goodwill impairments.

Sometimes investors have difficulty detecting the true economic situation behind accounting information. For example, the financial reports of many banks and insurance companies are so opaque that it is difficult for investors to assess those businesses' true returns on capital and risks. To be fair, the true profitability and risk of many such businesses may be genuinely unclear at the time they report results because product or trading payoffs may be spread over several years (as with mortgages, life insurance, or trading positions) and contingent on many different factors (for example, rates of default, interest, mortality, and foreign exchange). However, some companies, including Enron and WorldCom, have misled stock markets by purposely manipulating their financial statements. But all managers should understand that markets can be mistaken or fooled for only so long. Sooner or later, cash flows must justify share prices.

Different Accounting Standards Do Not Lead to Different Values

Share price data for companies that report different accounting results in different stock markets provide evidence that stock markets do not take reported earnings at face value. Non-U.S. companies that have securities listed in the United States and do not report under U.S. generally accepted accounting principles (GAAP)[23] or International Financial Reporting Standards (IFRS), for example, are required to report equity and net profit under U.S. GAAP. These can give results that differ significantly from the equity and net profit reported under their domestic accounting standards. If stock prices depended

---

[23] Since March 2008, non-U.S. companies reporting under IFRS are no longer required to reconcile financial statements to U.S. GAAP in their Securities and Exchange Commission (SEC) filings.

EXHIBIT 16.5 **No Clear Impact of U.S. GAAP Reconciliations**

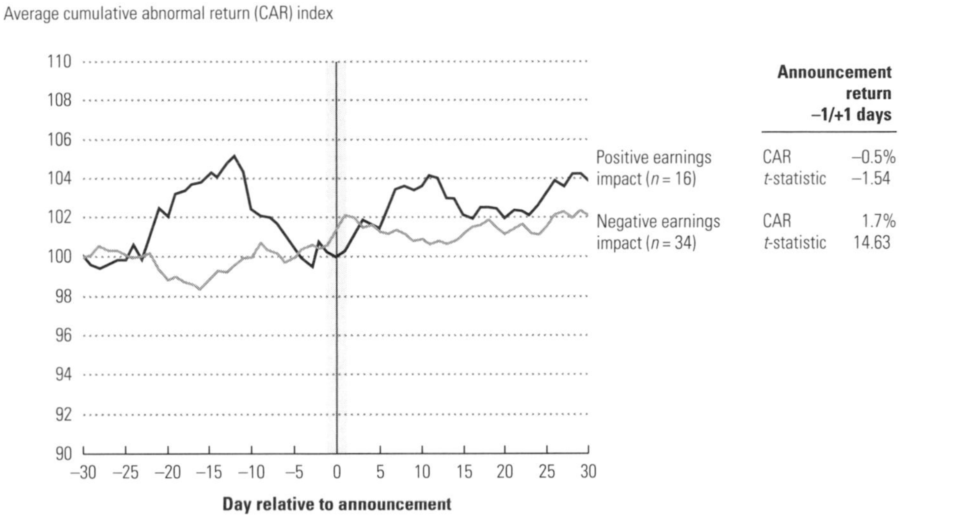

Average cumulative abnormal return (CAR) index

		Announcement return −1/+1 days
Positive earnings impact (n = 16)	CAR	−0.5%
	t-statistic	−1.54
Negative earnings impact (n = 34)	CAR	1.7%
	t-statistic	14.63

Day relative to announcement

Source: SEC filings, Datastream, Bloomberg, McKinsey Corporate Performance Center analysis.

on reported earnings, investors would care which set of earnings they looked at—those reported under U.S. GAAP or domestic accounting standards. But they don't. Investors care about a company's underlying performance, not its choice of accounting standards.

To prove the point, we analyzed a sample of 50 European companies that began reporting reconciliations of equity and profit to U.S. GAAP after obtaining U.S. listings between 1997 and 2004. The differences between net income and equity under U.S. and local accounting standards were often quite large; in more than half the cases, the gap was more than 30 percent. Many executives probably worried that lower earnings under U.S. GAAP would translate directly into a lower share price. But this was not the case. As shown in Exhibit 16.5, even though two-thirds of the companies in our sample reported lower earnings following U.S. disclosure, the stock market reaction to their disclosure was positive. At that time, following U.S. GAAP standards also generally meant disclosing more information than required by local standards. Evidently, improved disclosure outweighed any artificial accounting effects.

Treatment of Goodwill Does Not Affect Share Price

Since 2001 under U.S. GAAP and since 2005 under IFRS goodwill is no longer amortized on the income statement according to fixed schedules. Instead, companies must write off goodwill only when it is impaired according to business valuations produced by independent auditors. What effect did these changes in accounting for goodwill have on share prices? Not a lot, according to our analyses.

We looked at their impact on share prices in two ways. First, we investigated the price reactions for companies that stopped amortizing significant amounts of goodwill. These companies showed an increase in reported EPS after this change, since they were no longer charging goodwill amortization to the income statement. We analyzed the share price reaction for a sample of 54 such U.S. companies that had significant goodwill on the day in July 2001 when the abolition of goodwill amortization in the United States was announced.[24] The implied increase in EPS for these companies initially boosted their average share prices, but within two weeks the prices had returned to normal. The market realized that the accounting treatment of goodwill amortization does not affect cash flows. Furthermore, as shown in Exhibit 16.6, the initial share price reaction was not necessarily related to each company's relative amount of goodwill: for about a third of the sample, share prices actually declined on the announcement.

We also looked at 54 companies in the United States and Europe that had written off significant amounts of impaired goodwill against their profit since January 2002.[25] In this case, as shown in Exhibit 16.7, we did not find a statistically significant drop in share prices on the day a write-off was announced. Why not? The markets had already anticipated the lower benefits from past acquisitions and had reduced the stock price by an average 35 percent in the six months preceding the write-off announcement.

Time Warner, for example, announced on January 7, 2002, that it would write off $54 billion in goodwill. Time Warner's stock returns, plotted in Exhibit 16.7, show that the share price actually moved up somewhat on the day of the announcement, relative to major market indexes. However, Time Warner's stock had lost as much as 37 percent of its value over the six months preceding the announcement. The significant changes in reported earnings caused by the changes in accounting for goodwill therefore had no immediate impact on share prices. The markets looked beyond the effect of the accounting treatment on current earnings to the underlying long-term cash flow.

These findings should come as no surprise, given overwhelming evidence that the stock market also looked beyond goodwill amortization in the past when assessing pooling versus purchasing accounting for mergers and acquisitions.[26] In fact, goodwill amortization as such has never much mattered to market value—neither when it showed up in the financial statements nor when it disappeared.

---

[24] The sample consists of selected U.S. companies for which annual goodwill amortization was at least 1 percent of the market capitalization.

[25] The sample comprises selected U.S. and European companies with a market capitalization of at least $500 million and an impairment charge of at least 2 percent of market capitalization.

[26] See, for example, E. Lindenberg and M. Ross, "To Purchase or to Pool: Does It Matter?," *Journal of Applied Corporate Finance* 12, no. 2 (Summer 1999): 32–47.

EXHIBIT 16.6 No Consistent Market Reaction to SFAS-142 Goodwill Announcement

Abnormal return on announcement date, percent

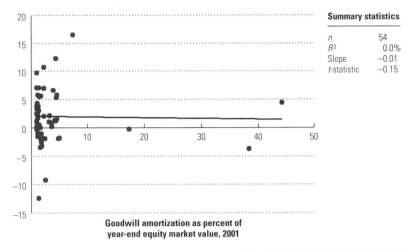

Summary statistics

n	54
R^2	0.0%
Slope	−0.01
t-statistic	−0.15

Goodwill amortization as percent of
year-end equity market value, 2001

Source: Datastream, McKinsey Corporate Performance Center analysis.

Accounting for Employee and Management Stock Options Is Irrelevant to Market Value

The introduction of rules requiring employee stock options to be expensed in the income statement caused much concern in the early 2000s. The discussion centered on whether the resulting negative impact on earnings would drive

EXHIBIT 16.7 No Market Reaction to Announcement of Goodwill Impairment

Cumulative abnormal return (CAR) index, $n = 54$

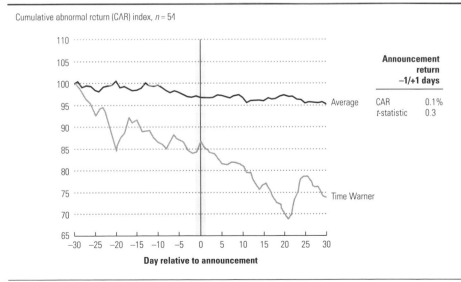

Announcement
return
−1/+1 days

CAR	0.1%
t-statistic	0.3

Day relative to announcement

Source: SEC filings, Datastream, Bloomberg, McKinsey Corporate Performance Center analysis.

stock prices lower. From a capital-market perspective, the answer is clear: as long as investors have sufficient information on the amount, terms, and conditions of the options granted, new expensing rules will not drive down share prices. In fact, research has found that companies that voluntarily planned to begin expensing their employee options *before* it became mandatory saw their share prices rise when they announced their intention, despite its negative implications for reported earnings.[27] The rise was especially strong when companies said they were expensing their options to boost transparency. The same researchers found that the stock market takes account of options values in its valuation of companies that give full information about their options schemes—even when these values are not explicitly expensed in the companies' income statements.[28]

We came to a similar conclusion after examining 120 U.S. companies that began voluntarily expensing their stock options in their income statements between July 2002 and May 2004. Their share prices did not fall when the effect of this choice showed up in their subsequent earnings announcements; on the contrary, their prices rose on the announcement day. Furthermore, as shown in Exhibit 16.8, there was no relationship between the impact on net income of option expensing and any abnormal returns during the days surrounding the new policy's announcement. This makes sense because the market already had the relevant information on the option plans and was not confused by a change in reporting policy.

LIFO versus FIFO Affects Market Values—But Not Because of Earnings Impact

The impact of different inventory accounting methods on cash flow and profits under U.S. tax laws provides a clear example of how much more investors care about economic fundamentals than accounting treatments. During periods when prices are rising, changing from FIFO to LIFO can decrease accounting profits yet lead to higher free cash flows. As prices rise, the LIFO inventory method results in lower earnings than FIFO, since the cost of goods sold is based on more recent, higher costs. But lower pretax earnings mean lower income taxes. Since the pretax cash flow is the same regardless of the accounting method, LIFO accounting leads to a higher after-tax cash flow than FIFO accounting, despite the lower reported earnings.

Any manager mistakenly focused solely on earnings would argue that switching from FIFO to LIFO will result in a lower share price as investors react to lower reported earnings. Yet research shows that, as the DCF model

---

[27] D. Aboody, M. Barth, and R. Kasznik, "Firms' Voluntary Recognition of Stock-Based Compensation Expense," *Journal of Accounting Research* 42, no. 2 (December 2004): 251–275.
[28] D. Aboody, M. Barth, and R. Kasznik, "SFAS No. 123 Stock-Based Compensation Expense and Equity Market Values," *Accounting Review* 79, no. 2 (2004): 251–275.

EXHIBIT 16.8 **Voluntary Option Expensing: No Impact on Share Price**

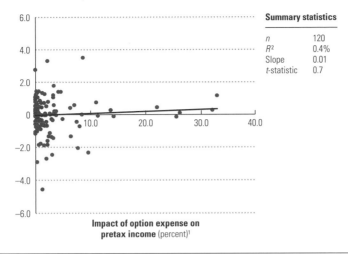

Abnormal return on announcement date, percent

Impact of option expense on
pretax income (percent)[1]

Summary statistics	
n	120
R^2	0.4%
Slope	0.01
t-statistic	0.7

[1] Defined as the absolute value of option expense divided by the pretax earnings before option expense.

Source: SEC filings, Datastream, Bloomberg, McKinsey Corporate Performance Center analysis.

would predict, switching from FIFO to LIFO in fact lifts share prices because it increases cash flow: after adjusting for movements in the broad market and other contemporary effects, companies switching to LIFO have experienced significant increases in share prices, whereas firms switching to FIFO have seen their share prices fall (see Exhibit 16.9). One study found that the larger the reduction in taxes following the switch to LIFO, the greater the share price increase attributable to the change.[29]

TECHNICAL TRADING FACTORS ARE IRRELEVANT FOR VALUE

Conventional wisdom has long held that companies can capture benefits for their shareholders without any improvements to underlying cash flows by listing their stock in multiple markets, splitting their stocks, having more analyst coverage, being included in a key market index, or providing earnings guidance. True, a company from an emerging market in Asia securing a U.S. listing or a little-known European company joining a leading global stock index might get some appreciable uplift. But well-functioning capital markets are entirely focused on the fundamentals of cash flow and revenue growth. Therefore, it does not matter how large, established companies in developed economies package and present their shareholders' claims on future cash flows. Whether

[29] G. Biddle and F. Lindahl, "Stock Price Reactions to LIFO Adoptions: The Association between Excess Returns and LIFO Tax Savings," *Journal of Accounting Research* 20, no. 2 (1982): 551–588.

EXHIBIT 16.9 **Inventory Accounting Change: Impact on Share Price**

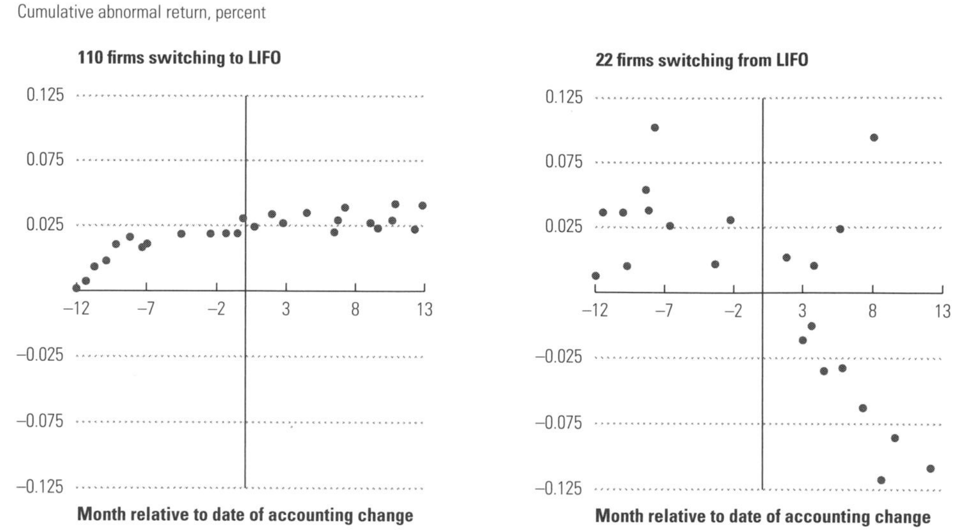

Cumulative abnormal return, percent

110 firms switching to LIFO

22 firms switching from LIFO

Month relative to date of accounting change

Month relative to date of accounting change

Source: S. Sunder, "Relationship between Accounting Changes and Stock Prices: Problems of Measurement and Some Empirical Evidence,"
Empirical Research in Accounting: Selected Studies, 1973.

the share is traded in one or multiple locations; denominated in securities of 1, 10, or 10,000 euros (or dollars or pounds sterling for that matter); or part of a major U.S., European, or Asian stock index is irrelevant.

This section provides examples of the negligible effects on value of three such changes in form rather than substance: stock splits, index inclusions/exclusions, and cross-listings. The evidence clearly shows that mature markets do not reward such repackaging or changes in presentation—unless there is an associated change in corporate performance.

True Impact of Stock Splits

In the United States alone, each year hundreds of companies increase their number of shares through a stock split.[30] From an economic perspective, a stock split is irrelevant because the size of the pie available to the shareholders remains the same. So, for example, after a two-for-one stock split, a shareholder who owned two shares worth $5 apiece ends up with four shares, each worth $2.50.

Yet in many cases, a stock split is accompanied by positive abnormal returns to shareholders. Exhibit 16.10 shows the typical return pattern, as estimated in

---

[30] R. D. Boehme and B. R. Danielsen report over 6,000 stock splits between 1950 and 2000: "Stock-Split Post-Announcement Returns: Underreaction or Market Friction?," *Financial Review* 42 (2007): 485–506. D. Ikenberry and S. Ramnath report over 3,000 stock splits between 1988 and 1998: "Underreaction to Self-Selected News Events: The Case of Stock Splits," *Review of Financial Studies* 15 (2002): 489–526.

EXHIBIT 16.10 **Cumulative Average Abnormal Returns around Stock Splits**

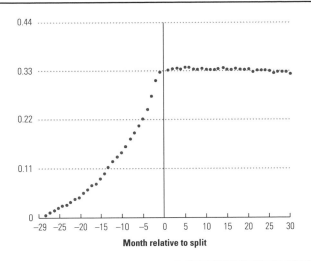

Source: E. Fama, L. Fisher, M. Jensen, and R. Roll, "The Adjustment of Stock Prices to New Information," *International Economic Review* 10 (1969): 1–21.

the seminal article on this topic by Eugene Fama and his colleagues.[31] Some managers and academics claim that this pattern shows how stock splits create value because they bring a company's share price back into the "optimal trading range." The theory is that lowering the price of a share makes it more attractive for capital-constrained investors, thereby increasing demand for the stock after a split and improving liquidity. However, there is ample evidence to show that this is not the case. After a split, trading volumes typically decline, and brokerage fees and bid-ask spreads increase, indicating lower liquidity, if anything.[32]

In fact, rising share prices around the time of a stock split have nothing to do with the split as such. Rather, the evidence shows they are a function of two factors: self-selection and the signaling of changes in a company's economic fundamentals. Self-selection is the tendency of companies to split their stocks into lower denominations because of a prolonged rise in their share price, as shown in Exhibit 16.10. As a result, we should expect any sample of companies that have split their stocks to show positive abnormal returns in the months preceding the split announcement, which is usually one to two months before the effective split date.[33] Thus, to argue that stock splits lead to share price run-ups would be to confuse cause with effect.

---

[31] E. Fama, L. Fisher, M. Jensen, and R. Roll, "The Adjustment of Stock Prices to New Information," *International Economic Review* 10 (1969): 1–21.

[32] T. Copeland, "Liquidity Changes Following Stock Splits," *Journal of Finance* 34, no. 1 (March 1979): 115–141.

[33] Boehme and Danielsen, "Stock-Split Post-Announcement Returns," report an average of 54 days from announcement to effective date in the years between 1962 and 1974. For the period between 1988 and 2000, this dropped to 24 days.

When managers announce a stock split, they are also signaling that they expect a continuation of the improvement in economic fundamentals to which the market is already responding. As the data in Exhibit 16.10 reveal, signaling an improvement in fundamentals gives an extra boost to share prices around the date of the split announcement. Researchers have found that the abnormal return is statistically significant for the three days around the date of the stock split announcement, at about 3 percent.[34] This effect is not a result of the announcement itself but of the announcement's implicit message that management is confident in the company's performance outlook.[35] Indeed, two-thirds of companies reported higher than expected earnings and dividends in the year following a stock split. When performance improvements actually occurred after the split, the stock market did not react, indicating that investors had already factored them into their decisions at the time of the stock split announcement. Consistent with this pattern, companies that did not improve performance as expected in the year after a stock split saw their share prices fall.[36]

Over the past decade, some researchers have reported positive abnormal returns not only in the days around a split announcement but also for the entire year following the split announcement.[37] These researchers conclude that the market is underreacting to stock splits and therefore is inefficient. But other researchers find that the abnormal returns do not lead to any arbitrage opportunities, so there is no question of market inefficiency.[38] Whichever way this debate goes, it does not change our conclusion: the stock market reacts positively to stock split announcements because they signal higher future cash flows. That is the substance that the market values. It has nothing to do with form.

Index Membership Does Not Matter to Value

Becoming a member of leading stock market indexes such as the S&P 500 or FTSE-100 appeals to managers because many large institutional investors track these indexes. Once a stock is added to the index, the argument goes, demand will increase dramatically—along with the share price—as institutional

---

[34] M. Grinblatt, R. Masulis, and S. Titman, "The Valuation Effects of Stock Splits and Stock Dividends," *Journal of Financial Economics* 13 (1984): 461–490. Interestingly enough, Grinblatt et al. find a similar 4.9 percent announcement effect for stock dividends, which are economically comparable to stock splits, as they also increase the number of shares without any change in the total claims for shareholders.

[35] M. Brennan and T. Copeland, "Stock Splits, Stock Prices, and Transaction Costs," *Journal of Financial Economics* 22 (1988): 83–101.

[36] See Fama, Fisher, Jensen, and Roll, "Adjustment of Stock Prices."

[37] Ikenberry and Ramnath, "Underreaction to Self-Selected News Events."

[38] The frictions do not lead to any arbitrage opportunities, according to Boehme and Danielsen, "Stock-Split Post-Announcement Returns." Following J. Conrad and G. Kaul, "Long-Term Market Overreaction or Biases in Computed Returns?," *Journal of Finance* 48 (1993): 39–63, they argue that the abnormal returns are mainly formed in the period between announcement and effective date of the split, during which trading frictions for shares ex- and presplit lead to a bias in return measurement.

EXHIBIT 16.11 **Effects of Inclusion Disappear after 45 Days**

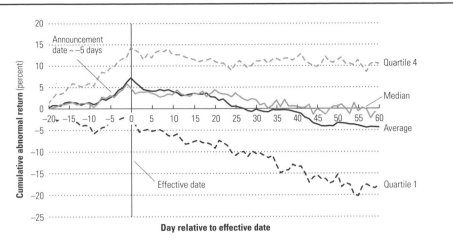

investors rebalance their portfolios to reflect the change of index membership. As long as that demand continues, so will the premium.

Anecdotal evidence appears to confirm this view. In 2001, Nortel, Shell, Unilever, and four other companies based outside the United States were removed from the S&P 500 index and replaced by the same number of U.S. corporations. The departing companies lost, on average, nearly 7.5 percent of their value in the three days after the announcement. The stock prices of the new entrants—including eBay, Goldman Sachs, and UPS—increased by more than 3 percent in the same period.

But empirical evidence shows that such changes in share price are typically short-lived. Academic research has found that share prices of companies excluded from a major stock index do indeed decrease after the announcement, but this fall is fully reversed within one or two months.[39] Surprisingly, the evidence on the impact of index inclusions appears less conclusive; several publications report that price increases occurring immediately after an inclusion are only partly reversed over time.[40]

We analyzed the effect on share price of 103 inclusions and 41 exclusions from the S&P 500 between December 1999 and March 2004.[41] For these, we plotted abnormal stock returns over an 80-day test period, from 20 days before the effective date of inclusion or exclusion to 60 days afterward. Exhibit 16.11

[39] H. Chen, G. Noronha, and V. Singal, "The Price Response to S&P 500 Index Additions and Deletions: Evidence of Asymmetry and a New Explanation," *Journal of Finance* 59, no. 4 (August 2004): 1901–1929.
[40] See also, for example, L. Harris and E. Gurel, "Price and Volume Effects Associated with Changes in the S&P 500: New Evidence for the Existence of Price Pressures," *Journal of Finance* 41 (1986): 815–830; and R. A. Brealey, "Stock Prices, Stock Indexes, and Index Funds," *Bank of England Quarterly Bulletin* (2000): 61–68.
[41] For further details, see M. Goedhart and R. Huc, "What Is Stock Membership Worth?," *McKinsey on Finance*, no. 10 (Winter 2004): 14–16.

shows the abnormal returns for the new entrants to the index. These companies all experienced a share price run-up in the months preceding the index inclusion, which is evidence of self-selection: they were included in the index because of their rapidly rising share prices. But the new entrants did not enjoy any permanent positive returns as a result. Indeed, though abnormal returns increased in the 10 days prior to the effective date—to an average of around 7 percent and a median of about 5 percent—they went back to zero within 45 days of inclusion. Statistically significant positive returns disappeared after only 20 days.

Looking at 41 companies ejected from the S&P 500 over the same period, we found similar patterns of temporary price change. The pressure on their prices following exclusion from the index lifted after two to three weeks.

The results are consistent with the phenomenon of liquidity pressure, which drives up share prices initially as investors adjust their portfolios to changes in the index. Prices revert to normal once portfolios are rebalanced. In the end, our evidence showed, as fundamental valuation theory would predict, that in most cases, new entrants to the S&P 500 did not enjoy permanent price premiums, and the prices of companies excluded did not suffer over the long term. Capital markets prove to be quite efficient, underlining the fact that the value of a stock is ultimately determined by its cash flow potential, not by membership in major equity indexes.

Cross-Listing Does Not Affect Market Value

For years, many academics, executives, and analysts believed companies cross-listing their shares on exchanges in the United States, London, and Tokyo could realize a higher share price and a lower cost of capital.[42] Cross-listed shares would benefit from more analyst coverage, a broader shareholder base, improved liquidity, higher governance standards, and better access to capital. In the 1980s and 1990s, hundreds of companies from around the world duly cross-listed their shares.

Such benefits may well have existed in the past before capital markets became more liquid and integrated, and investors more global. But our analysis of recent data shows that this does not hold today for companies in the developed markets of North America, Western Europe, Japan, and Australia.[43] Indeed, since 2002, the number of cross-listings by companies based in the developed world has been steadily declining in key capital markets in New York

[42] For example, see C. Doidge, A. Karolyi, and R. Stulz, "Why Are Foreign Firms That List in the U.S. Worth More?," *Journal of Financial Economics* 71, no. 2 (2004): 205–238; and M. King and U. Mittoo, "What Companies Need to Know about International Cross-Listing," *Journal of Applied Corporate Finance* 19, no. 4 (Fall 2007): 60–74.
[43] For further details, see R. Dobbs and M. Goedhart, "Why Cross-Listing Shares Doesn't Create Value," *McKinsey on Finance*, no. 29 (Autumn 2008): 18–23.

and London. Between May 2007 and May 2008, 35 large European companies, including household names such as Ahold, Air France, Bayer, British Airways, Danone, Fiat, and KPN terminated their cross-listings on stock exchanges in New York as the requirements for deregistering from U.S. markets became less stringent.[44]

In line with earlier research, we found that cross-listed European companies have more analyst coverage than those that are not cross-listed.[45] But after correcting for size, the difference is marginal: on average, a large cross-listed European company has 22 analysts versus 20 for its peers listed in a single market. In addition, institutional investors from the United States do not require the foreign companies in which they want to invest to be listed in the United States. CalPERS, for instance, a large U.S. investor, has an international equity portfolio of around 2,400 companies, but less than 10 percent of them have a U.S. cross-listing. Cross-listings do not make much difference to a stock's liquidity, either. The trading volumes of the cross-listed shares of European companies in the United States—American depositary receipts (ADRs)—typically account for less than 3 percent of these companies' total trading volumes. For Japanese and Australian companies, the percentage is even lower. Any advantages resulting from higher corporate governance standards once gained from a cross-listing in the United States or the United Kingdom hardly exist today for companies from developed countries, as corporate governance standards have converged across the developed world. Local stock markets have provided a sufficient supply of equity capital to companies in the developed economies of the European Union and Japan. In fact, three-quarters of the U.S. cross-listings of companies from these economies have never involved raising any new capital in the United States.[46]

Not surprisingly, we did not find any significant impact on shareholder value from cross-listings for companies from North America, Western Europe, Japan, and Australia. We analyzed the stock market reactions to 229 voluntary delistings by Western European, Japanese, and Australian companies from U.S. and U.K. stock exchanges since 2002.[47] We found no declines in share price in response to the delisting announcements. As Exhibit 16.12 shows,

---

[44] Since March 2007, foreign companies have been allowed to deregister with the U.S. Securities and Exchange Commission if less than 5 percent of global trading in their shares takes place on U.S. stock exchanges.

[45] See, for example, M. Lang, K. Lins, and D. Miller, "ADRs, Analysts, and Accuracy: Does Cross Listing in the U.S. Improve a Firm's Information Environment and Increase Market Value?," *Journal of Accounting Research* 41, no. 2 (May 2003): 317–345.

[46] This figure is based on 420 depositary receipt issues on the New York Stock Exchange, NASDAQ, and American Stock Exchange from January 1970 to May 2008 (www.adrbny.com).

[47] We focused our analysis on delisting rather than listing announcements. Listing announcements are frequently revoked at a later stage, when companies decide to defer or not go ahead with a cross-listing. As a result, listing announcements could be expected to trigger very limited share price reaction. We included only voluntary delistings; involuntary delistings also occur—for example, as a result of bankruptcies, mergers, and takeovers.

EXHIBIT 16.12 **Delisting from U.S./U.K. Exchanges: No Value Impact on Companies from Developed Markets**

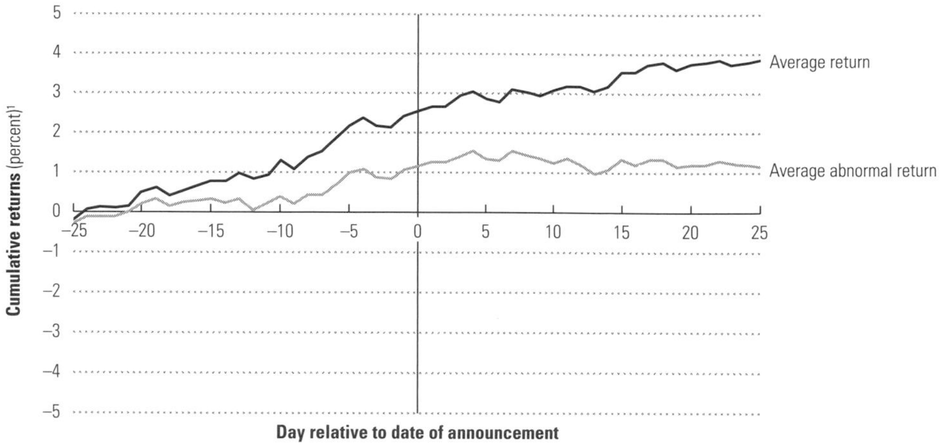

¹ Sample of 229 delistings from New York Stock Exchange, NASDAQ, or London International Main Market. Announcement dates between December 31, 2002, and December 31, 2007.

Source: Reuters, Bloomberg, Datastream, New York Stock Exchange (NYSE), London Stock Exchange.

there was no break in the abnormal return pattern in the three days before and after the delisting announcement. In fact, most announcements in our sample produced hardly any reaction from analysts and investors. The announcement by Dutch telecom player KPN that it planned to delist from the New York Stock Exchange (NYSE) was barely commented on in the Dutch newspapers.

Comparing the 2006 valuations of some 200 cross-listed companies with those of more than 1,500 comparable companies without foreign listings confirms our conclusion that cross-listing does not affect market value. Using multiple regression, we estimated the extent to which a cross-listing influenced a company's valuation as measured by the ratio between enterprise value and invested capital and the ratio between enterprise value and earnings before interest, taxes, depreciation, and amortization (EBITDA). We also took into account the company's return on invested capital, consensus growth projections, industry sector, and geographic region. As Exhibit 16.13 shows, whether a company was cross-listed in New York did not matter for its valuation level, when its return on capital was taken into account. The coefficients for a cross-listing were not statistically significant in any of the regressions. For companies with cross-listings in London, we found almost identical results. A cross-listing has no impact on a company's share price.

For companies from the emerging world, however, the story might be different. The reason is that their market conditions concerning, for example, governance practices, liquidity, investor sophistication, and access to global capital markets generally differ from the largely convergent conditions in developed

EXHIBIT 16.13 **U.S. Cross-Listing: No Impact on Valuation of Developed-Market Companies**

U.S.-listed and non-U.S.-listed companies in Western Europe, Japan, Canada, Australia, New Zealand

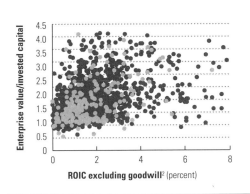

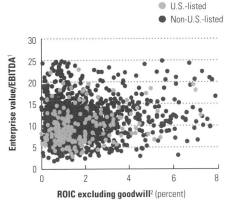

[1] Enterprise value at 2006 year-end divided by 2006 EBITDA.
[2] Average ROIC for 2004–2006.

Source: New York Stock Exchange, NASDAQ, Bloomberg, Datastream, McKinsey Corporate Performance Center analysis.

markets and vary a lot between countries. In general, therefore, these companies can realize some clear benefits from cross-listing in a well-functioning capital market. Cross-listed shares may represent as much as a third of their total trading volume, for example. Furthermore, some of these companies have succeeded in issuing large amounts of new equity through cross listings in U.S. or U.K. equity markets—something that might have been impossible at home. Finally, compliance with the more stringent U.S. or U.K. corporate governance requirements and stock market regulations rather than local ones could generate real benefits for shareholders.[48]

SUMMARY

Markets see through most illusions of value creation. Research demonstrates that markets are not fooled by earnings management; there is no reward for companies that generate stable earnings or consistently meet earnings targets. On the contrary, investors penalize companies that try to achieve earnings targets by manipulating their results. Markets reward or punish positive or negative short-term earnings surprises only when these coincide with an increase or decline in long-term return and growth expectations.

Markets are also quite capable of seeing the economic fundamentals behind accounting information. Empirical evidence clearly shows that share prices

[48] See R. Newell and G. Wilson, "A Premium for Good Governance," *McKinsey Quarterly*, no. 3 (2002): 20–23.

remain unchanged if accounting results do not reflect any cash flow changes or if the market had already anticipated such changes—for example, in the case of changes in accounting standards, options expensing, or most goodwill impairments. Capital markets are also able to see through any change in packaging or presentation of shareholder claims on a company's cash flows, unless there is an associated change in fundamental performance. Research shows that companies cannot boost their share price by merely listing their stock in multiple markets (if they are already listed in a well-developed stock market), splitting the stock, or being included in a key market index.

REVIEW QUESTIONS

1. Many corporate executives focus on earnings per share (EPS) and attempt to manage reported earnings in order to meet analysts' expectations. Can managers succeed in protecting the stock price of their company by managing these accounts?

2. Give an example of how to boost reported quarterly earnings by using accruals, and describe the implications for reported earnings in the next quarter. What is the risk involved in using accruals to boost earnings?

3. If a company's value is not driven by its short-term earnings, why do investors spend so much time analyzing a company's annual or even quarterly earnings announcements?

4. What risk does a company run once it starts to manage its earnings to meet analysts' targets year after year?

5. Empirical research shows that goodwill impairments have no impact on a company's share price. But these impairments do reflect an auditor's best estimate of the value lost in an acquisition by the company. Does the stock market not care about such losses?

6. Explain how changing from last-in first-out (LIFO) to first-in first-out (FIFO) might lead to a change in a company's intrinsic value in some countries but not in others.

7. As a rule, cross-listings for companies with a home listing in a mature capital market do not offer material benefits. Discuss how and why this might be different for companies based in emerging capital markets.

8. In the past, a fast-growing mobile telecommunications company has always capitalized its customer acquisition costs. For the next few years, management expects growth in its customer base to slow significantly, probably turning negative at some point. Explain what will happen to profits if revenues and cash costs per customer remain unchanged. Should management consider switching to expensing customer acquisition costs?

17

Emotions and Mispricing in the Market

Chapters 15 and 16 set out the evidence that stock market valuations correctly reflect underlying economic fundamentals in almost all cases and nearly all the time. But what about those episodes when markets appear to part company with reality? We agree with proponents of behavioral finance that emotions can get the better of investors at certain moments. But turning to the evidence again, we find such moments do not last very long and rarely involve more than a few companies or sectors. For the U.S. and European stock markets, we find the following patterns:

- Individual company share prices deviate significantly from the company's fundamental value only in rare circumstances—typically when barriers to trading, such as too limited a free float of shares, prevent rational investors from moving in to correct the price.

- Market-wide price deviations from fundamental valuations, as in the dot-com boom of the late 1990s or the soaring prices triggered by expectations of unsustainable corporate profits in 2007, are even less frequent, although they may appear to be becoming more so.

- In the vast majority of cases, price deviations from fundamentals are temporary. Market-wide deviations are typically corrected within three years. Company-specific deviations usually last only as long as the barriers preventing a price correction.

Although random deviations from intrinsic value can occur in stocks from time to time, managers are still best off assuming that the market will correctly reflect the intrinsic value of their decisions. What managers must be alert to, however, are systematic deviations from intrinsic value. These may affect strategic financial decisions, such as whether and when to issue new shares or pursue acquisitions. Managers who understand the potential causes of such deviations may exploit them to create more long-term value for their shareholders (see Chapter 18).

EMOTIONS RARELY DRIVE STOCK MARKET VALUES

Since the seminal article by Werner DeBondt and Richard Thaler in 1985,[1] some finance academics and practitioners have argued that stock markets are *not* efficient—that they do not necessarily reflect economic fundamentals.[2] According to this behavioral point of view, significant and lasting deviations from intrinsic value occur in market valuations.[3] We find that behavioral finance offers some valuable insights, chief among them that markets are not always right, because market imperfections prevent rational investors from correcting mispricing by irrational investors. But how often do these deviations arise? How long do they last? And are they so significant that they should affect how managers make their financial decisions? Scrutiny of the evidence shows that significant deviations from intrinsic value are in fact rare, and markets typically revert to the economic fundamentals rapidly enough to ensure that managers should continue to base their business decisions on discounted cash flow (DCF) analyses.

As we understand it, behavioral finance theory proposes that markets fail to reflect economic fundamentals under the following three conditions:

1. *When individual investors behave irrationally:* Investors are irrational if they do not process all available information correctly when forming their expectations of a stock's future performance. Studies of the investment behavior of professional fund managers and analysts show various forms of such irrationality. For example, individual investors attach too much importance to recent events and results, so they overprice companies with strong recent performance. Also, some individuals are overly conservative in updating their expectations, so they persist in underpricing stocks that have released positive news on earnings.

2. *When systematic patterns of irrational behavior emerge among investors:* If a few individual investors decide to buy or sell without reference to

---

[1] W. DeBondt and R. Thaler, "Does the Stock Market Overreact?" *Journal of Finance* 40, no. 3 (1985): 793–805.

[2] We loosely define efficient markets here as markets reflecting economic fundamentals, following Fischer Black, "Noise," *Journal of Finance* 41, no. (3) (1986): 533..

[3] For an overview of behavioral finance, see N. Barberis and R. Thaler, "A Survey of Behavioral Finance," in *Handbook of the Economics of Finance,* ed. G. M. Constantinides et al. (Boston: Elsevier Science, 2003): 1054–1123; and J. Ritter, "Behavioral Finance," *Pacific-Basin Finance Journal* 11, no. 4 (September 2003): 429–437.

economic fundamentals, the impact on share prices is limited. Only when large groups of investors start showing the same nonrational patterns of investment behavior—that is, when they behave irrationally in a systematic fashion—should persistent price deviations occur. Behavioral finance theory argues that habits of overconfidence, overreaction, and overrepresentation are common to many investors, resulting in groups large enough to prevent prices from reflecting underlying economic fundamentals at least for some stocks, some of the time.

3. *When there are limits to arbitrage in financial markets:* If there are no barriers to arbitrage, then any rational investors in a market can exploit emerging systematic patterns of irrational behavior, which will therefore have no lasting effects on market valuations. In reality, such arbitrage is not always possible. Transaction costs and risks are involved in setting up and running the arbitrage positions in some market conditions.

Let's consider the third condition in more detail. Say a company's share price has dramatically increased over the past few months because the company surprised the market with better-than-expected results. Solely on the basis of this strong recent performance, individual investors might believe the company will continue to exceed market expectations, and they may start bidding for shares. According to behavioral finance theory, many investors will demonstrate this type of myopic behavior, creating upward pressure on the share price. In theory, as long as enough far-sighted investors can identify and take short positions against overpricing created by these myopic investors, the share price will soon return to its fundamental level.

In practice, however, this may not happen; the costs, complexity, and risks involved in setting up a short position may be too high for those who invest on economic fundamentals. The biggest impediment to short selling, apart from regulatory constraints, is so-called noise trader risk. This risk arises from traders who take bets on short-term price movements without reference to fundamental valuations. It can prolong the movement of a share price in an irrational direction, making it difficult to gauge how long price deviations will persist and whether they will increase before finally disappearing. If fundamental investors have to abandon their positions before the share price returns to its fundamental value, they will incur a loss.

To illustrate this anomaly, suppose a rational investor believes a company's shares are worth $50. Because they are priced in the market at $100, the rational investor sells short 10,000 shares for $1 million, anticipating that the price must go down again. If the share price does in fact drop to $50 eventually, the investor then stands to make a profit of $500,000. The complication is that he or she had to borrow 10,000 shares to set up the short position at the outset. Banks won't lend shares for nothing; typically they require some collateral—let's say in this case a deposit of $1 million of government bonds. That works fine as long as the share price steadily declines, but not if it first rises to $200 before declining to $50. When the share price hits $200, the borrowed shares are worth $2 million, so the bank asks for an additional $1 million deposit to match the value of the shares. If the investor cannot provide the deposit, he or she is out of business, and the bank takes the collateral. Even though the investor's assessment about the ultimate value of the shares was correct, he or she could still lose $1 million instead of gaining $500,000.

When these three conditions all apply, behavioral finance predicts that pricing biases in financial markets can be both significant and persistent. In the next section, we discuss some familiar types of company mispricing to explore whether or how these conditions should change our perspectives on how finance theory applies to real-world decision making by corporate managers.

COMPANY MISPRICING: CARVE-OUTS AND DUAL LISTINGS

One type of market deviation often cited in support of behavioral finance theory is the mispricing of carve-outs and dual-listed companies. (See Chapter 22 for more details on carve-outs.) A well-documented example is the price differential that appeared between 3Com and Palm shares after Palm was carved out of 3Com in March 2000. On that date, 3Com floated 5 percent of its subsidiary Palm in anticipation of a complete spin-off within the next nine months. Yet immediately after the Palm carve-out, the market capitalization of Palm was higher than the entire market value of 3Com, implying that 3Com's other businesses had negative value (see Exhibit 17.1). Given the size and profitability of its other businesses, this observation clearly implied mispricing.

So why did rational investors not exploit the mispricing by going short in Palm shares and long in 3Com shares? The answer is they could not, because the free float of Palm shares was too small after the carve-out to accommodate such arbitrage: 95 percent of all the shares were still held by 3Com. Establishing a short position in Palm would have required borrowing the shares from a Palm shareholder. As the share supply via short sales increased steadily over the months following the carve-out (because arbitrageurs were eventually able to borrow shares from Palm shareholders), the price gap gradually decreased.[4]

Other documented cases of mispricing for parent companies and their carved-out subsidiaries involve similar difficulties in setting up short positions to exploit price differences.[5] Such difficulties allow mispricing to persist for several weeks or months until the full spin-off takes place or is abandoned. These anomalous price differences appear to be inconsistent with efficient

---

[4] See J. Cochrane, "Stocks as Money: Convenience Yield and the Tech-Stock Bubble," NBER Working Paper 8987, National Bureau of Economic Research (2002).

[5] O. Lamont and R. Thaler, "Can the Market Add and Subtract? Mispricing in Tech Stock Carve-Outs," *Journal of Political Economy* 111, no. 2 (2003): 227–268; and M. Mitchell, T. Pulvino, and E. Stafford, "Limited Arbitrage in Equity Markets," *Journal of Finance* 57, no. 2 (2002): 551–584.

EXHIBIT 17.1 **Market Value of 3Com versus Value of Palm Ownership by 3Com**

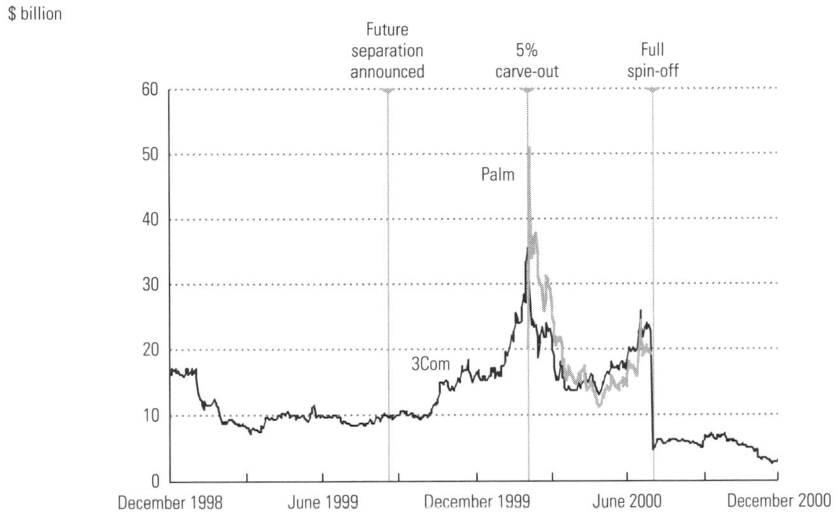

Source: Datastream.

markets (at least in the sense that relevant price information is not quickly and correctly processed). In all cases, however, these price differences were resolved within several months, as soon as the structural barriers to arbitrage disappeared.

A similar type of apparent mispricing occurs when the shares of dual-listed companies trade at different values on different exchanges. A notable example is the price disparity between the shares of Royal Dutch Petroleum and Shell Transport & Trading (T&T), which were traded separately on the Amsterdam and London stock markets, respectively, until 2005, although the two companies together formed a single group. These twin shares were entitled to a fixed 60:40 portion of the dividends of the combined Royal Dutch/Shell Group. Thus, one would expect that the prices of the Royal Dutch and Shell T&T shares would be priced in a fixed ratio of 60:40.

Over long periods, however, this has not been the case.[6] In fact, for several similar twin-share structures (such as Unilever and Reed-Elsevier), there have been prolonged periods of mispricing, as shown in Exhibit 17.2. This phenomenon occurs because, for some reason, investors prefer one of the twin shares over the other and are prepared to pay a premium. However, the arbitrage opportunity from going short in the overpriced share and long in the underpriced share is not exploited by rational investors.

---

[6] K. Froot and A. Perold, "Global Equity Markets: The Case of Royal Dutch and Shell," Harvard Business School Case 9-296-077; and K. Froot and E. Dabora, "How Are Stock Prices Affected by the Location of Trade?," *Journal of Financial Economics* 53, no. 2 (1999): 189–216.

EXHIBIT 17.2 **Share Price Disparity of Dual-Listed Companies**

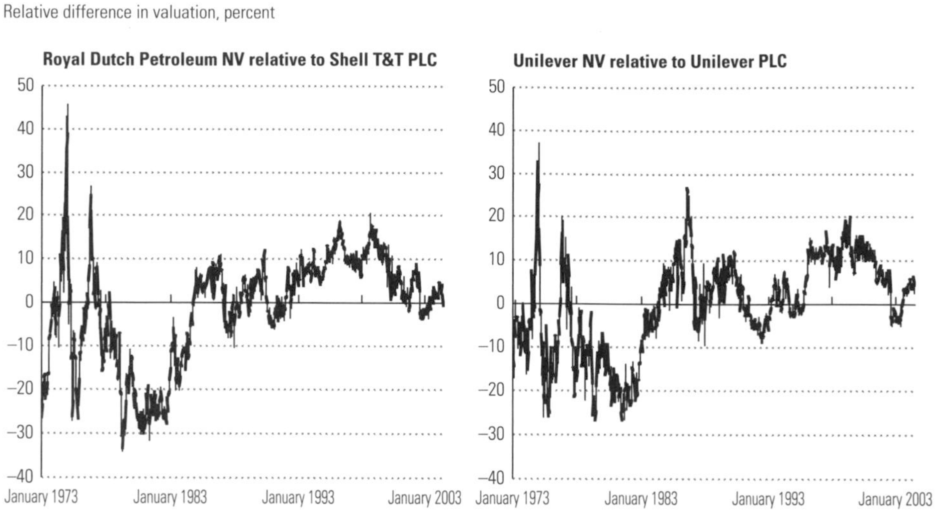

Relative difference in valuation, percent

Source: Datastream.

Not only have such price differentials persisted, but they have sometimes been as large as 30 percent. One explanation is that because of noise trader risk, the arbitrage opportunity around dual-listed stocks is actually a risky strategy.[7] Arbitrage investors cannot be sure that prices will converge in the near term; the price gap could even widen.

Long-Term Capital Management (LTCM), which collapsed in 1998, was the victim of just such an occurrence. The hedge fund bet that the Royal Dutch Petroleum–Shell T&T price gap would eventually disappear, so it bought shares of Shell and sold short shares of Royal Dutch. Most of LTCM's positions were based on identifying investments whose relative values were out of equilibrium. LTCM also used massive leverage, financing its investments with $25 of debt for every dollar of equity. When Russia defaulted on its debts in 1998, the financial markets behaved erratically, and a number of LTCM's positions, including Royal Dutch/Shell, generated paper losses. Because of LTCM's high leverage, lenders and counterparties reduced their willingness to lend to the fund in this environment, forcing it to liquidate some of its positions. LTCM liquidated its Royal Dutch/Shell position when the Royal Dutch premium had actually increased to 22 percent, generating a cash loss for LTCM of about $150 million.

Do such examples indict the market's ability to price? We do not think so. In recent years, the price differences for Royal Dutch and stocks with similar underlying Anglo-Dutch corporate structures have shrunk or even disappeared

[7] A. de Jong, L. Rosenthal, and M. van Dijk, "The Risk and Return of Arbitrage in Dual-Listed Companies," *Review of Finance* 13 (2009): 495–520.

as those underlying structures were abandoned. Some of these twin-share structures have been terminated on the formal merger of the two corporations, as was the case when Royal Dutch and Shell T&T merged in July 2005 and unified their shares. The price disparity between the two shares disappeared just after the merger was announced in October 2004; as soon as a formal date was set for definitive price convergence, arbitrageurs stepped in to correct any difference.[8] The fact that prices of twin shares converge on the announcement of a formal merger underlines not only the importance of noise trader risk, but also the argument that such mispricing occurs under special circumstances only—and is by no means a common or long-lasting phenomenon.

COMPANY MISPRICING: OVERREACTION AND UNDERREACTION, REVERSAL AND MOMENTUM

Over the past decades, two well-known patterns of price deviations from fundamental values in stock markets have received considerable attention in academic studies: long-term reversal in share prices and short-term momentum. Long-term reversal means that the high-performing stocks of the past few years typically become the low-performing stocks over the next few years.[9] Momentum describes when positive returns for stocks over the past several months are typically followed by several months of continued positive returns.[10] The literature on behavioral finance offers several explanations for these deviant price patterns, but the debate remains far from settled.

Some behaviorists argue that reversal is caused by overreaction: investors put too much weight on companies' recent performance. When companies have performed well in preceding years, investors are inclined to extrapolate that success into the future, and push up share prices too much. When cash flows fail to meet their optimistic expectations, investors sharply adjust them, bringing on a reversal. Thus, the winning stocks of the past become the low-performing stocks of the future. The same effect may also be responsible for the well-known phenomenon of low returns following initial public offerings (IPOs) and seasoned offerings.[11] Typically, companies issuing new stock previously demonstrated strong business performance, which in turn provides a

---

[8] See de Jong, Rosenthal, and van Dijk, "Risk and Return of Arbitrage."

[9] First documented by DeBondt and Thaler, "Does the Stock Market Overreact?"

[10] See, for example, N. Jegadeesh and S. Titman, "Returns to Buying Winners and Selling Losers: Implications for Stock Market Efficiency," *Journal of Finance* 48, no. 1 (1993): 65–92; and N. Jegadeesh and S. Titman, "Profitability of Momentum Strategies: An Evaluation of Alternative Explanations," *Journal of Finance* 56, no. 2 (2001): 699–720.

[11] See, for example, J. Ritter, "The Long Run Performance of Initial Public Offerings," *Journal of Finance* 46, no. 1 (1991): 3–28; T. Loughran and J. Ritter, "The New Issues Puzzle," *Journal of Finance* 50, no. 1 (1995): 23–51; and B. Dharan and D. Ikenberry, "The Long-Run Negative Drift of Post-Listing Stock Returns," *Journal of Finance* 50, no. 5 (1995): 1547–1574.

reason to exploit a favorable track record and issue stock. However, their future performance often turns out weaker than anticipated.[12]

Momentum may be explained by systematic underreaction: overly conservative investors are too slow in adjusting their expectations after new information becomes available. Investors may underestimate the true impact of earnings changes, divestitures, share repurchases, and so on.[13] The result is that stock prices do not instantaneously react to good or bad news. This could give rise to short-term momentum in stock returns, enabling stocks that have outperformed the market as a whole for several months to continue that trend over the next couple of months.

But academics are still debating whether irrationality among investors is truly what drives the long-term reversal and short-term momentum patterns found in stock returns. Eugene Fama and Kenneth French,[14] for example, believe that long-term reversals can be explained by risk premiums determined by market-to-book ratio and size. These can be interpreted as indicators of liquidity or distress risk, in addition to the traditional market or beta risk.[15] In Chapter 11, we discuss how such additional risk premiums can affect the cost of capital.

Similarly, short-term momentum in share price returns is not necessarily driven by irrational investors. Profits from exploiting these patterns are relatively limited after deducting transaction costs.[16] Thus, these small momentum biases could persist even if all investors were rational, and disappear as soon as they become large enough for rational investors to make material gains from trading on them.

Furthermore, behavioral finance cannot yet explain why investors overreact under some conditions (such as IPOs) and underreact in others (such as earnings announcements). Fama considers this puzzle a further indication that markets are efficient: there is no systematic way to predict when markets will over- or underreact.[17] Across all studies, the expected value of an abnormal return is therefore probably still zero. This would imply that managers should

---

[12] E. Fama, "Market Efficiency, Long-Term Returns, and Behavioral Finance," *Journal of Financial Economics* 49, no. 3 (1998): 283–306.

[13] Documented by V. Bernard and J. Thomas, "Evidence That Stock Prices Do Not Fully Reflect the Implications of Current Earnings for Future Earnings," *Journal of Accounting and Economics* 3, no. 4 (1990): 305–340; J. Lakonishok and T. Vermaelen, "Anomalous Price Behavior around Repurchase Tender Offers," *Journal of Finance* 45, no. 2 (1990): 455–478; and H. Desai and P. Jain, "Long-Run Common Stock Returns Following Stock Splits and Reverse Splits," *Journal of Business* 70, no. 3 (1997): 409–433.

[14] E. Fama and F. French, "Multifactor Explanation of Asset Pricing Anomalies," *Journal of Finance* 51, no. 1 (1996): 55–84.

[15] See, for example, J. Cochrane, *Asset Pricing* (Princeton, NJ: Princeton University Press, 2001), chap. 20.

[16] Cochrane, ibid., argues that momentum can be explained by a very small autocorrelation in stock returns combined with high volatility and that momentum predictability is too small to be exploited when transaction costs are taken into account.

[17] E. Fama, "Market Efficiency, Long-Term Returns, and Behavioral Finance," *Journal of Financial Economics* 49, no. 3 (1998): 283–306.

still make their decisions based on traditional DCF analyses and efficient market assumptions.

MARKET MISPRICING: BUBBLES AND BURSTS

There have been periods when deviations from economic fundamentals were more significant and widespread than those just described for individual company shares. However, such broader deviations are rare and short-lived, and the market usually corrects itself within a few years. In the following sections, we take a closer look at two recent examples: the high-tech bubble that burst in 2000 and the credit bubble that collapsed in 2007. Although the stock market as a whole suffered in the aftermath of both bubbles, the mispricing was in fact concentrated in a few particular sectors rather than market-wide.

The high-tech and credit-fueled bubbles had similar impacts on key market indexes in both the United States and Europe (see Exhibit 17.3), bringing the market up to unprecedented peaks and down again over the course of just a few years. But there were important differences. The high-tech bubble was a valuation bubble, in which the stock market priced companies at levels that were unjustified by underlying performance and growth; expectations of future earnings far above current earnings levels were unrealistic. The credit bubble was not a valuation bubble but an earnings bubble. Given the preceding performance and growth of companies, stock market values were not unreasonable. Unfortunately, that level of underlying performance was unsustainable—a fact that stock markets did not take sufficiently into account.

EXHIBIT 17.3 **U.S. and European Equity Markets in High-Tech and Credit Bubbles**

U.S. and European stock indexes TRS, index (December 1989 = 100)

Source: Datastream.

High-Tech Bubble Driving Up Market Expectations

When Netscape Communications became a public company in 1995, it saw its market capitalization soar to $6 billion on an annual revenue base of just $85 million. The financial world quickly became convinced that the Internet would change the world. Investors flocked to the market during the late 1990s, sending the Standard & Poor's (S&P) 500 index to a new peak of more than 1,500 in 2000. By 2001, the index had tumbled back to half that level.

Although the valuation of the market as a whole was affected, the high-tech bubble was concentrated in technology stocks and certain very large stocks in other sectors (so-called megacaps). Exhibit 17.4 shows what happened. Before and after the bubble, the price-to-earnings (P/E) ratios of the 30 largest companies were the same on average as those of the other 470 companies in the index. However, in 1999, the average top-30 company had a P/E of 46 times, compared with an average of 23 times for the other 470 companies. As a result, the weighted average P/E for the market overall reached 30 times.

Most of the large-capitalization companies with high P/Es were clustered in just three sectors: technology, media, and telecommunications (TMT). In most other U.S. sectors, P/Es were significantly lower. Thus, the American stock market bubble of the late 1990s was largely driven by the valuation of the TMT sectors. To illustrate how aggressively investors were valuing the prices of some of these TMT stocks, we analyzed the value of the 10 highest market capitalization U.S. technology companies. At the end of 1999, these 10 companies had a combined market capitalization of $2.4 trillion, annual revenues of $240 billion, and net income of $37 billion, resulting in an aggregate P/E of 64 times!

The high-tech market boom is a classic example of a valuation bubble, in which stocks are priced at earnings multiples that underlying fundamentals cannot justify. To illustrate, we built a simple DCF model that estimated what

EXHIBIT 17.4 **Impact of Largest Stocks on Overall Market Valuation**

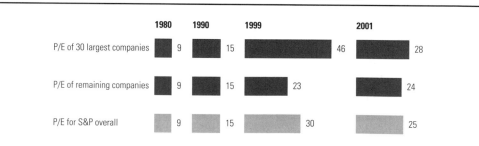

	1980	1990	1999	2001
P/E of 30 largest companies	9	15	46	28
P/E of remaining companies	9	15	23	24
P/E for S&P overall	9	15	30	25

Note: 12-month trailing price-earnings ratios.

Source: Compustat, McKinsey Corporate Performance Center analysis.

performance would be required from those companies in the future to justify their market value at the end of 1999. For investors to earn an 11 percent return, these companies would have needed to grow their revenues to approximately $2.7 trillion and their net income to about $450 billion by 2014. To put this in perspective, assuming the gross domestic product (GDP) grew at a healthy rate from 1999 through 2014 and corporate profits remained at a stable percentage of GDP (as they have for at least the past 80 years), the total corporate profits of all U.S. companies would be about $1.3 trillion to $1.5 trillion by 2014, implying that these 10 companies would need to earn about one-third of all the profits earned by all U.S. companies.

Of course, there was a kernel of real substance feeding the hype that fueled the rise in share values. Many of the companies born in this era (including Amazon.com, eBay, and Yahoo!) have created and are likely to continue to create substantial profits and economic value. But for every solid, innovative new business idea, there were dozens of companies that forgot or purposely threw out fundamental rules of economics.

One example was the concept of network effects, a variant of increasing returns to scale.[18] The concept is well illustrated by Microsoft's Office software, which provides word processing, spreadsheets, and graphics. Once Office had gained a critical share of the software market, software customers became unwilling to purchase and use incompatible competing products because they needed to share their work with others. As the installed base grew bigger, it became ever more attractive for customers to use Office software, creating an almost insurmountable barrier to competition. Without vigorous competition to push down margins, returns on capital for Microsoft in this marketplace have increased rather than decreased with scale.

Such network effects apply to very few products, as the economic theory behind them predicts.[19] But during the Internet bubble, investors misinterpreted the rule to mean that merely getting big faster than your competitors in a given market would result in enormous profits. Some analysts applied this winner-takes-all thinking to mobile-phone service providers, even though customers can and do easily switch from provider to provider, forcing providers to compete largely on price. Even Internet grocery delivery services were thought to gain from network effects, although when these services attract more customers, they also need more drivers, trucks, warehouses, and inventory, putting pressure on their return on capital. In reality, very few companies went on to enjoy real, long-term network effects. Much of the overinvestment in others during the high-tech bubble was based on a misunderstanding of their potential to create fundamental value.

---

[18] C. Shapiro and H. Varian, *Information Rules: A Strategic Guide to the Network Economy* (Boston: Harvard Business School Press, 1999).
[19] Shapiro and Varian, ibid., describe the conditions. For Microsoft Office, a key driver is the desire for compatibility to share documents.

EXHIBIT 17.5 **Aggregate versus Median Market-to-Capital Ratios**

Enterprise value/Invested capital[1] for S&P 500 companies

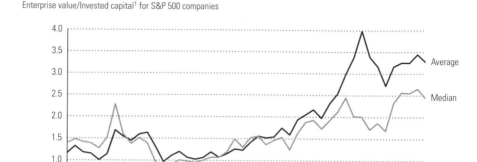

[1] For financial institutions: market capitalization/book value of equity.

Source: Standard & Poor's, Institutional Brokers' Estimate System, McKinsey Corporate Performance Center analysis.

Credit Bubble Driving Up Corporate Earnings

By 2007, stock markets around the world had more than recovered from the high-tech fallout, and the S&P 500 reached a new peak value in excess of 1,500. During the 1990s, investor euphoria and a highly speculative atmosphere had raised price-earnings ratios to heights that made valuations unsustainable. In contrast, the 2007 market P/E was about 40 percent lower than in 2000 and broadly in line with the P/Es of the 1960s, when inflation and interest rates were at similar levels.[20] This time, the market rode to its peak on the back of an earnings bubble. The largest property boom and credit expansion in U.S. and European history drove corporate earnings to exceptional levels that ultimately proved unsustainable. The extent of the bubble is best illustrated not by the price-earnings ratio but by the market-to-capital ratio, which soared from a long-term average of around $1^1/_2$ to 2 to well over 3.5 by 2007 (see Exhibit 17.5).[21]

Aggregate return on equity (ROE) had shot up to 23 percent in 2006, well above the 13.6 percent median ROE from 1962 to 2006. Combined with exceptional growth, the record returns on capital caused the ratio of total profits to GDP to jump to an unprecedented 5.7 percent in 2006—much higher than the historical average of about 2.3 percent, and easily surpassing the previous record of 4.5 percent, set in 2000.[22] But in mid-2007, a financial crisis

[20] P/E in this case is the median forward P/E as of the end of July 2007.

[21] For more details on the drivers of the 2007 market boom, see M. Goedhart, B. Jiang, and T. Koller, "Market Fundamentals: 2000 versus 2007," *McKinsey on Finance*, no. 25 (Autumn 2007): 8–11.

[22] Defined for the companies on the S&P 500 index as total net income before extraordinary items.

started to unfold that would drive the world's economy into its steepest downturn since the 1930s. As corporate profits dived, stock markets across the world lost more than half of their value from their peak levels in 2007 over the next year and a half.

Although all companies were affected, this bubble too was mainly driven by a few sectors producing massively inflated short-term earnings, which boosted overall market earnings levels. While for most U.S. sectors earnings growth from 2000 to 2006 resembled the rate of growth over the whole of the previous decade, the financial sector and the energy, utilities, and materials sector grew much faster (see Exhibit 17.6). Their sharp increases elevated their share of total S&P earnings from 41 percent in 1997 to 51 percent in 2006. In fact, the share of financial sector net income in total GDP for the United States jumped up from 0.8 percent to 2.4 percent over the same period. As an example, the capital base of Citigroup alone grew 130 percent over the period, while reaching an all-time high return on capital of almost 23 percent. As a result, Citigroup's earnings jumped from $14 billion in 2000 to $25 billion in 2006. By this time, investors had reduced the earnings multiples for both sectors in anticipation of declining results, but their downward adjustment was by no means sufficient.

Before the crash, these sectors had benefited the most from several underlying economic trends that contributed to accelerated earnings growth for all companies:

- *Growth of Asian economies:* Since the turn of the century, spectacular growth of large emerging economies, especially China and India, had boosted global demand and therefore prices for oil, gas, and other commodities. This trend pushed up earnings in the energy, utilities, and materials sector. It also generated a historic global savings surplus led by emerging-market economies, which further fueled already overheated credit markets.

- *Expansion of credit markets:* Since the 1970s, credit growth had gone hand in hand with economic growth. But after 2000, the global savings surplus and other factors such as innovative financial instruments and loose monetary policy were pushing credit growth in developed economies to levels that could not be sustained by accompanying rates of economic growth. Financial innovations in the form of structured and securitized finance instruments provided lenders with the opportunity to repackage and redistribute individual loans across many investors.[23] Central banks in the United States and Europe had kept interest rates low to stimulate economic recovery in the wake of the high-tech fallout of 2001. By 2007,

---

[23] Of course, such instruments as credit default swaps, collateralized debt obligations, and other asset-backed instruments had been around for years, but their application really took off in the late 1990s.

EXHIBIT 17.6 **Financial and Commodity Sectors out of Balance**

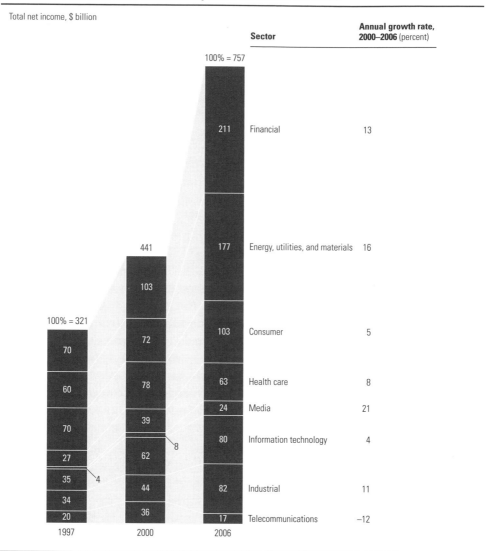

Total net income, $ billion

Sector	Annual growth rate, 2000–2006 (percent)
Financial	13
Energy, utilities, and materials	16
Consumer	5
Health care	8
Media	21
Information technology	4
Industrial	11
Telecommunications	−12

100% = 757

211
177
103
63
24
80
82
17
2006

441

103
72
78
39
62
44
36
8
2000

100% = 321

70
60
70
27
35
34
20
4
1997

[1] Net income before extraordinary items and adjusted for goodwill impairment.

total private-sector debt relative to GDP had increased sharply to historic peaks in both the United States and the European Union.[24]

- *Rise in housing prices:* In parallel, property prices soared, inflated by readily available credit. In the United States and many European countries,

[24] In the United States, debt almost doubled, rising from $22 trillion to $42 trillion, or 291 percent of GDP in 2008 (versus 222 percent in 2000). For the European economies, the growth of private-sector borrowing relative to GDP was comparable. See "Global Capital Markets: Entering a New Era," *McKinsey Global Institute*, September 2009.

housing prices roughly doubled between 2000 and 2006, bringing mortgage default rates to historical lows. Given the opportunities to transfer mortgage default risk via innovative instruments to other banks around the world, lenders believed that the risk/return trade-off on mortgage investments had permanently shifted. They continued to loosen mortgage standards. Mortgages were issued to increasingly risky borrower segments (so-called subprime loans), their risks camouflaged by rising housing prices and mortgage-repackaging structures.

By 2007, this apparently virtuous spiral had sent earnings in the financial sector to record levels. In addition, continually rising house prices made consumers wealthier, giving them access to more easy credit. The boom in debt-financed consumer spending accelerated earnings growth across all sectors.

But the spiral inevitably changed direction as basic economic laws started to prevail; credit must be repaid with interest at some point, and consumer wealth cannot outgrow GDP forever. U.S. housing prices started to fall, which led to a rapid rise in mortgage default rates. Because of the complex and international structures into which most mortgages had been repackaged, lenders were uncertain who would ultimately suffer the losses from mortgage defaults. Banks around the world simultaneously tried to unwind any positions with exposure to U.S. mortgages. The opacity of many credit instruments and their complex interconnections meant few buyers could be found. Prices for assets backed by mortgages and other forms of credit plummeted, bringing more and more financial institutions into distress. Lehman Brothers collapsed in September 2008. Many players, such as American International Group (AIG) and Citigroup in the United States, Royal Bank of Scotland in the United Kingdom, and Fortis and ING Groep in the Netherlands, survived only thanks to government support. The crisis resulted in the largest asset write-offs in history at around $2 trillion to $3 trillion for lenders in the United States and Europe alone, sending the rest of the economy into a deep recession and the stock market into its steepest decline since the 1930s. Earnings expectations plummeted, sending the S&P 500 to an intraday low of 667 in March 2009. Before the recession bottomed out, the stock market had largely corrected itself in the fall of 2009 to valuation levels that were more in line with sustainable, lower profit levels.

SUMMARY

While the stock market generally reflects fundamentals and sees through illusions, there is no denying that emotions can run away with parts of the market. But this occurs only under exceptional circumstances and typically does not last very long.

Company-specific deviations usually last only as long as the particular barriers preventing intrinsic investors from correcting them. This can be months, as in the case of 3Com and Palm, or sometimes years, as in the case of Shell and Royal Dutch. Market-wide price deviations from fundamentals are even less frequent, but they do occur. In the high-tech bubble of the late 1990s, excessive price-earnings multiples could not be justified by underlying economic fundamentals. In the credit bubble of the late 2000s, record-level corporate earnings were not sustainable. In these and all other cases, the market corrected itself, and within a few years, valuations returned to levels justified by underlying fundamentals.

REVIEW QUESTIONS

1. Under what conditions might the stock market fail to reflect economic fundamentals?

2. In which of the following markets would you expect market mispricing to be more likely or less likely to occur: the market for equity stocks, fine arts, foreign currency, securitized debt obligations, or copper? Give reasons for your answers.

3. Over the past five years, the highest share price for Google was around $700 and its lowest price was around $175. Exxon's highest and lowest share prices over the same period were $94 and $32. Do such wide ranges mean that the stock market is reflecting emotions more than fundamentals?

4. Discuss the possible factors underlying differences in price for the same stock on two different markets, such as the spread between the London and New York prices for a share of Shell's common equity stock.

5. Why is it much more risky to take a short position in a stock than a long position? What does that mean for the likelihood of over- versus undervaluation of a company's share price?

6. Discuss the key differences between the stock market downturn in 2001 and the one in 2008.

7. Discuss the pros and cons of introducing regulatory restrictions on short selling in an equity market.

8. What are the key strategic and tactical opportunities for an industrial company in case of general stock market overvaluation (and undervaluation)? What is typically preventing companies from capturing such opportunities?

18

Investors and Managers in Efficient Markets

The evidence presented in Chapter 15 demonstrated that stock markets are efficient, in the sense that share prices typically reflect the economic fundamentals of the companies whose shares are traded on those markets.[1] In this chapter, we explain how markets manage to generate efficient prices even though not all investors act rationally, as Chapter 17 explored. It is the interaction between investors with different strategies—some rational, some not—that can result in the observable market pattern of volatile prices that are still generally in line with intrinsic values.

We use a straightforward model to illustrate how market trading by both rational and irrational investors will produce markets that are both generally efficient and volatile. Empirical research using a new investor classification confirms that real investors do indeed fall into rational and less rational categories, but the more rational type—those who are well informed and focused on companies' economic fundamentals—are the ones who ultimately set market prices.

The implications of market efficiency for managers are clear.

- Managers should focus on driving return on invested capital (ROIC) and growth to create maximum value for shareholders, because ultimately stock market values are driven by those fundamental measures, too. As Chapter 16 demonstrates, market efficiency means there is no point in managers pursuing quarterly earnings growth or making share repurchases or cross-listings, because such cosmetic measures do not affect intrinsic value and will therefore have no lasting impact on share prices.

[1] We follow the definition of market efficiency given by Fischer Black, "Noise," *Journal of Finance* 41, no. 3 (1986): 533.

- Managers need to understand their investor base, so they can communicate their company's strategy for value creation effectively to different investor segments.

- Managers should not be distracted from their efforts to drive ROIC and growth by any short-term price volatility—that is, any temporary deviation in their share price from its intrinsic value—because such deviations are likely to occur from time to time, even in the most efficient stock market.

INVESTORS IN EFFICIENT MARKETS

If the relationship between market prices and intrinsic value were perfect, then there would be little point in trading, because all new information would be immediately and fully reflected in share prices.[2] In real life, however, the relationship between market prices and intrinsic value is often imperfect, especially in the short run, and we discussed some examples in Chapters 16 and 17.[3] Even investors who are rational, in the sense that they make investment decisions on the basis of intrinsic value as determined by risk/return trade-offs, may have different degrees of access to information or transaction costs that prohibit constant trading, and these may prevent market price levels from immediately and fully reflecting new information.[4] Other price deviations may occur because not all investors are rational. Fischer Black explained these kinds of market price deviations by what he called noise, referring to many small events whose combined effect on price setting in markets may exceed the impact of rarer large events. Some investors buy a company's stock because they like the company's products, noticed that its price went up the day before, or simply heard that other investors were buying. They may trade on similar small and frequent events because they believe these represent material information. Such noise could therefore have a bigger impact on prices than the company's announcement of large events such as acquisitions or new product development programs. Indeed, noise is inherent to financial markets because without it there would be very little trading. But because noise is, in fact, immaterial, price deviations from intrinsic values are also inherent to financial markets.[5]

Nevertheless, these price deviations are not large or enduring enough to overturn our conclusion that stock markets price companies efficiently. By saying the stock market is efficient, we do not mean that it sets prices to within

[2] See, for example, Sanford J. Grossman and Joseph E. Stiglitz, "On the Impossibility of Informationally Efficient Markets," *American Economic Review* 70, no. 3 (June 1980): 393–408.

[3] The evidence discussed in Chapter 16 from event studies on stock splits, index changes, and accounting changes illustrates that markets do reflect fundamentals—but not always instantaneously.

[4] See, for example, Stephen Figlewski, "Market 'Efficiency' in a Market with Heterogeneous Information," *Journal of Political Economy* 86, no. 4 (August 1978): 581–597.

[5] "Noise makes financial markets possible, but also makes them imperfect." Ibid., 530.

1 or 2 percent of intrinsic value. After all, intrinsic values are, like market prices, fairly variable estimates. For example, an increase in forecast sales margin of one percentage point for a retail business can make the company's estimated intrinsic value go up by 15 percent or more. While we would not go as far as Fischer Black, who would define a market as efficient if prices were within a factor of 0.5 to two times intrinsic values, we believe that a price bandwidth of plus or minus 20 percent of the intrinsic value of stocks at any given time makes a stock market efficient enough to provide the critical outcome of efficiency—namely, meaningful signals about the cost of capital that managers can use to make investment decisions. Given that all other business information on which managers base such decisions also is imprecise, this degree of latitude in our definition of market efficiency seems justified.

A Model of the Market

In this section, we illustrate how a stock market is able to produce the empirical patterns we found in the previous chapters: prices that are generally in line with intrinsic value but still volatile, and that may even deviate significantly from intrinsic value under specific (but rare) conditions.

There is a wide body of literature on the analysis and modeling of investor behavior and market pricing outcomes.[6] The general conclusion is that markets ultimately reflect the beliefs of traders who have the most accurate information. Because of their superior information, these traders will make more trading profits and accumulate more capital. This will increase their influence on stock prices over time and eventually make stock prices and intrinsic value converge. Only under very specific circumstances could the less informed or uninformed so-called noise traders have a lasting influence on prices.[7]

A simple model can illustrate how the interaction between investors with different strategies can result in the combination of volatile prices that are still generally in line with intrinsic value observable in real stock markets. Assume a basic market where only one company's stock and a risk-free asset (for comparison) are traded. Two types of investors trade in this market:

1. *Informed investors* develop a point of view about the intrinsic value of the company's shares based on its underlying fundamentals, such as return on capital and growth, and then make rational buy and sell decisions. They do not necessarily all agree on the exact value of the shares, because of differences in the information they can access. Some may believe the

---

[6] See, for example, the early publication by E. Fama, "The Behavior of Stock-Market Prices," *Journal of Business* 38, no. 1 (1965); and a recent overview, L. Blume and D. Easley, "Market Selection and Asset Pricing," in *Handbook of Financial Markets: Dynamics and Evolution*, ed. T. Hens and K. Hoppe (Amsterdam: Elsevier, 2009).

[7] See J. De Long, A. Shleifer, L. Summers, and R. Waldman, "The Survival of Noise Traders in Financial Markets," *Journal of Business* 64, no. 1 (1991): 1–19.

shares of the company trading the single stock on the market are worth $40, others $50, and others $60, giving not a single point but a range of $40 to $60 for the intrinsic value. Because the informed investors also have transaction costs and lack perfect information, they will start trading only if the stock price deviates by more than 10 percent from their estimated intrinsic value.

2. *Noise traders* do not care about intrinsic value and trade on any small event that may not constitute material new information. In that sense, they are irrational. Let us assume, for example, that they base their trades only on previous price movements: when shares are going up, they buy, assuming the price will continue to increase, and when prices are going down, they sell.[8]

Both types of investors invest in either the stock or the risk-free asset.

Say trading starts when the price of the single share in the market is $30. Informed investors start buying shares because they believe the shares should be worth $40 to $60. Their purchases begin to drive up the share price. The noise traders notice the rising share price and begin to purchase shares as well. This accelerates the share price increase, attracting more and more noise traders to jump on the bandwagon. As the share price increases, the informed investors gradually slow their purchases. At $36, the most pessimistic investors stop buying; at $44, they are convinced the shares are overvalued and begin to sell. As the price rises, more informed investors stop buying, and more start to sell. Once the price passes $66, all informed investors are selling. As more informed investors sell, momentum declines. Some of the noise traders sense the declining momentum and begin to sell as well. Eventually the selling pressure is greater than the buying pressure, and the stock price begins to fall. The noise investors accelerate the fall, but this slows as more and more informed investors begin to buy until, at $36, all informed investors are buying again. Eventually, noise traders will pick up the decrease of downward momentum and start to buy again as well, thereby stopping the price decline.

The pattern continues, with the share price oscillating within a band whose boundaries are set by the informed investors, as shown in Exhibit 18.1. If the noise traders act not only on price movements but also on random, insignificant events, there will also be price oscillations within the band.

Note that there are two bandwidths. One is set by the range of intrinsic values calculated by informed investors ($40 to $60), and the other is the trading

---

[8] Our two investor groups serve as an abstract illustration, but they are quite similar to feedback traders and smart money investors, as identified by Goetzmann and Massa in their analysis of two years of daily account information for 91,000 investors in an S&P 500 index fund. See William N. Goetzmann and Massimo Massa, "Daily Momentum and Contrarian Behavior of Index Fund Investors," *Journal of Financial and Quantitative Analysis* 37, no. 3 (September 2002): 375–389.

EXHIBIT 18.1 **Model of the Stock Market**

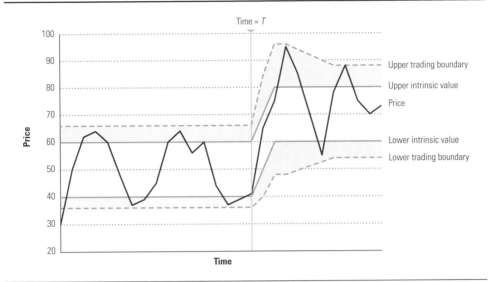

range, bounded by the prices at which all informed investors are either buying or selling ($36 and $66). The trading range depends on informed traders' transaction costs and their confidence in the reliability of their valuations. When informed traders are less confident in their valuations, they will sell at a higher margin above these estimates and buy at a lower margin below them than when they are more confident. Uncertainty about a company's intrinsic value is likely to vary over time as the company develops new business, launches new products, and announces plans for or results of research and development (R&D) projects, mergers, or divestments. At such times, informed investors will increase the trading bandwidth around their intrinsic-value estimates. Informed investors will never be so certain and uniform in their valuations as to leave no room for noise traders.[9]

Suppose that at time T the stock trades at $42, and the company announces the launch of a new product that no investors anticipated. Two things change now: the informed investors revise their estimates of the company's value to the range of $60 to $80, and at the same time, they increase their individual trading ranges from 10 to, say, 20 percent either side of their intrinsic valuation because of their uncertainty about the prospects for this new product. Even the most pessimistic informed investors will begin buying at a market price of $42, well below their buy threshold of $48 (20 percent below $60). Their buying causes the share price to begin a new cycle, but oscillating around a higher level and within a relatively wider trading range (see Exhibit 18.1). Thus,

[9] See J. De Long, A. Shleifer, L. Summers, and R. Waldmann, "Noise Trader Risk in Financial Markets," *Journal of Political Economy* 98, no. 4 (1990): 703; and R. Shiller, "From Efficient Markets Theory to Behavioral Finance," *Journal of Economic Perspectives* 17, no. 1 (2003): 83–104.

price volatility temporarily increases when informed investors are absorbing new information. Assuming that the confidence of the informed investors in their intrinsic estimates gradually increases as they digest news about the new product, their individual trading bands will gradually return to 10 percent either side of their intrinsic values.

In this model, prices will move within the bandwidth if there is sufficient informed capital in the market that is prepared to act when prices move outside the bandwidth boundaries. This mechanism can break down, however, in certain rare situations. For example, when informed investors are vastly outnumbered by noise traders,[10] their sales of stocks might not be able to stop a price rally. But as we will see in the next section, this circumstance is unlikely, given the amounts of capital managed by sophisticated, professional—that is to say, informed—investors today.[11] In addition, when there are real or perceived barriers to short selling, even a minority of noise traders could drive up prices above the bandwidth. Real barriers exist when there are simply insufficient underlying stocks to borrow for short selling, as was the case for the 3Com-Palm mispricing discussed in Chapter 17. Perceived barriers arise when investors decline to sell short for fear of losing significant amounts before prices revert to higher levels. Perceived barriers are more likely to occur when informed investors have less confidence in their own valuation estimates—for example, because there is still significant uncertainty around the company's future.

This model is simple but nevertheless demonstrates some important aspects of the stock market:

- Share prices are roughly in line with intrinsic values, because informed investors ultimately set the price boundaries in the market.

- The boundaries for share prices either side of intrinsic value are wider when there is more uncertainty about a stock's valuation.

- Share prices can be significantly volatile within the bounds set by informed investors even at times when no new information about a company has been revealed.

- Price deviations beyond the boundaries set by informed investors using intrinsic valuations occur only under rare conditions—for example, when informed traders are outnumbered or when institutional barriers or extreme uncertainty prevents them from selling the stock in question short.

---

[10] Outnumbered in terms of capital.

[11] This is also what the academic literature predicts: informed investors outweigh and ultimately survive noise traders. See, for example, Blume and Easley, "Market Selection and Asset Pricing."

Classification of Investors

The model we have just described assumes there are only two types of investors. In reality, there are, of course, many types of investors and investment strategies. The important question is whether in reality we can observe a category or categories of investors that perform the role of the informed investors in the model: focusing on intrinsic value and commanding sufficient funds to drive a company's share price.

Retail investors do not qualify, because they rarely matter when it comes to influencing a company's share price. In spite of collectively holding around 40 percent of U.S. equity, they do not move prices, because they do not trade very much. The real drivers of share prices are institutional investors, who manage hedge funds, mutual funds, or pension funds and can hold significant positions in individual companies. But which of these institutional investors matter most—and do they focus on intrinsic value?

Common approaches to understanding institutional investors are not helpful in answering this question. For example, sometimes investors are labeled as growth or value investors depending on the type of stocks or indexes they invest in. Most growth and value indexes, like that of Standard & Poor's, use market-to-book ratios to categorize companies as either value or growth: companies with high market-to-book ratios are labeled growth companies, and those with low market-to-book ratios are value companies. However, growth is only one factor driving differences in market-to-book ratios. In fact, we have found no difference in the distribution of growth rates between so-called value and growth stocks.[12] As we would expect, differences in market-to-book ratios derive mainly from differences in return on capital. The median return on capital for so-called value companies was 15 percent, compared with 35 percent for the growth companies. So the companies classified as growth did not grow faster, but they did have higher returns on capital.

A more useful way to categorize and understand investors is to classify them by their investment strategy. Do they develop a view on the value of a company, or do they look for short-term price movements? Do they do extensive research and make a few big bets, or do they make lots of small bets with less information? Do they build their portfolios from the bottom up, or do they mirror an index?

Using this approach, we classify institutional investors into three types: intrinsic investors, traders, and mechanical investors.[13] These groups differ in their investment objectives and how they build their portfolios. As a result, their portfolios vary along several important dimensions, including turnover

---

[12] See T. Koller and B. Jiang, "The Truth about Growth and Value Stocks," *McKinsey on Finance*, no. 22 (Winter 2007): 12–15.

[13] See R. Palter, W. Rehm, and J. Shih, "Communicating with the Right Investors," *McKinsey on Finance*, no. 27 (Spring 2008): 1–5.

EXHIBIT 18.2 **Investors Segmented by Investment Strategies**

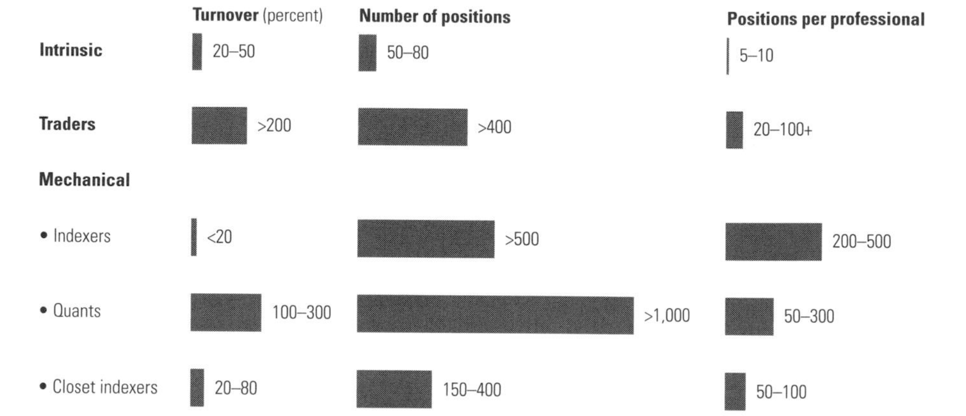

	Turnover (percent)	Number of positions	Positions per professional
Intrinsic	20–50	50–80	5–10
Traders	>200	>400	20–100+
Mechanical			
• Indexers	<20	>500	200–500
• Quants	100–300	>1,000	50–300
• Closet indexers	20–80	150–400	50–100

Source: McKinsey Corporate Performance Center analysis.

rate, number of shares held, and the number of positions held per investment professional (see Exhibit 18.2).

Intrinsic investors   Intrinsic investors take positions in companies only after undertaking rigorous due diligence of their inherent ability to create long-term value. This scrutiny typically takes more than a month. The depth of their research is manifested by the fact that they typically hold fewer than 80 stocks at any time, and their investment professionals manage only a few positions each, usually between 5 and 10. Portfolio turnover is low, as intrinsic investors typically accept that price-to-value discrepancies may persist for up to three or four years before disappearing again. We estimate that these investors hold around 20 to 25 percent of institutional U.S. equity and contribute 10 percent of the trading volume in the U.S. stock market.

Examples of intrinsic investors include Legg Mason Value Fund. This fund holds less than 50 stocks in its portfolio at any time and has a turnover rate of less than 10 percent. From the hedge fund world, Maverick Capital and Hermes Capital are good examples of intrinsic investors. Lee Ainslie, Maverick's managing director, is proud that Maverick holds only five positions per investment professional, and many of his staff have followed a single industry for 10, 20, or more years.[14]

Traders   Institutional/professional traders seek profits by betting on short-term movements in share prices, typically based on announcements about the

[14] R. Dobbs and T. Koller, "Inside a Hedge Fund: An Interview with the Managing Partner of Maverick Capital," *McKinsey on Finance*, no. 19 (Spring 2006): 6–11.

company or technical factors, like the momentum of the company's share price. The typical investment professional in this segment has 20 or more positions to follow and trades in and out of them quickly to capture small gains over short periods—as short as a few days or even hours. We estimate that traders own about 35 to 40 percent of institutional equity holdings in the United States.

Traders don't need to develop a point of view on a company's intrinsic value, just on whether its shares will go up or down in the very short term. For example, traders may develop a view that a drug company is about to announce good news about a product trial that will boost the company's share price. The trader would buy the shares, wait for the announcement and the subsequent rise in the share price, and then immediately unwind the position. Some traders are in and out of the same stock many times during the year. This does not mean traders don't understand the companies or industries they invest in; on the contrary, they follow the news about these companies closely and often approach companies directly, seeking nuances or insights that could matter greatly in the short term. However, they don't take a view on companies' long-term strategies and business performance.

Mechanical investors   Controlling about 35 to 40 percent of institutional equity in the United States, mechanical investors make decisions based on strict criteria or rules. Index funds are the prototypical mechanical investor, merely building their portfolios by matching the composition of an index such as the S&P 500. Another group of mechanical investors are the so-called quants, who use mathematical models to build their portfolios and make no qualitative judgments on a company's intrinsic value. Finally, closet indexers, although they are promoted as active managers, have portfolios that look like an index. Basing their portfolio on an index and making some adjustments, they hold a great many stocks: An investment professional in this category holds some 50 to 100 positions and hasn't the time to do in-depth research on them.[15] By contrast, intrinsic investors know every company in their portfolios in depth and build their portfolios from scratch, without taking their cue from any index.

Intrinsic Investors Drive Valuation Levels

Which of these investors matter most for the stock price? Analyzing the trading behavior of all three investor groups in more detail, we find support for the idea that intrinsic investors are the ultimate drivers of long-term share prices.

Exhibit 18.3 helps make the case, although at face value, traders show up as the most likely candidates for driving share price in the market. They own 35 to 40 percent of the institutional U.S. equity base, and as the first two

---

[15] For more on closet index funds, see Martijn Cremers and Antti Petajist, "How Active Is Your Fund Manager? A New Measure That Predicts Performance," FA Chicago Meetings Paper, January 15, 2007.

EXHIBIT 18.3 **Intrinsic Investors Have Greatest Impact on Share Price**

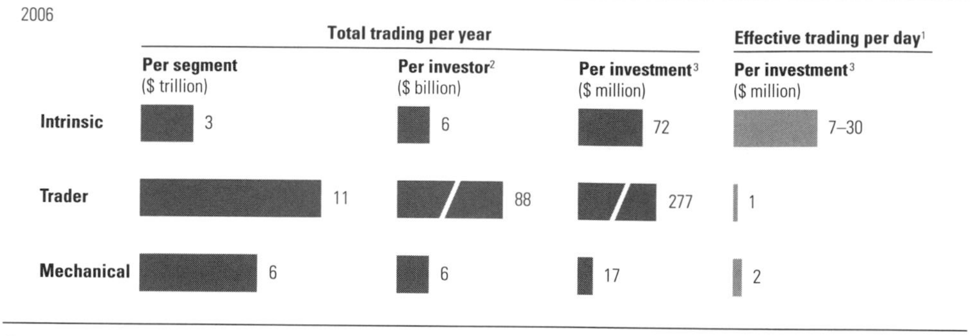

2006

	Total trading per year			Effective trading per day[1]
	Per segment ($ trillion)	Per investor[2] ($ billion)	Per investment[3] ($ million)	Per investment[3] ($ million)
Intrinsic	3	6	72	7–30
Trader	11	88	277	1
Mechanical	6	6	17	2

[1] Trading activity in segment per day that trade is made.
[2] Per investor in segment.
[3] Per investor in segment per investment

Source: R. Palter, W. Rehm, and J. Shih, "Communicating with the Right Investors," *McKinsey on Finance*, no. 27 (Spring 2008): 1–5.

columns show, they are much more active in the market than intrinsic and mechanical investors. Their overall transaction volume is made up of many more trades—of which many are trades in the same stock within relatively short time periods. The average professional trader bought and sold over $80 billion worth of shares in 2006, more than 12 times the amount traded by the typical intrinsic or mechanical investor. Similarly, as shown in the third column, the typical trader also buys or sells around $277 million in each equity stock he or she holds—far more per stock than the average intrinsic investor. Mechanical investors trade the lowest amount per stock, reflecting the high number of stocks they hold and their relatively infrequent trading.

But the last column in the exhibit, which shows the value of effective daily trading per investment on the days that an investor traded at all, is the figure that discloses the real impact of each investor group on share prices in the market. Effective daily trading is highest by far among intrinsic investors: *When* intrinsic investors trade, they buy or sell in much larger quantities than traders or mechanical investors. Although they trade much less frequently than the other investor groups, they hold much larger percentages of the companies in their portfolios, so when they do trade, they can move the prices of these companies' shares. Ultimately, therefore, intrinsic investors are the most important investor group for setting prices in the market.

The importance of intrinsic investors tells us that there are indeed investors who perform the role of the informed trader in our basic model: focusing on underlying fundamentals and driving the long-term share price toward intrinsic value. Other parties in the stock market trade more often and make share prices move in the short term. But in the long run, the intrinsic investors set the boundaries for price movements. This helps us understand why and how the stock market reflects economic fundamentals in the long run but not necessarily on a day-by-day basis.

MANAGERIAL IMPLICATIONS

Some managers point to the stock market's volatile prices to justify a belief that the market behaves irrationally. Others say that arguments supporting the discounted cash flow (DCF) approach do not square with the real world, basing their case on the market inefficiencies cited by academics.

Although academic research does indeed support the view that markets can be inefficient in the short term, in the sense that prices sometimes temporarily deviate from fundamental values, this does not make DCF valuation superfluous for strategic management decisions. As we have seen in this and the preceding three chapters, over the long term, stock market prices and intrinsic values do coincide, which means that markets price companies efficiently. In this section, we discuss the implications for managers of market efficiency itself (demonstrated in Chapters 15 and 16), the role of intrinsic investors in driving market efficiency (just explained), and temporary deviations from intrinsic value (explained in Chapter 17).

Focus on Intrinsic Value

The evidence presented in Chapters 15 to 17 strongly suggests that in the long term, the market reflects intrinsic value and prices in line with the fundamental value drivers of return on capital and growth. The overriding implication of such market efficiency for managers is that they should at all times focus on creating intrinsic value, because that is what matters to markets in the long term.

For strategic business decisions, short-term share price deviations from intrinsic value are also irrelevant. Short-term market deviations may represent an opportunity for investors to make money, depending on the practical difficulties and risks of setting up an arbitrage position. Once these inefficiencies become known, however, they usually disappear,[16] and evidence suggests that no investment fund has been able systematically to outperform the market as a whole over the last decades.[17] Apparently, any market inefficiencies are not frequent or significant enough to provide investors with systematic excess returns over extended periods.

Managers therefore should look to the long-term behavior of a company's share price, not whether it is 5 or 10 percent undervalued this week. They can safely assume that share prices equal intrinsic value and should therefore continue to make decisions based on DCF and economic profit. Managers who use the DCF approach to valuation, with their focus on increasing long-term free cash flow, will ultimately be rewarded with higher share prices.

[16] See, for example, S. Ross, "Neoclassical Finance, Alternative Finance and the Closed End Fund Puzzle," *European Financial Management* 8, no. 2 (2002): 129–137.
[17] M. Rubinstein, "Rational Markets: Yes or No? The Affirmative Case," *Financial Analysts Journal* 57, no. 3 (2001): 15–29.

This relationship helps the manager put the company's resources to their best use—and create maximum value for shareholders.

Not only does the stock market reward intrinsic value creation, but it also does a good job of seeing through any illusions of value, as Chapter 16 shows. Markets do not reward companies for stable or predictable earnings patterns, so managers should not try to smooth earnings over time or manage earnings toward analyst target levels, themselves often set arbitrarily. Stock markets are not distracted by the way accounting information represents a company's underlying fundamentals, so managers need not worry about goodwill impairments, stock option expensing, or new accounting rules. Finally, investors are interested in the substance rather than the form of their shareholdings. So managers in developed economies should not expect significant returns from splitting their stocks, listing in other markets, or stock index membership.

Understand Your Shareholder to Tailor Investor Communications

Although markets are efficient, not all investors are rational in the sense of focusing on intrinsic value and trading off risk against return in their investment decisions. As a result, share prices can fluctuate significantly even when no new, relevant information becomes available. As we saw in this chapter, so-called noise traders might trade on insignificant events or historical price patterns, thereby triggering additional trades by other noise traders. In the short term, this can lead to share price oscillations around the intrinsic value of stocks. Normally, however, informed investors will intervene and trade the share price back to a reasonable range around intrinsic value, depending on their transaction costs and risk appetites. In reality, such informed investors indeed exist and can be identified. This fact offers executives an important opportunity to improve the targeting, content, and impact of their investor communications.

The investors we term intrinsic focus on a company's intrinsic value and trade infrequently, but when they trade, they make significant moves and have significant impact on share prices. Other institutional investors, such as traders and mechanical investors (e.g., index funds), make more trades and might even be more prominent on road shows or in interactions with companies, but they have far less impact on prices.

Understanding how intrinsic investors think can help managers make better decisions. Intrinsic investors are essentially sophisticated businesspeople. Funds such as Legg Mason and Hermes Capital have an investment horizon of several years, conduct in-depth research on a company's value creation potential, and take significant stakes in relatively few companies. They understand the industry that the company is operating in and are perfectly aware of everyday challenges for managers such as balancing the interests of different stakeholders in a company. They are the last ones to be distracted by the illusions mentioned in Chapter 16 and are not interested in earnings accretion, quarterly target misses, or goodwill impairments as such: they don't care what the headline and bottom-line numbers are but want to know what is underneath in terms of business performance and growth.

Managers should know who the intrinsic investors are in their shareholder base, focus more of their investor communication time and effort on these investors, address their key concerns head-on, and give more weight to their opinions than to traders or retail or mechanical investors. In Chapter 24, we discuss in more detail how to communicate effectively with investors.

Be Cautious about Deviations

While keeping their focus on long-term value, corporate managers must remain alert to the development of any systematic deviations in their company's price from intrinsic value, in case these provide opportunities for tactical advantage in reaching strategic goals. For instance, systematic deviations can affect strategic financial decisions such as whether and when to issue new shares or pursue acquisitions. Paradoxically, the fact that such market deviations do from time to time occur makes it even more important for corporate managers and investors to understand the true, intrinsic value of their companies; otherwise, they will be unsure how to exploit any market deviations, if and when they occur.

There are several ways that corporate managers can benefit from timing the implementation of strategic decisions in line with short-term market deviations:

- Issuing additional share capital at times when the stock market is attaching too high a value to the company's shares relative to intrinsic value.

- Repurchasing company shares when the stock market underprices them relative to the intrinsic value.

- Paying for acquisitions with shares instead of cash when the stock market overprices the shares relative to intrinsic value.

- Divesting particular businesses at times when trading and transaction multiples in those sectors are higher than can be justified by underlying fundamentals.

Two caveats are important to note concerning these examples. First, we would not recommend basing a decision to issue or repurchase stock, divest or acquire businesses, or settle in cash or shares for transactions exclusively on a perceived difference between market value and intrinsic value. Instead, these decisions should be grounded in a sound strategic and business rationale that is expected to create value for shareholders. Market deviations are more relevant as tactical considerations regarding the timing and execution details of such decisions—that is, when to issue additional capital or how to pay for a particular transaction.

Second, corporate managers should be critical of analysts claiming to find such market deviations for their company's shares. After careful analysis, most of the alleged deviations that we have come across in our client experience turned out to be insignificant or even nonexistent. Market deviations are rare and typically short-lived. Thus, the evidence for deviations should be supported by sound analysis of intrinsic value before managers act on it. Deviations should be significant in both size and duration before they prompt managers to act, given the cost of strategic decisions and the time they take to execute.

REVIEW QUESTIONS

1. Why do executives spend so much time and effort on communicating with noise traders if intrinsic investors ultimately drive a company's share price?

2. Would a company's share price benefit from having fewer traders and more fundamental investors among the company's shareholders?

3. Following the investor model presented in this chapter, what returns do noise traders make on their investments in the long term: negative returns, returns around zero, or positive returns? What returns do fundamental investors make?

4. Why do noise traders have limited impact on a company's share price even when they make the largest volume of trades in the company's stock over a given time period?

5. Consider two companies that are identical except for their shareholder base. One company's shareholders comprise mostly noise traders, with mechanical investors making up the remainder. The other's shareholders are mainly fundamental investors, with a few mechanical investors. Discuss the possible implications of these differences in ownership for the two companies' expected levels of share price and share price volatility.

6. Why could it be important for executives to understand the composition of their company's shareholder base?

7. Do you think it is possible for a company to shape its shareholder base to maximize its share price? What would a company have to do?

8. Assuming that fundamental investors ultimately set a company's share price, name two reasons why you could still expect the price to show significant volatility.

Managing for Value

19

Corporate Portfolio Strategy

Part Four, beginning with this chapter, looks at value creation from a management perspective. At the heart of a company's corporate strategy—its blueprint for creating value—lie decisions about what businesses it should own. The principle for guiding such decisions is straightforward: the owner that can generate the highest cash flows from a business is the owner that will create the most value. A corollary is that no business has an inherent value. The amount of value it creates will always depend on who owns it.

General Mills' purchase of Pillsbury from Diageo in 2001 illustrates the point. Shortly after buying Pillsbury for $10.4 billion, General Mills increased the business's pretax cash flows by more than $400 million per year, increasing Pillsbury's operating profits by roughly 70 percent. Diageo's core business is in alcoholic beverages, while both General Mills and Pillsbury sell packaged foods. Under Diageo, Pillsbury was run entirely separately from Diageo's core business, because the two companies' manufacturing, distribution, and marketing operations rarely overlapped. In contrast, General Mills substantially reduced costs in Pillsbury's purchasing, manufacturing, and distribution, because significant costs were duplicated in their operations. On the revenue side, General Mills boosted Pillsbury's revenues by introducing Pillsbury products to schools in the United States where General Mills already had a strong presence. And the synergies worked both ways: for instance, Pillsbury's refrigerated trucks were used to distribute General Mills' newly branded refrigerated meals.

Pillsbury therefore had at least two values at the time of the sale: its value to General Mills and its value to Diageo. For General Mills to consider the deal attractive, the value of Pillsbury under General Mills' ownership had to be greater than the $10.4 billion price that General Mills paid. For Diageo to consider the deal attractive, Pillsbury's offer had to represent more than the value Diageo expected to create from Pillsbury in the future.

Clearly, General Mills was a better owner of Pillsbury than Diageo from a value-creating perspective. In reality, we can never pinpoint a company's ideal owner. We can only identify the best among potential owners in any given circumstances. Theoretically, some company other than General Mills could have generated even higher cash flows as the owner of Pillsbury. But this example illustrates how much impact a different owner can make to a company's value: 70 percent in this case. Best ownership also helps the economy by redirecting resources to their highest-value use. Significant activities can be carried out at much lower cost, freeing up capital and human resources for other activities.

This chapter explains what makes the best owner for a company and how the corporations that qualify as best owner may change over time. It also discusses how a business portfolio evolves and how to construct a portfolio, and it dispels some myths about diversification.

WHAT MAKES AN OWNER THE BEST

To identify the best owner of a business in any given industry circumstances, you first have to understand the sources of value on which potential new owners might draw. Some owners add value by linking a new business with other activities in their portfolio—for example, by using existing sales channels to access additional customers, or by sharing an existing manufacturing infrastructure. Others add value through distinctive skills such as operational or marketing excellence, or by providing better governance and incentives for the management team, or by having a better insight into how a market will develop. And finally, some add value through having more influence on critical stakeholders in a particular market—for instance, governments, regulators, or customers. Of course, in some cases, the best owner may be able to draw on two or more of these potential sources of new value, but let's examine them one at a time.

Unique Links with Other Businesses

The most straightforward way that owners add value is through links to other businesses within their portfolio, especially when only the parent company can make such links. Suppose, for instance, a mining company has the rights to develop a coal field in a remote location far from any rail lines or other infrastructure. Another mining company already operates a coal mine just 10 miles away and has built the necessary infrastructure, including the rail line. The second mining company would be a better owner of the new mine because its incremental costs to develop the mine are much lower than anyone else's. It can afford to purchase the undeveloped mine at a higher price than any other firm in the market and still earn an attractive return on invested capital (ROIC). Such unique links can be made across the value chain, from research and development (R&D) to manufacturing to distribution to sales. For instance, a large pharmaceutical company with a sales force dedicated to oncology might be the best owner of a small pharmaceutical company with a promising new oncology drug but no sales force.

In many cases, a potential parent company might be able to make the same kind of link to multiple possible subsidiaries. IBM, for one, has successfully acquired many small software companies to exploit its unique global sales force. IBM was a better owner of all these companies because it could accelerate the global revenue growth of these companies' products.

Distinctive Skills

Better owners may have distinctive functional or managerial skills from which the new business can benefit. Such skills may reside anywhere in the business system, including product development, manufacturing processes, and sales and marketing. But to make a difference, any such skill has to be a key driver of success in the industry. For example, a company with great manufacturing skills probably wouldn't be a better owner of a consumer packaged-goods business, because the latter company's manufacturing costs aren't large enough to affect its competitive position.

In consumer packaged goods, distinctive skills in developing and marketing brands are more likely to make one company a better owner than another. Take Procter & Gamble (P&G), which in 2009 had 23 billion-dollar brands in terms of net sales and 20 half-billion-dollar brands spread across a range of product categories, including washing-machine soap, beauty products, pet food, and diapers. Almost all of P&G's billion-dollar brands rank first or second in their respective markets. What makes P&G special is that it developed these brands in different ways. Some, including Tide and Crest, have been P&G brands for decades. Others, including Gillette and Oral-B, were acquired in the past 10 years. Finally, Febreze and Swiffer were developed from scratch in the past 10 years. As a group, these brands generated sales growth averaging 11 percent a year from 2001 to 2009.

Better Governance

Better owners can also add value through their better overall governance of a business, without necessarily running its day-to-day operations. Better governance refers to the way the company's owners (or their representatives) interact with the management team to create maximum value in the long term. For example, the best private equity firms don't just recapitalize companies with debt; they improve the companies' performance through improved governance.

Two of our colleagues analyzed 60 successful investments by 11 leading private equity firms. They found that in almost two-thirds of the transactions, the primary source of new value was improvement in the operating performance of the company relative to peers through fruitful interaction between the owners and the management team.[1] The use of financial leverage and clever timing of investments were not the most important sources of their success, even though critics have often claimed they were.

Private equity firms don't have the time or skills to run their portfolio companies day to day, but the higher-performing private equity firms do govern these companies very differently from the way listed companies are governed, and this is a key source of their outperformance. Typically, the private equity firms introduce a stronger performance culture and make quick management changes when necessary. They encourage managers to abandon any sacred cows, and they give managers leeway to focus on a longer horizon, say five years, rather than the typical one-year horizon for a listed company. Also, the boards of private equity companies spend three times as many days on their roles as do those at public companies. Most of their time is spent on strategy and performance management, rather than compliance and risk avoidance, the focus of boards of public companies.[2]

Better Insight and Foresight

Companies that have insight into how a market and industry will evolve and then act on that insight to expand existing businesses or develop new ones can be better owners because they capitalize on their innovative ideas. One example is Intuit, which noticed in the late 1990s that many small businesses were using its Quicken software, originally designed to help consumers manage personal finances. The observation led to an important insight: most business accounting software was too complex for the small business owner. So Intuit designed a new product expressly for small business accounting and within two years had claimed 80 percent of this burgeoning market.

While many companies in the mid-1980s saw that fiber-optic networks would be the future of communications, Williams Companies, an oil and natural gas company, had an additional insight: fiber-optic cable could be installed into its decommissioned oil and gas pipelines at a fraction of the cost that most competing cable network companies would have to pay. Combining its own network with those acquired from others, Williams eventually controlled 11,000 miles of cable, transmitting digital signals from one end of the United States to the other. Williams's insight combined with its pipeline infrastructure made it a good or possibly the best owner of this network in the emerging

---

[1] Conor Kehoe and Joachim Heel, "Why Some Private Equity Firms Do Better," *McKinsey Quarterly*, no. 1 (2005): 24–26.

[2] Viral Acharya, Conor Kehoe, and Michael Reyner, "The Voice of Experience: Public versus Private Equity," *McKinsey on Finance* (Spring 2009): 16–21.

digital communications industry. Williams also reduced its stake in fiber-optic cable at the right time, when prices were highly inflated. It sold most of its telecommunications businesses in 1994 for $25 billion.

Influence on Critical Stakeholders

The advantage from influence on critical stakeholders applies primarily to companies in emerging markets. Running these companies is complicated by a relatively small pool of managerial talent from which to hire, undeveloped capital markets, and governments that are heavily involved in business as customers, suppliers, and regulators. In such markets, large-scale diversified conglomerates such as Tata and Reliance in India and Samsung and Hyundai in Korea can be better owners of many businesses because they are more attractive employers, allowing them to skim off the best talent. Also, they have more capital than smaller competitors and know how to work with key stakeholders such as governments.

In less constrained markets, however, diversification rarely creates additional value for companies, as we explain in the final section of this chapter.

THE BEST-OWNER LIFE CYCLE

The definition of *best owner* isn't static, and best owners themselves will change over time as a business's circumstances change. Thus, a business's best owner could at different times be a larger company, a private equity firm, a government, a sovereign wealth fund, a family, the business's customers, its employees, or shareholders whenever a business becomes an independent public company listed on a stock exchange.

Furthermore, the parties vying to become best owners are continually evolving in different ways in different parts of the world. In the United States, most large companies are either listed or owned by private equity funds. They tend to go public earlier than companies elsewhere, so they rarely involve the second generation of a founding family. In Europe, government ownership also plays an important role. In Asia and South America, large companies are often controlled for several generations by members of their founding families, and family relationships also create ownership links between different businesses. Capital markets in these regions aren't as well developed, so founders are more concerned about ensuring that their firms stay true to their legacy after they have retired.

Consider an example of how the best owner for a company might change with its circumstances. Naturally, a business's founders will almost always be its first best owners. The founders' entrepreneurial drive, passion, and tangible commitment to the business are essential to getting the company off the ground.

Then as a business grows, it will probably need more capital, so it may sell a stake to a venture capital fund that specializes in helping new companies to grow. At this point, it's not unusual for the fund to put in new managers who supplant or supplement the founders, bringing skills and experience better suited to managing the complexities and risks of a larger organization.

To provide even more capital, the venture capital firm may take the company public, selling shares to a range of investors and, in the process, enabling itself, the founders, and the managers to realize the value of the company they created. As a public company, it shifts control to an independent board of directors (though the founders will still have important influence if they continue to own substantial stakes).

As the industry evolves, the company might find that it cannot compete with larger companies because, for instance, it needs distribution capability far beyond what it can build by itself in a reasonable time to challenge global competitors. Other external factors, such as regulatory or technological changes, also can create a similar need to change owners. In response to this limitation, the company may sell itself to a larger company that has the needed capability. In this way, it becomes a product line or business within a division of a multi-business corporation. Now the original company will merge with the manufacturing, sales, distribution, and administrative functions of the division.

As the markets mature for the businesses in the division where the original company now operates, its corporate owner may decide to focus on other, faster-growing businesses. So the corporation may sell its division to a private equity firm. Now that the division stands alone, the private equity firm can see how it has amassed an amount of central overhead that is inconsistent with its slower growth. So the private equity firm restructures the division to give it a leaner cost structure. Once the restructuring is done, the private equity firm sells the division to a large company that specializes in running slow-growth brands.

At each stage of the company's life, each best owner took actions to increase the company's cash flows, thereby adding value. The founder came up with the idea for the business. The venture capital firm provided capital and professional management. Going public provided the early investors with a way to realize the value of the founders' groundwork and raised more cash. The large corporation accelerated the company's growth with a global distribution capability. The private equity firm restructured the company's division when growth slowed. The company that became the final best owner applied its skills in managing slow-growth brands. All these changes of ownership made sense in terms of creating value.

CONSTANTLY EVOLVING PORTFOLIO OF BUSINESSES

Applying the best-owner sequence, executives must continually look for and acquire companies where they could be the best owner, and must divest businesses where they used to be the best owner but that another company could now own better. Since the best owner for a given business changes with time, a company needs to have a structured, regular corporate strategy process to review and renew its list of potential acquisition targets, and to test whether any of its existing businesses have reached their sell-by date.

For acquisitions, applying the best-owner principle often leads potential acquirers toward targets that are very different from those produced by traditional screening approaches. Traditional approaches often focus on finding potential targets that perform well financially and are somehow related to the parent's business lines. But through the best-owner lens, such characteristics might be less important or irrelevant.

Potential acquirers might do better to seek a financially weak company that has great potential for improvement, especially if the acquirer has proven expertise in improving performance. Focusing attention on tangible opportunities to reduce costs, or on identifying common customers, may be more rewarding in the long run than investigating a target for the vaguer reason that it is somehow related to your company.

Companies following the best-owner philosophy are as active in divesting as they are in acquiring; they sell and spin off companies regularly and for good reasons. To illustrate, 50 years ago, many pharmaceutical and chemical companies were combined because they required similar manufacturing processes and skills. But as the two industries matured, their research, manufacturing, and other skills diverged considerably, to the extent that they became distant cousins rather than sister companies. Today the keys to running a commodity chemicals company are scale, operating efficiency, and management of costs and capital expenditures. In contrast, the keys to running a pharmaceutical company are managing an R&D pipeline, a sophisticated sales force, the regulatory approval process, and relations with government in state-run health systems that buy prescription drugs. So while it might once have made sense for the two types of business to share a common owner, it no longer does. This is why nearly all formerly combined chemical-pharmaceutical companies have split up. For instance, the pharmaceutical company Zeneca was split from Imperial Chemical Industries in 1993 and later merged with another pharmaceutical company to form AstraZeneca. Similarly, pharmaceutical company Aventis was split off from the chemical company Hoechst in 1999; it was later purchased by Sanofi Synthelabo to create Sanofi Aventis, forming a bigger pharma-only company.

Executives are often concerned that divestitures look like an admission of failure, will make their company smaller, and will reduce their stock market value. Yet the research shows that, on the contrary, the stock market consistently reacts positively to divestitures, both sales and spin-offs.[3] Research has

---

[3] J. Mulherin and A. Boone, "Comparing Acquisitions and Divestitures," *Journal of Corporate Finance* 6 (2000): 117–139.

EXHIBIT 19.1 **Steps in Constructing a Portfolio of Businesses**

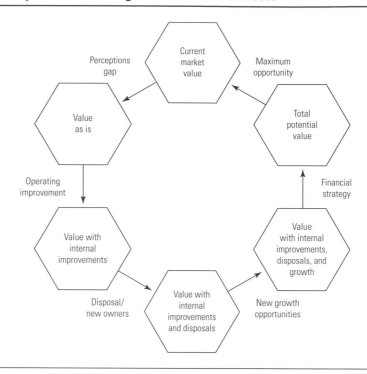

also shown that spun-off businesses tend to increase their profit margins by one-third during the three years after the transactions are complete.[4] Thus, planned divestitures are a sign of successful value creation.

CONSTRUCTING THE PORTFOLIO

Executives can apply the principles discussed in this chapter to construct a portfolio of businesses for their company. A typical large company already owns enterprises in a single business or has an existing collection of diverse businesses. So a logical starting place for constructing a more valuable portfolio would be to clean up the company's current portfolio. While there's no single right way to think through this task, we've found over the past 20 years that a systematic approach to constructing a company's portfolio of businesses is helpful. This section describes that approach, which is illustrated in Exhibit 19.1, as five analytical steps a company should pursue to develop its portfolio of

[4] P. Cusatis, J. Miles, and J. Woolridge, "Some New Evidence That Spinoffs Create Value," *Journal of Applied Corporate Finance* 7 (1994): 100–107.

businesses. Each step lands at a higher-level value, moving from current market value to total potential value:

1. Determine the company's current market value, and compare it with the company's value as is (its discounted cash flow [DCF] value estimated from cash flow projections based on existing business plans). Any gaps imply that the company managers have a different perspective on the value of the businesses than investors have.

2. Identify and value opportunities to improve operations internally—for example, by increasing margins, accelerating core revenue growth, and improving capital efficiency.

3. Evaluate whether some businesses should be divested.

4. Identify potential acquisitions or other initiatives to create new growth, and estimate their impact on value.

5. Estimate how the company's value might be increased through changes in its capital structure or other financial strategy changes. Adding these increases to the level of value after step 4 gives the total potential value of the company.

As an example, consider how the corporate strategy team at a real company (we'll call it EG Corporation) applied this approach. EG Corporation is a $10.65 billion company with six operating businesses, described in Exhibit 19.2. Consumerco, which manufactures and markets branded consumer packaged goods, was earning a high return on invested capital (ROIC), but its growth had barely kept up with inflation. Nevertheless, because of its size and high ROIC, it accounted for about 72 percent of EG's total enterprise value. Foodco operates a contract food service business. Its earnings had been growing, but ROIC was low because of high capital investment requirements in facilities. Woodco, a midsize furniture manufacturer, was formed through the acquisition of eight smaller companies, but their operations were still being consolidated. Woodco had suffered steadily declining returns. The other three businesses in the portfolio are a small newspaper, a small property development company, and a small consumer finance company.

As shown in Exhibit 19.2, the discounted cash flow (DCF) value of EG based on its business plans approximately matched its market value. A cash flow analysis showed that, while EG had been generating substantial discretionary (or free) cash flow in the Consumerco business, a large portion of that money had been sunk into Woodco and Foodco, and relatively little was reinvested in Consumerco. Moreover, little of the cash had found its way back to EG's shareholders. Over the previous five years, EG had, in effect, been borrowing to pay dividends to its shareholders.

The corporate strategy team analyzed each business unit to find opportunities to improve operations or possibly divest the business. While Consumerco

EXHIBIT 19.2 **EG Corporation: Current Situation**

	Sales ($ million)	EBITA ($ million)	Revenue growth (percent)	ROIC (percent)	DCF value of business plans ($ million)
Consumerco	6,300	435	3	30	6,345
Foodco	1,500	120	15	9	825
Woodco	2,550	75	19	6	1,800
Newsco	300	45	6	20	600
Propco	–	15	–	–	450
Finco	–	9	–	–	105
Corporate overhead	–	–	–	–	(1,275)
Total	10,650	699			8,850
Debt					(900)
Equity value					7,950
Less: Stock market value					7,200
Value gap					750
Percent of stock market value					10

had built strong brand names and most of its product lines had enjoyed a dominant market share, this analysis suggested it had room to increase revenue significantly and earn even higher margins:

- Consumerco had been cutting back on R&D and advertising spending to generate cash for EG's efforts to diversify and to buffer poor performance in other parts of EG's portfolio. Boosting investments in R&D and advertising would likely lead to higher sales volumes in existing EG products and encourage the introduction of additional high-margin products.

- Despite Consumerco's dominant position in its market categories, its prices were lower than for less popular brands. The value created by price increases would more than offset any losses in volume.

- Consumerco's sales force was less than half as productive as sales forces at other companies selling through the same channels. Sales productivity could increase to near the level of Consumerco's peers.

- Consumerco had room to cut costs, particularly in purchasing and inventory management. In fact, the cost of sales could easily be reduced by one percentage point.

When the team factored in these possibilities, they found that Consumerco's value could be increased by at least 37 percent.

Similar analysis of Foodco showed that it was clearly a candidate for divestiture. Foodco's ROIC was less than its cost of capital, so its growth was destroying value. Its industry as a whole was extremely competitive, although a few large players were earning respectable returns. However, even their returns were starting to decline. The Consumerco brand, which Foodco used, was found to be of little value in building the business, and Foodco would be unable to develop significant scale economies, at least in the near future. To make matters worse, Foodco had a voracious appetite for capital to build facilities but was not generating a return on new investment sufficient to cover the cost of the capital (its opportunity cost to the shareholders providing the capital). Last, Foodco was a particularly strong divestiture candidate because a new owner that was a larger, growing competitor could dramatically improve its performance.

Woodco, too, was in a position to improve on its performance dramatically as planned under EG's ownership, if it could achieve the same level of performance as other top furniture companies. This would likely require Woodco to focus less on growth and more on higher margins. To do this, Woodco would need to build better management information and control systems, and stick to its familiar mass-market products instead of striking out into new upmarket furnishings, as it had planned.

Although this analysis suggested that Woodco also might be sold (for instance, to a company that bought and improved smaller furniture firms), it would make little sense for EG to sell Woodco right away, midway through its consolidation, when potential buyers might be concerned that the business could fall apart. If the consolidation succeeded, EG could sell Woodco for a much higher price in 12 to 18 months, and EG's value could increase as a result by 33 percent.

Newsco and Propco were both subscale and could not attract top talent as part of EG. Furthermore, ready buyers existed for both, so divestiture was the clear choice.

The consumer finance sector had become so competitive that the spread between borrowing costs and the rates Finco earned on new loans did not cover the consumer finance company's operating costs. It turned out that the existing loan portfolio might be sold for more than the entire business was worth. In effect, each year's new business was dissipating some of the value inherent in the existing loan portfolio. The team recommended that the board decide to liquidate the portfolio and shut down Finco.

Looking for further internal improvements, the team found that EG's corporate staff had grown with the increasing complexity of its portfolio to the point where the business units had been obliged to add staff simply to interact with the corporate staff. By reducing the portfolio, EG would be able to cut corporate costs by 50 percent.

On the revenue side, EG had done little to take advantage of Consumerco's strong brands to incubate new businesses. A quick analysis showed that if EG could find new growth opportunities that generated $1.5 billion to $3 billion in sales, it could increase the market value of Consumerco by $2.4 billion or

EXHIBIT 19.3 **EG Corporation: Value Created through Restructuring**

	DCF value of business plans ($ million)	New corporate strategy ($ million)	Difference (percent)	Actions
Consumerco	6,345	8,700	37	Operating improvements
Foodco	825	1,050	27	Divest
Woodco	1,800	2,400	33	Consolidate/divest
Newsco	600	600	–	Divest
Propco	450	480	7	Divest
Finco	105	135	29	Liquidate
Corporate overhead	(1,275)	(675)	n/a	Streamline
Debt tax benefit	–	600	n/a	
Total	8,850	13,290	50	
Debt	(900)	(900)	–	
Equity value	7,950	12,390	56	
New growth opportunities	–	2,400+	–	
Equity value with new growth opportunities	7,950	14,790+	86	

more. While the immediate restructuring was the first priority, EG decided to keep generating new growth ideas as well.

Turning next to EG's financial strategy, the team found that EG had been pursuing a policy of maintaining an AA bond rating from Standard & Poor's, and prided itself on being a strong investment-grade company. However, its sizable and stable free cash flows meant that EG could support much higher debt. The Consumerco business, which generated the bulk of the cash, was recession-resistant. Also, not much reserve financial capacity would be needed, given the relative maturity of EG's core business and its limited need for capital. The company's executives also believed that EG could tap funding for a major expansion or acquisition, if it made economic sense. At a minimum, EG could raise $1.5 billion in new debt in the next six months and use the proceeds to repurchase shares or pay a special dividend. This debt would provide a more tax-efficient capital structure for EG, which would be worth about $600 million in present value to EG's shareholders (see Chapter 23).

Exhibit 19.3 summarizes EG's restructuring plan. All told, the restructuring could increase EG's value by 56 percent without the extra growth initiatives and by as much as 86 percent with successful growth initiatives, although these might be hard to realize (see Chapter 5).

THE MYTH OF DIVERSIFICATION

A perennial question in corporate strategy is whether companies should hold a diversified portfolio of businesses. The idea seemed to be discredited in the 1970s, yet some executives still say things like "It's the third leg of the stool that makes a company stable." Our perspective is that diversification is intrinsically neither good nor bad; it depends on whether the parent company adds more value to the businesses it owns than any other potential owner could, making it the best owner of those businesses in the circumstances.

Over the years, different ideas have been floated to encourage or justify diversification, but these theories simply don't hold water. Most rest on the idea that different businesses have different business cycles, so cash flows at the peak of one business's cycle will offset the lean cash years of other businesses, thereby stabilizing a company's consolidated cash flows. If cash flows and earnings are smoothed in this way, the reasoning goes, then investors will pay higher prices for the company's stock.

The facts refute this argument, however. First, we haven't found any evidence that diversified companies actually generate smoother cash flows. We examined the 50 companies from the S&P 500 with the lowest earnings volatility from 1997 to 2007. Fewer than 10 could be considered diversified companies, in the sense of owning businesses in more than two distinct industries. Second, and just as important, there is no evidence that investors pay higher prices for less volatile companies (see Chapter 16). In our regular analyses of diversified companies for our clients, we almost never find that the value of the sum of a diversified company's business units is substantially different from the market value of the consolidated company.[5]

Another argument is that diversified companies with more stable cash flows can safely take on more debt, thus getting a larger tax benefit from debt. While this may make sense in theory, however, we've never come across diversified companies that systematically used more debt than their peers.

Finally, a more nuanced argument is that diversified companies are better positioned to take advantage of different business cycles in different sectors. They can use cash flows from their businesses in sectors at the top of their cycle to invest in businesses in sectors at the bottom of their cycle (when their undiversified competitors cannot). Once again, we haven't found diversified companies that actually behave that way. In fact, we typically find the opposite: the senior executives at diversified companies don't understand their individual business units well enough to have the confidence to invest at the bottom of the cycle, when none of the competitors are investing. Diversified companies tend to respond to opportunities more slowly than less diversified companies.

While any benefits from diversification are elusive, the costs are very real. Investors can diversify their portfolios at lower cost than companies, because they only have to buy and sell stocks, something they can do easily and relatively cheaply many times a year. But substantially changing the shape of a portfolio of real businesses involves a diversified company in considerable transaction costs and disruption, and it typically takes many years. Moreover, the business units of diversified companies often perform less well than those of more focused peers, partly because of added complexity and bureaucracy.

---

[5] This assumes that the values of business units are based on peer businesses with similar performance.

Of course, diversification can be value-creating when the parent company is the best owner for all the businesses in its stable. For example, Danaher operates more than 40 businesses with combined revenues of more than $12 billion. From nanoscale microscopes to financial-transaction systems to drinking-water disinfection technologies, most of Danaher's businesses operate independently from each other, since they are inherently diverse and span such a wide range of industries. What Danaher's businesses share is its proven system for controlling quality, delivery, and cost, and for spawning innovation. Danaher buys only companies that it believes can benefit from applying this business system—typically, medium-sized companies that haven't yet tried a systematic approach to cost reduction and quality improvement. When Danaher purchases a company, it immediately sends in managers from other Danaher businesses to transform the new company, using the knowledge from other businesses they have improved. While a company in, say, the financial-transaction business could surely vie for best ownership of a credit card business, a firm like Danaher, which has honed its skills in creating value from acquisitions, could possibly be the better owner.

SUMMARY

The key to constructing a portfolio of value-creating businesses is to analyze whether the company is currently the best owner of each business in the portfolio from a value-creating viewpoint. If another company would be a better owner for a business, then the business is a candidate for divestment. Conversely, if you identify businesses from which the company could create more value than their present owners can, those businesses are appropriate acquisition targets.

The owner that qualifies as best for a business may change over the course of the business's life cycle and varies with its geography. A company in the United States, for instance, is likely to start up owned by its founders and to end its days in the portfolio of a conglomerate that specializes in extracting cash from businesses in declining sectors. In between, the business may have passed through a whole range of owners.

These facts about businesses have three critical implications for managers. First, divestitures may be as value-creating as acquisitions, so managers should not shrink from divesting businesses in their portfolio that another company might own better. Divestitures are not a sign of failure. Second, the process of scrutinizing the portfolio for possible additions and subtractions should be continual, because the definition of *best owner* for any business changes so much during its life cycle. Last, diversification is neither intrinsically good nor bad for any company. If the company is the best owner for a set of diverse businesses in its portfolio, then its diversification is by definition value-creating—and the reverse is also true.

REVIEW QUESTIONS

1. Explain why the value of a business may differ under different owners.
2. What are the potential sources of value that the best owner brings to a business? Share examples.
3. What are some impediments to matching the best potential owner to a business?
4. Provide examples of how the best owner of a business has changed over time. Give reasons for these changes.
5. Explain how and why the best owner of a business might change over time.
6. What are the steps involved in constructing a portfolio? Discuss potential hurdles in executing the analytic approach.
7. Should a company operate a diversified portfolio of businesses? What are the arguments for and against?
8. What are the benefits to society when a business is owned by its best owner?

20

Performance Management

The overall value that a company creates is the sum of the outcomes of innumerable business decisions taken by its managers and staff at every level, from choosing when to open the door to customers to deciding whether to acquire a new business. A company needs systems to ensure that all decisions affecting value are consistent with its short- and long-term objectives. Such performance management systems enable management to see clearly the impact of those myriad decisions on value creation.

Performance management systems typically include long-term strategic plans, short-term budgets, capital budgeting systems, performance reporting and reviews, and compensation frameworks. Successful value creation requires that all components of the performance management system be aligned with the company's strategy, so that they encourage decisions that maximize value. For example, if product development is important to the strategic plan, the short-term budget and capital budget must include enough spending in the current year to develop the new products, and performance reviews must evaluate progress on new products, not just short-term profits.

The success or failure of performance management depends not so much on the system—the metrics, corporate meeting calendars, scorecards, and so on—as on the rigor and honesty with which everyone engages in the process. Do the senior management team members really understand the economics of the business units they oversee? Can they negotiate performance targets that are both challenging and achievable? Are trade-offs between the short term and the long term transparent? Are managers sufficiently rewarded for focusing on long-term value?

When performance management is working well, it helps the layers of the organization communicate frankly and effectively. It gives managers space to manage, while assuring their bosses that agreed-on levels of performance will be achieved. In many companies, communication between layers of management revolves entirely around profit targets, whether they are hit or missed.

With a good performance management system, just as much attention is paid to the long-term value-creating intent behind short-term profit targets, and people across the company are in constant dialogue about what adjustments need to be made to stay in line with long-term performance goals.

We approach performance management from both an analytical and an organizational perspective. The analytical perspective focuses first on ensuring that companies use the right metrics: as well as historical performance measures, companies need to use diagnostic metrics that help them understand and manage their ability to create value over the longer term. Second, we analyze how to set appropriate targets, giving examples of analytically sound performance measurement in action. The organizational perspective describes the mind-sets and processes needed to support effective performance management.

CHOOSING THE RIGHT METRICS

Companies need metrics that will monitor their long-term health as well as their short-term performance. They also need to set appropriate targets in these dimensions. In this section, we describe how they might achieve both analytical tasks, and we give some examples of the potential benefits.

Identifying Value Drivers

Think of a patient visiting his doctor. The patient may be feeling fine, in the sense of meeting requirements for weight, strength, and energy. But if his cholesterol is above the target level that medical science has established as safe, he may need to take corrective action now to prevent future heart disease. Similarly, if a company shows strong growth and return on invested capital (ROIC), it still needs to know whether that performance is sustainable. Comparing readings of company health indicators against meaningful targets can tell us whether a company has achieved impressive past financial results at a cost to its long-term health, perhaps crippling its ability to create value in the future.

To see the critical difference between companies' recorded performance and their long-term health, consider the pharmaceutical industry. In the year after the patent on a drug expires, sales of that drug often decline by 50 to 75 percent or more, as generic producers lower prices and steal market share. When a major product will be going off patent in a couple of years with no replacement on the horizon, investors know future profits will suffer. In such a case, the company could have strong current performance but a poor performance outlook reflected in a low market value, because market values reflect long-term health, not just short-term profits. To take another example, retail chains can sometimes maintain apparently impressive margins by scrimping

EXHIBIT 20.1 **Value Creation Tree**

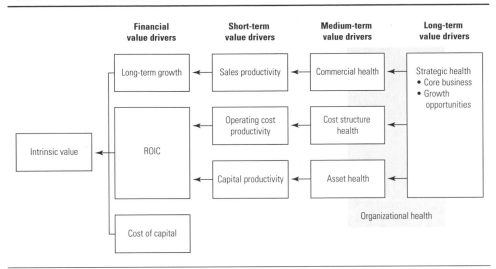

on store refurbishment and brand building, to the detriment of their future competitive strength.

We can gain insight into a company's health by examining the drivers of long-term growth and ROIC, the key drivers of value creation for all companies. A value driver tree, as shown in Exhibit 20.1, illustrates how performance on layers of related subordinate company value drivers feed into the key value drivers on the left-hand side. The generic subordinate value drivers are broken down into short-, medium-, and long-term categories. The choice of particular value drivers, along with targets for testing and strengthening each one, should vary from company to company, reflecting each company's different sectors and aspirations.

This framework shares some elements with the "balanced scorecard" introduced in a 1992 *Harvard Business Review* article by Robert Kaplan and David Norton.[1] Numerous nonprofit and for-profit organizations have subsequently advocated and implemented the balanced scorecard idea. Its premise is that financial performance is only one aspect of performance. As important to long-term value creation, Kaplan and Norton point out, are customer satisfaction, internal business processes, learning, and revenue growth.

Although our concept of value drivers resembles Kaplan and Norton's nonfinancial metrics, we differ in advocating that companies choose their own set of metrics for the outermost branches of the tree, under the generic headings set out here, and tailor their choice to their industry and strategy. Such tailoring is critical to setting the right strategic priorities. For example, product

---

[1] Robert S. Kaplan and David P. Norton, "The Balanced Scorecard: Measures That Drive Performance," *Harvard Business Review* 80, no. 1 (January 1992): 71–79.

innovation may be important to companies in one industry, while to companies in another, tight cost control and customer service may matter more, and their respective prioritization of value drivers should reflect the difference. Similarly, an individual company will have different value drivers at different points in its life cycle.

Every company will need to develop its own appropriate value driver metrics, but using the eight generic categories presented in Exhibit 20.1 as a starting point for analysis will ensure that a company systematically explores all the important ones.

Short-term value drivers   Short-term value drivers are the immediate drivers of historical ROIC and growth. They are typically the easiest to quantify and monitor frequently (monthly or quarterly). They are indicators of whether current growth and ROIC can be sustained, will improve, or will decline over the short term. They might include cost per unit for a manufacturing company or same-store sales growth for a retailer.

Following the growth and ROIC framework in Exhibit 20.1, short-term value drivers fall into three categories:

1. *Sales productivity* metrics are the drivers of recent sales growth, such as price and quantity sold, market share, the company's ability to charge higher prices relative to peers (or charge a premium for its product or services), sales force productivity, and for a retailer, same-store sales growth versus new-store growth.

2. *Operating cost productivity* metrics are typically drivers of unit costs, such as the component costs for building an automobile or delivering a package. UPS, for example, is well known for charting out the optimal delivery path of its drivers to enhance their productivity and for developing well-defined standards on how to deliver packages.

3. *Capital productivity* measures how well a company uses its working capital (inventories, receivables, and payables) and its property, plant, and equipment. Dell provides an example of highly productive working capital. The company revolutionized the personal computer (PC) business by building to order so it could minimize inventories. Because the company kept inventory levels so low and had few receivables to boot, it could, on occasion, operate with negative working capital.[2]

When assessing short-term corporate performance, separate the effects of forces that are outside management's control (both good and bad) from things management can influence. For instance, upstream oil company executives

---

[2] Since Dell has expanded beyond PCs into other businesses such as notebook computers and services that cannot use the same capital approach as the PC business, its aggregate capital is no longer negative.

shouldn't get much credit for higher profits that result from higher oil prices, nor should real estate executives for higher real estate prices (and the resulting higher commissions). Oil company performance should be evaluated with an emphasis on new reserves and production growth, exploration costs, and drilling costs. Real estate brokerages should be evaluated primarily on the number of sales, not whether housing prices are increasing or decreasing.

Medium-term value drivers Medium-term value drivers look forward to indicate whether a company can maintain and improve its growth and ROIC over the next one to five years (or longer for companies, such as pharmaceutical manufacturers, that have long product cycles). These metrics may be harder to quantify than short-term measures and are more likely to be measured annually or over even longer periods.

The medium-term value drivers fall into three categories:

1. *Commercial health* metrics indicate whether the company can sustain or improve its current revenue growth. These metrics include the company's product pipeline (talent and technology to bring new products to market over the medium term), brand strength (investment in brand building), and customer satisfaction. Commercial health metrics vary widely by industry. For a pharmaceutical company, the obvious priority is its product pipeline. For an online retailer, customer satisfaction and brand strength may be the most important components of medium-term commercial health.

2. *Cost structure health* metrics measure a company's ability to manage its costs relative to competitors over three to five years. These metrics might include assessments of programs such as Six Sigma, a method made famous by General Electric and adopted by other companies to reduce costs continually and maintain a cost advantage relative to their competitors across most of their businesses.

3. *Asset health* measures how well a company maintains and develops its assets. For a hotel or restaurant chain, the average time between remodeling projects may be an important driver of health.

Long-term strategic value drivers Metrics for gauging long-term strategic health show the ability of an enterprise to sustain its current operating activities and to identify and exploit new growth areas. A company must periodically assess and measure the threats—including new technologies, changes in customer preferences, and new ways of serving customers—that could make its current business less profitable. In assessing a company's long-term strategic health, it can be hard to identify specific metrics; those situations require more qualitative milestones, such as progress in selecting partners for mergers or for entering a market.

Besides guarding against threats, companies must continually watch for new growth opportunities, whether in related industries or in new geographies.

Organizational health   This final element of corporate well-being measures whether the company has the people, skills, and culture to sustain and improve its performance. Diagnostics of organizational health typically measure the skills and capabilities of a company, its ability to retain its employees and keep them satisfied, its culture and values, and the depth of its management talent. Again, what is important varies by industry. Pharmaceutical companies need deep scientific innovation capabilities but relatively few managers. Retailers need lots of trained store managers, a few great merchandisers, and in most cases, store staff with a customer service orientation.

Benefits of Understanding Your Business's Value Drivers

Clarity about a business's value drivers has several advantages. First, if managers know the relative impact of their company's value drivers on long-term value creation, they can make explicit trade-offs between pursuing a critical driver and allowing performance against a less critical driver to deteriorate. This is particularly helpful for choosing between activities that deliver short-term performance and those that build the long-term health of the business. These trade-offs are material: increasing investment for the long term will cause short-term returns to decline, as management expenses some of the costs, such as R&D or advertising, in the year they occur rather than the year the investments achieve their benefits. Other costs are capitalized but will not earn a return before the project is commissioned, so they too will suppress overall returns in the short term. Understanding the long-term benefits of sacrificing short-term earnings in this way should help corporate boards to support managers in making investments that build a business's long-term capability to create value.

Clarity about value drivers also enables the management team to prioritize actions so that activities expected to create substantially more value take precedence over others. Setting priorities encourages focus and often adds more to value than efforts to improve on multiple dimensions simultaneously. Without an explicit discussion of priorities and trade-offs, different members of the management team could interpret and execute the business strategy in numerous ways.

In general, distinctive planning and performance management systems promote a common language and understanding of value drivers that shape the way top management and employees think about creating value at each level of the organization. For example, in a pharmaceutical company, distinctive performance management would encourage discussion and coordinated action across the organization about specific steps to increase the speed of product launches and so accelerate value creation.

EXHIBIT 20.2 **Simple Value Driver Tree: Manufacturing Company**

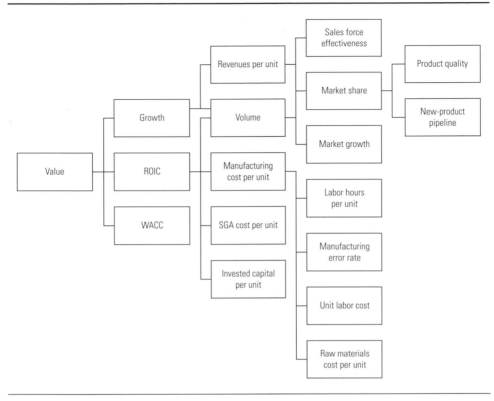

Tailoring Value Driver Trees to Specific Companies

The value driver tree is a systematic method for analytically and visually linking a business's unique value drivers to financial metrics and shareholder value. Each element of financial performance is broken down into value drivers. Exhibit 20.2 shows a simple value driver tree developed for a manufacturing company.

Our experience has taught us that developing different initial versions of trees based on different hypotheses and business knowledge will stimulate the identification of unconventional sources of value. The information from these versions should then be integrated into one tree (or in some cases, a few trees) that best reflects the understanding of the business.

To illustrate this process, we apply it to a temporary-help company. Exhibit 20.3 shows four different approaches used to develop the short-term portion of a value driver tree for this company. Exhibit 20.4 is a summary short-term value driver tree, created by adopting the most useful insights provided by the other trees. A tree based on profit-and-loss structure often seems to managers to be the most natural and easiest to complete. Such a tree, however, is unlikely

EXHIBIT 20.3 **Value Trees from Four Perspectives: Temporary-Help Company**

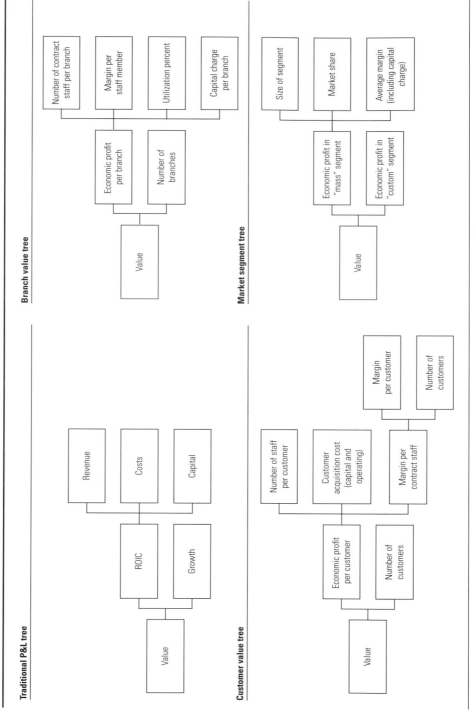

Traditional P&L tree

Branch value tree

Customer value tree

Market segment tree

436

EXHIBIT 20.4 **Summary Short-Term Value Tree: Temporary-Help Company**

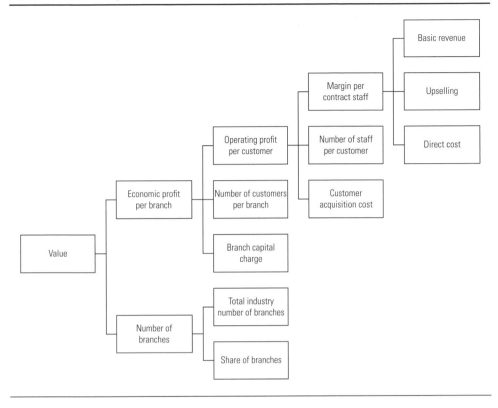

to provide the insight gained by looking at the business from a customer's perspective, from that of a branch of the company, or from some other relevant vantage point.

When you develop value driver trees, pay particular attention to the drivers of growth, because of the lags between investing in developing a growth opportunity and the eventual payoff. These will differ between opportunities. Continuing the example of the temporary-help company, Exhibit 20.5 illustrates a value tree created for developing business in a new geographic market. Important value drivers include building the client base and developing the staff capabilities in the new country, both of which take considerable time to achieve.

Every tip of a value tree is a potential value driver, so a full disaggregation would result in a large number of value drivers, more than could possibly be helpful for running the company. To be sure that the system is practical and effective, managers need to decide at this stage which drivers are the most important to value creation, and focus on them.

EXHIBIT 20.5 **Summary Medium-Term Value Tree: Temporary-Help Company, New Geographic Market**

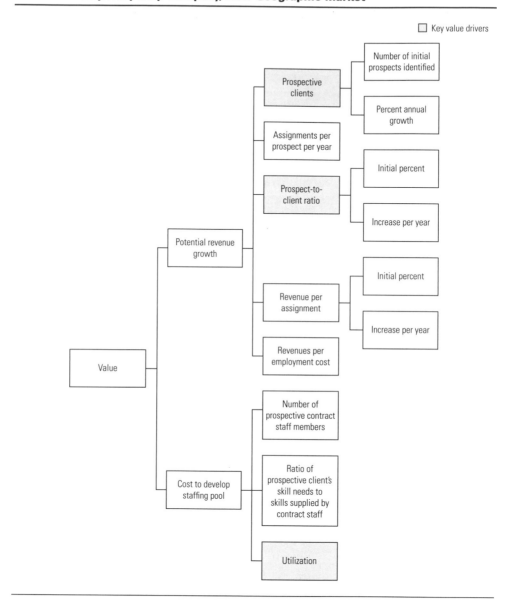

Setting Effective Targets

To make best use of their understanding of key value drivers and safeguard their company's future health, managers need to agree what reading they are targeting on each one. Targets need to be both challenging and realistic enough to be owned by the managers responsible for meeting them.

Businesses can identify realistic opportunities and targets by studying world-class competitors' performance on a particular value metric or milestone and comparing it with their own potential, or looking at the performance of high-performing firms from a different but similar sector. For instance, a petroleum company might benchmark product availability in its service station shops against a grocery retailer's equivalents. This is in part how lean manufacturing approaches developed by automakers have been successfully transplanted into many other industries, including retailing and services.

Businesses can also learn from internal benchmarks taken from comparable operations in different businesses controlled by the same parent. These may be less challenging than external benchmarks, as they do not necessarily involve looking at world-class players. However, internal benchmarks deliver several benefits. The data are likely to be more readily available, since sharing the information poses no competitive or antitrust problems. Also, unearthing the causes of differences in performance is much easier, as the unit heads can visit the benchmark unit. Finally, these comparisons facilitate peer review.

Most performance targets are a single point, but a range can be more helpful. General Electric, for example, sets base and stretch targets. The base target is set by top management based on prior-year performance and the competitive environment. The company expects managers to meet the base target under any circumstance; those who do not meet it rarely last long. The stretch target is a statement of the aspiration for the business and is developed by the management team responsible for delivery. Those who meet their stretch targets are rewarded, but those who miss them are seldom penalized. Using base and stretch targets makes a performance management system much more complex, but it allows the managers of the business units to communicate what they dream of delivering (and what it would take for them to achieve that goal) without committing them to delivery.

The Right Metrics in Action

Choosing the right performance metrics can give new insights into how a company might improve its performance in the future. For instance, Exhibit 20.6 illustrates the most important value drivers for a pharmaceutical company. The exhibit shows the key value drivers, the company's current performance relative to best- and worst-in-class benchmarks, its aspirations for each driver, and the potential value impact from meeting its targets. The greatest value creation would come from three areas: accelerating the rate of release of new products from 0.5 to 0.8 per year, reducing from six years to four the time it takes for a new drug to reach 80 percent of peak sales, and cutting cost of goods sold from 26 percent to 23 percent of sales. Some of the value drivers (such as new-drug development) are long-term, whereas others (such as reducing cost of goods sold) have a shorter-term focus.

EXHIBIT 20.6 **Key Value Drivers: Pharmaceutical Company**

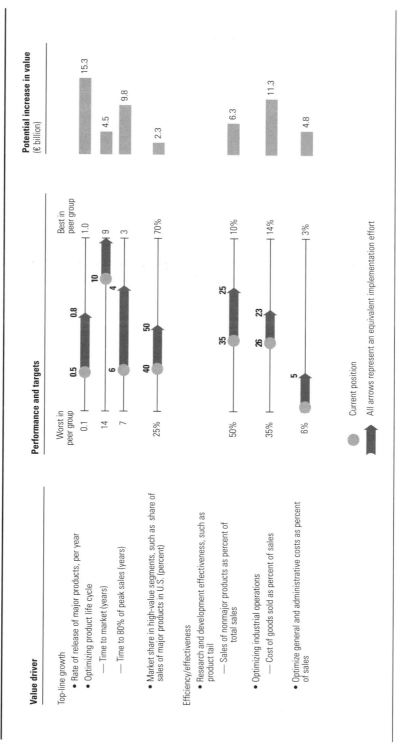

Similarly, focusing on the right performance metrics can help reveal what may be driving underperformance. A consumer goods company we know illustrates the importance of having a tailored set of key value metrics. For several years, a business unit showed consistent double-digit growth in economic profit. Since the financial results were consistently strong—in fact, the strongest across all the business units—corporate managers were pleased and did not ask many questions of the business unit. One year, the unit's economic profit unexpectedly began to decline. Corporate management began digging deeper into the unit's results and discovered that for the preceding three years the unit had been increasing its profit by raising prices and cutting back on product promotion. That created the conditions for competitors to take away market share. The unit's strong short-term performance was coming at the expense of its long-term health. The company changed the unit's management team, but lower profits continued for several years as the unit recovered its position with consumers.

A well-defined and appropriately selected set of key value drivers ought to allow management to articulate how the organization's strategy creates value. If it is impossible to represent some component of the strategy using the key value drivers, or if some key value driver does not serve as a building block in the strategy, then managers should reexamine the value trees. Similarly, managers must regularly revisit the targets they set for each value driver. As their business environment changes, so will the limits of what they can achieve.

ORGANIZATIONAL SUPPORT

Performance metrics give managers information about how well their company is performing now and its likely future performance. But without the right mechanisms to support managers in acting on this information, an elaborate performance measurement system is useless. Indeed, the measurements are less important than how they are used by the organization. We've found that the following ingredients lead to more effective organizational support for corrective action.

Buy-In to Performance Management at All Levels

Companies that succeed at performance management instill a value-creating mind-set throughout the business. Their employees at all levels understand the core principles of value creation (see Chapter 2), know why it matters, and make decisions that take into account the impact on value. They achieve this understanding if their top managers consistently reinforce the importance of the value mind-set in all their communications, build the capabilities to understand value creation, and (as discussed at the end of this section) link value creation to the reward process. Midlevel managers are unlikely to buy into managing for longer-term value creation if top management regularly cuts R&D, advertising, or employee development to make short-term profit targets. Without leadership from the top, a company cannot build a successful performance management system.

Motivating Targets

Managers and staff responsible for meeting targets need to be involved in setting them, so they understand the targets' purpose and will strive to deliver them. Consider the experience of one global consumer goods company. When the corporate technical manager ordered that all the company's bottling lines should achieve 75 percent operating efficiency regardless of their current level, some plant operators rebelled. Operators at one U.S. plant concluded that at 53 percent utilization their plant was running as well as it had ever run, and they refused to aim for higher performance. Then the plant launched a process permitting the operators to set their own performance goals. The same U.S. plant managed to raise efficiency above the 75 percent target over a period of only 14 months.

Higher-level managers also need to be seen to embrace the whole set of targets and be able to explain their interrelation. Otherwise, the targets may simply appear as a set of arbitrary aspirations imposed from above.

Fact-Based Performance Reviews

In too many performance reviews, senior management does not understand enough about the business to assess whether a business unit's performance resulted from the management team's cleverness and hard work or simply from good or bad luck. They need to base performance reviews on facts in order to ensure honest appraisal and make corrective action effective.

The best way to record facts for performance reviews is on a scorecard incorporating the key value metrics from the value driver analysis. Managers may be tempted to think financial reports alone can serve as the basis for performance discussions. Financial results are only part of the review process, however. Key value metrics show the operating performance behind the financial results.

Corporate centers may find it convenient to impose one scorecard on all business units, but this is shortsighted. Although a single scorecard makes it easier to compare units, management forgoes the chance to understand each unit's unique value drivers. Ideally, companies should have tailored scorecards that cascade through each business, so that each manager can monitor the key value drivers for which he or she is accountable.

Managers should use performance reviews as problem-solving sessions to determine the root causes of bad performance and how to fix them, rather than identifying who is to blame. To succeed, reviewers must first prepare thoroughly for reviews. They should then turn traditionally one-sided discussions ("boss tells, subordinate does") into collaborative sessions. Bringing groups together for performance reviews will introduce even more well-informed insights and perspectives, making problem solving more effective, increasing a sense of accountability, and deflecting potential sandbagging. Orchestrated with care, a performance review—even when results are below expectations—can help motivate frontline managers and employees, rather than deflating them.

Appropriate Rewards

The final element of successful performance management is giving appropriate rewards to individual managers and employees. Rewards today are typically financial and, according to some critics, have become excessive. Certainly in the late 1990s, as the long bull market extended, executives received extraordinary rewards, particularly in stock options, that had little to do with their own performance and everything to do with factors beyond their reach, such as declining interest rates. When the stock market fell, companies maintained the higher level of rewards.

Many have argued that current compensation systems remain broken because they rarely link compensation to the company's long-term value creation. Several ideas are emerging on how better to align the two. Here are several of the proposals:

- Linking stock-based compensation to the specific performance of the company, stripping out broad macro and industry effects (see Chapter 3).
- Tying some portion of compensation for senior executives to corporate results several years after the year of the review, even if that means deferring payment of that portion until after the executive's departure from the company.
- Linking bonuses as much to long-term company health metrics as to short-term financial results.
- Moving away from formulaic compensation to a more holistic system that incorporates performance against both quantifiable and nonquantifiable value drivers, even if it requires more judgment by the evaluator.
- Harnessing the power of nonfinancial incentives, such as career progression. Identifying and adhering to a distinctive set of values is another way that companies can attract and motivate employees who find working somewhere in tune with their beliefs to be a powerful incentive.

SUMMARY

For many companies, performance management is the most important driver of value creation. Yet performance management is difficult to describe, let alone execute well. The rewards, however, are great for companies that can build a value creation mind-set, clarify the business's short- and long-term value drivers, set stretch targets that people believe are achievable, conduct fact-based performance reviews, and motivate their people effectively.

REVIEW QUESTIONS

1. Compare and contrast the value driver approach to performance measurement with the balanced scorecard approach.
2. What is the goal of setting performance targets? What are some of the pitfalls inherent in the way companies sometimes set targets?
3. Provide some examples of potential short-term operating metrics for a company that you are familiar with.
4. Provide some examples of potential medium-term value drivers for a company that you are familiar with.
5. Construct three different value driver trees for a company, using different branches.

21

Mergers and Acquisitions

Mergers and acquisitions (M&A) are an important element of a dynamic economy. At different stages of an industry's or a company's life span, resource decisions that once made economic sense can become problematic. For instance, the company that invented a groundbreaking innovation may not be best suited to exploit it. As demand falls off in a mature industry, companies that have been in it a long time are likely to have excess capacity. At any time in a business's history, one group of managers may be better equipped to manage the business than another. At moments like these, acquisitions are often the best or only way to reallocate resources sensibly.

Acquisitions that reduce excess capacity or put companies in the hands of better owners or managers typically create substantial value both for the economy as a whole and for investors. You can see this effect in the increase in the combined cash flows of the many companies involved in acquisitions. Even though acquisitions overall create value, however, the distribution of any value they create tends to be lopsided, with the selling companies' shareholders capturing the bulk. In fact, most empirical research shows that one-third or more of acquiring companies destroy value for their shareholders because they transfer all the benefits of the acquisition to the selling companies' shareholders.

The challenge for managers, therefore, is to ensure that their acquisitions are among those that *do* create value for their shareholders. To that end, this chapter provides a framework for analyzing how to create value from acquisitions and summarizes the empirical research. It discusses the archetypal strategies that are most likely to create value, as well as some more difficult strategies that are often attempted. It provides practical advice on how to estimate and achieve operating improvements and whether to pay in cash or in stock. Last, it reminds managers that stock markets respond to the expected impact of acquisitions on intrinsic value, not accounting results.

VALUE CREATION FRAMEWORK

The conservation of value principle (detailed in Chapter 2) helps explain in theory how to create value from acquisitions. Acquisitions create value when the cash flows of the combined companies are greater than they would have otherwise been. If the acquirer doesn't pay too much for the acquisition, some of that value will accrue to the acquirer's shareholders.

The value created for an acquirer's shareholders equals the difference between the value received by the acquirer and the price paid by the acquirer:

$$\text{Value Created for Acquirer} = \text{Value Received} - \text{Price Paid}$$

The value received by the acquirer equals the intrinsic value of the target company as a stand-alone company run by its former management team plus the present value of any performance improvements to be achieved after the acquisition, which will show up as improved cash flows for the target's business or the acquirer's business. The price paid is the market value of the target plus any premium required to convince the target's shareholders to sell their shares to the acquirer:

$$
\begin{aligned}
\text{Value Created for Acquirer} = {} & (\text{Stand-Alone Value of Target} \\
& + \text{Value of Performance Improvements}) \\
& - (\text{Market Value of Target} \\
& + \text{Acquisition Premium})
\end{aligned}
$$

Exhibit 21.1 uses this framework to illustrate a hypothetical acquisition. Company A buys Company B for $1.3 billion, which includes a 30 percent premium over its market value. Company A expects to increase the value of

EXHIBIT 21.1 **Acquisition Evaluation Framework**

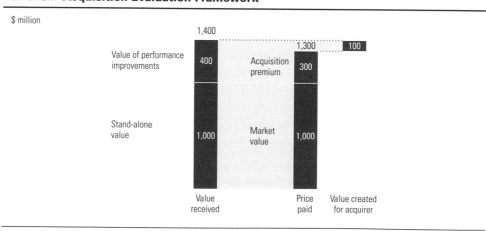

EXHIBIT 21.2 **Value Creation for Given Performance Improvements and Premium Paid**

Value creation as percent of deal value

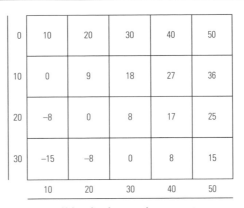

	0	10	20	30	40	50
10		0	9	18	27	36
20		−8	0	8	17	25
30		−15	−8	0	8	15
		10	20	30	40	50

Premium paid as percent of stand-alone value

Value of performance improvements as percent of stand-alone value

B by 40 percent through various operating improvements, so the value of B to A is $1.4 billion. Subtracting the purchase price of $1.3 billion from the value received of $1.4 billion leaves $100 million of value created for Company A's shareholders.

In the case where the stand-alone value of the target equals its market value, then value is created for the acquirer's shareholders only when the value of improvements is greater than the premium paid:

Value Created = Value of Improvements − Acquisition Premium

Examining this equation, it's easy to see why most of the value created from acquisitions goes to the seller's shareholders: If a company pays a 30 percent premium, then it must increase the value of the target by at least 30 percent to create any value.

Exhibit 21.2 shows the value created for the acquirer's shareholders relative to the amount invested in acquisitions at different levels of premiums and operating improvements. For example, Company A, from above, paid a 30 percent premium for Company B and improved B's value by 40 percent, so the value created for the acquirers' shareholders represents 8 percent of the amount Company A invested in the deal.

If we further assume that Company A was worth about three times Company B at the time of the acquisition, this major acquisition would be expected to increase Company A's value by only about 3 percent: $100 million of value creation (see Exhibit 21.1) divided by Company A's value of $3 billion. As this example shows, it is difficult for an acquirer to create a substantial amount of value from acquisitions.

EXHIBIT 21.3 **Selected Acquisitions: Significant Improvements**

percent

	Year	Present value of announced performance improvements /	Target value	Premium paid	Net value created from acquisition /	Purchase price
Kellogg/Keebler	2000	45–70		15	30–50	
PepsiCo/Quaker Oats	2000	35–55		10	25–40	
Clorox/First Brands	1998	70–105		60	5–25	
Henkel/National Starch	2007	60–90		55	5–25	

While a 40 percent performance improvement sounds steep, that's what acquirers often achieve. Exhibit 21.3 presents estimates of the value created from four large deals in the consumer products sector. To estimate the gross value creation, we discounted the announced actual performance improvements at the company's weighted average cost of capital (WACC). The performance improvements were substantial, typically in excess of 50 percent of the value of the target. In addition, Kellogg and PepsiCo paid unusually low premiums for their acquisitions, allowing them to capture more value.

EMPIRICAL RESULTS

Acquisitions and their effects on value creation are a perennial topic of interest to researchers. Empirical studies of acquisitions have yielded useful insights into when they occur, whether they create value, and for whom they create value.

Acquisitions tend to occur in waves, as shown in Exhibit 21.4. Several factors drive these waves: We tend to see more acquisitions when stock prices are rising and managers are optimistic (though to maximize the amount of value created, they should really make acquisitions when prices are low). Low interest rates also stimulate acquisitions, especially heavily leveraged acquisitions by private equity firms. Finally, one large acquisition in an industry encourages others in the same industry to acquire something, too.

The question of whether acquisitions create value has been studied by academics and other researchers for decades. Not surprisingly, given the benefits of acquisitions described in this chapter's introduction, researchers have shown that acquisitions collectively do create value for the shareholders of both the acquirer and the acquired company. According to McKinsey research on 1,415 acquisitions from 1997 through 2009, the combined value of the acquirer and target increased by about 4 percent on average.[1]

---

[1] Werner Rehm and Carsten Buch Siverstsen, "A Strong Foundation for M&A in 2010," *McKinsey on Finance*, no. 34 (Winter 2010): 17–22.

EXHIBIT 21.4 **Historical M&A Activity: U.S. and European Transactions**

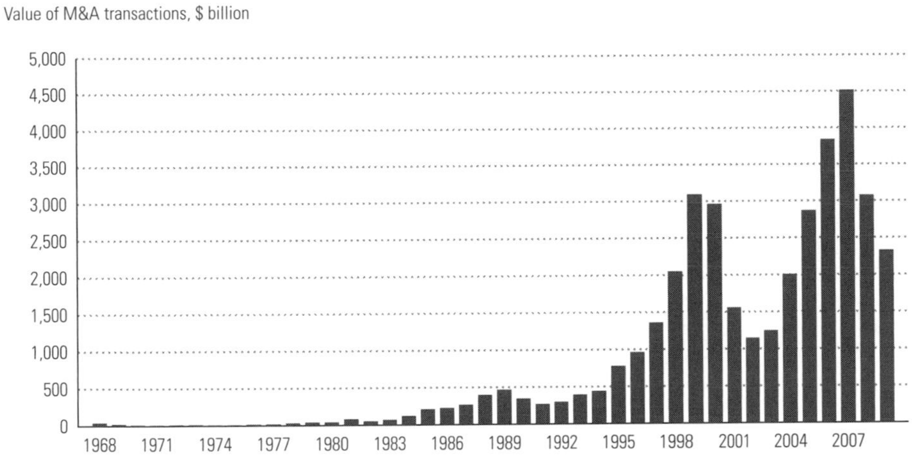

Value of M&A transactions, $ billion

Source: Dealogic, Capital IQ, Mergerstat, Thomson Reuters, McKinsey Corporate Performance Center analysis.

However, the evidence is also overwhelming that, on average, acquisitions do not create much if any value for the acquiring company's shareholders. Empirical studies examining the reaction of capital markets to M&A announcements find that the value-weighted average deal lowers the acquirer's stock price between 1 and 3 percent.[2] Stock returns following the acquisition are no better. Mark Mitchell and Erik Stafford have found that acquirers underperform comparable companies on shareholder returns by 5 percent during the three years following the acquisitions.[3]

Another way to look at the question is to estimate what percentage of deals create any value at all for the acquiring company's shareholders. McKinsey research found that one-third created value, one-third did not, and for the final third, the empirical results were inconclusive.[4]

These studies typically examine the stock market reaction to an acquisition within a few days of its announcement. Many have criticized using announcement effects to estimate value creation. However, additional research has shown that the initial market reactions are persistent and indicate future performance quite accurately (at least for the first year), as shown in Exhibit 21.5.[5]

Nevertheless, although studies of announcement effects give useful results for large samples, the same approach cannot be applied to individual

[2] S. B. Moeller, F. P. Schlingemann, and R. M. Stulz, "Do Shareholders of Acquiring Firms Gain from Acquisitions?" (NBER Working Paper W9523, Ohio State University, 2003).
[3] M. L. Mitchell and E. Stafford, "Managerial Decisions and Long-Term Stock Price Performance," *Journal of Business* 73 (2000): 287–329.
[4] Rehm and Siverstsen, "Strong Foundation for M&A."
[5] Mark Sirower and Sumit Sahna, "Avoiding the Synergy Trap: Practical Guidance on M&A Decisions for CEOs and Boards," *Journal of Applied Corporate Finance* 18, no. 3 (Summer 2006): 83–95.

EXHIBIT 21.5 **Shareholder Returns from Acquisitions, 1995–2001**

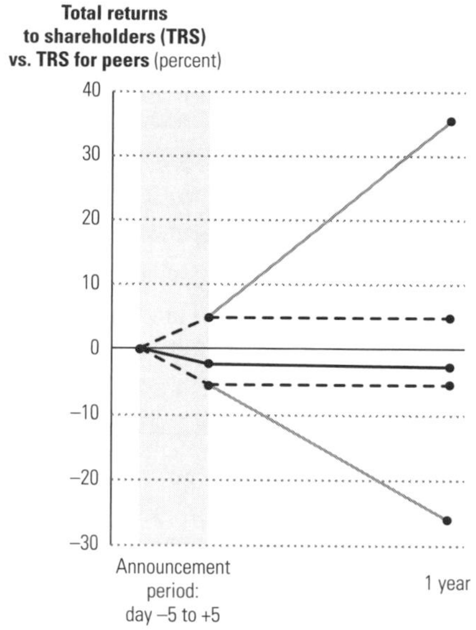

	Number of deals	Announcement return (percent)	1-year return (percent)
Persistent positive	52	5.6	33.1
Initial positive	103	5.7	4.9
Full sample	302	−4.1	−4.3
Initial negative	199	−9.2	−9.0
Persistent negative	133	−10.3	−24.9

Source: Mark Sirower and Sumit Sahna, "Avoiding the Synergy Trap: Practical Guidance on M&A Decisions for CEOs and Boards," *Journal of Applied Corporate Finance* 18, no. 3 (Summer 2006): 83–95.

transactions. While the market correctly assesses the results of transactions on average, that does not mean its initial assessment of a single transaction will always be correct. Another problem with studying announcement effects is that the analysis doesn't work for strings of small acquisitions, in which each individual deal isn't large enough to affect the parent's share price.

It comes as no surprise to find conclusive evidence that most or all of the value creation from acquisitions accrues to the shareholders of the target company, since the target shareholders are receiving, on average, such high premiums over their stock's preannouncement market price—typically about 30 percent.

Researchers have also tried to find whether specific factors could be identified that differentiate deals that are successful, in terms of the returns to the acquirer's shareholders, from unsuccessful ones. This research points to three characteristics that matter:

1. *Strong operators are more successful.* According to empirical research, acquirers whose earnings and share price grow at a rate above industry average for three years before the acquisition earn statistically significant positive returns on announcement.[6] Another study found similar

---

[6] R. Morck, A. Shleifer, and R. Vishny, "Do Managerial Objectives Drive Bad Acquisitions?" *Journal of Finance* 45 (1990): 31–48.

results using the market-to-book ratio as a measure of corporate performance.[7]

2. *Low transaction premiums are better.* Researchers have found that acquirers paying a high premium earn negative returns on announcement.[8]

3. *Being the sole bidder helps.* Several studies have found that acquirer stock returns are negatively correlated with the number of bidders; the more companies attempting to buy the target, the higher the price.[9]

Perhaps it is just as important to identify the characteristics that don't matter. There is no evidence that the following acquisition dimensions indicate either value creation or value destruction:

- Size of the acquirer relative to the target
- Whether the transaction increases or dilutes earnings per share
- The price-to-earnings (P/E) ratio of the acquirer relative to the target's P/E
- The relatedness of the acquirer and target, based on Standard Industrial Classification (SIC) codes

This empirical evidence is important because it shows that there is no magic formula to make an acquisition successful. Like any other business process, acquisitions are not inherently good or bad, just as marketing or research and development are not inherently good or bad. Each deal must have its own strategic logic. In our experience, acquirers in the most successful deals have well-articulated, specific value creation ideas going into each deal. The strategic rationales for less successful deals tend to be vague, such as to pursue international scale, fill in portfolio gaps, or build a third leg of the portfolio.

ARCHETYPES FOR VALUE-CREATING ACQUISITIONS

The empirical analysis is limited in its ability to identify specific acquisition strategies that create value, because of the wide variety of types and sizes of acquisitions and the lack of an objective way to classify acquisitions by strategy. Furthermore, the stated strategy may not be the real strategy. Companies

---

[7] H. Servaes, "Tobin's Q and the Gains from Takeovers," *Journal of Finance* 46 (1991): 409–419.

[8] M. L. Sirower, *The Synergy Trap* (New York: Free Press, 1997); and N. G. Travlos, "Corporate Takeover Bids, Methods of Payment, and Bidding Firms' Stock Return," *Journal of Finance* 42 (1987): 943–963. The result was statistically significant in Sirower but not significant in Travlos.

[9] Morck et al., "Do Managerial Objectives Drive Bad Acquisitions?"; and D. K. Datta, V. K. Narayanan, and G. E. Pinches, "Factors Influencing Wealth Creation from Mergers and Acquisitions: A Meta-Analysis," *Strategic Management Journal* 13 (1992): 67–84.

typically talk up all kinds of strategic benefits from acquisitions that are really all about cost cutting.

In the absence of empirical research, our suggestions for strategies that create value are based on our acquisitions work with companies. In our experience, the strategic rationale for an acquisition that creates value typically conforms to one of the following five archetypes:

1. Improve the performance of the target company.
2. Consolidate to remove excess capacity from an industry.
3. Create market access for the target's (or, in some cases, the buyer's) products.
4. Acquire skills or technologies more quickly or at lower cost than they could be built in-house.
5. Pick winners early and help them develop their businesses.

If an acquisition does not fit one or more of these archetypes, it's unlikely to create value.

The strategic rationale should be a specific articulation of one of these archetypes, not a vague concept like growth or strategic positioning. While growth and strategic positioning may be important, they need to be translated into something more tangible. Furthermore, even if your acquisition conforms to one of the archetypes, it still won't create value if you overpay.

Improve Target Company's Performance

Improving the performance of the target company is one of the most common value-creating acquisition strategies. Put simply, you buy a company and radically reduce costs to improve margins and cash flows. In some cases, the acquirer may also take steps to accelerate revenue growth.

Pursuing this strategy is what the best private equity firms do. Acharya, Hahn, and Kehoe studied successful private equity acquisitions where the target company was bought, improved, and sold with no additional acquisitions along the way.[10] They found that the operating profit margins of the acquired businesses increased by an average of about 2.5 percentage points more than at peer companies during the ownership of the private equity firm. That means many of the transactions increased operating profit margins even more.

Keep in mind that it is easier to improve the performance of a company with low margins and low return on invested capital (ROIC) than a high-margin, high-ROIC company. Consider the case of buying a company with a 6 percent operating profit margin. Reducing costs by 3 percentage points from 94 percent

---

[10] Viral V. Acharya, Moritz Hahn, and Conor Kehoe, "Corporate Governance and Value Creation: Evidence from Private Equity," Social Science Research Network Working Paper, February 17, 2010.

of revenues to 91 percent of revenues increases the margin to 9 percent and could lead to a 50 percent increase in the value of the company.

In contrast, if the company's operating profit margin is 30 percent, increasing the company's value by 50 percent requires increasing the margin to 45 percent. Costs would need to decline from 70 percent of revenues to 55 percent, a 21 percent reduction in the cost base. That expectation might be unreasonable.

Consolidate to Remove Excess Capacity from Industry

As industries mature, they typically develop excess capacity. For example, in chemicals, companies are constantly looking for ways to get more production out of their plants at the same time as new competitors (for example, Saudi Arabia in petrochemicals) continue to enter the industry. The combination of higher production from existing capacity with new capacity from new entrants often leads to more supply than demand. However, it is in no single competitor's interest to shut a plant. Companies often find it easier to shut plants across the larger combined entity resulting from an acquisition than, absent an acquisition, to shut their least productive plants and end up with a smaller company.

Reducing excess capacity is not limited to shutting factories but can extend to less tangible forms of capacity. For example, consolidation in the pharmaceutical industry has significantly reduced sales force capacity as merged companies' portfolios of products have changed and they have rethought how to interact with doctors. The pharmaceutical companies have also significantly reduced their research and development capacity as they have found more productive ways to conduct research and pruned their portfolios of development projects.

While there is substantial value to be created from removing excess capacity, nevertheless the bulk of the value often accrues to the seller's shareholders, not the buyer's.

Accelerate Market Access for Target's (or Buyer's) Products

Often, relatively small companies with innovative products have difficulty accessing the entire potential market for their products. For instance, small pharmaceutical companies typically lack the large sales forces required to access the many doctors they need to see in order to promote their products. Larger pharmaceutical companies sometimes purchase these smaller companies and use their own large-scale sales forces to accelerate the sales growth of the smaller companies' products.

IBM has pursued this strategy in its software business. Between 2002 and 2005, IBM acquired 39 companies for less than $500 million each. By pushing the products of these companies through IBM's global sales force, IBM estimated that it was able to increase the acquired companies' revenues by over 40 percent in the first two years after each acquisition and over 20 percent in the next three years.[11]

In some cases, the target can also help accelerate the acquirer's revenue growth. In Procter & Gamble's acquisition of Gillette, the combined company benefited because P&G had stronger sales in some emerging markets while Gillette had a bigger share of others. Working together, they were able to introduce their products into new markets much more quickly.

Get Skills or Technologies Faster or at Lower Cost Than They Can Be Built

Cisco Systems has used acquisitions of key technologies to assemble a broad line of network solution products and to grow very quickly from a single product line into the key player in Internet equipment. From 1993 to 2001, Cisco acquired 71 companies at an average price of approximately $350 million. Cisco's sales increased from $650 million in 1993 to $22 billion in 2001, with nearly 40 percent of its 2001 revenue coming directly from these acquisitions. By 2009, Cisco had more than $36 billion in revenues and a market capitalization of approximately $150 billion.

Pick Winners Early and Help Them Develop Their Businesses

The final winning acquisition strategy involves making acquisitions early in the life cycle of a new industry or product line, long before most others recognize that the industry will grow to a large size. Johnson & Johnson pursued this strategy in its early acquisitions of medical-device businesses. When Johnson & Johnson bought device manufacturer Cordis in 1996, Cordis had $500 million in revenues. By 2007, its revenues had increased to $3.8 billion, reflecting a 20 percent annual growth rate. J&J also purchased orthopedic-device manufacturer DePuy in 1996, when DePuy had $900 million of revenues. By 2007, DePuy's revenues had grown to $4.6 billion, also at an annual growth rate of 20 percent.

This acquisition strategy requires a disciplined approach by management in three dimensions. First, you need to be willing to make investments early, long before your competitors and the market see the industry's or company's potential. Second, you need to make multiple bets and expect some to fail. Third, you need to have the skills and patience to nurture the acquired businesses.

MORE DIFFICULT STRATEGIES FOR CREATING VALUE FROM ACQUISITIONS

Beyond the five main acquisition strategies just described, a handful of others can create value. However, these are more difficult to execute successfully.

---

[11] IBM Strategic Decisions Conference, 2007.

Roll-Up Strategy

Roll-up strategies are used to consolidate highly fragmented markets, where the current competitors are too small to achieve scale economies. An example is Service Corporation International's roll-up of the U.S. funeral business. Beginning in the 1960s, Service Corporation grew from one funeral home in Houston to over 1,400 funeral homes and cemeteries in 2008. Similarly, Clear Channel rolled up the radio station market in the United States, eventually owning more than 900 stations.

The strategy works when the businesses as a group can realize substantial cost savings or achieve higher revenues than the individual businesses. For example, Service Corporation's funeral homes in a single city can share vehicles, purchasing, and back-office operations. They can also coordinate advertising across a city to reduce costs and realize higher revenues.

Size per se is not what creates a successful roll-up. What matters is the right kind of size. For example, for Service Corporation, having multiple locations in the same city has been more important than simply having many branches spread over many cities, because the cost savings, such as sharing vehicles, can be realized only if the branches are near one another.

Because roll-up strategies are hard to disguise, they invite copycats. As others tried to copy Service Corporation's strategy, prices for some funeral homes were eventually bid up to levels that made additional acquisitions uneconomic.

Consolidate to Improve Competitive Behavior

Many executives in highly competitive industries hope consolidation will lead competitors to focus less on price competition, thereby improving the industry's ROIC. However, the evidence shows that unless an industry consolidates down to just three or four competitors and can keep entrants out, competitor pricing behavior does not change: there's often an incentive for smaller companies or new entrants to gain share through price competition. So in an industry with 10 competitors, lots of deals must be done before the basis of competition changes.

Enter into a Transformational Merger

A commonly mentioned reason for an acquisition or merger is to transform one or both companies. Transformational mergers are rare, however, because the circumstances have to be just right, and the management team needs to execute the strategy well. The best way to describe a transformational merger is by example. One of the world's leading pharmaceutical companies, Novartis of Switzerland, was formed by the $30 billion merger of Sandoz and Ciba-Geigy, announced in 1996. But this merger was much more than a simple combination of businesses: Under the leadership of the new CEO, Daniel Vasella, Sandoz and Ciba-Geigy were transformed into an entirely new company. Using the merger as a catalyst for change, Vasella and his management team not only captured $1.4 billion in cost synergies but also redefined the company's mission and strategy, portfolio and organization, and all key processes from research to sales. In all areas, there was no automatic choice for either the Ciba or the Sandoz way of doing things; instead, a systematic effort was made to find the *best* way of doing things.

Novartis shifted its strategic focus to innovation in its life sciences business (pharmaceuticals, nutrition, and agricultural) and spun off the $7 billion Ciba Specialty Chemicals business in 1997. Organizational changes included reorganizing research and development worldwide by therapeutic rather than geographic area, enabling Novartis to build up a world-leading oncology franchise. Across all departments and management layers, Novartis created a strong performance-oriented culture, supported by a change from a seniority-based to a performance-based compensation system for its managers.

Buy Cheap

The final way to create value from an acquisition is to buy cheap—in other words, at a price below the target's intrinsic value. In our experience, however, opportunities to create value by buying cheap are rare and relatively small.

Although market values revert to intrinsic values over longer periods, there can be brief moments when the two fall out of alignment. Markets sometimes overreact to negative news, such as the criminal investigation of an executive or the failure of a single product in a portfolio of many strong products. Such moments are less rare in cyclical industries, where assets are often undervalued at the bottom of the cycle. Comparing actual market valuations with intrinsic values based on a "perfect foresight" model, we found companies in cyclical industries could more than double shareholder returns (relative to actual returns) if they acquired assets at the bottom of a cycle and sold at the top.[12]

However, while markets do throw up occasional opportunities for companies to buy below intrinsic value, we haven't seen many cases. To gain control of the target, the acquirer must pay the target's shareholders a premium over the current market value. Although premiums can vary widely, the average premiums for corporate control have been fairly stable, near 30 percent of the preannouncement price of the target's equity.

For targets pursued by multiple acquirers, the premium rises dramatically, creating the so-called winner's curse. If several companies evaluate a given target and all identify roughly the same synergies, the one who

[12] T. Koller and M. de Heer, "Valuing Cyclical Companies," *McKinsey Quarterly*, no. 2 (2000): 62–69.

overestimates potential synergies the most will offer the highest price. Since the offer price is based on an overestimate of value to be created, the supposed winner overpays—and is ultimately a loser.[13] A related problem is hubris, or the tendency of the acquirer's management to overstate its ability to capture performance improvements from the acquisition.[14]

Since market values can sometimes deviate from intrinsic values, management must also be wary of the possibility that markets may be overvaluing a potential acquisition. Consider the stock market bubble during the late 1990s. Companies that merged with or acquired technology, media, and telecommunications companies saw their share prices plummet when the market reverted to earlier levels. Overpaying when the market is inflated is a serious concern because M&A activity seems to rise following periods of strong market performance. If (and when) prices are artificially high, large improvements are necessary to justify an acquisition, even when the target can be purchased at no premium to market value.

Premiums for private deals tend to be smaller, although comprehensive evidence is difficult to collect because publicly available data are scarce. Private acquisitions often stem from the seller's desire to get out, rather than the buyer's desire for a purchase.

ESTIMATION OF OPERATING IMPROVEMENTS

As we've been discussing, the main sources of value created through M&A are the cost and revenue improvements the combined company makes, and rarely a good deal made by the acquirer. Estimating potential improvements on the basis of limited information in the hectic context of a deal is tremendously difficult. But it is still worth the effort, given that the deal decision itself should be guided largely by the results. Here's a practical approach to making these estimates.

Estimating Cost Savings

Too often, managers estimate cost savings simply by calculating the difference in financial performance between the bidder and the target. Having an EBITA margin 200 basis points higher than the target, however, will not necessarily translate into better performance for the target. We find it helpful to use the company's business system as a guide for structuring the estimation of potential improvements. As an example, Exhibit 21.6 shows a generic business system, identifying potential savings related to research and development,

---

[13] K. Rock, "Why New Issues Are Underpriced," *Journal of Financial Economics* 15 (1986): 187–212.
[14] R. Roll, "The Hubris Hypothesis of Corporate Takeovers," *Journal of Business* 59 (1986): 197–216.

EXHIBIT 21.6 **Sample Framework for Estimating Cost Savings**

Function	Example savings
Research and development	• Stopping redundant projects • Eliminating overlap in research personnel • Developing new products through transferred technology
Procurement	• Pooled purchasing • Standardizing products
Manufacturing	• Eliminating overcapacity • Transferring best operating practices
Sales and marketing	• Cross-selling products • Using common channels • Transferring best practices • Lowering combined marketing budget
Distribution	• Consolidating warehouses and truck routes
Administration	• Exploiting economies of scale in finance/accounting and other back-office functions • Consolidating strategy and leadership functions

procurement, manufacturing, sales and marketing, distribution, and administration. The analysis should be structured using the following four steps:

1. Develop an industry-specific business system.

2. Develop a baseline for costs as if the two companies remained independent. Make sure the baseline costs are consistent with the intrinsic valuations.

3. Estimate the savings for each cost category based on the expertise of experienced line managers.

4. Compare resulting aggregate improvements with margin and capital efficiency benchmarks for the industry, to judge whether the estimates are realistic given industry economics.

An insightful business system will fulfill three criteria. First, it assigns every cost item of the target and each cost-saving idea to one (and only one) segment of the business system. This will assure that you examine the entire cost structure of the target without double-counting cost savings. Second, if you believe there will be cost savings in the bidder's organization, you must be able to assign these savings to the appropriate segments in the business system. Last, the business system should be designed such that each segment has sufficient detail. The analysis will not provide much insight if 90 percent of the cost savings are labeled "Administration." In this case, you should disaggregate the system further into organizational units such as finance, accounting, treasury, and investor relations.

Once the business system is completed, forecast baseline costs for both the acquirer and the target. The base level of costs equals the costs as if both companies had continued as stand-alone entities. For an accurate estimate of potential cost savings, tie the financial savings explicitly to operational activities in the business. For example, what is the equivalent head count reduction of cost savings in selling, general, and administrative (SG&A) expense? What is the resulting revenue per head count? How much will distribution costs fall when trucks are fully loaded, rather than partially loaded? Are revenues sufficient to guarantee fully loaded trucks?

When tying cost savings to operational drivers, involve experienced line managers in the process. An integrated team that includes both financial analysts and experienced line managers is more likely to be accurate than a pure finance team is. In addition, experienced line managers often will already know details about the target. If so, you will generate insights on capacity, quality issues, and unit sales not easily found in the public domain.

Consider one acquisition, where the head of operations took the lead in estimating the savings from rationalizing manufacturing capacity, distribution networks, and suppliers.[15] His in-depth knowledge about the unusual manufacturing requirements for a key product line and looming investment needs at the target's main plant substantially improved savings estimates. In addition, this manager conducted a due-diligence interview with the target's head of operations, learning that the target did not have an enterprise resource planning (ERP) system. Each of these facts improved negotiations and deal structuring, for example, by permitting management to promise that the target's main European location would be retained while maintaining flexibility about the target's main U.S. facility. Moreover, the involvement of the operations manager ensured that the company was prepared to act quickly and decisively to capture savings following the deal's closure.

After you complete the assessment, always compare the aggregate results for the combined companies with industry benchmarks for operating margins and capital efficiency. Ask whether the resulting ROIC and growth projections make sense given the overall expected economics of the industry. Only a fully developed integrated income statement and balance sheet will ensure that savings estimates are in line with economic reality. In particular, ensure that the ROIC for the new combination lands at the right level for the continuing value, a ROIC that is in line with the underlying competitive structure of the industry. The more difficult it is to sustain a competitive advantage, the more you need to scale down the synergies over the longer term.

---

[15] This and other examples can be found in S. A. Christofferson, R. S. McNish, and D. L. Sias, "Where Mergers Go Wrong," *McKinsey Quarterly*, no. 2 (2004): 93–99.

EXHIBIT 21.7 **Automotive Merger: Estimating Cost Savings**

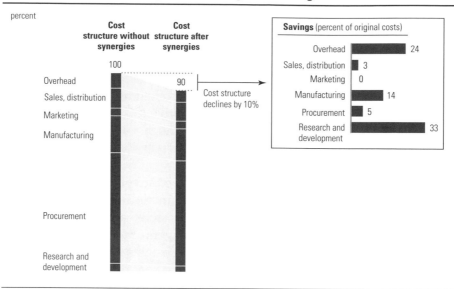

To illustrate the detail required in estimating synergies, Exhibit 21.7 presents the result of an outside-in synergy estimate for a merger in the automotive industry. Overall, the acquirer estimated that the combined entity could reduce total costs by about 10 percent. However, the relative savings varied widely by business system category. For example, although procurement costs are the single largest cost for automotive manufacturers, most companies already have the necessary scale to negotiate favorable contracts. Therefore, savings from procurement were estimated at only 5 percent. In contrast, research and development reductions were estimated at 33 percent, as the two companies consolidated new-product development, paring down the number of expected offerings. This reduction also had a follow-on effect in manufacturing, as product designs would move toward a common platform, lowering overall manufacturing costs. Finally, while sales and distribution expenses could be lowered, management decided to preserve the combined company's marketing budget.

Estimating Revenue Improvements

Although it is tempting to assume revenues for the newly combined company will equal stand-alone sales plus new cross-selling, the reality is often quite different. First, the merger often disrupts existing customer relationships, leading to a loss of business. Also, smart competitors use mergers as a prime opportunity to recruit star salespeople and product specialists. Some customers may have used the acquirer and target as dual sources, so they will move part of their business to another company to maintain a minimum of two suppliers.

Finally, customers who decide to stay during the merger will not be shy in asking for price and other concessions that salespeople will be eager to offer, for fear of losing the business.

Make sure to develop estimates of pricing power and market share that are consistent with market growth and competitive reality. As in the process for estimating cost savings, calibrate the pro forma assumptions against the realities of the marketplace. One global financial company estimated that an acquisition would net €1 billion in sales improvements within the next five years, including double-digit profit growth in the first year. However, overall market growth was limited, so the only way to achieve these sales goals was to lower prices. Actual profit growth was a mere 2 percent.

When estimating revenue improvements, be explicit about where any growth in revenues beyond base-case assessments is expected to originate. Revenue improvements will come from one or more of four sources:

1. Increasing each product's peak sales level
2. Reaching the increased peak sales faster
3. Extending each product's life
4. Adding new products (or features) that could not have been developed if the two companies had remained independent

Alternatively, revenue increases could come from higher prices, achievable because the acquisition reduces competition. In reality, however, antitrust regulations are in place precisely to prevent companies from using this lever, which would transfer value from customers to shareholders. Instead, any increase in price must be directly attributable to an increase in value to the customer and not to reduced choice.

We also suggest you project revenue improvements in absolute amounts per year or as a percentage of stand-alone revenues, rather than as an increase in the revenue growth rate. With the growth rate approach, you can easily overestimate the true impact of revenue improvements.

Evaluating the Quality and Accuracy of Improvement Estimates

We find that companies estimate their realized cost savings fairly well, especially when they acquire a business with similar characteristics. Estimated revenue improvements, however, are harder to realize. In Exhibit 21.8, we present the results of an analysis of 90 acquisitions conducted by McKinsey's Merger Management practice. In this sample, 86 percent of the acquirers were able to capture at least 70 percent of the estimated cost savings.[16] In contrast,

---

[16] S. A. Christofferson, R. S. McNish, and D. L. Sias, "Where Mergers Go Wrong," *McKinsey Quarterly*, no. 2 (2004): 93–99.

EXHIBIT 21.8 **Transaction Success at Capturing Projected Improvements**

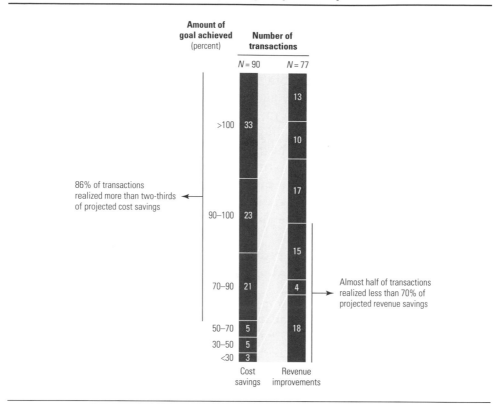

almost half of the acquirers realized *less* than 70 percent of the targeted revenue improvements, and in almost one-quarter of the observed acquisitions, the acquirer realized less than 30 percent of the targeted revenue improvements.

In our experience, too many managers in low-growth businesses believe they can create value merely by purchasing a high-growth business. This is not so; to create value, the transaction has to enable one or both of the companies to grow faster than originally expected. In fact, many companies have difficulty even maintaining the baseline revenue growth because, as noted in the discussion of estimating revenue improvements, a portion of the combined company's customers either leave due to uncertainty, demand larger discounts, or find a new source after two of their suppliers have merged.

Implementation Costs, Requirements, and Timing

Capturing synergies always incurs costs. Some are obvious, such as the costs to decommission a plant and the severance that must be paid to employees. Others are more subtle, such as rebranding campaigns when the name of the target is changed, integration costs for different information technology systems, and the retraining of employees. But these costs, often forgotten, must also be identified and estimated. It is not unusual for total implementation costs to be equivalent to a full year of cost savings or more.

Bear in mind that acquirers often make overly optimistic assumptions about how long it will take to capture synergies. Reality intervenes in many ways: ensuring stable supplies to customers while closing a plant can be more complicated than the acquirer expects, disparate customer lists from multiple sources can be tricky to integrate, and examining thousands of line items in the purchasing database almost always takes more hours than estimated, just to name a few possibilities.

Moreover, timing problems can affect whether the improvements are captured at all. Our experience suggests that improvements not captured within the first full budget year after consolidation may never be captured, as the drive to capture them is overtaken by subsequent events. Persistent management attention matters.

Neglecting the "use by" date of certain savings can be equally problematic. Many potential savings do not stay on the table forever. For example, one source of cost savings is eliminating cyclical excess capacity in a growing industry. But in these circumstances, the excess capacity will eventually be eliminated through natural growth. Thus, *incremental* savings from reducing capacity can be realized only if it is reduced during the expected duration of any capacity overhang.

HOW TO PAY: IN CASH OR IN STOCK?

Should the acquiring company pay in cash or in shares? Research evidence shows that, on average, an acquirer's stock returns surrounding the acquisition announcement are higher when the acquirer offers cash than when it offers shares. We hesitate, however, to draw a conclusion based solely on aggregate statistics; after all, even companies that offer cash can pay too much.

Assuming that the acquirer is not capital constrained, the real issue is whether the risks and rewards of the deal should be shared with the target's shareholders. When the acquiring company pays in cash, its shareholders carry the entire risk of capturing synergies and paying too much. If the companies exchange shares, the target's shareholders assume a portion of the risk.

Exhibit 21.9 outlines the impact on value of paying in cash rather than shares for a hypothetical transaction. Assume that the acquirer and the target have a market capitalization of $1 billion and $500 million, respectively. The acquirer pays a total price of $650 million, including a premium of 30 percent. We calculate the estimated discounted cash flow (DCF) values after the transaction under two scenarios: (1) the value of operating improvements is $50 million lower than the premium paid, and (2) the value of these improvements is $50 million higher. (To simplify, we assume that market value equals

EXHIBIT 21.9 **Paying with Cash versus Stock: Impact on Value**

Value to shareholders after transaction, $ million

Market value before deal	
Acquirer	1,000
Target	500
Price paid (30% premium)	650
Ownership ratio (stock deal)	39.4%/60.6%

	Downside scenario (Synergies = 100)	Upside scenario (Synergies = 200)
Consideration in cash		
Combined value	1,600	1,700
Price paid	(650)	(650)
Value of acquirer postdeal	950	1,050
Value of acquirer predeal	(1,000)	(1,000)
Acquirer value created (destroyed)	(50)	50
Consideration in stock		
Combined value	1,600	1,700
Target's share (39.4%)	(630)	(670)
Value of acquirer postdeal	970	1,020
Value of acquirer predeal	(1,000)	(1,000)
Acquirer value created (destroyed)	(30)	30

intrinsic value for both the target and the acquirer.) If the payment is entirely in cash, the target's shareholders get $650 million, regardless of whether the improvements are high enough to justify the premium. These shareholders do not share in the implementation risk. The acquirer's shareholders see the value of their stake increase by $50 million in the upside case and decrease by the same amount in the downside case. They carry the full risk.

Next, consider the same transaction paid for in shares. The target's shareholders participate in the implementation risk by virtue of being shareholders in the new combined entity.[17] In the upside case, their payout from the acquisition increases as improvements increase: They receive $670 million in value, as opposed to $650 million. Effectively, even more value has been transferred from the acquirer's shareholders to the target's shareholders. The acquirer's shareholders are willing to allow this form of payment, however, because they are protected if implementation goes poorly. If the deal destroys value, the target's shareholders now get less than before, but still a nice premium, since

---

[17] Target shareholders with small stakes can sell their shares in the public market to avoid implementation risk. Influential shareholders with large stakes, such as company founders and senior executives, will often agree not to sell shares for a specified period. In this case, they share the risk of implementation.

their portion of the combined company is worth $630 million, compared with the $500 million market value before the deal.

From this perspective, two key issues should influence your choice of payment: First, do you think the target and/or your company is overvalued or undervalued? During a bubble, you will be more inclined to pay in shares, as everybody will then share the burden of the market correction. In such a scenario, develop a perspective on relative overvaluation of the two businesses. If you believe your shares are more overvalued than the target's, they are valuable in their own right as transaction currency.[18] Second, how confident are you are in the ability of the deal to create value overall? The more confident you are, the more you should be inclined to pay in cash.

When weighing whether to pay in cash or in shares, you should also consider what your optimal capital structure will be. Can your company raise enough cash through a debt offering to pay for the target entirely in cash? Overextending credit lines to acquire a company can devastate the borrower. One company, an automotive supplier, borrowed cash to pay for a string of acquisitions. Operating improvements did not materialize as originally expected (partly because the postmerger plan was not executed rigorously), and the company ended up with a debt burden that it could not bear. In the end, the company was forced into bankruptcy.

If the capital structure of the combined entity cannot accommodate any extra debt incurred by paying cash for the acquisition, then you need to consider paying partially or fully in shares, regardless of any desire to share risk among the shareholders of the new entity.

FOCUS ON VALUE CREATION, NOT ACCOUNTING

Many managers focus on the accretion and dilution of earnings brought about by an acquisition, rather than the value it could create. They do so despite numerous studies showing that stock markets pay no attention to the effects of an acquisition on accounting numbers, but react only to the value that the deal is estimated to create. Focusing on accounting measures is therefore dangerous and can easily lead to poor decisions, as described in Chapter 16.

By 2005, both International Financial Reporting Standards (IFRS) and U.S. Generally Accepted Accounting Principles (GAAP) eliminated amortization of goodwill. This change meant earnings dilution in acquisitions with goodwill was smaller than under the old accounting rules. Furthermore, most acquisitions paid for with cash are now accretive, since a major source of dilution has vanished. In the case of share deals, the deal is accretive if the acquirer's price-to-earnings ratio is higher than the target's.

---

[18] The signaling effect of a share consideration is similar to that of share issuance. The capital markets will use this new information (that the shares might be overvalued) when pricing the shares.

EXHIBIT 21.10 **EPS Accretion with Value Destruction**

Impact on EPS	Cash deal	Stock deal
Net income ($ million)		
Net income from acquirer	80.0	80.0
Net income from target	30.0	30.0
Additional interest[1]	(19.5)	–
Net income after acquisition	90.5	110.0
Number of shares (million)		
Original shares	40.0	40.0
New shares	–	12.5
Number of shares	40.0	52.5
Earnings per share (dollars)		
EPS before acquisition	2.00	2.00
EPS accretion	0.26	0.10
EPS after acquisition	2.26	2.10

Assumptions	Acquirer	Target
Net income ($ million)	80.0	30.0
Shares outstanding (million)	40.0	10.0
EPS (dollars)	2.0	3.0
Preannouncement share price (dollars)	40.0	40.0
P/E ($ per share)	20.0	13.3
Market value ($ million)	1,600.0	400.0
Price paid ($ million)	–	500.0

[1] Pretax cost of debt at 6%, tax rate of 35%.

This is not as encouraging as it sounds. Many acquisitions are earnings accretive but destroy value. Consider the hypothetical deal in Exhibit 21.10. You are deciding whether to purchase a company currently priced in the market at $400 million for $500 million in cash. Your company, the acquirer, is worth $1.6 billion and has a net income of $80 million. For simplicity, assume there are no operating improvements to come from the deal. You decide to finance this deal by raising debt at a pretax interest rate of 6 percent. This deal destroys value: you overpay by $100 million (remember, no improvements). Even so, next year's earnings and earnings per share (EPS) actually increase because the after-tax earnings from the acquired company ($30 million) exceed the after-tax interest required for the new debt ($19.5 million).

How can a deal increase earnings yet destroy value? The acquirer is borrowing 100 percent of the deal value based on the combined cash flows of both companies. But the acquired business could not sustain this level of debt on its own. Since the acquirer puts an increased debt burden on the existing shareholders without properly compensating them for the additional risk, it is destroying value. Only when the ROIC (calculated as target profits plus improvements divided by the total purchase price) is greater than the cost of capital are shareholders appropriately compensated. In our hypothetical deal, the investment is $500 million, and the after-tax profit is $30 million—a mere 6 percent return on invested capital. While this is above the after-tax cost of financing the debt of 3.9 percent, it is below the cost of capital.

Now suppose the same target is acquired through an exchange of shares. The acquirer would need to issue 12.5 million new shares to provide the

EXHIBIT 21.11 **Market Reaction to EPS Impact of Acquisitions**

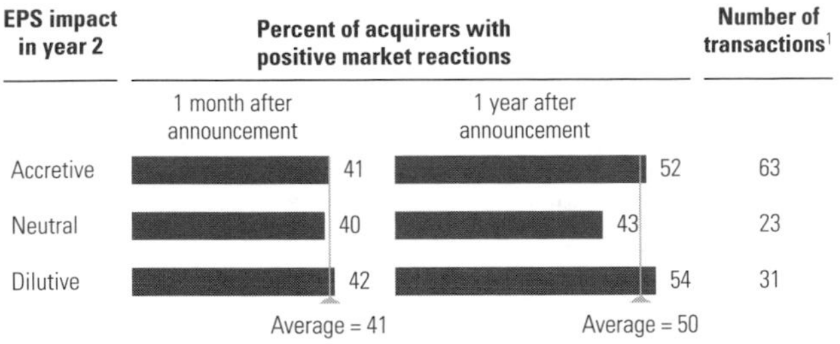

EPS impact in year 2	Percent of acquirers with positive market reactions		Number of transactions[1]
	1 month after announcement	1 year after announcement	
Accretive	41	52	63
Neutral	40	43	23
Dilutive	42	54	31
	Average = 41	Average = 50	

[1] The sample set included 117 transactions greater than $3 billion by U.S. companies between January 1999 and December 2000.

Note: The difference in returns between accretive and dilutive is not statistically significant. Returns were risk-adjusted using the capital asset pricing model (CAPM).

Source: Thomson, analyst reports, Compustat, McKinsey Corporate Performance Center analysis.

25 percent acquisition premium that the target company's shareholders demand.[19] After the deal, the combined company would have 52.5 million shares outstanding and earnings of $110 million. The earnings per share for the new company rise to $2.10, so the deal is again accretive without having created any underlying value. The new EPS is merely the weighted average of the two companies' EPS values, so the increase is a result of mathematics rather than value created by the deal.

Financial markets understand the priority of creating real value over results presented in accounts. In a study of 117 U.S. transactions larger than $3 billion that took place in 1999 and 2000, we found that earnings accretion or dilution resulting from the deals was not a factor in the market's reaction (see Exhibit 21.11). Regardless of whether the expected EPS was greater, smaller, or the same two years after the deal, the market's reaction was similar at one month after the announcement and one year after the announcement.

SUMMARY

Acquisitions are good for the economy when they allocate resources more efficiently between owners. However, empirical evidence shows that only a minority of acquisitions are good for the shareholders of the acquirers. Most acquisitions create more value for the shareholders of the target company than for those of the buyer. This is perhaps not surprising when we recall that acquisitions can create value for acquirers only if the target company's performance improves by more than the value of the premium over the target's

[19] The exchange ratio in this hypothetical deal is 1.25 shares of the acquiring company for each share of the target company. We assume that the capital market does not penalize the acquirer and that the exchange ratio can be set in relation to the preannouncement share price plus the 25 percent acquisition premium.

intrinsic value that the acquirer had to offer for the target in order to persuade its shareholders to part with it.

Managers can help to ensure that their acquisitions are among the minority that create value for all their shareholders by choosing one of the limited number of archetypal acquisition strategies that have created value for acquirers in the past. Success also depends critically on making realistic estimates of the cost and revenue improvements that the target company can realize under new ownership, taking into account the often substantial cost of implementing those improvements. Downside—and upside—risks can be shared with the target's shareholders if the buyer decides to pay for the acquisition in shares rather than cash, though managers need to weigh the implications of this decision carefully. Last, managers should bear in mind at all times that stock markets are interested only in the impact of acquisitions on the intrinsic value of the combined company. Whether an acquisition will increase or decrease earnings per share has no effect on the direction and extent of movements in the buyer's share price following the acquisition announcement.

REVIEW QUESTIONS

1. How can an acquisition create value for the combined entity's shareholders but not for the acquirer's shareholders?

2. What are the pros and cons of measuring the success or failure of an acquisition by immediate stock price reactions to its announcement? When is this approach most likely to provide insights?

3. Describe the five acquisition archetypes that often create value for both the acquirer and the seller. Based on situations with which you are familiar, rank these archetypal strategies from easiest to hardest to plan and execute.

4. What would it take for an acquisition to increase the acquirer's value by 10 percent? Give your answer in terms of size of deal, value of improvements, and premium paid.

5. Why do many value-destroying acquisitions increase earnings per share (EPS)?

6. Describe the circumstances under which the acquirer is better off paying in stock rather than cash. What are the implications for the acquirers' shareholders of paying in stock?

7. Why is it hard for acquirers simply to buy cheap?

8. Describe some important techniques for estimating potential operating improvements on the basis of only published information.

22

Creating Value
through Divestitures

As we described in Chapter 19, any program to create value should include periodically and systematically cleaning out your portfolio of businesses. But as we noted in that chapter, managers often mistakenly equate divestitures with failure. Therefore, the role that divestitures actually play in value creation programs is often very different from the role they *should* play.

Divestitures, like mergers and acquisitions (M&A), tend to occur in waves. In the decade following the conglomerate excesses of the 1960s and 1970s, many companies refocused their portfolios. These divestitures were generally sales to other companies or private buyout firms. Exhibit 22.1 shows that the divestiture wave of the late 1990s included more public ownership transactions, such as spin-offs, carve-outs, and tracking stocks. The mix of divestiture activities over the past 10 years indicates that public ownership transactions have become an established means for divesting businesses. Recent activity levels in divestitures and M&A also appear to show a more even balance in their volumes.

Evidence shows that divestitures create value for corporations in the short term around their announcement, as well as in the long term following the divestiture. Furthermore, companies employing a balanced portfolio approach to acquisition and divestiture have outperformed companies that rarely divest. This approach includes divesting businesses that are performing well but could do even better under different ownership. Despite their potential, divestitures usually occur in reaction to pressure from outside the corporation, rather than as part of a proactive and systematic divestiture program. Executives seem to shy away from divestitures and usually delay them too long. In their view, expanding the business portfolio is a clearer sign of success—and easier to

Special thanks to André Annema for coauthoring this chapter, and to Lee Dranikoff and Antoon Schneider, whose work on divestitures forms a core part of this chapter.

EXHIBIT 22.1 **Divestiture Volume vs. M&A Volume**

$ billion[1]

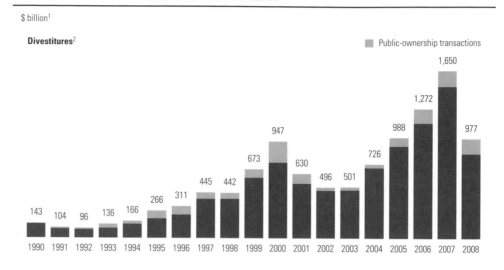

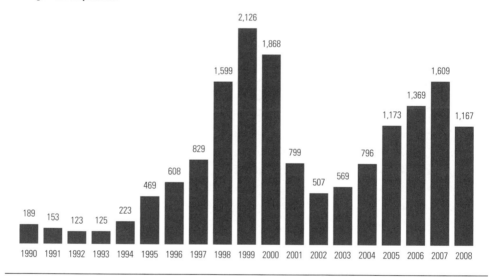

[1] Transactions with deal value above $50 million. Deals involving U.S. or European target and/or acquirer.
[2] Divestitures include sales of equity stakes greater than 50%, asset sales, and public ownership transactions (spin-offs, carve-outs, split-offs).

Source: Securities Data Company, Dealogic, McKinsey Corporate Performance Center analysis.

manage—than selling parts of it, especially profitable parts. Restructuring the portfolio and cutting the losses from a nonperforming business can look like admitting a mistake.

In this chapter, we focus on answering the following questions:

- What evidence is there that divestitures create value, and what drives that value creation?

- What is an effective approach to deciding on divestiture transactions?
- How should management choose the specific type of transaction for a divestiture?

VALUE CREATION FROM DIVESTITURES

Because divestitures create value for corporations in the short term around the announcement, as well as over the longer term following the transaction, executives should focus on divestitures' potential for creating value; they should not hold back from divestitures out of concerns about diluting earnings per share or making the corporation smaller. For several years, Siemens, based in Germany, has been pursuing a theme of profitable growth, including major portfolio initiatives. As part of this program, Siemens put its telecommunication carrier business into a 50–50 joint venture with Nokia in 2006, and a year later sold its Siemens VDO business (supplying parts and components as well as software to carmakers) to Continental. The two businesses had contributed over 25 percent of Siemens's sales in 2005. These transactions reflected a significant change in the group's portfolio orientation, but one that the company thought was needed in order to shift its focus onto the more attractive parts of its portfolio.

But why are divestitures value-creating? And given their value-creating potential, why do executives resist them? This section offers answers to these questions.

Evidence for Value from Divestitures

Academic research provides abundant evidence for divestitures' potential to create value.[1] A study of 370 private and public companies found significant positive excess returns around the announcement of different types of divestitures;[2] the results are summarized in Exhibit 22.2. Most of the companies the researchers studied were reactive in their use of divestitures, waiting until they had to respond to economic, technological, or regulatory shocks. For example, in August 2004, Agfa-Gevaert announced that it was selling its consumer film and photo labs division to focus on its more profitable activities in medical imaging and graphic arts. The increased popularity of digital cameras had

---

[1] See, for example, J. Miles and J. Rosenfeld, "The Effect of Voluntary Spin-Off Announcements on Shareholder Wealth," *Journal of Finance* 38 (1983): 1597–1606; K. Schipper and A. Smith, "A Comparison of Equity Carve-Outs and Seasoned Equity Offerings: Share Price Effects and Corporate Restructuring," *Journal of Financial Economics* 15 (1986): 153–186; K. Schipper and A. Smith, "Effects of Recontracting on Shareholder Wealth: The Case of Voluntary Spin-Offs," *Journal of Financial Economics* 12 (1983): 437–468; J. Allen and J. McConnell, "Equity Carve-Outs and Managerial Discretion," *Journal of Finance* 53 (1998): 163–186; and R. Michaely and W. Shaw, "The Choice of Going Public: Spin-Offs vs. Carve-Outs," *Financial Management* 24 (1995): 5–21.

[2] J. Mulherin and A. Boone, "Comparing Acquisitions and Divestitures," *Journal of Corporate Finance* 6 (2000): 117–139.

EXHIBIT 22.2 **Market-Adjusted Announcement Returns of Divestitures**[1]

	All	Spin-offs	Carve-outs	Asset sales
Mean (percent)	3.0	4.5	2.3	2.6
Median (percent)	1.8	3.6	0.9	1.6
Number of transactions	370	106	125	139

[1] Cumulative abnormal returns measured from 1 day before to 1 day after announcement.

Source: J. Mulherin and A. Boone, "Comparing Acquisitions and Divestitures," *Journal of Corporate Finance*, 6 (2000): 117–139.

caused a decline in sales of traditional rolls of film. Photo activities had been Agfa-Gevaert's original business, and according to the CEO, divesting them was not an easy decision, but with changing market conditions the company had to make a choice.

Most research looking at divestitures' impact on value has focused on the short term. But what about their impact over a longer term? A McKinsey study of 200 large U.S. companies over a 10-year period showed that companies with a passive portfolio approach—those that did not sell businesses or only sold poor businesses under pressure—underperformed companies with an active portfolio approach.[3] The best performers systematically divested as well as acquired companies. The process is natural and never-ending. A divested unit may very well pursue further separations later in its lifetime, especially in dynamic industries undergoing rapid growth and technological change.

General Dynamics, a U.S. defense company, provides an interesting example of an active portfolio approach that created considerable value. At the beginning of the 1990s, General Dynamics faced an unattractive industry environment. According to forecasts at that time, U.S. defense spending would be cut significantly, and General Dynamics—a broad and varied producer of weapons systems—was expected to be affected severely. When CEO William A. Anders took control in 1991, he initiated a series of divestitures. Revenues were halved in a period of two years, but shareholder returns were extraordinary: an annualized rate of 58 percent between 1991 and 1995, more than double the shareholder returns of General Dynamics' major peers. Then, starting in 1995, Anders began acquiring companies in attractive subsectors. Over the next seven years, General Dynamics' annualized return exceeded 20 percent, again more than double the typical returns in the sector.

Why Divestitures Create Value

Divesting a business unit creates value when other owners believe the unit is worth more under their ownership than the sellers believe the business is worth to themselves. To put it more opportunistically from a seller's perspective, a

[3] J. Brandimarte, W. Fallon, and R. McNish, "Trading the Corporate Portfolio," *McKinsey on Finance* (Fall 2001): 1–5.

divestiture creates value when someone else is willing to pay a price that exceeds the seller's estimated value of the business unit.

Chapter 19 introduced this "best owner" principle. Business units can be worth more in another ownership structure because the current structure may impose unique costs on the parent and/or business unit. Some of these costs can be hidden, such as when the parent company's culture is dominated by a mature business and limits innovation. In other cases, the costs can be more explicit—for example, when a company lacks core skills to be an effective operator in an industry. An active portfolio management approach creates value by avoiding, eliminating, or at least minimizing these costs.

Divestiture of underperforming businesses clearly avoids the direct costs of bearing deteriorating results. But divestiture of profitable and/or growing businesses can also benefit both the parent and the business unit. In these situations, a divestiture may create value because the subsidiary can become more competitive as a result of greater freedom to tailor financing and investment decisions, improved management incentives, or better focus. Capital structure was a key reason for the health care divestiture announced by Tyco International in January 2006. As Tyco CFO Chris Coughlin explains, "We were driving the capital structure of all of Tyco on the basis of what a company in the healthcare industry needed, but healthcare was only a quarter of our revenues. The other businesses clearly did not require that kind of a capital structure."[4] Divestitures also may create value by taking advantage of information asymmetry. For example, certain executives may recognize early on that upcoming technological changes or a shift in consumer behavior will change the potential value of particular activities, so they decide to exit through a divestiture before others start to recognize these trends.

Because of these potential benefits, companies should regularly review whether to divest businesses and may need to divest even good, healthy ones to allow the corporation to grow stronger and let the remaining businesses reach their full potential. Companies ripe for divestiture could be at any stage in their life cycle and might well include a profitable, cash-generating business or a business with relatively high growth potential. In many cases, the costs of holding on to supposedly healthy businesses far outweigh the benefits. Consider what some of these costs might be.

Costs to the parent   Well-established, mature businesses provide a company with stability and cash flows, but this stability can be a mixed blessing. The culture of the mature business unit may become incompatible with the culture that the parent company wants to create. For example, stable units may remove the impetus to innovate, when this impetus might be a critical driver of success for other, smaller businesses in the portfolio. Also, mature units typically are

---

[4] L. Corb and T. Koller, "When to Break Up a Conglomerate: An Interview with Tyco International's CFO," *McKinsey on Finance* (Autumn 2007): 12–18.

relatively large and may absorb a significant share of scarce management time that might be better spent on identifying growth opportunities. For example, Pactiv (a producer of specialty packaging products) sold its aluminum business in 1999, despite the business's strong cash flow. According to management, the aluminum business was using resources and management time that could have been more usefully deployed elsewhere. In addition, the cyclical nature of the aluminum business made the company as a whole more difficult for investors to understand.

Alternatively, cross-subsidization between business units does not give the right economic incentives and leads to suboptimal decision making. For example, unrestricted access to capital can result in a business pursuing investment opportunities with low value-creating potential. Conflicts of interest between business units can also distort decision making and be a reason to pursue divestment. During the early 1990s, Lucent—at that time a business unit of AT&T and a successful maker of telecom equipment—was selling its products to many of AT&T's competitors. To avoid conflict and to ease possible customer concerns, AT&T arranged to spin off Lucent in 1996.

Costs to the unit   A business unit's performance may be hampered by poor fit with the parent company, not just in strategy but also in terms of the parent company's core capabilities. All companies evolve through a life cycle, from start-up through expansion to maturity, and different skills and capabilities are needed to manage the business well at different moments in the cycle: from a focus on innovation in the start-up phase, when a viable business idea and platform are created, to cost management skills at maturity, when efficiency is the key driver of success. Many corporations lack the full breadth and depth of skills. Typically, they excel in only a few capabilities, which also tend to be fairly static over time. That explains why it makes sense to scrutinize the entire portfolio for potential divestitures, including good and bad businesses, at different stages of their life cycles.

For example, pharmaceutical company executives face the challenge of managing two different types of business. The major pharmaceutical companies emphasize innovation and typically have core skills in the discovery, development, and marketing of innovative drugs. These drugs require a specialized sales force but are patent-protected and can be highly profitable. As products approach the date when their patent protection will expire, generic competitors usually enter the market. Typically, prices for these products plummet, and the pharmaceutical company loses significant market share. The changed market dynamics require a very different set of skills—in particular, cost-effective manufacturing and sales. The question is whether the pharmaceutical majors that hold on to prescription drugs after their patents expire have enough of these skills to maximize value from such products.

According to Tyco's CFO, one of the positive impacts of the health care spin-off was that it helped that business attract new talent that most likely would not have joined the old Tyco: "They now see [the spun-off business] as a healthcare company with a very defined strategy, where people can advance while remaining in healthcare and playing a very significant role."

Depressed exit prices   Companies that hold on to seriously underperforming businesses too long risk bringing down the value of the entire corporation. By the time the company is forced to conduct a fire sale of the assets, it has already destroyed substantial value and generally will receive limited proceeds from the divestiture. Relative to outsiders, managers should be in a better position to determine a business's true performance prospects. Research has shown that as a business becomes more mature and competitive challenges increase, the level of future shareholder value it is expected to create generally declines, and its total returns to shareholders start to decline relative to the business's industry sector.[5] An opportune moment to divest the business is shortly before market valuations begin to reflect its lower future performance potential.

Why Executives Shy Away from Divestitures

Although an active portfolio approach recognizes the value to be created from divestitures, most executives seem to shy away from an active approach. The McKinsey study of 200 U.S. companies found a clear bias against divestitures. Almost 60 percent of the companies had executed two or fewer divestitures over the 10-year period. Furthermore, according to analysis of a random sub-sample of divestitures, at least 75 percent of the transactions were made in reaction to some form of pressure, such as underperformance of the corporate parent, the business unit, or both. In addition, the majority of reactive deals occurred only after the business had been underperforming for many years. Because underperformance (eventually) becomes transparent to the market, investors exert continuous pressure on the corporation to divest. In an analysis of voluntary asset sales, companies that decided to sell assets tended to be poor performers and were highly leveraged, suggesting that most voluntary asset sales are reactive rather than part of a proactive divestiture program.[6] Other researchers have confirmed that parent companies tend to hold on to underperforming businesses too long.[7]

In our experience, many managers dislike divestitures because these transactions dilute corporate earnings. However, if another party is willing to pay more for the subsidiary than the value the parent company expects to extract, the divestiture will create value and should be pursued. Although earnings

---

[5] R. Foster and S. Kaplan, *Creative Destruction* (New York: Doubleday, 2001).

[6] L. Lang, A. Poulsen, and R. Stulz, "Asset Sales, Firm Performance, and the Agency Costs of Managerial Discretion," *Journal of Financial Economics* 37 (1994): 3–37.

[7] D. Ravenscraft and F. Scherer, *Mergers, Sell-Offs, and Economic Efficiency* (Washington, DC: Brookings Institution, 1987), 167; and M. Cho and M. Cohen, "The Economic Causes and Consequences of Corporate Divestiture," *Managerial and Decision Economics* 18 (1997): 367–374.

EXHIBIT 22.3 **Earnings Dilution through Divestitures**

$ million

	Company	Divested business unit	Hold cash	Debt repayment	Share buyback
			Use of proceeds		
Operating value	2,500	400	2,100	2,100	2,100
Cash	–	–	500	–	–
Enterprise value	2,500	–	2,600	2,100	2,100
Debt	(600)	–	(600)	(100)	(600)
Market value of equity	1,900	–	2,000	2,000	1,500
Shares outstanding	100	–	100	100	75
Share price	19.0	–	20.0	20.0	20.0
EBIT	266.8	60.0	206.8	206.8	206.8
Interest income (2%)	–	–	10.0	–	–
Interest expense (6%)	(36.0)	–	(36.0)	(6.0)	(36.0)
Pretax income	230.8	60.0	180.8	200.8	170.8
Taxes (35%)	(80.8)	(21.0)	(63.3)	(70.3)	(59.8)
Net income	150.0	39.0	117.5	130.5	111.0
Earnings per share (dollars)	1.50	–	1.18	1.31	1.48
Price-to-earnings ratio	12.7	–	17.0	15.3	13.5

per share may fall, the company's price-to-earnings (P/E) ratio will rise, as the example in Exhibit 22.3 illustrates. The company described in the two left columns receives an offer to sell a mature business for $500 million in cash. In the hands of the parent company, the value of the business is estimated to be $400 million. Such a divestiture creates value, no matter how the parent company uses the proceeds:

- *Holding cash:* If the parent company simply holds on to the proceeds, it will dilute its earnings per share. The reason is straightforward: The interest rate earned on the cash is lower than the earnings yield (earnings relative to value) of the divested business unit. In other words, the interest income earned is lower than the forgone earnings of the business unit. This is just simple mathematics. However, the equity value increases, and the company's P/E is higher than before.

- *Repaying debt:* If the company uses the proceeds to repay some debt instead, earnings per share will still be lower than before the divestiture if the interest rate on the debt is lower than the earnings yield of the divested business. However, dilution is less than in the scenario of holding on to the proceeds, because the interest rate on debt is usually higher than the investment yield on cash holdings.

- *Buying back shares:* If the company uses the proceeds to buy back shares, earnings per share will be diluted if the ratio of sales proceeds to earnings of the divested business unit is lower than the P/E of the remaining business. The relative change in earnings is less than the relative change in the number of shares outstanding. Because divested units are typically the most mature businesses in a company's portfolio, divestitures often lead to earnings dilution. In the example shown, the sale proceeds and the amount used for buybacks would have to increase to about $530 million in order for it to become earnings accretive.

Against this background of executive resistance, it is perhaps not surprising that a change in corporate leadership seems to be one of the key triggers for divestitures. Among the previously mentioned 200 companies researched, about half of their major divestitures (those reported on the front page of the *Wall Street Journal*) took place in companies when the chief executive officer was fairly new.

HOW TO APPROACH DIVESTITURES

A value-creating approach to divestitures may result in divesting good and bad businesses at any stage of their life cycle. Clearly, divesting a good business is often not an intuitive choice and may be hard for managers. It therefore makes sense to enforce some discipline in active portfolio management, for example, by holding regular dedicated business exit review meetings, to ensure that the topic remains on the executive agenda, and by giving units a "date stamp," or estimated time of exit. This practice has the advantage of obliging executives to evaluate all businesses as their sell-by date approaches, although executives may decide to retain businesses after their sell-by date. Other disciplined approaches include setting a limit on the number of businesses in the corporate portfolio or aiming for a target balance in acquisitions and divestitures. Such practices help transform divestitures from evidence of failure into shrewd strategies for building value.

The principle that a business's potential to create value and the parent company's ability to realize that value should determine divestiture decisions provides a strong framework for initially assessing a corporate portfolio (see Chapter 19). However, various practical challenges may complicate decisions on whether and how to divest. In this section, we focus on what these practical challenges might be.

Synergies and Shared Assets, Services, or Systems

Because synergies and shared assets, services, or systems can significantly influence the economics of the parent company following a divestiture, they are an important driver of net value creation. Therefore, when analyzing a divestiture, you must understand what is being sold, what the implications are for the remaining businesses, and what the divestiture means in terms of net value creation for the parent company.

When a company divests a business unit, it may lose with it certain synergy benefits. For example, if a business unit gives cross-selling opportunities to other units, this benefit will be lost when the unit is sold. Likewise, a corporation may bundle its procurement for various businesses globally so that it enjoys significant discounts. A reduction in volumes after a divestiture can result in lower discounts and higher costs for the remaining businesses, as well as for the divested business unit itself.

Shared assets, services, and systems pose similar issues. For example, a single manufacturing facility can consist of production lines of products from different business units. When a corporation sells a business unit, it will not necessarily transfer the production facility. This means the corporation may retain the same total fixed-cost base supported by a smaller overall business volume. The same may hold for all kinds of support services and processes that are centralized for the group in one (low-cost) location rather than decentralized at the business unit level. These stranded costs for the parent company should not be ignored when analyzing value creation potential. Reducing the cost base to the same level relative to business volume as before the divestiture might take quite some time, and additional cost. The parent may therefore consider including, for example, a service contract in the transaction to keep business volume closer to its level before the deal.

Financing and Fiscal Changes

Combining various businesses with different operating risk profiles may result in a group with a higher relative debt capacity than some of the businesses individually are able to sustain. For example, an integrated electricity player that divests its (regulated) transmission and/or distribution network business and keeps a portfolio of generation and supply units will have a very different risk profile after the divestiture and consequently a different debt capacity and corresponding value from tax shields.

Fiscal changes may be more difficult to assess without knowing the details of a proposed deal structure, but they too can have real impact on the postdeal economics. When Cadbury Schweppes demerged into a global confectionary and an Americas beverages business in 2008, the company indicated that the effective corporate tax rate for the Americas beverages business would increase from 32 percent within the Cadbury Schweppes group to 37 percent on a stand-alone basis. Differences in fiscal regimes also play a role. In the European Union, the Parent-Subsidiary Directive requires member states to refrain from taxing profit (including capital gains) distributions from subsidiaries to parents; in addition, profit distributions from subsidiaries to parents must be exempt from withholding taxes. In the United States, corporations do not enjoy this so-called participation exemption for capital gains on divested subsidiaries and are at a disadvantage from that perspective.

Legal, Contractual, or Regulatory Barriers

The divestment process may be complicated by legal, contractual, or regulatory barriers. These are typically not large enough to distort the value creation potential but can seriously slow down the process and add to the amount of work to be done—and therefore increase the time and resources required to come to closure. This holds not only for large divestments such as the Cadbury example, but also for smaller divestments. These are often structured as asset transactions, which can be complex because they require extensive documentation and contracts with respect to all the different categories of assets involved.

Contractual issues typically come as unpleasant surprises, often discovered after companies have started the process of a divestiture. Examples include the need to create transitional service agreements between buyer and seller to guarantee continuity of the business unit, or change-of-ownership clauses that are activated at divestiture, rendering the existing contract or agreement invalid when ownership in the business transfers. This can, for example, be the case for procurement contracts, long-term contracts with customers, and loan agreements.

Pricing and Liquidity of the Assets

Challenges in these areas can eventually frustrate a divestiture, even one with strong value creation potential. As discussed in Chapter 15, market valuation levels are generally in line with intrinsic value potential in the long term but can deviate in the short term. Executives should use their superior insight into their businesses to assess such possible value gaps with regard to divestiture. If the market currently attaches more value to a business than its intrinsic value estimated by management, then a near-term divestiture looks like a good idea.

The example of Cadbury Schweppes shows that changes in external market conditions can work against original divestment plans. In March 2007, Cadbury Schweppes announced the separation of its global confectionary business and its Americas beverages business in order to "provide both management teams the focused opportunity to extract the full potential inherent in the businesses." Initial plans were to sell the beverages business through an auction among (primarily) private equity bidders, with the resulting proceeds to be returned to shareholders as a special dividend. As the credit crunch unfolded in 2008 and private equity interest dried up, Cadbury had to change its plan from a sale of Americas Beverages to a demerger of the corporate group into two listed entities without any special dividend paid to its shareholders. Cadbury pushed ahead with a demerger after its initial auction plan fell through, but many other companies canceled their divestments plans entirely during the financial crisis. Although external market factors may lower potential proceeds from a divestiture, management should balance this against the (hidden) costs of continuing with the status quo—namely, the costs of carrying the assets. Obviously, when a company needs to divest in order to prevent financial distress, it has much less freedom over the timing of its decision.

Even when valuation levels in the market seem undistorted and a company has received an offer that would create value, a lack of other potential buyers may make the seller reluctant to pursue the transaction. An academic study concluded that liquidity is a key driver in explaining the difference in divestment behavior between companies that seem to have similar fundamental reasons to divest.[8] The more liquid a market for particular assets, the better the price setting is expected to be. In other words, more competing buyers are likely to produce a better price for the seller.

DECIDING ON TRANSACTION TYPE

Once a corporation has identified businesses for divestiture, it must decide what transaction structure to use. There are different types of private and public transaction structures. Which transaction type to use depends on the availability of strategic or financial buyers, the need to raise cash, and the benefits of retaining some level of control during the first phase of the separation. Although the reason for pursuing a divestiture should be to increase the value of the corporation, a parent's urgent need for cash may lead it to choose a transaction type that delivers the maximum amount of cash, rather than one that maximizes value.

In the remainder of this chapter, we provide a brief overview of different transaction types and discuss the trade-offs among alternative forms of public ownership transactions, their impact on long-term performance, and the dynamics of ownership structures over time.

Public and Private Forms of Divestiture

Executives can choose from many types of transaction structures for private and public transactions:

Private transactions

- *Trade sale:* sale of part or all of a business to a strategic or a financial investor

---

[8] F. Schlingemann, R. Stulz, and R. Walkling, "Divestitures and the Liquidity of the Market for Corporate Assets," *Journal of Financial Economics* 64 (2002): 117–144.

- *Joint venture:* a combination of part or all of a business with other industry players, other companies in the value chain, or venture capitalists

Public transactions

- *Initial public offering (IPO):* sale of all shares of a subsidiary to new shareholders in the stock market
- *Carve-out:* sale of part of the shares in a subsidiary to new shareholders in the stock market
- *Spin-off (or demerger):* distribution of all shares in a subsidiary to existing shareholders of the parent company
- *Split-off:* an offer to existing shareholders of the parent company to exchange their shares in the parent company for shares in the subsidiary
- *Tracking stock:* a separate class of parent shares that is distributed to existing shareholders of the parent company through a spin-off or sold to new shareholders through a carve-out

In most cases, companies should choose a private transaction if they can identify other parties that are better owners of the business. Private transactions allow the company to sell the business unit at a premium and capture value immediately. In most situations, the counterparties will be strategic buyers, that is, other industry players. However, the company should also consider financial buyers. Fiscal implications may affect this decision in practice, because asset sales for cash typically generate a taxable profit and therefore may turn out to be less favorable.

If the company cannot identify better owners, it will have to choose a public restructuring alternative. All the public transactions in the preceding list involve the creation of a new public security, but not all of them actually result in cash proceeds. Full IPOs and carve-outs result in cash proceeds as securities are sold to new shareholders. In spin-off and split-off transactions, new securities are offered to existing shareholders, sometimes in exchange for other existing shares (split-offs). When industry consolidation is expected, a public transaction may be more beneficial for the shareholders in the long term if the newly floated business unit would drive the consolidation or would be a takeover candidate. In that case, shareholders do not earn a premium from the divestiture itself, but significant value may be created for shareholders in the future. In the following subsections we comment on the most common forms of public transactions.

Spin-offs   The commonest form of public ownership transaction is a spin-off. In this case, the parent company gives up control over the business unit by distributing the subsidiary shares to the parent shareholders. This full separation maximizes the strategic flexibility of the subsidiary, provides the greatest freedom to improve operations by sourcing from more competitive companies (instead of the former parent), and avoids conflicts of interest between the parent company and the business unit. Spin-offs are usually carried out to improve operating performance of the business units.

Many spin-offs are executed in two steps: a minority IPO (carve-out) followed by a full spin-off relatively shortly thereafter. A one-step spin-off is typically less complex and does not depend on market circumstances, as no shares need to be issued. However, a two-step spin-off has benefits as well. The minority IPO already establishes dedicated equity coverage, creates market making in the shares, and may reduce the risk of flow-back by developing an interested investor base.

According to McKinsey's research on operating and capital market performance after completion of the transaction, spin-offs typically meet or exceed expectations for value creation. Analysis of parent and subsidiary performance of a sample of spin-off transactions shows that the operating margin of a spun-off subsidiary improves by one-third on average during the three years after completion of the transaction. Operating margins of the parent companies on average show a very modest increase. Academic research confirms the improvements in operating performance, with larger improvements for the subsidiary than for the parent company.[9] Some research concludes that operating improvements were significant only for focus-improving spin-offs (transactions where the business spun off was different from the parent's core line of business).[10]

Post-transaction total returns to shareholders (TRS) for spin-off parents and subsidiaries are consistent with the results on operating improvements. As Exhibit 22.4 shows, market index-adjusted TRS during a two-year period after completion are positive for both parents and spun-off subsidiaries. However, the positive performance of the subsidiaries is driven by focus-improving spin-offs. Transactions that did not improve focus had mostly negative post-transaction returns.[11]

Carve-outs   Sometimes parent companies do not want to give up control over a business unit. The reason could be a desire to maintain some synergies between parent and subsidiary or to shelter the subsidiary from market forces such as mergers and acquisitions. If the company does not want to give up control, it should consider a minority carve-out or possibly a tracking stock.

When thinking about partially separating ownership of a business unit through a carve-out, executives need to plan for full separation. Although a

[9] P. Cusatis, J. Miles, and J. Woolridge, "Some New Evidence That Spinoffs Create Value," *Journal of Applied Corporate Finance* 7 (1994): 100–107.

[10] L. Daley, V. Mehrotra, and R. Sivakumar, "Corporate Focus and Value Creation: Evidence from Spinoffs," *Journal of Financial Economics* 45 (1997): 257–281.

[11] Cusatis, Miles, and Woolridge, "Some New Evidence" (see note 9) find similar shareholder returns for parents and subsidiaries.

EXHIBIT 22.4 **Long-Term Market Performance of Spin-Offs**

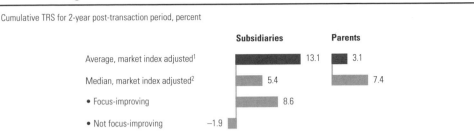

Cumulative TRS for 2-year post-transaction period, percent

[1] Adjusted for either U.S. or European market index.
[2] Adjusted for median return of index constituents over similar measurement period.

Source: Datastream, Compustat, McKinsey Corporate Performance Center analysis.

minority carve-out might initially shelter the unit from market forces such as acquisitions, it is very unlikely that the parent can hold on to its majority stake for long. In most situations, the separation is irreversible. The separated businesses may attract new equity financing to fund their growth or perhaps pursue acquisitions, both of which will most likely dilute the parent's stake in the carved-out business, ultimately leading to loss of control.

Carve-out subsidiaries typically have higher growth rates than their parents but do not differ much in terms of operating performance. For high-growth subsidiaries, a carve-out results in proceeds that can be used to fund this growth.

The downside of ownership restructuring where the parent retains a controlling stake in the subsidiary is the possibility of unclear governance. If the parent enforces a minimum stake to retain control, this may restrict growth and value creation by the separated business, which would destroy the benefits that the carve-out was intended to deliver. In addition, these companies risk further conflicts as the carved-out business unit's executives pursue the best interests of their own company and shareholders.

France Telecom's carve-out of mobile-phone operator Orange provides an example of these conflicts. In 2001 France Telecom carved out a 14 percent stake of Orange after acquiring the business from Vodafone, which had to divest it after acquiring Mannesman. The carve-out's main objective was to raise cash to reduce France Telecom's high leverage at the time. In a consolidating industry, Orange could not use its equity for acquisitions without further diluting France Telecom's stake. Using debt financing for acquisitions would have worsened France Telecom's balance sheet. Early in 2004, France Telecom reacquired the Orange shares from the market. The delisting supported the implementation of France Telecom's new integrated fixed-mobile operator strategy at a time when the rationale for a separate listing was becoming unclear. Valuations had come down, and incorporating Orange's cash flows into the group structure would deliver financing and fiscal benefits.

On average, the market-adjusted long-term performance for carve-out parents and subsidiaries is negative. For a variety of reasons, however, performance among carve-out transactions diverges significantly. Research indicates that carve-outs from financially distressed parent companies on average show negative market-adjusted returns, whereas other carve-out companies earn positive market-adjusted returns.[12] The subsidiaries from distressed parents continue to have relatively low operating performance, indicating that they were partly contributing to the distress. Additional evidence suggests that market performance is better for carve-out transactions that improve the focus of both entities.[13]

In addition, there is a clear relationship between carve-out subsidiaries' success in the capital markets and the evolution of their ownership structure. Research on a relatively small sample found that virtually all minority carve-outs were either fully sold or reacquired at a later stage.[14] Carve-out subsidiaries that were reacquired earned negative shareholder returns in the period between the first issue and parent reacquisition. In our research on more than 200 carve-outs announced before 1998, the majority of the carve-out entities did not last.[15] As shown in Exhibit 22.5, only 8 percent of the carve-out subsidiaries we analyzed remained majority-controlled by the parent. The majority of the subsidiaries were spun off further, acquired, or merged with other players. Most of these acquisitions or parent buybacks happened within a four-year period after the carve-out. During the two years after completion, shareholder returns of the carve-out entities showed a clear performance difference. Carve-outs with positive shareholder returns, when adjusted for market returns, were typically spun off. Carve-outs with negative returns were usually acquired or bought back by the parent, suggesting they were less successful than had been anticipated, or perhaps were executed for the wrong reasons.

Academic research over a period of 20 years on 91 carve-outs with subsequent reacquisitions confirms the underperformance of the subsidiaries.[16] According to the same research, the parent companies that engage in reacquisitions actually experience a negative share price effect at announcement of the carve-out, suggesting that the market views the carve-out as a mistake. While the parent and business unit experience positive effects around the reacquisition, the returns of the parent following the reacquisition are positive when the units are fully reacquired and negative when the units are partially reacquired. Other research found evidence that the initial market reaction to a carve-out

[12] J. Madura and T. Nixon, "The Long-Term Performance of Parent and Units Following Equity Carve-Outs," *Applied Financial Economics* 12 (2002): 171–181.

[13] A. Vijh, "Long-Term Returns from Equity Carveouts," *Journal of Financial Economics* 51 (1999): 273–308.

[14] A. Klein, J. Rosenfeld, and W. Beranek, "The Two Stages of an Equity Carve-Out and the Price Response of Parent and Subsidiary Stock," *Managerial and Decision Economics* 12 (1991): 449–460.

[15] A. Annema, W. Fallon, and M. Goedhart, "Do Carve-Outs Make Sense?" *McKinsey on Finance* (Fall 2001): 6–10.

[16] K. Gleason, J. Madura, and A. K. Pennathur, "Valuation and Performance of Reacquisitions Following Equity Carve-Outs," *Financial Review* 41 (2006): 229–246.

EXHIBIT 22.5 **Typical Carve-Out Trajectories**

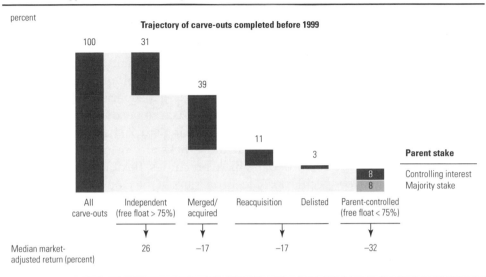

Source: Datastream, Factiva, McKinsey Corporate Performance Center analysis.

announcement includes anticipation of the secondary events such as spin-offs, M&A, and reacquisition.[17]

Examples of parent buybacks are France Telecom's Wanadoo and Deutsche Telekom's T-Online. Both telecom companies had previously carved out minority stakes in their Internet service providers. France Telecom floated a minority stake in Wanadoo around midyear 2000 at €9 per share; the shares peaked at around €22 in September 2000, and then France Telecom reacquired the minority stake in early 2004 at €8.9 per share. Deutsche Telekom floated a minority stake in T-Online in early 2000 at €27 per share; the shares peaked at around €47 in May 2000, and then Deutsche Telekom announced an offer to buy back the shares in October 2004 at €9 per share. The independence of these Internet businesses no longer fitted with the strategy of their telecom parents to integrate Internet operations with the fixed-line business to spur growth.

Carve-outs that lasted as parent-controlled companies with a free float of less than 75 percent showed significant negative returns (see Exhibit 22.5). In our research, these carve-out subsidiaries typically had lower growth rates than other carve-outs. This underperformance may indicate that the rationale of the carve-out was flawed; the carve-outs may have happened for opportunistic reasons unrelated to value creation. The parent companies most likely did not intend to fully separate these businesses when they were carved out. The low market returns could have resulted from the subsidiary lacking the opportunity to maximize its potential under continued parent control, or the parent taking

[17] M. Otsubo, "Gains from Equity Carve-Outs and Subsequent Events," *Journal of Business Research* 62 (2008): 1207–1213.

advantage of high market valuation levels at the time, without considering real ongoing benefits of full separation.

Tracking stock   An alternative form of public ownership restructuring is the issuance of tracking stock. Tracking stock offers a parent the advantage of maintaining control over a separated subsidiary, but it often complicates corporate governance. Because there is no formal, legal separation between the subsidiary and the parent, a single board of directors needs to decide on potentially competing needs of common and tracking stock shareholders.

In addition to competing needs, tracking stocks also result in both entities being liable for each other's debt, which precludes flexible capital raising. Although there may be specific tax or legal barriers in the way of separation that would favor the use of a tracking stock alternative, the evidence for tracking stock is far from convincing. In an analysis of tracking stocks, this kind of transaction appeared to destroy value in the long term.[18] On the elimination of tracking stock, the announcement effect for the parent was positive, reflecting the market's relief that the structure had been discontinued. Furthermore, tracking stock is used far less often than carve-out and spin-off transactions, implying that this form of ownership restructuring fails to bring the benefits executives are looking for.

SUMMARY

As businesses go through their life cycles, they pose new challenges to the structure of their parent corporation's portfolio. An active portfolio approach that pays as much attention to divestiture opportunities as to potential acquisitions is integral to a corporation's program to create value.

A good example of these ownership dynamics is AT&T, as shown in Exhibit 22.6. After the company's original breakup in the 1980s, AT&T continued the process of ownership separation in 1996, leading to five new public companies within five years. AT&T first spun off Lucent Technologies (telecom equipment and networking), which in 2000 spun off Avaya (communication networks) and executed a carve-out of Agere Systems (semiconductors), which was acquired by LSI Logic in 2007. AT&T also spun off NCR (information technology hardware and software) in 1996 and carved out AT&T Wireless in 2000. NCR itself spun off Teradata (computer software) in 2007.

In the fall of 2000, AT&T had originally announced it was going to split itself into four units: AT&T Wireless, AT&T Broadband, AT&T Consumer, and AT&T Business. The company carved out AT&T Wireless in 2000, followed by a full spin-off of Wireless in 2001. AT&T Wireless was acquired by Cingular Wireless (a joint venture of SBC Communications and BellSouth) in 2004.

---

[18] M. Billett and A. Vijh, "The Wealth Effects of Tracking Stock Restructurings," *Journal of Financial Research* 27 (2004): 559–583.

EXHIBIT 22.6 **AT&T: Dynamics of Ownership Restructuring**

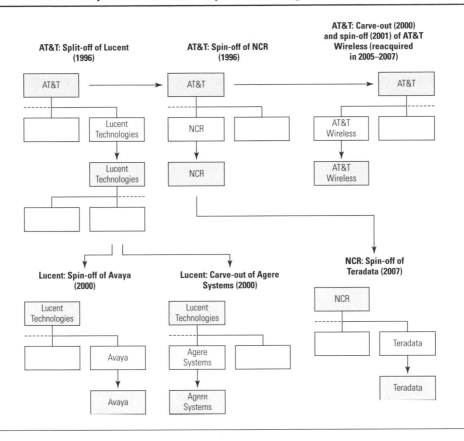

Through the acquisitions of SBC and BellSouth in 2005 and 2007, respectively, AT&T regained control of the wireless business. AT&T did not establish AT&T Broadband as originally planned, by combining the company's broadband/cable assets with Liberty Media Corporation, a stand-alone entity with its own tracking stock that had been acquired in 1998 as part of TCI. Instead, it eventually spun off the existing tracking stocks on Liberty Media in 2001 to make it a fully independent business and sold its other broadband/cable assets to Comcast in 2002. The implementation of the tracking stock for AT&T Consumer to separate it from AT&T Business never happened.

In contrast to AT&T, most corporations divest businesses only after resisting shareholder pressure. In delaying, they risk forgoing the potentially significant value they could create by taking an active approach to divestitures. Ideally, executives should pursue an ongoing, proactive divestiture program to evaluate the corporate portfolio continually as its businesses evolve through their life cycles and the industry itself changes.

Senior executives should prepare the organization for this cultural shift to a more active approach. They should deliver the message that their new approach will entail divesting good businesses, and such divestitures should not be considered failures. Because divesting good businesses may be hard for managers, corporations should build forcing mechanisms into their divestiture programs. Successful divestitures require executives to take a thorough look at the implications for the economics of the remaining businesses so they can take these into consideration when structuring a divestiture agreement. They should not underestimate the time and effort required to complete a divestiture.

REVIEW QUESTIONS

1. Explain under what conditions a divestiture will lead to EPS dilution or accretion if the proceeds from the divestiture are used: (1) to repay debt; (2) to repurchase shares. How do your answers affect value created by a divestiture?

2. Describe the key reasons why divesting a business can create value for shareholders, even when the business is still in the early stages of its life cycle.

3. Identify and explain the significance of four factors that complicate a manager's decision to divest a business unit.

4. A company intends to sell one if its larger business units to a strategic buyer. The company's controller is concerned because the sale would result in overcapacity of 25 percent in the company's information technology (IT) center. He proposes that the company be compensated for these stranded costs by an increase in the sale price. Discuss what reaction you expect from the buyer. How would you propose to resolve the stranded costs issue?

5. An executive is reluctant to sell a high-performing business unit, arguing that the sale would dilute the company's ROIC to a level below the WACC and make the company value-destroying. Discuss.

6. Identify and describe two private transaction approaches to corporate divestiture and two public transaction approaches. When are private transactions likely to create more value than public transactions?

7. An oil company wants to divest its low-growth chemicals division, which has an estimated stand-alone value of around $5 billion and represents around 40 percent of the entire oil company's value. What do you think could be the most promising transaction approaches and why?

8. An electronics conglomerate intends to divest its high-growth solar energy business, which develops and manufactures solar panels and has an estimated value of $250 million, around 5 percent of the total value of the conglomerate. What do you think could be the most promising transaction approaches and why?

23

Capital Structure

Careful design and management of a company's capital structure do more to prevent value destruction than to boost value creation. When managers make decisions about capital structure, they usually have much more to lose than to gain in terms of value—as underlined by the sharp increases in bankruptcies following the burst of the high-tech bubble in 2001 and the credit crisis in 2007.

In this chapter, we discuss tools and frameworks that can help managers make three levels of decisions about capital structure. The first level is strategic: How much funding does the company need to support its core strategic plans? And how much flexibility does it need, on the one hand, to make additional investments as opportunities arise and, on the other, to provide robustness to withstand any downturn in the business cycle and other adverse economic conditions? The second level concerns the company's target capital structure: What mix of debt and equity best fits the company's needs for core funding, flexibility, and robustness? At the third level, decisions are about the tactical, short-term steps required to adjust the capital structure in line with meeting these long-term targets. For instance, should the company hold on to excess cash or pay it out by increasing dividends or repurchasing shares?

This chapter addresses the following topics in detail:

- The impact of capital structure on value creation for shareholders
- The role of credit ratings in capital structure decisions
- Choosing the short-term steps to manage a capital structure
- Establishing long-term capital structure targets
- Creating value from financial engineering

CAPITAL STRUCTURE AND VALUE CREATION

Today, companies can choose from a wide variety of financing instruments, ranging from traditional common equity and straight debt to more exotic instruments such as convertible preferred equity, convertible and commodity-linked debt, and many others. But the fundamental question in designing a company's capital structure remains simply the choice between debt (which represents a fixed claim on the enterprise value) and equity (the residual claim). We can further simplify this choice to asking what the company's leverage should be, measured as the ratio of debt to total enterprise value.

Trade-Offs in Capital Structure Design

Although academic researchers have investigated the issue for decades, there is still no clear model for deciding a company's optimal leverage ratio, the leverage that would create most value for shareholders.[1] There is evidence that leverage delivers key benefits in the form of reductions in taxes and avoidance of overinvestment, but leverage is also associated with costs arising from business erosion and conflicts of interest among investors.

Tax savings   The most obvious benefit of debt over equity is reduced taxes. Interest charges for debt are tax deductible, whereas payments to shareholders as dividends and share repurchases are not. Replacing equity with debt reduces taxable income and therefore increases the value of the firm.[2] However, this tax effect does not make 100 percent debt funding optimal. More debt funding may reduce corporate taxes but could actually lead to higher taxes for investors. In many countries, investor taxes are higher on interest income than on capital gains on shares, a circumstance that could make equity funding more attractive, depending on the relevant tax rates for corporations and investors.[3]

Reduction of corporate overinvestment   According to the *free-cash-flow hypothesis*,[4] debt can help impose investment discipline on managers, as private equity firms have known well for decades. Especially in companies with strong cash flows and few growth opportunities, managers may be tempted to loosen controls and increase corporate spending on perks or investment projects and acquisitions that will boost growth at the expense of value. If share ownership is widely dispersed, it is difficult and costly for shareholders to assess when managers are engaging in such overinvestment. Debt curbs such managerial behavior by forcing the company to pay out free cash flow according to

---

[1] For an overview of the literature, see M. Barclay and C. Smith, "The Capital Structure Puzzle: Another Look at the Evidence," *Journal of Applied Corporate Finance* 12, no. 1 (1999): 8–20.
[2] For an overview, see M. Grinblatt and S. Titman, *Financial Markets and Corporate Strategy*, 2nd ed. (New York: McGraw-Hill, 2002), chap. 14; and R. Brealey, S. Myers, and F. Allen, *Principles of Corporate Finance*, 9th ed. (New York: McGraw-Hill, 2008), chap. 19.
[3] M. Miller, "Debt and Taxes," *Journal of Finance* 32, no. 2 (1977): 261–275.
[4] M. Jensen, "Agency Costs of Free Cash Flow, Corporate Finance and Takeovers," *American Economic Review* 76, no. 2 (1986): 323–339.

scheduled interest and principal obligations before they can make any additional investments.

Costs of business erosion and bankruptcy   However, higher levels of debt also give rise to costs from business erosion.[5] Highly leveraged companies are more likely to forgo investment opportunities or reduce budgets for research and development (R&D) and other costs for which the payoffs are further in the future, since they need to have cash available to repay their debts on time. As a result, these companies may miss significant opportunities to create value. Furthermore, companies with higher leverage are more likely to lose customers, employees, and suppliers because of their higher risk of financial distress. For example, suppliers to highly indebted retailers typically demand up-front payment, creating a negative cycle of lower stocks leading to lower sales leading to more difficulty in meeting debt schedules, and so on. The risk of losing customers is particularly high when the products require long-term service and maintenance. For example, Chrysler and General Motors (including its European subsidiary Opel) lost considerable market share to Japanese and European competitors as they faced financial distress during the 2008 credit crisis. Ultimately, business erosion can lead to bankruptcy, triggering additional legal and administrative costs of liquidating or restructuring the company for the debt holders after it has defaulted on its debt. Academic research indicates that these direct bankruptcy costs are relatively small, around 3 percent of a company's market value before it becomes distressed.[6]

Costs of investor conflicts   Higher leverage may cause additional loss of value as a result of conflicts of interest among debt holders, shareholders, and managers,[7] particularly through the measures that debt holders take to protect their interests. When companies come close to defaulting on their debt, shareholders will prefer to take out any cash rather than invest it in value-creating opportunities that would primarily benefit the debt holders. The shareholders' preference leads to corporate underinvestment. Shareholders also may have more to gain from high-risk investments with short-term payoffs than from low-risk investments with longer-term payoffs, even though the latter could generate more value. This preference leads to asset substitution (the usual finance theory term for exchanging lower-risk assets for higher-risk assets). Of course, debt holders will try to protect themselves from these and other conflicts of interest with shareholders. For example, they may insist on various

---

[5] We prefer the term *business erosion* to the more often used *financial distress* because the associated costs arise very gradually and long before there may be an actual distress event, such as nonperformance on debt.

[6] See, for example, L. Weiss, "Bankruptcy Resolution: Direct Costs and Violation of Priority of Claims," *Journal of Financial Economics* 27, no. 2 (1990): 285–314.

[7] See, for example, S. Ross, R. Westerfield, and J. Jaffe, *Corporate Finance*, 6th ed. (New York: McGraw-Hill, 2001), 427–430.

EXHIBIT 23.1   **Impact of Capital Structure on Value**

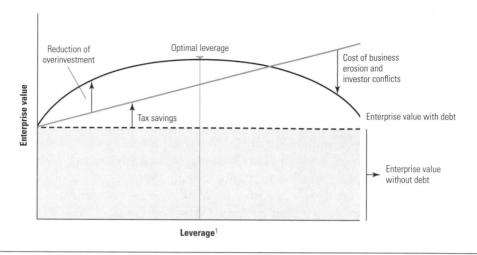

¹ Defined as debt divided by enterprise value.

types of restrictive covenants and monitor management actions. All of these measures have costs that are ultimately borne by the company's shareholders.

Exhibit 23.1 summarizes the combined influence of all these factors on a company's value. As leverage increases, a company's value goes up because it captures additional tax savings from interest payments and gains value from management's improved discipline, which guards against overinvestment. But as debt continues to rise, these benefits are gradually countered by the expected costs of business erosion and bankruptcy and conflicts of interest among investors. Beyond the point of optimal leverage, these costs start to outweigh the benefits, so any further increase in leverage decreases the company's value.

In theory, the optimal pattern of leverage will differ between companies, depending on their characteristics. The higher a company's returns, the lower its growth and business risk, and the more fungible its assets and capabilities, the more highly it should be leveraged. Such companies are more likely to benefit from tax savings, because they have stable profits. Imposing discipline on their management is more important, because for low-growth companies, the cost of overinvesting is likely to be high. And the expected costs of business erosion are lower, because the company's assets and capabilities have alternative uses; even after a bankruptcy, the assets and capabilities would have significant value to new owners. This explains why airlines can sustain high leverage:[8] in spite of their low returns and high risk, airplanes are easily deployed for use by other airline companies in the event of a bankruptcy.

[8] Specifically, leverage is high when the operating leases of aircraft are taken into account.

Leverage should be lower for companies with lower returns, higher growth potential and risk, and highly specific assets and capabilities. In these companies, the potential tax savings are small, because taxable profits are low in the near term. Management needs more financial freedom, because investments are essential to capture future growth. In addition, because of the high growth and the unique nature of the assets and capabilities of growth companies, the expected costs of eroding business through high leverage are high, too. If such companies go into bankruptcy, they lose valuable growth opportunities, and any remaining assets have very little value to third parties.

There is ample evidence from academic research to show that companies adopt these patterns of leverage in practice. The most highly leveraged industries are indeed typically mature and asset intensive; examples are steel, paper, and cement. Industries with the lowest leverage, such as software, biotech, and high-tech start-ups, have larger opportunities for growth and investment. Companies with extensive tangible assets usually sustain greater debt, because they have more assets that can serve as collateral, reducing the costs of business erosion and bankruptcy.[9] Companies with more volatile earnings and higher advertising and R&D costs tend to be financed with less debt.[10] Leverage also proves to be higher for companies with more fungible assets and lower for companies producing durable goods, such as machinery and equipment, requiring long-term maintenance and support.[11]

Pecking-order theory An alternative to the view that there are trade-offs between equity and debt is a school of thought in finance theory that sees a pecking order in financing.[12] According to this theory, companies meet their investment needs first by using internal funds (from retained earnings), then by issuing debt, and finally by issuing equity. One of the causes of this pecking order is that investors interpret financing decisions by managers as signals of a company's financial prospects. For example, investors will interpret an equity issue as a signal that management believes shares are overvalued. Because of this interpretation, rational managers will turn to equity funding only as a last resort because it could cause the share price to fall. An analogous argument holds for debt issues, although the overvaluation signal is much smaller because the value of debt is much less sensitive to a company's financial success.[13]

---

[9] R. Rajan and L. Zingales, "What Do We Know about Capital Structure? Some Evidence from International Data," *Journal of Finance* 50, no. 5 (1995): 1421–1460.

[10] M. Bradley, G. Jarell, and E. Kim, "On the Existence of an Optimal Capital Structure: Theory and Evidence," *Journal of Finance* 39, no. 3 (1984): 857–878; and M. Long and I. Malitz, "The Investment-Financing Nexus: Some Empirical Evidence," *Midland Corporate Finance Journal* 3, no. 3 (1985): 53–59.

[11] See Barclay and Smith, "Capital Structure Puzzle"; and S. Titman and R. Wessels, "The Determinants of Capital Structure Choice," *Journal of Finance* 43, no. 1 (1988): 1–19.

[12] See G. Donaldson, "Corporate Debt Capacity: A Study of Corporate Debt Policy and the Determination of Corporate Debt Capacity," Harvard Graduate School of Business, Boston (1961); and S. Myers, "The Capital Structure Puzzle," *Journal of Finance* 39, no. 3 (1974): 575–592.

[13] An exception is, of course, the value of debt in a financially distressed company.

According to the theory, companies will have lower leverage when they are more mature and profitable, simply because they can fund internally and do not need any debt or equity funding. However, evidence for the theory is not conclusive. For example, mature companies generating strong cash flows are among the most highly leveraged, whereas the pecking-order theory would predict them to have the lowest leverage. High-tech start-up companies are among the least leveraged, rather than debt-loaded, as the theory would predict.[14] Recent research,[15] confirmed by surveys among financial executives,[16] shows how the signaling hypotheses underlying the pecking-order theory are more relevant to financial managers in selecting and timing specific funding alternatives than for setting long-term capital structure targets.

Is There an Optimal Capital Structure?

Although the costs and benefits of leverage are clear, the way to determine the optimal capital structure for a given company is less certain. How should managers decide on the best target leverage for their companies? The bad news is that there seems to be no exact answer. But there is good news, too. First, for most companies, the answer is less critical for shareholder value than some practitioners think. Second, managers can find meaningful indications of an *effective* capital structure—that is, a structure that is hard to improve on in terms of creating shareholder value.

Leverage matters less than we think   How critical is leverage for shareholder value, anyway? Exhibit 23.2 shows the distribution of credit ratings for all U.S. and European companies with a market capitalization over $1 billion according to Standard & Poor's. The ratings, which serve as indicators of a company's credit quality, range between AAA (highest quality) and D (defaulted). Ratings of BBB– and higher indicate so-called investment-grade quality. The vast majority of the companies in Exhibit 23.2 are in the rating categories of A+ to BBB–. Credit ratings are fairly stable over time, so most companies probably do not move in and out of this range. We interpret this distribution of ratings as evidence that, for most companies, the range from A+ to BBB– is an effective rating level, meaning it cannot clearly be improved upon in terms of creating value for shareholders. Few companies are at rating levels of AA–, because

---

[14] See Barclay and Smith, "Capital Structure Puzzle"; and M. Baker and J. Wurgler, "Market Timing and Capital Structure," *Journal of Finance* 52, no. 1 (2002): 1–32.

[15] See also A. Hovakimian, T. Opler, and S. Titman, "The Debt-Equity Choice," *Journal of Financial and Quantitative Analysis* 36, no. 1 (2001): 1–24, for evidence that the pecking-order theory predicts short-term movements in corporate debt levels but that long-term changes are more in line with the trade-offs discussed earlier in this section.

[16] J. Graham and H. Campbell, "How Do CFOs Make Capital Budgeting and Capital Structure Decisions?" *Journal of Applied Corporate Finance* 15, no. 1 (2002): 8–23.

EXHIBIT 23.2   **Credit Ratings for Large Companies: Mostly between A and BBB**

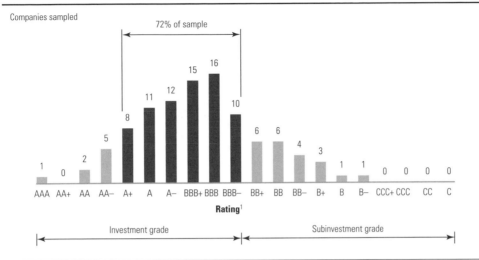

[1] Standard & Poor's credit ratings for all U.S. and European companies with a market capitalization over $1 billion.

Source: Datastream, Bloomberg, McKinsey Corporate Performance Center analysis.

too little leverage would leave too much value on the table in the form of tax savings and management discipline. At the other extreme, below the rating level of BBB–, the costs of business erosion and investor conflicts associated with high leverage become too onerous: interest rates would sharply increase, and access to funding would be limited because many investors cannot invest in debt that is not investment grade, especially when credit is tight, as demonstrated by the 2008 credit crisis.

As the next section of this chapter shows, however, this does not mean that all companies have a similar capital structure. On the contrary, companies with the same credit rating can have very different capital structures across industry sectors because of their different business risk.

Within the range from A+ to BBB–, shareholder value does not vary much with a company's capital structure. This is especially true when we compare the impact on shareholder value of credit rating with the impact of key value drivers such as return on invested capital (ROIC) and growth. To illustrate, consider a simple example that focuses on only the tax savings resulting from increased debt financing. Exhibit 23.3 shows how the multiple of enterprise value over earnings before interest, taxes, and amortization (EBITA) for an average company in the S&P 500 would change with changes in the amount of its debt financing, as measured by the interest coverage ratio.[17] The EBITA multiple is estimated using the basic value driver formula as presented in

---

[17] This is the ratio of EBITA to interest expenses, which is widely used by managers and credit raters to measure financial health; see the next section for more details.

EXHIBIT 23.3   **Capital Structure's Limited Impact on Enterprise Value**

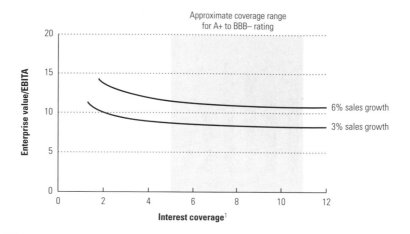

Chapter 2 and applied using an adjusted present value (APV) methodology.[18] We assume a long-term ROIC of 14 percent and an unlevered cost of capital of 9 percent—typical scores for a middle-of-the-road S&P 500 company.

As Exhibit 23.3 shows, enterprise value does not change dramatically with the level of debt funding except at very low levels of interest coverage (below 2). But at such low levels of coverage, the company will likely have a credit rating below investment grade, and two additional factors will make the real value impact of additional debt less advantageous than it appears in this simple model. First, the costs of business erosion and investor conflicts will become significant and offset some of the tax savings. Second, the expected value of any tax savings will itself decline because of the growing probability that the company will not capture these savings in the first place. The impact on real

---

[18] Applying the APV methodology to the value driver formula and discounting the tax shield on interest at the unlevered cost of equity results in the following formula:

$$\text{Value} = \text{NOPLAT} \times \frac{1 - \dfrac{g}{\text{ROIC}}}{k_u - g} + \sum_{t=1}^{\infty} \frac{k_D \times T \times D_t}{(1 + k_u)^t}$$

where k_u is the unlevered cost of equity, D_t is the debt in year t, k_D is the cost of debt, T is the tax rate, and all other symbols are as defined in Chapter 3.

If we make the additional assumption that companies finance with debt while maintaining a stable interest coverage ratio, the formula can be simplified as follows:

$$\text{Value} = \text{NOPLAT} \times \frac{\left(1 - \dfrac{g}{\text{ROIC}} + \dfrac{T}{1 - T} \times \dfrac{\text{Interest}}{\text{EBITA}}\right)}{k_u - g}$$

where EBITA/Interest is the target coverage ratio.

value will therefore be less than predicted by the value driver formula at low coverage ratios, so the true curve would be even flatter than shown here.

Capital structure therefore is not a big value booster, especially when compared with additional growth (also shown in the exhibit) or improvements in return on invested capital (ROIC). So it is not surprising that most companies have credit ratings in the range of A+ to BBB–, roughly corresponding to coverage ratios of 5 to 11 times interest.

Of course, capital structure can make a big difference for companies at the far ends of the interest coverage spectrum. Companies with strong earnings and cash flows but without any debt probably fail to capture significant value for their shareholders. Well-documented examples include pharmaceutical companies such as American Home Products (renamed Wyeth in 2002 and acquired by Pfizer in 2009), which had almost no debt for more than 30 years until 1989. The forgone tax shields on debt amounted to an estimated $1.7 billion over that period.[19] At the other extreme, companies with very high levels of debt at an interest coverage of 2 and less probably do not render their shareholders a great service, either. Such leverage levels are unsustainable and more likely to destroy shareholder value, due to a high probability of business erosion, investor conflicts, and ultimately bankruptcy. Recent empirical evidence confirms that the cost of overleveraging is much higher than the cost of underleveraging.[20]

Setting an effective capital structure   Difficult as it may be to determine an optimal capital structure, it is much easier to find an effective structure—that is, one that cannot clearly be improved upon in terms of shareholder value creation because it is somewhere in the relatively flat range of the valuation curves of Exhibits 23.1 and 23.3. To find such an effective structure, you can use several reference points.

Peer group comparison: An industry peer group is a good starting point. The key value trade-offs in designing capital structure laid out earlier—among growth, return, and asset specificity—are largely industry-specific. If these characteristics are fairly similar across a peer group of companies, market forces will drive these companies toward an effective capital structure. By analyzing what capital structure most companies in the peer group have, you obtain at least some understanding of what a reasonable capital structure could be. Furthermore, the approach also makes sense from a competitive perspective: as long as your capital structure is not too different, you have at least not given away any competitive advantage derived from capital structure (nor have you gained any). For example, there is academic evidence that high-leverage

---

[19] See T. Opler, M. Saron, and S. Titman, "Corporate Liability Management: Designing Capital Structure to Create Shareholder Value," *Journal of Applied Corporate Finance* 10, no. 1 (1997): 21–32.

[20] J. Van Binsbergen, J. Graham, and J. Yang, "The Cost of Debt," EFA 2007 Ljubljana Meetings Paper, WFA 2007, Big Sky, Montana.

companies sometimes fall victim to price wars started by financially stronger competitors.[21]

Credit-rating analysis: Peer group comparisons offer meaningless conclusions if many companies in the sector are not at their targeted capital structure—in other words, if the companies in a group are making the same mistakes. For example, many players in the telecommunications sector had too much debt in the early 2000s as a result of aggressive acquisitions and investments in mobile communication. In such circumstances, it is more revealing to analyze only peers with investment-grade credit ratings and determine what it takes to achieve such a rating. This allows you not only to set a target structure but also to assess how your credit rating would be affected if you deviated from that target structure. Since the 1960s, a body of evidence has been recorded showing company credit ratios clustering around industry-specific averages, further indicating that each industry has its own effective capital structure.[22]

Cash flow analysis: Although external comparisons of capital structure and credit ratings are important, each company will face specific challenges arising from its particular investment needs, dividend policy, and other considerations. You should therefore carefully analyze future cash inflows and outflows for your company and the capital structure implications. Test a given capital structure under different scenarios to analyze how credit quality will develop over time and what future funding deficits or surpluses to expect. Assess the company's financial *flexibility*: What capital structure will enable you to undertake planned acquisitions or make planned capital expenditures? Also test for financial *robustness*: What levels of risk—for example, from business or sector downturns—could the company absorb with a given capital structure? Finally, set a capital structure target that accommodates both sufficient flexibility and robustness. Later in this chapter, we illustrate this approach with a numerical example.

CREDIT RATINGS AND CAPITAL STRUCTURE

Before managers can set a capital structure target for their company, they need to understand its likely impact on the company's credit rating. It is important to understand this impact for three reasons:

1. Ratings are a useful summary indicator of capital structure health; lower ratings reflect higher probabilities of default. Exhibit 23.4 shows the average probability of default associated with each credit-rating category

---

[21] See, for example, P. Bolton and D. Scharfstein, "A Theory of Predation Based on Agency Problems in Financial Contracting," *American Economic Review* 80, no. 1 (1990): 93–106.

[22] E. Schwarz and R. Aronson, "Some Surrogate Evidence in Support of the Concept of Optimal Financial Structure," *Journal of Finance* 22, no. 1 (1967): 10–18.

EXHIBIT 23.4   **Corporate Bond Ratings and Default Probabilities**

percent

Standard & Poor's	Default probability[1]	Moody's	Default probability[2]	
AAA	0.12	Aaa	0.12	Investment grade
AA	0.33	Aa	0.24	
A	0.75	A	0.54	
BBB	3.84	Baa	2.16	
BB	14.45	Ba	11.17	
B	33.02	B	31.99	Subinvestment grade
CCC	61.35	Caa	60.83	
CC		Ca		
C		C		

[1] Percentage defaulting within 5 years based on default rates between 1981 and 2003.
[2] Percentage defaulting within 5 years based on default rates between 1970 and 2003.

Source: Standard & Poor's RatingsDirect database, *Statistical Review of Moody's Rating Performance, 1920–2003* (Moody's, 2004), McKinsey Corporate Performance Center analysis.

for Standard & Poor's and Moody's. From these numbers, it is evident that a capital structure rated B or lower is probably not a wise leverage target because of the very high probability of default.

2. Ratings largely determine the company's access to the debt markets. Below investment-grade BBB ratings, the opportunities for debt funding are much smaller because many investors are barred from investing in sub-investment-grade debt.

3. Credit ratings are nowadays important elements in the communication to shareholders. Managers should be able to explain whether their company can or should maintain its current rating. The stock market bubble of the 1990s and the 2008 credit crisis have underlined the importance of a company's credit quality to equity investors as well as debt providers.

Drivers of Credit Ratings: Coverage and Size

The process of setting a credit rating for a company is elaborate and relies considerably on qualitative assessment of the historical and likely future performance of a company's management and business. Nevertheless, empirical evidence shows that credit ratings are primarily related to two financial indicators:[23] (1) *size* in terms of sales or market capitalization and (2) interest *coverage* in terms of EBITA; earnings before interest, taxes, depreciation, and amortization (EBITDA); or debt divided by interest expenses.[24]

[23] See, for example, J. Pettit, C. Fitt, S. Orlov, and A. Kalsekar, "The New World of Credit Ratings," UBS research report (September 2004).
[24] Standard & Poor's also uses measures such as free flow from operations (FFO), which differs somewhat from EBITDA but essentially also is aimed at capturing operational cash flow.

Size is especially relevant in its extremes: for example, all companies with AAA ratings have market capitalizations higher than $50 billion. One explanation for this relationship is that larger companies are more likely to diversify their risk. But the relationship between size and credit rating does not help managers set capital structure policy, because size is not really within their control and makes a difference only for very large or very small companies.

Coverage is much more relevant when setting capital structure targets. A company's interest coverage is a straightforward indicator of its ability to comply with its short-term debt service obligations. Interest coverage is defined as follows:

$$\text{Coverage} = \frac{\text{EBITA}}{\text{Interest}} \text{ or } \frac{\text{EBITDA}}{\text{Interest}} \text{ or } \frac{\text{Net Debt}}{\text{EBITDA}}$$

EBITA interest coverage measures how many times a company could pay its interest commitments out of its ongoing operational cash flow if it invested only an amount equal to its annual depreciation charges to keep business running. When expressed as EBITDA to interest, interest coverage measures available cash flow before any capital expenditures and taxes. Debt coverage—net debt to EBITDA—is sometimes used instead of interest coverage to measure the company's ability to service its debt in the short term as it gives deeper insight when companies use large amounts of convertibles or low-interest, short-term debt. In terms of straightforward EBIT(D)A interest coverage, the companies' financial health might look very strong. However, when they need to roll over their convertible or low-interest debt into regular debt funding at higher rates, their interest coverage will plummet. Under these circumstances, net debt to EBITDA will give a more accurate picture than EBIT(D)A interest coverage.

Many models have attempted to explain credit ratings or default probabilities from a company's financial and business characteristics.[25] From our own analyses, we find that a limited number of credit ratios explain credit rating fairly well, with interest coverage as the single most significant indicator.[26] Exhibit 23.5 summarizes the results for a sample containing all U.S. and European companies rated by Standard & Poor's (excluding financial institutions). It shows how interest coverage is a key explanatory variable for the Standard & Poor's credit ratings, with more than 45 percent of rating differences explained by interest coverage alone.

Analyzing the data further, we also find that coverage for a given credit rating differs by industry in a predictable way. In Exhibit 23.6, we show how

---

[25] For an overview, see R. Cantor, "An Introduction to Recent Research on Credit Ratings," *Journal of Banking and Finance* 28, no. 11 (2004): 2565–2573; and E. Altman, "Financial Ratios, Discriminant Analysis, and the Prediction of Corporate Bankruptcy," *Journal of Finance* 23, no. 4 (1968): 589–609.
[26] This holds for EBITA as well as EBITDA coverage measures.

EXHIBIT 23.5 **Interest Coverage Explaining Credit Rating**

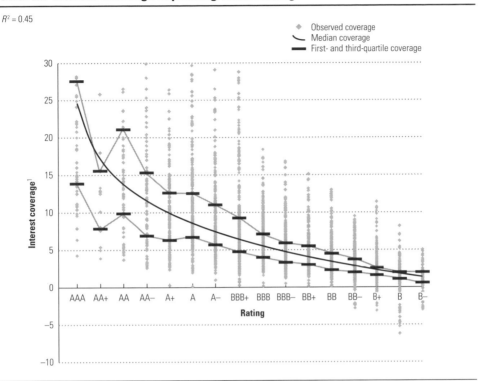

$R^2 = 0.45$

◆ Observed coverage
⌣ Median coverage
━ First- and third-quartile coverage

[1] EBITA/interest.

Source: Standard & Poor's RatingsDirect database, McKinsey Corporate Performance Center analysis.

coverage ratios differ across sectors for a given credit rating. For example, telecom companies will have better credit ratings than steel companies at the same level of coverage. To understand why this is the case, we estimated the volatility of EBITDA over the five years preceding the date of the credit rating.[27] Industries with more volatile EBITDAs need higher coverage to attain a given credit rating, as the exhibit shows. This makes sense: for a given level of interest coverage, more volatility makes it more probable that a company will lack sufficient cash flow to service its interest commitment in the future. As a result, the credit rating will be lower.

By taking into account the different interest coverage requirements across sectors, it is possible to develop an estimate in any sector of a company's likely credit rating for a given level of operating profit and interest. Obviously, we could further refine the analysis by including more explanatory ratios, such as net debt to EBITDA, free flow from operations (FFO) to interest, solvency, and

[27] EBITDA volatility is measured here as the average standard deviation of relative annual changes in EBITDA for the largest 25 companies in each sector in terms of market capitalization.

EXHIBIT 23.6 **Interest Coverage and Credit Rating for Selected Industry Sectors**

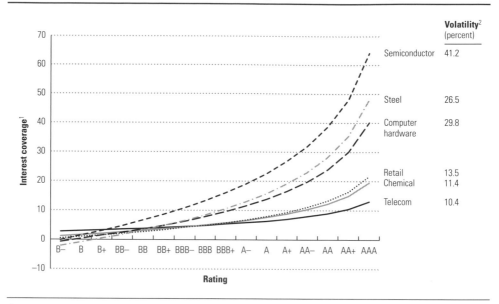

¹ EBITDA/interest.
² Median volatility of EBITDA over the prior 5 years for the largest 25 companies in each sector.

Source: Standard & Poor's RatingsDirect database, McKinsey Corporate Performance Center analysis.

more. However, these ratios are often highly correlated, so calculating them does not always add explanatory power.

Credit Spreads from Credit Ratings

From a company's credit rating, you can estimate the interest rate payable on its debt funding. The difference between the yields on corporate bonds and risk-free bonds—the *credit spread*—is greater for companies with lower credit ratings, because their probability of default is higher. Exhibit 23.7 plots cumulative default probabilities against the credit ratings over 5 and 10 years and the average credit spreads for each rating between 1992 and 2004.

Notice that the probability of default does not increase in a straight line with descending credit rating; the difference in default probability between AAA and BBB is much smaller than the difference between a BBB and a B rating. Spreads reflect the increasing default probabilities almost proportionally. However, after the investment-grade benchmark of BBB, the spread increases more sharply, although this effect is less pronounced when the three years immediately following the peak of the bubble in 2000 are excluded. One explanation is that, as noted earlier in this chapter, some institutional investors cannot invest in debt that is below investment grade (BBB–), so the debt market is considerably smaller for below-investment-grade debt, and interest rates

EXHIBIT 23.7 **Default Probability and Credit Spread**

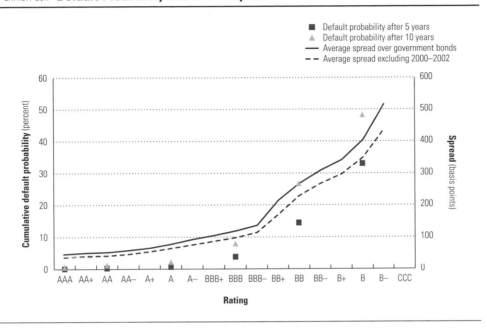

Source: Bloomberg, Standard & Poor's RatingsDirect database, McKinsey Corporate Performance Center analysis.

correspondingly higher. Apart from this turning point at the investment-grade level, spreads appear to follow changes in default probabilities fairly closely.

Leverage and Solvency versus Coverage

The leverage measure used in the academic literature is leverage in terms of market value, defined as the market value of debt (D) over the market value of debt plus equity (E):

$$\text{Leverage} = \frac{D}{D+E}$$

This ratio measures how much of the company's enterprise value is claimed by debt holders and is an important concept for estimating the benefits of tax shields arising from debt financing. It is therefore also a crucial input in calculating the weighted average cost of capital (WACC; see Chapter 10 on capital structure weights).

Leverage, however, suffers from several drawbacks as a way to measure and target a company's capital structure. First, companies could have very low leverage in terms of market value but still be at a high risk of financial distress if their short-term cash flow is low relative to interest payments. High-growth companies usually have very low levels of leverage, but this does not mean their debt is low-risk. A second drawback is that market value can change radically (especially for high-growth, high-multiple companies), making leverage a fast-moving indicator. For example, several European telecom companies, including Royal KPN Telecom and France Telecom, had what appeared to be reasonable levels of debt financing in terms of leverage during the stock market boom of the late 1990s. Credit providers appeared willing to provide credit even though the underlying near-term cash flows were not very high relative to debt service obligations. But when their market values plummeted in 2001, leverage for these companies shot up, and financial distress loomed. Thus, it is risky to base a capital structure target on a market-value-based measure.

This does not mean that leverage and coverage are fundamentally divergent measures. Far from it: they actually measure the same thing but over different time horizons. For ease of explanation, consider a company that has no growth in revenues, profit, or cash flows. For this company, we can express the leverage and coverage as follows:[28]

$$\text{Leverage} = \frac{D}{D+E}$$

$$= \frac{\text{Interest}_1 + \text{PV}(\text{Interest}_2) + \cdots + \text{PV}(\text{Interest}_\infty)}{\text{NOPLAT}_1 + \text{PV}(\text{NOPLAT}_2) + \cdots + \text{PV}(\text{NOPLAT}_\infty)}$$

$$\text{Coverage} = \frac{\text{EBITA}}{\text{Interest}} = \frac{1}{(1-T)} \times \frac{\text{NOPLAT}}{\text{Interest}}$$

where
D = market value of debt
E = market value of equity
NOPLAT_t = net operating profit less adjusted taxes in year t
Interest_t = interest expenses in year t
T = tax rate

The market value of debt captures the present value of all future interest payments, assuming perpetual rollover of debt financing. The enterprise value $(E + D)$ is equal to the present value of future NOPLAT, because depreciation equals capital expenditures for a zero-growth company. A leverage ratio therefore measures the company's ability to cover its interest payments over a very long term. The problem is that short-term interest obligations are what mainly get a company into financial distress. Coverage, in contrast, focuses only on the short-term part of the leverage definition, keeping in mind that NOPLAT roughly equals EBITA $\times$ $(1 - T)$. Coverage indicates how easily a company can service its debt in the near term.

Both measures are meaningful, and they are complementary. For example, if market leverage were very high in combination with strong current interest

---

[28] The simplifying no-growth assumption is for illustration purposes only. For a growing company, the same point holds.

coverage, this could indicate the possibility of future difficulties in sustaining current debt levels in, for example, a single-product company faced with rapidly eroding margins and cash flows because the product is approaching the end of its life cycle. Despite very high interest coverage today, such a company might not be given a high credit rating, and its capacity to borrow could be limited.

Solvency measures of debt over total assets or debt over book value of equity are seldom as meaningful as coverage or leverage. The key reason is that these book value ratios fail to capture the company's ability to comply with debt service requirements in either the short or the long term. Market-to-book ratios can vary significantly across sectors and over time, making solvency a poor proxy for long-term ability to service debt. The Dutch publishing company Wolters-Kluwer, for example, had low book equity for years because under Dutch Generally Accepted Accounting Principles (GAAP) it had written off all goodwill on acquisitions directly against equity. In spite of very low solvency, with a ratio of equity to total assets below 20 percent, Wolters-Kluwer had a credit rating around A, well within investment grade.

Solvency becomes more relevant in times of financial distress, when a company's creditors use it as a rough measure of the available collateral. Higher levels of solvency usually indicate that debt holders stand better chances of recovering their principal and interest due—assuming that asset book values are reasonable approximations of asset liquidation values. However, in a going concern, solvency is much less relevant for deciding capital structure than coverage and leverage measures.

Market-Based Rating Approach

Alternative approaches to credit assessment have been developed based on the notion that equity can be modeled as a call option on the company's enterprise value, with the debt obligations as the exercise price.[29] Using option valuation models and market data on price and volatility of the shares, these approaches estimate the future probability of default, that is, the probability that enterprise value will be below the value of debt obligations.[30] The advantage is that all information captured by the equity markets is directly translated into the default estimates. Traditional credit ratings tend to lag changes in a company's performance and outlook because they aim to measure credit quality "through the cycle"[31] and are less sensitive to short-term fluctuations in quality.

---

[29] This is because equity is a residual claim on the enterprise value after payment of principal and interest for debt. It has value only to the extent that enterprise value exceeds debt commitments. See R. Merton, "On the Pricing of Corporate Debt: The Risk Structure of Interest Rates," *Journal of Finance* 29 (1974): 449–470; or, for an introduction, R. Brealey and S. Myers, *Principles of Corporate Finance*, 7th ed. (New York: McGraw-Hill, 2003), chap. 24.

[30] See P. Crosbie and J. Bohn, "Modeling Default Risk," Moody's KMV White Paper (December 2003).

[31] See E. Altman and H. Rijken, "How Rating Agencies Achieve Rating Stability," *Journal of Banking and Finance* 28, no. 11 (2004): 2679–2714.

The disadvantage of market-based ratings is that no fundamental analysis is performed on the company's underlying business and financial health. If equity markets have missed some critical information, the resulting estimates of default probability do not reflect their omission. As we discussed in Chapter 17, markets reflect company fundamentals most of the time, but not always. When they do not, the market-based rating approaches would incorrectly estimate default risk as well, as happened in the case of Royal KPN Telecom, which took the equity market (and the traditional rating agencies, for that matter) by surprise in 2001, suffering a sudden decline in both share prices and credit ratings.[32]

SHORT-TERM STEPS TO MANAGE CAPITAL STRUCTURE

Empirical analyses have demonstrated that companies actively manage their capital structure and stay within certain leverage boundaries. Companies are much more likely to issue equity when they are overleveraged relative to this target, and much less likely when they are underleveraged.[33] They make adjustments to regain their target capital structure after they have missed it for one or two years, rather than immediately after each change in leverage; continual adjustment would be impractical and costly due to share price volatility and transaction costs.[34] This is also the pattern we would expect to find if companies were targeting interest coverage: changes in share price and leverage typically precede changes in operating cash flows and therefore any increase in coverage.

When managing their capital structures, companies need to take account of the transaction costs and signaling effects associated with different adjustments. Transaction costs are easier to assess than signaling effects: in general, equity issues are more expensive than bond issues, which in turn are more expensive than bank loans. For adjustments in all categories of capital, there are powerful economies of scale, because the costs are largely fixed (see Exhibit 23.8). Thus, from the perspective of transaction costs, equity becomes effective only for larger amounts. For smaller funding amounts, bank loans are the typical solution.

For listed companies, capital structure decisions are complicated by the fact that they send the capital markets signals about a company's prospects. Investors assume that managers possess more information than themselves about the company's true business and financial outlook. Of course, managers

---

[32] See Crosbie and Bohn, "Modeling Default Risk," 23.

[33] P. Marsh, "The Choice between Equity and Debt: An Empirical Study," *Journal of Finance* 37, no. 1 (1982): 121–144.

[34] See, for example, M. Leary and M. Roberts, "Do Firms Rebalance Their Capital Structures?" *Journal of Finance* 60, no. 6 (2005): 2575–2619.

EXHIBIT 23.8 **Transaction Costs for Equity and Debt Financing**

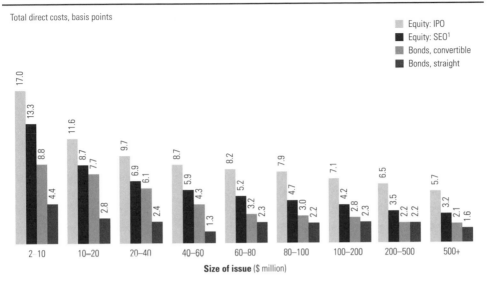

Total direct costs, basis points

- Equity: IPO
- Equity: SEO[1]
- Bonds, convertible
- Bonds, straight

Size of issue ($ million)

[1] Seasoned equity offering.

Source: L. Inmoo, S. Lochhead, J. Ritter, and Q. Zhao, "The Costs of Raising Capital," *Journal of Financial Research* 19, no. 1 (1996): 59–74. Analysis of transaction costs of around 4,500 equity and bond issues, 1990–1994.

can and do communicate directly with investors, but investors tend to give less credence to words than to actions. Therefore, they analyze management's decisions on offerings or repurchases of debt and equity and on dividends for any signals of the company's financial prospects. Managers should be aware of giving out such signals before adjusting capital structures. However, keep in mind that although these signals may lead to short-term price reactions, they do not increase or decrease intrinsic value as such. Managers should ensure that sooner or later they can meet any value expectations they have set in the capital markets. Signaling unrealistically rosy prospects will ultimately backfire.

Signaling effects, coming on top of any effect on intrinsic value made by a change in capital structure, may dampen but could also amplify that effect. For example, cutting dividends not only provides a signal of lower future cash flows but also decreases leverage, thereby reducing tax shields on interest and giving management more slack in discretionary investments, making the cut's impact on share price even more likely to be negative.

There are some key trade-offs among alternative financing instruments used to resolve funding shortages and surpluses. In principle, increasing leverage and returning cash to investors typically meets with positive market reactions. Decreasing leverage and asking investors for more capital typically leads to negative price reactions.

Raising Additional Funds

Consider three fundamental ways to resolve funding needs: cutting dividends, issuing new equity, or issuing new debt. Obviously, companies can choose from many more instruments to raise cash, including preferred stock, convertibles, warrants, and more exotic hybrid forms of capital. However, the signaling effects of these instruments derive from the essential trade-offs discussed here.

If a company already has too much debt relative to its long-term leverage target, it probably has no alternative but to raise equity. If management does have a choice, it should probably first consider issuing debt, which gives the least negative signals. Issuing equity comes second because it stimulates more negative price reactions—and higher transaction costs unless large amounts are raised. Dividend cuts are more a measure of last resort because they send a highly negative signal to the capital markets, typically causing share prices to fall substantially. This order of preference corresponds with survey findings on how CFOs make capital structure decisions.[35]

Cutting dividends   In our experience, companies are extremely reluctant to cut dividends to free up funding for new investments, because the stock market typically interprets such reductions as a signal of lower future cash flows. Share prices on average decline around 9 percent on the day a company announces dividend cuts or omissions.[36] Furthermore, some investor groups count on dividends being paid out every year, and skipping these dividends will force them to liquidate parts of their portfolios, leading to unnecessary transaction costs. Investors are likely to react negatively to dividend cuts unless management has very compelling arguments for withholding dividends to invest in future growth. (Some research does indeed suggest that companies with better growth opportunities are less severely punished by the stock market.[37]) Finally, the amount of funding freed up by cutting dividends is limited, so dividend cuts alone are unlikely to resolve more substantial funding shortages.

Issuing equity   Issuing equity also is likely to lead to a drop in share prices in the short term. Typically, share prices decline by around 3 percent on announcements of seasoned equity offerings.[38] Because investors assume that managers have superior insights into the company's true business and financial outlook, they believe managers will issue equity only if a company's shares

---

[35] See Graham and Campbell, "How Do CFOs Make Decisions?"

[36] P. Healey and K. Palepu, "Earnings Information Conveyed by Dividend Initiations and Omissions," *Journal of Financial Economics* 21, no. 2 (1988): 149–175.

[37] L. Lang and R. Litzenberger, "Dividend Announcements: Cash Flow Signaling versus Free Cash Flow Hypothesis," *Journal of Financial Economics* 24, no. 1 (1989): 181–192.

[38] See, for example, B. Eckbo and R. Masulis, "Seasoned Equity Offerings: A Survey," in *Handbooks in Operations Research and Management Science* 9, ed. R. Jarrow, V. Maksimovic, and W. Ziemba (Amsterdam: Elsevier, 1995); and C. Smith, "Investment Banking and the Capital Acquisition Process," *Journal of Financial Economics* 15, no. 1/2 (1986): 3–29.

are overvalued in the stock market. Therefore, the share price will decrease in the short term on the announcement of an equity issuance, even if it is not actually overvalued.

Issuing debt   There is ample evidence showing that investors interpret the issuance of new debt much more positively than equity offerings. Because companies commit to fixed future interest payments that can be withheld only at considerable cost, investors see the issuance of debt as a strong signal that future cash flows will be sufficient. Investors also know that debt is more likely to be issued when management perceives a company's share price to be undervalued. As managers are assumed to be better informed on the company's future, share prices typically respond less negatively than when new equity is issued. Empirical evidence shows that the price reaction is typically flat.[39]

Redeeming Excess Funds

Turning to funding surpluses, consider three basic alternatives for handling excess cash: dividend increases, share repurchases or extraordinary dividends, and debt repayments. Assuming there is no need to pay down debt to target levels, managers should probably first consider share repurchases or extraordinary dividends, since these send a favorable signal to capital markets. Voluntary debt repayments do not represent a positive signal, unless the company is close to or in financial distress. Increasing the dividend payout ratio provides the strongest signal. However, this is an attractive measure only if the company can indeed deliver against the investor expectations for higher, ongoing dividends.

The major caveats surrounding the return of cash to investors concern the market's growth expectations for the company in question and potential tax implications for investors. High-growth companies could face negative reactions if the market interprets returning cash as a signal that management has lowered growth expectations (although in our experience, cash returns are rarely unexpected). Regular or extraordinary dividend payouts could lead to higher taxable income for shareholders, depending on the jurisdiction and their individual tax position.

Dividend increases   Companies increasing their dividends generally receive positive market reactions of around 2 percent on the day of announcement.[40]

---

[39] See, for example, W. Mikkelson and M. Partch, "Valuation Effects of Security Offerings and the Issuance Process," *Journal of Financial Economics* 15, no. 1/2 (1986): 31–60; and Smith, "Investment Banking and the Capital Acquisition Process."

[40] See, for example, S. Benartzi, R. Michaely, and R. Thaler, "Do Changes in Dividends Signal the Future or the Past?" *Journal of Finance* 52, no. 3 (1997): 1007–1034; and J. Aharony and I. Swarey, "Quarterly Dividends and Earnings Announcements and Stockholders," *Journal of Finance* 35, no. 1 (1980): 1–12.

For companies that initiate dividend payments, the impact is even greater.[41] In general, investors interpret dividend increases as good news about the company's long-term outlook for future earnings and cash flows. On average they are right, according to the evidence. Most companies that increase their dividend payout usually do so after strong earnings growth and when they are able to maintain such high levels of earnings in the year following the dividend increase. Companies that start paying dividends for the first time typically continue to experience high rates of earnings growth.

The drawback of increasing dividends is that investors interpret this action as a long-term commitment to higher payouts. As noted earlier, the stock market severely penalizes companies for cutting dividends from customary long-term levels. Managers should be confident that future cash flows from operations will be sufficient to pay for capital expenditures as well as higher dividends. In other words, dividend increases are useful to handle structural cash surpluses over time but much less suitable for a one-time surplus payout.

Higher dividends are not necessarily good news for investors. They can also signal that companies have permanently lower future investment opportunities. They could herald declining share prices if the stock market had expected the company to continue to invest strongly in valuable growth opportunities.

Share repurchases   In the 1990s, share repurchases gained notable importance as an alternative way to distribute cash to shareholders. In 1999, for example, share repurchases totaled $181 billion, close to the $216 billion in regular dividend payments for companies listed on the New York Stock Exchange.[42] Even in the wake of the stock market downturn in 2000, major companies in different sectors have continued to repurchase shares on a large scale; examples include Unilever, Marks & Spencer, ExxonMobil, IBM, and Viacom.

Investors typically interpret share repurchases positively for several reasons. First, buying back shares indicates to investors that management believes the company's shares are undervalued. If shares were overvalued, management should pay down debt instead, to return cash to the capital markets. If management itself buys back shares, this effect is reinforced. Second, a share buyback shows that managers are confident that future cash flows are strong enough to support future investments and debt commitments. Third, it signals that the company will not spend its excess cash on value-destroying investments. Fourth, share buybacks can result in lower taxes for investors than dividend payments in countries where capital gains are taxed at lower rates. In the United States, this is the case for most investors, which partly explains the

---

[41] Healey and Palepu, "Earnings Information."
[42] See J. Pettit, "Is a Share Buyback Right for Your Company?" *Harvard Business Review* 79, no. 4 (2001): 141–147.

more prominent role of buybacks in the United States than in some European countries.

Contrary to widespread belief among analysts and managers, share buybacks or dividend increases do not create intrinsic value by themselves.[43] As we pointed out in Chapter 2, most companies' share repurchases lead to an increase in earnings per share (EPS). But that does not mean that any value is created. In the process, the company's price-to-earnings ratio drops by the same percentage so that the price per share does not change. What matters is the signaling, not the EPS accretion. Research shows that share prices on average increase 2 to 3 percent on the day of announcement for smaller repurchase programs (in which less than 10 percent of shares outstanding are acquired through open-market transactions).[44] For far less frequent larger repurchase programs, in which usually around 15 percent of shares are bought back through tender offers, price increases are even stronger, at around 16 percent on announcement.[45]

In contrast to dividend increases, share buyback programs are not seen as long-term commitments, so buybacks are more suitable for one-off cash distributions. Sometimes companies have built up very high cash positions because of strong historical earnings combined with decreased investment opportunities. For example, in 2004 Microsoft announced that it would repay a record $75 billion over the next four years in cash to its shareholders, mostly in share repurchases. In other cases, companies end up with large cash balances after portfolio divestments, as IBM did in the second half of the 1990s, and they use the cash proceeds to repurchase shares.

As an alternative to share repurchases, a company could declare an extraordinary dividend payout, as Microsoft did in 2004 as part of its cash return program. Microsoft paid out a significant portion in the form of an extraordinary dividend because of its concern that the share repurchase was so massive that it would swamp the liquidity in the market for Microsoft stock. The drawback of extraordinary dividends, compared with share repurchases, is that the dividend forces the cash payout on all shareholders, regardless of their preferences for capital gains or dividends. A share repurchase program at least leaves this decision to the shareholder, who is in the best position to decide whether it would be more beneficial to receive cash or hold on to capital gains.

---

[43] We abstract here from any value created by higher leverage. For most share repurchases and dividend increases, this value is typically small (see also note 18 in this chapter).

[44] In smaller programs, companies typically buy their own shares at no premium or a limited premium in so-called open-market purchases. Larger programs are often organized in the form of tender offers in which companies announce that they will repurchase a particular amount of shares at a significant premium. See, for example, R. Comment and J. Jarrell, "The Relative Signaling Power of Dutch-Auction and Fixed Price Self-Tender Offers and Open-Market Repurchases," *Journal of Finance* 46, no. 4 (1991): 1243–1272.

[45] T. Vermaelen, "Common Stock Repurchases and Market Signaling: An Empirical Study," *Journal of Financial Economics* 9, no. 2 (1981): 138–183.

In most cases, announcements of share repurchase programs and extraordinary dividends are no surprise to the stock market. But in those cases where they are a surprise, they tend to signal insufficient valuable growth opportunities for the company. An interesting example is that of Merck, one of the largest pharmaceutical companies worldwide.[46] In 2000, it announced a $10 billion share repurchase, which led to a 15 percent fall in its share price in the next four weeks (although the initial price reaction was favorable). Investors apparently assumed that Merck had been unable to find interesting research and development opportunities and could no longer maintain its long-term earnings growth target of 20 percent.

Debt repayment   The third option to reduce excess cash balances is to repay debt—for example, by buying back corporate bonds in the market. Unless the company needs to pay down debt to recover from financial distress, this typically does not meet with positive stock market reactions. First, it is hard to interpret this as an indication of undervaluation of bonds or debt. Bonds are less likely to be undervalued than stocks unless the company is in financial distress. Thus, buying back bonds is more likely to indicate to investors that management believes stocks are overvalued; otherwise, management would buy back stocks. Second, it signals that future cash flows may not be sufficient to support current levels of debt and that management therefore needs to reduce the corporate debt burden now, while it has the cash to do so. Third, as for all cash returns to investors, debt repayments could signal a lack of investment opportunities.

For financially distressed companies, buying back bonds can send a positive signal to the equity markets. For such companies, bond prices go up and down with the enterprise value, just as share prices do. In this situation, a bond buyback could therefore also be a credible signal that management believes the bonds are undervalued (and because in this case bonds are similar to equity, this must also mean that shares are undervalued). For example, when the Swiss-Swedish engineering company ABB announced a €775 million bond buyback in July 2004, its share price increased 4 percent on the day of the announcement. The stock market apparently saw the buyback as further evidence that the company was on a trajectory to recover from an earlier financial crisis.

DESIGNING A LONG-TERM CAPITAL STRUCTURE

We recommend a straightforward approach to developing a long-term capital structure that works hand in hand with the business strategy. It consists of

---

[46] For this and more examples of share repurchases, see Pettit, "Is a Share Buyback Right for Your Company?" (note 42).

three stages: (1) project the funding surplus or deficit; (2) develop a target capital structure; and (3) decide on tactical measures, such as share repurchases, changes in dividend payout, and share or debt issuance. As we describe each of these stages in detail, we will illustrate the approach with a straightforward numerical example.

Project Funding Surplus or Deficit

It is important to understand a company's strategy and its implications for future cash flows before setting out to develop a capital structure. The structure should support the strategy by providing enough funding for business operations and planned investments, enough flexibility to capture unexpected investment opportunities, and enough robustness to withstand adverse business conditions. Surveys among financial executives show that they put more emphasis on preserving financial robustness and flexibility than on minimizing the cost of capital.[47] As we noted earlier, this is a sound approach: the potential harm to a company's operations and business strategy from a bad capital structure is greater than the potential benefits from tax shields and managerial discipline.

Estimate expected operating and investment cash flows   Based on a company's strategy and business plans, estimate the expected future cash flows from operations and the requirements for future capital expenditures and acquisitions, net of any planned divestments.

Analyze exposure to business risks   Understand the uncertainty around the cash flow projections. The more cash flows fluctuate across the business cycle, the more you should aim for a robust target capital structure. As an example, try to estimate how quickly and how far earnings have dropped over the past years in a typical downturn. In the semiconductor industry, for example, companies maintain large buffers above targeted credit ratings and coverage ratios so that they remain financially sound in a cycle downturn.

Scope potential for unexpected investment opportunities   Sometimes, acquisition and investment opportunities are hard to predict or quantify. In such cases, a target capital structure should allow for more flexibility, leaving excess funding capacity over and above targeted credit rating and ratios. An example can be found in cyclical industries, such as commodity chemicals, where investment spending typically follows profits, leading to excess capacity when the new plants come on line simultaneously. Over the cycle, a company can substantially outperform its competitors if it develops a countercyclical strategic capital structure and maintains less debt than might otherwise be optimal.

---

[47] See Graham and Campbell, "How Do CFOs Make Decisions?"

During bad times, it will then have the flexibility to make investments when its competitors cannot.[48]

Project as-is financing surplus or deficit   Project the free cash flows from operations and investments as well as the financing cash flows resulting from the current capital structure as if unchanged. Project the resulting future funding deficit or surplus flow, and assume it is balanced by additional short-term debt or excess cash, respectively.

A simple example can illustrate (see Exhibit 23.9). Assume a company called CashWise is planning for its capital structure over the 2010–2015 period. In 2009, it realized sales of €10 billion per year and a healthy earnings before interest and taxation (EBIT) margin on sales of 15 percent with a pretax ROIC of 30 percent. CashWise currently has a BBB– credit rating and an EBIT-to-interest coverage ratio of 6.1. It has developed investment plans for the next six years to boost its sales growth from a current level of 3.5 percent per year to an average of more than 8 percent per year until 2015. The net investment requirements are accordingly high, amounting to more than €3 billion in net property, plant, and equipment (net PP&E) and working capital over that same period. Furthermore, CashWise is looking out for interesting acquisition opportunities among its smaller competitors. A meaningful acquisition of one of the smaller peers would require an investment outlay of around €1 billion. The capital structure should provide enough flexibility to allow for an add-on acquisition while staying well within investment grade. Based on an analysis of earnings fluctuations over the past 10 years, a typical downturn sees an operating profit decline of around 20 percent.

The as-is financing surplus and deficit projections based on CashWise's business plan are shown in Exhibit 23.10. Clearly, the operating cash flows are more than sufficient to support the planned level of investments for growth. Because CashWise has limited commitments to repay existing debt, the cumulative surplus until 2015 amounts to €2 billion. As a working assumption, assume that this is all invested in excess cash.

Develop Target Capital Structure

Given the estimates for a company's funding requirements, you can start to develop a target capital structure for the next five to 10 years.

Set target credit ratios   Although leverage and coverage ratios all point in the same direction, interest coverage targets are more appropriate for setting

---

[48] T. Augat, E. Bartels, and F. Budde, "Multiple Choice for the Chemical Industry," *McKinsey Quarterly*, no. 3 (2003): 126–136.

EXHIBIT 23.9 **CashWise: Projections of Operational Cash Flows—Expectations, Risks, and Opportunities**

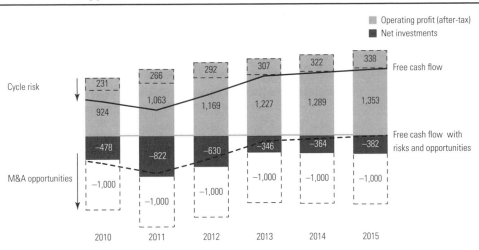

€ million	2009	2010	2011	2012	2013	2014	2015
Income statement							
Revenues	10,000	11,000	12,650	13,915	14,611	15,341	16,108
Cost of goods sold, SG&A	(8,500)	(9,350)	(10,753)	(11,828)	(12,419)	(13,040)	(13,692)
Operating profit (EBIT)	1,500	1,650	1,898	2,087	2,192	2,301	2,416
Interest on existing debt	(245)	(244)	(240)	(230)	(228)	(225)	(222)
Interest on excess cash	–	14	10	20	63	110	161
Profit before taxes	1,255	1,420	1,007	1,877	2,027	2,106	2,355
Taxes[1]	(402)	(426)	(500)	(563)	(608)	(656)	(707)
Net income	853	994	1,167	1,314	1,419	1,530	1,649
Invested capital							
Working capital	1,500	1,628	1,872	2,059	2,162	2,271	2,384
Net PP&E	3,500	3,850	4,428	4,870	5,114	5,369	5,638
Invested capital	5,000	5,478	6,300	6,930	7,276	7,640	8,022
Cash flow statement							
Operating profit (EBIT)		1,650	1,898	2,087	2,192	2,301	2,416
Taxes on operating profit		(495)	(569)	(626)	(657)	(690)	(725)
(Increase) decrease in working capital		(128)	(244)	(187)	(103)	(108)	(114)
(Increase) decrease in invested capital		(350)	(578)	(443)	(244)	(256)	(268)
Free cash flow		677	507	831	1,188	1,247	1,309
Key ratios (percent)							
Revenue growth	3.5	10.0	15.0	10.0	5.0	5.0	5.0
Operating margin	15.0	15.0	15.0	15.0	15.0	15.0	15.0
Pretax ROIC	30.0	30.1	30.1	30.1	30.1	30.1	30.1

[1] Corporate tax rate of 30 percent assumed from 2010 onward.

EXHIBIT 23.10 **CashWise: Projections of As-Is Financing Surplus/Deficit**

€ million

	2009	2010	2011	2012	2013	2014	2015
Balance sheet							
Working capital	1,500	1,628	1,872	2,059	2,162	2,271	2,384
Net PP&E	3,500	3,850	4,428	4,870	5,114	5,369	5,638
Invested capital	5,000	5,478	6,300	6,930	7,276	7,640	8,022
(Excess cash)	–	(198)	(143)	(283)	(905)	(1,578)	(2,295)
Short-term debt	–	–	–	–	–	–	–
Existing debt	3,500	3,480	3,430	3,280	3,255	3,220	3,165
Equity	1,500	2,196	3,013	3,933	4,926	5,997	7,152
Investor funds	5,000	5,478	6,300	6,930	7,276	7,640	8,022
Cash flow statement							
Free cash flow		677	507	831	1,188	1,247	1,309
After-tax interest on existing debt		(171)	(168)	(161)	(159)	(158)	(155)
Existing debt repayment		(20)	(50)	(150)	(25)	(35)	(55)
Dividends		(298)	(350)	(394)	(426)	(459)	(495)
Cash flow existing financing		(489)	(568)	(705)	(610)	(652)	(705)
Funding surplus (deficit)		188	(62)	126	577	595	605
Excess cash investment		(198)	55	(140)	(622)	(672)	(717)
After-tax interest on excess cash		10	7	14	44	77	112
Equity issuance (repayment) and extraordinary dividends		–	–	–	–	–	–
Short-term debt issuance (repayment)		–	–	–	–	–	–
After-tax interest on net short-term debt		–	–	–	–	–	–
New funding		(188)	62	(126)	(577)	(595)	(605)

long-term capital structure targets. As we saw earlier in this chapter, they are more closely correlated with credit ratings and follow directly from projections of future interest (or debt) and operating earnings (or cash flow).[49]

Returning to the CashWise example, the CFO wants to develop a capital structure that justifies a single-A credit rating. This rating target would require an EBIT-to-interest coverage of approximately 9.5 in CashWise's industry. In addition, the CFO wants the structure to be robust enough in a typical business downturn for the company to retain at least a minimum rating of BBB+, giving it unrestricted access to debt markets. To be that robust, CashWise's interest coverage should not drop below 7.5, even in the face of a 20 percent earnings decline. The CFO also wants enough flexibility to make an acquisition of around €1 billion and retain the minimum credit rating.[50] For other credit ratios, no targets are set at the moment, but if any covenants are in place for existing debt, these requirements should of course be observed when setting any target ratios.

---

[49] Leverage ratios require an estimate of debt relative to enterprise value going forward.

[50] We assume that this flexibility for acquisitions is not required in an earnings downturn scenario.

Develop target capital structure over business cycle First identify and understand the key drivers of the financing surpluses (or deficits). The familiar value drivers—growth and return on invested capital—determine uses and sources of *free cash flow from operations.* Higher growth in general leads to greater cash requirements, as investments in net PP&E and working capital usually go up with growth. CashWise is investing €3 billion in growth until 2015, with growth levels peaking at 15 percent in 2011. Higher ROIC leads to lower cash requirements from either higher operating margins over sales or higher turnover of invested capital.[51] As long as CashWise's margins remain at 15 percent, the company can easily support its investments in growth.

In terms of the drivers of *financing cash flow*, the existing debt requires interest and principal payments according to a fixed schedule. By 2015, €335 million of CashWise's existing debt needs to be paid down, with a peak repayment of €150 million in 2012. CashWise has established a fairly conservative policy of paying out about 30 percent of profits in shareholder dividends.

Now you can develop some initial ideas about CashWise's future capital structure. Exhibit 23.11 summarizes its projected coverage over time, relative to the target A and minimum BBB+ rating, and illustrates the structure's robustness and flexibility. The exhibit shows the estimated credit ratings for different combinations of EBITA and net debt.[52] Moving from the bottom right to the upper left in the chart leads to stronger ratings. Furthermore, you can assess a structure's robustness by measuring the vertical distance down to a particular rating line, as this reflects the amount of EBIT that could be lost without falling below that particular rating. Flexibility can be estimated from the horizontal distance to the left of a particular rating line (which represents the amount of additional debt that could be raised without additional earnings). Under the as-is projections, CashWise significantly overshoots its targeted (and minimum) coverage ratios. This is because it retains all excess funding, pushing its net debt position rapidly to below €1 billion by 2015. Given the key drivers just described, the company could consider further increasing its growth and capital spending and/or returning more cash to shareholders by paying out more dividends or repurchasing equity shares.

We assume that total market growth is low and that increasing market share is unlikely to create a lot of value for CashWise, so more aggressive growth is not a realistic strategic option. But by returning more cash to shareholders, CashWise could set a target capital structure that would better fit its strategy. For example, the target projections of EBIT and net debt shown in Exhibit 23.11 lead to an A credit rating if business plans are fully realized.

---

[51] But capital turnover increases have stronger short-term cash impact than margin increases, for the same change in ROIC.

[52] As we discussed in the previous section, more factors drive a credit rating than EBIT and net debt alone. But assuming other key factors such as the company's business risk and management quality are constant, the ratio of EBIT to net debt is a reasonable basis for estimating a company's credit rating. (Note that the EBIT-to-debt ratio is simply the EBIT-to-interest ratio multiplied by the interest rate.)

EXHIBIT 23.11 **CashWise: Capital Structure Coverage Trajectories**

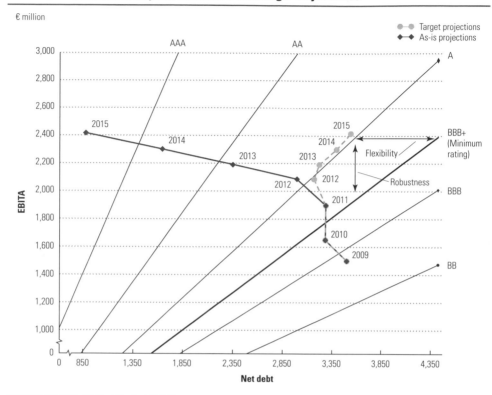

Following these target projections, the cash flow from operating profit could support a net debt position of around €3.5 billion in 2015—almost €2.7 billion more than anticipated in the as-is scenario.

But where does CashWise then stand in terms of robustness and flexibility? How would it get along if the business were to face tighter margins? How much debt could it raise to fund an acquisition if an opportunity arose in the next few years? As the vertical arrows in the chart indicate, CashWise has sufficient robustness to withstand a 20 percent decline in EBIT from 2011 onward so that it would still be rated BBB+ across the cycle. Given the opportunities to scale down growth plans if necessary and reduce dividend payout ratios, its capital structure seems robust enough. Following the horizontal arrows, there is also ample flexibility to maintain such a minimum rating even if the company raised some €1 billion of new debt for a potential acquisition—in addition to any debt capacity in the acquisition target itself.[53]

[53] To be precise, €1 billion of debt capacity is available to finance the equity value of an acquisition, assuming that any debt would be supported by the acquisition's own operations.

Decide on Tactical Measures

The next step is to decide in more detail which instruments to use and when, in order to move toward the targeted trajectory in Exhibit 23.11. In the current example, CashWise needs to decide how and when to return cash to its shareholders. Should it increase its regular dividends, repurchase shares, or pay out an extraordinary dividend?

Increasing regular dividends sends the strongest signal to the stock market that CashWise's outlook is healthy. But any reductions of dividends lead to very negative signals, so you need to be quite sure that an increased dividend can be sustained for many years. Furthermore, dividend increases may lead to higher taxes for certain groups of shareholders. CashWise is cautious about increasing dividends, going for a limited increase from 30 to 35 percent of net income as of 2012. Thus, CashWise retains some flexibility to cover any unforeseen business losses, as it could stop increasing dividends in any future year. Using regular dividends, it can pay out an additional €200 million to shareholders over the next five years.

Repurchasing shares sends a weaker signal on the company's underlying value but gives management more flexibility to change the amounts paid out over the years. Furthermore, in contrast to dividend payments, it offers shareholders the choice of whether to receive any cash. Depending on jurisdiction, share buybacks might also be more tax efficient for the shareholders than dividend payouts. CashWise therefore decides to return the bulk of the excess cash in a €2 billion share repurchase program, starting in 2012. The CFO does not want to exceed this amount over the next years because of concerns that it could distort regular trading in the stock.

Paying out an extraordinary dividend is similar to repurchasing shares in terms of signaling and flexibility. But such payouts give shareholders less freedom to take or leave any cash returns and could be less tax efficient for them. CashWise decides to distribute any remaining cash beyond €2.0 billion in the form of extraordinary dividends. According to current estimates, this would be approximately €200 million between 2013 and 2015.

Exhibit 23.12 shows the projections of CashWise's financial statements, including the targeted cash return measures. Note that until 2012, there is no need to return additional cash to shareholders, because CashWise's investments for growth absorb most of its cash flow and it first needs to step up its interest coverage. As a result, CashWise still has some flexibility for its final decision on how exactly to adjust its capital structure.

Bear in mind that the decision to return cash to shareholders follows from the target capital structure; these decisions should not be made the other way around. As we discussed in the prior section, returning cash to shareholders does not create value in itself. At best, it could send signals to the market about the company's underlying value, thereby possibly accelerating the realization

EXHIBIT 23.12 **CashWise: Projections of Targeted Capital Structure**

€ million

	2010	2011	2012	2013	2014	2015
Balance sheet						
Working capital	1,628	1,872	2,059	2,162	2,271	2,384
Net PP&E	3,850	4,428	4,870	5,114	5,369	5,638
Invested capital	5,478	6,300	6,930	7,276	7,640	8,022
(Excess cash)	(198)	(143)	(112)	(35)	–	–
Short-term debt	–	–	–	–	175	375
Existing debt	3,480	3,430	3,280	3,255	3,220	3,165
Equity	2,196	3,013	3,762	4,056	4,245	4,482
Investor funds	5,478	6,300	6,930	7,276	7,640	8,022
Cash flow statement						
Operating profit (EBIT)	1,650	1,898	2,087	2,192	2,301	2,416
Taxes on operating profit	(495)	(569)	(626)	(657)	(690)	(725)
(Increase) decrease in working capital	(128)	(244)	(187)	(103)	(108)	(114)
(Increase) decrease in invested capital	(350)	(578)	(443)	(244)	(256)	(268)
Free cash flow	677	507	831	1,188	1,247	1,309
After-tax interest on existing debt	(171)	(168)	(161)	(159)	(158)	(155)
Debt repayment	(20)	(50)	(150)	(25)	(35)	(55)
Dividends	(298)	(350)	(457)	(482)	(506)	(531)
Cash flow existing financing	(489)	(568)	(768)	(666)	(698)	(741)
Funding surplus (deficit)	188	(62)	63	521	549	568
Excess cash investment	(198)	55	31	77	35	–
After-tax interest on excess cash	10	7	5	2	–	–
Equity issuance (repayment)	–	–	(100)	(600)	(650)	(650)
Extraordinary dividends	–	–	–	–	(100)	(100)
Short-term debt issuance (repayment)	–	–	–	–	175	200
After-tax interest on net short-term debt	–	–	–	–	(9)	(18)
New funding	(188)	62	(63)	(521)	(549)	(568)

of that value in the share price. It should never drive a company's capital structure.

CREATING VALUE FROM FINANCIAL ENGINEERING

Financial engineering means different things to different people. We define it pragmatically as managing a company's capital structure for maximum shareholder value with financial instruments beyond straight debt and equity. It typically involves more complex and sometimes even exotic instruments such as synthetic leasing, mezzanine finance, securitization, commodity-linked debt, commodity and currency derivatives, and balance sheet insurance.

In general, companies can create much more value for shareholders in their business activities than in financial engineering. As we pointed out in Part

Three, capital markets typically do a good job of pricing financial instruments, and companies will have difficulty boosting their share prices by accessing so-called cheap funding, however complex the funding structures are.

Nevertheless, financial engineering can create shareholder value under specific conditions, both directly (through tax savings or lower costs of funding) and indirectly (for example, by increasing a company's debt capacity so that it can raise funds to capture more value-creating investment opportunities). However, as we discuss in the remainder of this chapter, such benefits need to outweigh any potential unintended consequences that inevitably arise with the complexity of financial engineering.

In this section, we consider three basic tools of financial engineering: derivative instruments that transfer company risks to third parties, off-balance-sheet financing that detaches funding from the company's credit risk, and hybrid financing that offers new risk-return financing combinations.

Derivative Instruments

With derivative instruments, such as forwards, swaps, and options, a company can transfer particular risks to third parties that can carry these risks at a lower cost. For example, many airlines hedge their fuel costs with derivatives to be less exposed to sudden changes in oil prices. Of course, this does not make airlines immune to prolonged periods of high oil prices, because the derivative positions must be renewed at some point in time. But derivatives at least give the airlines some time to prepare business measures such as cost cuts or price increases. Derivatives are not relevant to all companies, and there are many examples where the complexity around the use of derivatives has been badly managed.[54] In general, derivatives are useful tools for financial managers when risks are clearly identified, derivative contracts are available at reasonable prices because of liquid markets, and the total risk exposures are so large that they could seriously harm a corporation's health.

Off-Balance-Sheet Financing

A wide range of instruments fall under the umbrella of off-balance-sheet financing. These include operating leases, synthetic leases, securitization, and project finance. Although the variety of these instruments is huge, they have the common element that companies effectively raise debt funding without carrying the debt on their own balance sheets.

In most cases, off-balance-sheet financing is used to capture tax advantages. For example, many of the largest hotel companies in the United States don't

---

[54] In the 1990s, some high-profile scandals—for example, at Metallgesellschaft, Procter & Gamble, and Orange County, California—underlined the need for such caution.

own most of the hotels they operate. Instead, the hotels themselves are owned by other companies, often structured as partnerships or real estate investment trusts (REITs). Unlike corporations, partnerships and REITs don't pay U.S. income taxes; taxes are paid only by their owners. Therefore, in the United States, placing hotels in partnerships and REITs eliminates an entire layer of taxation. With ownership and operations separated in this manner, total income taxes are lower, so investors in the ownership and operating companies are better off as a group because their aggregate cash flows are higher.

However, these deals are very complex, because they need to ensure that the interests of the owner and management company are aligned. For example, the deals need to define in advance how the REITs and the hotel companies will make decisions about renovating the hotels, terminating the leases, and other situations where the interests of both parties could conflict. Unfortunately, such potential conflicts are sometimes overlooked or are simply too complex to cover in advance. The owners of Mervyn's (a clothing retail chain in the United States) tried to do something similar in 2004 but failed to align the interests of the real estate company and the operating company.[55] While Mervyn's had plenty of other problems, this structure exacerbated the difficulty of improving the company's performance. Mervyn's filed for bankruptcy in 2008. All its stores were closed and its assets liquidated in 2009.

In other cases, off-balance-sheet financing aims primarily at enabling a company to attract debt funding on terms that would have been impossible to realize for traditional forms of debt. A well-known example is the large-scale securitization of customer receivables undertaken by Ford Motor Company and General Motors. Both companies sold large sums of their receivables to fully owned but legally separate entities.[56] Because the receivables represented relatively sound collateral, these entities had better credit ratings and credit terms than their parent companies. This effectively enabled both companies to tap large sums of debt for investments that otherwise would have been difficult to obtain at similar terms—although one can question whether the investments made by Ford and GM resulted in any value creation. More successful examples include the use of project financing for building and running large infrastructure projects such as gas pipelines, toll bridges, or tunnels. Companies (or sometimes governments) in emerging markets and with low credit ratings may have difficulty attracting large sums of debt. But they can use project financing to raise cash for the initial investments; once the infrastructure asset is operational, the interest and principal on the debt are paid to the lender directly from the cash flows from the asset's revenues. In this way, the debt service is assured, even if the company itself goes bankrupt.

---

[55] Emily Thornton, "What Have You Done to My Company?" *BusinessWeek*, December 8, 2008, 40–44.
[56] These represent examples of a so-called special-purpose entity (SPE) or, as it is referred to under U.S. Generally Accepted Accounting Principles, a variable-interest entity (VIE).

Some managers find off-balance-sheet financing attractive because it re-duces the amount of assets shown on the balance sheet and increases the reported return on assets. That is not a good reason to do it. Investors will see through accounting representations, as we discussed in Chapter 16. Fur-thermore, following the latest requirements of U.S. Generally Accepted Ac-counting Principles (GAAP) and International Financial Reporting Standards (IFRS), special-purpose entities for off-balance-sheet financing need to be fully consolidated and shown on the balance sheet.

Hybrid Financing

Hybrid financing involves forms of funding that share some elements of both equity and debt. Examples are convertible debt, convertible preferred stock, and callable perpetual debt. In particular, convertible debt has been widely used in the past decades. The total volume of convertibles issued worldwide amounted to $145 billion in 2003—almost 8 percent of total new debt issuances in that year.[57]

Convertible debt (debt that may be exchanged for common stock in a given proportion within or after a specified period) can make sense when investors or lenders differ from managers in their assessment of the company's credit risk.[58] When the discrepancy is great, it may become difficult or even impossible to achieve agreement on the terms of credit. But a company's credit risk has less impact on credit terms if the debt is convertible. The key reason is that higher credit risk makes the straight-debt component of the convertible less attractive and the warrant component more attractive, so the two components balance each other to an extent. Overall, convertible debt is less sensitive to differences in credit risk assessment and may therefore facilitate agreement on credit terms that are attractive to both parties. This also explains why high-growth companies use this instrument much more than other companies; they usually face more uncertainty about their future credit risk.

Do not issue convertible debt just because it has a low coupon. The coupon is low because the debt also includes a conversion option. It is a fallacy to think that convertible debt is cheap funding. And avoid issuing convertible debt simply because it is a way to issue equity against the current share price at some point in the future when share prices will be much higher. That future value is already priced into the conversion options. Furthermore, if the company's share price does not increase sufficiently, the convertible debt will not be converted to equity, and the company will end up with interest-bearing debt instead.

---

[57] D. Viazza and D. Aurora, "Global Convertibles to Decelerate from Torrid Pace," *Standard & Poor's Research Report*, March 24, 2004.
[58] See M. Brennan and E. Schwartz, "The Case for Convertibles," *Journal of Applied Corporate Finance* 1, no. 2 (1988): 55–64.

SUMMARY

Although a poorly managed capital structure can lead to financial distress and value destruction, capital structure is not a key value driver: For companies whose leverage is already at reasonable levels, the potential to add value is limited, especially relative to the impact of improvements in returns on invested capital and growth. Rather than fine-tuning for the optimal capital structure, managers should make sure the company has enough financial flexibility to support its strategy while at the same time minimizing the risk of financial distress.

REVIEW QUESTIONS

1. Define optimal capital structure. What is the relationship between optimal capital structure, corporate value, and cost of capital? How does the concept of effective capital structure differ from optimal capital structure?

2. Some companies carry essentially no long-term debt and only a minimal amount of short-term debt in their capital structure. Review the balance sheets of Google and Novartis. Provide an explanation for why well-managed and profitable companies appear to undervalue the benefits associated with an optimal capital structure.

3. The degree of company financial risk is measured and reported by independent rating agencies such as Standard & Poor's and Moody's. What factors do these rating agencies evaluate when determining a company's financial risk classification? In what range of financial risk classification do we find most companies?

4. Explain why companies with the same credit rating can have very different capital structures.

5. Describe a process a manager should employ to establish an effective capital structure target.

6. Start-up companies typically have little or no debt. Discuss if and how this fits with value maximization given the cost-benefit trade-offs between different levels of debt and tax savings, overinvestment, business disruption, and investor conflicts.

7. Discuss the importance of the "pecking order" theory for managing the capital structure of a company, in terms of both short-term, tactical financing decisions and long-term, strategic decisions.

8. For which company would you think the issuance of a convertible bond makes more sense: BMW or Tesla? Explain why.

24

Investor Communications

Previous chapters in Part Four explored how to manage a company to create value. The final element of value creation is ensuring that the company's stock market price truly reflects its potential to create value. Many executives still believe that the purpose of investor communications is to achieve the highest possible share price. But the overriding objective of investor communications must be to align a company's share price with management's perspective on the intrinsic value of the company.

A gap between a company's market value and its intrinsic value brings significant disadvantages to all the company's stakeholders. If a company's stock price exceeds its intrinsic value, the price will eventually fall as the company's real performance becomes evident to the market. When that fall comes, employee morale will suffer, and management will have to face a concerned board of directors who may not understand why the price is falling so far and so fast. Too high a share price may also encourage managers to keep it high by adopting short-term tactics, such as deferring investments or maintenance costs, that will hamper value creation in the long run. Conversely, too low a share price has drawbacks as well, especially the threat of takeover. In addition, it makes paying for acquisitions with shares an unattractive option, and may demoralize managers and employees.

Nevertheless, executives worry constantly that their market value isn't high enough or that markets don't understand their company properly. CEOs and CFOs are deeply concerned by their company's share price and spend a large and growing portion of their time on investor communications. They express frustration at the amount of time this effort absorbs and the nature of their interactions with some investors and analysts who are obsessively focused on short-term earnings.

Special thanks to Robert Palter and Werner Rehm for their support and insights on this chapter. We drew heavily on their article "Opening Up to Investors," *McKinsey on Finance* (Spring 2009): 26–31.

Until recently, most companies have approached investor communications in an ad hoc way. Executives receive advice from investor relations consultants, whose backgrounds are typically in public relations rather than finance. But the academic community has recently begun to research investor composition and communications more comprehensively, providing the data from which to construct a systematic approach to investor communications that can help executives align the market price of their company's shares with the company's intrinsic value—the proper goal of investor relations. In addition, a systematic approach helps executives communicate with investors more effectively and efficiently, so it saves them time.

While there are no hard-and-fast formulas for achieving good investor communications, we find that companies can improve in several areas. First, companies need to know whether there really is a material discrepancy between their intrinsic value and their market value that their investor communications should aim to close. Many companies do not analyze the possible gap systematically; they base complaints about their share price on more superficial indicators of value. In fact, for about 80 percent of the thousands of companies we've analyzed over the years, either the market value has been reasonably close to an objective, thorough assessment of the company's intrinsic value, or any gap has been attributable to the market's misvaluation of an entire industry, not just one company. In these cases, better communications cannot be expected to move the company's share price.

A second area of improvement is for companies to understand their investor base. At present, many don't understand their investor base well enough to anticipate how different investor segments are likely to react to their announcements of strategic moves and how the moves of different segments will likely affect their share price.

Finally, many companies don't tailor their communications to the investors who matter most to their share price: the sophisticated intrinsic investors who drive the long-term value of the shares. These sophisticated investors want more transparency and more thoughtful guidance about the future than simple earnings per share (EPS) projections.

INTRINSIC VALUE VERSUS MARKET VALUE

Senior executives often claim that the stock market undervalues or "doesn't appreciate" their company. They say this not just in public, where you would expect them to, but also in private: they really believe that if only they had different investors or if only the investors or analysts understood their company better, then the company would have a higher share price. Yet in many cases these senior executives have not developed their own rigorous, detailed perspective on what their company's share price should be. Their optimistic belief is based on some high-level analysis of price-to-earnings ratios (P/Es) or a stray comment by an analyst that the shares are undervalued.

Any good strategy must begin with an honest assessment of the situation, and a strategy for investor communications is no different. It should start with an estimate of the size of the gap, if any, between management's view of the company's intrinsic value and the stock market value. But in practice, after some thoughtful analysis and probing, we typically find that no significant gap exists or that any gap can be explained by the company's historical performance relative to shareholders' expectations. We will illustrate using two disguised examples, which we call Chemco and PharmaCo.

Example 1: Chemco

Chemco, a large specialty chemicals company, has earned attractive returns on capital, but its product lines are in slow-growth segments, so Chemco's revenue growth has been low. Chemco recently adopted a strategy to buy small companies in faster-growing areas of the industry. The company intends to apply its manufacturing and distribution skills to improve the performance of the acquired companies. The faster-growth segments also have higher returns on invested capital (ROICs). Currently, 18 months since the company made its first acquisitions under this strategy, 5 percent of Chemco's revenues are from the fast-growth segments.

Chemco's managers were concerned that the company's price-to-earnings ratio trailed the P/Es of many companies with which it compared itself. They wondered whether factors such as the company's old-fashioned name or the small number of analysts covering the industry were the cause of the low value.

We began analyzing the apparent discrepancy by assessing Chemco's value relative to companies it thought of as its peers. Some of the supposed peers were 100 percent involved in the fast-growth segments, far more than Chemco, with only 5 percent of its revenues coming from fast-growth segments. Also, some of its peers were going through substantial restructurings, so current earnings were very low. When we segmented Chemco's peers, we found that its earnings multiple (enterprise value divided by earnings before interest, taxes, and amortization—EBITA) was in line with those of its close peers but behind those of the companies in the fast-growing segment (see Exhibit 24.1). A third set of companies had high multiples because of current low earnings due to restructuring. Exhibit 24.1 also shows that Chemco and its closest peers had lower ROICs and much lower growth rates than the other companies. So from a historical performance perspective, Chemco's value was aligned with its performance relative to its closest peers.

Next, we reverse engineered the share price of Chemco and its peers by building a discounted cash flow (DCF) model for each company and estimating what levels of future performance would be consistent with the current share price. Exhibit 24.2 shows that if Chemco increased its revenues at 2 percent per year and maintained its most recent level of margins and capital turnover, its DCF value would equal its current share price. This growth rate was in line

EXHIBIT 24.1 **Chemco: Valuation in Line with Close Peers**

	Enterprise value/EBITA	ROIC, 2009 (percent)	Organic growth, 2007–2009 (percent)
Chemco	8.6	20.5	2.0
Close-peer companies			
California Co.	8.5	19.5	3.1
Texas, Inc.	8.0	12.2	2.5
Florida Associates	6.8	16.1	1.9
Peers in fast-growth segments			
Vermont, Inc.	9.7	33.0	10.0
Montana Co.	11.2	33.9	11.8
Restructuring companies			
Bretagne Co.	9.3	10.0	3.4
Normandy, Inc.	12.2	5.1	1.2

with the implicit growth of its closest peers and lower than the companies in the fast-growing segment.

Finally, we used a DCF model to value management's announced growth aspirations. If Chemco achieved its growth aspirations of 6 percent per year, its DCF value would be $19 billion, suggesting a value gap of 36 percent relative to its current equity value of $14 billion. Thus, there was a gap between management's view of Chemco's intrinsic value and its market value. But could better communication close the gap? Investors were valuing Chemco in line with its closest peers, so Chemco would need to convince investors that the growth strategy was feasible. But there was little evidence the strategy would succeed. Chemco's managers had been in place for at least five years and

EXHIBIT 24.2 **Chemco: Implicit Revenue Growth in Current Share Price Using DCF Model, 2010–2020**

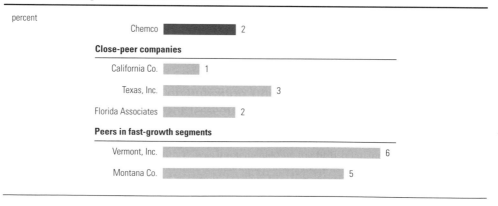

percent	
Chemco	2
Close-peer companies	
California Co.	1
Texas, Inc.	3
Florida Associates	2
Peers in fast-growth segments	
Vermont, Inc.	6
Montana Co.	5

had spent most of that time dealing with issues in its core business. The new strategy required Chemco to grow faster than the industry in its core businesses and to acquire and integrate companies in faster-growth product areas, a very difficult task. It is not surprising that the market had adopted a wait-and-see attitude to rewarding Chemco for its new strategy.

Example 2: PharmaCo

PharmaCo makes specialty pharmaceuticals and has been increasing revenues at around 5 percent per year. PharmaCo's managers believed the company was not fairly valued by the capital market. PharmaCo had a strong product pipeline, with several products coming to market very soon. Management and stock analysts alike expected 23 percent revenue growth for the next three years. Management then expected 13 percent per year for the following 10 years and also expected to maintain its high margins and ROICs.

The DCF value of PharmaCo's management projections was $65 billion, 60 percent more than its market value of $40 billion. To determine the source of this gap, we also valued PharmaCo's closest peers. We used a DCF model to estimate the long-term growth rates implicit in their share prices. The implied long-term growth rate for PharmaCo was 12 percent per year, while the implied long-term growth rate for its peers ranged from 2 percent to 6 percent. So the market had already embedded in PharmaCo's share price a growth premium that was substantial relative to its peers—just not as high as PharmaCo hoped. It is doubtful that better communication could close the value gap, given PharmaCo's already high valuation, both in absolute terms (12 percent expected growth) and relative to peers (twice the expected growth of the next best company).

UNDERSTANDING THE INVESTOR BASE

Does it matter who your investors are? It is not clear whether one investor base is better than another in the sense of helping to align the share price with a company's intrinsic value. But understanding the company's investor base can give managers insights that might help them anticipate how the market will react to important events and strategic actions, as well as help managers improve the effectiveness and efficiency of their investor relations activities.

Most investor classification systems yield only a shallow understanding of how investors actually construct their portfolios. For example, shares of companies that have relatively high book value or earnings multiples are designated "growth" stocks by agencies like Standard & Poor's, which prepare indexes on various classes of stock. Shares of companies outside this group are labeled "value" stocks by the investor community. Similarly, investors and investment funds that tend to invest primarily in growth stocks are called growth

EXHIBIT 24.3 **Growth and Value Stocks: Sales Growth and ROIC**

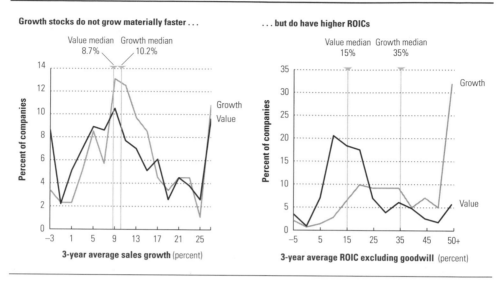

Source: McKinsey Corporate Performance Center analysis.

investors or growth funds, while those that invest primarily in value stocks are called value investors or value funds. And all executives want their shares to be sought out by growth investors, because they believe this will increase their share prices.

Yet, the labels "growth" and "value" are misleading. Most companies classified as growth stocks, as designated by the agencies, and with a high proportion of growth investors don't actually grow their revenues or earnings any faster than value stocks. Not surprising to us, a more important differentiator is ROIC. Growth stocks do have higher ROICs than value stocks. That's why a modestly growing company, like the tobacco company Philip Morris International, ends up on the growth stock list. Their high valuation multiples are not due to high growth; they are due to high ROIC. Exhibit 24.3 shows the distribution of growth versus value stocks on both revenue growth and ROIC. The distributions across revenue growth levels are similar, whereas the distributions across ROIC levels are markedly different.

A common fallacy believed by executives is that they can increase their share price (and valuation multiple) by marketing their shares better to growth investors, because growth investors tend to own shares with higher valuation multiples. But the causality runs in reverse: in our analysis of companies whose stock prices have recently increased enough to shift them from the value classification to the growth classification, what precipitated the rise in their market value was clearly not an influx of growth investors. Rather, growth investors responded to higher multiples, moving into the stock only after the share price had already risen.

In Chapter 18, we introduced an investor classification system based on differences among investors' portfolio-building strategies, which offers a better understanding of which investors drive share prices. We found that the investor category with the most influence on share price movements (except for short-term volatility triggered by company announcements) is the category of intrinsic investors. Compared with others, these investors typically have many fewer companies in their portfolios, so they are able to do deeper and more detailed research on the intrinsic value of each of their investments. They also tend to have longer horizons, so they hold stocks for longer periods.

Based on their research, intrinsic investors form a view of what a stock is worth. If the price rises by a given margin above that value, the intrinsic investor will sell. If a stock's value falls well below what an intrinsic investor considers its real worth, this type of investor will buy in considerable volume, setting a floor to the price. The variation in views on company values held by different intrinsic investors tends to set the upper and lower limits of the trading range of particular stocks. (See Chapter 18 for a more detailed explanation of this effect.)

Companies should therefore focus their investor communications on intrinsic investors. If intrinsic investors form a view of the value of your company consistent with your own, then the market as a whole is likely to value your company as you do, because of intrinsic investors' role in driving share prices. Their understanding of long-term value creation also means they are more likely than other investors to hold on to a stock through periods of short-term volatility (so long as they believe these periods do not reflect a material change in the underlying value of the company) and thus support the management team. They are the investors you should listen to when you want to understand what the market thinks of your company.

COMMUNICATING TO INTRINSIC INVESTORS

Intrinsic investors are sophisticated: they want transparency about results, management's candid assessment of the company's performance, and insightful guidance about the company's targets and strategies. Their role in determining stock prices makes it worth management's while to meet these needs in their investor communications and to avoid oversimplifying.

Transparency

Legislation and accounting rules continually require more transparency. Results can be transparent enough to meet today's regulatory requirements, however, and still fail to meet the standard of transparency that satisfies intrinsic investors. Companies within an industry typically start to disclose information more useful to such investors in response to the investors' explicit demands or the leadership of one or more industry pioneers. For example, the petroleum industry has for many years published detailed fact books that describe oil production and reserves by geography, key parameters that investors want to know when valuing petroleum companies. In pharmaceuticals, companies provide detailed information about their product pipelines at every stage of research and development. In these industries, any company that failed to disclose what others disclose would likely lose the market's trust.

In most industries, however, the level of disclosure and transparency has been less standardized, so management must choose how transparent it wants to be. In these cases, managers are too often cowed by fears that a detailed discussion of the issues and opportunities facing their company will reveal sensitive information to competitors or make it harder to put the best gloss on their results.

In our experience, however, a company's competitors, customers, and suppliers already know more about any business than its managers might expect. For example, there is a cottage industry of photographers dedicated to searching for and publicizing new car models that automotive manufacturers have not yet formally acknowledged. In addition, a company's competitors will be talking regularly to the company's customers and suppliers, who won't hesitate to share information about the company whenever that is in their interest. So revealing details about themselves is unlikely to affect companies as adversely as they might expect, and they should assess the competitive costs and benefits of greater transparency with that in mind.

In some situations, companies might even be able to gain an advantage over their competitors by being more transparent. Suppose a company has developed a new technology, product, or manufacturing process that management feels sure will give the company a lead over competitors. Furthermore, managers believe competitors will be unable to copy the innovation. At a strategic level, disclosing the innovation might discourage competitors from even trying to compete if they believe the company has too great a lead. From an investor's perspective, disclosure of the innovation could increase the company's share price relative to its competitors, thus making it more attractive to potential partners and key employees and reducing the price of stock-based acquisitions.

Sophisticated investors build up their view of a company's overall value by summing the values of its discrete businesses. So they are not much concerned with aggregate results: these are simply averages, providing little insight into how the company's individual businesses might be positioned for future growth and returns on invested capital. At many companies, management teams that desire a closer match between their company's market value and their own assessment might achieve this by disclosing more about the performances of their individual businesses.

One large global electronics company, for example, reports gross margins for both its product and services businesses. But nowhere does it provide operating margins for the different units—information that is crucial to helping investors value businesses with differing levels of expenditure on R&D and selling, general, and administrative costs. Failing to report such information often gives investors the impression that management is trying to obscure some underlying performance issues. In another case, a U.S. media conglomerate provides detailed information by business unit on the income statement but leaves it to investors to sort out the balance sheet by business unit.

How much detail is enough? Concerning financial data, it depends on whether the information is critical for assessing how much value a business can create. For instance, IBM discloses revenue growth in constant currency terms below the business unit level. Nestlé does so at a product and regional level. This kind of detailed financial information is very helpful to investors and gives competitors no insight into business models or sources of strategic advantage that they wouldn't already have learned from competitive intelligence and their own results. As a rule of thumb, companies should provide a detailed income statement for each business unit, down to the level of earnings before interest, taxes, and amortization (EBITA) at least. They should also provide all operating items in the balance sheet—such as property, plant, and equipment (PP&E), accounts receivable, inventories, and accounts payable—reconciled with the consolidated reported numbers. Even companies with a single line of business can improve their disclosures without giving away strategically sensitive information. Whole Foods Market, a U.S. grocery chain, provides ROIC by age of store (see Exhibit 24.4). This gives investors deeper insights into the company's economic life cycle.

Concerning operational data, what to disclose depends on the key value drivers of a business or business unit. Ideally, these should be the metrics that management uses to make strategic or operational decisions. For example, each quarter, the information technology research firm Gartner Group discloses a narrow but highly relevant set of metrics for each of its three business units. As Gartner's CFO explains, the firm publishes only the most important of the metrics that management uses to examine the performance of the business. Companies in some industries, such as steel and airlines, likewise regularly disclose volumes and average prices, as well as the use and cost of energy,

EXHIBIT 24.4 **Whole Foods: ROIC by Age of Store**

Comparable stores (Q1 2008)	Number of stores	Average size (square feet)	Comps (percent)	ROIC (percent)
Over 11 years old	64	28,300	5.4	78
Between 8 and 11 years old	28	33,400	4.0	55
Between 5 and 8 years old	41	33,900	8.3	41
Between 2 and 5 years old	41	44,600	11.7	22
Less than 2 years old (including 5 relocations)	15	58,100	37.7	−2

Source: Whole Foods Annual Report 2007, March 2008 investor presentation, and WholeFoods.com.

EXHIBIT 24.5 **Lowe's: Customer Transactions and Average Ticket Size**

Other metrics	2007	2006	2005
Comparable store sales (decrease)/increase (percent)	5.1	–	6.1
Customer transactions (in millions)	720	680	639
Average ticket	$67.05	$68.98	$67.67
At end of year			
Number of stores	1,534	1,385	1,234
Sales floor square feet (in millions)	174	157	140
Average store size, selling square feet (in thousands)	113	113	113
Return on average assets (percent)	9.5	11.7	11.9
Return on average shareholders' equity (percent)	17.7	20.8	21.5

Source: Company SEC filings.

which are the key drivers of value in these sectors. Lowe's (the hardware retailer) provides helpful information about key value drivers such as the number of transactions and the average ticket size (see Exhibit 24.5).

A common mistake among companies disclosing operating data is to provide different metrics from quarter to quarter, depending on which reflect best on the company. This approach probably hurts more than it helps, because consistency matters to investors: they rightly wonder why management has stopped providing the figures for any given metric and probably assume the figures are worse now than they were when the company published them—and they are probably right.

To make sound investment decisions, intrinsic investors require executives to be honest in their public assessments of their company and its businesses. Yet executives typically approach public announcements less candidly. Most management presentations and publications offer only a celebration of the past year's performance and a less than comprehensive assessment of shortfalls. Very few discuss the impact of strategic trade-offs on the numbers—for instance, how a pricing initiative drove growth at the expense of margins. Companies that openly discuss what happened during the year and disclose where management has identified pockets of underperformance even in good times will help investors assess the quality of the executive team and thus the potential for future value creation. More important, when strategic decisions go bad, investors want to understand what management has learned. Intrinsic investors, in particular, understand that business requires taking risks and that not all of them pay off. Such investors value forthrightness and will probably support a company through a course correction if they have been given enough information previously to develop faith in management's judgment.

Consider the case of Progressive Insurance. In the third quarter of 2006, the company lowered its policy rates to encourage faster growth, making what

CEO Glenn Renwick described as "an explicit trade-off of margin for longer-term customer growth." He acknowledged that "while we will never know the outcome of alternative decisions, we feel very good about the focus on customer growth." When the strategy did not work out as planned, Renwick addressed the subject directly in the first two sentences of his letter to the shareholders in the 2007 annual report: "Profitability and premium growth are both down and they directly reflect the pricing strategy we enacted," he wrote. That strategy "did not produce the aggregate revenue growth we had hoped for." Long-term investors look for this kind of candid assessment when they decide to bet on a management team.

Becoming more transparent can be difficult. Some companies that have preferred greater discretion are not sure whether to change. These are often strongly performing companies with good track records. Over many years, that performance record (frequently a series of steady earnings increases) has permitted them to rebuff investors' demands for more transparency. But it is the nature of every business's life cycle to see growth slowing after years of success as the business matures or markets become more competitive. At that juncture, new strategies are called for if the company is to continue creating value for its shareholders, and these changes of direction need to be communicated to investors if the market price is to continue to reflect the company's true worth, the goal of every investor communications strategy.

In one situation, a large company did not disclose that most of its profits came from aging, low-growth products with a large installed base, while its newer high-growth products were far less profitable due to competition and new technologies. In another case, a consumer products company kept its earnings growing by selectively reducing investments in advertising and promotion. Because of both companies' long histories of success, any sudden disclosure of these changes would surely have caused stock prices to decline, most likely sharply: academic research suggests that when companies in these circumstances fall, they fall hard.[1] Executives at such companies need to decide whether their current predicament is temporary and short-lived or the days of strong growth and high returns are in fact over for the company. If the latter, they clearly need a quick transition plan. If the former, they need to assess whether they should defer greater transparency and the likely price volatility it will cause until they have returned to their growth path.

Guidance

In the view of many companies' executives, the ritual of issuing guidance on their likely earnings per share (EPS) in the next quarter or year is a necessary,

[1] Douglas J. Skinner and R. G. Sloan, "Earnings Surprises, Growth Expectations, and Stock Returns" (working paper, 2002). See also Linda A. Myers and Douglas J. Skinner, "Earnings Momentum and Earnings Management" (working paper, 2002).

EXHIBIT 24.6 **Consumer Packaged Goods: Similar Multiples for Guiders and Nonguiders**

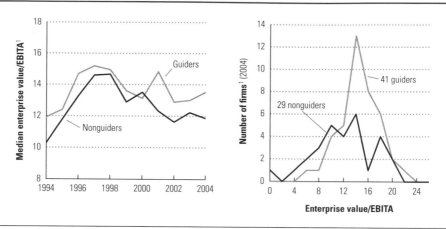

[1] Among companies in packaged foods and meats, personal products, household products, soft drinks, and brewers.

Source: Thomson First Call, McKinsey Corporate Performance Center analysis.

if sometimes onerous, part of communicating with financial markets. We surveyed executives about guidance and found that they saw three primary benefits of issuing earnings guidance: higher valuations, lower share price volatility, and improved liquidity. Yet our analysis found no evidence that those expected benefits materialize. Instead of EPS guidance, we believe executives should provide investors with the broader operational measures shaping company performance, such as volume targets, revenue targets, and initiatives to reduce costs.[2] They can present this information at the beginning of the financial year and issue updates if there are significant changes.

To test whether companies giving EPS guidance were rewarded with higher valuations, we compared the earnings multiples of companies that provided guidance with those that did not, industry by industry. For most industries, the underlying distributions of the two sets of companies were statistically indistinguishable. Exhibit 24.6 shows this pattern for the consumer packaged-goods industry. The left side shows the median multiple of enterprise value to earnings before interest, taxes, and amortization (EBITA) for companies providing guidance and those that didn't each year from 1994 to 2004. The right side shows the distribution across companies for guiders and nonguiders. Although the median for guiders is slightly higher, the graph on the right side shows that the distributions of multiples are similar.

Furthermore, in the year companies begin to offer guidance, contrary to what they must have hoped, their total returns to shareholders (TRS) are no different from those of companies that don't offer it at all, as shown in

[2] Peggy Hsieh, Timothy Koller, and S. R. Rajan, "The Misguided Practice of Earnings Guidance," *McKinsey on Finance* (Spring 2006): 1–5.

EXHIBIT 24.7 **Minimal Impact of Guidance on TRS**

Number of first-year guider firms with returns at given level relative to industry[1]

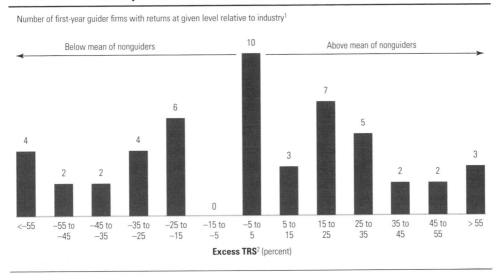

[1] 50 firms in guiding sample, all from the consumer packaged-goods sector.
[2] Excess TRS for a firm is defined as TRS in year of starting guidance minus median TRS in same year for nonguiding firms. At the 99% confidence level, the mean of the underlying distribution is not different from zero. Results are similar for the year after starting guidance.

Source: Thomson First Call, McKinsey Corporate Performance Center analysis.

Exhibit 24.7. Returns to shareholders are just as likely to be above the market as below the market in the year a company starts providing guidance.

On the issue of share price volatility, we found that when a company begins to issue earnings guidance, the likelihood of volatility in its share price increasing or decreasing is just the same as it is for companies that don't issue guidance. Finally, we found that when companies do begin issuing earnings guidance, they do indeed experience an increase in trading volumes relative to companies that don't provide it, as their management anticipates. However, the effect wears off the next year.

When we asked executives about stopping guidance, many feared that their share price would decline and its volatility would increase. But when we analyzed 126 companies that had discontinued issuing guidance, we found they were just about as likely to see higher or lower shareholder returns as the rest of the market. Of the 126 companies, 58 had higher returns than the overall market in the year they stopped issuing guidance, and 68 had lower returns. Furthermore, our analysis showed that the lower-than-market returns of companies that discontinued guidance resulted from poor underlying performance and not the act of ending guidance itself. For example, two-thirds of the companies that stopped guidance and experienced lower returns on capital saw lower TRS than the market. For companies that increased ROIC, only about one-third had delivered lower TRS than the market.

Our conclusion was that issuing guidance offers companies and investors no real benefits. On the contrary, it can trigger real costs and unfortunate unintended consequences. The difficulty of predicting earnings accurately, for example, frequently causes management teams to endure the painful experience of missing quarterly forecasts. That, in turn, can be a powerful incentive for management to focus excessive attention on the short term, at the expense of longer-term investments, and to manage earnings inappropriately from quarter to quarter to create the illusion of stability. Moreover, according to our research with intrinsic investors, they realize that earnings are inherently unpredictable. For that reason, they prefer that companies not issue quarterly EPS guidance.

When Coca-Cola stopped issuing guidance in late 2002, its executives had concluded that providing short-term guidance prevented management from concentrating on strategic initiatives to build its businesses and succeed over the long term. Instead of indicating weak earnings, Gary Fayard (then CFO) believed that the move signaled a renewed focus on long-term goals. The market seemed to agree and did not react negatively: Coke's share price held steady.[3]

As an alternative, we believe executives will gain advantages from providing guidance at the start of the financial year on the real short-, medium-, and long-term value drivers of their businesses, giving ranges rather than point estimates. They should update this guidance whenever there is a meaningful change in their targets. For example, companies as diverse as General Electric and Arrow Electronics provide target ranges for returns on capital. Other companies provide a range of possibilities for revenue growth under a variety of assumptions about inflation, and they discuss the growth of individual business units when that matters. Some companies also provide information on value drivers that can help investors assess the sustainability of growth. Humana, for example, provides guidance on estimated membership in its health plans—including plans whose membership the company expects will decline. Gartner sets out a range of long-term goals, such as growth targets by business unit, margin improvement targets, and capital spending goals.

The value drivers a business chooses to publicize will depend on the unique characteristics of the business. For example, a leading project-based company provides details on the performance of individual current projects, plus the timing and expected returns of potential projects. One European company provides investors with a tax estimation tool, which uses the investors' assessments of regional growth rates to provide a best guess on the tax rates the company will face.

Ideally, companies would provide the kind of information that would help investors make their own projections of the companies' performance based on their assessment of external factors. For example, in resource extraction industries, the prices for the commodities extracted, such as gold, copper, or oil, are volatile. For such companies, a management team's view on future

---

[3] David M. Katz, "Nothing but the Real Thing," *CFO* (March 2003), http://cfo.com.

prices is not necessarily better than that of their investors. Production targets would therefore be more useful to investors in these industries than revenue targets. Similarly, exchange rates are unpredictable, yet they can affect the profits of multinationals by 5 percent or more in a given year. Companies should therefore avoid predicting exchange rates and locking them into EPS targets. Rather, they should discuss their targets at constant currency rates. This would give investors a much clearer picture of their expected performance.

SUMMARY

The issues that currently surround investor communications will remain unresolved for some time. Traditionally, there have been two camps: those who believe you can talk up your share price and those who believe companies shouldn't spend much time or effort on investor communications at all, because it won't make any difference to their market value. Our view is that investors can more accurately value a company if they have the right information, and a market value aligned with the true value of your company is the best outcome of your investor communications strategy. Moreover, even if you do manage to talk up the stock in the short term, this is unlikely to be the best thing for the company in the long run.

You can improve the alignment of your company's value with its intrinsic value by applying some of the systematic approaches described in this chapter for understanding your value, understanding your current and potential investors, and communicating with investors. These principles also can help managers use their scarce time for investor communications more efficiently and effectively.

REVIEW QUESTIONS

1. What is the purpose of investor communications? What do managers often believe the purpose is?
2. Why does a gap between a company's intrinsic value and its market value raise issues for the company's executives?
3. Do companies typically have a substantial gap between their market value and their intrinsic value? Give reasons for your answer.
4. What are the three main areas where a company can focus its attention in order to improve its investor communications?
5. How does classifying investors into segments help a company?

6. Company shares are often categorized as growth stocks or value stocks by certain agencies. Why are these labels misleading? What is the difference between growth and value stocks?

7. What are the key differences between intrinsic investors and traders?

8. Why is it beneficial for a company to provide more information to the investors than is required by regulators and GAAP?

9. What do executives believe are the benefits of issuing EPS guidance? Are these benefits actually realized by companies?

Part Five

Advanced Valuation Issues

25

Taxes

In Chapter 7, the company's income statement and balance sheet are reorganized into operating items, nonoperating items, and financing items. Using the reorganized financial statements, we build return on invested capital (ROIC) and free cash flow (FCF), which in turn drive the company's valuation. One complex line item that typically combines all three categories (operating, nonoperating, and financing items) is reported taxes. Unfortunately, company disclosures rarely provide all the information required to build the operating taxes necessary to project free cash flow. However, you can reverse engineer operating taxes by combining assumptions about marginal tax rates with a clever analysis of the company's tax reconciliation tables.

Once you have computed operating taxes, we recommend converting them from an accrual basis to a cash basis for valuation, because accrual taxes typically do not reflect the cash taxes actually paid. For instance, growing companies with fixed assets tend to pay lower cash taxes than those reported on the income statement, since the government allows accelerated depreciation on new fixed assets. To convert operating taxes to operating cash taxes, adjust operating taxes by the increase in operating deferred tax liabilities (net of operating tax assets). To assure that operating cash taxes are independent of nonoperating items, such as taxes related to unfunded pensions, you need to separate deferred taxes into operating and nonoperating categories. Again, company disclosures do not easily lend themselves to determining operating-related deferred tax assets and liabilities.

Any deferred taxes you classify as operating will flow through cash taxes, net operating profit less adjusted taxes (NOPLAT), and consequently free cash flow (FCF). Deferred taxes classified as nonoperating will not be included in an FCF valuation and therefore must be valued either as part of their corresponding accounts (as in the case of pensions), valued separately (as in the case of net operating loss carry-forwards), or ignored as accounting conventions (as in the case of nondeductible amortization).

In this chapter, we go through the steps of estimating operating taxes, converting operating taxes to operating cash taxes, and incorporating deferred taxes into a corporate valuation. We start with the calculation of operating taxes.

OPERATING TAXES ON THE REORGANIZED INCOME STATEMENT

To determine operating taxes, we need to remove the effects of nonoperating and financing items from reported taxes. Although this sounds straightforward, it can be challenging because of the complexity of tax accounting and the need for data that companies do not typically disclose. To show the steps involved in computing operating taxes, we introduce a hypothetical company so we can present complete information about its internal financials; with full information, operating taxes can be computed without error. Next, we present only the information about taxes that would typically be found in an annual report and use that information to compare alternative methodologies for estimating operating taxes from public data. Then we compare results from these methods with the actual value of operating taxes calculated on the basis of complete information.

Exhibit 25.1 presents the internal financials of a global company for a single year. The company generated $2,000 million in domestic earnings before interest, taxes, and amortization (EBITA) and $500 million in foreign EBITA. The company amortizes intangible assets held domestically at $400 million per year. Thus, domestic earnings before interest and taxes (EBIT) are $1,600 million. The company holds debt locally and deducts interest ($600 million) on its domestic statements. It recently sold an asset held in the foreign market and recorded a gain of $50 million. The company pays a statutory (domestic)

EXHIBIT 25.1 **Income Statement by Geography**

$ million

	Domestic subsidiary	Foreign subsidiary	R&D tax credits	One-time credits	Company
EBITA[1]	2,000	500	–	–	2,500
Amortization	(400)	–	–	–	(400)
EBIT[1]	1,600	500	–	–	2,100
Interest expense	(600)	–	–	–	(600)
Gains on asset sales	–	50	–	–	50
Earnings before taxes	1,000	550	–	–	1,550
Taxes	(350)	(110)	40	25	(395)
Net income	650	440	40	25	1,155
Tax rates (percent)					
Statutory tax rate	35.0	20.0	–	–	–
Effective tax rate	–	–	–	–	25.5

[1] EBITA is earnings before interest, taxes, and amortization; EBIT is earnings before interest and taxes.

EXHIBIT 25.2 **Operating Taxes and NOPLAT by Geography**

$ million

	Domestic subsidiary	Foreign subsidiary	R&D tax credits	One-time credits	Company
EBITA	2,000	500	–	–	2,500
Operating taxes	(700)	(100)	40	–	(760)
NOPLAT[1]	1,300	400	40	–	1,740
Tax rates (percent)					
Statutory tax rate	35.0	20.0	–	–	–
Operating tax rate	–	–	–	–	30.4

[1] Net operating profit less adjusted taxes.

tax rate of 35 percent on earnings before taxes, but only 20 percent on foreign operations.

The majority of taxes are related to earnings, but the company also generates $40 million in *ongoing* research and development (R&D) tax credits (credits determined by the amount and location of the company's R&D activities), which are expected to grow as the company grows. The company also has $25 million in *one-time* tax credits, such as tax rebates related to historical tax disputes. All told, the company pays an effective tax rate on pretax profits of 25.5 percent, well below its statutory domestic rate of 35 percent.[1]

Operating taxes are computed as if the company were financed entirely with equity. Exhibit 25.2 calculates operating taxes and NOPLAT for our hypothetical company. To compute operating taxes, apply the local marginal tax rate to each jurisdiction's EBITA, before any financing or nonoperating items.[2] In this case, apply 35 percent to domestic EBITA of $2,000 million and 20 percent to $500 million in foreign EBITA. Since R&D tax credits are related to operations and expected to grow with revenue, they are included in operating taxes as well. The corporation as a whole pays $760 million in operating taxes on EBITA of $2,500 million, resulting in an operating tax rate of 30.4 percent. Note how the operating tax rate does not equal either the statutory tax rate (35 percent) or the effective tax rate from Exhibit 25.1 (25.5 percent).

Computing Operating Taxes Using Public Statements

In practice, companies do not give a full breakout of the income statement by geography, but provide only the corporate income statement and a tax

[1] The effective tax rate, as computed in most annual reports, equals reported taxes divided by earnings before taxes. It will differ from the company's domestic statutory tax rate because foreign income is typically taxed at a rate different from the company's statutory income rate. Differences will also arise because of tax credits unrelated to current income.

[2] The interest tax shield is valuable. Rather than being valued as part of income, however, it is typically valued as part of the weighted average cost of capital (WACC) or separately in adjusted present value. Since amortization is typically nondeductible for tax purposes, it has no value. Therefore, operating taxes are calculated as a function of EBITA, rather than EBIT.

EXHIBIT 25.3 **Income Statement and Tax Reconciliation Table**

Company income statement		Tax reconciliation table (in notes)	
$ million		percent	
EBITA	2,500	Taxes at statutory rate	35.0
Amortization	(400)	Foreign-income adjustment	(5.3)
EBIT	2,100	R&D tax credits	(2.6)
		Audit revision, etc.	(1.6)
Interest expense	(600)	Effective tax rate	25.5
Gains on asset sales	50		
Earnings before taxes	1,550		
Taxes	(395)		
Net income	1,155		

reconciliation table. Exhibit 25.3 presents the income statement and tax reconciliation table for our hypothetical company. The income statement matches the company-wide income statement in Exhibit 25.1. The tax reconciliation table, which is found in the notes of the annual report, reconciles the taxes reported on the income statement with the taxes that would be paid at the company's domestic statutory rate. For instance, the company paid 5.3 percent ($82.5 million) less in taxes than under the statutory rate of 35 percent because foreign geographies were taxed at only 20 percent.[3] The tax table plays a critical role in determining operating taxes.

The most comprehensive method for computing operating taxes from public data is to begin with reported taxes and undo financing and nonoperating items one by one. In most cases, start by converting the tax reconciliation table from percentages to millions of dollars.[4] To do this, multiply each reported percentage on the tax reconciliation table by "earnings before taxes" found on the income statement. Here are the results when we apply this conversion to the amounts from Exhibit 25.3:

$ million	
Taxes at statutory rate	542.5
Foreign-income adjustment	(82.5)
R&D tax credit	(40.0)
Audit revision, etc.	(25.0)
Reported taxes	395.0

[3] At a statutory tax rate of 35 percent, a company would pay taxes of $192.5 million on $550 million of income. In actuality, our hypothetical company paid only $110 million, a difference of $82.5 million. Dividing $82.5 million by corporate earnings before taxes ($1,550 million) equals 5.3 percent.

[4] Most companies report the tax reconciliation in percentages; however, some companies do report the tax reconciliation table in millions of dollars. In that case, use the figures provided.

EXHIBIT 25.4 **Comprehensive Approach for Estimating Operating Taxes**

$ million

Reported taxes	395	Remove nonoperating taxes
Audit revision, etc.	25	found in reconciliation table
Reported taxes: Operating only	420	
Plus: Amortization tax shield (at 35%)	140	Remove taxes related to
Plus: Interest tax shield (at 35%)	210	nonoperating income or expense
Less: Taxes on gains (at 20%)	(10)	at appropriate marginal tax rate
Operating taxes	760	
Operating tax rate on EBITA (percent)	30.4	

Next, use the dollar-based tax reconciliation table to eliminate one-time and nonoperating taxes from reported taxes. One-time items are excluded for valuation purposes because they have no effect on future tax obligations. Nonoperating items should be valued separately or in conjunction with the corresponding nonoperating asset or liability. Determining what constitutes a one-time or nonoperating tax requires judgment. Our hypothetical company recently concluded a tax audit with the government for past overpayments. Since the tax credit is not expected to recur, we deem it nonoperating. In Exhibit 25.4, reported taxes of $395 million are adjusted by $25 million to remove the effect of the audit revision. Reported taxes related to operations equal $420 million.

In the final step, adjust reported taxes for each nonoperating item the company reports on its income statement between EBITA and earnings before taxes. In our hypothetical company, the three nonoperating items between EBITA and earnings before taxes are amortization, interest expense, and gains on an asset sale. Since intangibles and debt are held domestically, the amortization tax shield and interest tax shield are computed at 35 percent of the corresponding line item. For instance, the interest tax shield equals $210 million ($600 million × 0.35). Subtract any incremental taxes on nonoperating gains (add taxes related to losses), again at the appropriate marginal tax rate.[5] By applying these adjustments to reported operating taxes in Exhibit 25.4, we arrive at an operating tax of $760 million, which matches the operating taxes found in Exhibit 25.2.

This is the most theoretically sound method for computing operating taxes. However, it relies heavily on properly matching each nonoperating item with the appropriate marginal tax rate—a very difficult achievement in practice. In some cases, the annual report will provide pre- and posttax nonoperating charges. For instance, in Lockheed Martin's 2007 10-K, the company reports, "In the second quarter of 2007, we sold our remaining 20% interest in Comsat

---

[5] If a nonoperating gain or loss on the income statement is not taxed at the statutory rate, the tax reconciliation table will reflect the difference. Be careful not to adjust twice (once from the reconciliation table and again from the nonoperating item at the actual marginal rate).

International. The transaction resulted in a gain, net of state income taxes, of $25 million which we recorded in Other income (expenses) and an increase in Net earnings of $16 million." In most cases, however, companies will not explicitly report marginal taxes related to nonoperating items. It therefore becomes necessary to assume the marginal rate for each nonoperating item. We discuss this next.

Computing Operating Taxes: Simple Methods to Contend with Incomplete Data

If marginal tax rates on nonoperating items are not reported (as is usually the case), you will have to make an assumption about the tax jurisdiction in which nonoperating items are held. In such cases, simpler, more intuitive methods are available.

If you believe the company records interest expenses and other nonoperating items domestically (typical for companies in countries with high tax rates), multiply the statutory tax rate by EBITA, and then adjust for other operating taxes. In Panel A of Exhibit 25.5, the domestic statutory rate (35 percent) is applied to EBITA ($2,500 million), resulting in statutory taxes on EBITA of $875 million. Using data from the converted tax reconciliation table computed earlier, subtract the dollar-denominated foreign-income adjustment ($83 million) and the R&D tax credit ($40 million) from statutory taxes on EBITA ($875 million) to determine operating taxes.

The estimate for operating taxes, $753 million, is close but not equal to the $760 million computed using the comprehensive method. The difference is explained by the fact that gains on the asset sales of $50 million were taxed at 20 percent, not at the statutory rate. Had gains on asset sales been taxed at 35 percent, the two methods would yield identical results.

EXHIBIT 25.5 **Simple Approach for Estimating Operating Taxes**

$ million

Panel A		Panel B	
Assumption: Nonoperating items recognized domestically		Assumption: Nonoperating items recognized globally	
Statutory tax rate (percent)	35.0	Blended global rate (percent)[1]	29.7
× EBITA	2,500.0	× EBITA	2,500.0
Statutory taxes on EBITA	875.0	Global taxes on EBITA	741.9
Foreign-income adjustment	(82.5)		
R&D tax credit	(40.0)	R&D tax credit	(40.0)
Estimated operating taxes	752.5	Estimated operating taxes	701.9
Estimated operating tax rate (percent)	30.1	Estimated operating tax rate (percent)	28.1

[1] Blended global rate equals 35.0 percent statutory rate minus 5.3 percent from the foreign-income adjustment.

If you believe the company reports interest expense and other nonoperating items in various geographies proportional to each geography's profits (typical for companies in countries with low tax rates), multiply a blended global rate by EBITA, and adjust for other operating taxes. In Panel B of Exhibit 25.5, a blended global rate of 29.7 percent is applied to $2,500 million in EBITA. The blended global rate is the statutory tax rate (35 percent) adjusted by the foreign-income adjustment (–5.3 percent) found in the company's tax reconciliation table in Exhibit 25.3. Next, work through the reformatted tax reconciliation table for other operating taxes beyond the foreign-income adjustment. For our hypothetical company, subtracting $40 million in R&D tax credits from global taxes on EBITA of $742 million leads to an estimate of $702 million in operating taxes. Once again, estimated operating taxes are not quite equal to actual operating taxes. This is because the majority of nonoperating items are recognized domestically, in violation of the assumption that they were distributed across geographies in line with profits.

If these two methods lead to incorrect assessments of operating taxes, why use them? Because for most companies, the marginal tax rate on nonoperating items is not disclosed, making the comprehensive method presented in Exhibit 25.4 unusable. In our experience, you are likely to make fewer implementation errors using the simplified method based on an assumption about the provenance of nonoperating items than if you try to use the comprehensive method based on inadequate information. In Chapter 7, we estimated Home Depot's operating tax rate using the simple approach presented in Panel A of Exhibit 25.5.

Unsuitable Alternatives for Computing Operating Taxes

Two alternatives that are incorrect yet common in practice are to use either the company's statutory tax rate or the company's effective rate *with no adjustments*. These shortcuts work for straightforward companies that operate only domestically, but in most other cases, they lead to volatile, often biased estimates of operating taxes.

Computing operating taxes by multiplying operating profit by the company's statutory tax rate typically leads to an upward-biased estimate of operating taxes, because it fails to recognize that foreign earnings are often taxed at different levels. For example, the operating tax rate at Hasbro, a toy company with extensive foreign earnings, is consistently below 30 percent, even though the company's statutory rate hovers near 37.5 percent (federal rates plus state rates). In fact, 46.8 percent of profitable S&P 500 companies had effective tax rates between 20 percent and 35 percent in 2008.

Alternatively, applying the effective tax rate to operating profit handles foreign earnings properly but does not exclude one-time nonoperating items. This can lead to biased (and volatile) estimates of operating taxes. For instance, in 2004, the U.S. Congress passed legislation allowing companies to

EXHIBIT 25.6 **Deferred Tax Assets and Liabilities**

$ million

	Prior year	Current year
Deferred tax assets[1]		
Tax loss carry-forwards	550	600
Warranty reserves	250	300
Deferred tax assets (DTAs)	800	900
Deferred tax liabilities		
Accelerated depreciation	3,600	3,800
Pension and postretirement benefits	850	950
Nondeductible intangibles	2,200	2,050
Deferred tax liabilities (DTLs)	6,650	6,800

[1] Deferred tax assets are consolidated into a single line item on the balance sheet. If small, they are typically included in other assets.

repatriate foreign earnings at a small incremental tax if domestic investments were made. Many companies used this opportunity to repatriate significant earnings, leading to unusually high effective tax rates in 2005. Since this is a one-time tax, it should be evaluated separately and not as part of operating taxes.

CONVERTING OPERATING TAXES TO OPERATING CASH TAXES

In the previous section, we estimated *accrual-based* operating taxes as if the company were all-equity financed. In actuality, many companies will never pay (or at least will significantly delay paying) accrual-based taxes. Consequently, a cash tax rate (one based on the operating taxes actually paid in cash to the government) represents value better than accrual-based taxes.

To convert operating taxes to operating cash taxes, subtract the increase in net operating deferred tax liabilities from operating taxes.[6] To determine the portion of deferred taxes related to ongoing operations, investigate the income tax footnote. This is the same footnote in which the tax reconciliation table appears. In Exhibit 25.6, we present the footnote for deferred tax assets (DTAs)

---

[6] Given the complexity of today's deferred tax accounting, using the change in deferred taxes is insufficient. For instance, Coca-Cola reported an increase of $1,259 million in net deferred tax liabilities ($1,615 million less $356 million) in 2007, although it actually deferred only $109 million. The large change in net deferred tax liabilities was caused by arcane accounting related to acquisitions. Another example is Tiffany's, the American gem retailer. In 2008, net deferred tax assets rose from $112 million to $229 million on only $522 million in income and $191 million in taxes. This dramatic rise in deferred tax assets was related to the sale/leaseback of its flagship stores in Tokyo and London, and not a systematic deferral of operating taxes.

and deferred tax liabilities (DTLs) for our hypothetical company. The company has two operating-related DTAs and DTLs:

1. *Warranty reserves (a DTA):* The company records an expense (and takes a tax deduction) for promised warranties when it sells the product. The government recognizes a deductible expense only when a product is repaired, so cash taxes tend to be higher than accrual taxes. Thus, accrual-based taxes typically understate the actual cash taxes paid.

2. *Accelerated depreciation (a DTL):* The company uses straight-line depreciation for its GAAP/IFRS reported statements and accelerated depreciation for its tax statements (because larger depreciation expenses lead to smaller taxes). For a growing company, accelerated depreciation is typically larger than straight-line depreciation, so accrual-based taxes typically overstate the actual cash taxes paid.

In addition, the company has three nonoperating DTAs and DTLs:

1. *Tax loss carry-forwards (a DTA):* When a company loses money, it does not receive a cash reimbursement from the government (as the investor statement would imply), but rather a credit toward future taxes. Given that past losses are typically unrelated to current profitability, they should not be included as operating. Since tax loss carry-forwards are valuable, they must be valued separately.

2. *Pension and postretirement benefits (a DTA):* In the United States, the government provides tax relief only when cash contributions are made to pension plans. Thus, deferred taxes arise when reported pension expense differs from cash contributions. Since underfunded pensions are treated as nonoperating, deferred taxes related to pensions also are nonoperating.

3. *Nondeductible intangibles (a DTL):* When a company buys another company, it typically recognizes intangibles that are separable and identifiable (such as customer lists). Since amortization is deductible on the investor's statement but is nondeductible for tax purposes, the company will record a DTL during the year of the acquisition and then draw down the DTL as the intangible amortizes. Since operating taxes (computed in Exhibit 25.4) exclude the amortization tax shield from the investor's statement, no adjustment for deferrals related to such intangible assets should be made to operating taxes. Instead, treat deferred taxes related to amortization of intangibles as nonoperating.

Exhibit 25.7 reorganizes the items in the note about deferred tax assets and liabilities into operating and nonoperating items. Deferred tax assets (such as

EXHIBIT 25.7 **Deferred Tax Asset and Liability Reorganization**

$ million

	Prior year	Current year
Operating DTLs, net of operating DTAs		
Accelerated depreciation	3,600	3,800
Warranty reserves	(250)	(300)
Operating DTLs, net of operating DTAs	3,350	3,500
Nonoperating DTAs		
Tax loss carry-forwards	550	600
Nonoperating DTAs	550	600
Nonoperating DTLs		
Pensions and postretirement benefits	850	950
Nondeductible intangibles	2,200	2,050
Nonoperating DTLs	3,050	3,000

those related to warranties) are netted against deferred tax liabilities (such as those related to accelerated depreciation). This reorganization makes the components of operating taxes, the reorganized balance sheet, and ultimately the final valuation more transparent and less prone to error.

To convert accrual-based operating taxes into operating cash taxes, subtract the increase in net operating DTLs (net of DTAs) from operating taxes. We compute the increase in net operating DTLs by subtracting last year's net operating DTLs ($3,350 million) from this year's net operating DTLs ($3,500 million), presented in Exhibit 25.7. During the current year, operating-related DTLs increased by $150 million. Thus, to calculate cash taxes, subtract $150 million from operating taxes of $760 million (computed in Exhibit 25.4):

$ million	Current Year
Operating taxes	760
Decrease (increase) in net operating DTLs	(150)
Operating cash taxes	610

Operating cash taxes equal $610 million. The operating cash tax rate equals operating cash taxes divided by EBITA, or $610 million divided by $2,500 million, which equals 24.4 percent. The operating cash tax rate can be applied to forecasts of EBITA to determine future free cash flow.

DEFERRED TAXES ON THE REORGANIZED BALANCE SHEET

One critical component of a well-structured valuation model is a properly reorganized balance sheet. As outlined in Chapter 7, the accountant's balance

EXHIBIT 25.8 **Reorganized Balance Sheet: Treatment of Deferred Taxes**

$ million

Total funds invested: uses		Total funds invested: sources	
Operating assets	12,000	Short-term debt	500
Operating liabilities	(3,000)	Long-term debt	2,100
Invested capital without intangibles	9,000	→ Pension and postretirement benefits (DTL)	950
		Debt and debt equivalents	3,550
Intangibles	8,000		
→ Nondeductible intangibles (DTL)	(2,050)	→ Accelerated depreciation (DTL)	3,800
Invested capital with intangibles	14,950	→ Warranty reserves (DTA)	(300)
		Owners' equity	8,500
		Equity and equity equivalents	12,000
→ Tax loss carry-forwards (DTA)	600		
Total funds invested	15,550		
		Total funds invested	15,550

sheet is reorganized into invested capital, nonoperating items, and sources of financing. As a general rule, DTAs and DTLs are *not* considered part of invested capital. Since operating DTAs and DTLs flow through NOPLAT via cash taxes, they are considered equity equivalents. Why equity? When we convert accrual taxes to cash taxes, income is adjusted, and the difference becomes part of retained earnings, making it an equity equivalent.[7]

Exhibit 25.8 presents a reorganized balance sheet that includes the five deferred tax items from Exhibit 25.7. There are two adjustments to the left side of total funds invested: nondeductible intangibles ($2,050 million) and tax loss carry-forwards ($600 million). Debt equivalents include a DTL related to pension and postretirement benefits ($950 million). Equity equivalents include two equity equivalents: the accelerated depreciation DTL ($3,800 million) and the warranty reserves DTA ($300 million). Since warranty reserves lead to an operating DTA, they are netted against operating DTLs.

Most DTLs are classified as either debt (if they are nonoperating) or equity (if they are operating) equivalents. Nondeductible amortization related to intangibles requires special treatment. When a company buys another company, it typically recognizes intangible assets for intangibles that are separable and identifiable (such as customer lists). Since amortization is deductible on the investor's statement but is nondeductible for tax purposes, the company will record a DTL (often quite large) during the year of the acquisition and then draw down the DTL as the intangible amortizes. To keep the balance sheet balanced, the company will increase intangibles (known in accounting as "grossing up") by the DTL. Since the grossed-up intangible and deferred tax

---

[7] If mistakenly included as part of invested capital, operating DTAs and DTLs could be double-counted in free cash flow: once in NOPLAT via cash taxes and again when taking the change in invested capital. As discussed in Chapter 7, equity equivalents are not part of invested capital.

liability are purely accounting conventions, they should be netted against one another by lowering the intangible.

One practical difficulty with DTAs and DTLs is finding them. Sometimes they are explicitly listed on the balance sheet, but often they are embedded within other assets and other liabilities. Where they are included is often detailed in the tax footnote. For instance, in its 2007 annual report, Coca-Cola describes embedded DTAs and DTLs as follows:

> Noncurrent deferred tax assets of $66 million and $168 million were included in the consolidated balance sheets line item other assets at December 31, 2007 and 2006, respectively. Current deferred tax assets of $238 million and $117 million were included in the consolidated balance sheets line item prepaid expenses and other assets at December 31, 2007 and 2006, respectively. Current deferred tax liabilities of $29 million and $33 million were included in the consolidated balance sheets line item accounts payable and accrued expenses at December 31, 2007 and 2006, respectively.

VALUING DEFERRED TAXES

Deferred tax assets and liabilities classified as operating will flow through NOPLAT via cash taxes. As part of NOPLAT, they are also part of free cash flow, and therefore are not valued separately. The remaining nonoperating DTAs and DTLs are either valued as part of the corresponding nonoperating account (as for pensions and convertible bonds), valued separately (as for net operating loss carry-forwards), or ignored as an accounting convention (as for intangible assets). For each deferred tax account, there are four valuation methodologies:

1. *Value as part of NOPLAT and subsequently enterprise value:* Any DTA or DTL used to convert operating into cash taxes will flow through free cash flow and subsequently be valued as part of enterprise value. In our hypothetical example, DTAs related to warranties and DTLs related to accelerated depreciation are valued as part of free cash flow.

2. *Value as part of a corresponding nonoperating asset or liability:* The value of DTAs and DTLs related to pensions, convertible debt, and sale/leasebacks should be incorporated into the valuation of their respective accounts. How this is done depends on the nuances of the account. As an example, deferred taxes related to pensions arise when pension expense differs from the cash contribution. But the deferred tax account recognized on the balance sheet reflects accumulated *historical* differences and not future tax savings. Therefore, to value the tax shield associated with unfunded pensions, you should multiply the current

unfunded liability by the marginal tax rate.[8] Do not use the book value of the deferred tax account.

3. *Value as a separate nonoperating asset:* When a DTA such as tax loss carry-forwards, commonly referred to as net operating losses (NOLs), does not have a corresponding balance sheet account like pensions, it must be valued separately. To value NOLs, tie the forecast of tax savings directly to expected future taxes, and discount at the unlevered cost of equity—the cost of debt is too conservative. Be careful to check with local tax experts, since NOLs can be applied only in certain circumstances and for certain lengths of time. For instance, NOLs can be applied only in the country where they are generated. Therefore, a company with an NOL in one country yet significant profits in another cannot use the credit. In addition, do not become overly reliant on the valuation of NOLs found in the company's annual report. Accounting rules dictate that NOLs be valued using an all-or-nothing approach, whereas in discounted cash flow we apply the probability of realization to determine an NOL's expected value.

4. *Ignore as an accounting convention:* Some DTLs, such as the kind of non-deductible amortization described earlier in this chapter, arise because of accounting conventions and are not an actual cash liability. These items should be valued at zero.

REVIEW QUESTIONS

1. Exhibit 25.9 presents the tax reconciliation table for ToyCo, a $5 billion designer and distributor of children's toys. Convert the tax table from percent to $ millions. Separate the converted tax table into three groups: taxes attributable to domestic income, other operating taxes, and nonoperating taxes. Treat "Other, net" as nonoperating.

2. Exhibit 25.5 presents two approaches for estimating operating taxes. Use both methods to determine the operating taxes for ToyCo in year 3. What are ToyCo's statutory rate, effective tax rate, and operating tax rate (under both approaches)?

3. When a company incorporated in a country with a high tax rate does business in countries with lower tax rates, it will report an effective tax rate below its statutory rate. Is the difference sustainable into the future? What

---

[8] Under U.S. law, only cash contributions are deductible, not pension expense. To value pensions, there is no need to value cash contributions. Instead, expected cash contributions should match expected service costs (the economic benefits given to employees) plus current underfunding. Since service cost is part of EBITA, its related tax savings will be part of operating taxes. The remaining piece, underfunding, and its tax shield are valued separately.

EXHIBIT 25.9 **ToyCo: Tax Reconciliation Table**

percent

	Year 1	Year 2	Year 3
Statutory income tax rate	35.0	35.0	35.0
State and local income taxes, net	1.1	1.0	0.7
Repatriation of foreign earnings	–	3.5	–
Liabilities settleable in common stock	3.4	–	–
Tax on international earnings	(6.5)	(7.9)	(7.5)
Exam settlements	(6.5)	(0.8)	(0.5)
Other, net	1.5	(0.4)	1.5
Effective tax rate	28.0	30.4	29.2
Profits (millions of dollars)			
Operating profit (EBITA)	587.1	572.6	673.6
Earnings before taxes	462.3	441.1	529.7

occurs if the company decides to repatriate earnings? How should operating taxes be computed in the year of repatriation? How is ROIC distorted by foreign taxation and repatriation?

4. Exhibit 25.10 presents deferred tax assets and liabilities for ToyCo. Using Exhibit 25.7 as a guide, reorganize the deferred tax table into three categories: net operating deferred tax liabilities (net of operating deferred tax assets), nonoperating deferred tax assets, and nonoperating deferred tax liabilities. In year 3, ToyCo generated $200.7 million in operating taxes on $673.6 million of EBITA. Using this information, what are the cash taxes in year 3? What is the percent of operating taxes that were deferred and what is the operating cash tax rate?

5. ToyCo has working capital of $400 million, fixed assets equal to $800 million, and debt equal to $600 million. Use this data and the reorganized deferred

EXHIBIT 25.10 **ToyCo: Deferred Tax Assets and Liabilities**

$ million

	Year 1	Year 2	Year 3
Deferred tax assets			
Accounts receivable	20.5	16.8	17.3
Inventories	24.6	20.2	15.9
Losses and tax credit carry-forwards	39.1	34.4	29.6
Pension	10.0	34.1	26.6
Deferred tax assets	94.2	105.5	89.4
Deferred tax liabilities			
Convertible debentures	40.2	47.6	56.8
Depreciation of long-lived assets	47.7	121.5	120.3
Equity method investment	–	–	26.9
Deferred tax liabilities	87.9	169.1	204.0

taxes in Question 4 to create invested capital and total funds invested for year 3. Use equity as the plug to get total funds invested to reconcile.

6. One of the most common deferred tax liabilities occurs because of accelerated depreciation. When is the difference between reported taxes and cash taxes likely to be greatest? When will it be smallest? Can it reverse? That is, can cash taxes be higher than reported taxes?

26

Nonoperating Expenses, One-Time Charges, Reserves, and Provisions

To project future cash flows from ongoing operations, you would typically focus on expenses above earnings before interest, taxes, and amortization (EBITA), such as cost of sales, distribution expenses, selling expenses, and administrative expenses. But what about nonoperating expenses, such as business realignment expenses, goodwill impairment, and extraordinary items? Nonoperating expenses are infrequent or unusual charges that are indirectly related to the company's typical activities and not expected to recur. The conventional wisdom is to ignore nonoperating expenses in discounted cash flow (DCF) calculations as backward-looking, one-time costs. Yet research shows that the type and accounting treatment of nonoperating expenses can affect future cash flow and must be incorporated into operating cash flow.

In addition to making forecasts more precise, adjustments for nonoperating expenses will also make assessments of past performance more accurate. For instance, before 2009, purchased in-process R&D for U.S. companies was written off at the time of purchase.[1] This artificially lowered acquired intangibles and retained earnings. To assess historical return on invested capital (ROIC) properly, you need to make adjustments for this type of nonoperating item.

This chapter analyzes nonoperating expenses that appear between EBITA and earnings before taxes. Typical nonoperating expenses include *amortization*

---

[1] Statement of Financial Accounting Standards (SFAS) No. 141(R), *Business Combinations*, requires that companies recognize acquired in-process R&D as an indefinite-lived intangible asset. Before 2009, companies expensed purchased in-process R&D. SFAS 141(R) brings in-process R&D accounting into line with International Financial Reporting Standards (IFRS) requirements.

expense, restructuring charges, unusual charges (such as litigation expense), *asset write-offs, goodwill impairments,* and *purchased R&D.* Although interest expense, interest income, and income from associates are nonoperating, they are ongoing. Therefore, analyze interest expense as part of financing (see Chapter 11), and analyze interest income and income from associates in conjunction with the asset that generates the income (see Chapter 12).

For *noncash* nonoperating expenses, such as restructuring charges, a corresponding reserve will be recognized on the balance sheet. This reserve is typically nonoperating and therefore is treated as a debt equivalent. But not every reserve is nonoperating. This chapter outlines a classification system for provisions, categorizing them into ongoing operating provisions, long-term operating provisions, nonoperating provisions, and provisions used to smooth income. We describe the process for reorganizing the income statement and balance sheet to reflect the true effect of such provisions, if any, on company value, and show how to treat them in free cash flow (FCF) and equity valuation. We begin the chapter by analyzing nonoperating expenses and one-time charges.

NONOPERATING EXPENSES AND ONE-TIME CHARGES

Given their infrequent nature, nonoperating expenses and one-time charges can distort a company's historical financial performance and consequently bias our view of the future. It is therefore critical to separate one-time nonoperating expenses from ongoing operating expenses. The idea sounds simple, but implementation can be tricky. Nonoperating expenses are often spread across the income statement, and some nonoperating expenses are hidden in the company's notes. And even after being properly identified, the job is not done. Each nonoperating expense must be carefully analyzed to determine its impact on future operations, and, if necessary, forecasts must be adjusted to reflect any information embedded in the expense.

To assess the impact of nonoperating expenses and incorporate their information in cash flow forecasts, we recommend a three-step process:

1. *Reorganize the income statement into operating and nonoperating items.* This process requires judgment. As a general rule, treat items that grow in line with revenues and are related to the core business as operating. For line items that are lumpy but only tangentially related to core operations, test the impact of each line item on long-term ROIC.
2. *Search the notes for embedded one-time items.* Not every one-time charge will be disclosed in the consolidated income statement. Sometimes the

management discussion and analysis (MD&A) section of the annual report will disclose additional information on one-time items.

3. *Analyze each extraordinary item for its impact on future operations.* Line items not included in EBITA will not be included in free cash flow (FCF), so they are not part of core operating value. Therefore, it is critical to analyze each nonoperating line item separately and determine whether the charge is likely to continue in the future, in which case it should be incorporated into FCF projections.

Reorganizing the Income Statement

Income statements typically include a line item that reads "Operating profit/loss." For example, in Exhibit 26.1, the income statement for Boston Scientific, a medical equipment manufacturer, shows that in 2008 the company reported an operating loss of $1,505 million. But is this loss an accurate reflection of the company's long-run earnings potential? The accountant's definition of operating profit differs from our definition of EBITA, in that the accounting standards for classifying items as nonoperating (i.e., to be recorded below operating profit/loss) are extremely strict. For us to benchmark core operations effectively, EBITA and net operating profit less adjusted taxes (NOPLAT) should include only items related to the ongoing core business, regardless of their classification by accounting standards.

EXHIBIT 26.1 **Boston Scientific: Income Statement**

$ million

Accounting income statement

	2006	2007	2008
Net sales	7,821	8,357	8,050
Cost of products sold	(2,207)	(2,342)	(2,469)
Gross profit	5,614	6,015	5,581
SG&A expenses	(2,675)	(2,909)	(2,589)
R&D expenses	(1,008)	(1,091)	(1,006)
Royalty expense	(231)	(202)	(203)
Amortization expense	(530)	(641)	(543)
Impairment of goodwill	–	–	(2,790)
Purchased R&D expenses	(4,119)	(85)	(43)
Restructuring charges	–	(176)	(78)
Litigation-related charges	–	(365)	(334)
(Loss) gain on assets sales	–	(560)	500
Operating (loss) income	(2,949)	(14)	(1,505)

Reorganized income statement

	2006	2007	2008
Net sales	7,821	8,357	8,050
Cost of products sold	(2,207)	(2,342)	(2,469)
Gross profit	5,614	6,015	5,581
SG&A expenses	(2,675)	(2,909)	(2,589)
R&D expenses	(1,008)	(1,091)	(1,006)
Royalty expense	(231)	(202)	(203)
EBITA	1,700	1,813	1,783
EBITA margin (percent)	21.7	21.7	22.1

Source: Boston Scientific annual report, 2008.

Boston Scientific reports several "operating" expenses that are in fact non-operating. Amortization of intangibles ($543 million in 2008), impairment of goodwill ($2,790 million), and purchased R&D expenses ($43 million) are all noncash reductions in the value of intangible assets; they differ only in their timing and regularity. Other nonoperating expenses include restructuring charges ($78 million), litigation charges ($334 million), and gains on asset sales ($500 million). For valuation purposes, such nonoperating expenses should not be deducted from revenue to determine EBITA.

The right side of Exhibit 26.1 presents the calculation of EBITA for Boston Scientific. Only operating expenses that grow in line with revenue—such as cost of products sold; selling, general, and administrative (SG&A) expense; R&D expense; and royalty expense—are included in the calculation of EBITA. Note how the accountant's definition of operating income fluctuates wildly (a loss of $14 million in 2007 and a loss of $1,505 million in 2008), while EBITA is relatively stable ($1,813 million in 2007 and $1,783 million in 2008).

As we have already stated, classifying items as operating or nonoperating requires judgment. Operating expenses tend to be ongoing and tied to revenue, so a long-term perspective is critical. For instance, treat a plant closure that occurs every 10 years as nonoperating.[2] Conversely, treat a retailer's expenses related to closing stores every year or two years as operating.

For Boston Scientific, we classify royalty payments as operating because royalties are a fundamental part of the medical devices industry and grow in line with revenue. In contrast, litigation expenses tend to be lumpy and sporadic. For instance, Boston Scientific recognized $700 million in litigation expenses related to a single patent infringement case ($365 million in 2007 and $334 million in 2008). In the previous five years, however, Boston Scientific recorded only one other major litigation charge. We could treat the litigation expenses as operating, but this would artificially depress ROIC in the years that the expense was recognized, rather than in the years when the corresponding benefits were reaped. When classification is unclear, measure ROIC with and without the expense. If the expense is lumpy, smooth the expense over the period in which the expense was generated.

Searching the Notes for Hidden One-Time Items

Not every nonoperating expense or one-time charge is explicitly reported in the income statement. Nonoperating expenses and one-time charges can also be embedded in cost of sales or selling expenses. To find embedded expenses, read the MD&A section in the company's annual report. This section details the changes in cost of sales and other expenses from year to year and will

[2] For example, in 2005, Hasbro took an $18 million charge for a plant closure in Valencia, Spain; it was the only such charge Hasbro reported between 1998 and 2007. During the same time period, the Foot Locker closed stores every year.

sometimes report unusual items. In 2006, Boston Scientific reported such an expense:

> In 2006, our SG&A expenses increased by $861 million, or 47 percent, as compared to 2005 . . . including $65 million of acquisition-related costs associated primarily with certain Guidant integration and retention programs.

Whether you make an adjustment to NOPLAT for such an expense depends on whether the charge is large enough to affect perceptions of performance. Do not bother if it is not, as an adjustment could make your analysis overly complex and time-consuming.

Analyzing Each Extraordinary Item for Impact on Future Operations

In Kodak's 2007 annual report, the company writes, "Restructuring actions are expected to generate future annual cost savings of approximately $295 million, $274 million of which are expected to be future annual cash savings." If credible, such projections should be incorporated into your forecast of future cash flow. More broadly, academic researchers have been examining the predictive component of special items and one-time charges. Early research pointed to the low persistence of special items, indicating that they are in fact transitory and should not be incorporated into forecasts. However, this early research examined persistence only on a year-to-year basis. In 2007, researchers from George Mason University extended the window to multiple years and found persistence in special items for companies with strong core profits.[3] In other words, a highly profitable company that reports a series of, say, restructuring charges is likely to continue with similar charges in the future. Persistence was low for companies with little operating profit.

One reason special items may persist year after year for profitable companies is that management may be shifting ongoing operating costs into special items to meet certain earnings targets, as many academic researchers believe they do. This belief also appears common among research analysts, as they decrease their earnings forecasts following the disclosure of a special item.[4] Although the research showing that special items are used to manage earnings is persuasive, it remains unclear how to relate the research results to an individual company. Again, judgment is required: pay close attention to companies disclosing special items, and if the special items seem likely to recur, especially in a challenging economy, adjust your forecasts accordingly.

[3] Patricia M. Fairfield, Vicki Wei Tang, and Karen A. Kitching, "The Persistence of Special Items," Social Science Research Network (May 2007).
[4] P. K. Chaney, C. E. Hogan, and D. C. Jeter, "The Effect of Reporting Restructuring Charges on Analysts' Forecast Revisions and Errors," *Journal of Accounting and Economics* 27 (1999): 261–284.

A comprehensive list of nonoperating items and one-time charges is impractical, but the following items are the most common: amortization expense, asset write-offs including write-offs of goodwill and purchased R&D, restructuring charges, litigation charges, and gains and losses on asset sales. Since each of these nonoperating items requires a particular adjustment, we will work through them one by one.

Amortization expense   In 2002, FASB 142 and IFRS 3 changed the accounting standards for acquisitions. The premium paid for acquisitions is no longer classified solely as goodwill, but instead is separated into intangible assets and goodwill. To be classified as an intangible asset, the asset must be separable and identifiable. If it is not, it is classified as goodwill.[5] Goodwill is tested annually and impaired when the carrying amount of goodwill exceeds its implied fair market value.

Although accounting standards require amortization of acquired intangibles, in most circumstances you should *not* deduct amortization from operating profit to determine NOPLAT. As an alternative to expensing amortization, use EBITA (not EBIT) to determine operating profits. Since amortization is excluded from operating profit, remember to include the cumulative excluded amortization in your total for intangible assets on the balance sheet. A corresponding entry should be made to equity (titled cumulative amortization) to balance total funds invested.

Why not amortize intangibles? The idea of recognizing an intangible asset and then amortizing its use over time is a good one. Yet current accounting standards do not allow companies to take this approach consistently across all intangibles. Today, only *acquired* intangibles are capitalized and amortized, while *internally generated* intangible assets, such as brand and distribution networks, are expensed when they are created. Thus, the EBIT of a company that acquires an intangible asset and then replenishes the asset through internal investment will be penalized twice on its financial statements, once through SG&A and again through amortization. In fact, to expense the creation of new intangible assets while amortizing old intangibles would be tantamount to mixing capital expenditures and depreciation on the income statement, a clearly undesirable characteristic. For valuation purposes, avoid mixing amortization and expensing by maintaining goodwill and acquired intangibles at their original values. To do this, compute operating profit before amortization, and add cumulative amortization to the current value of goodwill and intangible assets.

Exhibit 26.2 demonstrates the effect of amortization on margins of four companies in the medical devices industry. The most pronounced difference between EBITA and EBIT is for Boston Scientific. As a result of the company's

---

[5] For example, patents are considered separable and identifiable, whereas management talent is not. Thus, patents are classified as an intangible asset, while management talent is aggregated with other unidentifiable assets and titled "goodwill." Only intangible assets are amortized.

EXHIBIT 26.2 **EBITA and EBIT Margins in the Medical Devices Industry, 2008**

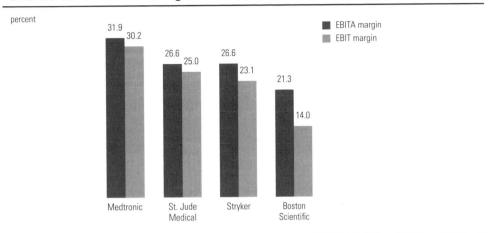

purchase of its large rival Guidant, amortization expense equals 7.7 percent of revenue. On an EBITA basis, Boston Scientific earns within a few percent of the majority of its rivals. After taking into account amortization, however, this gap widens greatly. The gap occurs because Boston Scientific's EBIT includes investments required to replenish intangible assets (via SG&A) as well as an amortization charge. This double penalty artificially lowers the company's EBIT.

The only situation in which it is appropriate to deduct amortization is when intangibles can be capitalized (versus expensed) consistently. For instance, a company that has no sales force and instead purchases customer contacts from a third party will capitalize the contracts. Since sales outlays are never expensed via SG&A, they must be amortized to arrive at a meaningful measure of operating profitability. Otherwise, the income statement would not accurately reflect the cost of selling expenses.

Asset write-offs If the value of an asset falls below its book value, accounting standards dictate the asset should be written down (sometimes entirely) to its fair value. Although write-downs and write-offs give lenders insight into the diminished value of their collateral, the resulting balance sheet value understates the historical investment made by shareholders. Thus, ROIC can artificially rise dramatically following a write-down. To counteract this effect, treat asset write-downs and write-offs as nonoperating, and *add* cumulative write-downs to invested capital. To balance total funds invested, create a corresponding equity equivalent.

Two categories of asset write-offs are common:

1. *Goodwill impairments:* Treat goodwill impairments as nonoperating, and add back cumulative impairments to goodwill on the balance

sheet.[6] Since the purpose of computing ROIC with goodwill is to measure historical performance *including* all past acquisition premiums, goodwill should remain at its original level.

2. *Purchased R&D expenses:* Before 2009, when one company purchased another company that had R&D for products not yet completed, U.S. accounting principles allowed the acquirer to allocate a portion of the purchase price to purchased R&D (also known as in-process R&D). The fair value of the purchased R&D was recorded as an asset and then immediately written off against earnings. However, since this asset has value (as proven by the purchasing company), do not include the write-off in operating profits. Instead, treat in-process R&D as nonoperating, and add back cumulative write-offs to goodwill (and equity). Starting in 2009, Statement of Financial Accounting Standards (SFAS) No. 141(R), *Business Combinations*, requires that companies recognize acquired in-process R&D as an intangible asset of indefinite life. SFAS 141(R) brings in-process R&D accounting into line with International Financial Reporting Standards (IFRS) requirements.

Restructuring charges   As business changes, companies must adapt. Major changes often require plant closures, employee layoffs, inventory write-downs, asset write-offs, and other restructuring charges. If a restructuring charge is unlikely to recur, treat the charge as nonoperating. If, however, a pattern of ongoing restructuring charges emerges, further analysis is required.

Exhibit 26.3 presents the restructuring charges for Eastman Kodak between 2001 and 2008. During this period, Kodak's restructuring charges averaged $462 million per year, or 4.0 percent of revenues. These expenses are reported separately from cost of sales and SG&A. Restructuring charges for Eastman Kodak have been significant, averaging twice the company's capital expenditures.

Given their size and persistence, Eastman Kodak's restructuring charges should be analyzed to determine what portion of them represents cash (such as severance payments), whether any cash restructuring charges are likely to continue, and for how long. According to management disclosure in the company's annual report, a major restructuring program was announced in 2004 and was expected to continue for "a three year period ending in 2006." In December 2008, the company announced a new round of restructuring charges "in the range of $250 million to $300 million" for termination benefits and other exit costs. Since Eastman Kodak's product markets remain soft, analysts project the company to continue shrinking. As revenues decline, continued

---

[6] For a discussion of current accounting standards related to business combinations and goodwill impairment, see the previous section on amortization expense.

EXHIBIT 26.3 **Eastman Kodak: Restructuring Charges**

$ million

659, 98, 479, 695, 665, 416, 543, 140

2001 2002 2003 2004 2005 2006 2007 2008

Average restructuring charge $462 million

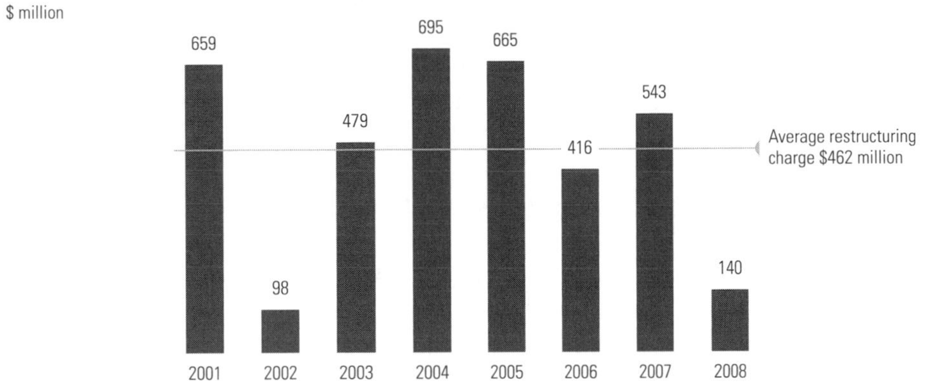

Source: Eastman Kodak annual reports.

eliminations are likely. With severance averaging $50,000 per employee,[7] material restructuring charges are likely to continue.

Many restructuring charges are recorded before any cash is spent. If this is the case, a corresponding reserve will be recorded in the liabilities section of the balance sheet. In the next main section, we consider treatment of various reserves, including those related to restructuring charges.

Litigation charges   When there is likely to be a legal judgment against a company, the company will recognize a litigation charge. If the litigation charge recurs frequently and grows with revenue, treat the charge as operating. For instance, most hospital systems frequently have to defend themselves against malpractice lawsuits. Since these lawsuits are a cost of doing business, the litigation costs should be treated as operating costs for valuation and projected forward. However, if a litigation cost is truly a one-time expense, treat it as nonoperating, and value any claims against the company separately from core operations.

Gains and losses on the sale of assets   When an asset's sale price differs from its book value, the company will recognize a gain or loss. Since current gains and losses are backward-looking (value has been created or destroyed in the past), treat them as nonoperating. Additionally, double-check to make sure projected free cash flow will not be distorted by the asset recently sold. For instance, make sure future depreciation reflects only the remaining assets.

---

[7] According to Kodak's 2007 annual report, severance costs at Kodak totaled $1,398 million, and the company eliminated 27,560 positions between 2004 and 2007.

Although gains and losses should not be included in operating profit, past asset sales may provide insight about the level of cash generated by future asset sales. Again, be careful to value future asset sales (and their corresponding gains and losses) only when the assets do not generate free cash flow. Otherwise, the resulting double-counting will overstate the company's value.

PROVISIONS AND THEIR CORRESPONDING RESERVES

Provisions are noncash expenses that reflect future costs or expected losses. Companies take provisions by reducing current income and setting up a corresponding reserve as a liability (or deducting the amount from the relevant asset).

For the purpose of analyzing and valuing a company, we categorize provisions into one of four types: ongoing operating provisions, long-term operating provisions, nonoperating restructuring provisions, or provisions created for the purpose of smoothing income (transferring income from one period to another). Based on the characteristics of each provision, adjust the financial statements to reflect the company's true operating performance. For example, ongoing operating provisions are treated the same way as any other operating expense, whereas restructuring provisions are converted from an accrual to a cash basis and treated as nonoperating. Exhibit 26.4 summarizes the four types of provisions.

Although reclassification leads to better analysis, the way you adjust the financial statements should not affect the company's valuation, because the

EXHIBIT 26.4 **Treatment of Provisions and Reserves**

Classification	Examples	Treatment in NOPLAT	Treatment in invested capital	Treatment in valuation
Ongoing operating provisions	Product returns and warranties	Deduct provisions from revenue to determine NOPLAT.	Deduct reserve from operating assets to determine invested capital.	Provision is part of free cash flow.
Long-term operating provisions	Plant decommissioning costs and unfunded retirement plans	Deduct operating portion from revenue to determine NOPLAT, and treat interest portion as nonoperating.	Treat reserve as a debt equivalent.	Deduct reserve's present value from the value of operations.
Nonoperating provisions	Restructuring charges, such as expected severance due to layoffs	Convert accrual provision into cash provision, and treat as nonoperating.	Treat reserve as a debt equivalent.	Deduct reserve's present value from the value of operations.
Income-smoothing provisions	Provisions for the sole purpose of income smoothing	Eliminate provision by converting accrual provision into cash provision.	Treat reserve as an equity equivalent.	Since income-smoothing provisions are noncash, there is no effect.

EXHIBIT 26.5 **Provisions and Reserves in the Financial Statements**

$ million

	Today	Year 1	Year 2	Year 3	Year 4
Income statement					
Revenue	–	1,000	1,200	1,400	1,600
Operating costs	–	(550)	(660)	(910)	(880)
Provision for product returns	–	(100)	(120)	(140)	(160)
Provision for plant decommissioning	–	(24)	(27)	(30)	–
Income-smoothing provision	–	(40)	(40)	80	–
EBITA	–	286	353	400	560
Provision for restructuring	–	–	(30)	–	–
Net income	–	286	323	400	560
Balance sheet					
Operating assets	700	840	980	1,120	–
Reserve for product returns	150	180	210	240	–
Reserve for plant decommissioning	119	144	170	–	–
Reserve for restructuring	–	–	30	–	–
Reserve for income smoothing	–	40	80	–	–
Equity	431	476	490	880	–
Liabilities and shareholders' equity	700	840	980	1,120	–

valuation depends on how and when cash flows through the business, not on accrual-based accounting.

Adjustments for the Provisions

In Exhibit 26.5, we present the abbreviated financial statements for a hypothetical company that recognizes four types of provisions: a provision for future product returns, an environmental provision for decommissioning the company's plant in four years, a provision for smoothing income, and a restructuring provision for future severance payments. In this example, we reorganized forecast statements rather than historical statements to demonstrate how each type of provision would be treated from a valuation perspective. (Historical statements should be adjusted in the same way as forecast statements.) For simplicity, we assume the company pays no taxes and has no debt.

The process for adjusting the financial statements depends on the type of provision. We use Exhibit 26.6 to discuss the treatment for each provision for our hypothetical company. In the following discussion, all numbers in parentheses refer to the year 1 reorganized financial statements.

Provisions related to ongoing operations   When a company warranties a product, expects that some products will be returned, or self-insures a service,

EXHIBIT 26.6 **ROIC with Provisions and Reserves**

$ million

	Today	Year 1	Year 2	Year 3	Year 4
NOPLAT					
Reported EBITA	–	286	353	400	560
Interest associated with plant decommissioning	–	12	14	17	–
Increase (decrease) in income-smoothing reserve	–	40	40	(80)	–
NOPLAT	–	337	407	337	560
Reconciliation to net income					
Net income	–	286	323	400	560
Interest associated with plant decommissioning	–	12	14	17	–
Increase (decrease) in income-smoothing reserve	–	40	40	(80)	–
Provision for restructuring	–	–	30	–	–
NOPLAT	–	337	407	337	560
Invested capital					
Operating assets	700	840	980	1,120	–
Reserve for product returns	(150)	(180)	(210)	(240)	–
Invested capital	550	660	770	880	–
Reserve for plant decommissioning	119	144	170	–	–
Reserve for restructuring	–	–	30	–	–
Reserve for income smoothing	–	40	80	–	–
Equity	431	476	490	880	–
Invested capital	550	660	770	880	–
ROIC (on beginning-of-year capital, percent)	–	61.4	61.7	43.8	63.6

it must create a corresponding liability when that product or service is sold. If the reserve is related to the ongoing operations and grows in step with sales, the reserve should be treated the same as other non-interest-bearing liabilities (e.g., accounts payable). Specifically, the provision should be deducted from revenues to determine EBITA, and the reserve ($180 million) should be netted against operating assets ($840 million). Since the provision and reserve are treated as operating items, they appear as part of free cash flow and should not be valued separately.

Long-term operating provisions Sometimes, when a company decommissions a plant, it must pay for cleanup and other costs. Assume our hypothetical company owns a plant that operates for 10 years and requires $200 million in decommissioning costs. Rather than expense the cash outflow in a lump sum at the time of decommissioning, the company builds a reserve as if it borrowed the money gradually over time. Thus, if the company borrowed $12.5 million annually at 10 percent, the debt (recorded as a reserve) would grow to $200 million by the plant's final year of operation.

If the provision is material, it will be recorded in the company's footnotes as follows:

Balance sheet	Today	Year 1	Year 2	Year 3
Starting reserve	96.8	119.1	143.5	170.4
Plant-decommissioning expense (1)	12.5	12.5	12.5	12.5
Interest cost (2)	9.7	11.9	14.4	17.0
Decommissioning payout	0.0	0.0	0.0	(200.0)
Ending reserve	119.1	143.5	170.4	0.0
Income statement				
Reported provision (1 + 2)	22.2	24.5	26.9	29.6

In year 1, two years before decommissioning, the reported provision is $24.5 million. The provision consists of the $12.5 million annual decommissioning expense and $11.9 million in hypothetical interest expense (the interest that would have been paid if the company had gradually borrowed the decommissioning expense). Therefore, when calculating adjusted EBITA, add back $11.9 million to reported EBITA to remove the interest charges.

To measure NOPLAT and invested capital consistently, treat the reserve ($143.5 million in year 1) as a source of debt-based capital (and do not net against operating assets to determine invested capital). When you treat the plant closure reserve as a debt equivalent, the final payment will not flow through free cash flow. Therefore, for companies that use the present-value methodology to determine reserves, subtract the current reported reserve ($119.1 million as of today) from the value of operations ($1,607 million) to determine equity value. The value of operations is converted into equity value at the bottom of Exhibit 26.7.

One-time restructuring provisions   When management decides to restructure a company, it will often recognize certain future expenses (e.g., severance) immediately. We recommend treating one-time provisions as nonoperating and treating the corresponding reserve as a debt equivalent. In year 2, our hypothetical company declared a $30 million restructuring provision, which will be paid in year 3. Since the restructuring is nonoperating, it is not deducted from revenues to determine NOPLAT. Rather, it is included in the reconciliation to net income. Because we plan to value the provision on a cash basis, the noncash reserve is treated as a debt equivalent and is not netted against operating assets to determine invested capital.

Since nonoperating income (and expenses) does not flow through free cash flow, the restructuring expense must be valued separately on a cash basis. To convert accrual-based restructuring expenses to cash, start with the restructuring expense, and subtract the increase in the restructuring reserve. This leads

EXHIBIT 26.7 **Enterprise DCF with Provisions and Reserves**

$ million

	Today	Year 1	Year 2	Year 3	Year 4	
NOPLAT	–	337	407	337	560	
Net investment in invested capital	–	(110)	(110)	(110)	880	
Free cash flow	–	227	297	227	1,440	
From the investor's perspective						
Provision for restructuring	–	–	30	–	–	
(Increase) decrease in restructuring reserve	–	–	(30)	30	–	
Cash-based restructuring provision	–	–	–	30	–	Present value at 10% = 23
Interest associated with plant decommissioning	–	12	14	17	–	
(Increase) decrease in plant closure reserve	–	(24)	(27)	170	–	
Dividends	–	240	310	10	1,440	
Free cash flow	–	227	297	227	1,440	
Free cash flow						
Free cash flow	–	227	297	227	1,440	
Discount factor (at 10%)	–	0.91	0.83	0.75	0.68	
Discounted cash flow	–	207	246	171	984	

Valuation		**Source**
Value of operations	1,607	Summation of discounted cash flow
Value of restructuring provision	(23)	Present value at 10% (debt equivalent)
Reserve for plant decommissioning	(119)	Reported as of today (debt equivalent)
Equity value	1,465	

to a cash-based restructuring provision of $0 in year 2 and $30 million in year 3 (see Exhibit 26.7). The estimated present value of the nonoperating cash flow stream equals $23 million, which must be deducted from the value of operations to determine equity value.

Income-smoothing provisions   In some countries, provisions can be manipulated to smooth earnings. In Exhibit 26.5, our hypothetical company was able to show a smooth growth in reported EBITA and net income by using a smoothing provision. Although we title the account "income-smoothing provision," actual companies use subtler wording, such as "other provisions." For our hypothetical company, a provision was recorded in years 1 and 2 and was reversed in year 3. By using an income-smoothing provision, the company hid its year 3 decline in operating performance (operating costs rose from 70 percent to 80 percent of sales).

To evaluate the company's performance properly, eliminate any income-smoothing provisions. Do this by adding the income-smoothing provision back to reported EBITA (essentially undoing the income-smoothing provision). In this way, we are converting the provision to cash, rather than accounting for it as an accrual, and subsequently need to treat the reserve as an equity equiv-alent (using a process identical to the one for deferred taxes). Since income-smoothing provisions are entirely noncash, they should result in no adjustment to the company's valuation.

Provisions and Taxes

In most situations, provisions are tax deductible only when cash is dispersed, not when the provision is reported. Thus, most provisions will give rise to deferred-tax assets.[8] For operating-related provisions, we recommend using cash, rather than accrual taxes. For nonoperating provisions, net the deferred tax asset against the corresponding provision. For an in-depth discussion on deferred taxes, see Chapter 25.

REVIEW QUESTIONS

1. Using an Internet search tool, locate Procter & Gamble's investor relations web site. Under "Financial Reporting," you will find the company's 2009 annual report. Procter & Gamble has a very simple income statement. Only selling, general, and administrative expenses and cost of products sold are deducted from revenue to determine operating income. In Note 1, Summary of Significant Accounting Policies, you will find a discussion of the preceding two expenses. Does either embed nonoperating expenses? If so, adjust P&G's operating income to create a clean measure of EBITA.

2. ValueCo generates $10 million in after-tax operating profit on $100 million in assets. The company has $20 million in accounts payable, $15 million in product warranty reserves, $5 million in severance reserves, $30 in long-term debt, and $30 million in equity. What is ValueCo's ROIC?

3. In year 0, SmoothCo has $50 million in cash and $50 million in inventory, financed by $100 million in equity. In year 1, the company records $100 million in revenue, $80 million in operating costs, and $10 million in litiga-tion provisions for a case yet to be resolved. Based on the preceding data, build a balance sheet for year 1. Assume inventory remains constant and no dividends are paid. What is the return on equity in year 1? In year 2, the company records $100 million in revenue and $90 million in operating costs. The case started in year 1 is resolved for $5 million in cash. Because man-agement overestimated the amount of litigation charges, SmoothCo takes a

---

[8] For instance, a $30 million noncash restructuring charge would lead to a $30 million restructuring reserve. If the restructuring charge is tax deductible on the GAAP income statement, retained earnings would drop by only $21 million (assuming a 30 percent tax rate). Since the increase in the restructuring reserve does not match the drop in retained earnings, the balance sheet will not balance. To plug the difference, a deferred tax asset is recognized for $9 million.

$5 million gain in year 2. What is ROE in year 2? How is ROE distorted by the litigation expense?

4. Companies in highly competitive industries often see a number of consecutive restructuring charges. In these cases, should restructuring be treated as operating or nonoperating? From a valuation perspective, what are the important issues that should be considered?

27

Leases, Pensions, and Other Obligations

When a company borrows money to purchase an asset, the asset is listed on the company's balance sheet matched by a corresponding obligation. Over the past 20 years, however, clever use of existing accounting rules has allowed companies to keep many assets and their corresponding debts "off balance sheet." Instead of recognizing these assets and their corresponding debts, companies may record just the rental and transaction fees on the income statement, disclosing the real nature of these transactions only in the footnotes.

The two most common forms of off-balance-sheet debt are operating leases and securitized receivables. From an economic perspective, operating leases and securitized receivables are no different from traditional asset ownership and debt. When the assets and related borrowings do not appear on the balance sheet, this omission biases nearly every financial ratio, including return on invested capital (ROIC). In fact, because of the distortions caused by operating leases in particular, these leases are now under scrutiny by the Securities and Exchange Commission (SEC), Financial Accounting Standards Board (FASB), and International Accounting Standards Board (IASB). The issue is significant. One SEC study found that 77 percent of U.S. traded public companies have operating leases and these total $1.25 trillion in undiscounted future cash obligations. In response to these staggering numbers, the FASB and IASB formed a joint task force to examine whether companies should capitalize operating leases on the balance sheet.

Another well-known type of off-balance-sheet item is unfunded pension liabilities. The reporting of these liabilities also has been under recent scrutiny by the global accounting community. Historically, companies were allowed to recognize pension shortfalls gradually. This caused the recorded amount of pension shortfalls to differ from their market values. Following a change in policy, British and U.S. companies are now required to report underfunding of pensions at their market values;[1] under IASB doctrine, the recognition of pension shortfalls at their market values is still optional. But for all three standards, income statement distortions are still prevalent, as a company can record lower pension expenses even when it is raising employee benefits and losing money in its pension fund. This is because only expected returns (and not actual returns) on pension investments flow through the income statement, and the rate of expected returns is selected at the discretion of company management.

Unless and until the rules change, analysts comparing corporations' performance must carefully investigate these off-balance-sheet items. Without appropriate adjustments, off-balance-sheet items can bias return on invested capital (ROIC) dramatically upward, making competitive benchmarking unreliable. Yet only financial analysis is affected by the treatment of off-balance-sheet debt. Valuation will be identical whether or not it is adjusted for off-balance-sheet debt, as long as corresponding adjustments are made to the cost of capital and the level of debt.

In the first two parts of this chapter, we demonstrate how to investigate the footnotes to find off-balance-sheet items, focusing on operating leases and securitized receivables. We show how to recapitalize each item on the balance sheet, compute the new ROIC, and compare the result with the raw calculations. In the third part of the chapter, we work through an example of the pension footnote to show how to build a clean pension expense that accurately reflects the economic benefits given to employees.

It is important to note that not every company will have these off-balance-sheet obligations. Operating leases tend to be most prevalent in industries such as airlines and hospitals that use large, easily transferable assets. Securitized receivables tend to be found in companies with few fixed assets. Unfunded pensions are often associated with established companies, such as automobile manufacturers and steel companies, because companies founded within the past 20 years typically provide defined-contribution plans rather than traditional defined-benefit pensions.

OPERATING LEASES

When a company borrows money to purchase an asset, the asset and debt are recorded on the company's balance sheet, and interest is deducted from operating profit to determine net income. If, instead, the company leases that same asset from another organization (the lessor) and the lease meets certain criteria, the company (or lessee) records only the periodic rental expense

---

[1] Financial Reporting Standard (FRS) 17 was implemented by the British Financial Reporting Council in 2000. Statement of Financial Accounting Standards (SFAS) 158 was passed in 2006 by U.S.-based FASB, and International Accounting Standard (IAS) 19 is currently under consideration for revision by the IASB.

associated with the lease.[2] Therefore, a company that chooses to lease its assets will have artificially low *operating* profits (because rental expenses include an implicit interest expense) and artificially high capital productivity (because the assets do not appear on the lessee's balance sheet). Although these two effects counteract one another, the net effect is an artificial boost in ROIC, because the reduction in operating profit by rental expense is typically smaller than the reduction in invested capital caused by omitting assets. The result is especially dramatic for profitable companies that lease a substantial portion of their fixed assets, as is typical of retailers and airlines.

This section outlines how to adjust the financial statements and valuation to reflect the real economics of operating leases. Adjusting the financial statement makes return on capital and free cash flow once again independent of capital structure choices, specifically whether to lease, own, or borrow. Although ROIC and leverage ratios will change following the adjustment, the company's valuation should not. A drop in ROIC will be accompanied by a corresponding drop in the cost of capital and increase in debt equivalents. The net effect will leave the equity valuation unchanged.

The process for adjusting financial statements and valuation for operating leases consists of three steps:

1. Reorganize the financial statements to reflect operating leases appropriately. Capitalize the value of leased assets on the balance sheet, and make a corresponding adjustment to long-term debt. Adjust operating profit upward by removing the implicit interest in rental expense.

2. Build a weighted average cost of capital (WACC) that reflects adjusted debt-to-enterprise value. To do this, use an adjusted debt-to-value ratio that includes capitalized operating leases. If unlevered industry betas are used to determine the cost of equity, lever them at the adjusted debt-to-value ratio to determine the levered cost of equity.

3. Value the enterprise by discounting free cash flow (based on the newly reorganized financial statements) at the adjusted cost of capital. Subtract traditional debt and the current value of operating leases from enterprise value to determine equity value.

Adjusting for Operating Leases: An Example

In Exhibit 27.1, we present the financial statements of a hypothetical company. The company is profitable and growing, with short-term assets and liabilities funded by a mix of debt and equity. To avoid the complexities of continuing

---

[2] SFAS 13 details certain situations when leases must be capitalized (the asset and associated debt must be recorded on the balance sheet). For example, if the asset is transferred to the lessee at the end of the lease, the lease must be capitalized. At the time of this writing, a joint task force of the FASB and IASB is examining whether all leases should be capitalized.

EXHIBIT 27.1 **Leasing Example: Financial Statements**

$ million

Income statement

	Today	Year 1	Year 2	Year 3
Revenues	900.0	1,000.0	1,150.0	1,265.0
Expenses	–	(800.0)	(920.0)	(1,012.0)
Rental expense	–	(106.4)	(115.4)	(118.1)
Operating income	–	93.6	114.6	134.9
Interest	–	(7.1)	(7.7)	(7.9)
Earnings before taxes	–	86.5	106.9	127.0
Taxes	–	(21.6)	(26.7)	(31.7)
Net income	–	64.9	80.2	95.2

Supplemental disclosure

Rental expense	n/a	106.4	115.4	118.1
Value of operating leases[1]	710.6	769.2	787.8	–

Balance sheet

	Today	Year 1	Year 2	Year 3
Short-term assets	360.0	400.0	345.0	–
Long-term assets	189.4	230.8	362.2	–
Operating assets	549.4	630.8	707.2	–
Operating liabilities	180.0	200.0	230.0	–
Debt	118.4	128.2	131.3	–
Equity	251.0	302.6	345.9	–
Liabilities and equity	549.4	630.8	707.2	–

[1] The value of operating leases is not typically disclosed. A method for estimating the value of leased assets is presented later in this chapter.

value, we assume the company liquidates in the final year. Debt is retired, and a liquidating dividend is paid.

A significant portion of the company's assets, $710.6 million, is leased.[3] Since the leases are classified as operating leases, the leased assets are not included on the company's balance sheet, where only $549.4 million in operating assets are reported. Instead, the company reports $106.4 million in rental expenses in year 1. Typically, rental expense is not explicitly shown as a separate line item on the income statement, but instead is disclosed in the company's footnotes.

The values of the leased assets are also shown in Exhibit 27.1. Under current accounting standards, the actual value of leased assets is typically not disclosed, but there are various methods for estimating the value of leased assets, which we outline later in the chapter. For the purpose of this adjustment example, we assume the value of the leased assets has already been estimated.

Reorganize financial statements to reflect operating leases appropriately

Exhibits 27.2 and 27.3 show how to adjust the financial statements to reflect operating leases. On the left side of the exhibits, the financial statements are reorganized *without* an adjustment for operating leases; on the right side, the reorganized financial statements reflect adjustments for leases. To assure consistency, net operating profit less adjusted taxes (NOPLAT) is reconciled to

[3] To highlight the adjustments for operating leases, we assume a significant portion of the assets is leased. Although significant leases are common in airlines and retail, most industries use operating leases in moderation.

EXHIBIT 27.2 **Leasing Example: NOPLAT Calculation**

$ million

NOPLAT (direct from financial statements)

	Year 1	Year 2	Year 3
Revenues	1,000.0	1,150.0	1,265.0
Operating expenses	(800.0)	(920.0)	(1,012.0)
Rental expense	(106.4)	(115.4)	(118.1)
Operating income	93.6	114.6	134.9
Operating taxes	(23.4)	(28.7)	(33.7)
NOPLAT	70.2	86.0	101.1

Reconciliation

Net income	64.9	80.2	95.2
After-tax interest expense	5.3	5.8	5.9
NOPLAT	70.2	86.0	101.1
ROIC (on beginning-of-year capital, percent)	19.0	20.0	21.2

NOPLAT (adjusted for leases)

	Year 1	Year 2	Year 3
Revenues	1,000.0	1,150.0	1,265.0
Operating expenses	(800.0)	(920.0)	(1,012.0)
Lease depreciation	(70.9)	(76.9)	(78.8)
Operating income	129.1	153.1	174.3
Operating taxes	(32.3)	(38.3)	(43.6)
NOPLAT	96.8	114.8	130.7

Reconciliation

Net income	64.9	80.2	95.2
After-tax interest expense	5.3	5.8	5.9
After-tax lease interest	26.6	28.8	29.5
NOPLAT	96.8	114.8	130.7
ROIC (on beginning-of-year capital, percent)	9.0	9.6	10.3

EXHIBIT 27.3 **Leasing Example: Invested Capital Calculation**

$ million

Invested capital (direct from financial statements)

	Today	Year 1	Year 2	Year 3
Operating assets	549.4	630.8	707.2	—
Operating liabilities	(180.0)	(200.0)	(230.0)	—
Invested capital	369.4	430.8	477.2	—
Reconciliation				
Debt	118.4	128.2	131.3	—
Equity	251.0	302.6	345.9	—
Invested capital	369.4	430.8	477.2	—

Invested capital (adjusted for leases)

	Today	Year 1	Year 2	Year 3
Operating assets	549.4	630.8	707.2	—
Capitalized operating leases	710.6	769.2	787.8	—
Adjusted operating assets	1,260.0	1,400.0	1,495.0	
Operating liabilities	(180.0)	(200.0)	(230.0)	—
Invested capital	1,080.0	1,200.0	1,265.0	—
Reconciliation				
Debt	118.4	128.2	131.3	—
Capitalized operating leases	710.6	769.2	787.8	—
Equity	251.0	302.6	345.9	—
Invested capital	1,080.0	1,200.0	1,265.0	—

EXHIBIT 27.4 **Leasing Example: Current Capital Structure**

Capital structure (unadjusted for leases)			Capital structure (adjusted for leases)		
	$ million	percent of total		$ million	percent of total
Debt value	118.4	25	Debt value	118.4	10
Market value of equity	355.3	75	Market value of equity	355.3	30
Enterprise value	473.7	100	Value of operating leases	710.6	60
			Enterprise value	1,184.3	100

net income, and invested capital is computed from both sources and uses of invested capital. The adjustments are as follows:

- The value of capitalized operating leases ($710.6 million) is added to book assets to long-term debt. The corresponding adjustments increase both sources and uses of invested capital.

- Implicit lease interest expense is removed from operating profit. To compute the implicit interest expense, multiply the value of operating leases ($710.6 million) by the cost of secured debt, which we assume is 5 percent.[4] The remaining rental expense is renamed lease depreciation (the other major component of rental expense). Since depreciation is not related to capital structure, it remains as an operating expense.

Operating income rises from $70.2 million to $96.8 million in year 1 after the numbers have been adjusted (see Exhibit 27.2). Invested capital rises from $430.8 million to $1,200.0 million in year 1 (see Exhibit 27.3). Although it appears the two might offset one another, this is not the case, because invested capital rises by a greater proportion than operating profit. The return on invested capital (ROIC) of 19.0 percent in year 1 for the unadjusted financial statements is more than double the 9.0 percent ROIC in year 1 of the properly adjusted financial statements; what appears to be the creation of above-average returns is merely an artifact of off-balance-sheet leverage.

Build a cost of capital that reflects adjusted debt-to-enterprise value   Although the return on capital drops when leases are capitalized, this does not necessarily mean the company is destroying value. The cost of capital must be adjusted for operating leases as well, and it will drop after adjustment.

To determine the cost of capital, we start by computing how the company is financed. Exhibit 27.4 presents the unadjusted and adjusted capital structure for our leasing example. To determine unadjusted enterprise

---

[4] The secured cost of debt can be proxied by the yield to maturity on AA-rated 10-year bonds.

EXHIBIT 27.5 **Leasing Example: Weighted Average Cost of Capital (WACC) Calculation**

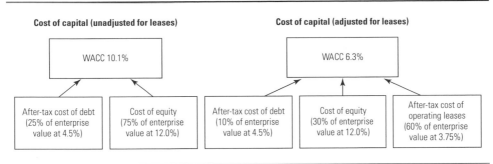

value, sum the value of debt and equity. Debt value equals the book value of debt ($118.4 million) presented in Exhibit 27.1. The market value of equity ($355.3 million) is reported by financial data providers, such as Bloomberg. On an unadjusted basis, debt comprises 25 percent of enterprise value and equity value comprises 75 percent of enterprise value. To adjust capital structure for operating leases, add the value of operating leases ($710.6 million) to unadjusted enterprise value. On an adjusted basis, debt comprises 10 percent of enterprise value, equity comprises 30 percent of enterprise value, and the value of operating leases comprises 60 percent of enterprise value.

Exhibit 27.5 presents the cost of capital adjusted and unadjusted for operating leases. The unadjusted cost of capital is computed as a weighted average of debt and equity. For instance, in our example, 25 percent of the $473.7 million enterprise value is financed at a 6 percent cost of debt. At a tax rate of 25 percent, the after-tax cost of debt is 4.5 percent. The remaining 75 percent is funded by equity at 12 percent cost of equity. This leads to a weighted average cost of capital (WACC) of 10.1 percent. The adjusted cost of capital weights the after-tax cost of debt (4.5 percent) by 10 percent, the cost of equity (12 percent) by 30 percent, and the after-tax cost of operating leases (3.75 percent) by 60 percent. This leads to a lower WACC of 6.3 percent.

In our hypothetical company, the cost of equity was given at 12 percent. In practice, the cost of equity must be estimated using the capital asset pricing model (CAPM) and beta. When you use an unlevered industry beta as the starting point for calculating the cost of equity, lever the beta using the capital structure implied by the operating lease treatment. In our example, the implied adjusted ratio of debt ($118.4 million plus $710.6 million) to equity ($355.3 million) is 2.33 times. If you are using a raw beta directly from a regression, no adjustments are necessary.

Value the enterprise   Although NOPLAT, invested capital, and ROIC are affected by the accounting treatment of off-balance-sheet financing, the

EXHIBIT 27.6 **Leasing Example: Free Cash Flow and Equity Valuation**

$ million

Free cash flow (unadjusted for leases)

	Year 1	Year 2	Year 3
NOPLAT	70.2	86.0	101.1
(Increase) decrease in invested capital	(61.3)	(46.4)	477.2
Free cash flow	8.9	39.5	578.4
Reconciliation			
After-tax interest	5.3	5.8	5.9
Cash flows to debt	(9.8)	(3.1)	131.3
Cash flows to equity	13.3	36.9	441.2
Reconciliation of free cash flow	8.9	39.5	578.4
Discount factor	1.101	1.213	1.336
Discounted cash flow	8.0	32.6	433.1

Valuation

Enterprise value	473.7
Debt	(118.4)
Equity value	355.3

Free cash flow (adjusted for leases)

	Year 1	Year 2	Year 3
NOPLAT	96.8	114.8	130.7
(Increase) decrease in invested capital	(120.0)	(65.0)	1,265.0
Free cash flow	(23.2)	49.8	1,395.7
Reconciliation			
After-tax interest	5.3	5.8	5.9
After-tax lease interest	26.6	28.8	29.5
Cash flows to debt	(9.8)	(3.1)	131.3
Cash flows to lease debt	(58.7)	(18.6)	787.8
Cash flows to equity	13.3	36.9	441.2
Reconciliation of free cash flow	(23.2)	49.8	1,395.7
Discount factor	1.063	1.130	1.201
Discounted cash flow	(21.8)	44.1	1,162.0

Valuation

Enterprise value	1,184.3
Debt	(118.4)
Operating leases	(710.6)
Equity value	355.3

company's value is not.[5] In Exhibit 27.6, free cash flow and enterprise valuation are computed using the reorganized financial statements. The reconciliation of free cash flow is also provided. On the left side of Exhibit 27.6, free cash flow is computed without adjustment for operating leases. On the right side, adjustments for operating leases are made.

To build adjusted free cash flow, do not add lease depreciation back to NOPLAT to compute gross cash flow. Although depreciation is a noncash charge for the lessor, it is a cash charge for the lessee. Year-to-year changes in operating leases are part of adjusted invested capital, so they are part of free cash flow. Although NOPLAT is consistently higher after adjustments for leases, free cash flow is not. This is because free cash flow is a function of NOPLAT (which is higher) less capital investments (which are often higher as well). Do not include after-tax lease interest (an outflow of $26.6 million in year 1) and the change in lease obligations (an inflow of $58.7 million) as part of free cash flow; they are sources of financing.

To value the enterprise, discount free cash flow at the appropriate cost of capital: 10.1 percent for unadjusted free cash flow and 6.3 percent for

---

[5] Equity valuation is independent of the *accounting treatment* of operating leases, but not the use of operating leases themselves. Similar to debt, operating leases have tax advantages relative to asset purchases financed by equity. Relative to bank loans, operating leases offer the potential advantage that monitoring and maintenance by the lessor may lower moral hazard problems when the asset is redeployed.

lease-adjusted free cash flow. To convert enterprise value to equity value, subtract today's value of debt ($118.4 million) and lease obligations ($710.6 million) from enterprise value. As shown in Exhibit 27.6, the equity value ($355.3 million) is unchanged when the financial statements are adjusted for operating leases.

Since valuation is not affected by the treatment of operating leases, you may wonder why it is worth the effort to adjust the financial statements. The answer is that capitalizing operating leases is a critical step in competitive benchmarking. Companies that use more operating leases will have higher raw ROICs, leading to misperceptions of their relative performance. Thus, even if you choose not to adjust the valuation for operating leases because this will not affect your final figures, always benchmark performance with adjusted numbers.

Estimating the Value of Leased Assets

Companies seldom disclose the value of their leased assets, but you need to estimate their value to adjust for operating leases. We recommend the following estimation process using rental expense, the cost of secured debt, and an estimated asset life. To see why, examine the determinants of rental expense. To compensate the lessor properly, the rental expense includes compensation for the cost of financing the asset (at the cost of secured debt, denoted by k_d in the following equations) and the periodic depreciation of the asset (for which we assume straight-line depreciation). The following equation solves for periodic rental expense:

$$\text{Rental Expense}_t = \text{Asset Value}_{t-1} \left(k_d + \frac{1}{\text{Asset Life}} \right) \tag{27.1}$$

To estimate the asset's value, rearrange equation (27.1) as follows:

$$\text{Asset Value}_{t-1} = \frac{\text{Rental Expense}_t}{k_d + \dfrac{1}{\text{Asset Life}}} \tag{27.2}$$

Rental expense is disclosed in the footnotes, and the cost of debt can be estimated using AA-rated yields. (Remember, the operating lease is secured by the underlying asset, so it is less risky than the company's unsecured debt.) This leaves only the asset life, which is unreported. To estimate asset life, Lim, Mann, and Mihov propose using property, plant, and equipment (PP&E) divided by annual depreciation. In their research, they examined 7,000 firms over 20 years and computed the median asset life at 10.9 years.[6]

---

[6] Steve C. Lim, Steven C. Mann, and Vassil T. Mihov, "Market Evaluation of Off-Balance Sheet Financing: You Can Run but You Can't Hide," EFMA 2004 Basel Meetings Paper (December 1, 2003).

There are several other approaches for computing asset value. The most common alternative is to compute the present value of required lease payments, which can be found in the company's footnotes. Although this method is used by rating agencies such as Standard & Poor's, it systematically undervalues the asset, since it ignores the residual value returned at the end of the lease contract. For example, most would agree that a $1 million asset leased for two years is worth more than the present value of two payments of $100,000 per year.

A second alternative for computing the asset value of operating leases is the perpetuity method. In this method, the rental expense is divided by the cost of debt. But the perpetuity method systematically overvalues leased assets. Why? The method is identical to the depreciation-adjusted perpetuity proposed in equation (27.2) using an infinite asset life. Since the asset life is in fact finite, the perpetuity method understates the denominator and thus overstates the asset value, especially for short-lived assets.

A final possibility is to multiply rental expense by a capitalization rate. Many in the investment banking community multiply rental expenses by 8 times to approximate asset value. Although this method is quite simplistic, the multiplier is based on reasonable assumptions: Using the depreciation-adjusted perpetuity from equation (27.2) with a cost of debt of 6 percent and an asset life of 15 years leads to a multiplier of 8 times.[7] But be careful. As the actual cost of debt or asset life deviates from these values, the 8 times multiplier could lead to incorrect assessments.

Research on Operating Leases as a Form of Debt

To analyze our hypothetical company, we treated off-balance-sheet leases no differently than traditional debt. But is this the practice of investors, lenders, and the rating agencies? To address this question, researchers have examined the use of off-balance-sheet leases and their effects on credit ratings and interest rates.

In one study, Lim, Mann, and Mihov examined the effect of operating leases on debt ratings and bond yield premiums for 7,000 companies over 20 years.[8] They found that when companies used more operating leases, they were, in fact, awarded lower credit ratings by rating agencies. These ratings and the use of operating leases subsequently led to higher required yields on new public bond issuances. In a second study, researchers at Ohio State University examined more than 2,500 bank loans to test whether credit statistics adjusted for operating leases explained the interest rates charged better than unadjusted

[7] Asset value equals rental expense times a capitalization rate, such that the capitalization rate equals 1 divided by the sum of the cost of debt and 1 divided by the asset life. If the cost of debt is 0.06 and 1 divided by the asset life equals 0.067 (i.e., $\frac{1}{15}$), the capitalization rate equals 7.9.
[8] Ibid.

statistics did.[9] They found that interest rates for unrated, unsecured debt were indeed explained better by credit statistics adjusted for operating leases. The evidence is clear. Investors, lenders, and rating agencies all treat operating leases the same as traditional debt. Thus, a thoughtful financial analysis will adjust the financial statements for operating leases.

SECURITIZED RECEIVABLES

A less common form of off-balance-sheet debt is receivables securitization, a process where the company sells its accounts receivable to another company. In some cases, the receivables are sold to a third party, but in many cases, they are sold to a subsidiary. Although the receivables are legally owned by someone else, the original company continues to process and collect them.

By selling a portion of its receivables, the company will reduce accounts receivable on the balance sheet and increase cash flow from operations on the accountant's cash flow statement. But the improved accounting metrics are misleading. In reality, the company pays a fee for the arrangement, reduces its borrowing capacity, and pays higher interest rates on unsecured debt—all characteristics of raising traditional debt. Some may argue that receivables securitization is a cheaper form of borrowing, since interest rates tend to be low, but this also is misleading. Interest rates are low because the collateral is short-term and generally recoverable compared with the company's traditional unsecured debt.

To determine return on capital, free cash flow, and leverage consistently, add back securitized receivables to the balance sheet, and make a corresponding increase to short-term debt. Any fees paid for securitizing receivables should be treated as interest. Data necessary to make the adjustments will appear in the footnotes to company accounts.

Consider the footnotes on receivables securitized by Crown Cork & Seal:

> The Company had no outstanding borrowings under its $758 revolving credit facility at December 31, 2008 and had $234 of securitized receivables.... The Company recorded expenses related to the securitization facilities of $14, $17, and $15, respectively, as interest expense, including commitment fees of 0.25% on the unused portion of the facilities.

To make the adjustment for Crown Cork & Seal, $234 million should be added to accounts receivable and short-term debt. Since operating profit remains unchanged (fees are part of interest) and invested capital rises, ROIC will

---

[9] Jennifer Lynne M. Altamuro, Rick M. Johnston, Shail Pandit, and Haiwen (Helen) Zhang, "Operating Leases and Credit Assessments," Ohio State University working paper (April 2008).

be lower. Leverage ratios such as debt to value will rise, but interest coverage ratios will remain unchanged.

In some cases, fees are included in selling, general, and administrative (SG&A) expense, rather than interest expense. In these situations, the fees must be moved from SG&A expense to interest expense. For example, Hasbro includes securitization fees in its selling expenses:

> As of December 30, 2008 and December 31, 2007 the utilization of the receivables facility was $250,000. During 2008, 2007, and 2006, the loss on the sale of the receivables totaled $5,302, $7,982, and $2,241, respectively, which is recorded in selling, distribution, and administration expenses in the accompanying consolidated statements of operations.

For Hasbro, $250 million should be added to accounts receivable and short-term debt, and $5.3 million should be moved from SG&A expense to interest expense, raising operating profits. An upward adjustment should also be made to operating taxes at the marginal tax rate. (Interest tax shields will be valued as part of the cost of capital.)

PENSIONS AND OTHER POSTRETIREMENT BENEFITS

Each year, thousands of companies promise future retirement benefits to their employees. In many cases, these companies set aside investments in a separate trust to fund future obligations. But if future obligations are greater than the value of investments held, the company must report unfunded retirement obligations. Although pension shortfalls are universal, their magnitudes vary across nations. For instance, in Germany, companies are not required to prefund retirement obligations, so companies' unfunded liabilities are quite large. In the United States, regulations limit the amount of pension underfunding. These regulations do not cover other retirement benefits such as medical expenses, so even U.S. companies can have significant unfunded liabilities.

Today, under U.S. Generally Accepted Accounting Principles (GAAP), U.S. companies report the market value of pension shortfalls (and excess pension assets) on the balance sheet.[10] Before 2006, the market value of a pension shortfall was only recognized in the pension footnote. The balance sheet instead recognized a smoothed figure averaged over many years. Consequently, a company that had an overfunded plan in the past but was currently experiencing a shortfall could continue to show an overfunded pension asset for years, even though, in reality, a large liability existed. Starting in December 2006, FASB Statement of Financial Accounting Standards (SFAS) No. 158

---

[10] Not every company reports prepaid pension assets and unfunded pension liabilities as a separate line item. Many companies consolidate prepaid pension assets in other long-term assets, and unfunded pension liabilities in other long-term liabilities.

eliminated pension smoothing on the balance sheet. Companies are now required to report excess pension assets and unfunded pension obligations on the balance sheet *at their current values*, not as smoothed values as in the past.[11] Unfortunately, SFAS 158 addressed only deficiencies on the balance sheet. The idiosyncrasies of pension accounting still distort operating profitability and can even be manipulated by management to enhance margins artificially.

In this section, we outline how to incorporate excess pension assets and unfunded pension liabilities into enterprise value, and how to adjust the income statement to eliminate accounting distortions. The process consists of the following three steps:

1. Identify excess pension assets and unfunded liabilities on the balance sheet. If the company does not separate pension accounts, search the pension footnote for their location. Excess pension assets should be treated as nonoperating, and unfunded pension liabilities should be treated as a debt equivalent.

2. Add excess pension assets to and deduct unfunded pension liabilities from enterprise value. Valuations should be done on an after-tax basis.

3. To reflect accurately the economic expenses of pension benefits given to employees, remove the accounting pension expense from cost of sales, and replace it with the service cost and amortization of prior service costs reported in the notes. The pension expense, service cost, and amortization of prior service costs are reported in the company's notes.

Analyzing and Valuing Pensions: DuPont Example

To demonstrate the proper treatment of pensions and other postretirement benefits, we examine the accounts of the global chemicals company DuPont. This example shows how, following the passage of SFAS 158, including excess pension assets and pension retirement liabilities in enterprise value has become (somewhat) simpler for U.S. companies. Historically, values reported on the balance sheet did not accurately reflect pension surpluses or liabilities. In DuPont's pension footnote, shown in Exhibit 27.7, the funded status indicates that in 2005, DuPont's pension plans were *underfunded* by $3.1 billion. Yet on the balance sheet, DuPont reported *excess* pension assets of $3.3 billion in other assets and a cumulative net surplus of $2.3 billion (the net amount recognized). This discrepancy occurred because balance sheet reporting lagged fund performance and was adjusted over long periods. Under the

---

[11] IAS 19 currently gives companies a choice on whether to smooth pension assets and liabilities on the balance sheet. If companies choose not to smooth, then gains and losses on pension funds should be recognized either directly in the income statement or in accumulated comprehensive income. At the time of this writing, IASB is proposing to eliminate smoothing on the balance sheet as well.

EXHIBIT 27.7 **DuPont: Pension Note in Annual Report, Funded Status**

$ million

	Pension benefits			Other benefits		
	2005	**2006**	**2007**	**2005**	**2006**	**2007**
Benefit obligation at end of year	22,935	22,849	22,206	4,089	4,255	3,796
Fair value of plan assets at end of year	19,792	21,909	22,618	–	–	–
Funded status	(3,143)	(940)	412	(4,089)	(4,255)	(3,796)
Amounts recognized in the consolidated balance sheet						
Other assets	3,280	1,040	2,187	–	–	–
Intangible assets	28	–	–	–	–	–
Other accrued liabilities	(60)	(136)	(112)	(350)	(338)	(315)
Other liabilities	(1,750)	(1,844)	(1,663)	(4,311)	(3,917)	(3,481)
Accumulated other comprehensive loss	843	–	–	–	–	–
Net amount recognized	2,341	(940)	412	(4,661)	(4,255)	(3,796)
	↓	↓		↓	↓	
	Before SFAS 158	After SFAS 158		Before SFAS 158	After SFAS 158	

Source: DuPont 2007 annual report.

new U.S. standards, the balance sheet must match the actual funding status in every period. Thus, funded status matches net amount recognized in 2006 and beyond. The same holds true for other retirement liabilities, such as retiree medical expenses. For example, in 2007, DuPont had no investments set aside to support $3.8 billion in future medical liabilities (labeled by DuPont as "other benefits"). As this case illustrates, whenever you value companies reporting under IFRS or accounting standards other than U.S. GAAP from 2006 onward, you should refer to the footnotes to find the fair value of the pension assets and liabilities.

Identify excess pension assets and unfunded pension liabilities   Not every company reports prepaid pension assets and unfunded pension liabilities as a separate line item. Many companies consolidate prepaid pension assets in other long-term assets and unfunded pension liabilities as part of other long-term liabilities, making them difficult to identify. In the pension footnote, the company typically reports the location of any excess pension assets and unfunded liabilities on the balance sheet. For instance, in 2007, DuPont includes excess pension assets of $2,187 million as a component of other assets (see the "other assets" line in Exhibit 27.7). Note how excess assets and unfunded liabilities are reported separately. This is because pension assets from one plan are *not* netted against underfunding from another.

When reorganizing the balance sheet and income statement, separate operating assets from pension assets, and treat excess pension assets as nonoperating. Unfunded pension liabilities should be treated as a debt equivalent and,

EXHIBIT 27.8 **DuPont: Pension Note in Annual Report, Pension Expense**

$ million

	2005	2006	2007	
Service cost	349	388	383	→ Operating
Amortization of prior service cost	37	29	18	
Interest cost	1,160	1,192	1,228	
Expected return on plan assets	(1,416)	(1,648)	(1,800)	
Amortization of loss	303	227	117	→ Nonoperating
Other	(1)	3	–	
Net periodic (benefit) cost	432	191	(54)	

Source: DuPont 2007 annual report.

as such, should not be deducted from operating assets to determine invested capital.

Value excess pension assets and unfunded pension liabilities   For an ongoing enterprise, excess pension assets can be netted against unfunded liabilities to determine net assets (liabilities) outstanding.[12] To incorporate pensions for a company with net excess assets, add (1 – marginal tax rate) × net pension assets to enterprise value, as excess pension assets will lead to fewer required contributions in the future. Not every country provides tax relief on pension contributions, so check local tax law to determine the marginal tax rate for contributions. To value companies with net unfunded liabilities, deduct (1 – marginal tax rate) × net pension liabilities from enterprise value.

In 2007, DuPont recognized $412 million in excess pension assets and $3,796 million in unfunded other benefits, for a net total liability of $3,384 million. Assuming a marginal tax rate of 35 percent, the after-tax liability equals $2,200 million. To determine equity value, deduct the after-tax liability from enterprise value.

Adjust the income statement for pensions   Pension expenses are composed of four primary items: service cost, interest cost on plan liabilities, expected return on plan assets, and recognized gains and losses (amortization of loss). Exhibit 27.8 presents the pension expense breakout for DuPont. To determine the portion of pension expense that is compensation to employees (and not gains and losses on pension investments), combine service cost and

---

[12] Most countries charge a significant penalty for withdrawing excess funds from pension plans. If the company is being valued for liquidation or the pension plan is being terminated, net unfunded liabilities cannot be netted against excess pension assets. Instead, add after-tax excess pension assets at the penalty rate, and deduct after-tax unfunded pension liabilities at the marginal tax savings for pension contributions.

amortization of prior service cost to arrive at today's value of promised retirement payments.[13] In 2007, DuPont had $383 million in service cost and $18 million in prior service cost, giving a total operating expense of $401 million.

The remaining items—interest cost, expected return on plan assets, and amortization of loss—are related to the performance of the plan assets, not the operations of the business.[14] Therefore, they should not be included in cost of sales to determine NOPLAT. (Pension expense is typically embedded in cost of sales.)

For companies with significant pension plans, failure to adjust pension expense for nonoperating items can distort profit dramatically. In the middle of this century's first decade, strong stock returns drove pension assets up; this raised the expected dollar return on plan assets, driving down reported pension expense. This rising market added nearly $500 million to DuPont's operating profit between 2005 and 2007 (nonoperating pension expenses fell from $46 million in 2005 to a nonoperating profit of $455 million in 2007). DuPont's 2007 expected dollar returns were so large, in fact, that the company reported a net pension gain of $54 million (the net periodic benefit in Exhibit 27.8) as part of earnings before interest, taxes, and amortization (EBITA), rather than a net expense!

To remove plan performance from operating expenses, remove pension expense—in DuPont's case, a $54 million gain in 2007 (subtract gains, add back expenses)—and replace it with the service cost ($383 million) and amortization of prior service cost ($18 million). These adjustments are shown in the middle section of Exhibit 27.9. Making these adjustments lowers EBITA in 2007 by $455 million, more than 10 percent of pretax operating profits.

As shown in the bottom section of Exhibit 27.9, the unadjusted EBITA margins for DuPont fell from 14.9 percent in 2005 to 13.4 percent in 2006, recovering to 14.3 percent in 2007. This rebound, however, was an illusion based on pension expense accounting and the strengthening stock market. After operating margins are adjusted for pension effects (as a result of removing pension expense and replacing it with service cost), operating margins drop from 15.1 percent in 2005 to 12.6 percent in 2006 with little recovery the following year. Free cash flow forecasts based on the unadjusted 14.3 percent margins could inflate value.

---

[13] Service cost represents the present value of retirement promises given to the company's employees in a particular year. Prior service costs are additional *retroactive* benefits given to employees from an amendment to the pension plan. Prior service costs are not expensed immediately. Instead, they are amortized over the expected lifetimes of employees. For more on pension accounting, see D. Kieso, J. Weygandt, and T. Warfield, *Intermediate Accounting*, 13th ed. (Hoboken, NJ: John Wiley & Sons, 2010), Chapter 20, "Accounting for Pensions and Postretirement Benefits."

[14] Interest cost represents the present value of service cost growing into the actual retiree payout. Expected return on plan assets equals the expected return based on asset mix. Amortization of gains and losses represents the gradual recognition of past gains and losses of the pension fund.

EXHIBIT 27.9 **DuPont: Adjusted Operating Profits**

$ million

	2005	2006	2007	
Operating profits, unadjusted				
Revenues	28,491	29,982	30,653	
Operating costs	(24,242)	(25,966)	(26,267)	
Operating profits, unadjusted	4,249	4,016	4,386	
Operating profits, adjusted				
Revenues	28,491	29,982	30,653	
Operating costs	(24,242)	(25,966)	(26,267)	
Net periodic (benefit) cost	432	191	(54)	
Less: service cost	(349)	(388)	(383)	→ –$455 in 2007
Less: amortization of prior service cost	(37)	(29)	(18)	
Operating profits, adjusted	4,295	3,790	3,931	
Operating margin (percent)				
Operating margin, unadjusted	14.9	13.4	14.3	
Operating margin, adjusted	15.1	12.6	12.8	

Expected Return and Earnings Manipulation

To avoid volatility in the income statement, accounting standards allow companies to include "expected returns" on pension plan assets in pension expense rather than actual returns.[15] This enables companies to smooth pension returns from year to year, because the rate of expected returns is determined by the company's financial staff.

Since expected return is unverifiable, company management has discretion over the rate used—a license that management may sometimes take advantage of to manipulate accounting profitability. Bergstresser, Desai, and Rauh find that management increases expected rates of return to increase profitability immediately before acquiring other firms and before exercising stock options.[16] They also find that companies with the weakest shareholder protections tend to use the highest estimates for expected return. In another study, Comprix and Muller find that managers use higher expected rates of return when their compensation committees place greater emphasis on pension income in CEO compensation.[17] It is not clear whether the market recognizes and discounts

[15] Between 2005 and 2007, DuPont used an 8.74 percent expected return on plan assets to determine pension expense.
[16] Daniel B. Bergstresser, Mihir A. Desai, and Joshua Rauh, "Earnings Manipulation, Pension Assumptions, and Managerial Investment Decisions," *Quarterly Journal of Economics* 121, no. 1 (February 2006): 157–195. For more on shareholder protection indexes, see P. Gompers, J. Ishii, and A. Metrick, "Corporate Governance and Equity Prices," *Quarterly Journal of Economics* 118, no. 1 (2003): 107–155.
[17] Joseph Comprix and Karl A. Muller III, "Asymmetric Treatment of Reported Pension Expense and Income Amounts in CEO Cash Compensation Calculations," *Journal of Accounting and Economics* 42, no. 3 (December 2006): 385–416.

this kind of manipulation. Coronado and Sharpe find evidence that earnings associated with changed pension assumptions are capitalized into prices to the same degree as regular operating earnings.[18] This is surprising, given the market's resistance to other means of manipulating earnings (see Chapter 17). One explanation could be the continuing complexities of pension accounting; for robust valuations, these must be understood.

REVIEW QUESTIONS

1. Casher Industries leases a significant portion of its assets, expecting $25 million in rental expense next year. Casher Industries can borrow at 7 percent and the average life of leased assets is seven years. Estimate the value of leased assets. If you misestimate the average life to be 10 years, how large will the valuation error be?

2. Casher Industries expects to earn $25 million in operating profit next year. The company pays an operating tax rate of 30 percent and a marginal tax rate of 35 percent. Using the lease data provided in Question 1, what is the after-tax operating profit adjusted for capitalized operating leases?

3. Many financial analysts estimate the value of operating leases by discounting rental payments provided in the annual report at the cost of debt. Is this method likely to overestimate or underestimate the value of leased assets? Why?

4. Many companies securitize their accounts receivable. Name two ways the cost for securitizing receivables is recognized. If you decide to capitalize securitized receivables, when is an expense adjustment required?

5. Using an Internet search tool, locate Procter & Gamble's investor relations web site. Under "Financial Reporting," you will find the company's 2009 annual report. In Note 8 of the annual report (which is titled Postretirement Benefits and Employee Stock Ownership Plan), P&G reports a breakout of its pension expense. Use this breakout to eliminate nonoperating income related to pensions from operating income reported in P&G's income statement.

6. Using an Internet search tool, locate Procter & Gamble's investor relations web site. Under "Financial Reporting," you will find the company's 2009 annual report. In the balance sheet, there is no report of prepaid pension assets or unfunded pension liabilities. Does this mean that P&G's pension plan is fully funded?

---

[18] J. Coronado and S. Sharpe, "Did Pension Plan Accounting Contribute to a Stock Market Bubble?" (mimeo, Board of Governors of Federal Reserve System, 2003).

28

Capitalized Expenses

When a company builds a plant or purchases equipment, the asset is capitalized on the balance sheet and depreciated over time. Conversely, when a company creates an intangible asset, such as a brand name, distribution network, or patent, accounting rules dictate that the entire outlay must be expensed immediately. For firms with significant intangible assets, such as technology companies and pharmaceutical firms, failure to recognize intangible assets can lead to significant underestimation of a company's invested capital and, thus, overstatement of return on invested capital (ROIC). To illustrate why and how to capitalize expenses, in this chapter we focus on one category, research and development (R&D) expenses.

For the purposes of measuring a company's economic performance, any expense with benefits lasting more than a year should be treated as an investment, since it has created a durable intangible asset. We recommend capitalizing R&D expenses for three reasons:

1. *To represent historical investment more accurately:* By expensing items with long-term benefits, the accounting statements will understate the company's historical investment. This understatement of capital can artificially boost ROIC in later years, making a business appear more attractive than it really is. (In the example to follow, ROIC drops from 42 percent to 13 percent when R&D expenses are appropriately capitalized.)

2. *To prevent manipulation of short-term earnings:* When R&D is expensed, reductions in current R&D flow immediately through the income statement, so under traditional accounting, a manager looking to meet short-term earnings targets can simply reduce R&D. When R&D is capitalized, however, short-term earnings are unaffected by changes in R&D. Only long-run earnings are affected, through amortization. Thus, reducing R&D will lead to improved profitability only if long-term operating performance improves.

3. *To improve performance assessments of long-term investments:* Many companies set R&D budgets at a fixed percentage of revenue. For companies with stable costs and a fixed R&D budget, operating margins will remain constant, regardless of the company's growth rate. If growth is falling, however, expensing R&D masks the resulting drop in true performance. For management to assess the true performance of long-term investments, these must be capitalized.

Although changing the accounting treatment of R&D can change perceptions of a company's performance, it will not affect the company's valuation. Cash outflows related to R&D will appear either in the income statement when expensed or in the investing section when capitalized. Thus, free cash flow (FCF) and, consequently, valuation are unaffected by how R&D is treated.

To start the chapter, we construct a hypothetical example to demonstrate how accounting choice affects ROIC. The length of asset life you choose will affect your assessment of performance, so we also present a sensitivity analysis to show the impact of choosing different asset lifetimes. Next, we set out in detail the capitalization process, using Adobe Systems, an American software company, as an example. Using the newly adjusted financial statements for Adobe Systems, we show the impact of capitalizing R&D expense on the company's ROIC and FCF. We conclude the chapter with a brief discussion of other expenses suitable for capitalization.

EXPENSING VERSUS CAPITALIZATION

In Exhibit 28.1, we present the reorganized financial statements for PharmaCo, a hypothetical company founded in 1995. The company grew rapidly during its first 15 years, generating nearly $900 million in revenue by 2010. PharmaCo

EXHIBIT 28.1 **PharmaCo: Reorganized Financial Statements**

$ million

	2005	2006	2007	2008	2009	2010	
Revenues	587.0	662.6	730.9	791.2	843.3	887.9	
Cost of sales	(352.2)	(397.6)	(438.5)	(474.7)	(506.0)	(532.7)	← Fixed at 60%
R&D expense	(108.0)	(119.4)	(129.6)	(138.7)	(146.5)	(153.2)	
Operating profit	126.7	145.6	162.7	177.8	190.8	202.0	
Operating taxes	(50.7)	(58.3)	(65.1)	(71.1)	(76.3)	(80.8)	
NOPLAT[1]	76.0	87.4	97.6	106.7	114.5	121.2	
Invested capital	195.7	220.9	243.6	263.7	281.1	296.0	← Revenue to capital fixed at 3×

[1] Net operating profit less adjusted taxes.

consistently spends 60 percent of revenues on raw materials, direct labor, and marketing expenses. To renew its product pipeline as it grows, the company spends $20 million in fixed research plus incremental R&D set to 15 percent of revenues.

Since PharmaCo's expense structure forms a constant proportion of revenues, the company generates stable after-tax margins of 13.5 percent. And with revenue fixed at three times invested capital, return on invested capital also is stable at just above 40 percent. But does a 40 percent return on capital represent the company's true performance? No. Invested capital computed directly from the balance sheet includes only purchased capital and not the intellectual capital created internally.

An alternative to expensing is to capitalize R&D on the balance sheet in a manner identical to the practice for capital expenditures.[1] Exhibit 28.2 compares ROIC when R&D is expensed with ROIC when R&D is capitalized. In this example, R&D is capitalized and then amortized over an eight-year period.

In the firm's early years, capitalized R&D leads to higher ROICs than expensed R&D. To capitalize R&D, R&D expense is replaced with amortization of historical R&D. Since R&D expense is greater than amortization in the company's formative years, this keeps early margins and consequently ROICs high. ROIC falls as the firm matures and growth slows, however, because amortizing historical R&D lowers profits and accumulated R&D increases capital. ROIC computed with capitalized R&D stabilizes at 13 percent, dramatically lower than the 42 percent ROIC computed on the unadjusted financial statements.

From the example illustrated in Exhibit 28.2, it is clear that the accounting treatment of R&D matters. Whether the returns on capital are 42 percent or 13 percent has major implications for resource allocation, performance assessments, and competitive behavior. For instance, if the cost of capital is 15 percent, is the company creating or destroying value when it reaches maturity in 2020? Since capitalized R&D better reflects the underlying economics, the company is in fact destroying value, and management should question continued investment. Competitors should question the validity of entering the company's product markets. The margins may be high, but required investment is large.

The impact of capitalizing R&D on any performance assessment will depend on your estimation of asset life, a subjective judgment. In the PharmaCo example, we assumed an asset life of eight years. In Exhibit 28.3, we stress-test this assumption by varying asset life between two and 12 years. Even an asset life of just two years dramatically reduces PharmaCo's ROIC from 42.0 percent when R&D is expensed to 22.6 percent when it is capitalized. Increasing the asset life continues to lower ROIC, but by relatively smaller amounts as asset life

---

[1] As a reminder, R&D should only be expensed for performance analysis. U.S. GAAP and IFRS require companies to expense most research and development for external reporting. Both standards allow for the capitalization of certain development expenses. IFRS is more liberal than U.S. GAAP on capitalization criteria.

EXHIBIT 28.2 **PharmaCo: Return on Invested Capital**

percent
50
40
30
20
10
0
−10
−20
−30
−40
1999 2001 2003 2005 2007 2009 2011 2013 2015 2017 2019
ROIC with R&D expensed
ROIC with R&D capitalized

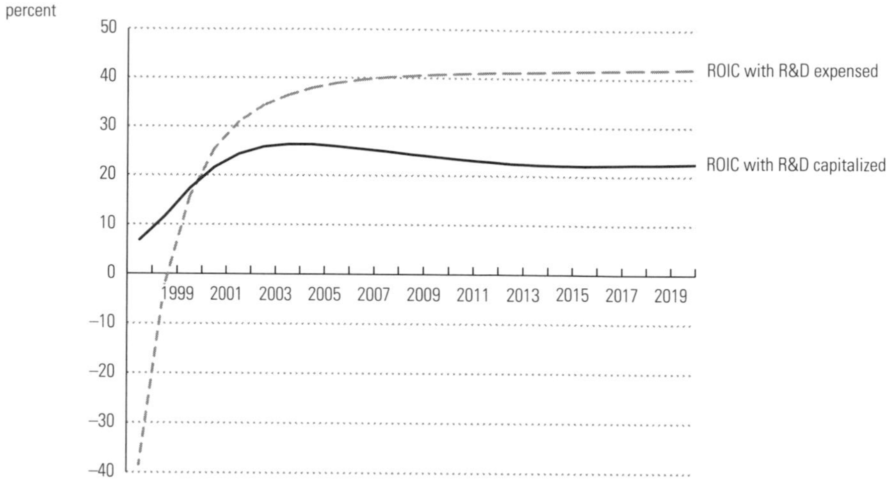

increases. So choosing an asset life of eight rather than 12 years (a reasonable range for the life of most R&D assets) does not materially affect perceptions of performance (ROIC would be 12.8 percent versus 11.7 percent, respectively).

For companies that spend a smaller percentage of revenues on R&D, the drop in ROIC that results from capitalizing R&D will be smaller but still pronounced. For example, a company spending only 5 percent of revenue on R&D would see ROIC drop from 42.0 percent to 19.8 percent.

EXHIBIT 28.3 **PharmaCo: Return on Invested Capital in 2020**

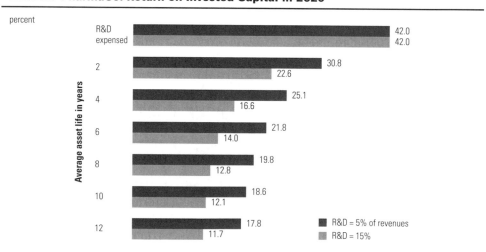

percent
Average asset life in years
R&D expensed
42.0
42.0
2
30.8
22.6
4
25.1
16.6
6
21.8
14.0
8
19.8
12.8
10
18.6
12.1
12
17.8
11.7
R&D = 5% of revenues
R&D = 15%

PROCESS FOR CAPITALIZING R&D

To estimate ROIC when R&D has been capitalized, use the following three-step process:

1. Build and amortize the R&D asset, using an appropriate asset life.
2. Adjust invested capital upward by the historical cost of the R&D asset.
3. Adjust net operating profit less adjusted taxes (NOPLAT) by replacing R&D expense with R&D amortization. Since R&D expense is tax deductible, do *not* adjust operating taxes.

As a reminder, free cash flow will *not* change if R&D is capitalized. Changes in NOPLAT will be offset by changes in invested capital. We next apply the three-step process to Adobe Systems.

Building and Amortizing the R&D Asset

To build the R&D asset, choose a starting year, and begin accumulating R&D expenses. Choose the earliest year feasible, as the model requires accumulated R&D to reach a steady state before the adjusted ROIC calculation becomes meaningful. Exhibit 28.4 presents historical R&D expenses for Adobe Systems between 1987 and 2008. In 1987, Adobe spent $4.1 million of R&D on revenues of $39.3 million. By 2008, R&D grew to $662.1 million on revenues of $3.6 billion.

Using 1987 as a starting year, set the R&D asset value to zero, as shown in the bottom section of Exhibit 28.4. To this value, add $4.1 million of R&D expense. Since the starting asset is zero, no amortization is recorded in the first year. Next, set the starting balance in 1988 equal to 1987's ending balance. To this value, add 1988's R&D expense of $7.3 million. Since intangible assets

EXHIBIT 28.4 **Adobe Systems: Capitalization of R&D**[1]

$ million

	1987	1988	1989	...	2006	2007	2008
Partial income statement							
Revenue	39.3	83.5	121.4	...	2,575.3	3,157.9	3,579.9
R&D expense	4.1	7.3	13.4	...	539.7	613.2	662.1
Capitalized R&D asset							
R&D intangible, starting	–	4.1	11.0	...	1,806.3	2,165.3	2,562.1
R&D expense	4.1	7.3	13.4	...	539.7	613.2	662.1
Amortization	–	(0.4)	(1.1)	...	(180.6)	(216.5)	(256.2)
R&D intangible, ending	4.1	11.0	23.4	...	2,165.3	2,562.1	2,967.9

[1] Estimated asset life = 10 years.

Source: Adobe Systems annual reports.

EXHIBIT 28.5 **Adobe Systems: Adjusted Invested Capital**

$ million

	2004	2005	2006	2007	2008
Invested capital					
Operating working capital	(224)	(192)	(168)	(378)	(50)
Property, plant, and equipment	100	104	227	290	313
Investment in lease receivable	127	127	127	207	207
Other assets, net	2	(2)	(19)	(8)	(35)
Invested capital without goodwill	4	36	168	111	435
→ Capitalized R&D asset	1,601	1,806	2,165	2,562	2,968
Adjusted invested capital without goodwill	1,605	1,842	2,333	2,673	3,403
Goodwill	110	119	2,149	2,148	2,135
Other intangibles	16	16	506	403	215
Cumulative amortization of acquired intangibles	21	60	300	542	729
Adjusted invested capital	1,751	2,037	5,289	5,766	6,482

Source: Adobe Systems annual reports.

created by R&D have a limited life, reduce the starting figure by an appropriate amortization amount. Assuming straight-line amortization and a 10-year asset life, subtract amortization of $0.4 million (the starting balance of $4.1 million times 10 percent).[2] This leads to an ending balance in 1988 of $11.0 million. Repeat this process for every year through 2008. For Adobe, the R&D asset grows to nearly $3 billion by 2008.

Adjusting Invested Capital for Capitalized Expenses

Exhibit 28.5 presents the adjustment to invested capital for Adobe Systems. Using the method outlined in Chapter 7, we first compute invested capital by reorganizing the balance sheet. In 2008, Adobe had $435 million in invested capital without goodwill—primarily facilities and equipment. But could a competitor replicate Adobe's business for under $500 million? No. Adobe Systems generates profitability not through the ownership of its fixed assets, but rather through its intellectual capital, so you must include the value of this intangible asset in Adobe Systems' invested capital to calculate a meaningful ROIC.

To adjust invested capital for capitalized expenses, add the capitalized R&D asset (computed following the method outlined earlier in Exhibit 28.4) to invested capital. In 2008, add $2,968 million in capitalized R&D to $435 million

[2] In this model, we compute amortization at 10 percent of the preceding year's ending balance. Advanced models will straight-line amortize actual R&D expense. Based on simulated data, we believe the simplicity of using an ending balance to determine amortization outweighs any improvements arising from straight-line amortization.

EXHIBIT 28.6 **Adobe Systems: Net Operating Profit Less Adjusted Taxes**

$ million

	2004	2005	2006	2007	2008
Unadjusted NOPLAT					
Revenues	1,667	1,966	2,575	3,158	3,580
Cost of revenue	(104)	(113)	(292)	(355)	(363)
Selling, general, and administrative	(638)	(721)	(931)	(1,090)	(1,308)
→ R&D expense	(311)	(365)	(540)	(613)	(662)
EBITA[1]	613	767	812	1,100	1,247
Operating taxes	(160)	(200)	(223)	(279)	(284)
NOPLAT	453	568	589	821	963
Adjusted NOPLAT					
Revenues	1,667	1,966	2,575	3,158	3,580
Cost of sales	(104)	(113)	(292)	(355)	(363)
Selling expenses	(638)	(721)	(931)	(1,090)	(1,308)
→ Amortization of R&D asset	(143)	(160)	(181)	(217)	(256)
EBITA	781	973	1,171	1,497	1,653
Operating taxes	(160)	(200)	(223)	(279)	(284)
NOPLAT	621	773	948	1,218	1,369

[1] Earnings before interest, taxes, and amortization.

Source: Adobe Systems annual reports.

in invested capital for an adjusted invested capital of $3,403 million.[3] Adding goodwill and intangibles leads to invested capital with goodwill of $6,482 million. Not unexpectedly, more than 90 percent of Adobe's capital comes in the form of capitalized R&D and intangibles acquired during acquisitions.

Adjusting NOPLAT for Capitalized Expenses

Exhibit 28.6 presents the adjustment to NOPLAT for Adobe Systems. To adjust NOPLAT, replace R&D expense ($662.1 million in 2008) with R&D amortization ($256.2 million), computed as outlined in Exhibit 28.4. Operating taxes remain unchanged, because R&D expense is tax deductible at its full amount, so using R&D amortization would overstate the company's tax burden.[4] For Adobe, replacing expense with amortization raises NOPLAT in 2008 from $963 million to $1,369 million. This is quite common for growth firms, as current R&D is typically higher than the amortization of historical R&D. As the company's

[3] By adding capitalized R&D to operating assets, total funds invested will no longer balance. To balance total funds invested, add capitalized R&D to equity equivalents. For more on total funds invested and their reconciliation, see Chapter 7.

[4] The treatment of the R&D tax shield appears inconsistent with the earlier treatment of interest expense and its associated tax shield. In discounted cash flow valuation, the interest tax shield is removed from operating taxes but is either valued as a reduction to the cost of capital or valued separately. Since R&D is related to operations and not financing, a comparable adjustment is inappropriate.

growth rate tapers off, however, amortization will catch up with expense, and NOPLAT adjustments will be small.

One benefit of capitalizing R&D is that reductions in current R&D will not affect *current* operating profits. This limits managers' ability to manipulate short-term profits at the expense of long-term investment. For instance, had Adobe cut R&D in 2008 from $662 million to $300 million, adjusted operating profit in that year would remain the same, since R&D amortization is based on historical R&D spend, not current R&D expense. Cutting R&D today would lead to lower future R&D amortization, but lower amortization does not guarantee higher future profits, since future profits result from today's investments.

ROIC AND FREE CASH FLOW WITH CAPITALIZED R&D

To measure performance or allocate capital properly, you must have an accurate assessment of return on capital. Given the level of R&D spending at Adobe Systems, it would be impossible to arrive at a realistic ROIC without capitalizing R&D. Exhibit 28.7 presents ROIC between 2004 and 2008 with R&D expensed (as required by accounting rules). Computed on a raw basis, ROIC without goodwill has fluctuated between 221.5 percent and 12,707.7 percent. These extreme and volatile returns occur because Adobe uses very little physical capital. Small year-to-year differences in capital lead to dramatic changes in ROIC yet have no real economic impact. In contrast, capitalizing R&D for Adobe Systems eventually leads to stable ROICs without goodwill near 40 percent. With goodwill, ROICs dropped dramatically after Adobe's purchase of Macromedia in 2005. Returns on capital have improved slightly since then and have stabilized at 21.1 percent.

Unlike ROIC, free cash flow (FCF) will not change when expenses are capitalized. When an expense is capitalized, the expense is merely moved from gross cash flow to gross investment. Free cash flow remains unaffected because both are components of FCF. Since amortization is noncash, it also has

EXHIBIT 28.7 **Adobe Systems: Return on Invested Capital**

percent

	2004	2005	2006	2007	2008
Without goodwill					
ROIC with R&D expensed	12,707.7	1,574.8	351.5	740.6	221.5
ROIC with R&D capitalized	38.7	41.9	40.6	45.6	40.2
With goodwill					
ROIC with R&D expensed	301.2	245.6	18.8	25.6	27.4
ROIC with R&D capitalized	35.4	37.9	17.9	21.1	21.1

EXHIBIT 28.8 **Adobe Systems: Free Cash Flow (excluding Goodwill and Acquired Intangibles)**

$ million

	2005	2006	2007	2008
R&D expensed (unadjusted)				
NOPLAT	568	589	821	963
Depreciation	44	68	73	83
Gross cash flow	611	656	895	1,047
Investments in working capital	(32)	(24)	210	(328)
Capital expenditures	(40)	(191)	(136)	(107)
Other operating investments	4	16	(91)	27
Free cash flow	535	457	878	639
R&D capitalized (adjusted)				
→ Adjusted NOPLAT	773	948	1,218	1,369
Depreciation	44	68	73	83
→ Amortization of R&D	160	181	217	256
Gross cash flow	977	1,196	1,508	1,709
Investments in working capital	(32)	(24)	210	(328)
Capital expenditures	(48)	(191)	(136)	(107)
Other operating investments	4	16	(91)	27
→ Investment in R&D	(365)	(540)	(613)	(662)
Free cash flow	535	457	878	639

no effect (it is deducted to compute NOPLAT but added back to calculate gross cash flow). Thus, capitalizing R&D should have no effect on valuation beyond the degree to which it changes your perceptions of the company's ability to create value in the future.

Exhibit 28.8 shows how to compute FCF when R&D is capitalized and compares this with its calculation when R&D is expensed. Adjusted FCF differs from unadjusted FCF in three ways. First, adjusted NOPLAT ($1,369 million in 2008) is computed with R&D amortization rather than R&D expense. Second, R&D amortization ($256 million) is added to NOPLAT to compute gross cash flow. Third, R&D expense ($662 million) is subtracted from gross cash flow in the investment section. These three adjustments lead to FCF of $639 million in 2008, irrespective of the choice of accounting treatment for R&D. Since FCF remains unchanged, the choice of R&D treatment will not affect valuation, either. It affects only performance measurement.

OTHER EXPENSES SUITABLE FOR CAPITALIZATION

In this chapter, we limited ourselves to the process of capitalizing R&D, because few other intangible investments are publicly reported. But if you have internal company data, you can apply the same process to any expense resulting in long-term benefits. Management can build a second set of economic accounts (besides GAAP or IFRS reporting) that assist in measuring the return on capital of building a brand, expanding distribution channels, or developing internal talent.

Take a beer company that is considering how it might extend its distribution network. Management is questioning whether the company should expand to new geographic regions or to smaller pubs. If costs related to expanding distribution are expensed immediately, this makes it impossible to compute returns on investment for past decisions. Managers are left with only a gut feeling about the true performance of their alternatives. With internal capitalization of up-front costs, however, management can systematically rank alternatives that best utilize resources at hand.

While these insights are valuable, managers must take care when capitalizing expenses that create long-term assets. Left unchecked, managers will have an incentive to classify all expenses as investments, even those with no long-term benefits, because this will maximize *reported* short-term performance. They will also be reluctant to write off investments that prove worthless. For instance, a distribution channel may be kept open merely to avoid a write-down on the manager's economic balance sheet. Ultimately, however, there is no advantage to be gained from giving way to these temptations, because doing so would only serve to obscure the true picture of the company's economic performance.

REVIEW QUESTIONS

1. ResearchCo is a medical devices company, producing equipment for diagnosing and treating heart disease. The company currently generates $100 million in revenues and is expected to grow 10 percent per year. ResearchCo maintains cost of sales at 50 percent of revenue, maintains research and development (R&D) at 15 percent of revenue, and pays an operating tax rate of 30 percent. To generate 10 percent growth, ResearchCo will reinvest 20 percent of NOPLAT each year. Last year's invested capital equaled $75 million. Using the preceding data, forecast five years of NOPLAT and five years of invested capital. What is the ROIC on year-end capital by year? Do not capitalize R&D.

2. Your colleague argues that R&D for ResearchCo should be capitalized and amortized. If R&D is capitalized, what is the starting R&D asset, investment in R&D, amortization of R&D, and ending R&D asset by year? Use straight-line amortization over three years, with the first amortization charge deducted the following year.

3. Use the R&D capitalization table developed in Question 2 to modify NOPLAT and invested capital from Question 1. What is the ROIC on year-end capital by year? How does this compare to the ROIC computed in Question 1?

4. Compute the annual free cash flow for ResearchCo with and without the capitalization of R&D. How do the two sets of free cash flows differ? Assume no depreciation of physical assets.

29

Inflation

Sound analysis and forecasting of the financial performance of companies in high-inflation environments is challenging. Inflation distorts the financial statements, adding to the difficulty of making year-to-year historical comparisons, ratio analyses, and performance forecasts.

Although all the familiar tools described in Part Two still apply in times of high inflation, such times cause some particular complications that we discuss in this chapter:

- History shows that inflation leads to lower value creation in companies, because it erodes real-terms free cash flow (FCF) and increases the cost of capital.
- Historical analysis of a company's performance when inflation is high requires additional metrics in real terms.
- Financial projections of a company's future performance should be made in both nominal and real terms whenever possible.

As we explain in this chapter, when inflation is high, analysis and valuation depend on insights from both nominal- and real-terms approaches. Nominal indicators are sometimes not meaningful (e.g. for capital turnover), and in other cases, real indicators are problematic (e.g., when determining corporate income taxes). But when properly applied, valuations in real and nominal terms should yield an identical value.

INFLATION LEADS TO LOWER VALUE CREATION

Since the 1980s, inflation has generally been mild in the developed economies of Europe and North America at levels around 2 to 3 percent per year. But this does not mean inflation has become irrelevant. As Exhibit 29.1 shows, the

EXHIBIT 29.1 **Historical Inflation in Developed Economies**

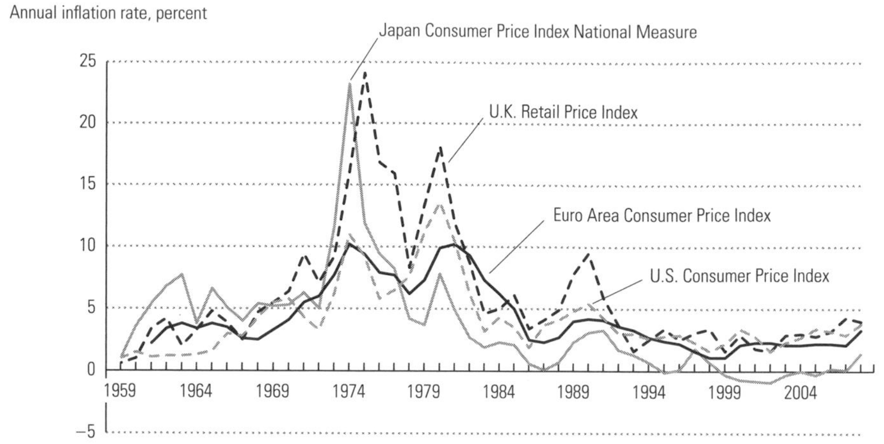

Annual inflation rate, percent

Source: Bureau of Labor Statistics, Office for National Statistics, Eurostat, Statistics Bureau of the Ministry of Internal Affairs and Communication (MIC), Japan.

situation was quite different in the 1970s, when inflation hovered around 10 percent for the same economies. Some economists warn of a return of such inflation levels, as government deficits have risen rapidly across developed economies.[1] And in many of the emerging economies of Latin America and Asia, inflation has been at double-digit levels for many years. In stark contrast, Japan has experienced extremely low inflation and even deflation since the early 1990s.

Inflation is often persistent, stretching out over several years as in the 1970s and 1980s, because suppressing it requires strict and unpopular government measures. For example, curbing inflation caused by overheating in the economy typically requires increasing interest rates and reducing public spending to dampen growth. In most cases, such measures are undertaken only when everything else has failed and when inflation has become too high to ignore—but even more difficult to fix.

You need to take account of persistent inflation in analysis and valuation because a large body of academic research clearly shows that inflation is negatively correlated with returns in the stock market.[2] To illustrate, as inflation increased from around 2 to 3 percent in the late 1960s to around 10 percent in the second half of the 1970s, the average price-to-earnings (P/E) ratio for companies in the United States declined from around 18 to below 10. When

---

[1] See, for example, M. Feldstein, "The Fed Must Reassure Markets on Inflation," *Financial Times*, June 28, 2009.

[2] See, for example, E. Fama and G. Schwert, "Asset Returns and Inflation," *Journal of Financial Economics* 5 (1977): 115–146; and J. Ritter and R. Warr, "The Decline of Inflation and the Bull Market of 1982–1999," *Journal of Financial and Quantitative Analysis* 37, no. 1 (2002): 29–61.

inflation finally came down from 1985 onward, P/E ratios returned to their historical levels.

There are several explanations for why inflation is bad for value creation; some of these point to the cost of capital, and others to cash flows. Academic research has found evidence that investors often misjudge inflation, which pushes up the cost of capital in real terms and depresses market valuations.[3] Inflation can also affect the real-terms cash flows generated by companies both directly and indirectly. The *direct effect* of an inflation increase is a one-off loss in value for companies with so-called net monetary assets—that is, asset positions that are fixed in nominal terms.[4] For example, a balance of receivables loses 10 percent in value when inflation unexpectedly increases by 10 percent. The reverse holds for net monetary liabilities, such as fixed-rate debt. Depending on the relative size of its receivables, payables, and debt, the direct effect for a particular company could be positive or negative.

The *indirect cash flow effects* of inflation typically depress value most, as these can lead to ongoing losses as long as inflation lasts. First, companies suffer a loss on their depreciation tax shields if depreciation charges cannot be inflation-adjusted for tax purposes—and this is typically the case. Second, most companies cannot pass on to their customers the whole of any cost increases arising from inflation without losing sales volume. As a result, they fail to maintain profitability in real terms.

To understand how significant the challenge of passing on cost increases can be, consider this simple example. Assume a company generates steady sales of $1,000 per year. Earnings before interest, taxes, and amortization (EBITA) are $100, and invested capital is $1,000. Without loss of generality, assume the asset base is evenly spread across 15 groups with remaining lifetimes of 1 to 15 years. Gross property, plant, and equipment (PP&E) is $1,875, and annual capital expenditures equal depreciation charges at $125.[5] The company's key financials would be as shown in Exhibit 29.2.

If the cost of capital is 8 percent, the discounted cash flow (DCF) value at the start of year 2—or any year—equals:

$$DCF = \frac{100}{(8\% - 0\%)} = 1,250$$

Now assume that in year 2, inflation suddenly increases to 15 percent and stays at that level in perpetuity, affecting costs and capital expenditures

---

[3] See, for example, F. Modigliani and R. Cohn, "Inflation, Rational Valuation, and the Market," *Financial Analysts Journal* 35 (1979): 24–44.

[4] See, for example, H. Hong, "Inflation and the Market Value of the Firm: Theory and Test," *Journal of Finance* 32, no. 4 (1977): 1031–1048.

[5] At the end of each year, after replacement of the asset group that is fully depreciated, the average remaining life of assets is exactly eight years. Annual depreciation is therefore $1,000 ÷ 8 = $125, and gross PP&E equals 15 × $125 = $1,875.

EXHIBIT 29.2 **Financial Projections without Inflation**

dollars

	Year 1	Year 2	Year 3	Year 4 ...	Year 16	Year 17 ...
Sales	1,000	1,000	1,000	1,000 ...	1,000	1,000 ...
EBITDA[1]	225	225	225	225 ...	225	225 ...
Depreciation	(125)	(125)	(125)	(125) ...	(125)	(125) ...
EBITA[2]	100	100	100	100 ...	100	100 ...
Gross property, plant, and equipment	1,875	1,875	1,875	1,875 ...	1,875	1,875 ...
Cumulative depreciation	(875)	(875)	(875)	(875) ...	(875)	(875) ...
Invested capital	1,000	1,000	1,000	1,000 ...	1,000	1,000 ...
EBITDA	225	225	225	225 ...	225	225 ...
Capital expenditures	(125)	(125)	(125)	(125) ...	(125)	(125) ...
Free cash flow (FCF)	100	100	100	100 ...	100	100 ...
EBITA growth (percent)	–	–	–	– ...	–	– ...
EBITA/sales (percent)	10.0	10.0	10.0	10.0 ...	10.0	10.0 ...
Return on invested capital (percent)	10.0	10.0	10.0	10.0 ...	10.0	10.0 ...
FCF growth (percent)	–	–	–	– ...	–	– ...

[1]Earnings before interest, taxes, depreciation, and amortization.
[2]Earnings before interest, taxes, and amortization.

equally. The company manages to keep its sales margin at around 10 percent by increasing prices for its products while keeping sales volume and physical production capacity constant. In the process, it even succeeds in lifting its return on invested capital (ROIC) to almost 20 percent after 15 years (see Exhibit 29.3).

Although these results may be impressive at first sight, a closer inspection of the summary financials reveals significant value destruction. Free cash flow declines in the first years, because the capital expenditures grow at the rate of inflation of 15 percent, roughly twice the earnings before interest, taxes, depreciation, and amortization (EBITDA) growth of around 7 to 8 percent. Free cash flow (FCF) growth only gradually rises to the rate of inflation in year 17, so that it drops significantly in real terms.[6] In combination with a cost of capital increase to 24 percent,[7] this makes the company's value plummet. An explicit DCF valuation with continuing value estimated as of year 17 would show the value at the start of year 2 as low as $481.

To pass on inflation to customers in full without losing sales volume, the company should increase its *cash flows*, not its earnings, at 15 percent per year

[6] Given our assumption of an asset lifetime of 15 years, FCF growth gradually increases from 0 to 15 percent until year 17, when a new steady state is reached if inflation remains constant.
[7] With inflation at 15 percent, the cost of capital increases from 8 percent to $(1 + 8\%) \times (1 + 15\%) - 1 = 24\%$.

EXHIBIT 29.3 **Financial Projections with Inflation and Incomplete Inflation Pass-On**

dollars

	Year 1	Year 2	Year 3	Year 4 ...	Year 16	Year 17 ...
Sales	1,000	1,131	1,283	1,460 ...	7,516	8,644 ...
EBITDA	225	240	259	281 ...	1,210	1,392 ...
Depreciation	(125)	(125)	(126)	(129) ...	(397)	(456) ...
EBITA	100	115	132	152 ...	814	936 ...
Gross property, plant, and equipment	1,875	1,894	1,934	1,999 ...	6,840	7,866 ...
Cumulative depreciation	(875)	(875)	(876)	(880) ...	(2,082)	(2,394) ...
Invested capital	1,000	1,019	1,058	1,119 ...	4,758	5,472 ...
EBITDA	225	240	259	281 ...	1,210	1,392 ...
Capital expenditures	(125)	(144)	(165)	(190) ...	(1,017)	(1,170) ...
Free cash flow (FCF)	100	96	93	91 ...	193	222 ...
EBITA growth (percent)	–	15.0	15.0	15.0 ...	15.0	15.0 ...
EBITA/sales (percent)	10.0	10.2	10.3	10.4 ...	10.8	10.8 ...
Return on invested capital (percent)	10.0	11.5	13.0	14.4 ...	19.7	19.7 ...
FCF growth (percent)	–	–3.7	–3.2	–2.4 ...	14.3	15.0 ...

(see Exhibit 29.4). In this case, the DCF value at the start of year 2 is fully preserved:

$$\mathrm{DCF} = \frac{115}{(24\% - 15\%)} = 1{,}250$$

But having all cash flows grow with inflation implies that the company's reported financial performance increases sharply. As the summary financials show, EBITA growth is now more than 33 percent in year 2. In the same year, the sales margin (EBITA divided by sales) increases from 10.0 to 11.6 percent, and ROIC increases from 10.0 to 13.4 percent. After 15 years of constant inflation, the sales margin and ROIC would end up at 17.6 percent and 34.7 percent, respectively. The ROIC needs to rise this far to keep up with inflation and the higher cost of capital.

The reason is that invested capital and depreciation do not grow with inflation immediately. For example, in year 2, annual capital expenditures increase by 15 percent, but this adds only $15\% \times \$125 = \$18.75$ to invested capital. Annual depreciation changes in year 3 by only a small amount:[8] $\frac{1}{15} \times 19 = 1.25$. In each year, the company replaces only $\frac{1}{15}$ of assets at inflated prices, so it takes 15 years of constant inflation to reach a steady state

---

[8] We are assuming that assets are acquired at the end of each year and depreciated for the first time in the next year.

EXHIBIT 29.4 **Financial Projections with Inflation and Full Inflation Pass-On**

dollars

	Year 1	Year 2	Year 3	Year 4	...	Year 16	Year 17	...
Sales	1,000	1,150	1,323	1,521 ...		8,137	9,358 ...	
EBITDA	225	259	298	342 ...		1,831	2,105 ...	
Depreciation	(125)	(125)	(126)	(129) ...		(397)	(456) ...	
EBITA	100	134	171	213 ...		1,434	1,649 ...	
Gross property, plant, and equipment	1,875	1,894	1,934	1,999 ...		6,840	7,866 ...	
Cumulative depreciation	(875)	(875)	(876)	(880) ...		(2,082)	(2,394) ...	
Invested capital	1,000	1,019	1,058	1,119 ...		4,758	5,472 ...	
EBITDA	225	259	298	342 ...		1,831	2,105 ...	
Capital expenditures	(125)	(144)	(165)	(190) ...		(1,017)	(1,170) ...	
Free cash flow (FCF)	100	115	132	152 ...		814	936 ...	
EBITA growth (percent)	–	33.7	28.1	24.5 ...		15.1	15.0 ...	
EBITA/sales (percent)	10.0	11.6	13.0	14.0 ...		17.6	17.6 ...	
Return on invested capital (percent)	10.0	13.4	16.8	20.2 ...		34.7	34.7 ...	
FCF growth (percent)	–	15.0	15.0	15.0 ...		15.0	15.0 ...	

where capital and depreciation grow at the rate of inflation. As the example shows, sales margin and ROIC increase in each year until the steady state in year 17.

Although this example is stylized, the conclusion applies to all companies: after each acceleration in inflation, we should expect reported earnings to outpace inflation and reported sales margin and ROIC to increase—even though, in real terms, nothing has changed. Unfortunately, history shows that in periods of inflation, companies do not achieve such big improvements in reported return on invested capital. As we discussed in Chapter 4, ROICs have been remarkably stable at around 10 percent in the United States, including during the 1970s and 1980s, when inflation was at 10 percent or more. If companies had succeeded in passing on inflation effects, they should have reported much higher ROICs in those years. Instead, they hardly managed to keep returns at preinflation levels.

One likely cause is that companies cannot pass on the cost increases to customers by increasing prices without losing volume, or can pass on increases only with some time lag. This is especially costly when inflation is high: a half-year delay in passing on 15 percent inflation implies that revenues are always 7.5 percent too low, making margins plummet. Another reason could be that managers do not sufficiently adjust targets for growth of earnings and sales margin when faced with inflation. If a company keeps its sales margins and ROIC constant in times of inflation, cash flows and value are eroding in real terms. EBIT growth in line with inflation is also insufficient for sustaining a company's value, and this holds even truer for a leveraged indicator such as earnings per share.

Whatever the exact reason, history shows that companies do not manage to pass on inflation in full. As a result, their cash flow in real terms declines. In addition, there is empirical evidence that in times of inflation, investors increase the cost of capital in real terms. Lower cash flow and higher cost of capital are a proven recipe for lower share prices, just as we saw in the 1970s and 1980s.

HISTORICAL ANALYSIS IN TIMES OF HIGH INFLATION

In countries experiencing extreme inflation (more than 25 percent per year), companies often report in year-end currency. In the income statement, items such as revenues and costs that were booked throughout the year are restated at year-end purchasing power. Otherwise, the addition of these items would not be meaningful. The balance sheet usually has adjustments to fixed assets, inventory, and equity; the accounts payable and receivable are already in year-end terms.

In most countries, however, financial statements are not adjusted to reflect the effects of inflation. If inflation is high, this leads to distortions in the balance sheet and income statement. In the balance sheet, nonmonetary assets, such as inventories and property, plant, and equipment (PP&E), are shown at values far below current replacement value if they are long-lived. In the income statement, depreciation charges are too low relative to current replacement costs. Sales and costs in December and January of the same year are typically added as if they represent the same purchasing power.

As a result, many financial indicators typically used in historical analyses can be distorted when calculated directly from the financial statements in high-inflation economies. In such circumstances, companies often index their internal management accounts to overcome these issues. If they do not, or if you are doing an outside-in analysis, at least correct for the following distortions:

- Growth is overstated in times of inflation, so restate it in real terms by deflating with an annual inflation index if sales are evenly spread across the year. If sales are not spread evenly, use quarterly or monthly inflation indexes to deflate the sales in each corresponding interval.

- Capital turnover is typically overstated because operating assets are carried at historical costs. You can approximate the current costs of long-lived assets by adjusting their reported values with an inflation index for their estimated average lifetimes. Or consider developing ratios of real sales relative to physical-capacity indicators appropriate for the sector—for example, sales per square meter in consumer retail. Inventory levels also need restating if turnover is low and inflation is very high.

- Operating margins (operating profit divided by sales) can be overstated because depreciation is too low and slow-moving inventories make large nominal holding gains. Corrections for depreciation charges follow from adjustments to PP&E. You can estimate cash operating expenses at current-cost basis by inflating the reported costs for the average time held in inventory. Alternatively, use historical EBITDA-to-sales ratios to assess the company's performance relative to peers; these ratios at least do not suffer from any depreciation-induced bias.

- Use caution in interpreting credit ratios and other indicators of capital structure health. Distortions are especially significant in solvency ratios such as debt to equity or total assets, because long-lived assets are understated relative to replacement costs, and floating-rate debt is expressed in current currency units. As we advised in Chapter 23, use coverage ratios such as EBITDA to interest expense.[9] These are less exposed to accounting distortions, because depreciation has no impact on them and debt financing is mostly at floating rates or in foreign currency when inflation is persistent.

FINANCIAL PROJECTIONS IN REAL AND NOMINAL TERMS

When you make financial projections of income statements and balance sheets for a valuation in a high-inflation environment, keep in mind that accounting adjustments cannot affect free cash flow. Thus, for valuation purposes, we project financial statements without making any accounting adjustments for inflation. We can make the projections in either nominal or real terms. Exhibit 29.5 summarizes the major advantages and shortcomings of each approach.

Neither is perfect. On the one hand, projecting in real terms makes it difficult to calculate taxes correctly, as tax charges are often based on nominal financial statements. Furthermore, you need to project explicitly the effects of working-capital changes on cash flow because these do not automatically follow from the annual change in working capital. On the other hand, using nominal cash flows makes future capital expenditures difficult to project, because the typically stable relationship between revenues and fixed assets does not hold in times of high inflation. This means depreciation charges and EBITA also are difficult to project.

To prepare consistent financial projections, you therefore need to use elements of both nominal and real forecasts. We illustrate in this section how to combine the two approaches in a DCF valuation. In the example, we consider a company whose revenues grow at 2 percent in real terms while the annual

---

[9] Distortions occur in the ratio of EBITA to interest coverage if operating profit is overstated due to low depreciation charges and low costs of procured materials.

EXHIBIT 29.5 **Combining Real and Nominal Approaches to Financial Modeling**

✓ Preferred application

Estimates	Modeling approach	
	Real	**Nominal**
Operational performance		
Sales	✓	✓
EBITDA	✓	✓
EBITA	✓	–
Capital expenditures	✓	–
Investments in working capital	✓[1]	✓
Income taxes	–	✓
Financial statements	✓[2]	✓
Continuing value	✓[1]	✓

[1] If inflation impact on investments in working capital is explicitly included.
[2] If inflation corrections are separately modeled and included in income statement and balance sheet.

inflation rate is 20 percent in the first forecast year and 10 percent thereafter (see Exhibit 29.6). To simplify, we assume that all cash flows occur at the end of the year. At extremely high, fluctuating levels of inflation, however, this assumption could distort financial projections, because the cash flows that accumulate throughout the year are subject to different inflation rates. So in such cases, split the year into quarterly or even monthly intervals, project cash flows for each interval, and discount the cash flows at the appropriate discount rate for that interval.

In practice, financial projections for high-inflation valuations raise many more issues than in this simplified example. Nevertheless, it is useful for showing how to address some key issues when developing a cash flow forecast

EXHIBIT 29.6 **DCF under Inflation: Operational and Financial Assumptions**

		Forecasts					
	Year 1	Year 2	Year 3	Year 4	Year 5	...	Year 25
Operational assumptions							
Real growth rate (percent)	2	2	2	2	2		–
Real revenues	1,000	1,020	1,040	1,061	1,082	...	1,608
Real EBITDA	300	306	312	318	325	...	483
Net working capital/revenues (percent)	20	20	20	20	20	...	20
Real net PP&E/real revenues (percent)	40	40	40	40	40	...	40
Lifetime of net PP&E	5	–	–	–	–	...	–
Financial assumptions							
Inflation rate (percent)	–	20	10	10	10	...	10
Inflation index	1.00	1.20	1.32	1.45	1.60	...	10.75
Tax rate (percent)	35	35	35	35	35	...	35
Real WACC (percent)	–	8.0	8.0	8.0	8.0	...	8.0
Nominal WACC (percent)	–	29.6	18.8	18.8	18.8	...	18.8

Note: Adjusted formula for real-terms continuing value.

in periods of inflation. Using the following step-by-step approach leads to the real and nominal valuation results shown in Exhibit 29.7. (Note that the projections in nominal terms, in contrast to those in real terms, show capital turnover increasing over time because nominal revenues grow faster than net property, plant, and equipment (PP&E) in a high-inflation environment.)

Step 1: Forecast Operating Performance in Real Terms. To the extent possible, convert historical nominal balance sheets and income statements into real terms (usually at the current year's currency value). At a minimum, make a real-terms approximation of the historical development of the key value drivers—growth and return on capital—and the underlying capital turnover and EBITA margin, so you can understand the true economics of the business. With these approximations, forecast the operating performance of the business in real terms:

- Project future revenues and cash expenses to obtain EBITDA forecasts.[10]
- Estimate property, plant, and equipment (PP&E) and capital expenditures from your assumptions for real-terms capital turnover.
- Working capital follows from projected revenues and assumptions on days of working capital required.
- From projected net PP&E and assumptions on the lifetime of the assets, derive the annual depreciation to estimate real-terms EBITA.

Step 2: Build Financial Statements in Nominal Terms. Nominal projections can be readily derived through the following steps, which convert the real operating projections into nominal terms:[11]

- Project nominal revenues, cash expenses, EBITDA, and capital expenditures by multiplying their real-terms equivalents by an estimated inflation index for the year.
- Estimate net PP&E on a year-by-year basis from the prior-year balance plus nominal capital expenditures minus nominal depreciation (which is estimated as a percentage of net PP&E according to the estimated asset lifetime).
- Working capital follows from revenues and days of working capital required.
- Subtract the nominal depreciation charges from EBITDA to obtain nominal EBITA.

---

[10] This step assumes that all expenses included in EBITDA are cash costs.

[11] As noted, these projections are made for valuation purposes and not necessarily in accordance with local or international accounting standards prescribing any inflation or monetary corrections for particular groups of assets and liabilities under, for example, inflation accounting. Note that free cash flows would not be affected by such adjustments.

EXHIBIT 29.7 **DCF under Inflation: Real and Nominal Models**

	Real projections						Nominal projections					
	Year 1	Year 2	Year 3	Year 4	Year 5 ...	Year 25	Year 1	Year 2	Year 3	Year 4	Year 5 ...	Year 25
NOPLAT												
Revenues	1,000	1,020	1,040	1,061	1,082 ...	1,608	1,000	1,224	1,373	1,541	1,729 ...	17,283
EBITDA	300	306	312	318	325 ...	483	300	367	412	462	519 ...	5,185
Depreciation	(80)	(80)	(82)	(83)	(85) ...	(126)	(80)	(80)	(85)	(92)	(100) ...	(926)
EBITA	220	226	231	235	240 ...	356	220	287	327	370	419 ...	4,259
Taxes	(77)	(84)	(87)	(89)	(92) ...	(139)	(77)	(101)	(114)	(130)	(147) ...	(1,491)
NOPLAT[1]	143	142	144	146	148 ...	218	143	187	212	241	272 ...	2,768
Free cash flow												
NOPLAT	143	142	144	146	148 ...	218	143	187	212	241	272 ...	2,768
Depreciation	80	80	82	83	85 ...	126	80	80	85	92	100 ...	926
Capital expenditures	(80)	(88)	(90)	(92)	(93) ...	(139)	(80)	(106)	(118)	(133)	(149) ...	(1,491)
Investment in net working capital	–	(37)	(23)	(23)	(24) ...	(35)	–	(45)	(30)	(34)	(38) ...	(376)
Free cash flow	–	97	113	114	116 ...	170	–	116	149	166	185 ...	1,827
Invested capital												
Net PP&E (beginning of year)	400	400	408	416	424 ...	631	400	400	426	459	500 ...	4,631
Depreciation	(80)	(80)	(82)	(83)	(85) ...	(126)	(80)	(80)	(85)	(92)	(100) ...	(926)
Capital expenditures	80	88	90	92	93 ...	139	80	106	118	133	149 ...	1,491
Net PP&E (end of year)	400	408	416	424	433 ...	643	400	426	459	500	549 ...	5,196
Net working capital	200	204	208	212	216 ...	322	200	245	275	308	346 ...	3,457
Invested capital	600	612	624	637	649 ...	965	600	670	734	808	895 ...	8,653
Ratios (percent)												
Net PP&E/revenues	–	40	40	40	40 ...	40	–	35	33	32	32 ...	30
Net working capital/revenues	–	20	20	20	20 ...	20	–	20	20	20	20 ...	20
ROIC	–	24	24	23	23 ...	23	–	31	32	33	34 ...	36
FCF growth rate	–	–	-7	1	1 ...	2	–	–	28	11	12 ...	12
DCF valuation												
Free cash flow	–	97	113	114	116 ...	170	–	116	149	166	185 ...	1,827
Continuing value (value driver formula)[2]	–	–	–	–	– ...	2,891	–	–	–	–	– ...	31,063
Continuing value (cash flow perpetuity formula)	–	–	–	–	– ...	2,891	–	–	–	–	– ...	31,064
Present value factor	–	0.93	0.86	0.79	0.74 ...	0.16	–	0.77	0.65	0.55	0.46 ...	0.01
DCF value	1,795	–	–	–	– ...	–	1,795	–	–	–	– ...	–

[1] Net operating profit less adjusted taxes
[2] Adjusted formula for real-terms continuing value.

- Calculate income taxes on nominal EBITA without inflation corrections, unless tax laws allow for such corrections.

In this example, we did not build a complete balance sheet and income statement. Complete financial statements would be needed for major decisions concerning, for example, dividend policy and capital structure, debt financing, and share repurchase. Developing complete financial statements would require the following additional steps:

- Forecast interest expense and other nonoperating income statement items in nominal terms (based on the previous year's balance sheet).
- Equity should equal last year's equity plus earnings, less dividends, plus or minus any share issues or repurchases.
- Balance the balance sheet with debt or marketable securities.

Step 3: Build Financial Statements in Real Terms. Most of the operating items for the real-terms income statement and balance sheet were already estimated in step 1. Now include the real-terms taxes on EBITA by deflating the nominal taxes as estimated in step 2. For full financial statements, use the inflation index to convert debt, marketable securities, interest expense, income taxes, and nonoperating terms from the nominal statements into real terms. The real-terms equity account is a plug to balance the balance sheet. To make sure you have done this correctly, be sure the real equity account equals last year's equity plus earnings, less dividends, plus or minus share issues or repurchases, and plus or minus inflationary gains or losses on the monetary assets (such as cash, receivables, payables, and debt).

Step 4: Forecast Free Cash Flows in Real and Nominal Terms. Forecast the future free cash flows in real and nominal terms from the projected income statements and balance sheets. Follow the general approach described in Chapter 9. The only difference is that the real-terms investment in net working capital (NWC^R) is equal to the increase in working capital plus a monetary loss due to inflation:[12]

$$\text{Investment in } NWC_t^R = \text{Increase in } NWC_t^R + NWC_{t-1}^R \left(1 - \frac{IX_{t-1}}{IX_t}\right)$$

where IX_t is the inflation index for the year t.

---

[12] Even for assets held at constant levels in real-terms balance sheets, replacement investments are required at increasing prices in an inflationary environment. These replacement investments represent a cash outflow, also in real terms, but do not show up from real-terms balance sheet differences from year to year. In contrast, the nominal investment cash flow does follow from the nominal balance sheet differences from year to year.

To check for consistency, use the inflation index to convert the free cash flows from the nominal projections to real terms. These should equal the free cash flows from the real-terms projections in each year.

Step 5: Estimate DCF Value in Real and Nominal Terms. When discounting real and nominal cash flows under high inflation, you must address three key issues:

1. Ensure that the weighted average cost of capital estimates in real terms ($WACC^R$) and nominal terms ($WACC^N$) are defined consistently with the inflation assumptions in each year:

$$1 + WACC_t^N = (1 + WACC_t^R)(1 + Inflation_t)$$

2. The value driver formula as presented in Chapter 10 should be adjusted when estimating continuing value in real terms in high-inflation environments. The returns on capital in real-terms projections overestimate the economic returns in the case of positive net working capital. The free cash flow in real terms differs from the cash flow implied by the value driver formula by an amount equal to the annual monetary loss on net working capital:

$$FCF_t^R = \left(1 - \frac{g_t^R}{ROIC_t^R}\right) NOPLAT_t^R - NWC_{t-1}^R \left(1 - \frac{IX_{t-1}}{IX_t}\right)$$

The real-terms value driver formula is adjusted for this monetary loss, reflecting the perpetuity assumptions for inflation (i) and the ratio of net working capital to invested capital (NWC^R/IC^R):

$$CV^R = \frac{\left(1 - \frac{G^R}{ROIC^R}\right) NOPLAT^R}{WACC^R - g^R}$$

where $G^R = g^R - \left[\frac{NWC^R}{IC^R}\left(\frac{i}{1+i}\right)\right]$

The resulting continuing-value estimate is the same as that obtained from an FCF perpetuity formula. After indexing for inflation, it also equals the continuing-value estimates derived from nominal projections.

3. When using the continuing-value formulas, make sure the explicit forecast period is long enough for the model to reach a steady state with constant growth rates of free cash flow. Because of the way inflation affects capital expenditures and depreciation, you need a much longer horizon than for valuations with no or low inflation.

SUMMARY

To analyze and value companies in high-inflation countries, we use the same tools and approaches as introduced in Part Two. However, their application can be somewhat different. When analyzing a company's historical performance, you should be aware that persistent inflation can distort many familiar financial indicators, such as growth, capital turnover, operating margins, and solvency ratios. Ensure that you make appropriate adjustments to these ratios. When making financial projections, use a combined nominal- and real-terms approach, because real-terms and nominal-terms projections both offer relevant insights and can be used for cross-checking your results. When discounting cash flows, use inflation assumptions in the weighted average cost of capital that are fully consistent with those underlying your cash flow projections.

REVIEW QUESTIONS

1. Why does high inflation typically destroy value for companies?
2. Which company's ROIC would you expect to go up more in times of inflation: a company with long-lived assets or one with short-lived assets, everything else being equal?
3. Describe the impact of high inflation on the financial statements of a company. What unique challenges does inflation present for analysis of historical performance?
4. Explain how an increase in inflation affects a company's tax shields from depreciation and the resulting impact on the company's value.
5. Why should you construct both real and nominal corporate forecasts when doing a valuation in high-inflation conditions?
6. Describe the five-step approach to combining nominal and real forecasts.
7. Assume that inflation unexpectedly increases by 10 percent. Explain why a company's ROIC then needs to increase by more than 10 percent to preserve its shareholder value.
8. Assume a high-inflation scenario in which a manufacturing company does not grow in real terms, and maintains its inventory of raw materials constant relative to sales. Does the company need to invest in inventories or not, given no change in either sales volume or inventory volume? Give a nominal and real-terms example and discuss.

9. In conditions of high inflation, nonmonetary assets tend to be stated on the balance sheet at values far below their replacement costs. Inventory accounting can further complicate historical analysis for companies in such an environment. Which accounting methodology would better represent the true value of the inventory in periods of high inflation: last-in first-out (LIFO) or first-in first-out (FIFO)? How would this change in a period of deflation?

30

Foreign Currency

To value businesses, subsidiaries, or companies in foreign countries, follow the same principles and methods that we presented in Part Two. Fortunately, such valuations have become simpler over the past few years as international accounting differences have rapidly diminished. Most of the world's major economies have now adopted either International Financial Reporting Standards (IFRS) or U.S. generally accepted accounting principles (GAAP), and these two standards are rapidly converging. Also, remember that if you follow the recommendations for rearranging financial statements in Chapter 7, you will get identical results regardless of which accounting principles you follow to prepare the financial statements.

Nevertheless, the following issues arising in cross-border valuations still need special attention:

- Forecasting cash flows in foreign currency (the currency of the foreign entity to be valued) and domestic currency (the home currency of the person doing the valuation).
- Estimating the cost of capital in foreign currency.
- Incorporating foreign-currency risk in valuations.
- Using translated foreign-currency financial statements.

For each of these issues, this chapter highlights the steps that require special analyses.

FORECASTING CASH FLOWS IN FOREIGN AND DOMESTIC CURRENCY

To value a company with international operations, first forecast the components of cash flow in their most *relevant* currency. This means forecasting the British-pound cash flows in British pounds, the Swiss-franc cash flows in Swiss francs, and so on, before combining them into a set of financials for the entire company.

A company valuation should always result in the same intrinsic value regardless of the currency or mix of currencies in which cash flows are projected. To achieve this consistent outcome, you need to use consistent monetary assumptions and one of the following two methods for forecasting and discounting foreign-currency cash flows:

1. *Spot rate method:* Project foreign cash flows in the foreign currency, and discount them at the foreign cost of capital. Then convert the present value of the cash flows into domestic currency, using the spot exchange rate.

2. *Forward rate method:* Project foreign cash flows in the foreign currency, and convert these into the domestic currency using the relevant forward exchange rates. Then discount the converted cash flows at the cost of capital in domestic currency.

We first illustrate both methods with a simple example. Assume you want to estimate the value of a Swiss subsidiary for its German parent company as of 2009. Exhibit 30.1 shows the cash flow projections for the subsidiary in the foreign currency (Swiss francs). The nominal cash flows grow at 3 percent per year in real terms plus inflation, which is projected to increase from 0.5 to 1.5 percent per year until 2015. Note that this inflation projection is consistent with the interest rates shown. For example, in 2011, the forward interest rate equals the real interest rate plus the expected inflation rate for that year:

$$(1 + 3.00\%)\,(1 + 1.00\%) - 1 = 4.03\%$$

And the two-year interest rate (yield) as of 2009 is the geometric average of the first- and second-year nominal forward interest rates:

$$[(1 + 3.52\%)\,(1 + 4.03\%)]^{1/2} - 1 = 3.77\%$$

Using the *spot rate method*, simply project cash flows in Swiss francs, and discount them at the Swiss risk-free interest rates. (We assume the subsidiary's beta is zero.) The resulting present value is 589.9 Swiss francs. Converting this value at the spot exchange rate of 1.200 Swiss francs per euro results in a discounted cash flow (DCF) value of €491.6 million:

Spot rate method		Year					
		2010	2011	2012	2013	2014	2015
Cash flow (millions of Swiss francs)		103.0	106.6	110.9	115.4	120.1	124.9
Discount factor		0.966	0.929	0.888	0.850	0.813	0.777
Present value of cash flow		99.5	99.0	98.6	98.1	97.6	97.1
DCF value (millions of Swiss francs)	589.9						
DCF value (millions of euros)	**491.6**						

EXHIBIT 30.1 **Projecting and Discounting Foreign Cash Flows**

		2010	2011	2012	2013	2014	2015
Foreign currency (Swiss francs)	**Cash flows**						
	Nominal cash flow	103.0	106.6	110.9	115.4	120.1	124.9
	Real cash flow	102.5	105.6	109.3	113.7	118.3	123.1
	Inflation (percent)	0.50	1.00	1.50	1.50	1.50	1.50
	Interest rates (percent)						
	Real interest rate	3.00	3.00	3.00	3.00	3.00	3.00
	Nominal forward interest rate	3.52	4.03	4.55	4.55	4.55	4.55
	Nominal interest yield	3.52	3.77	4.03	4.16	4.24	4.29
Foreign exchange rates (Swiss francs per euro)	Spot exchange rate 1.200						
	Forward exchange rate	1.194	1.188	1.177	1.165	1.154	1.137
Domestic currency (euros)	**Interest rates** (percent)						
	Nominal interest yield	4.03	4.29	4.71	4.93	5.06	5.23
	Nominal forward interest rate	4.03	4.55	5.58	5.58	5.58	6.09
	Real interest rate	3.00	3.00	3.00	3.00	3.00	3.00
	Inflation (percent)	1.00	1.50	2.50	2.50	2.50	3.00
	Cash flows						
	Real cash flow	85.4	88.4	92.0	96.7	101.5	106.7
	Nominal cash flow	86.3	89.8	94.3	99.1	104.1	109.9

The *forward-rate method* is more complex. The projected cash flows in Swiss francs should be converted to euros on a year-by-year basis using forward rates and then discounted at euro interest rates. For most currencies, however, forward exchange rates are not available beyond 18 months. This means you need to estimate synthetic forward exchange rates using interest rate parity theory.

According to this theory, changes in foreign exchange rates follow the ratio of expected inflation rates between two currencies. Exhibit 30.2 plots the relationship between domestic inflation and domestic interest rates for 38 countries from 1995 to 2004. The exhibit shows that inflation differences explain most of the difference in nominal interest rates.

EXHIBIT 30.2 **Relationship between Inflation and Interest Rates**

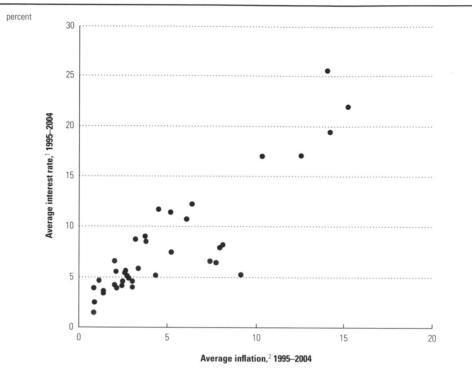

[1] Money market rate.
[2] Consumer price inflation.
Note: Sample of 38 countries in North and Latin America, Western and Eastern Europe, and Asia Pacific.
Source: International Monetary Fund International Financial Statistics.

Following interest rate parity theory, the forward foreign-exchange rate in year t, X_t, equals the current spot rate, X_0, multiplied by the ratio of nominal interest rates in the two currencies over the forecast interval, t:

$$X_t = X_0 \left[\frac{1 + r^F}{1 + r^D} \right]^t$$

where r^F is the interest rate in foreign currency and r^D is the interest rate in domestic currency.

In Exhibit 30.1, the euro–Swiss franc forward exchange rates are consistent with interest rate parity. For example, as of January 2010, a German company can borrow four-year money in Switzerland at a 4.16 percent nominal interest rate, r^F, while the borrowing rate in euros, r^D, is 4.93 percent for the same period. The spot exchange rate, X_0, is 1.200 Swiss francs per euro. We can use interest rate parity to estimate the three-year forward rate, X_3:

$$X_3 = 1.200 \left[\frac{1 + 4.16\%}{1 + 4.93\%} \right]^4 = 1.165$$

As these calculations show, whether a company borrows in Swiss francs or euros has no impact on value (unless there are any tax implications). If a German company borrows 1,200 Swiss francs today, it has to repay the loan with interest of 4.16 percent a year, totaling 1,412 Swiss francs in 2013. It can convert this total into a €1,212 payment in 2013 at today's four-year forward exchange rate (1,412 ÷ 1.165). Converting the borrowed amount of 1.200 Swiss francs at the current spot rate, the German company has effectively taken up a €1.000 loan, which is to be repaid with 4.93 percent annual interest, the euro interest rate on four-year money, totaling €1.212 in 2013.

In the forward-rate method, the Swiss-franc cash flow projections are converted to euro cash flows by using the forward exchange rates (see Exhibit 30.1). Using the euro interest rates to discount the converted cash flows, we obtain a present value of €491.6 million, exactly the same value as we obtained under the spot rate method:

	Year					
Forward-rate method	2010	2011	2012	2013	2014	2015
Cash flow at forward exchange rate (millions of euros)	86.3	89.8	94.3	99.1	104.1	109.9
Discount factor	0.961	0.919	0.871	0.825	0.781	0.737
Present value of cash flow (millions of curos)	82.9	82.5	82.1	81.7	81.3	80.9
DCF value (millions of euros)	**491.6**					

Of course, you could also derive the forward exchange rate in year t, X_t, from the current spot rate, X_0, multiplied by the ratio of the rates of inflation for the two currencies over the forecast interval:

$$X_t = X_0 \left[\frac{(1 + i_1^F) \times (1 + i_2^F) \times \ldots \times (1 + i_t^F)}{(1 + i_1^D) \times (1 + i_2^D) \times \ldots \times (1 + i_t^D)} \right]$$

where i_t^D is the inflation rate in year t in domestic currency and i_t^F is the inflation rate in year t in foreign currency. For example, in Exhibit 30.1, the three-year forward rate equals

$$X_3 = 1.200 \left[\frac{(1.005) \times (1.010) \times (1.015)}{(1.010) \times (1.015) \times (1.025)} \right] = 1.177$$

After conversion, the Swiss subsidiary's cash flows in euros differ from the original cash flows in Swiss francs by exactly the difference in inflation rates between the two currencies. Thus, the forward Swiss-franc-to-euro exchange rates are tied not only to the Swiss franc and euro interest rates, but also to the differences in Swiss and euro expected future inflation rates.

In other words, when you project and discount cash flows in different currencies, you cannot make independent assumptions for inflation, interest rates, and forward exchange rates across currencies. To ensure that your valuation results do not change with the choice of currency of denomination for a business's cash flows, you need to ensure that your monetary assumptions for all the currencies involved are consistent as follows:

- Inflation assumptions underlying cash flow projections in a specific currency need to be consistent with inflation assumptions underlying interest rates in that currency.
- Forward exchange rates between two currencies need to be consistent with inflation and interest rate differences between those currencies.
- Cash flow projections need to be converted from one currency into another at forward exchange rates.

ESTIMATING THE COST OF CAPITAL IN FOREIGN CURRENCY

As when you are forecasting cash flows in different currencies, the most important rule when you are estimating costs of capital for foreign businesses is to have consistent monetary assumptions. The expected inflation that determines the foreign-currency cash flows should equal the expected inflation included in the foreign-currency weighted average cost of capital (WACC) through the risk-free rate. In all other respects, estimating the WACC for a foreign entity is the same as estimating the WACC for a domestic entity. Nevertheless, we regularly come across foreign-currency valuations that mistakenly use the domestic-currency WACC—for instance, when parent companies use their own WACC to value the foreign-currency cash flow projections of their subsidiaries.

The cost of capital is best estimated from the perspective of a global investor (see Chapter 11). This means that both the market risk premium and beta should be measured against a global market portfolio and not against a local (foreign or domestic) market portfolio. We recommend this approach because capital markets have become global, in the sense that a considerable share of all equity trades is now international, and global traders, primarily large institutional investors, draw their capital from and invest it all over the world. If premiums for risk were significantly different across countries, capital would flow from countries with lower-than-average premiums to those with higher-than-average premiums, thereby reequalizing premiums.

Application of a global market risk premium also makes intuitive sense. Consider the consumer goods companies Procter & Gamble and Unilever. Both sell their household products around the world and have roughly the same geographic spread. The shares of both are traded in the United States

EXHIBIT 30.3 **Comparing Realized Returns, 1900–2008**

Annualized returns, percent

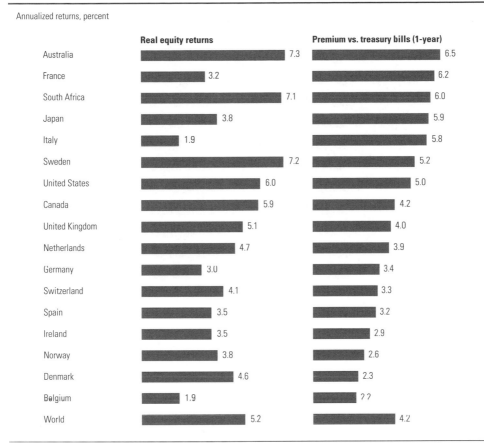

	Real equity returns	Premium vs. treasury bills (1-year)
Australia	7.3	6.5
France	3.2	6.2
South Africa	7.1	6.0
Japan	3.8	5.9
Italy	1.9	5.8
Sweden	7.2	5.2
United States	6.0	5.0
Canada	5.9	4.2
United Kingdom	5.1	4.0
Netherlands	4.7	3.9
Germany	3.0	3.4
Switzerland	4.1	3.3
Spain	3.5	3.2
Ireland	3.5	2.9
Norway	3.8	2.6
Denmark	4.6	2.3
Belgium	1.9	??
World	5.2	4.2

Source: E. Dimson, P. Marsh, M. Staunton, and J. Wilmot, *Credit Suisse Global Investment Returns Yearbook 2009* (London: Credit Suisse Research Institute, February 2009).

and Europe. The primary difference is that Procter & Gamble is domiciled in the United States, and Unilever is domiciled in the United Kingdom and the Netherlands. With such similar business profiles and investor bases, it would be odd if the two companies had different costs of capital.

Despite this reasoning, some comparisons of market data across countries do show differences in realized premiums, but this is mainly because the markets compared have different industry compositions. For example, Exhibit 30.3 compares the realized premiums on stock market indexes with government bond returns for several countries and the world, using numbers from Dimson, Marsh, Staunton, and Wilmot's analysis of long-term average returns on equities, corporate bonds, and short-term government bonds.[1] Realized returns vary considerably across markets, depending on the time period over

[1] E. Dimson, P. Marsh, M. Staunton, and J. Wilmot, *Credit Suisse Global Investment Returns Yearbook 2009* (London: Credit Suisse Research Institute, 2009).

EXHIBIT 30.4 **Share of Equity Returns Explained by Industry Composition of Index**

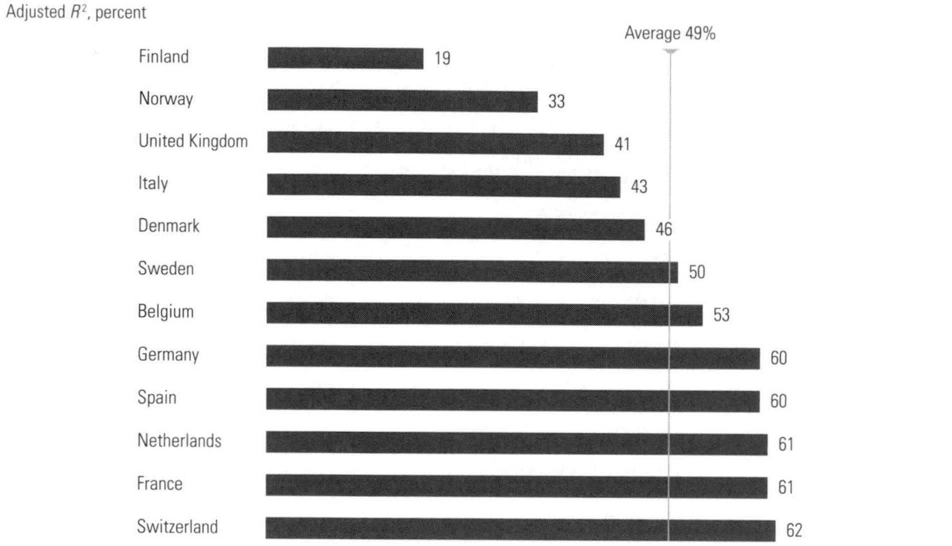

Adjusted R^2, percent

Average 49%

Finland	19
Norway	33
United Kingdom	41
Italy	43
Denmark	46
Sweden	50
Belgium	53
Germany	60
Spain	60
Netherlands	61
France	61
Switzerland	62

Source: R. Roll, "Industrial Structure and the Comparative Behaviour of International Stock Market Indexes," *Journal of Finance* 47, no. 1 (1992): 3–42.

which they are measured. Exhibit 30.3 shows that even for a 100-year period, realized returns can still vary a lot. One reason is the variation in levels of economic development over the past century among the countries listed. Furthermore, data from some of the markets may reflect their limited integration with international capital markets in the past. Therefore, the historical data may not properly represent the current situation.

More importantly, many of these market indexes do not represent large, diversified portfolios. In particular, the key stock market indexes in most European countries, which account for the majority of their stock markets' total capitalization, typically include only 25 to 40 companies, often from a limited range of industries. Indeed, research has shown that a large fraction of the variation in returns on European market indexes could be explained by their industry composition (see Exhibit 30.4).[2] Exhibit 30.5 shows some recent data comparing the 10 largest global stock markets that have market capitalizations exceeding $1 trillion with 10 smaller markets that have capitalizations between $100 billion and $200 billion. The smaller stock markets are dominated by particular stocks and sectors, whereas the larger markets—in particular, Japan and the United States—are much more diversified.

We maintain, therefore, that ideally the global market risk premium should be based on a global market index such as the MSCI World Index. Unfortunately, global indexes rarely go far back in time, so long-term estimates

[2] R. Roll, "Industrial Structure and the Comparative Behavior of International Stock Market Indexes," *Journal of Finance* 47, no. 1 (1992): 3–42.

EXHIBIT 30.5 **Comparing Stock Market Concentration**

2009, percent

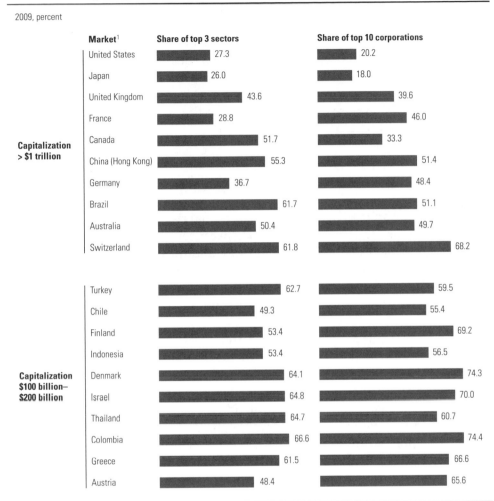

Market[1]	Share of top 3 sectors	Share of top 10 corporations
United States	27.3	20.2
Japan	26.0	18.0
United Kingdom	43.6	39.6
France	28.8	46.0
Canada	51.7	33.3
China (Hong Kong)	55.3	51.4
Germany	36.7	48.4
Brazil	61.7	51.1
Australia	50.4	49.7
Switzerland	61.8	68.2
Turkey	62.7	59.5
Chile	49.3	55.4
Finland	53.4	69.2
Indonesia	53.4	56.5
Denmark	64.1	74.3
Israel	64.8	70.0
Thailand	64.7	60.7
Colombia	66.6	74.4
Greece	61.5	66.6
Austria	48.4	65.6

Capitalization > $1 trillion applies to the upper group (United States through Switzerland).
Capitalization $100 billion–$200 billion applies to the lower group (Turkey through Austria).

[1] Ranked by total market capitalization in U.S. dollars.

Source: Datastream.

of historical market risk premiums are not readily available. Therefore, we generally resort to specially compiled series, as shown in Exhibit 30.3. These include estimates for the global market risk premium or the well-diversified U.S. market as a basis for a global market risk premium. Correlation between the S&P 500 and global market indexes (such as the MSCI World Index) has, so far, been very high, making the S&P 500 a good proxy. Estimates from both sources are typically not far apart, falling in the range of 4 to 5 percent (see also Chapter 11).

Since we are using a global market risk premium, we should also use a global beta. As we just noted, the local market indexes of many countries are biased toward certain companies and/or industries. Therefore, a beta derived from a local market index does not necessarily represent the risk contribution of that stock to a diversified, global portfolio.

Although many practitioners make ad hoc adjustments to the discount rate to reflect political risk, foreign-investment risk, or foreign-currency risk, we do not recommend this. As explained in Chapter 33 on emerging markets, political or country risk is best handled by adjusting expected cash flows and weighting them by the probability of various scenarios. Meanwhile, any premiums for foreign-currency risk are already captured in the spot and forward exchange rates, as we discuss in the following section.

INCORPORATING FOREIGN-CURRENCY RISK IN VALUATIONS

We do not support the inclusion of an additional risk premium in the discount rate to cover for perceived currency risk, because any currency risk premium will already have been included in the spot and forward exchange rates used to translate currencies. The extent to which financial markets actually price currency risk in spot and forward exchange rates is still an open debate among academics.[3] But these risk premiums—if any—are likely to be small.[4]

This should not come as a surprise. Basic finance theory tells us that there is no value in a company managing currency risk for its shareholders when the shareholders can manage this risk themselves simply by diversifying their portfolios.

Keep in mind that nominal currency risk is irrelevant if exchange rates immediately adjust to differences in inflation rates. The only relevant currency risk is real currency risk as measured by changes in relative purchasing power. Analysis of purchasing power parity indicates that currencies indeed revert to parity levels following changes in relative rates of inflation, but not immediately. Short-term deviations from exchange rates that give purchasing power parity can be significant and potentially leave corporations exposed to real currency risk. However, shareholders are typically able to diversify this real currency risk.

To see how, consider Exhibit 30.6, which shows the monthly volatility of real exchange rates for a selection of Latin American and Asian currencies plus the British pound, and four currency portfolios. Although some of the currencies are highly volatile, holding a regional portfolio already eliminates a lot of the resulting real currency risk, as shown by the lower volatility of the regional portfolios. Combining a developing markets portfolio with a British pounds portfolio diversifies the real risk even further. If shareholders can disperse most

---

[3] See, for example, B. Solnik, *International Investments*, 4th ed. (Reading, MA: Addison-Wesley, 1999), chap. 5.
[4] P. Sercu and R. Uppal, *International Financial Markets and the Firm* (Cincinnati, OH: South-Western, 1995), chap. 14.

EXHIBIT 30.6 **Diversification of Real Currency Risk**

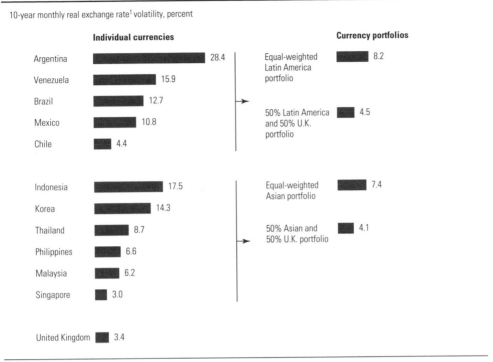

10-year monthly real exchange rate[1] volatility, percent

[1] Exchange rates to U.S. dollar.
Source: International Monetary Fund.

real currency risk by diversifying, there is no need for a currency risk premium of any significance in the company's cost of capital.

USING TRANSLATED FOREIGN-CURRENCY FINANCIAL STATEMENTS

Analysis of the historical performance of foreign businesses is best done in the foreign currency. But sometimes this is not possible—for example, when the business's statements have been translated into its parent company's currency and included (or consolidated) in the parent's accounts. A British subsidiary of a European corporate group will always prepare financial statements in British pounds, and when the European parent company prepares its financial statements, it will translate the British pounds in the statements of the British subsidiary at the current euro-pound exchange rate. However, if the exchange rate fluctuates from year to year, the European parent company will report the same asset at a different euro amount each year, even if the asset's value in British pounds has not changed. This change in the value of the British asset in the parent's reporting currency would suggest a cash expenditure, but no cash has been spent because the change is solely due to a change in the exchange

EXHIBIT 30.7 **Currency Translation Approaches**

	U.S. GAAP	IFRS
Moderate inflation	Current method	Current method
Hyperinflation	Temporal method	Inflation-adjusted current method

rate. Therefore, following the guidelines from Chapter 7, you need to make a correction to the cash flow estimated from the financial statements that is equal to the gains/losses from the currency translation.

Between them, U.S. GAAP and IFRS approve three approaches to translating the financial statements of foreign subsidiaries into the parent company's currency: the current method, temporal method, and inflation-adjusted current method. The correct approach to use depends on which standard you follow and the inflation rate in the country in question. Exhibit 30.7 shows the approach recommended by each standard for countries with moderate inflation and those with hyperinflation.

For subsidiaries in moderate-inflation countries, translating the financial statements into the currency of the parent company is fairly straightforward. Both U.S. GAAP and IFRS apply the current method, which requires translating all balance sheet items except equity at the year-end exchange rate. Translation gains and losses on the balance sheet are recognized in the equity account, so they do not affect net income. The average exchange rate for the period is used to translate the income statement.

For subsidiaries where inflation rates are higher, IFRS and U.S. GAAP differ in what they define as hyperinflation, whether to adjust statements for inflation, and what approach to use for translating the financial statements. U.S. GAAP defines hyperinflation as cumulative inflation over three years of approximately 100 percent or more. IFRS states that this is one indicator of hyperinflation but suggests considering other factors as well, such as the degree to which local investors prefer to keep wealth in nonmonetary assets or stable foreign currencies.

U.S. GAAP requires companies to use the temporal method for translating financial statements of subsidiaries in hyperinflation countries into the parent's currency. To use this method, you must translate all items in the financial statements at the exchange rate prevailing at the relevant transaction date. This means using historical exchange rates for items carried at historical cost, current exchange rates for monetary items, and year-average or other appropriate exchange rates for other balance sheet items and the income statement. Any resulting currency gains or losses are reported on the income statement of the parent.

The IFRS approach to currency translation for subsidiaries in hyperinflation countries is similar to that for moderate-inflation countries. The key difference is that IFRS requires the hyperinflation country statements to be restated in current (foreign) currency units based on a general price index before they are translated into the parent company's currency. All except some monetary items need to be restated to account for the estimated impact of very high inflation on values over time. This generally requires some judgment on the part of the translator and will also depend on the details of specific agreements and contracts; for example, any debt-financing agreements may or may not already be linked to an index. This restatement will result in a gain or loss on the subsidiary's income statement. Because the full statements are restated in current (year-end) foreign-currency units, the year-end exchange rate should be used to translate both the balance sheet and the income statement into the parent company's currency. Any translation gains or losses will be included in the equity account of the parent.

Exhibit 30.8 shows an example for a U.S. parent company using all three approaches to currency translation. In this example, the exchange rate has changed from 0.95 at the beginning of the year to 0.85 at the end of the year, consistent with 14 percent inflation in the foreign country during the year and U.S. inflation of 2 percent. The average exchange rate for the year is 0.90. As the exhibit illustrates, the three approaches can result in significantly different amounts for net income and equity in the parent company's currency. Of course, these differences should not affect your estimate of free cash flow for the subsidiary.

SUMMARY

You should apply the DCF valuation approach to foreign companies in just the same way you apply it to domestic companies. Nevertheless, some difficult issues can arise in valuing foreign companies or domestic companies with foreign operations. You need to understand and reflect local accounting in your analysis, but the adjustments are typically straightforward, following the general guidelines from Chapter 7. Because IFRS and U.S. GAAP are now the dominant accounting standards, however, any difficulties arising from international accounting differences have been greatly reduced.

Cash flows for foreign businesses can be projected in foreign or domestic currency as long as you apply your chosen method of currency translation—spot rate or forward rate—consistently. The approach for estimating the cost of

EXHIBIT 30.8 **Currency Translation**

| | Local currency | Current method | | Temporal method | | Inflation-adjusted currency method | | |
		Foreign-exchange rate	U.S. dollars	Foreign-exchange rate	U.S. dollars	Adjusted	Foreign-exchange rate	U.S. dollars
Balance sheet								
Cash and receivables	100	0.85	85	0.85	85	100	0.85	85
Inventory	300	0.85	255	0.90	270	321	0.85	273
Net fixed assets	600	0.85	510	0.95	570	684	0.85	581
	1,000	–	850	–	925	1,105	–	939
Current liabilities	265	0.85	225	0.85	225	265	0.85	225
Long-term debt	600	0.85	510	0.85	510	684	0.85	581
Equity								
Common stock	100	0.95	95	0.95	95	100	0.95	95
Retained earnings	35	–	32	–	95	56	–	48
Foreign-currency adjustment	–	–	(12)	–	–	–	–	(10)
	1,000	–	850	–	925	1,105	–	939
Income statement								
Revenue	150	0.90	135	0.90	135	161	0.85	137
Cost of goods sold	(70)	0.90	(63)	0.93	(65)	(75)	0.85	(64)
Depreciation	(20)	0.90	(18)	0.95	(19)	(23)	0.85	(20)
Other expenses, net	(10)	0.90	(9)	0.90	(9)	(11)	0.85	(9)
Foreign-exchange gain/(loss)	–	–	–	–	66	20[1]	0.85	17
Income before taxes	50	–	45	–	108	72	–	61
Income taxes	(15)	0.90	(13)	0.90	(13)	(16)	0.85	(13)
Net income	35	–	32	–	95	56	–	48

[1] Gain from restatement.

capital should be the same for any company anywhere in the world, although estimating some of the parameters (particularly market risk premium) can be controversial. Considering the global integration of capital markets, we also recommend using a single market risk premium for companies around the world. Similarly, currency risk does not require a separate premium to be added to the cost of capital.

REVIEW QUESTIONS

1. Is the cost of risk-free financing the same or different in different countries?
2. Many companies use economists' forecasts of foreign exchange rates to translate cash flow projections denominated in foreign currency. What are the possible drawbacks of using such forecasts?

3. Why do local market risk premiums differ across national stock markets? Do the differences mean that some markets are more attractive to invest in than others?

4. Are there conditions under which you should consider using a local market risk premium and a local beta estimate for a valuation rather than a global risk premium and beta?

5. What impact does the globalization of capital markets have on a manager's judgment of the appropriate cost of capital to employ when estimating the value of a subsidiary headquartered in a foreign country?

6. U.S. GAAP and IFRS accounting standards are converging. Since this is the case, why would a manager need to understand the historical differences between these standards?

7. Discuss the differences between the current, temporal, and inflation-adjusted current methods for translating the financial statements of acquisitions or divisions located in moderately inflationary and hyperinflationary economic environments.

8. The forward rate and spot rate methods for discounting foreign currency cash flows are equivalent if interest rate parity holds. Assume that interest rate parity does not hold for a specific currency because it is pegged to the dollar at a fixed exchange rate and capital flows are controlled by the monetary authorities in the country in question. Which method would apply in that case and why?

31

Case Study: Heineken

This chapter applies the tools and techniques from Part Two and the previous chapters in Part Five by presenting a case study that develops an external perspective on the performance and valuation of Heineken as of January 2009. [1] The case study parallels the kind of outside-in analysis and valuation that a sophisticated investor might undertake, but the steps are the same as for making an internal, company-wide analysis and valuation to support executive decisions.

Based in the Netherlands, the Heineken Group is the world's third largest beer company, behind Anheuser-Busch InBev (AB InBev) and SABMiller. Its main brands are the popular Heineken and Amstel beers. The company is an international brewer; only 4 percent of its volume comes from the Netherlands. Heineken earns 49 percent of net revenues in Western Europe, 26 percent in Central and Eastern Europe, 12 percent in Africa and the Middle East, 11 percent in North America, and the remaining 2 percent in the Asia-Pacific region. In 2007, Heineken joined Danish brewer Carlsberg to acquire British competitor Scottish & Newcastle (S&N). The €13.5 billion acquisition, in which it took over 45 percent of S&N, was a major move for Heineken in the global consolidation of the beer industry. After this acquisition, Heineken generated revenues of €14.3 billion and employed more than 56,000 people worldwide in 2008. [2]

We start with a short industry description, after which we rearrange Heineken's financial statements according to the methodology derived in Chapter 7, with special attention to the impact of the S&N acquisition. Then we analyze Heineken's historical profitability and growth rates, following the method described in Chapter 8. Next, we derive scenarios for future

The authors would like to thank Martijn Olthof for his contribution to this chapter.
[1] Because this is an illustration, we also analyzed and adjusted items that are immaterial for the valuation of Heineken, but could be significant for the valuation of other companies.
[2] Heineken's January 2010 acquisition of the beer division of Fomento Económico Mexicano S.A.B. de C.V. (FEMSA) is not reflected in this case study.

performance and growth of Heineken and corresponding cash flow projections. We estimate Heineken's cost of capital to derive the continuing value and discounted cash flow (DCF) of operations for each scenario. Finally, we estimate Heineken's value per share, following the approach set out in Chapter 12.

INDUSTRY DEVELOPMENTS

The worldwide beer industry has long been fragmented and regional, and has experienced slow to average growth. Over the five years leading to 2008, the volume of worldwide beer consumption grew 4.3 percent annually. Growth expectations for the period from 2008 to 2014 are around 2.6 percent per year, with low or negative growth in developed markets and the main source of growth in emerging markets (see Exhibit 31.1).

In the past few years, the beer industry has experienced a couple of large mergers and acquisitions, making it a little less fragmented than before. The

EXHIBIT 31.1   **Growth Expectations for the Worldwide Beer Market**

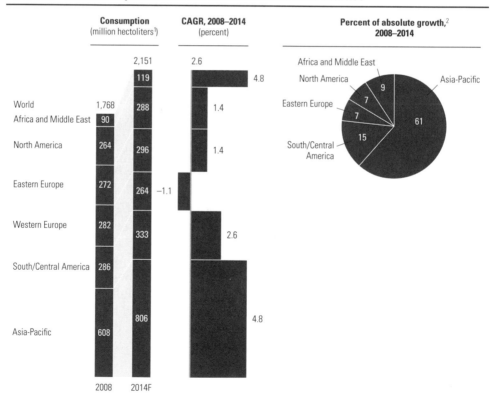

[1] 1 hectoliter = 100 liter.
[2] Excludes Western Europe due to negative growth prospect.

Source: Canadean 2009 Global Beer Report.

EXHIBIT 31.2 **Beer Industry: National Market Share**

percent

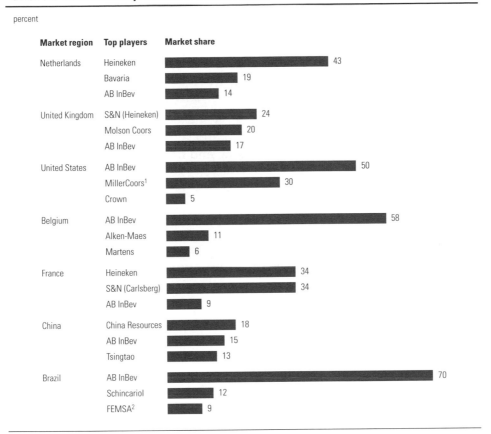

Market region	Top players	Market share
Netherlands	Heineken	43
	Bavaria	19
	AB InBev	14
United Kingdom	S&N (Heineken)	24
	Molson Coors	20
	AB InBev	17
United States	AB InBev	50
	MillerCoors[1]	30
	Crown	5
Belgium	AB InBev	58
	Alken-Maes	11
	Martens	6
France	Heineken	34
	S&N (Carlsberg)	34
	AB InBev	9
China	China Resources	18
	AB InBev	15
	Tsingtao	13
Brazil	AB InBev	70
	Schincariol	12
	FEMSA[2]	9

[1] Joint venture between Molson Coors and SABMiller.
[2] Acquired by Heineken in 2010.

Source: Canadean 2009 Global Beer Report

top three brewers have a combined market share of 30 percent worldwide (up from 23 percent in 2003), and the top 20 brewers have a combined market share of 70 percent. Although the global market is fragmented, many regional markets are oligopolies. For example, in the top 20 markets by size, the top two players have an average combined market share of 69 percent. However, the leading players vary from country to country (see Exhibit 31.2).

Although the major brewers have expanded outside their home markets, competition has remained predominantly local because of consumer preference for local brands and tastes, high government tariffs, regulations, and limited opportunities for economies of scale or scope across national borders. As a result, when brewers have entered new markets, they typically have focused on transferring skills, such as marketing, rather than building globally integrated businesses. The strength of local competition has kept the pace of industry consolidation slow, as local brewers did not feel the need to sell their businesses to the majors to remain competitive. As tastes converge, technology improves, transportation costs decline, and brewers learn how to leverage their expertise and brand names better, the industry has slowly begun to reach consumers on a global scale.

REORGANIZING FINANCIAL STATEMENTS

As explained in Chapter 7, to analyze Heineken's historical performance, we need to reorganize the balance sheet and income statement to separate the operating items from the nonoperating and financing items. Exhibits 31.3 through 31.10 detail the reorganization of Heineken's financials. Exhibits 31.3

EXHIBIT 31.3 **Heineken: Historical Income Statements**

€ million

	2004 restated	2005 reported	2006 reported	2007 reported	2007 restated	2008 reported
Revenues	10,062	10,796	11,829	12,564	11,245	14,319
Other income	–	–	379	30	28	32
Raw materials, consumables, and services	(6,101)	(6,657)	(7,376)	(8,162)	(7,320)	(9,548)
Personnel expenses	(1,957)	(2,180)	(2,241)	(2,165)	(1,951)	(2,415)
Earnings before interest, taxes, depreciation, and amortization (EBITDA)	2,004	1,959	2,591	2,267	2,002	2,388
Depreciation[1]	(615)	(647)	(706)	(694)	(615)	(741)
Amortization of operating intangibles[1]	(28)	(29)	(17)	(20)	(17)	(34)
Amortization of acquired intangibles[1]	(8)	(8)	(11)	(11)	(8)	(72)
Impairment of goodwill and acquired intangibles[1]	(2)	(15)	(18)	(21)	(4)	(275)
Impairments of PP&E and operating intangibles[1]	(3)	(11)	(34)	(18)	6	(84)
Results from operating activities	1,348	1,249	1,805	1,503	1,364	1,182
Interest income	78	60	52	67	64	91
Interest expense	(243)	(199)	(185)	(168)	(155)	(469)
Other net finance expenses	(165)	25	11	(26)	(4)	(107)
Profit before income tax	1,018	1,135	1,683	1,376	1,269	697
Income tax expenses	(306)	(300)	(365)	(429)	(394)	(248)
Share of profit of associates and joint ventures[2]	21	34	27	25	54	(102)
Minority interest	(91)	(108)	(134)	(165)	(122)	(138)
Net profit	642	761	1,211	807	807	209
Shareholders' equity						
Position as of January 1	2,782	3,256	3,969	5,009	5,009	5,404
Net profit	642	761	1,211	807	807	209
Other net recognized income and expense	5	148	35	(71)	(71)	(779)
Dividends	(173)	(196)	(196)	(333)	(333)	(363)
Purchase of own shares	–	–	(14)	(15)	(15)	(11)
Share-based payments	–	–	4	7	7	11
Position as of December 31	3,256	3,969	5,009	5,404	5,404	4,471

[1] Depreciation, amortization, and impairments separated according to the information in the footnotes.
[2] In Heineken's annual report, this item is presented above the "profit before income tax" line.

EXHIBIT 31.4 **Heineken: Historical Balance Sheets**

€ million

	2004 restated	2005 reported	2006 reported	2007 reported	2007 restated	2008 reported
Inventories	782	883	893	1,007	883	1,246
Trade and other receivables	1,646	1,787	1,917	1,873	1,769	2,504
Prepayments and accrued income	–	–	–	123	110	231
Cash and cash equivalents	678	585	1,374	715	560	698
Other investments	26	23	12	105	14	14
Assets classified as held for sale	–	–	41	21	21	56
Total current assets	3,132	3,278	4,237	3,844	3,357	4,749
Property, plant, and equipment	4,773	5,067	4,944	5,362	4,673	6,314
Intangible assets	1,837	2,380	2,449	2,541	2,110	7,109
Investments in associates and joint ventures	134	172	186	214	892	1,145
Other investments	632	646	786	671	606	987
Deferred tax assets	269	286	395	336	316	259
Total noncurrent assets	7,645	8,551	8,760	9,124	8,597	15,814
Total assets	10,777	11,829	12,997	12,968	11,954	20,563
Bank overdrafts	517	351	747	282	251	94
Loans and borrowings	429	709	494	873	787	875
Trade and other payables	2,025	2,451	2,496	2,806	2,525	3,846
Tax liabilities	30	141	149	89	71	85
Provisions	43	100	122	143	143	158
Total current liabilities	3,044	3,752	4,008	4,193	3,777	5,058
Loans and borrowings	2,638	2,233	2,091	1,521	1,295	9,084
Employee benefits	680	664	665	646	586	688
Provisions	298	273	242	184	158	344
Deferred tax liabilities	384	393	471	478	427	637
Total noncurrent liabilities	4,000	3,563	3,469	2,829	2,466	10,753
Equity attributable to equity holders of the company	3,256	3,969	5,009	5,404	5,404	4,471
Minority interests	477	545	511	542	307	281
Total shareholders' equity	3,733	4,514	5,520	5,946	5,711	4,752
Total liabilities and shareholders' equity	10,777	11,829	12,997	12,968	11,954	20,563

and 31.4 present Heineken's income statements and balance sheets for the years 2004 through 2008, keeping as close as possible to the line item naming and structure of the company's 2008 annual report. Exhibits 31.5 through 31.10 present the calculations of Heineken's net operating profit less adjusted taxes (NOPLAT), invested capital, and free cash flow (FCF) for each year plus backup calculations and information on specific issues, such as pensions, goodwill, and deferred taxes.

In 2008, Heineken changed from proportional consolidation of its joint ventures to the equity method, which makes a direct comparison of the reported financials for 2007 and 2008 less meaningful. Therefore, we show both the reported 2007 results and the restated 2007 results from the 2008 annual report. For the FCF calculation for 2008, which uses year-on-year changes in balance sheet items, we use the restated 2007 figures. For the same reasons, we use the restated 2004 figures under International Financial Reporting Standards (IFRS) accounting from the 2005 annual report, rather than the original 2004 reported results under Dutch generally accepted accounting principles.

In our analysis and reorganization of Heineken's financial statements, the following accounting issues merit special attention.

Income Statement and NOPLAT

First we deal with issues of interpretation arising from analysis of the income statement (Exhibit 31.3) to calculate NOPLAT (Exhibit 31.5).

Depreciation, amortization, and impairments   To calculate NOPLAT, we separate the depreciation of property, plant, and equipment (PP&E) from amortization and impairments, which Heineken reports as a single item on the income statement. Within amortization, we further separate amortization of acquired intangibles (which is nonoperating, as discussed in Chapter 7) from operating amortization, which relates mostly to software. We separate any impairments from income on nonconsolidated investments, notably the €214 million impairment included in the €102 million loss from associates and joint ventures in 2008 ("nonconsolidated investments" refers to 'associates and joint ventures' in Heineken's financial statements).

Other income   According to notes to Heineken's financial statements, the item "other income" relates to gains on the sale of fixed assets. Therefore, in the NOPLAT statement, we classify it as a nonoperating gain (loss) on disposals.

Raw materials   To adjust raw materials, we take out a €219 million fine from the European Commission (EC) in 2007 and a €16 million loss on disposals in 2008. These are included as nonoperating results in the NOPLAT statement.

Personnel expenses   We remove the following items from personnel expenses:

- *Nonoperating pension expenses:* We take out the entire reported pension expense and recognize only the current and past service costs under personnel expenses. Exhibit 31.6 shows that the total pension expense includes several nonoperating items, such as interest on the pension obligation and expected return on plan assets. These are included as (nonoperating) pension adjustments in the NOPLAT statement.
- *Additions to nonoperating provisions (net of reversals):* From the notes to the financial statements, we find that most of Heineken's provisions are

EXHIBIT 31.5 **Heineken: NOPLAT Calculation**

€ million

	2004 restated	2005 reported	2006 reported	2007 reported	2007 restated	2008 reported
Revenues	10,062	10,796	11,829	12,564	11,245	14,319
Raw materials, as reported	(6,101)	(6,657)	(7,376)	(8,162)	(7,320)	(9,548)
Remove: EC fine	–	–	–	219	219	–
Remove: Loss on disposals	–	–	–	–	–	16
Raw materials, adjusted	(6,101)	(6,657)	(7,376)	(7,943)	(7,101)	(9,532)
Personnel expense, as reported	(1,957)	(2,180)	(2,241)	(2,165)	(1,951)	(2,415)
Remove: Reported pension expense	96	96	100	84	82	78
Add: Current and past pension service costs	(80)	(82)	(84)	(73)	(72)	(80)
Remove: Additions to nonoperating provisions	–	102	99	76	76	161
Personnel expense, adjusted	(1,941)	(2,064)	(2,126)	(2,078)	(1,865)	(2,256)
Adjusted EBITDA	2,020	2,075	2,327	2,543	2,279	2,531
Depreciation, as reported	(615)	(647)	(706)	(694)	(615)	(741)
Remove: Gain on sale of fixed assets	(26)	(58)	–	–	–	–
Depreciation, adjusted	(641)	(705)	(706)	(694)	(615)	(741)
Amortization of operating intangibles	(28)	(29)	(17)	(20)	(17)	(34)
Adjusted EBITA	1,351	1,341	1,604	1,829	1,647	1,756
Operating cash taxes	(414)	(406)	(431)	(447)	(396)	(463)
NOPLAT	937	935	1,173	1,382	1,251	1,293
Operating cash taxes						
Statutory domestic tax rate	34.5%	31.5%	29.6%	25.5%	25.5%	25.5%
Income tax at statutory domestic rate	466	422	475	466	420	448
Tax effect of foreign operations	(72)	(28)	(50)	18	5	16
Income tax at blended global rate	394	394	425	484	425	464
Increase (decrease) in operating deferred tax liability	20	12	6	(37)	(29)	(1)
Operating cash taxes	414	406	431	447	396	463
Operating cash tax rate	30.7%	30.3%	26.9%	24.4%	24.1%	26.4%
Reconciliation with net profit						
Net profit	642	761	1,211	807	807	209
EC fine	–	–	–	219	219	–
Loss (gain) on disposals	(26)	(58)	(379)	(30)	(28)	(16)
Pension adjustments to personnel expenses	16	14	16	11	10	(2)
Additions to nonoperating provisions	–	102	99	76	76	161
Decrease (increase) in operating deferred tax liability	(20)	(12)	(6)	37	29	1
Amortization of acquired intangibles	8	8	11	11	8	72
Impairment of goodwill and acquired intangibles	2	15	18	21	4	275
Impairments of PP&E and operating intangibles	3	11	34	18	(6)	84
Interest income	(78)	(60)	(52)	(67)	(64)	(91)
Other net finance expenses	165	(25)	(11)	26	4	107
Nonoperating taxes	(88)	(94)	(60)	(55)	(31)	(216)
Income from nonconsolidated investments	(21)	(34)	(27)	(25)	(94)	(112)
Impairments of nonconsolidated investments	–	–	–	–	40	214
Adjusted net profit	603	628	854	1,049	974	686
Interest expense	243	199	185	168	155	469
Minority interest	91	108	134	165	122	138
NOPLAT	937	935	1,173	1,382	1,251	1,293

EXHIBIT 31.6 **Heineken: Pension Expense Recognized in Income Statement**

€ million

	2007	2008
Current service costs	71	75
Past service costs	1	5
Operating pension costs	72	80
Interest on obligation	133	258
Expected return on plan assets	(129)	(241)
Actuarial gains and losses recognized	2	(1)
Effect of any curtailment or settlement	4	(18)
Nonoperating pension costs	10	(2)
Total pension costs in income statement	82	78

for restructuring costs. We assume that additions to these nonoperating provisions flow through personnel expenses in the income statement. For example, the additions to provisions (net of reversals) for 2008 were €161 million, which is very close to the €166 million of exceptional restructuring charges included in personnel expenses.

Asset disposals   For 2004 and 2005, we correct the depreciation charges on property, plant, and equipment (PP&E) for any gains on asset disposals, which were included in this line item in the financial statements. We include these items in nonoperating loss (gain) on disposals in the NOPLAT statement.

Operating cash taxes   We use the simple method explained in Chapter 25, assuming that nonoperating items are taxed domestically, because the financial reports include insufficient information about Heineken's tax situation to do a comprehensive estimate of operating taxes. Exhibit 31.5 shows how operating taxes equal the sum of income taxes at the blended global rate plus the change in the operating deferred taxes. Income taxes at the blended global rate are simply earnings before interest, taxes, and amortization (EBITA) times the domestic tax rate net of any tax effects of foreign operations.

The change in the operating deferred taxes is estimated using additional information from the notes to Heineken's financial statements, which detail the components of the deferred tax assets and liabilities in the balance sheet (see Exhibit 31.7):

- *Operating deferred taxes* are assumed to be those related to PP&E, inventory, and other undisclosed items. They are treated as equity equivalents in invested-capital calculations (see Exhibit 31.8). Annual changes in operating deferred taxes are included in NOPLAT as part of operating cash taxes if the changes were (1) recurring and (2) charged or credited to the

EXHIBIT 31.7 **Treatment of Deferred Tax Liabilities (DTLs) and Deferred Tax Assets (DTAs)**

€ million

Net deferred tax assets	2007	2008	Treatment in invested capital[1]	Change in net deferred tax assets 2008	Treatment in free cash flow	2008
Operating[2]					NOPLAT[3]	(1)
					Change in operating DTA/DTL[4]	(60)
Property, plant, and equipment	(329)	(470)	Operating			(61)
Inventories	15	6	DTA/DTL (EE)	(61)		
Other items	26	115				
Total	(288)	(349)				
Nonoperating						
Investments	1	(3)				
Loans and borrowings	–	1	Nonoperating		Change in nonoperating	
Employee benefits	113	146	DTA/DTL (DE)	81	DTA/DTL	81
Provisions	49	100				
Total	163	244				
			Intangibles		Investment in goodwill	
Intangible assets	–	(422)	adjustment (NOA)[5]	(422)	and intangibles	(422)
Tax loss carry-forwards	14	149	Tax loss carry-		Change in tax loss	
			forwards (NOA)	135	carry-forwards	135
Total net assets (liabilities)	(111)	(378)		(267)		(267)
Recognized as assets	316	259				
Recognized as liabilities	427	637				
Total net assets (liabilities)	(111)	(378)				

[1] EE is equity equivalent; DE is debt equivalent; NOA is nonoperating asset.
[2] Assuming all temporary differences correspond to operating assets/liabilities.
[3] Items booked through P&L and recurring (e.g., origination, reversal of depreciation differences).
[4] Items booked through P&L and not recurring (e.g., changes in future tax rates).
[5] Netted out against grossed-up intangibles.

income statement. Examples are changes in deferred taxes driven by depreciation differences in net property, plant, and equipment (NPPE). But most changes in Heineken's operating deferred taxes are nonrecurring (e.g., changes as a result of tax rate revisions) or did not pass through the income statement (e.g., changes as a result of acquisitions). Only €1 million in operating deferred tax changes are included in NOPLAT.

- *Deferred tax items for nonoperating assets or liabilities* such as investments, loans and borrowings, employee benefits, and provisions are treated as debt equivalents or nonoperating assets in the invested-capital calculation and do not affect NOPLAT.

- *Deferred taxes for intangibles* are netted out in the invested-capital statement as an adjustment to acquired intangibles (listed in Exhibit 31.8 as a €422 million reversal of intangibles value adjustment in 2008). This tax position results from the nondeductible amortization of a step-up of acquired intangibles, which is purely an accounting convention, as shown in Chapter 25, and does not affect NOPLAT.

EXHIBIT 31.8 **Heineken: Invested-Capital Calculation**

€ million

	2004 restated	2005 reported	2006 reported	2007 reported	2007 restated	2008 reported
Working cash	201	216	237	251	225	286
Trade receivables	1,499	1,682	1,779	1,873	1,680	2,401
Inventories	782	883	893	1,007	883	1,246
Prepayments and accrued income	147	94	91	123	110	231
Operating current assets	2,629	2,875	3,000	3,254	2,898	4,164
Trade payables	804	1,049	1,039	1,170	1,043	1,570
Accruals and deferred income	330	445	603	688	573	738
Other current operating liabilities	869	964	930	941	890	1,356
Operating current liabilities	2,003	2,458	2,572	2,799	2,506	3,664
Operating working capital	626	417	428	455	392	500
Net property, plant, and equipment	4,773	5,067	4,944	5,362	4,673	6,314
Operating intangibles	46	30	33	38	32	73
Invested capital excluding intangibles	5,445	5,514	5,405	5,855	5,097	6,887
Goodwill and acquired intangibles	1,791	2,350	2,416	2,503	2,078	7,036
Cumulative amortization and unrecorded goodwill	3,155	3,178	3,207	3,237	3,199	3,542
Reversal of intangibles value adjustment	–	–	–	–	–	(422)
Invested capital including intangibles	10,391	11,042	11,027	11,595	10,374	17,043
Excess cash	477	369	1,137	464	335	412
Nonconsolidated investments	134	172	186	214	892	1,145
Other financial assets	658	618	876	775	709	1,073
Tax loss carry-forwards	22	19	11	17	14	149
Total funds invested	11,682	12,220	13,238	13,065	12,324	19,822
Shareholders' equity	3,256	3,969	5,009	5,404	5,404	4,471
Dividends payable	14	31	29	36	32	76
Operating deferred tax liabilities	351	342	304	326	288	349
Cumulative amortization and unrecorded goodwill	3,155	3,178	3,207	3,237	3,199	3,542
Equity and equivalents	6,776	7,520	8,549	9,003	8,923	8,438
Short-term debt	946	1,060	1,241	1,155	1,038	969
Long-term debt	2,638	2,233	2,091	1,521	1,295	9,084
Interest payable	38	41	34	38	37	104
Retirement-related liabilities	680	664	665	646	586	688
Nonoperating provisions	341	373	364	327	301	502
Nonoperating deferred tax liabilities (assets)	(214)	(216)	(217)	(167)	(163)	(244)
Minority interest	477	545	511	542	307	281
Debt and equivalents	4,906	4,700	4,689	4,062	3,401	11,384
Total funds invested	11,682	12,220	13,238	13,065	12,324	19,822

- *Tax loss carry-forwards* are unrelated to any other balance sheet item and treated as a separate nonoperating asset in invested-capital calculations. They do not affect NOPLAT.

The operating taxes are reconciled to reported taxes by the item called nonoperating taxes in the reconciliation with net profit on the NOPLAT statement.

Balance Sheet and Invested Capital

Next we show how we exclude any financial assets and nonoperating assets shown on the balance sheet (Exhibit 31.4) from the calculation of invested capital (Exhibit 31.8).

Trade and other receivables On the balance sheet, Heineken includes several nonoperating items in trade and other receivables. We exclude from invested capital derivatives used for hedging from trade receivables and payables and group these under other financial assets (€1,073 million in 2008). Gains or losses on these derivatives are reported by Heineken as net finance expenses in the income statement or changes in hedging reserves in shareholders' equity.

Other investments and assets held for sale Other investments and assets held for sale, which include advances to customers, are nonoperating. In the invested-capital statement, they are included in other financial assets. Because Heineken classified advances to customers as financial assets until 2006, we assume they are interest-bearing.

Trade and other payables We separate Heineken's reported trade and other payables (on the balance sheet given as €3,846 million in 2008) into derivatives used for hedging (€87 million reclassified under other financial assets), dividends payable (€76 million), interest payable (€104 million), trade payables (€1,570 million), other current operating liabilities (€1,271 million), and accruals and deferred income (€738 million). We have added the short-term tax liabilities (€85 million) to other current operating liabilities.

Intangible assets We split intangible assets as reported into operating intangibles (e.g., software) and goodwill and acquired intangibles, so that we can estimate return on invested capital (ROIC) including and excluding goodwill and acquired intangibles. As explained in Chapter 7, we add back cumulative historical amortization and impairments to the amount of goodwill and acquired intangibles reported in the balance sheet, amounting to around €10 billion in 2008 (see Exhibit 31.9).

The goodwill amortization and impairment adjustment for Heineken is complex because of two changes in accounting treatment. Until 2002, Heineken used to write off any amount of goodwill directly against equity. The total

EXHIBIT 31.9   **Heineken: Adjustments to Goodwill and Acquired Intangibles**

€ million

	2004 restated	2005 reported	2006 reported	2007 reported	2007 restated	2008 reported
Goodwill and acquired intangibles	1,791	2,350	2,416	2,503	2,078	7,036
Accumulated goodwill directly written off against equity (pre-2003)	3,027	3,027	3,027	3,027	3,027	3,027
Accumulated goodwill amortized (2003–2004)	117	117	117	117	117	117
Accumulated goodwill impaired (2005–2008) plus accumulated amortization and impairments of acquired intangibles	11	34	63	93	55	398
Total adjusted goodwill and acquired intangibles	4,946	5,528	5,623	5,740	5,277	10,578

cumulative amount written off until 2002 is not reported, but we made an estimate by adding up all the annual goodwill write-offs (net of reversals) since 1980. This amounts to around €3 billion. After 2002, Heineken switched to amortization of goodwill and charged a total of €117 million in amortization to the income statement in 2003 and 2004. After 2004 and the introduction of International Financial Reporting Standards (IFRS), Heineken stopped amortizing goodwill. Since 2004, the total amount of goodwill impaired plus acquired intangibles amortized or impaired cumulates to €398 million as of 2008.

Provisions   We assume all of Heineken's current and noncurrent provisions are nonoperating, according to the methodology explained in Chapter 26, since these mainly concern restructuring costs. Note that all retirement-related provisions are separately reported as employee benefits in the balance sheet.

Free Cash Flow Statement

For the next step, calculating free cash flow, we add back depreciation and amortization costs to NOPLAT and deduct investments in invested capital (see Exhibit 31.10).

Changes in foreign-currency translation reserve   When calculating gross investments, we deduct the increase in the foreign-currency translation reserve from capital expenditures to obtain the actual cash spent on capital investments. Details on the changes in the translation reserve are in Heineken's statement of recognized income and expense in the notes to the annual report.

Impairments   All impairments are added to the increases in property, plant, and equipment (PP&E), operating intangibles, and nonconsolidated investments when calculating the corresponding investment cash flows.

EXHIBIT 31.10 **Heineken: Free Cash Flow Calculation**[1]

€ million

	2005	2006	2007	2008
NOPLAT	935	1,173	1,382	1,293
Depreciation and amortization of operating intangibles	734	723	714	775
Gross cash flow	1,669	1,896	2,096	2,068
Investment in operating working capital	209	(11)	(28)	(108)
Capital expenditures (net of disposals)	(1,012)	(603)	(1,137)	(2,457)
Impairments of PP&E and operating intangibles	(11)	(34)	(18)	(84)
Increase (decrease) in foreign-currency translation reserve	201	(84)	(100)	(645)
Gross investment	(613)	(732)	(1,283)	(3,294)
Free cash flow before goodwill	1,056	1,164	813	(1,226)
Investments in goodwill and acquired intangibles	(582)	(95)	(119)	(4,883)
Free cash flow after goodwill	474	1,069	694	(6,109)
Interest income	60	52	67	91
Income from nonconsolidated investments	34	27	25	112
FC fine	–	–	(219)	–
Gain (loss) on disposals	58	379	30	16
Other net finance expenses	25	11	(26)	(107)
Nonoperating taxes	94	60	55	216
Decrease (increase) in tax loss carry-forwards	3	8	(6)	(135)
Increase (decrease) in operating deferred tax liabilities[2]	3	(32)	(15)	60
Increase (decrease) in nonoperating provisions	(70)	(108)	(113)	40
Increase (decrease) in retirement-related liabilities	(30)	(15)	(30)	104
Net investment in nonconsolidated investments	(38)	(14)	(28)	(253)
Impairments of nonconsolidated investments	–	–	–	(214)
Net investment in other financial assets	40	(258)	101	(364)
Decrease (increase) in excess cash	100	(768)	674	(77)
Nonoperating cash flow	287	(658)	515	(511)
Cash flow available to investors	761	411	1,209	(6,620)
Interest expense	199	185	168	469
Decrease (increase) in short-term debt	(117)	(174)	82	2
Decrease (increase) in long-term debt	405	142	570	(7,789)
Flow to (from) debt holders	487	153	820	(7,318)
Dividends to shareholders	196	196	333	363
Decrease (increase) in dividends payable	(17)	2	(7)	(44)
Decrease (increase) in share capital	–	10	8	–
Adjustments to retained earnings[3]	(5)	(87)	(18)	177
Dividends to minority interest holders	86	101	117	148
Other decrease (increase) in minority interest	12	35	6	(27)
Decrease (increase) in nonoperating deferred taxes	2	1	(50)	81
Flow to (from) equity holders	274	258	389	698
Cash flow available to investors	761	411	1,209	(6,620)

[1] 2008 changes in balance sheet items calculated based on 2007 restated balance sheet.
[2] Without the change in operating deferred tax liabilities that is included in operating cash taxes.
[3] Adjustments to retained earnings are net of the change in foreign-currency translation reserves.

Investments in goodwill and acquired intangibles The amount of investments in goodwill and acquired tangibles equals the annual change in the sum of goodwill and acquired intangibles and reversal of intangibles value adjustments in the invested-capital statement plus the sum of amortization of acquired intangibles and impairment of acquired intangibles and goodwill for the year from the NOPLAT statement.

ANALYZING HISTORICAL PERFORMANCE

The next task is to analyze Heineken's historical performance so we can make a rational forecast of the company's future cash flows. Exhibit 31.11 summarizes Heineken's key performance indicators for 2004 to 2008, including all

EXHIBIT 31.11 **Heineken: Historical Performance Ratios**

percent

	2005	2006	2007	2008	Proforma 2008[3]
Operating ratios					
Adjusted EBITA/revenues	12.4	13.6	14.6	12.3	11.9
Raw materials/revenues[1]	61.7	62.4	63.2	66.6	67.3
Personnel expenses/revenues[1]	19.1	18.0	16.5	15.8	15.6
Depreciation/revenues[1]	6.8	6.1	5.7	5.4	5.2
Return on invested capital (average)					
Tangible fixed assets/revenues[2]	45.9	42.6	41.3	38.7	41.1
Operating working capital/revenues	4.8	3.6	3.5	3.1	3.8
Revenues/invested capital (times)	2.0	2.2	2.2	2.4	2.2
Pretax ROIC	24.5	29.4	32.5	29.3	26.5
Operating cash tax rate	30.3	26.9	24.4	26.4	26.4
After-tax ROIC	17.1	21.5	24.5	21.6	19.5
After-tax ROIC including goodwill	8.7	10.6	12.2	9.4	8.0
Growth rates					
Revenue growth rate	7.3	9.6	6.2	27.3	−4.6
Adjusted EBITA growth rate	(0.7)	19.6	14.2	6.6	–
NOPLAT growth rate	(0.2)	25.5	18.0	3.4	–
Invested capital growth rate	6.3	(0.1)	5.1	64.3	–
Net income growth rate	18.5	59.1	(33.4)	(74.1)	–
Investment rates					
Gross investment rate	36.7	38.6	61.2	159.3	–
Net investment rate	(13.0)	0.7	41.2	194.8	–
Financing					
Coverage (adjusted EBITA/interest)	6.7	8.7	10.9	3.7	–
Cash coverage (gross cash flow/interest)	8.4	10.2	12.5	4.4	–
Debt/total book capitalization	38.5	35.4	31.1	57.4	–

[1] Adjusted to exclude nonoperating and nonrecurring items.
[2] Net property, plant, and equipment plus operating intangibles.
[3] Proforma adjusted figures reflecting full-year ownership of S&N by Heineken.

the preceding adjustments to the financial statements. We have included an additional column for 2008 showing some of the key indicators corrected for the effects of the S&N acquisition, as we explain in the next section.

Pro Forma Adjustments for Scottish & Newcastle Acquisition

Before analyzing Heineken's historical financial results, we make a pro forma adjustment in NOPLAT and invested capital to account for the acquisition of Scottish & Newcastle in 2008 (see Exhibit 31.12). In revenues on the NOPLAT statement for 2008, we include four more months of the acquired business, because Heineken consolidates it as of the end of April 2008. Because we don't have the income statement for the first four months of 2008 for the part of Scottish & Newcastle that was acquired by Heineken, we base the adjustment on a separate press release that provides full-year 2007 figures. As a proxy for the first four months of 2008, we have taken $\frac{4}{12}$ of these figures to gross up the income statement for Heineken in 2008. In the 2007 invested-capital statement, we include the invested capital of the acquired business so that we can eventually calculate a 2008 ROIC estimate based on average invested capital for 2007 and 2008. Because we don't have a balance sheet for the acquired business as of 2007 year-end, we base the adjustment on the balance sheet at the time of acquisition, as disclosed in Heineken's 2008 annual report (on page 94).

EXHIBIT 31.12 **Heineken: Scottish & Newcastle (S&N) Proforma Adjustment**

€ million

	As reported	S&N adjustment	Proforma
NOPLAT 2008 adjustment			
Revenues	14,319	1,251	15,570
Raw materials	(9,532)	(946)	(10,478)
Personnel expenses	(2,256)	(173)	(2,429)
EBITDA	2,531	132	2,663
Depreciation	(775)	(37)	(812)
Adjusted EBITA	1,756	96	1,852
Operating cash taxes	(463)	(25)	(488)
NOPLAT	1,293	70	1,364
Invested capital 2007 adjustment			
Operating working capital	392	261	653
Net property, plant, and equipment	4,673	1,705	6,378
Operating intangibles	32	–	32
Invested capital excluding intangibles	5,097	1,966	7,063
Goodwill and acquired intangibles	2,078	4,764	6,842
Cumulative amortization and unrecorded goodwill	3,199	–	3,199
Invested capital including intangibles	10,374	6,730	17,104

EXHIBIT 31.13 **Heineken: Revenue Growth Analysis**

percent

	2004	2005	2006	2007	2008	CAGR[1] 2004–2008
Organic volume growth	1.1	0.2	4.3	4.2	7.0	3.3
Price increase/mix change	1.4	2.0	2.8	3.1	0.4	1.9
Organic growth at constant currency	2.5	2.2	7.1	7.3	7.4	5.3
Acquisitions: First-time consolidations	9.1	4.5	2.0	0.4	21.0	7.2
Currency movements	−3.4	0.6	0.5	−1.5	−0.9	(1.0)
Accounting changes, other	−0.1	0.6	−0.0	0.0	−13.5	(2.8)
Nominal revenue growth (euros-based)	8.1	7.9	9.6	6.2	14.0	9.1

[1] Compound annual growth rate.

Growth and ROIC Analysis

To evaluate Heineken's financial performance, we compare it with other large, publicly traded beer companies: Anheuser-Busch InBev, SABMiller, Molson Coors, and Carlsberg. From 2004 through 2008, Heineken increased its revenues by 9.1 percent per year (see Exhibit 31.13). However, organic growth (volume, price increase, and product mix) has driven only 5.3 percent per year of this growth. Acquisitions have added 7.2 percent per year. The remaining difference is due to currency effects and accounting changes. In 2008 Heineken changed its accounting for joint ventures from proportional to equity accounting, which caused a 13.5 percent drop in reported sales.

Exhibit 31.14 compares Heineken's revenue growth with that of its peers. Overall growth from 2004 to 2008 varies from 9.1 percent for Heineken to 18.4 percent for Anheuser-Busch InBev. However, these results are not comparable, due to acquisitions, accounting changes, and currency effects. The

EXHIBIT 31.14 **Beer Industry: Revenue Growth Analysis, 2004–2008**

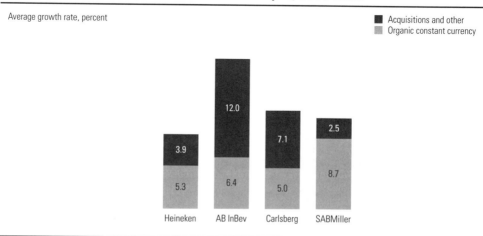

Source: Company annual reports and analyst presentations.

distribution of organic growth was narrower, ranging from 5.0 percent to 8.7 percent, with Heineken at 5.3 percent.

As most of the companies have similar organic growth rates, the most important driver for explaining the differences in value across peers is return on invested capital (ROIC). Heineken increased its ROIC excluding goodwill from 16.3 percent in 2004 to 24.5 percent in 2007, after which ROIC fell in 2008 to 19.6 percent (see Exhibit 31.15). The decline was partly due to the lower returns from the acquired business from Scottish & Newcastle, which has lower margins. Heineken's EBITA margin declined from 14.6 percent in 2007 to 11.9 percent in 2008. Capital turnover has been stable for the past three years at 2.2 (remember that we used Heineken's acquisition-adjusted 2007 year-end invested capital in order to calculate the average invested capital for 2008).

We also estimate Heineken's ROIC including goodwill to see the impact of acquisitions. Including goodwill cuts Heineken's ROIC roughly in half. The

EXHIBIT 31.15 **Beer Industry: Value Drivers**

percent

	2004	2005	2006	2007	2008
ROIC (including goodwill)[1]					
Heineken	9.4	8.7	10.6	12.2	8.0
AB InBev	9.1	10.1	10.9	12.0	5.9
SABMiller	14.0	9.7	8.4	8.5	8.0
Molson Coors	8.4	6.1	4.5	4.7	4.4
Carlsberg	5.9	5.5	6.8	7.5	6.5
ROIC (excluding goodwill)[1]					
Heineken	16.3	17.1	21.5	24.5	19.5
AB InBev	19.9	25.0	29.7	35.7	28.4
SABMiller	41.4	32.2	30.1	27.8	22.0
Molson Coors	16.1	19.1	18.0	19.3	18.3
Carlsberg	9.0	10.1	13.3	14.3	18.1
EBITA margin					
Heineken	13.4	12.4	13.6	14.6	11.9
AB InBev	17.3	21.3	24.6	27.2	23.2
SABMiller	20.2	21.5	21.9	21.9	22.5
Molson Coors	8.7	12.0	12.5	13.1	13.8
Carlsberg	8.3	8.6	10.0	10.3	11.9
Capital turnover (excluding goodwill)[1]					
Heineken	1.8	2.0	2.2	2.2	2.2
AB InBev	1.7	1.8	1.8	2.0	1.9
SABMiller	3.1	2.5	2.3	2.1	1.6
Molson Coors	2.8	2.7	2.4	2.5	2.2
Carlsberg	1.6	1.6	1.8	1.9	2.0

[1] Using average invested capital.

Scottish & Newcastle acquisition causes an even larger difference, with ROIC including goodwill down to 8 percent in 2008.

Anheuser-Busch InBev and SABMiller had the best underlying operating performances, with 2008 ROICs before goodwill of 28.4 percent and 22.0 percent, respectively. For both players, the driver of the high ROIC is high margins, with Anheuser-Busch InBev increasing its margin from 17.3 percent in 2004 to 23.2 percent in 2008 and SABMiller improving from 20.2 percent to 22.5 percent in the same period. SABMiller's capital turnover declined significantly, however, from 3.1 in 2004 to 1.6 in 2008. Including goodwill paid for acquisitions changes the picture: Heineken is tied with SABMiller for the highest ROIC at 8 percent. For all these companies except Carlsberg, ROIC including goodwill dropped significantly throughout the years for all peers as a result of large acquisitions as the industry consolidated.

Stock Market

As a final assessment of historical performance, we compare the stock market performance of these companies using two indicators: total returns to shareholders (TRS) and the ratio of market value to invested capital. Of course, the impact of the economic recession weighed heavily on Heineken and its peers. Given that share prices across the industry recovered after 2008, we can interpret Heineken's stock market performance indicators only relative to its peers.

In terms of TRS, Heineken has struggled over the past five years. Both Heineken and Carlsberg had negative TRS when measured over the one, three, and five years to 2008 (see Exhibit 31.16). Over that period, Heineken's shareholder returns have averaged –0.4 percent per year, much lower than for Molson Coors, at 11.4 percent, and SABMiller, at 10.6 percent. (These returns are all measured in euros to reflect the viewpoint of international investor.) The market set high standards for Heineken. Unfortunately, Heineken has been unable to keep pace with expectations.

We also compare Heineken's ratio of market value to invested capital with those of its peers. Market value to invested capital compares the company's market value (both debt and equity) to the amount of capital that has been invested in the company (fixed assets, working capital, and investments in intangibles from acquisitions); it measures the market's perception of the company's ability to create wealth. The matrix on the bottom of Exhibit 31.16 shows TRS and the ratio of market value to invested capital simultaneously. Heineken's value places it in line with all peers except Carlsberg at a market-value-to-invested-capital ratio of 1.2. This means the market assigns a value of €1.20 for every euro invested in the company. Carlsberg is the only company that was really valued below peers' levels, with a market-value-to-invested-capital ratio of 0.7.

As of 2008, Heineken is valued in line with Anheuser-Busch InBev, Molson Coors, and SABMiller, but the market historically had high expectations for

EXHIBIT 31.16 **Beer Industry: Stock Market Performance**

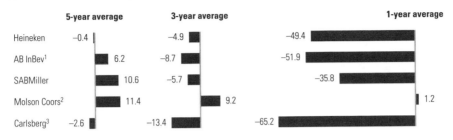

TRS, period ended December 31, 2008, percent (measured in euros)

Relative valuations, December 31, 2008

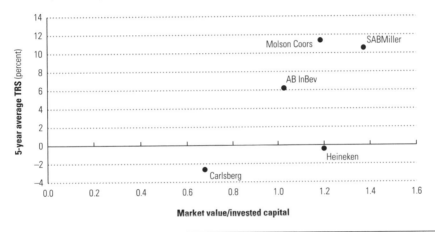

¹ Only InBev before the merger.
² Only Coors before the merger.
³ Based on the B share, for which there is a more liquid market than for the A share.

Heineken, so its TRS is lower. Molson Coors and SABMiller had high value to invested capital as well as high TRS.

Heineken is valued at 11.0 times EBITA, in line with all peers except SAB-Miller, which is lower (see Exhibit 31.17). As the exhibit shows, since earnings multiples are in line for most peers, market-value-to-capital differences are mainly a result of differences in ROIC.

FORECASTING PERFORMANCE

We develop our performance forecast following the approach laid out in Chapter 9. First, we offer a strategic perspective on Heineken and describe several scenarios. We then translate the base-case scenario into a financial forecast. For this case study, we use a five-year detailed forecast, followed by a summary

EXHIBIT 31.17 **Beer Industry: Value Multiples**

	Value/invested capital[1]	Operating value/EBITA	2008 ROIC[2] (percent)	2004–2008 ROIC (percent)
Excluding goodwill				
Heineken[3]	3.0	11.0	19.6	19.8
AB InBev[3]	5.3	10.9	28.4	27.7
SABMiller	3.3	8.6	22.0	30.7
Molson Coors	5.1	12.2	18.3	18.2
Carlsberg	2.3	11.3	18.1	13.0
Including goodwill				
Heineken[3]	1.2	11.0	8.0	9.8
AB InBev[3]	1.0	10.9	5.9	9.6
SABMiller	1.4	8.6	8.0	9.7
Molson Coors	1.2	12.2	4.4	5.6
Carlsberg	0.7	11.3	6.5	6.4

[1] December 31, 2008.
[2] Using average invested capital.
[3] ROIC adjusted to include acquisitions for a full year.

forecast for 10 years. The continuing value follows after the 15-year explicit forecast period (discussed in Chapter 10).

Creating Scenarios

For valuing Heineken, we develop three scenarios that can describe the company's potential strategy and business climate:

1. *Business as usual:* Under the business-as-usual scenario, the industry experiences no major shocks, Heineken continues to grow organically at a modest rate, and its margins and capital efficiency remain constant at 2008 levels (pro forma including a full year of Scottish & Newcastle acquisition).

2. *Aggressive acquisition:* Heineken and its competitors accelerate their growth through more acquisitions. This strategy drives up acquisition prices, reducing returns on capital.

3. *Operating improvement:* In this scenario, Heineken focuses on improving its operations, ultimately managing to increase the margins of Scottish & Newcastle to a level at which the total group margin returns to preacquisition levels of 2007.

For the remainder of this section, we analyze only the business-as-usual scenario in detail. The resulting valuations of the other two scenarios are summarized at the end of this chapter.

Short-Term Forecasting

We typically create an explicit forecast of 10 to 15 years, so the company can reach a steady-state financial performance before we apply a continuing value. We divide the explicit forecast period into two subperiods. For the first subperiod (five years in Heineken's case), we forecast complete income statements and balance sheets. For the remaining subperiod (10 years in Heineken's case), we use a condensed forecast.

As with most forecasts, we derive most income statement and balance sheet line items from the revenue forecast. The detailed forecast assumptions for the first five years are laid out in Exhibit 31.18 for the income statement items and Exhibit 31.19 for the balance sheet items.

- *Revenue:* The projected revenue growth rate is the sum of volume growth, price and product mix changes, currency effects, and growth from acquisitions. For the next five years, we project an initial slowdown of volume growth and price increases due to the economic recession. Toward 2013, we expect Heineken's underlying volume growth to pick up to around 2.0 percent per year, somewhat lower than the industry because of Heineken's stronger presence in the slower-growing developed markets. The geographic mix of sales affects average prices realized, since prices are lower in emerging markets. We forecast effective price increases to stay at their long-term average of 2.8 percent. Finally, we assume no acquisitions for Heineken in the base case.

- *Operating expenses:* We forecast operating expenses as a percentage of revenues. The acquisition of Scottish & Newcastle makes historical comparisons difficult. For raw materials, personnel expenses, depreciation, and the amortization of acquired intangibles, we therefore assume cost ratios to be constant at postacquisition 2008 levels. The ratio of amortization of operating intangibles is not meaningful in 2008, however, since we cannot make a detailed pro forma adjustment for this item. For the next five years, we assume this ratio to be equal to average 2005–2007 levels.

- *Interest expense and income:* We estimate each year's interest expense based on the level of debt at the beginning of that year, rather than the average for the year, to avoid circular calculations. We forecast the interest rate on Heineken's debt to be 5 percent, its current borrowing rate. To estimate the interest rate on excess marketable securities, we use the average interest rate on one-year euro-denominated bonds (3 percent).

- *Taxes:* We estimate that Heineken's marginal tax rate as 25.5 percent, the statutory tax rate in the Netherlands. Heineken's effective tax rate on operating profits is expected to remain at its 2008 level of 26.4 percent, with cash taxes equal to that proportion of operating profit.

EXHIBIT 31.18   **Heineken: Income Statement Forecast Assumptions**

	Historical				Forecast				
	2005	2006	2007	2008	2009	2010	2011	2012	2013
Revenue growth (percent)									
Organic volume growth	0.2	4.3	4.2	7.0	0.5	1.0	1.5	2.0	2.0
Price increase and mix change	2.0	2.8	3.1	0.4	0.5	1.0	2.0	2.8	2.8
Organic growth at constant currency	2.2	7.1	7.3	7.4	1.0	2.0	3.5	4.8	4.8
Acquisitions: First-time consolidations	4.5	2.0	0.4	21.0	–	–	–	–	–
Currency movements	0.6	0.5	–1.5	–0.9	–	–	–	–	–
Accounting changes, other	0.6	–	–	–13.5	–	–	–	–	–
Nominal revenue growth (euros-based)	7.9	9.6	6.2	14.0	1.0	2.0	3.5	4.8	4.8
Operating expense ratios (percent)									
Raw materials/revenues	61.7	62.4	63.2	67.3	67.3	67.3	67.3	67.3	67.3
Personnel expenses/revenues	19.1	18.0	16.5	15.6	15.6	15.6	15.6	15.6	15.6
Depreciation/assets	14.8	13.9	14.0	12.2	12.2	12.2	12.2	12.2	12.2
Amortization of operating intangibles/assets	63.0	56.7	60.6	106.3	60.1	60.1	60.1	60.1	60.1
Amortization of acquired intangibles/assets	4.9	5.2	5.0	5.5	5.5	5.5	5.5	5.5	5.5
Interest rates (percent)									
Interest income/excess cash	12.6	14.1	5.9	17.7	3.0	3.0	3.0	3.0	3.0
Interest expense/financial debt	6.0	5.6	6.3	4.7	5.0	5.0	5.0	5.0	5.0
Net interest/retirement liability	2.8	1.1	0.8	2.7	3.0	3.0	3.0	3.0	3.0
Taxes (percent)									
Statutory domestic tax rate	31.5	29.6	25.5	25.5	25.5	25.5	25.5	25.5	25.5
Blended global tax rate	29.4	26.5	26.5	26.4	26.4	26.4	26.4	26.4	26.4
Operating cash tax rate	30.3	26.9	24.4	26.4	26.4	26.4	26.4	26.4	26.4
Minority interest (percent)									
Minority interest/profit before income tax	9.3	7.7	10.1	12.0	12.0	12.0	12.0	12.0	12.0
Dividends (€ million)									
Dividends to shareholders	196	196	333	363	363	363	363	363	363
Dividends to minority interest holders	86	101	117	148	148	148	148	148	148
Other									
Share of profit in associates/Investments in associates	25.4	15.7	13.4	10.2	10.2	10.2	10.2	10.2	10.2
Other net finance expenses (€ million)	25	11	(26)	(107)	–	–	–	–	–
Pretax exceptionals (€ million)	(39)	271	(52)	(126)	–	–	–	–	–
After-tax exceptionals (€ million)	(26)	(52)	(258)	(573)	–	–	–	–	–

- *Minority interest:* We assume that minority interest will remain at about 12 percent of profits before taxes.
- *Dividends:* Heineken maintains a conservative dividend policy, so we assume that its dividend will remain constant over the next five years.
- *Share of profits in associates:* The share of profits in associates and joint ventures represents Heineken's share of the income of nonconsolidated investments in affiliates and joint ventures. In 2008, Heineken

EXHIBIT 31.19 **Heineken: Balance Sheet Forecast Assumptions**

	Historical				Forecast				
	2005	2006	2007	2008	2009	2010	2011	2012	2013
Working capital									
Working cash (percent of revenues)	2.0	2.0	2.0	2.0	2.0	2.0	2.0	2.0	2.0
Trade receivables (days)	56.9	54.9	54.4	56.3	56.3	56.3	56.3	56.3	56.3
Inventories (days)	29.9	27.6	29.3	29.2	29.2	29.2	29.2	29.2	29.2
Prepayments and accrued income (days)	3.2	2.8	3.6	5.4	5.4	5.4	5.4	5.4	5.4
Trade payables (days)	35.5	32.1	34.0	36.8	36.8	36.8	36.8	36.8	36.8
Accruals and deferred income (days)	15.0	18.6	20.0	17.3	17.3	17.3	17.3	17.3	17.3
Other current operating liabilities (days)	32.6	28.7	27.3	31.8	31.8	31.8	31.8	31.8	31.8
Net working capital (percent of revenues)	3.9	3.6	3.6	3.4	3.4	3.4	3.4	3.4	3.4
Fixed assets (percent of revenues)									
Net property, plant, and equipment	46.9	41.8	42.7	40.6	40.6	40.6	40.6	40.6	40.6
Operating intangibles	0.3	0.3	0.3	0.5	0.5	0.5	0.5	0.5	0.5
Other assets (€ million)									
Investment in associates	172	186	214	1,145	1,145	1,145	1,145	1,145	1,145
Other financial assets	618	876	775	1,073	1,073	1,073	1,073	1,073	1,073
Tax loss carry-forwards	19	11	17	149	149	149	149	149	149
Investments in goodwill and acquired intangibles	526	75	118	135	–	–	–	–	–
Other liabilities									
Dividends payable (percent of dividends)	13.1	10.3	12.1	18.2	18.2	18.2	18.2	18.2	18.2
Interest payable (percent of debt)	1.1	1.0	1.1	1.1	1.1	1.1	1.1	1.1	1.1
Retirement-related liabilities (percent of revenues)	6.2	5.6	5.1	4.4	4.4	4.4	4.4	4.4	4.4
Nonoperating provisions (€ million)	373	364	327	502	502	502	502	502	502
Operating deferred tax liabilities (percent of revenues)	3.2	2.6	2.6	2.2	2.2	2.2	2.2	2.2	2.2

reported a loss of €102 million from nonconsolidated investments. Most of this, however, was due to an impairment. The ongoing profit of €112 represented about 10.2 percent of the balance sheet account for nonconsolidated investments. We assume that future income will remain at 10.2 percent of the balance sheet amount.

- *Working capital:* Between 2005 and 2008, net working capital has been relatively stable at around 3.5 percent of revenues. We forecast that net working capital will remain at 2008 levels of 3.4 percent of net revenues. To simplify later analysis, we express individual working-capital items forecasts in days' sales.

- *Fixed assets:* In 2008, after the acquisition of Scottish & Newcastle, the ratio of net PP&E to revenues declined a bit compared with the previous year and reached 40.6 percent. We forecast that this ratio, indicating the amount of PP&E required to generate each euro of revenues, will remain at this level. Note that this simplified forecast approach might not hold for a high-growth company or one operating in an inflationary environment. We keep the level of operating intangible assets, such as software, at 0.5 percent of revenues.

- *Investments in associates and joint ventures:* We keep the value of investments in associates and joint ventures (nonconsolidated investments) equal to 2008, since we do not forecast further expansion of Heineken's equity holdings.

- *Other financial assets:* Other financial assets consist of investments and loans to customers. We assume these remain constant.

- *Goodwill:* Since our forecast of revenue growth in the base case does not include acquisitions, we forecast no investments in goodwill or intangibles associated with the acquisitions.

- *Retirement-related liabilities:* The retirement-related liabilities are equal to the difference between the company's retirement assets and the actuarial liability for current and former employees. We assume this grows with revenues.

- *Short- and long-term debt:* Short-term debt includes both debt due within one year and the current portion of long-term debt. We assume that short-term debt is held constant for the next five years, while any financing need or surplus is reflected in the change in long-term debt.

- *Nonoperating provisions:* We project that Heineken will keep its nonoperating provisions at the same level as in 2008.

- *Minority interest:* Minority interest on the balance sheet increases each year by the minority interest on the income statement less an assumed dividend of €148 million, which we assume continues for the next five years.

Exhibits 31.20 to 31.25 show the resulting projected income statements, balance sheets, and calculations of NOPLAT, invested capital, free cash flow, and economic profit for the years 2008 to 2013. For 2008, we use the pro forma adjusted financial statements to reflect a full year of the Scottish & Newcastle acquisition. Note that we reverse the effect of this adjustment on Heineken's equity to start at the actual, unadjusted 2008 year-end equity level (see Exhibit 31.20 in the overview of changes in shareholders' equity).

Midterm Forecasting

For the years 2014 to 2023, we use a streamlined model, projecting only core value drivers such as net revenue growth, EBITA margin, and the ratio of revenues to invested capital. Our forecast assumes that Heineken reaches a steady state, with constant growth, margins, and ROIC beginning in 2014.

EXHIBIT 31.20 **Heineken: Forecast Income Statement**

€ million

	Historical	Forecast				
	2008 proforma[1]	2009	2010	2011	2012	2013
Revenues	15,570	15,726	16,041	16,602	17,399	18,234
Raw materials	(10,478)	(10,583)	(10,794)	(11,172)	(11,709)	(12,271)
Personnel expenses	(2,429)	(2,453)	(2,502)	(2,590)	(2,714)	(2,845)
Net interest on pension deficit	(17)	(21)	(21)	(21)	(22)	(23)
EBITDA	2,646	2,669	2,723	2,819	2,954	3,096
Depreciation	(778)	(770)	(778)	(793)	(821)	(860)
Amortization of operating intangibles	(34)	(44)	(44)	(45)	(47)	(49)
Amortization of acquired intangibles	(72)	(90)	(85)	(81)	(76)	(72)
EBIT	1,763	1,765	1,816	1,900	2,010	2,115
Interest income	91	12	–	–	–	–
Interest expense	(469)	(503)	(455)	(428)	(402)	(376)
Other net finance expenses	(107)	–	–	–	–	–
Pretax exceptionals	(126)	–	–	–	–	–
Profit before income tax	1,152	1,274	1,361	1,472	1,608	1,739
Income tax expenses	(273)	(337)	(359)	(389)	(425)	(459)
Share of profit of associates and joint ventures	128	117	117	117	117	117
After-tax exceptionals	(573)	–	–	–	–	–
Minority interest	(138)	(153)	(163)	(176)	(193)	(208)
Net profit	295	902	956	1,024	1,108	1,188
Shareholders' equity						
Position as of January 1	5,404	4,471	5,010	5,603	6,264	7,009
Net profit	295	902	956	1,024	1,108	1,188
Other net recognized income and expense	(779)	–	–	–	–	–
Dividends	(363)	(363)	(363)	(363)	(363)	(363)
Purchase of own shares	(11)	–	–	–	–	–
Share-based payments	11	–	–	–	–	–
Adjustment for S&N acquisition[1]	(86)	–	–	–	–	–
Position as of December 31	4,471	5,010	5,603	6,264	7,009	7,834

[1] Proforma adjusted figures reflecting full-year ownership of S&N by Heineken.

We could have applied the continuing value at this point but instead present the 10-year forecast to illustrate what the streamlined forecast looks like. The assumptions are laid out in Exhibit 31.26, and the resulting summary financial statements appear in Exhibit 31.27.

Check for Reasonableness

Exhibit 31.28 summarizes Heineken's performance in the business-as-usual scenario. Heineken's growth falls slightly from its historically high level, as we do not include any acquisitions in the base case. ROIC excluding goodwill is a bit below the 2005–2007 average and does not reach its 2007 levels of around

EXHIBIT 31.21   **Heineken: Forecast Balance Sheet**

€ million

	Historical	Forecast				
	2008 proforma[1]	2009	2010	2011	2012	2013
Inventories	1,246	1,258	1,284	1,329	1,392	1,459
Trade receivables	2,401	2,425	2,474	2,560	2,683	2,812
Prepayments and accrued income	231	233	238	246	258	271
Working cash	311	315	321	332	348	365
Excess cash	387	–	–	–	–	–
Total current assets	4,576	4,231	4,316	4,467	4,681	4,906
Net property, plant, and equipment	6,314	6,377	6,505	6,732	7,055	7,394
Operating intangibles	73	74	75	78	82	85
Goodwill	5,393	5,393	5,393	5,393	5,393	5,393
Acquired intangibles	1,643	1,553	1,467	1,387	1,310	1,238
Reversal of intangibles value adjustment	(422)	(398)	(376)	(354)	(334)	(315)
Cumulative amortization and unrecorded goodwill	3,542	3,632	3,718	3,798	3,875	3,947
Investments in associates and joint ventures	1,145	1,145	1,145	1,145	1,145	1,145
Other financial assets	1,073	1,073	1,073	1,073	1,073	1,073
Tax loss carry-forwards	149	149	149	149	149	149
Total noncurrent assets	18,910	18,998	19,149	19,401	19,748	20,109
Total assets	23,486	23,229	23,465	23,868	24,429	25,016
Short-term debt	969	969	969	969	969	969
Trade payables	1,570	1,586	1,617	1,674	1,754	1,839
Dividends payable	76	93	93	93	93	93
Interest payable	104	109	99	93	88	82
Accruals and deferred income	738	745	760	787	825	864
Other current operating liabilities	1,356	1,370	1,397	1,446	1,515	1,588
Total current liabilities	4,813	4,872	4,936	5,062	5,244	5,435
Long-term debt	9,084	8,126	7,590	7,071	6,548	5,947
Retirement-related liabilities	688	695	709	734	769	806
Nonoperating provisions	502	502	502	502	502	502
Nonoperating deferred tax liabilities (assets)	(244)	(244)	(244)	(244)	(244)	(244)
Operating deferred tax liabilities	349	350	351	352	353	354
Total noncurrent liabilities	10,379	9,428	8,908	8,414	7,928	7,366
Shareholders' equity	4,471	5,010	5,603	6,264	7,009	7,834
Cumulative amortization and unrecorded goodwill	3,542	3,632	3,718	3,798	3,875	3,947
Minority interest	281	286	301	329	374	434
Total equity	8,294	8,928	9,621	10,391	11,257	12,215
Total liabilities and shareholders' equity	23,486	23,229	23,465	23,868	24,429	25,016

[1] Proforma adjusted figures reflecting full-year ownership of S&N by Heineken.

EXHIBIT 31.22   **Heineken: NOPLAT Forecast**

€ million

	Historical	Forecast				
	2008 proforma[1]	**2009**	**2010**	**2011**	**2012**	**2013**
Revenues	15,570	15,726	16,041	16,602	17,399	18,234
Raw materials	(10,478)	(10,583)	(10,794)	(11,172)	(11,709)	(12,271)
Personnel expenses	(2,429)	(2,453)	(2,502)	(2,590)	(2,714)	(2,845)
Adjusted EBITDA	2,663	2,690	2,744	2,840	2,976	3,119
Depreciation	(778)	(770)	(778)	(793)	(821)	(860)
Amortization of operating intangibles	(34)	(44)	(44)	(45)	(47)	(49)
Adjusted EBITA	1,852	1,876	1,922	2,001	2,108	2,210
Income tax at blended global rate	(489)	(496)	(508)	(529)	(557)	(584)
Increase (decrease) in operating deferred tax liability	1	1	1	1	1	1
Operating cash taxes	(488)	(495)	(507)	(528)	(556)	(583)
NOPLAT	1,364	1,382	1,415	1,474	1,553	1,627
Reconciliation to net profit						
Net profit	295	902	956	1,024	1,108	1,188
Interest income	(91)	(12)	–	–	–	–
Other net finance expenses	107	–	–	–	–	–
Income from nonconsolidated investments	(128)	(117)	(117)	(117)	(117)	(117)
Net interest on pension deficit	17	21	21	21	22	23
Amortization of acquired intangibles	72	90	85	81	76	72
Decrease (increase) in operating deferred tax liabilities	1	1	1	1	1	1
Nonoperating taxes	(216)	(159)	(148)	(140)	(132)	(124)
Exceptionals	699	–	–	–	–	–
Adjusted net profit	757	726	797	870	958	1,043
Interest expense	469	503	455	428	402	376
Minority interest	138	153	163	176	193	208
NOPLAT	1,364	1,382	1,415	1,474	1,553	1,627

[1] Proforma adjusted figures reflecting full-year ownership of S&N by Heineken.

25 percent anymore. Overall, the results are consistent with the scenario and current strategy we have described.

ESTIMATING COST OF CAPITAL

Our estimate of Heineken's weighted average cost of capital (WACC) is 7.6 percent, as shown in Exhibit 31.29. This estimate is based on a target market value capital structure of 15 percent debt to 85 percent equity, with the cost of equity at 8.3 percent and pretax cost of debt at 5.3 percent.

Our estimate of Heineken's target capital structure (15 percent debt to 85 percent equity) is based on historical analysis. Heineken's end-of-2008

EXHIBIT 31.23 **Heineken: Invested-Capital Forecast**

€ million

	Historical	Forecast				
	2008 proforma[1]	**2009**	**2010**	**2011**	**2012**	**2013**
Working cash	311	315	321	332	348	365
Trade receivables	2,401	2,425	2,474	2,560	2,683	2,812
Inventories	1,246	1,258	1,284	1,329	1,392	1,459
Prepayments and accrued income	231	233	238	246	258	271
Operating current assets	4,189	4,231	4,316	4,467	4,681	4,906
Trade payables	1,570	1,586	1,617	1,674	1,754	1,839
Accruals and deferred income	738	745	760	787	825	864
Other current operating liabilities	1,356	1,370	1,397	1,446	1,515	1,588
Operating current liabilities	3,664	3,701	3,775	3,907	4,094	4,291
Operating working capital	525	531	541	560	587	615
Net property, plant, and equipment	6,314	6,377	6,505	6,732	7,055	7,394
Operating intangibles	73	74	75	78	82	85
Invested capital excluding intangibles	6,912	6,982	7,121	7,370	7,724	8,095
Goodwill and acquired intangibles	7,036	6,946	6,860	6,780	6,703	6,631
Cumulative amortization and unrecorded goodwill	3,542	3,632	3,718	3,798	3,875	3,947
Reversal of intangibles value adjustment	(422)	(398)	(376)	(354)	(334)	(315)
Invested capital including intangibles	17,068	17,161	17,323	17,594	17,968	18,358
Excess cash	387	–	–	–	–	–
Nonconsolidated investments	1,145	1,145	1,145	1,145	1,145	1,145
Other financial assets	1,073	1,073	1,073	1,073	1,073	1,073
Tax loss carry-forwards	149	149	149	149	149	149
Total funds invested	19,822	19,528	19,690	19,961	20,335	20,725
Shareholders' equity	4,471	5,010	5,603	6,264	7,009	7,834
Dividends payable	76	93	93	93	93	93
Operating deferred tax liabilities	349	350	351	352	353	354
Cumulative amortization and unrecorded goodwill	3,542	3,632	3,718	3,798	3,875	3,947
Equity and equivalents	8,438	9,086	9,765	10,508	11,330	12,229
Short-term debt	969	969	969	969	969	969
Long-term debt	9,084	8,126	7,590	7,071	6,548	5,947
Interest payable	104	109	99	93	88	82
Retirement-related liabilities	688	695	709	734	769	806
Nonoperating provisions	502	502	502	502	502	502
Nonoperating deferred tax liabilities (assets)	(244)	(244)	(244)	(244)	(244)	(244)
Minority interest	281	286	301	329	374	434
Debt and equivalents	11,384	10,443	9,926	9,454	9,005	8,496
Total funds invested	19,822	19,528	19,690	19,961	20,335	20,725

[1] Proforma adjusted figures reflecting full-year ownership of S&N by Heineken.

EXHIBIT 31.24 **Heineken: Free Cash Flow Forecast**

€ million

	Forecast				
	2009	**2010**	**2011**	**2012**	**2013**
NOPLAT	1,382	1,415	1,474	1,553	1,627
Depreciation and amortization of operating intangibles	814	822	838	868	909
Gross cash flow	2,195	2,237	2,312	2,420	2,537
Investment in operating working capital	(5)	(11)	(19)	(27)	(28)
Capital expenditures (net of disposals)	(878)	(951)	(1,069)	(1,195)	(1,252)
Gross investment	(883)	(962)	(1,088)	(1,221)	(1,280)
Free cash flow before goodwill	1,313	1,276	1,225	1,199	1,256
Investments in goodwill and acquired intangibles	–	–	–	–	–
Free cash flow after goodwill	1,313	1,276	1,225	1,199	1,256
Interest income	12	–	–	–	–
Income from nonconsolidated investments	117	117	117	117	117
Nonoperating taxes	159	148	140	132	124
Increase (decrease) in retirement-related liabilities[1]	(14)	(7)	4	13	14
Decrease (increase) in excess cash	387	–	–	–	–
Nonoperating cash flow	661	259	261	263	256
Cash flow available to investors	1,973	1,534	1,486	1,462	1,512
Interest expense	503	455	428	402	376
Decrease (increase) in short-term debt	(5)	10	6	6	6
Decrease (increase) in long-term debt	958	536	519	523	600
Flow to (from) debt holders	1,456	1,001	953	930	982
Dividends to shareholders	363	363	363	363	363
Decrease (increase) in dividends payable	(17)	–	–	–	–
Dividends to minority interest holders	148	148	148	148	148
Decrease (increase) in nonoperating deferred taxes	–	–	–	–	–
Decrease of intangibles adjustment	24	23	21	20	19
Flow to (from) equity holders	518	534	532	531	530
Cash flow available to investors	1,973	1,534	1,486	1,462	1,512

[1] Changes that have not flowed through the income statement.

capital structure using market values is 44 percent debt to 56 percent equity, as shown in Exhibit 31.30. Heineken historically has had around 13 percent debt. Its debt-to-equity ratio in 2008 is higher because of the recent acquisition of Scottish & Newcastle and its depressed share price at the time (which recovered significantly in 2009). In light of Heineken's significant cash flow and conservative dividend, we expect the company to reduce its debt levels significantly within a few years in order to reduce this ratio back toward historical levels. Therefore, we select a conservative long-term capital structure of 15 percent debt.

EXHIBIT 31.25 **Heineken: Forecast Economic Profit**

€ million

	Historical	Forecast				
	2008 adjusted[1]	2009	2010	2011	2012	2013
Before goodwill						
After-tax ROIC (percent)	19.3	20.0	20.3	20.7	21.1	21.1
WACC (percent)	7.6	7.6	7.6	7.6	7.6	7.6
Spread (percent)	11.7	12.4	12.7	13.1	13.5	13.5
Invested capital (beginning of year)	7,063	6,912	6,982	7,121	7,370	7,724
Economic profit	827	856	885	933	993	1,040
NOPLAT	1,364	1,382	1,415	1,474	1,553	1,627
Capital charge	(537)	(525)	(531)	(541)	(560)	(587)
Economic profit	827	856	885	933	993	1,040
After goodwill						
After-tax ROIC (percent)	8.0	8.1	8.2	8.5	8.8	9.1
WACC (percent)	7.6	7.6	7.6	7.6	7.6	7.6
Spread (percent)	0.4	0.5	0.6	0.9	1.2	1.5
Invested capital (beginning of year)	17,104	17,068	17,161	17,323	17,594	17,968
Economic profit	64	84	111	157	216	262
NOPLAT	1,364	1,382	1,415	1,474	1,553	1,627
Capital charge	(1,300)	(1,297)	(1,304)	(1,317)	(1,337)	(1,366)
Economic profit	64	84	111	157	216	262

[1] To reflect the fact that Heineken did not own the S&N business for a full year.

Capital Structure

Even though we did not use Heineken's year-end 2008 capital structure, we present its calculation in Exhibit 30.30 as follows:

- *Short-term debt:* Short-term debt matures within one year, so in most cases, book value approximates market value.
- *Long-term debt:* None of Heineken's debt is publicly traded, so market quotes were unavailable. Given Heineken's sound capital structure, even after the Scottish & Newcastle transaction, we assume that the book value of the long-term debt approximates market value.
- *Retirement-related liabilities:* As Exhibit 31.31 shows, Heineken's balance sheet position includes an actuarial loss of €143 million in 2008. To estimate the market value of the retirement-related liabilities, we exclude this actuarial loss and apply Heineken's statutory tax rate to the resulting deficit.

EXHIBIT 31.26 **Heineken: Medium-Term Operating Ratios**

percent

	Historical						Forecast									
	2008	**2009**	**2010**	**2011**	**2012**	**2013**	**2014**	**2015**	**2016**	**2017**	**2018**	**2019**	**2020**	**2021**	**2022**	**2023**
Revenue growth	14.0	1.0	2.0	3.5	4.8	4.8	3.0	3.0	3.0	3.0	3.0	3.0	3.0	3.0	3.0	3.0
Adjusted EBITA margin	11.9	11.9	12.0	12.1	12.1	12.1	12.1	12.1	12.1	12.1	12.1	12.1	12.1	12.1	12.1	12.1
Operating cash tax rate	26.4	26.4	26.4	26.4	26.4	26.4	26.4	26.4	26.4	26.4	26.4	26.4	26.4	26.4	26.4	26.4
Revenues/average invested capital (times)	2.2	2.3	2.3	2.3	2.3	2.3	2.3	2.3	2.3	2.3	2.3	2.3	2.3	2.3	2.3	2.3
Revenues/end-of-year invested capital (times)	2.3	2.3	2.3	2.3	2.3	2.3	2.3	2.3	2.3	2.3	2.3	2.3	2.3	2.3	2.3	2.3
Pretax ROIC	26.5	27.0	27.3	27.6	27.9	27.9	27.7	27.7	27.7	27.7	27.7	27.7	27.7	27.7	27.7	27.7
After-tax ROIC	19.5	19.9	20.1	20.3	20.6	20.6	20.4	20.4	20.4	20.4	20.4	20.4	20.4	20.4	20.4	20.4
After-tax ROIC including goodwill	8.0	8.1	8.2	8.4	8.7	9.0	9.1	9.2	9.4	9.5	9.7	9.8	10.0	10.1	10.3	10.4

EXHIBIT 31.27 **Heineken: Medium-Term Forecasts**

€ million

	Historical			Forecast												
	2008	2009	2010	2011	2012	2013	2014	2015	2016	2017	2018	2019	2020	2021	2022	2023
Revenues	15,570	15,726	16,041	16,602	17,399	18,234	18,781	19,344	19,925	20,523	21,138	21,772	22,426	23,098	23,791	24,505
Adjusted EBITA	1,852	1,876	1,922	2,001	2,108	2,210	2,276	2,344	2,415	2,487	2,562	2,638	2,718	2,799	2,883	2,970
Operating cash taxes	(488)	(495)	(507)	(528)	(556)	(582)	(600)	(618)	(636)	(656)	(675)	(695)	(716)	(738)	(760)	(783)
NOPLAT	1,364	1,382	1,415	1,474	1,553	1,627	1,676	1,726	1,778	1,831	1,886	1,943	2,001	2,061	2,123	2,187
Invested capital excluding intangibles	6,912	6,982	7,121	7,370	7,724	8,095	8,338	8,588	8,846	9,111	9,384	9,666	9,956	10,254	10,562	10,879
Invested capital including intangibles	17,068	17,161	17,323	17,594	17,968	18,358	18,601	18,851	19,108	19,374	19,647	19,929	20,219	20,517	20,825	21,142
Free cash flow before goodwill	785	1,313	1,276	1,225	1,199	1,256	1,433	1,476	1,520	1,566	1,613	1,661	1,711	1,763	1,816	1,870
Free cash flow after goodwill	666	1,313	1,276	1,225	1,199	1,256	1,433	1,476	1,520	1,566	1,613	1,661	1,711	1,763	1,816	1,870

EXHIBIT 31.28 **Heineken: Business-as-Usual Scenario Summary**

percent

| | Historical | | | | |
	2005–2007	2008	2009	2010–2013	2014–2023
Revenue growth					
Organic	5.5	7.4	1.0	3.8	3.0
Acquisitions	2.3	21.0	–	–	–
Other	0.1	–14.4	–	–	–
Total revenue growth	7.9	14.0	1.0	3.8	3.0
Adjusted EBITA growth	11.0	6.6	1.3	4.2	3.0
Invested capital growth	2.5	–2.1	1.0	3.8	3.0
Adjusted EBITA/revenues	13.5	11.9	11.9	12.1	12.1
Turnovers/invested capital (times)	2.1	2.2	2.3	2.3	2.3
Tax rate on EBITA	27.2	26.4	26.4	26.4	26.4
ROIC after taxes, before goodwill	21.0	19.5	19.9	20.4	20.4
ROIC after taxes, after goodwill	10.5	8.0	8.1	8.6	9.7

EXHIBIT 31.29 **Heineken: Weighted Average Cost of Capital**

percent

	Target capital structure	Cost	Tax benefit	Weighted cost
Debt	15.0	5.3	25.5	0.6
Common equity	85.0	8.3		7.0
Total	100.0			7.6

EXHIBIT 31.30 **Heineken: Capital Structure**

	Book value (€ million)	Percent of total book value	Market value (€ million)	Percent of total market value
Short-term debt	686	3.6	686	2.9
Long-term debt	9,083[1]	47.7	9,083	38.7
Retirement-related liabilities	542[1]	2.8	619	2.6
Nonoperating provisions	402[1]	2.1	374	1.6
Excess cash	(387)	(2.0)	(387)	(1.6)
Total debt	10,327	54.2	10,376	44.2
Shareholders' equity	8,438	44.3	10,730	45.8
Minority interest	281	1.5	2,342	10.0
Total equity	8,719	45.8	13,073	55.8
Total	19,046	100.0	23,449	100.0

[1] Book values are shown net of deferred tax assets.

EXHIBIT 31.31 **Heineken: Pension Liability Recognized in the Balance Sheet**

€ million

	2007	2008
Present value of unfunded obligations	287	266
Present value of funded obligations	2,571	4,697
Total present value of obligations	2,858	4,963
Fair value of plan assets	(2,535)	(4,231)
Present value of net obligations	323	732
Actuarial (losses) gains not recognized	171	(143)
Recognized liability for defined-benefit obligations	494	589
Other long-term employee benefits	92	99
Total	586	688

- *Nonoperating provisions:* We estimate the market value of the nonoperating provisions by taking the book value and applying the statutory tax rate of 25.5 percent.

- *Shareholders' equity:* At year-end 2008, the market value of Heineken's equity was €10.7 billion.

- *Minority interest:* To estimate a market value for minority interest, we apply a peer-average price-earnings (P/E) multiple of 17.0 to Heineken's minority interest income in 2008. Given minority interest income in 2008 of €138 million, we estimate the market value of minority interest to be €2.3 billion.

Cost of Debt

Heineken is not rated by Standard & Poor's or Moody's Investors Service. We assume that if it were rated, it would have a BBB rating, similar to other beer companies. In the Netherlands, the default premium for BBB-rated, investment-grade companies has historically been around 100 basis points. Since the euro risk-free rate was 4.3 percent on average over the years leading up to 2009, we estimate the cost of debt for Heineken at 5.3 percent before taxes, or 3.9 percent after taxes.

Cost of Equity

Using the capital asset pricing model, we estimate Heineken's cost of equity to be 8.3 percent based on a euro risk-free rate of 4.3 percent, a market risk premium of 5.3 percent, and a levered beta of approximately 0.75. The levered beta is based on the median of the unlevered betas for a sample of brewers (0.64) relevered to Heineken's target capital structure (debt-to-value ratio of 15 percent). To unlever and relever the betas, we use the formula $\beta l = \beta u \times (1 + D/E)$, as explained in Chapter 9. In the brewing industry, the range of unlevered betas was 0.20 to 1.16, and the median and mean were almost identical (0.64 versus 0.63). As we mentioned earlier, individual companies' betas are difficult to measure, so we typically use the industry median rather than a company's measured beta unless we have specific reasons to believe that the company's beta should differ from that of the industry.

ESTIMATING CONTINUING VALUE

We use the value driver model to estimate Heineken's DCF continuing value. For the business-as-usual scenario, the values of the parameters are estimated as follows.

The first year of the continuing-value period is 2024 (one year after the last forecast year). We project Heineken's 2024 NOPLAT to be €2,252 million.

Heineken's WACC is projected to remain at 7.6 percent. We do not foresee any significant change in Heineken's target capital structure or business risk.

Heineken's return on new invested capital (RONIC) before goodwill beyond 2024 is forecast to be 19.0 percent. This is consistent with the forecast performance in the years leading up to 2024 in this scenario. This forecast for RONIC implies that Heineken, like other branded consumer product companies, owns brands that will allow it to achieve returns above its cost of capital for a long time.

We expect that Heineken's NOPLAT will grow at 3 percent, based on 1.5 percent volume growth, 1.5 percent price increases, and constant margins. This forecast for growth is less than nominal gross domestic product (GDP) growth but consistent with the earlier years in the forecast.

By using these parameters in the recommended continuing-value formula, we obtain an estimated continuing value (CV) of €41,235 million in 2024:

$$CV = \frac{\text{NOPLAT}_{2024} \left(1 - \dfrac{g}{\text{RONIC}}\right)}{\text{WACC} - g}$$

$$= \frac{2{,}252 \left(1 - \dfrac{3.0\%}{19\%}\right)}{7.6\% - 3.0\%}$$

$$= 41{,}235 \text{ million}$$

Using the economic-profit approach and the same parameters, we obtain a continuing value of economic profit after 2023 equal to €30,356 million, calculated as follows:

$$\text{CV of Economic Profit} = \frac{\text{Economic Profit}_{2024}}{\text{WACC}}$$

$$+ \frac{\text{NOPLAT}_{2024}\left(\dfrac{g}{\text{RONIC}}\right)(\text{RONIC} - \text{WACC})}{\text{WACC}(\text{WACC} - g)}$$

$$= \frac{1{,}426}{7.6\%} + \frac{2{,}252\left(\dfrac{3.0\%}{19\%}\right)(19\% - 7.6\%)}{7.6\%(7.6\% - 3.0\%)}$$

$$= 30{,}356 \text{ million}$$

The continuing value is a large portion of Heineken's value, because Heineken is expected to earn more than its cost of capital during and after the explicit forecast. However, the economic-profit continuing value is smaller than the DCF continuing value. Adding the amount of invested capital at the end of 2023 to the continuing value of economic profit gives a total continuing value of €41,235 million, the same value calculated using the DCF approach:

$$\begin{aligned}\text{CV} &= \text{Invested Capital}_{2023} + \text{CV of Economic Profit} \\ &= 10{,}879 \text{ million} + 30{,}356 \text{ million} \\ &= 41{,}235 \text{ million}\end{aligned}$$

CALCULATING AND INTERPRETING RESULTS

To complete and analyze the Heineken valuation, we first calculate the equity value of Heineken for the business-as-usual scenario. We then value the other two scenarios we developed. Finally, we estimate a probability-weighted value.

Value in the Business-as-Usual Scenario

Exhibits 31.32 and 31.33 show the calculation of the value of Heineken's operations as of January 2009, using the DCF and economic-profit approaches, respectively. Under both methods, the value of Heineken's operations is €27,447 million.

The value of operations includes a midyear adjustment equal to one-half of a year's value discounted at Heineken's WACC. This is to adjust for the fact that we conservatively discounted the free cash flows and economic profits as if they were entirely realized at the end of each year, when, in fact, cash flows occur (cycles notwithstanding) evenly throughout the year. The six-month factor assumes that cash flows will come in on average in the middle of the year.

EXHIBIT 31.32 **Heineken: DCF Valuation**

€ million

	Free cash flow (FCF)	Discount factor	Present value of FCF
2009	1,313	0.9294	1,220
2010	1,276	0.8637	1,102
2011	1,225	0.8027	983
2012	1,199	0.7460	894
2013	1,256	0.6933	871
2014	1,433	0.6444	923
2015	1,476	0.5988	884
2016	1,520	0.5565	846
2017	1,566	0.5172	810
2018	1,613	0.4807	775
2019	1,661	0.4468	742
2020	1,711	0.4152	711
2021	1,763	0.3859	680
2022	1,816	0.3586	651
2023	1,870	0.3333	623
Continuing value	41,235	0.3333	13,743
Operating value			26,460
Midyear adjustment factor			1.04
Operating value, discounted to current month			27,447

EXHIBIT 31.33 **Heineken: Economic Profit Valuation**

€ million

	Economic profit (EP)	Discount factor	Present value of EP
2009	850	0.9294	706
2010	885	0.8637	764
2011	933	0.8027	749
2012	993	0.7460	740
2013	1,040	0.6933	721
2014	1,061	0.6444	684
2015	1,093	0.5988	654
2016	1,125	0.5565	626
2017	1,159	0.5172	600
2018	1,194	0.4807	574
2019	1,230	0.4468	549
2020	1,267	0.4152	526
2021	1,305	0.3859	503
2022	1,344	0.3586	482
2023	1,384	0.3333	461
Continuing value	30,356	0.3333	10,117
Present value of economic profit			19,547
Invested capital excluding intangibles (beginning of forecast)			6,912
Less: Present value of investments in goodwill			–
Value of operations			26,460
Midyear adjustment factor			1.04
Operating value, discounted to current month			27,447

EXHIBIT 31.34 **Heineken: Value of Equity**

€ million

	Book value	Market value
Value of operations	–	27,447
Excess cash	387	387
Nonconsolidated investments	1,145	2,173
Other financial assets[1]	1,070	1,070
Tax loss carry-forwards	149	149
Enterprise value		31,225
Short-term debt[2]	(1,073)	(1,073)
Long-term debt[1]	(9,083)	(9,083)
Retirement-related liabilities[1]	(542)	(619)
Nonoperating provisions[1]	(402)	(374)
Value of outstanding options	–	–
Minority interest	(281)	(2,342)
Equity value		17,733
Number of shares outstanding (million)		490
Value per share (euros)		36.19

[1] Book value is net of deferred tax assets and liabilities.
[2] Book value is net of interest payable.

Under the business-as-usual scenario, Heineken's equity value is €17,733 million, or €36.19 per share, as shown in Exhibit 31.34. To calculate the market equity value, we add the market value of nonoperating assets such as excess cash, financial fixed assets, and nonconsolidated investments to the value of operations; this sum is the enterprise value. We then subtract debt, retirement liabilities, minority interest, and nonoperating provisions to obtain the equity value.

Heineken's enterprise value includes three nonoperating assets:

1. Other financial assets of €1,070 million are primarily receivables from customers, available-for-sale investments, and investments held to maturity. We value these at book value.

2. Nonconsolidated investments are equity holdings in other companies (also called associates and joint ventures) where Heineken does not have economic control (typically holdings of 50 percent or less of those companies' equity). We value these at a multiple of income from these investments, similar to the multiples for all brewers. Heineken's share of income from these companies was €128 million in 2008 (pro forma adjusted for the Scottish & Newcastle acquisition), which we multiply by a typical brewer's P/E multiple of 17 to estimate the value of Heineken's interest at €2,173 million.

3. Heineken's excess cash of €387 million is valued at book value.

By adding the nonoperating assets to the value of operations, we determine an enterprise value of €31,225 million. The value of Heineken's debt, minority interest, retirement-related liabilities, and nonoperating provisions were estimated in the section on cost of capital earlier in the chapter.

The value of operations for the business-as-usual case is about four times the invested capital (excluding goodwill). This is consistent with Heineken's projected ROIC being about 2.5 times its cost of capital with modest growth. (With zero growth, the ratio of DCF value to invested capital will equal the ratio of ROIC to WACC.)

Additional Scenarios and Probability Weighting

We also valued the other two scenarios for Heineken: the operating-improvement scenario and the aggressive-acquisition scenario. The results are summarized in Exhibit 31.35.

In the operating-improvement scenario, we project that Heineken could improve margins and capital turnover near to the peak levels it achieved in 2007, before acquiring Scottish & Newcastle. This brings Heineken's ROIC up to 25 percent by the end of the forecast, versus 20 percent in the business-as-usual scenario. Under the operating-improvement scenario, Heineken's value is €47.35 per share, a 31 percent premium to the business-as-usual scenario.

For the aggressive-acquisition scenario, we forecast growth from acquisitions at the five-year average historical level of 6 percent from 2009 to 2013. Under this scenario, competition for acquisitions heats up, and Heineken is forced to pay high premiums to continue its acquisition growth. We forecast goodwill to increase to 200 percent of revenues from acquisitions during the acquisition year. Operating performance remains constant. Under the

EXHIBIT 31.35 **Summary of Scenario Values**

	Scenario		
	Operating improvement	Business as usual	Aggressive acquisition
Average revenue growth, 2009–2013 (percent)	3.2	3.2	9.2
Average EBITA/revenues, 2009–2013 (percent)	13.5	12.0	12.3
Average ROIC excluding goodwill, 2009–2013 (percent)	22.7	20.3	21.3
Enterprise value (€ billion)	32.9	27.4	25.4
Equity value (€ billion)	23.2	17.7	15.7
Equity value per share (euros)	47.35	36.19	32.08
Probability (percent)	25	60	15
Expected value per share (euros)		38.36	

aggressive-acquisition scenario, Heineken's value is €32.08 per share, an 11 percent discount relative to the business-as-usual case.

Finally, we weight the scenario values with probabilities and arrive at an estimated value of €38.36 per share, as shown in Exhibit 31.35. Heineken's €22 share price at the end of 2008 was considerably lower, but before the economic recession in the first half of 2008 the share price had been in a range of €35 to €40. At the time of writing this book, the price had already recovered to almost €35 per share. We assign a higher probability to the upside scenario because we believe the pressures on operating performance will force Heineken management to focus on operating improvement rather than acquisition growth. That said, the temptation of growth through acquisitions is always lurking and may overcome the focus on operations.

While the scenario approach estimates a value relatively close to the early 2008 and late 2009 market values, the real insight from the scenario approach is the spread of values. Even in the case of a profitable but modestly growing company like Heineken, the spread of values per share of €32 to €47 across the scenarios indicates a substantial opportunity (or risk) for both investors and managers.

Part Six

Special Situations

32

Valuing Flexibility

In valuing companies with the standard discounted cash flow (DCF) approaches outlined in Part Two, we did not consider the value of managerial flexibility. Managers react to changes in the economic environment by adjusting their plans and strategies. For example, they may choose to scale back or abandon an investment project that delivers poor results, or to expand or extend the project if it is highly successful. Such flexible changes of plan can take many different forms, and each may have a substantial impact on value. A standard DCF approach based on a single cash flow projection, or even multiple cash flow scenarios, cannot calculate what that impact is.

Managerial flexibility is not the same as uncertainty. Companies or projects with highly uncertain futures involving a single management decision, such as business start-ups with high growth potential, can indeed be valued using a standard DCF approach under different scenarios (see, for example, Chapter 34). Flexibility refers to choices between alternative plans that managers may make in response to events. For example, if they have planned to stage their investments in the business start-up, they may decide whether to proceed or not at each stage, depending on information arising from the stage before. For cases where managers expect to respond flexibly to events, we need a special, contingent valuation approach.

Company-wide valuation models rarely take flexibility into account. To analyze and model flexibility accurately, you must be able to describe the set of specific decisions managers could make in response to future events, and include the cash flow implications of those decisions. In valuing a company, flexibility therefore becomes relevant only in cases where management responses to specific events may change the course of the whole company. For example, to value Internet or biotech companies with a handful of promising new products in development, you could project sales, profit, and investments for the company as a whole that are conditional on the success of product development.[1] Another example is a company that has built its strategy around buying up smaller players and integrating them into a bigger entity, capturing synergies along the way. The first acquisitions may not create value in their own right but may open opportunities for value creation through further acquisitions.

Flexibility is typically more relevant in the valuation of individual businesses and projects, as it mostly concerns detailed decisions related to production, capacity investment, marketing, research and development, and so on. In this chapter, we concentrate on how to value flexibility when valuing projects.

We explore two contingent valuation approaches: real-option valuation (ROV), based on formal option-pricing models, and decision tree analysis (DTA). Although they differ on some technical points, both boil down to forecasting, implicitly or explicitly, the future free cash flows contingent on the future states of the world and management decisions, and then discounting these to today's value.

You should learn both the ROV and the DTA approaches, because each has advantages depending on the types of risks involved. Valuing flexibility does not always require sophisticated, formal option-pricing models. The DTA approach is an effective alternative for valuing flexibility related to, for example, technological risk but not commodity risk. Furthermore, if you have no reliable estimates on the value and variance of the cash flows underlying the investment decision, there is little justification for using sophisticated ROV approaches. In addition, the DTA approach is more transparent to managers than is ROV, which most managers cannot easily decipher.

Real-option valuation is theoretically superior to DTA, but it is not the right approach in every case. By definition, it cannot replace traditional discounted cash flow, because valuing an option using ROV still depends on knowing the value of the underlying assets. Unless the assets have an observable market price, you will have to estimate that value using traditional DCF. Because commodity prices are observable, the ROV approach is especially well suited to decisions in commodity-based businesses, such as investments in oil and gas fields, refining facilities, chemical plants, and power generators.[2]

This chapter is limited to the basic concepts of valuing managerial flexibility and real options. We focus on the following topics:

- Fundamental concepts behind uncertainty, flexibility, and value (when and why flexibility has value)

[1] See, for example, E. S. Schwartz and M. Moon, "Rational Pricing of Internet Companies," *Financial Analysts Journal* 56, no. 3 (2000): 62–75; and D. Kellog and J. Charnes, "Real-Options Valuation for a Biotechnology Company," *Financial Analysts Journal* 56, no. 3 (2000): 76–84.

[2] See, for example, E. S. Schwartz and L. Trigeorgis, eds., *Real Options and Investment under Uncertainty: Classical Readings and Recent Contributions* (Cambridge, MA: MIT Press, 2001); T. Copeland and V. Antikarov, *Real Options: A Practitioner's Guide* (New York: Texere, 2003); or L. Trigeorgis, *Real Options: Managerial Flexibility and Strategy in Resource Allocation* (Cambridge, MA: MIT Press, 1996).

- Classification of flexibility in terms of real options to defer investments; make follow-on investments; and expand, change, or abandon production
- Comparison of DTA and ROV approaches to valuing flexibility, including situations when each approach is most appropriate
- A four-step approach to analyzing and valuing real options, illustrated with numerical examples using ROV and DTA

UNCERTAINTY, FLEXIBILITY, AND VALUE

To appreciate the value of flexibility and its key value drivers, consider a simple example:[3] Suppose you are deciding whether to invest $6,000 one year from now to produce and distribute a new pharmaceutical drug already under development. In the upcoming final development stage, the product will undergo clinical tests on patients for one year for which all investments have already been made, so these tests involve no future cash flows. The trials could have one of two possible outcomes. If the drug proves to be highly effective, it will generate an annual net cash inflow of $500 into perpetuity. If it is only somewhat effective, the annual net cash inflow will be $100 into perpetuity. These outcomes are equally probable.

Based on this information, the expected future net cash flow is $300, the probability-weighted average of the risky outcomes ($500 and $100). We assume that success in developing the new product and the value of the new product are unrelated to what happens in the overall economy, so this risk is fully diversifiable by the company's investors. Therefore, the cost of capital for this product equals the risk-free rate, say 5 percent (remember, only nondiversifiable risk requires a premium). Assuming that the company will realize its first year's product sales immediately upon completing the trials and at the end of each year thereafter, the net present value (NPV) of the investment is estimated as follows:

$$NPV = \frac{-6,000}{1.05} + \sum_{t=1}^{\infty} \frac{300}{(1.05)^t} = 286$$

To apply the NPV approach, we discount the incremental expected project cash flows at the cost of capital. Any prior development expenses are irrelevant because they are sunk costs. Alternatively, if the project is canceled, the NPV equals $0. Therefore, management should approve the incremental investment of $6,000.

---

[3] The example is inspired by A. Dixit and R. Pindyck, *Investment under Uncertainty* (Princeton, NJ: Princeton University Press, 1994), 26.

In this example of the NPV decision rule, undertaking development creates value. But there are more alternatives than deciding *today* whether to invest. Using an approach similar to the scenario approach described in Chapter 13, we can rewrite the previous NPV calculation in terms of the probability-weighted values of the drug, discounted to today:

$$NPV = 0.5 \left[\frac{-6,000}{1.05} + \sum_{t=1}^{\infty} \frac{500}{(1.05)^t} \right] + 0.5 \left[\frac{-6,000}{1.05} + \sum_{t=1}^{\infty} \frac{100}{(1.05)^t} \right]$$
$$= 0.5(4,286) + 0.5(-3,714) = 286$$

Here, the NPV is shown as the weighted average of two distinct results: a positive NPV of $4,286 following a favorable trial outcome and a negative NPV of –$3,714 for an unfavorable outcome. If the decision to invest can be deferred until trial results are known, the project becomes much more attractive. Specifically, if the drug proves to be less effective, the project can be halted, avoiding the negative NPV. You need invest only if the drug is highly effective, and the annual cash flow of $500 more than compensates for the incremental investment.

This flexibility is an option to defer the investment decision. To value the option, we can use a contingent NPV approach, working from right to left in the payoff tree shown in Exhibit 32.1:

$$NPV = 0.5 \times Max \left[\left(\frac{-6,000}{1.05} + \sum_{t=1}^{\infty} \frac{500}{(1.05)^t} \right), 0 \right] + 0.5$$
$$\times Max \left[\left(\frac{-6,000}{1.05} + \sum_{t=1}^{\infty} \frac{100}{(1.05)^t} \right), 0 \right]$$
$$= 0.5(4,286) + 0.5(0) = 2,143$$

The contingent NPV of $2,143 is considerably higher than the $286 NPV of committing today. Therefore, the best alternative is to defer a decision until

EXHIBIT 32.1 **Value of Flexibility to Defer Investment**

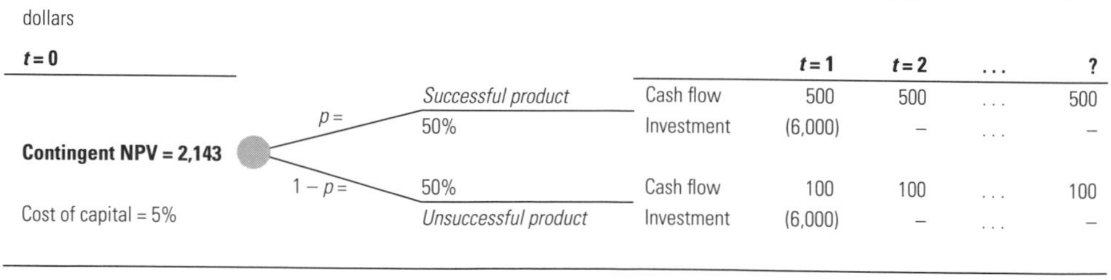

dollars

t = 0				t = 1	t = 2	...	?
		Successful product	Cash flow	500	500	...	500
	p =	50%	Investment	(6,000)	–	...	–
Contingent NPV = 2,143							
	1 – p =	50%	Cash flow	100	100	...	100
Cost of capital = 5%		*Unsuccessful product*	Investment	(6,000)	–	...	–

Note: *t* = time, in years
        p = probability

the trial outcomes are known. The value of the option to defer investment is the difference between the value of the project with flexibility and its value without flexibility: $2,143 − $286 = $1,857.

Based on this example, we can summarize the distinction between the standard and contingent NPVs. The standard NPV is the maximum, decided today, of the expected discounted cash flows or zero:

$$\text{Standard NPV} = \underset{t=0}{\text{Max}} \left[\frac{\text{Expected (Cash Flows)}}{\text{Cost of Capital}}, 0 \right]$$

The contingent NPV is the expected value of the maximums, decided when information arrives, of the discounted cash flows in each future state or zero:

$$\text{Contingent NPV} = \text{Expected}_{t=0} \left[\text{Max} \left(\frac{\text{Cash Flows Contingent on Information}}{\text{Cost of Capital}}, 0 \right) \right]$$

These two NPV approaches use information quite differently. Standard NPV forces a decision based on today's expectation of future information, whereas contingent NPV permits the flexibility of making decisions after the information arrives. Unlike standard NPV, it captures the value of flexibility. A project's contingent NPV will always be greater than or equal to its standard NPV.

The value of flexibility is related to the degree of uncertainty and the room for managerial reaction (see Exhibit 32.2). It is greatest when uncertainty is high and managers can react to new information. In contrast, if there is little uncertainty, managers are unlikely to receive new information that would alter future decisions, so flexibility has little value. In addition, if managers

EXHIBIT 32.2 **When Is Flexibility Valuable?**

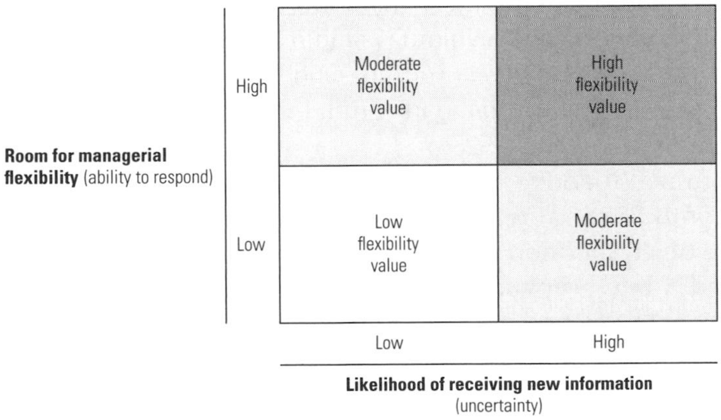

cannot act on new information that becomes available, the value of flexibility also is low.

Including flexibility in a project valuation is most important when the project's standard NPV is close to zero—that is, when the decision whether to go ahead with the project is a close call. Sometimes senior management intuitively overrules standard NPV results and accepts an investment project for strategic reasons. In these cases, the flexibility recognized in contingent valuation fits better with strategic intuition than the rigid assumptions of standard NPV approaches.

Drivers of Flexibility Value

To identify and value flexibility, you must understand what drives its value. Consider what happens if the range of possible annual cash flow outcomes (originally $500 versus $100 per year) increases to $600 versus $0. Since expected cash flows and cost of capital remain unchanged, the standard NPV is the same ($286).[4] However, the contingent NPV increases from its prior level of $2,143:

$$
\begin{aligned}
NPV = 0.5 \times \text{Max} & \left[\left(\frac{-6,000}{1.05} + \sum_{t=1}^{\infty} \frac{600}{(1.05)^t} \right), 0 \right] + 0.5 \\
& \times \text{Max} \left[\left(\frac{-6,000}{1.05} + \sum_{t=1}^{\infty} \frac{0}{(1.05)^t} \right), 0 \right] \\
& = 0.5(6,286) + 0.5(0) = 3,143
\end{aligned}
$$

The contingent NPV of $3,143 is almost 50 percent greater at this higher level of uncertainty. Why? The investment is made only if the drug is highly effective (that is, under a favorable trial outcome), so only the cash flows from the favorable outcome affect the contingent valuation. Since the cash flow projections contingent on the favorable outcome have increased by 20 percent and the required investment has not changed, the contingent NPV increases substantially. The value of the deferral option rises from $1,857 to $2,857 (computed as $3,143 − $286).

We can formally derive the key value drivers of real options by making an analogy with financial options and option-pricing theory. In our original example, the deferral option is identical to a call option with an exercise price of $6,000 and a one-year maturity on an underlying risky asset that has a current value of $6,000 and a variance determined by the cash flow spread of

---

[4] We assume that the trial outcome risk is uncorrelated with the overall economy.

EXHIBIT 32.3 **Drivers of Flexibility Value**

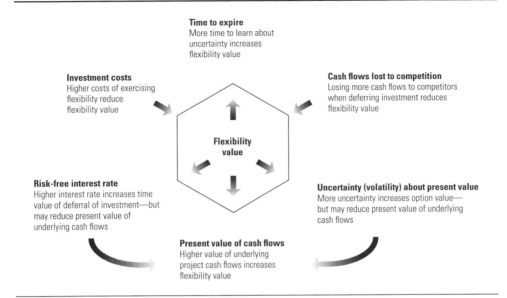

Time to expire
More time to learn about
uncertainty increases
flexibility value

Investment costs
Higher costs of exercising
flexibility reduce
flexibility value

Cash flows lost to competition
Losing more cash flows to competitors
when deferring investment reduces
flexibility value

**Flexibility
value**

Risk-free interest rate
Higher interest rate increases time
value of deferral of investment—but
may reduce present value of
underlying cash flows

Uncertainty (volatility) about present value
More uncertainty increases option value—
but may reduce present value of underlying
cash flows

Present value of cash flows
Higher value of underlying
project cash flows increases
flexibility value

$400 across outcomes.[5] As with financial options, the value of a real option depends on six parameters, summarized in Exhibit 32.3.

These drivers of value show how allowing for flexibility affects the valuation of a particular investment project. Holding other drivers constant, option value decreases with higher investment costs and more cash flows lost while holding the option. Option value increases with higher value of the underlying asset's cash flows, greater uncertainty, higher interest rates, and a longer lifetime of the option. With higher option values, a standard NPV calculation that ignores flexibility will more seriously underestimate the true NPV.

Be careful how you interpret the impact of value drivers when designing investment strategies to exploit flexibility. The impact of any individual driver described in Exhibit 32.3 holds only when all other value drivers remain constant. In practice, changes in uncertainty and interest rates not only affect the value of the option but usually change the value of the underlying asset as well. When you assess the impact of these drivers, you need to assess all their effects on the option's value, both direct and indirect. Take the case of higher uncertainty. In our example, we increased the uncertainty of future cash flow without changing its expectation or present value. But if greater uncertainty lowers the expected level of cash flows or raises the cost of capital, the impact on the value of the option could be negative, because the value of the underlying assets declines. The same holds for the impact of an interest rate increase.

---

[5] The current value of the underlying risky asset is the present value of expected annual cash flows of $300 into perpetuity, discounted at a 5 percent cost of capital.

Higher interest rates reduce the present value of required investment, thereby increasing the option value—if the value of the underlying asset is assumed constant. In reality, higher interest rates would also reduce the present value of cash flows on the underlying asset, which would lower the option's value.

CLASSIFYING FLEXIBILITY IN TERMS OF REAL OPTIONS

Contingent valuation is an important tool for helping managers make the right decisions to maximize shareholder value when faced with strategic or operating flexibility. However, in real life, that flexibility is never as well defined and straightforward as in the preceding examples. A lot depends on management's ability to recognize, structure, and manage opportunities to create value from operating and strategic flexibility. A detailed discussion is beyond the scope of this book,[6] but we provide some basic guidelines here.

To *recognize* opportunities for creating value from flexibility when assessing investment projects or strategies, managers should try to be as explicit as possible about the following details:

- *Events:* What are the key sources of uncertainty? Which events will bring new information and when? A source of uncertainty is key only if relevant new information about it is likely to trigger a change in decision. For example, investing in a pilot project for a product launch makes sense only if there is a chance that the pilot outcome would actually change the launch decision. Similarly, options to switch inputs for manufacturing processes are valuable only if the input prices can be expected to diverge significantly.

- *Decisions:* What decisions can management make in response to events? It is important that managers have some discretion to react to a relevant event. If, say, they would like to pull out of developing a product when intermediate results are disappointing but are prevented by contractual agreements, they do not have true management flexibility. Similarly, intense competition can make it unattractive for managers to defer a decision to launch a new product until they have more information about potential demand.

- *Payoffs:* What payoffs are linked to these decisions? Bear in mind that there should be a positive NPV to be captured in some realistic future state of the world. This NPV should be derived from sustainable competitive advantages. In the late 1990s, some established retail companies acquired Internet start-ups as options for future growth, expecting

---

[6] For a more in-depth discussion, see, for example, Copeland and Antikarov, *Real Options*; or Trigeorgis, *Real Options*.

them to make significant additional online sales. But in many cases, the retail companies failed to test adequately the competitive advantage and value creation potential of these start-ups under realistic future scenarios.

With regard to *structuring* flexibility, some projects or strategies have predefined, built-in flexibility. Take, for example, research and development (R&D) investments in pharmaceutical products where the outcomes of clinical or patient trials provide natural moments to decide whether to stop or proceed with investments. But in many other cases, flexibility can be structured into a project to create maximum value. Think of redesigning infrastructure investments in ports or airfields in stages such that future expansion takes place only if and when needed, or reshaping a growth strategy in such a way that it explicitly includes options to redirect resources as more information becomes available.

In the end, flexibility has value only if managers actually *manage* it—that is, use new information to make appropriate changes to their decisions. Therefore, companies should ensure that their managers face proper incentives to capture potential value from flexibility. For example, the option to pull out of a staged-investment project when intermediate results are disappointing does not have any value if managers do not act on the information, as is sometimes the case, "because we have made such enormous investments already." When a company bases its strategy on creating growth options through a string of acquisitions, those options generate maximum value only if the company delays further acquisitions until new, positive information about their potential arrives. The company leaves the option value on the table if it proceeds with additional acquisitions in the dark.

To help managers recognize, structure, and manage opportunities for capturing value from flexibility, we segment options into the categories described next.

Option to Defer Investment

The option to defer an investment is equivalent to a call option on stock. For example, assume a leaseholder of an undeveloped oil reserve has the right to develop the reserve by paying a lease-on-development cost. The leaseholder can defer development until oil prices rise. The expected development cost is equivalent to the exercise price.

Deferring investment is not without cost. The opportunity cost of deferring investment equals the difference between the current net proceeds per barrel of oil produced and the present value per barrel of developed oil reserves. If this opportunity cost is too high, the decision maker may want to exercise the option (e.g., develop the reserve) before its relinquishment date.

Abandonment Option

The option to abandon (or sell) a project, such as the right to abandon a coal mine, is equivalent to a put option on a stock. If a project proceeds poorly, the decision maker may abandon the project and collect the liquidation value. The expected liquidation (or resale) value of the project is equivalent to the exercise price. When the present value of the asset falls below the liquidation value, the act of abandoning (or selling) the project is equivalent to exercising a put. Because the liquidation value of the project sets a lower bound on the project's value, the option to liquidate is valuable. A project that can be liquidated is worth more than a similar project without the possibility of abandonment.

Follow-On (Compound) Option

Technically speaking, follow-on options are options on options (so-called compound options). An example would be phased investments, such as a factory that can be built in stages, each stage contingent on those that precede it. At each decision point, management can continue the project by investing additional funds (an exercise price) or abandon it for whatever it can fetch. Other examples are research and development programs, new-product launches, exploration and development of oil and gas fields, movie sequels, and an acquisition program where the first purchase is thought of as a platform for later acquisitions.

Option to Expand or Contract

The option to expand the scale of a project is equivalent to a call option on stock. For example, management may choose to build production facilities in such a way that they can be easily expanded if a product is more successful than was anticipated. An option to expand gives management the ability, but not the obligation, to make additional follow-on investments (e.g., to increase the production rate) if the project proceeds well. The option to contract the scale of a project's operation is conceptually equivalent to a put option. Projects should be engineered so that output can be contracted if necessary. The ability to forgo future spending on the project is equivalent to the exercise price of the put.

Option to Extend or Shorten

Companies that can extend the life of an asset or contract by paying a fixed amount of money (the exercise price) own a valuable option. This is also true if it is possible to shorten the life of an asset or a contract. The option to extend is a call option, and the option to shorten is a put option. Real estate leases often have clauses with an option to extend or shorten the lease.

Option to Increase or Decrease Scope

Scope is the number of activities covered in a project. An option related to scope is the ability to increase or decrease activities at a future decision point. Scope is like diversification: it is sometimes preferable to be able, at some exercise cost, to choose among a wider range of alternatives. An option to increase scope is similar to a call.

Switching Options

A project whose operation can be switched on and off (or switched between two distinct locations, and so on) is worth more than a similar project without this flexibility. Examples include a flexible manufacturing system that can produce two or more different products, peak-load power generation, and the ability to exit and reenter an industry. The option to switch project locations or choose among raw materials is a portfolio of call and put options. Restarting operations when a project is shut down is equivalent to a call option. Shutting down operations when unfavorable conditions arise is equivalent to a put option. The cost of restarting (or shutting down) operations may be thought of as the exercise price.

METHODS FOR VALUING FLEXIBILITY

As we mentioned earlier in this chapter, the two methods for contingent valuation are decision tree analysis (DTA) and real-option valuation (ROV) using formal option-pricing models. We will illustrate each method with a simple example: the opportunity to invest $105 at the end of one year in a mining project that has an equal chance of returning either $150 or $50 in cash flow, depending on the mineral price. The risk-free rate, r_f, is 5 percent, and the weighted average cost of capital (WACC) for the project is 10 percent. The present value (PV) of the cash flows today is:

$$PV = \frac{0.5(150) + 0.5(50)}{1.10} = 90.9$$

If an investment decision were required immediately, the project would be declined. The standard NPV of the mining project equals the discounted expected cash flow of $90.90 minus the present value of the investment outlay of $105 next year. Since the level of investment is certain, it should be discounted at the risk-free rate of 5 percent:

$$\text{Standard NPV} = 90.9 - \frac{105}{1.05} = 90.9 - 100 = -9.1$$

EXHIBIT 32.4 **Contingent Payoffs for Investment Project, Twin Security, and Risk-Free Bond**

dollars

		$t=1$				
			Project without flexiblilty	Project with flexiblilty	Twin security	Risk-free bond
$t=0$	Successful project	Cash flow	150	150		
$p=$ 50%		Investment	(105)	(105)		
NPV = ?		**Net cash flow**	**45**	**45**	**50**	**1.05**
$1-p=$ 50%	Unsuccessful project	Cash flow	50	50		
		Investment	(105)	(105)		
Risk-free rate = 5%		**Net cash flow**	**(55)**	**–**	**16.7**	**1.05**
WACC = 10%						

Note: t = time, in years
p = probability

The answer changes if management has flexibility to defer the investment decision for one year, allowing it to make the decision after observing next year's mineral price and the associated cash flow outcome (see Exhibit 32.4). The net cash flows in the favorable state are $150 – $105 = $45. In the unfavorable state, management would decline to invest, accepting net cash flows of $0. We first value this flexibility using an ROV approach.

Real-Option Valuation (ROV)

Option-pricing models use a *replicating portfolio* to value the project. The basic idea of a replicating portfolio is straightforward: If you can construct a portfolio of priced securities that has the same payouts as an option, the portfolio and option should have the same price. If the securities and the option are traded in an open market, this identity is required; otherwise arbitrage profits are possible. The interesting implication is that the ROV approach lets you correctly value complex, contingent cash flow patterns.

Returning to our $105 investment project, assume there exists a perfectly correlated security (or commodity in this example) that trades in the market for $30.30 per share (or unit).[7] Its payouts ($50 and $16.70) equal one-third of the payouts of the project, and its expected return equals the underlying project's cost of capital.

---

[7] You could also use this twin security to value the investment project without flexibility by means of a replicating portfolio. Because the twin security's cash flows are always exactly one-third of the project cash flows, the project without flexibility should be worth three times as much as the twin security, or 90.9 (= 3 × 30.3). The twin security is a basic concept that is implicitly used in standard DCF as well; you derive the beta of a project by identifying a highly correlated, traded security and use that security's beta as input for the cost of capital in the DCF valuation.

This twin security can be used to value the project, including the option to defer, by forming a replicating portfolio.[8] Consider a portfolio consisting of N shares of the twin security and B risk-free bonds with a face value of $1. In the favorable state, the twin security pays $50 for each of the N shares, and each bond pays its face value plus interest, or $(1 + r_f)$. Together, these payouts must equal $45. Applying a similar construction to the unfavorable state, we can write two equations with two unknowns:

$$50.0N + 1.05B = 45$$

$$16.7N + 1.05B = 0$$

The solution is $N = 1.35$ and $B = -\$21.43$. Thus, to build a replicating portfolio, buy 1.35 shares and short 21.43 bonds (shorting a bond is common language for selling a bond, or borrowing money).

This position pays off exactly the same cash flow as the investment project under both states of the world. Therefore, the value of the project, including the ability to defer, should equal the value of the replicating portfolio:

$$\text{Contingent NPV} = N(\text{Price of Twin Security}) - B(1)$$

$$= 1.35(30.3) - 21.43(1) = 19.5$$

The value of the deferral option is the difference between the total contingent NPV of the project and its standard NPV without flexibility: $19.50 - (-\$9.10) = \$28.60$ (remember, the standard NPV was negative).

Contingent NPV can also be determined with an alternative ROV approach called *risk-neutral valuation*. The name is somewhat misleading because a risk-neutral valuation does adjust for risk, but as part of the scenario probabilities rather than the discount rate. To value an option, weight the future cash flows by risk-adjusted (or so-called risk-neutral) probabilities instead of the actual scenario probabilities. The probability-weighted average cash flow is then discounted by the risk-free rate to determine current value. The risk-neutral probability of the favorable state, p^*, is defined as follows:[9]

$$p^* = \frac{1 + r_f - d}{u - d} = 0.45$$

---

[8] If the project itself were traded, you would not need a twin security but would construct a replicating portfolio with the traded value of the project itself.
[9] See, for example, Trigeorgis, *Real Options*, 75–76.

where

$$u = \frac{\text{FV(Favorable State)}}{\text{PV}} = \frac{50.0}{30.3} = 1.65$$

$$d = \frac{\text{FV(Unfavorable State)}}{\text{PV}} = \frac{16.7}{30.3} = 0.55$$

Solve by substituting:

$$p^* = 0.45$$

$$1 - p^* = 0.55$$

These probabilities implicitly capture the risk premium for investments perfectly correlated with the twin security. We discount the future cash flows weighted by the risk-neutral probabilities at the risk-free rate of 5 percent, arriving at exactly the same value determined using the replicating portfolio:

$$\text{Contingent NPV} = \frac{0.45(45) + 0.55(0)}{1.05} = 19.5$$

It is no coincidence that the replicating portfolio and risk-neutral valuation lead to the same result. They are mathematically equivalent, and both rely on the price of the twin security to derive the value of an investment project with an option to defer.

Valuation Based on Decision Tree Analysis (DTA)

A second method for valuing a project with flexibility is to use decision tree analysis (DTA). This leads to the right answer in principle, but only if we apply the *correct* cost of capital for a project's contingent cash flows.

One DTA approach is to discount the project's contingent payoffs net of the investment requirements. Unfortunately, we can only derive the correct cost of capital for these cash flows from the ROV results. Given the project's contingent NPV of $19.50 with equal chances of paying off $45 or $0, the implied discount rate from the ROV analysis is 15.5 percent.[10] This is significantly above the underlying asset's 10 percent cost of capital, because the contingent cash flows are more risky. The contingent NPV has an equal chance of increasing by 131 percent or decreasing by 100 percent. The value of the underlying asset ($90.90) has a 50–50 chance of going up 65 percent (to $150) or down by

---

[10] In this simplified example, there is one value for the cost of capital. In general, the cost of capital for the contingent cash flows is not constant. It changes with the risk of the option across time and states of the world.

45 percent (to $50). If we were to use the underlying asset's cost of capital of 10 percent, the DTA results would therefore be too high:

$$\text{Contingent NPV} = \frac{0.5(45) + 0.5(0)}{1.10} = 20.5$$

A better DTA approach separately discounts the two components of the contingent cash flows. The contingent payoffs from the underlying asset are discounted at the cost of capital of the underlying asset. The investment requirements are discounted at the risk-free rate. Using this DTA approach, the valuation now comes much closer to the correct result:

$$\text{Contingent NPV} = 0.5 \left[\frac{150}{1.10} - \frac{105}{1.05} \right] + 0.5(0) = 18.2 \tag{32.1}$$

We discuss in the next section how this second DTA approach can lead to the exact ROV outcome if the underlying risk is either diversifiable or non-diversifiable but too small to influence the future investment decision (i.e., if the project value would exceed the investment requirements even in the unfavorable state).

Comparing ROV and DTA Approaches

As summarized in Exhibit 32.5, the standard NPV approach undervalues our mining project. The ROV approach generates a correct value because it captures the value of flexibility by using a replicating portfolio or risk-neutral valuation. The DTA approach could lead to the same result and is actually quite close in this example, capturing almost the entire gap between the standard NPV valuation and the more granular ROV result. But the DTA results might be further off or closer to the ROV mark, depending on the project's payoffs and risks.

This example does not mean that ROV is the single best approach to valuing managerial flexibility. The stylized example did not take into account two important aspects of real-life investment decisions: the type of underlying risk and the availability of data on the value and variance of cash flows from the underlying asset. Exhibit 32.6 describes when each method is most suitable. As we explain next, ROV works best when the future cash flows are closely linked to traded commodities, securities, or currencies. Not surprisingly, real-option valuations are most often used for commodity-linked investments, such as in the mining and oil industries. In most other cases, we recommend the more straightforward DTA approach because (most of) the underlying risk is diversifiable or because only rough estimates are available for required inputs such as the underlying asset value and variance.

Underlying risk: Diversifiable versus nondiversifiable   Investment projects can be exposed to a wide range of risks, such as product price and demand risk, interest and currency risks, technological risk, and political risk. The question

EXHIBIT 32.5 **Valuation Result: Standard versus Contingent NPV**

dollars

Standard NPV		
	Cash flow	150
$p=$ 50%	Investment	(105)
NPV	**Net cash flow**	**45**
(9.1)		
$1-p=$ 50%	Cash flow	50
	Investment	(105)
Risk-free rate = 5%	**Net cash flow**	**(55)**
WACC = 10%		

Contingent NPV

Decision tree analysis[1]

	Cash flow	150
$p=$ 50%	Investment	(105)
NPV	**Net cash flow**	**45**
18.2		
$1-p=$ 50%	Cash flow	50
	Investment	(105)
	Net cash flow	**–**

Real-option valuation[2]

	Cash flow	150
p^* 45%	Investment	(105)
NPV	**Net cash flow**	**45**
19.5		
$1-p^*$ 55%	Cash flow	50
	Investment	(105)
	Net cash flow	**–**

Note: t = time, in years; p = probability; p^* = binomial (risk-neutral) probability.

[1] Discounting cash flows at the project's cost of capital of 10% and investments at the risk-free rate of 5%.

[2] Using risk-neutral valuation.

is which particular risk (or group of risks) could affect a project's cash flow to such an extent that it would change management's future decisions:

- If commodity prices, as in mining, the oil industry, or power generation, are keys to future investment decisions, the key *underlying risk is not diversifiable*. Other examples include interest or currency risks or risks

EXHIBIT 32.6 **Application Opportunities for ROV versus DTA**

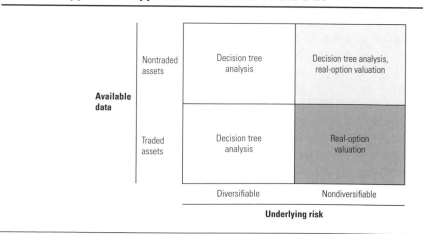

that are strongly correlated with overall economic activity. For some investments, these risks outweigh any technological, regulatory, or other diversifiable risks. For example, decisions to invest in the expansion of a power plant are typically driven by the difference in fuel and power prices and by overall demand for power.

- If technological risks such as a drug trial outcome are key, the *underlying risk is diversifiable* because the correlation of the outcome with overall economic activity is low. Other examples are geological risks such as the size of an undeveloped oil field, or even some forms of marketing risk such as consumer acceptance of a new product. These risks are sometimes more important for future investment decisions than nondiversifiable risks. For example, the driver of the decision to invest in drug development is whether the drug passes the trials, not whether the drug—once successfully developed—is worth more or less depending on general economic conditions.

When nondiversifiable risk is driving future investment decisions, only ROV leads to the theoretically correct valuation. The DTA approach might end up close but is difficult to apply because it is unclear how to discount the project's contingent cash flows (unless you know the implied cost of capital from the ROV results). This was illustrated in the second example in this chapter, where the difference in mining payoffs stemmed from changes in the mineral price. The ROV approach—using the mineral commodity to set up a replicating portfolio—provided the correct estimate of the project's value. The DTA approach could not provide a correct value, although it was quite close in that particular case.

For diversifiable underlying risk, a straightforward DTA is an effective tool for valuing flexibility. In this case, we can discount the project's payoffs in each scenario at the cost of capital of the underlying asset and discount the investment requirements at the risk-free rate (see the example in equation 32.1). A simple illustration is the pharmaceutical drug example from the beginning of the chapter. There was an implicit assumption that all the underlying risks in the development project were diversifiable, given that the cost of capital was equal to the risk-free rate. Therefore, we could use a simple DTA approach and still arrive at exactly the same (correct) value that an ROV approach would have produced.[11]

---

[11] To value the drug development project with an ROV approach, we build a replicating portfolio. Assume a twin security exists whose payoffs are perfectly correlated with the outcome of the drug trial, generating $52.50 when the outcome is favorable and $10.50 when it is unfavorable. Because its cash flows are driven by technological risk only, the security's market beta is zero, and its present value must be $30. A replicating portfolio consists of a long position of 107.1 of these securities and a short position of $1,071.40 in risk-free bonds. The ROV is therefore 107.1(30) − 1,071.4(1) = 2,143. See also Dixit and Pindyck, *Investment under Uncertainty*, 30–32, for a similar proof.

In reality, investment risks are rarely completely diversifiable. A developed drug's cost of capital typically exceeds the risk-free rate because demand and price for a drug are likely to vary at least somewhat with economic conditions. The key question is then whether the contingent investment decisions are driven by the diversifiable risk (e.g., the outcome of clinical trials) or the nondiversifiable risk in a project (e.g., as reflected in the beta of a successfully developed drug). We can effectively apply the DTA approach as long as the contingent decisions are predominantly driven by diversifiable underlying risk: discount the project's payoffs at the weighted average cost of capital and the investment layouts at the risk-free rate.

Toward the end of this chapter, we include a numerical example of a research and development project where the DTA approach leads to exactly the same value as an ROV approach because the nondiversifiable risk does not make a difference in the future investment decisions.

Data availability: Traded versus untraded assets   The results of an ROV (and DTA) valuation critically depend on well-grounded estimates for the value and the variance of cash flows from the underlying asset.

If the estimate for the *underlying asset value* is inaccurate, the flexibility value also will be inaccurate. Returning to our first example, if we misestimate the future cash flows generated by a highly effective drug, the value of the option to defer will be inaccurate. In this simple example, we assumed a no-growth cash flow perpetuity. In practice, you would have to estimate the value with a full-fledged DCF model projecting sales growth, operating margins, capital turnovers, and so on. All ROV (and DTA) approaches build on this valuation of the underlying asset.

A similar argument holds for estimates of the *variance* of the underlying asset's cash flows (called *volatility* in the option-pricing literature). Volatility can have a great impact on value, because real options typically have long lifetimes and are often "at the money" or close to it,[12] meaning the decision of whether to undertake the project is a close call.[13]

To illustrate the impact of volatility on such options, consider the value of a 10-year, at-the-money call option on a dividend-paying stock. Assume the risk-free rate is 5 percent, the dividend yield is 2.5 percent, and the current price for the underlying stock is $100. The value of the call option would be $27 based on a volatility of 20 percent and $35 for a volatility of 30 percent—an increase in value of almost 30 percent.[14] Likewise, in the drug development example,

---

[12] It follows from option-pricing theory that the sensitivity of option value to changes in variance (referred to as vega) increases as the option's lifetime increases and as the option is closer to the money. An option is at the money if its exercise price equals the value of the underlying asset.

[13] If the investment decision were a clear go or no-go, there would be little value in flexibility in the first place, and no need to consider the option value.

[14] The results were obtained with a Black-Scholes option-pricing model. See, for example, R. Brealey and S. Myers, *Principles of Corporate Finance,* 7th ed. (New York: McGraw-Hill, 2003), chap. 21.

changes in cash flow variance significantly affect the option's value. Still, for many managers and practitioners, volatility remains an abstract concept: How do you reasonably estimate the range of cash flow outcomes from the sale of a product that has yet to be released?[15]

Sometimes the underlying asset value and variance can be derived from traded assets. Examples include options to shut down gas-fueled power generation, abandon a copper mine, or defer production of an oil field. In such cases, because you can estimate the key inputs with reasonable accuracy, ROV should be more accurate than DTA. Even then, accurately estimating underlying value and variance is not straightforward. Although short-term volatility can be measured using commodity prices, it is often the long-term volatility that is important for real options (because they have long lifetimes). In fact, short-term volatility can be misleading because oil prices are mean-reverting. For example, high current volatility of spot prices for crude oil is not meaningful for the valuation of a long-term, oil-related option. Extrapolating high short-term volatility could suggest long-term future oil prices that are unrealistically high or low.

When estimates for the underlying asset valuation and variance (volatility) cannot be derived from traded assets and are largely judgmental, a DTA approach is more appropriate. It is more straightforward and transparent to decision makers than the ROV approach. Transparency is especially important when critical valuation assumptions require the decision maker's judgment. DTA captures the essence of flexibility value, and the theoretical advantage of ROV is less important if required inputs are unavailable.

FOUR-STEP PROCESS FOR VALUING FLEXIBILITY

To value flexibility, use the four-step process illustrated in Exhibit 32.7. In step 1, conduct a valuation of the investment project without flexibility, using a traditional discounted cash flow model. In step 2, expand the DCF model into an event tree, mapping how the value of the project evolves over time, using unadjusted probabilities and the weighted average cost of capital. At this stage, the model does not include flexibility, so the present value of the project, based on discounting the cash flows in the event tree, should equal the standard DCF value from the first step.

In step 3, turn the event tree into a decision tree by identifying the types of managerial flexibility that are available. Build the flexibility into the nodes of the tree. Multiple sources of flexibility are possible at a single decision node, such as the option to abandon and expand, but it is important to have clear priorities among them. Be careful in establishing the sequence of decisions regarding flexibility, especially when the decision tree has compound options.

---

[15] The range needs to include the associated probabilities to provide a variance estimate.

EXHIBIT 32.7   **Four-Step Process for Valuing Flexibility**

	Estimate NPV without flexibility	Model uncertainty in event tree	Model flexibility in decision tree	Estimate contingent NPV
Objectives	Compute base-case present value without flexibility	Understand how present value develops with respect to changing uncertainty	Analyze event tree to identify and incorporate managerial flexibility to respond to new information	Value total project using DTA or ROV approach
Comments	Standard NPV approach used for valuation of underlying asset	No flexibility modeled; valuation following event tree should equal standard NPV	Flexibility is incorporated into event tree, transforming it into decision tree	Under high uncertainty and managerial flexibility, contingent NPV will be significantly higher than standard NPV

Finally, step 4 entails recognizing how the exercise of flexibility alters the project's risk characteristics. If (most of) the risk driving the contingent cash flows is fully diversifiable, you need no special modeling and can use DTA, discounting investment cash flows at the risk-free rate and the underlying project's cash flows at the weighted average cost of capital, as in the pharmaceutical example in the next section. If the risk is (mostly) nondiversifiable and priced in the market, the appropriate risk-adjusted discount rate for the project's cash flows is no longer the weighted average cost of capital used in step 1. In that case, use an ROV approach for the project with flexibility, using a replicating portfolio or risk-neutral valuation.

Real-Option Valuation: A Numerical Example

Using the four-step process, we illustrate the ROV approach with a straight-forward binomial lattice for valuing flexibility that is assumed to be driven by nondiversifiable risk. The results are identical to alternative option-pricing models that use more complicated mathematics such as stochastic calculus or Monte Carlo simulation.

Step 1: Estimate net present value without flexibility   Assume that an investment in a project to build a factory generates cash flows whose present value (PV) equals $100, with volatility of 15 percent per year.[16] Its expected rate of return and cost of capital (k) equals 8 percent. The risk-free rate is 5 percent per year, and the cash outflow necessary to undertake the project, if we invest in it immediately, is $105. Thus, the standard NPV is –$5, and we would not undertake the project if we had to commit today.

---

[16] The standard deviation of the rate of change of the factory value.

EXHIBIT 32.8 **Event Tree: Factory without Flexibility**

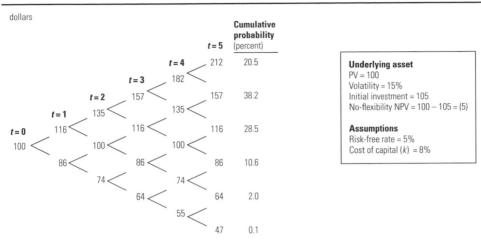

	Cumulative probability (percent)

dollars

Underlying asset
PV = 100
Volatility = 15%
Initial investment = 105
No-flexibility NPV = 100 − 105 = (5)

Assumptions
Risk-free rate = 5%
Cost of capital (*k*) = 8%

Step 2: Model uncertainty using event tree
The lattice that models the potential values of the underlying risky asset is called an event tree. It contains no decision nodes and simply models the evolution of the underlying asset. Exhibit 32.8 illustrates potential values the factory might take for each of next five years. Defining T as the number of years per upward movement and σ as the annualized volatility of the underlying factory value, determine the up-and-down movements by using the following formulas:[17]

$$\text{Up Movement} = u = e^{\sigma\sqrt{T}}$$

$$\text{Down Movement} = d = \frac{1}{u}$$

Substitute numerical values into these formulas:

$$u = e^{0.15\sqrt{1}} = 1.1618$$

$$d = \frac{1}{1.1618} = 0.8607$$

Based on traditional DCF using an 8 percent cost of capital, the probability of an up movement is 72.82 percent, and the probability of a down movement is

---

[17] J. Cox, M. Rubinstein, and S. Ross, "Option Pricing: A Simplified Approach," *Journal of Financial Economics* 7, no. 3 (1979): 229–263. As T becomes smaller, the binomial lattice results converge to the true value of the option. In this example, we have chosen $T = 1$ for ease of illustration.

27.18 percent.[18] As can be verified, the present value of any branch in the event tree equals the expected payout discounted at the 8 percent cost of capital. For example, take the uppermost branch in the fifth time period. Its present value is:

$$\text{PV}_{t=4} = \frac{E(\text{PV}_{t=5})}{(1+k)} = \frac{0.7282(211.7) + 0.2718(156.8)}{1.08} = 182.2$$

A similar calculation will produce any of the values in the event tree, resulting in a PV of the project of $100 at $t = 0$. That present value equals the result in step 1, so we know the tree is correct.

Step 3: Model flexibility using decision tree   When you add decision points to an event tree, it becomes a decision tree. Suppose the factory can be expanded for an additional $15. The expansion increases the factory's value at that node by 20 percent. The option can be exercised at any time during the next five years.

Exhibit 32.9 shows the resulting decision tree. To find the payouts at a given point on the tree, start with the final branches and work backward through time. Consider the uppermost branch in period 5. On the upward limb, the payout absent expansion would be 211.7, but with expansion, it is $1.20 \times 211.7 - 15 = 239.0$. Since the value with expansion is higher, we would decide to expand. On the lower limb of that same node, the payout with expansion is $1.20 \times 156.8 - 15 = 173.2$, versus 156.8 without expansion, so again we would expand.

Step 4: Estimate contingent net present value   To determine the value of the project with the flexibility to expand, work backward through the decision tree, using the replicating-portfolio method at each node. For the node highlighted in Exhibit 32.9, you can replicate the payoffs from the option to expand, using a portfolio of N units of the underlying project[19] and B units of $1 risk-free bonds:

$$116.2N + 1.05B = 124.4$$

$$86.1N + 1.05B = 88.3$$

Solving the equations, we find that $N = 1.2$, and $B = -14.3$. Therefore, a replicating portfolio consists of 1.2 units of the project without flexibility

---

[18] See the previous note for the derivation of the formula for estimating the upward probability:

$$\frac{(1+k)^T - d}{u - d} = \frac{(1+8\%) - 0.8607}{1.1618 - 0.8607} = 0.7282$$

[19] If the project itself is not traded but a traded twin security exists, we could construct the portfolio in a similar way with units of the twin security and risk-free bonds.

EXHIBIT 32.9 **Decision Tree: Option to Expand Factory**

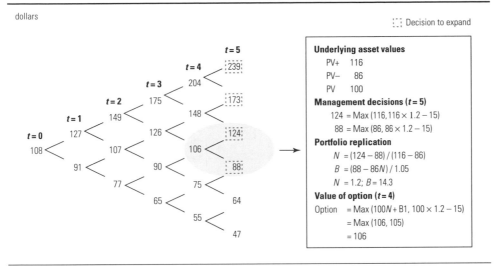

Note: t = time, in years
PV = present value
N = number of replicating securities
B = number of risk-free bonds

Incremental investment: $15
Incremental payoff: 20%

(at that node, valued at $100 in Exhibit 32.8), plus a short position of 14.3 bonds worth $1. As shown in Exhibit 32.9, the value of the option is then:

$$PV = 100N + 1B = 105.7$$

Work backward from right to left, node by node, to obtain a present value of $108.40 for a project that has an option to expand. As a result, the net present value of the project increases from –$5 to $3.40, so the option itself is worth $8.40. Note that the analysis also provides the value-maximizing decision strategy: management should expand the factory only after five years and only if the factory is worth $75 or more.[20]

If, instead, management had the option to abandon the factory at any node for a fixed liquidation value of $100, the valuation would be as shown in Exhibit 32.10. Again, work from right to left through the decision tree. For the highlighted node, the value of the underlying factory is $116.20 in the upward branch and $86.10 in the downward branch. Given the ability to do so, the company would abandon the project for $100 in the downward branch, so the

[20] This is analogous to a call option on a stock that does not pay dividends: it is never exercised prematurely. For example, in the node highlighted in Exhibit 32.10, the value in year 4 of deferring the expansion of the factory to year 5 is $105.70, as calculated in the preceding equation. The value of expanding in year 4 is $100 × 1.20 – $15 = $105. It is therefore optimal to defer expansion, as is the case for all nodes before year 5.

EXHIBIT 32.10 **Decision Tree: Option to Abandon Factory**

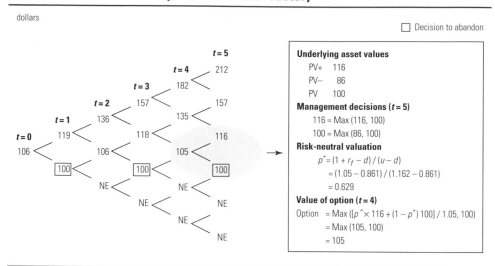

dollars

☐ Decision to abandon

Underlying asset values
PV+	116
PV−	86
PV	100

Management decisions ($t = 5$)
116 = Max (116, 100)
100 = Max (86, 100)

Risk-neutral valuation
$$p^* = (1 + r_f - d) / (u - d)$$
$$= (1.05 - 0.861) / (1.162 - 0.861)$$
$$= 0.629$$

Value of option ($t = 4$)
Option $= \text{Max} ([p^* \times 116 + (1 - p^*) 100] / 1.05, 100)$
$= \text{Max} (105, 100)$
$= 105$

Note: NE = nonexisting state
t = time, in years
PV = present value
p^* = binomial (risk-neutral) probability
u = upward movement of value
d = downward movement of value
r_f = risk-free rate

Liquidation value: $100

payoffs in the decision tree are $116.20 in the upward branch and $100 in the downward branch. Using risk-neutral valuation this time, the abandonment option can be valued in this node at $104.90, as shown in Exhibit 32.10 (the same result a replicating portfolio would have generated). Working backward through time, the value for a factory with the ability to abandon is $106.40, so that the abandonment option is worth $6.40. Now the value-maximizing decision strategy is to abandon the factory immediately in any year in which its value drops below $100.

Multiple sources of flexibility can be combined within a single decision tree, as illustrated in Exhibit 32.11, using risk-neutral valuation. The value of the project, including the options to abandon and expand, would be $113.50 rather than $100, its stand-alone value without flexibility. With these options, the correct decision would be to accept the project. Note that the value of the combined expansion-abandonment flexibility, $13.50, is less than the sum of the individual flexibility values ($8.40 + $6.40 = $14.80) but greater than either of them individually. The values of both options are not additive, because they interact in complex ways (for example, you cannot expand the factory once you have abandoned it). As indicated in Exhibit 32.11, the best decision strategy is to abandon the factory whenever its value drops below $100 and to expand only in year 5 if its value exceeds $75.

EXHIBIT 32.11   **Decision Tree: Option to Expand or Abandon Factory**

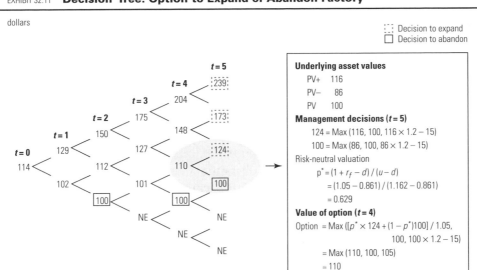

dollars

⋮⋮⋮ Decision to expand
☐ Decision to abandon

Underlying asset values
PV+   116
PV−   86
PV   100
Management decisions (t = 5)
124 = Max (116, 100, 116 × 1.2 − 15)
100 = Max (86, 100, 86 × 1.2 − 15)
Risk-neutral valuation
$p^* = (1 + r_f − d) / (u − d)$
   = (1.05 − 0.861) / (1.162 − 0.861)
   = 0.629
Value of option (t = 4)
Option = Max ([p^* × 124 + (1 − p^*)100] / 1.05,
                100, 100 × 1.2 − 15)
   = Max (110, 100, 105)
   = 110

Note: NE = nonexisting state
    t = time, in years
    PV = present value
    p^* = binomial (risk-neutral) probability
    u = upward movement of value
    d = downward movement of value
    r_f = risk-free rate
    Liquidation value: $100
    Incremental investment: $15
    Incremental payoff: 20%

REAL-OPTION VALUATION AND DECISION TREE ANALYSIS: A NUMERICAL EXAMPLE

In our next example, we apply both the DTA and the ROV approaches in the valuation of a research and development project. Assume a company needs to decide whether to develop a new pharmaceutical drug. In our simplified example,[21] the first step in development is a research phase of three years, in which the most promising chemical compounds are selected. The probability of success in the research phase is estimated at 15 percent. This is followed by a three-year testing phase, during which the compounds are tested in laboratory and clinical settings. The chance of successfully completing the testing phase is 40 percent. If there are successful results, the drug can be released in the market. On failure in any phase, the company terminates development, and the product dies worthless.

---

[21] Pharmaceutical R&D is much more complex and consists of more phases than shown in this example. For a more extensive example of valuing flexibility in pharmaceutical research and development, see Kellog and Charnes, "Real-Options Valuation for a Biotechnology Company."

DTA Approach: Technological Risk

The DTA approach presented next follows the four steps for the valuation of flexibility as described in the previous section. In the DTA valuation of the research and development project, we consider only the underlying technological risk relating to the research and testing outcomes. The commercial risk concerning the future profitability of the drug and the technological risk are jointly taken into account in the ROV approach discussed in the next section.

Step 1: Estimate present value without flexibility   If the development process succeeds, the drug will deliver substantial value in six years' time. Margins in the pharmaceutical industry are high because drugs are protected against competition through patents. A successful drug is expected to generate annual sales of $2,925 million and a 45 percent earnings before interest, taxes, depreciation, and amortization (EBITDA) margin on sales until its patent expires, 10 years after its market launch. (Because prices decline drastically after a patent expires, we do not count proceeds beyond that time.) Assuming a 30 percent tax rate and a 7 percent cost of capital, a marketable drug's present value at the launch date would therefore be $6,475 million. Unfortunately, the odds of successful development are small. The cumulative probability of success over the research and testing phase is only 6 percent (0.15 for research $\times$ 0.40 for testing). In addition, the investments needed to develop, test, and market a drug are high: $100 million in the research phase, $250 million in the testing phase, and $150 million in marketing.

If we had to commit to all three investments today, we should not proceed, because the NPV would be negative:

$$\text{Standard NPV} = \text{PV(Expected Cash Flows)} - \text{PV (Investments)}$$

$$= 0.06\frac{6,475}{(1.07)^6} - 100 - \frac{250}{(1.05)^3} - \frac{150}{(1.05)^6} = -169$$

However, if we take into account management's ability to abandon the project before completion, the value is significantly higher.

Step 2: Model uncertainty using event tree   In this development project, a key source of risk behind the diverging contingent cash flows is technological risk relating to the research and testing outcomes. You can model this uncertainty using a straightforward event tree (see Exhibit 32.12). Note that the tree shows all cash inflows and outflows at values discounted to today. For example, the expected value of a marketable drug after six years is shown at its present value as of today ($t = 0$) of $4,314 million (which equals the drug's value at

EXHIBIT 32.12 **Event Tree: R&D Option with Technological Risk**

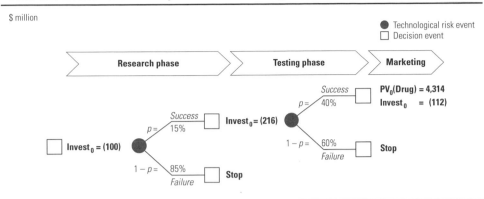

Note: PV_0(Drug) = present value of marketable drug discounted to $t = 0$ at WACC
Invest$_0$ = investment discounted to $t = 0$ at risk-free rate
p = probability of technological success

launch of $6,475 discounted over six years at 7 percent). Since the investment outlays are certain, they are discounted at the risk-free rate of 5 percent.[22]

Step 3: Model flexibility using decision tree   Next, include decision flexibility in the tree, working from right to left. At the end of the testing phase, we have the option to invest $150 million in marketing, which equals $112 million in today's dollars. We should invest only if testing has produced a marketable product. At the end of the research phase, we have the option to proceed with the testing phase. If the research phase fails, there is no point in proceeding, and if it is successful, we will proceed to testing only if the payoffs justify the incremental investment of $250 million (or $216 million discounted to today at the risk-free rate).

Step 4: Estimate value of flexibility   Because the technological risk is fully diversifiable, apply a DTA approach for the valuation of flexibility. Again, work from right to left in the tree (see Exhibit 32.13). At the end of the testing phase, we proceed with launching the product only if there is a marketable product. The value at this point in time is therefore $Max[(4,314 - 112), 0] = $4,202 million. The value of the option to proceed at the end of the research phase is calculated as follows:

$$PV \text{ (Option)} = Max[PV \text{ (Testing)} - Inv \text{ (Testing)}, 0]$$

---

[22] The assumption to discount investment outlays at the risk-free rate is also implicitly made in the ROV approach.

EXHIBIT 32.13   **Decision Tree: R&D Option with Technological Risk**

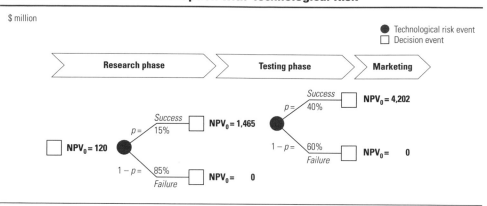

Note: NPV_0 = net present value of development project discounted to $t=0$
       p = probability of technological success

In this equation, PV(Testing) is the present value of proceeding with testing, which equals the probability-weighted future payoffs:

$$PV\ (Testing) = 0.40(4{,}202) + 0.60(0) = 1{,}681$$

Inv(Testing) is the investment requirement for the testing phase, which equals $250 million or $216 million discounted to $t = 0$. Substituting, find the present value of the development project prior to the testing phase:

$$PV\ (Option) = Max\ [(1{,}681 - 216), 0] = 1{,}465$$

These amounts need not be discounted further, because they already represent present value as of $t = 0$.

Working farther from right to left in the tree, we find the contingent NPV for the entire development project prior to the research phase:

$$PV\ (Option) = Max\ [PV\ (Research) - Inv\ (Research), 0]$$
$$= Max\ [0.15\ (1{,}465) + 0.85\ (0) - 100, 0] = \$120\ million$$

This value including flexibility is significantly higher than the standard NPV of –$169 million.

ROV Approach: Technological and Commercial Risk

Our analysis thus far did not include the other source of uncertainty in the development project: the commercial risk concerning the future cash flow potential of the successfully developed and marketed drug. ROV is necessary to handle both technological and commercial risk.

EXHIBIT 32.14 **Event Tree: R&D Option with Technological and Commercial Risk**

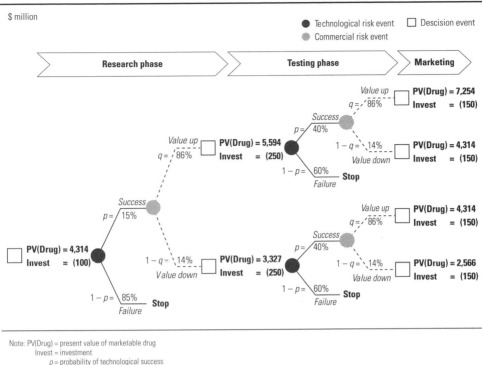

Note: PV(Drug) = present value of marketable drug
Invest = investment
p = probability of technological success
q = probability of drug value increase

Step 1: Estimate present value without flexibility   This step is identical for the DTA and ROV approaches.

Step 2: Model uncertainty using event tree   Both risks can be modeled in a combined event tree (see Exhibit 32.14). In contrast to the event tree in the DTA approach, the amounts in this tree do not represent present values but rather future values that will need to be discounted when you solve for the value of the option. For simplicity, we have chosen a one-step binomial lattice to describe the evolution of the drug value over each three-year period.[23] Assuming an annual volatility of 15 percent, we can derive the upward and downward movements, u and d, as follows:

$$u = e^{\sigma \sqrt{T}} = e^{0.15\sqrt{3}} = 1.30$$

$$d = \frac{1}{u} = \frac{1}{1.30} = 0.77$$

[23] With more nodes, the tree quickly becomes too complex to show in an exhibit, because it does not converge in the technological risk. We carried out the analysis with 10 nodes and found that doing so did not affect the results for this particular example.

The probability of an upward movement is 86 percent, and the probability of a downward movement is 14 percent.[24] The value of a marketable drug at the start of the research phase is $4,314 million. At the end of the research phase, there are three possible outcomes: failure leading to a drug value of $0, success combined with an increase in the value of a marketable drug to $5,594 million, and success combined with a decrease in the value of a marketable drug to $3,327 million. Following the same logic, there are six possible outcomes after the testing phase.

Step 3: Model flexibility using decision tree   The logic underlying the decision tree including commercial risk (see Exhibit 32.15) is the same as under the DTA approach. For example, the payoff at the end of the testing phase in the top branch equals Max[(7,254 − 150), 0] = 7,104. The primary difference is that the ROV version of the tree recognizes the ability to abandon development if the value of a marketable drug drops too much.

Step 4: Estimate contingent NPV   The commercial risk regarding the drug's future cash flows is not diversifiable,[25] so you need to use an ROV approach to include it in your valuation. This example uses risk-neutral valuation. Therefore, risk-adjust all probabilities of the upward and downward movements for the drug's value:

$$p^* = \frac{(1 + r_f)^T - d}{u - d} = \frac{1.05^3 - 0.77}{1.30 - 0.77} = 0.74$$

Having applied the risk-neutral probabilities, discount all contingent payoffs at the risk-free rate, working from right to left in the tree. Because the technological risk is fully diversifiable, there is no need to adjust the probabilities for success and failure in research or testing.

For example, from Exhibit 32.15, the value of the option at the end of a research phase showing a drop in the value of the drug is expressed as follows:

$$PV \text{ (Option)} = Max \text{ [PV (Testing)} - Inv \text{ (Testing), 0]}$$

[24] The formula for estimating the upward probability is:

$$\frac{(1 + k)^T - d}{u - d} = \frac{1.07^3 - 0.77}{1.30 - 0.77} = 0.86$$

where k is the expected return on the asset.

[25] Recall that we assumed the cost of capital for a marketed drug is 7 percent. Given our assumption for a risk-free rate of 5 percent, its beta must be different from zero.

EXHIBIT 32.15   **Decision Tree: R&D Option with Technological and Commercial Risk**

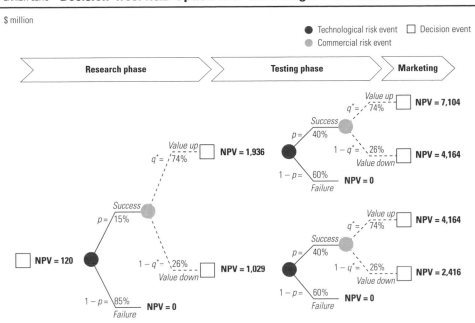

$ million

● Technological risk event   □ Decision event
● Commercial risk event

Note: NPV = net present value of project
      q^* = binomial (risk-neutral) probability of an increase in marketable drug value
      p = probability of technological success

In this equation, PV(Testing) represents the value of proceeding with testing at this node. It equals the value of the future payoffs weighted by risk-neutral probabilities and discounted at the risk-free rate:

$$PV\ (Testing) = \frac{0.40\,[0.74\,(4,164) + 0.26(2,416)] + 0.60(0)}{(1.05)^3} = 1,279$$

Inv(Testing) equals $250 million, so the value of the development project at this node is as follows:

$$PV\ (Option) = Max\ [(1,279 - 250),\ 0] = 1,029$$

Solve for the other nodes in the same way. Working backward through the tree, the contingent NPV is estimated at $120 million, the same result we obtained in the DTA approach without commercial risk.

This is not surprising. A closer look at the decision tree reveals that uncertainty about the future value of the drug if it is marketable is not significant enough to influence any of the decisions in the development process. In this example, the commercial risk makes no difference, even if we assume volatility as high as 50 percent (an amount that exceeds the volatility of many high-tech stocks). As we noted earlier, when nondiversifiable risk (the drug's commercial risk as measured by its beta) does not influence investment decisions, the DTA and ROV results are equivalent.

Moreover, in real situations, the key uncertainty in drug development is whether the drug proves to be an effective disease treatment without serious side effects. The commercial risk is far less relevant, because a truly effective drug almost always generates attractive margins. The example illustrates how in such cases it is more practical to focus on the technological risk entirely, using a DTA approach. Explicitly modeling the nondiversifiable (e.g., commercial) risk requires an ROV approach that is more complex and may not even affect the valuation results.

In general, when faced with multiple sources of underlying risk, carefully assess whether all these possible risks are important or whether one dominates all others. Sometimes you can focus the valuation approach on just one or two sources of uncertainty and greatly simplify the analysis.

SUMMARY

Managerial flexibility lets managers defer or change investment decisions as a business or project develops. Clearly, it can alter the value of the business or project substantially. Rigid use of standard DCF analysis fails to account for the impact that exercising flexibility has on present value.

Flexibility comes in many forms, such as the option to defer, expand, contract, or abandon projects or switch them on and off; this chapter has illustrated only a few applications. Contingent NPV analysis, in the form of decision tree analysis (DTA) or real-option valuation (ROV) models, correctly captures flexibility's impact on value. Although the ROV approach is theoretically superior to DTA, applying it is more complex. So ROV is often limited to valuing flexibility in commodity-based industries where commodity prices are measurable, making its application more straightforward. In most other cases, a careful DTA approach delivers results that are reasonably solid and can provide more valuable insights.

REVIEW QUESTIONS

1. Define contingent net present value (NPV). Outline and explain the differences between standard and contingent NPV.
2. Identify the value drivers embedded in a "real" option and how they might interact.
3. Assume a company runs a plant for which the value one year from now is either $1,000 if market growth is positive or $250 if market growth is

negative. The probability of positive market growth is 60%, and the probability is 40% for negative market growth. At any time, the company can choose to close the plant and collect the scrap value of $285 if scrapped today or $300 if scrapped in one year. The cost of capital for the plant is 10% and the risk-free rate is 5%. Estimate the value of the plant using the standard NPV, decision tree analysis (DTA), and real-option valuation (ROV) valuation models. Explain the differences in results.

4. Under what circumstances should a manager apply a standard NPV approach, a DTA approach, or an ROV approach to valuation?

5. It is often argued that the two most important real options available to a manager evaluating investment decisions are the option to defer an investment decision and the option to abandon an investment decision. Explain the significance of these two options. What insights could the ROV or the DTA model provide into these decisions?

6. The option to defer an investment reduces risk for a company because it does not need to commit the full investment outlay until there is more certainty about the true value of the underlying asset. But the implied cost of capital for the project including flexibility is higher than for the project without flexibility (see, e.g., Exhibit 32.5). Explain why this is the case.

7. When estimating the value of an option on a traded stock, the expected return on the stock is irrelevant—as proven in option pricing theory. For the valuation of an option on an asset that is not traded, such as in the numerical example introduced in Exhibit 32.8, the expected cash flow returns are required. Discuss how that is still consistent with option pricing theory.

8. Consider the example of the valuation of the pharmaceutical R&D project described in the final section of the chapter. Under the assumptions stated, the DTA value is identical to the ROV value. Calculate what volatility (as modeled in terms of parameters u and d) would make the ROV value differ from the DTA value, and discuss what drives this difference.

33

Valuation in
Emerging Markets

The emerging economies in Asia and South America will experience strong growth over the coming decades, possibly even recovering from the 2008 recession earlier and faster than many developed economies. Over the long term, many analysts see China and India moving into the ranks of the world's largest economies.[1] This sometimes spectacular economic development will produce many situations requiring sound analysis and valuation. In the rising number of privatizations, joint ventures, mergers, and acquisitions, local financial parties such as banks and capital markets will display growing sophistication. Institutional investors will also continue to diversify their portfolios, adding international holdings in emerging-market stocks.

In Chapters 29 and 30, we discussed the general issues around forecasting cash flows in a foreign currency, estimating cost of capital in a foreign currency, and incorporating high inflation into cash flow projections. In this chapter, we focus on the specific issues that arise in financial analysis and valuation of businesses in emerging markets. Valuation is typically more difficult in these environments because of various risks and possible obstacles to businesses. These include macroeconomic uncertainty, illiquid capital markets, controls on the flow of capital into and out of the country, less rigorous standards of accounting and disclosure, and high levels of political risk. It is impossible to generalize about these risks, as they differ by country and may affect businesses in different ways. Academics, investment bankers, and industry practitioners have yet to agree on how to address them. Methods vary considerably, and practitioners often make arbitrary adjustments based on intuition and limited empirical evidence.

The authors would like to thank André Annema for his contribution to this chapter.
[1] See, for example, D. Wilson and R. Purushothaman, "Dreaming with BRICs: The Path to 2050," Global Economics Paper 99, Goldman Sachs & Co. (October 2003).

Since emerging-market valuations are so complex and there is no agreed-upon method, we recommend a triangulation approach—comparing estimates of value derived from three different methods. First, we use discounted cash flows (DCFs) with probability-weighted scenarios that model the risks the business faces. Then we compare the value obtained from this approach with the results of two secondary approaches: a DCF valuation with a country risk premium built into the cost of capital, and a valuation based on comparable trading and transaction multiples. We illustrate the approach with the valuation of ConsuCo, a Brazilian retail company focusing on both food and durable consumer goods.[2]

The basics of estimating a DCF value are the same in emerging markets as elsewhere, so we follow the same steps in the valuation process as we did in Part Two: historical analysis, forecasting cash flows, estimating the cost of capital, and calculating and interpreting results. We also address two additional steps required for an emerging-market valuation:

1. Creating a consistent set of macroeconomic assumptions regarding, for example, foreign exchange rates, inflation, interest rates, and gross domestic product (GDP) growth

2. Incorporating country risk in the valuation

HISTORICAL ANALYSIS

Accounting conventions in emerging markets may differ substantially from those of developed markets, in which case understanding a company's economics may be difficult. Furthermore, in many countries, complicated tax credits and adjustments make cash taxes harder to estimate than in developed markets. However, large accounting and tax differences are frequently eliminated when the income statement and the balance sheet are brought together in the cash flow calculation, following the guidelines set out in Chapter 7. Nevertheless, you need to understand the possible differences before starting any valuation of an emerging-market company.

In the case of ConsuCo, there are no major accounting differences to adjust for. Brazilian Generally Accepted Accounting Principles (GAAP) changed at the end of 2006 and have become very similar to U.S. GAAP and International Financial Reporting Standards (IFRS) regarding, for instance, accounting for leases, derivatives, and stock-based compensation. To illustrate, before this change, ConsuCo treated all leases as off-balance-sheet operating

---

[2] This case illustration is a disguised example.

leases. It now applies the same standards as under U.S. GAAP for classifying leases as either operating or financial, including additional disclosure requirements. Although most leases still remain operating, this doesn't affect our assessment, because we make a standard capital adjustment for operating leases, following the approach described in Chapter 27. One area where a difference remains is goodwill, which can be amortized under Brazilian GAAP. In addition, any goodwill is measured relative to the book value of the relevant assets and liabilities, whereas U.S. GAAP typically uses their fair value. Again, our assessment for valuation is not affected, because we add back any goodwill amortization on a cumulative basis to calculate invested capital.

Having found no major accounting differences to manage, we analyzed ConsuCo's historical financial statements following the approach of Chapter 7, rearranging the balance sheet and the income statement to get the statements for net operating profit less adjusted taxes (NOPLAT), invested capital, and free cash flow. We then estimated some key financial ratios on an approximate real-terms basis. Although annual inflation in Brazil has been moderate since 1997 at an average level of 7 percent, ratios such as operating margin and capital turnover are likely to be biased by inflation when directly calculated from the financial statements. To offset this bias, we looked at trends in cash operating margins—that is, earnings before interest, taxes, depreciation, and amortization (EBITDA) over sales. In addition, we estimated sales in real terms per store and per square meter of store space over time, to understand the development of real-terms capital turnover.

The results are reflected in Exhibit 33.1. Between 2004 and 2008, ConsuCo's sales growth in real terms was highly volatile, with a compound annual growth rate of 3.4 percent, similar to the growth in the number of stores and very close to real GDP growth. This was very much driven by strong growth in 2008, which was mostly due to improved average store performance. Still, average growth since 2003 is relatively low compared with the preceding five years: the average real growth over the past 10 years was about 6 percent per year. The average level of sales per store in real terms has been quite stable, but this does not reflect the increasing store size. With average sales per square meter decreasing and store size increasing, profit margins and ROIC performance have deteriorated: EBITDA margin has decreased to around 7 percent since 2005, and ROIC is now about 6 percent.

Performance in 2008 suggests that recently launched initiatives to improve efficiency and productivity are starting to pay off, but a key question is how much further potential remains to be materialized and consequently what levels of long-term growth and return on invested capital (ROIC) are sustainable. Before we discuss our financial forecasts for ConsuCo in more detail, let us review some of the more technical points about assumptions that are fundamental to creating a financial forecast.

EXHIBIT 33.1   **ConsuCo: Key Historical Financial Indicators**

reais, million

	2004	2005	2006	2007	2008
Invested capital					
Current operating assets	4,769	4,833	5,194	5,936	6,133
Current operating liabilities	(2,650)	(2,953)	(3,596)	(4,051)	(4,304)
Net operating working capital	2,119	1,880	1,598	1,885	1,829
Net property, plant, and equipment	6,322	5,517	6,059	6,886	7,059
Other net operating assets	3,427	3,683	5,006	5,258	5,756
Operating invested capital (excluding goodwill)	11,868	11,080	12,662	14,028	14,645
Goodwill plus cumulative goodwill written off	2,067	2,104	1,940	2,221	2,319
Operating invested capital (including goodwill)	13,935	13,184	14,602	16,249	16,964
Excess marketable securities	1,326	2,061	1,434	1,094	1,807
Other nonoperating assets	818	652	449	451	518
Total investor funds	16,079	15,897	16,485	17,795	19,289
Total interest-bearing debt and operating leases	8,299	7,662	8,127	8,965	9,664
Other nonoperating liabilities	1,318	1,538	1,728	1,737	1,774
Adjusted equity	6,462	6,697	6,630	7,093	7,851
Total investor funds	16,079	15,897	16,485	17,795	19,289
NOPLAT					
Sales	17,950	19,162	19,829	21,290	25,762
Cost of goods sold	(12,702)	(13,483)	(14,233)	(15,321)	(18,971)
Other operating costs	(3,864)	(4,119)	(4,349)	(4,523)	(4,933)
EBITDA	1,384	1,560	1,247	1,447	1,858
Depreciation and amortization	(498)	(631)	(442)	(447)	(588)
Adjusted EBITA	886	929	805	1,000	1,269
Cash taxes	(43)	(207)	(324)	(179)	(329)
NOPLAT	844	722	481	821	940
Key financial ratios					
Nominal indicators (percent)					
Sales growth	16.3	6.8	3.5	7.4	21.0
Adjusted EBITA/sales	4.9	4.8	4.1	4.7	4.9
NOPLAT/sales	4.7	3.8	2.4	3.9	3.6
Invested capital (excluding goodwill)/sales	58	64	66	57	54
Invested capital (including goodwill)/sales	69	74	76	66	62
ROIC (excluding goodwill)	7.1	6.5	3.8	5.9	6.4
ROIC (including goodwill)	6.1	5.5	3.3	5.1	5.5
Approximate real indicators (percent)					
Sales growth (inflation-adjusted)	1.4	0.1	−3.1	3.0	16.8
Gross profit/sales	29.2	29.6	28.2	28.0	26.4
EBITDA/sales	7.7	8.1	6.3	6.8	7.2
Sales/store (reais million)	32.7	32.5	31.9	31.3	35.2
Sales/square meter (reais thousand)	15.8	15.0	14.4	13.5	15.5

CREATING A CONSISTENT SET OF ECONOMIC ASSUMPTIONS

Every forecast of a company's financial performance is based on a set of economic and monetary assumptions about, for instance, exchange rates, inflation
rates, and interest rates. In emerging markets, however, these parameters can
fluctuate wildly from year to year. It is therefore crucial to make sure not only
that each of these parameters is reflected in the financial forecasts of the company, but also that these assumptions are internally consistent. In Chapter 29,
we discussed how some fundamental monetary assumptions should be defined consistently to avoid any biases in the valuation results. This becomes
even more important when you value companies in emerging markets. We recommend creating one integrated set of economic and monetary assumptions
that include, among others, real GDP growth; price inflation (consumer prices,
wages, etc.); interest rates; exchange rates; and whatever other parameters are
deemed relevant (e.g., oil prices). The purpose is not so much to create the right
economic forecasts—these will always be uncertain—but rather to create one
or more sets of consistent assumptions to apply to the valuation.

An important parameter is the exchange rate. Like many international
companies, the cash flows of emerging-market companies can be denominated in several currencies. Consider a national oil company that exports oil.
Its revenues are determined by the dollar price of oil, while many of its costs,
especially labor and domestic purchases, are determined by the domestic currency. If foreign-exchange rates perfectly reflected inflation differentials (so
that purchasing power parity held), the company's operating margins and
cash flows in real terms would be unaffected. In that case, changes in exchange
rates would be irrelevant for valuation purposes.

When estimating the impact of exchange rate movements on cash flow
forecasts, keep in mind that the evidence shows that purchasing power parity
(PPP) does hold over the long run,[3] even between emerging and developed
economies. In other words, exchange rates ultimately do adjust for differences
in inflation between countries. For example, if you held $100 million of Brazilian
currency in 1964, by 2008 it would have been practically worthless in U.S.
dollars. Yet if we adjust for purchasing power, the value of the currency has
fluctuated around the $100 million mark during the 44-year period. Suppose
that, instead of holding $100 million of Brazilian currency, you held $100 million
of assets in Brazil whose value increased with inflation. In about half the years,
their value would have been within 15 percent of the original investment,
but in other years, it might have deviated much more, either positively or
negatively. For example, at the end of 2008, the assets would have been worth
approximately $150 million. Exhibit 33.2 shows the estimated real (inflation-
adjusted) exchange rate for the Brazilian currency, which explains this effect.

---

[3] For an overview, see Alan M. Taylor and Mark Peter Taylor, "The Purchasing Power Parity Debate,"
CEPR Discussion Paper 4495 (2004).

EXHIBIT 33.2 **Brazilian PPP-Adjusted Dollar Exchange Rate**

reais per U.S. dollar index, 1964 = 100

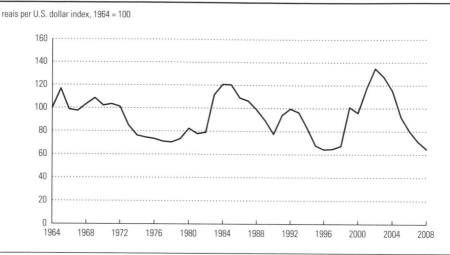

Source: MCM Consultants, IMF International Financial Statistics, Datastream.

Although PPP may hold in the long term, in the short run exchange rates can move far and fast. For example, in Argentina at the end of 2001, the exchange rate rose from one peso per U.S. dollar to nearly 1.9 pesos per U.S. dollar in 15 days, and to 3.1 pesos per dollar in less than four months. And as Exhibit 33.2 shows, during a period of just two weeks in 1999, Brazil's currency weakened by more than 50 percent relative to the U.S. dollar. Therefore, before making financial projections, assess whether the current exchange rate is over-valued or undervalued on a PPP basis and, if so, by how much. Then model the convergence of currency rates to purchasing power parity within your set of economic and monetary assumptions.

Regardless of any short- or long-term economic exposure to varying exchange rates, your valuation results should be independent of the currency or mix of currencies in which you forecast the company's cash flows. Use actual or synthetic forward exchange rates to convert any future cash flow into another currency. In many emerging economies, the forward-exchange market is nonexistent or illiquid, so actual forward rates provide little guidance on likely future exchange rate movements or inflation differentials. In that case, estimate a synthetic forward rate from your assumptions about future inflation and interest rates for the currencies concerned (see Chapter 30 for details).

In the case of ConsuCo, the underlying exchange rate exposure is limited, as the company has very few cash flows denominated in foreign currency. We have therefore not made any adjustments for a change in the exchange rate, even though the real (Brazilian currency) is at 70 percent of PPP. It might, however, be relevant to consider the indirect impact that a convergence of

EXHIBIT 33.3 **Economic and Monetary Assumptions**

percent

	2006	2007	2008	2009E	2010E	...	2014E
Real GDP growth							
Brazil	4.0	5.7	5.1	−0.7	3.5	...	3.7
United States	2.7	2.1	0.4	−2.7	1.5	...	2.1
Inflation (consumer prices)							
Brazil	4.2	3.6	5.7	4.8	4.1	...	4.5
United States	3.2	2.9	3.8	−0.4	1.7	...	2.2

Source: IMF World Economic Outlook.

the real and nominal exchange rates could have on the growth and potential profitability of the Brazilian consumer goods sector and ConsuCo.

Exhibit 33.3 shows the economic and monetary assumptions that we used for ConsuCo's valuation, focusing only on real GDP growth and inflation. Real GDP growth is expected to be between 3 and 4 percent a year, whereas annual inflation is expected to stay just above 4 percent.

FORECASTING CASH FLOWS

Historical analysis showed a turnaround in ConsuCo's performance during 2008. Based on the historical analysis and information from analyst reports up to September 2009, we made the operating and financial forecasts summarized in Exhibit 33.4 in real and nominal terms. We assumed that no major economic crisis will materialize in Brazil after 2010.

We believe that the turnaround of ConsuCo is genuine and sustainable. During the past few years, management of the company has changed, and current management has a strong track record in delivering the turnaround. The company has put a lot of effort into improving same-store sales growth in food, which first showed in 2008's results. In the nonfood segment (items such as furniture and electronics), ConsuCo is also well positioned by having various different formats and channels. These categories currently have a low penetration in Brazil and are expected to show double-digit growth over the years to come. Finally, through some portfolio changes, the company entered new regions in Brazil where it can roll out some of its existing formats.

We therefore assume that the company can deliver about 10 percent real sales growth in the short term, gradually declining to the longer-term historical average of 6 percent. In the very long term, we expect the Brazilian economic growth rate to be in line with average historical real GDP growth rates in the United States. We forecast limited improvement in operating margins. Despite

EXHIBIT 33.4   **ConsuCo: Summary Financial Projections, Base Case**

	2009	2010	2011	2012	2013	2014	...	2019	...	2024
Operating projections										
Sales growth (real, percent)	10.0	10.0	9.0	8.0	7.0	6.0	...	3.8	...	3.0
EBITDA/sales (percent)	7.4	7.6	7.8	7.8	7.8	7.8	...	7.8	...	7.8
Sales/square meter (reais, thousands)	16.0	16.7	17.1	17.4	17.6	17.6	...	17.6	...	17.6
Capital expenditures[1] (reais, millions)	591	671	727	788	853	789	...	1,044	...	1,250
Real projections										
Sales (reais, millions)	13,885	15,274	16,649	17,981	19,239	20,394	...	25,485	...	29,889
Adjusted EBITA/sales (percent)	5.9	6.0	6.1	6.0	6.0	5.9	...	5.6	...	5.3
NOPLAT/sales (percent)	4.3	4.3	4.3	4.1	4.0	3.9	...	3.6	...	3.4
Invested capital/sales (percent)[2]	56.1	55.8	55.7	55.9	56.3	56.3	...	58.8	...	61.2
ROIC (percent)[2]	7.6	7.6	7.7	7.4	7.1	6.9	...	6.2	...	5.6
Nominal projections										
Sales (reais, millions)	14,552	16,663	18,926	21,319	23,815	26,380	...	41,081	...	60,043
Adjusted EBITA/sales (percent)	6.1	6.2	6.4	6.4	6.4	6.4	...	6.3	...	6.2
NOPLAT/sales (percent)	4.4	4.5	4.6	4.5	4.4	4.4	...	4.4	...	4.3
Invested capital/sales (percent)[2]	54.1	52.6	51.4	50.6	50.1	49.2	...	48.2	...	48.2
ROIC (percent)[2]	8.1	8.5	9.0	9.0	8.9	9.0	...	9.1	...	9.0

[1] Inflation adjusted.
[2] Invested capital excluding goodwill.

continuing efficiency gains, we expect increasing competition for market share to put downward pressure on the margins at the same time and therefore are conservative about seeing further margin improvement in the continuing-value period.

Capacity requirements and expected capital expenditures are derived from real growth forecasts in combination with assumed increases in sales productivity. We expect sales productivity to improve again over the next few years, with sales per square meter of store space returning to a level similar to that of about five years ago. However, to realize sales productivity, ConsuCo will also have to invest in substantial reformatting of stores, resulting in an increase in total net property, plant, and equipment (net PP&E) per square meter. As a result, invested capital as a percent of sales will initially drop in real terms but slowly increase again in the longer term.

Although ROIC in real terms will increase until 2011 as a result of improved sales productivity, we expect it to come down after that to just under 6 percent in the continuing-value period. In contrast, the ROIC in nominal terms increases from 8 percent to 9 percent because of inflation's impact on capital turnover.

Strong growth in the first four years, combined with the reformatting and upgrading of stores, means that free cash flow is negative in those years because of the significant investments that this requires. If growth in capacity and revenues in 2010 were a few percentage points lower, the free cash flow would become positive.

INCORPORATING EMERGING-MARKET RISKS IN THE VALUATION

The major distinction between valuing companies in developed markets and in emerging markets is the increased level of risk in the latter. Not only do you need to account for risks related to the company's strategy, market position, and industry dynamics, as you would in a developed market, but you also have to deal with the risks caused by greater volatility in the local capital markets and macroeconomic and political environments.

There is no consensus on how to reflect this higher level of risk in a premium to the discount rate. The alternative is to model risks explicitly in the cash flow projections in what we call the *scenario DCF approach.* Both methodologies, if correctly and consistently applied, lead to the same result. We show this in the following example of an investment in two identical production plants, one in Europe and the other in an emerging economy (see Exhibit 33.5). However, the scenario DCF approach is analytically more robust and does a better job of showing the impact of emerging-market risks on value.

Scenario DCF Approach

The scenario DCF approach simulates alternative trajectories for future cash flows. At a minimum, model two scenarios: The first should assume that cash flow develops according to conditions reflecting business as usual (i.e., without major economic distress). The second should reflect cash flows assuming that one or more emerging-market risks materialize.

In the example, the cash flows for the European plant grow steadily at 3 percent per year into perpetuity. For the plant in the emerging market, the cash flow growth is the same under a business-as-usual scenario, but there is a 25 percent probability of economic distress resulting in a cash flow that is 55 percent lower into perpetuity. The emerging-market risk is taken into account, not in the cost of capital but in the lower expected value of future cash flows from weighting both scenarios by the assumed probabilities. The resulting value of the emerging-market plant (€1,917) is clearly below the value of its European sister plant (€2,222), using a weighted average cost of capital (WACC) of 7.5 percent.

We assumed for simplicity that if adverse economic conditions develop in the emerging market, they will do so in the first year of the plant's operation. In reality, of course, the investment will face a probability of domestic economic distress in each year of its lifetime. Modeling risk over time would require more complex calculations yet would not change the basic results. We also assumed

EXHIBIT 33.5   **Scenario DCF vs. Country Risk Premium DCF**

euros

Net present value for identical facilities in . . .

. . . a European market

Scenario approach

Cash flows in perpetuity[1]

	Probability	Year 1	2	3	4	...
"As usual"	100%	100	103	106	109	...
"Distressed"	0%					

Expected cash flows

	Year 1	2	3	4
	100	103	106	109

Cost of capital 7.5%
Net present value 2,222

Country risk premium approach

Cash flows in perpetuity[1]

	Year 1	2	3	4	...
"As usual"	100	103	106	109	...

Cost of capital 7.5%
Net present value 2,222

. . . an emerging market

Scenario approach

Cash flows in perpetuity[2]

	Probability	Year 1	2	3	4	...
"As usual"	75%	100	103	106	109	...
"Distressed"	25%	45	46	48	49	

Expected cash flows

	Year 1	2	3	4
	86	89	92	94

Cost of capital 7.5%
Net present value 1,917 → 86% of European NPV

Country risk premium approach

Cash flows in perpetuity[2]

	Year 1	2	3	4	...
"As usual"	100	103	106	109	...

Cost of capital 7.5%
Country risk premium 0.7%
Adjusted cost of capital 8.2%
Net present value 1,917 → 86% of European NPV

[1] Assuming perpetuity cash flow growth of 3%.
[2] Assuming perpetuity cash flow growth of 3% and recovery under distress of 45% of cash flows "as usual."

that the emerging-market business would face significantly lower cash flows in a local crisis but not wind up entirely worthless.

Country Risk Premium DCF Approach

The second approach is to add a country risk premium to the cost of capital for comparable investments in developed markets. You then apply the resulting discount rate to the cash flow projections in a business-as-usual scenario. The key drawback is that there is no objective way to establish the country risk premium. For our two-plant example, we can derive in hindsight what the premium should be to obtain the same result as under the scenario DCF approach. For us to arrive at a value of €1,917 for the emerging-market plant, the discount rate for the business-as-usual projections would have to be 8.2 percent, which translates to a country risk premium of 0.7 percent.

On occasion, practitioners make the mistake of adding the country risk premium to the cost of capital to discount the *expected* value of future cash flows, rather than to the promised cash flows of a business-as-usual scenario. The resulting value is too low because this approach accounts twice for the probability of a crisis.[4]

Scenario DCF as Prime Valuation Approach

Some surveys show that managers generally adjust for emerging-market risks by adding a risk premium to the discount rate.[5] Nonetheless, we recommend using the scenario DCF valuation as your primary approach and using the country risk premium and multiples approaches for triangulation. Scenario DCF valuation provides a more solid analytical foundation and a more robust understanding of the value than incorporating country risks in the discount rate.

One reason is that most country risks, including expropriation, devaluation, and war, are largely diversifiable (though not entirely, as the economic crises in 1998 and 2008 demonstrated). Consider the international consumer-goods player illustrated in Exhibit 33.6. Its returns on invested capital were highly volatile for individual emerging markets, but taken together, these markets were hardly more volatile than developed markets; the corporate portfolio diversified away most of the risks. Finance theory clearly indicates that the cost of capital should not reflect risk that can be diversified. This does not mean that diversifiable risk is irrelevant for a valuation: the possibility of adverse

[4] This is analogous to the error made by discounting the expected coupon and principal payments on a corporate bond at the promised yield (i.e., the yield to maturity) instead of the expected yield (i.e., the cost of debt).

[5] T. Keck, E. Levengood, and A. Longfield, "Using Discounted Cash Flow Analysis in an International Setting: A Survey of Issues in Modeling the Cost of Capital," *Journal of Applied Corporate Finance* 11, no. 3 (1998).

EXHIBIT 33.6 **Returns on Diverse Emerging-Market Portfolio**

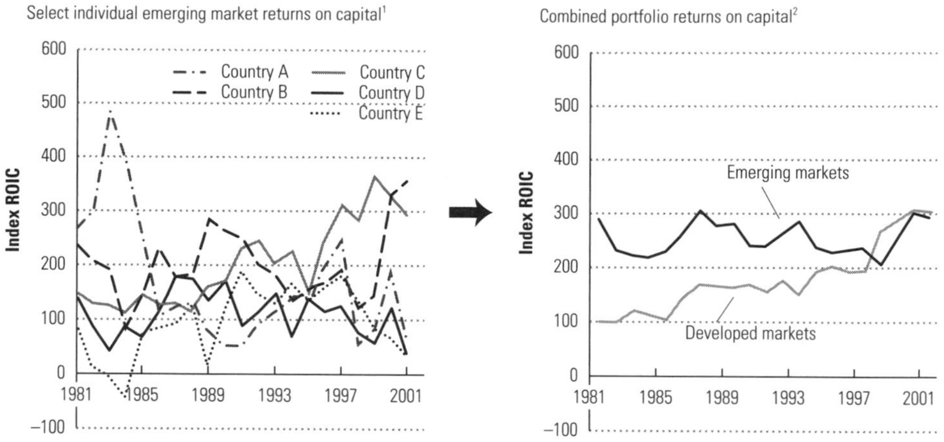

Select individual emerging market returns on capital[1]

Combined portfolio returns on capital[2]

[1] In stable currency and adjusted for local accounting differences.
[2] Combined portfolio included additional countries not reflected here.

Source: Company information.

future events will affect the level of expected cash flows, as in the example in Exhibit 33.5. But once this has been incorporated into the forecast for cash flows, there is no need for an additional markup of the cost of capital if the risk is diversifiable.

Another argument against a country risk premium is that many country risks apply unequally to companies in a given country. For example, banks are more likely to be affected than retailers. Some companies (raw-materials exporters) might benefit from a currency devaluation, while others (raw-materials importers) will be damaged. For the consumer goods company in Exhibit 33.6, economic crises had only a short-term impact on sales and profit as measured in the parent's domestic, stable currency. In most cases, after a year or two, sales and profits roughly regained their original growth trajectories. Applying the same risk premium to all companies in an emerging market could overstate the risk for some businesses and understate it for others.

Furthermore, there is no systematic method to calculate a country risk premium. In our example, we could reengineer this premium because the true value of the plant was already known from the scenario approach. In practice, the country risk premium is sometimes set at the spread of the local government debt rate[6] denominated in U.S. dollars and a U.S. government bond of similar

---

[6] This is also a promised yield rather than an expected yield on government bonds, further underlining the point that the cost of capital based on country risk premium should not be applied to expected cash flows, but to promised cash flows (those following a business-as-usual scenario in which no country risk materializes).

maturity. However, that is reasonable only if the returns on local government debt are highly correlated with returns on corporate investments.

From an operational viewpoint, when managers have to discuss emerging-market risks and their effect on cash flows in scenarios, they gain more insights than they would get from a so-called black-box addition to the discount rate. By identifying specific factors with a large impact on value, managers can plan to mitigate these risks. Last but not least, managers easily underestimate the impact that even a small country risk premium in the discount rate may have on valuations: in the example shown in Exhibit 33.6, setting a country risk premium of 3 percent would be equivalent to assuming a 70 percent probability of economic distress.

Constructing Cash Flow Scenarios and Probabilities

To use the scenario DCF approach, you need to construct at least two scenarios. The base case, or business-as-usual scenario, describes how the business will perform if no major crises occur. The downside scenario describes the financial results if a major crisis does occur.

We have already developed a set of macroeconomic and monetary assumptions for the ConsuCo base case. Now we need to do the same for the downside scenario. The major macroeconomic variables to forecast are GDP growth, inflation rates, foreign-exchange rates, and interest rates. These items must be linked in a way that reflects economic realities and should be included in the basic set of monetary assumptions underlying your valuation. For instance, when constructing a downside scenario with high inflation, make sure that the same inflation rates underlie the financial projections and cost of capital estimates for the company. Foreign-exchange rates should also reflect this pattern of inflation in the long run, because of purchasing power parity.

Given the assumptions for macroeconomic performance, you construct the industry scenarios largely in the same way as for valuations in developed markets. The major difference is the greater uncertainty involved in modeling outcomes under severe crises for which there may be no precedent.

To construct ConsuCo's downside scenario, we analyzed its performance under more adverse economic conditions in the past. Brazil has experienced several severe economic and monetary downturns, including an inflation rate that topped 2,000 percent in 1993. Judging by its key financial indicators, such as EBITDA to sales and real-terms sales growth, the impact on ConsuCo's business performance was significant. ConsuCo's cash operating margin was negative for four years, at around –10 to –5 percent, before recovering to its normal levels. In the same period, sales in real terms declined by 10 to 15 percent per year but grew sharply after the crisis. For the downside scenario projections, we assumed similar negative cash margins and a real-terms decline in sales for up to five years, followed by a gradual return to the long-term margins and

EXHIBIT 33.7 **ConsuCo: ROIC and Financials, Base Case vs. Downside Scenario**

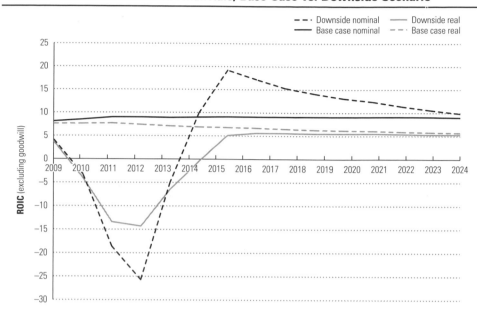

Financials (percent)	2009	2010	2011	2012	2013	2014
Nominal indicators: base case						
Sales growth	15.3	14.5	13.6	12.6	11.7	10.8
Adjusted EBITA/sales	6.1	6.2	6.4	6.4	6.4	6.4
NOPLAT/sales	4.4	4.5	4.6	4.5	4.4	4.4
Invested capital (excluding goodwill)/sales	54	53	51	51	50	49
Invested capital (including goodwill)/sales	62	59	57	56	55	54
ROIC (excluding goodwill)	8.1	8.5	9.0	9.0	8.9	9.0
Free cash flow (reais million)	(63)	(136)	(94)	(91)	(85)	113
Nominal indicators: downside scenario						
Sales growth	10.0	25.0	66.3	66.3	25.0	11.3
Adjusted EBITA/sales	3.1	−2.2	−8.0	−7.6	−1.1	3.3
NOPLAT/sales	2.3	−1.5	−5.8	−5.8	−1.1	2.2
Invested capital (excluding goodwill)/sales	55	47	31	22	21	22
Invested capital (including goodwill)/sales	63	54	35	25	23	24
ROIC (excluding goodwill)	4.2	−3.2	−18.6	−25.7	−5.0	9.9
Free cash flow (reais million)	(149)	(777)	(2,533)	(4,504)	(2,677)	(558)

growth assumed under the business-as-usual scenario. Exhibit 33.7 compares the nominal and real returns on invested capital under both scenarios.

In the downside scenario, the returns plummet and then increase as the recovery starts. After 2014, the nominal returns overtake those in the base case, as extreme inflation pushes up capital turnover. Of course, the nominal returns are artificially high, as a comparison with the real returns shows. The DCF value in the downside scenario will turn out to be just under half of the base case value. Free cash flow would be several billion reais negative, which would put a strong financing burden on ConsuCo: under such a scenario, ConsuCo would probably have to revise its growth strategy.

While estimating probabilities of economic distress for the cash flow scenarios is ultimately a matter of management judgment, there are indicators to suggest what probabilities would be reasonable. Historical data on previous crises can give some indication of the frequency and severity of country risk and the time required for recovery. Analyzing the changes in GDP of 20 emerging economies over the past 20 years, we found they had experienced economic distress about once in every five years (a real-terms GDP decline of more than 5 percent). This would suggest a 20 percent probability for a downside scenario.

Another source of information for estimating probabilities is prospective data from current government bond prices.[7] Recent academic research suggests that government default probabilities five years into the future in emerging markets such as Argentina were around 30 percent in nondistress years.[8] We estimated the probability of the downside scenario materializing for ConsuCo at around 30 percent.

ESTIMATING COST OF CAPITAL IN EMERGING MARKETS

Calculating the cost of capital in any country can be challenging, but for emerging markets, the challenge is an order of magnitude higher. In this section, we provide our fundamental assumptions, background on the important issues, and a practical way to estimate the components of the cost of capital.

Fundamental Assumptions

Our analysis adopts the perspective of a global investor—either a multinational company or an international investor with a diversified portfolio. Of course, some emerging markets are not yet well integrated with the global market, and local investors may face barriers to investing outside their home market. As a result, local investors cannot always hold well-diversified portfolios, and their cost of capital may be considerably different from that of a global investor. Unfortunately, there is no established framework for estimating the capital cost for local investors. Furthermore, as long as international investors have access to local investment opportunities, local prices will be based on an international cost of capital. Finally, according to empirical research, emerging markets have

[7] See, for example, D. Duffie and K. Singleton, "Modeling Term Structures of Defaultable Bonds," *Review of Financial Studies* 12 (1999): 687–720; and R. Merton, "On the Pricing of Corporate Debt: The Risk Structure of Interest Rates," *Journal of Finance* 29, no. 2 (1974): 449–470.

[8] See J. Merrick, "Crisis Dynamics of Implied Default Recovery Ratios: Evidence from Russia and Argentina," *Journal of Banking and Finance* 25, no. 10 (2001): 1921–1939.

become increasingly integrated into global capital markets.[9] We believe that this trend will continue and that most countries will gradually reduce foreign-investment restrictions for local investors in the long run.

Another assumption is that most country risks are diversifiable from the perspective of the global investor. We therefore need no additional risk premiums in the cost of capital for the risks encountered in emerging markets when discounting expected cash flows. Of course, if you choose to discount the promised cash flow from the business-as-usual scenario only, you should add a country risk premium.

Given these assumptions, the cost of capital in emerging markets should generally be close to a global cost of capital adjusted for local inflation and capital structure. It is also useful to keep some general guidelines in mind:

- *Use the capital asset pricing model (CAPM) to estimate the cost of equity in emerging markets.* The CAPM may be a less robust model for the less integrated emerging markets, but there is no better alternative model today. Furthermore, we believe it will become a better predictor of equity returns worldwide as markets continue to become more integrated.

- *There is no one right answer, so be pragmatic.* In emerging markets, there are often significant information and data gaps (e.g., for estimating betas or the risk-free rate in local currency). Be flexible as you assemble the available information piece by piece to build the cost of capital, and triangulate your results with country risk premium approaches and multiples.

- *Be sure monetary assumptions are consistent.* Ground your model in a common set of monetary assumptions to ensure that the cash flow forecasts and discount rate are consistent. If you are using local nominal cash flows, the cost of capital must reflect the local inflation rate embedded in the cash flow projections. For real-terms cash flows, subtract inflation from the nominal cost of capital.

- *Allow for changes in cost of capital.* The cost of capital in an emerging-market valuation may change, based on evolving inflation expectations, changes in a company's capital structure and cost of debt, or foreseeable reforms in the tax system. For example, in Argentina during the economic and monetary crisis of 2002, the short-term inflation rate was 30 percent. This could not have been a reasonable rate for a long-term cost of capital estimate, because such a crisis could not be expected to last forever.[10] In such cases, estimate the cost of capital on a year-by-year basis, following the underlying set of basic monetary assumptions.

---

[9] See, for example, C. Harvey, "The Drivers of Expected Returns in International Markets," *Emerging Markets Quarterly* (Fall 2000): 1–17.

[10] Annual consumer price inflation came down to around 5 percent in Argentina in 2004.

- *Don't mix approaches.* Use the cost of capital to discount the cash flows in a probability-weighted scenario approach. Do not add any risk premium, because you would then be double-counting risk. If you are discounting only future cash flows in a business-as-usual scenario, add a risk premium to the discount rate.

Estimating the Cost of Equity

To estimate the components of the cost of equity, use the standard CAPM described in Chapter 11.

Risk-free rate   In emerging markets, the risk-free rate is harder to estimate from government bonds than in developed markets. Three main problems arise. First, most of the government debt in emerging markets is not, in fact, risk free: the ratings on much of this debt are often well below investment grade. Second, it is difficult to find long-term government bonds that are actively traded with sufficient liquidity. Finally, the long-term debt that is traded is often in U.S. dollars, a European currency, or the Japanese yen, so it is not appropriate for discounting local nominal cash flows.

We recommend a straightforward approach. Start with a risk-free rate based on the 10-year U.S. government bond yield, as in developed markets. Add to this the projected difference over time between U.S. and local inflation, to arrive at a nominal risk-free rate in local currency.[11] Sometimes you can derive this inflation differential from the spread between local government bond yields denominated in local currency and those denominated in U.S. dollars.[12]

Beta   Sometimes practitioners calculate beta relative to the local market index. This is not only inconsistent from the perspective of a global investor, but also potentially distorted by the fact that the index in an emerging market will rarely be representative of a diversified economy. Instead, estimate industry betas relative to a well-diversified or global market index as recommended in Chapter 11.

To estimate the beta for ConsuCo, we examined its own beta and those of peer companies, just as we would in the case of a company from a developed market. We estimated the asset betas for retail companies in the United States and Europe but also for several larger retail companies in Latin America. We looked at long-term historical average betas to avoid distortion due to the recent economic crisis. The results are presented in Exhibit 33.8. The average beta of

---

[11] In this way, we do not model the U.S. term structure of interest rates. Technically, this should be included as well, but it will not make a large difference in the valuation.

[12] Technically, this is correct only if the emerging-market bonds are relatively low-risk, as for Chile and South Korea.

EXHIBIT 33.8 **ConsuCo: Estimating Beta**

Unlevered beta[1]

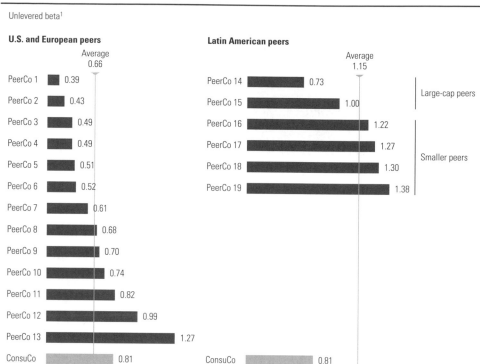

[1] Based on beta development since January 2005, with beta calculated from 5 years of monthly data in dollars.
Source: Datastream.

U.S. and European retail companies is around 0.7. For the Latin American peers, betas appear to be much higher, but large-cap retailers more similar in size to ConsuCo have betas in the range of 0.7 to 1.0. Given that ConsuCo's own beta estimate at 0.81 is also in that range, it seems appropriate to use a beta that is above the U.S. and European peer group. However, the Latin American peer group of large retailers is very small, because it is generally harder to find a sizable sample of publicly traded local peer companies in emerging markets. In this case, we suggest you triangulate your results as follows. First, identify the broader industry or sector index in the emerging market or region where the company is active. Second, examine whether there is any consistent markup over several years in the beta estimate for that index versus a U.S.-European index for the same sector. Third, add the estimated markup, if any, to the beta estimate for a sample of U.S.-European peer companies. We illustrate this process for ConsuCo next.

We examined the beta of the Brazilian market as a whole, as well as the broader consumer goods and services sector in Brazil (which includes more than retail companies). As shown in Exhibit 33.9, the Brazilian betas are in

EXHIBIT 33.9 **Equity Market and Consumer Sector Betas**

Global market index, U.S. dollars

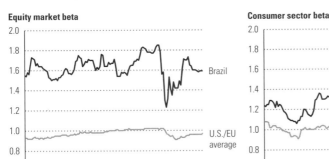

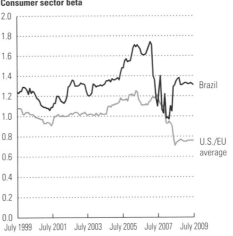

[1] Beta calculated from 5 years of monthly data in dollars.

Source: Datastream.

both cases well above the U.S. and European levels. The beta for the Brazilian market as a whole has been approximately 60 to 70 percent above the United States and Europe over the past decade. However, the industry composition of the Brazilian stock market is quite different from that of the United States and Europe, so this comparison does not reveal much. More meaningful is the comparison of the Brazilian consumer goods and services sector beta with the corresponding U.S. and European sectors. The same exhibit shows that in recent history, the beta for the Brazilian consumer goods and services sector was at a fairly consistent premium of around 25 percent relative to that of the United States and Europe.

Bringing all the evidence together, we estimate ConsuCo's beta at 0.8, which is in fact equal to its own beta estimate. It corresponds to a 25 percent premium[13] to the average asset beta for the U.S. and European retail peers and is in line with ConsuCo's larger Latin American peers.

Market risk premium As discussed in Chapter 30, excess returns of local equity markets over local bond returns are not a good proxy for the market

---

[13] Do not confuse this beta markup for Latin American retail companies with the country risk premium, discussed in the next section. The beta markup could reflect differences in business models or indeed a systematic component of country risk. In either case, it represents risk for which investors require a higher expected return. The recommended valuation approach remains unchanged: forecast future scenarios for cash flow and scenario probabilities, and then discount the expected future cash flows at the cost of capital based on your beta estimate.

EXHIBIT 33.10   **ConsuCo: Cost of Equity Estimate**

percent

	2009	2010	2011	2012	2013	2014	...	2019	...	2024
United States										
Inflation	0.1	1.1	1.3	1.5	1.7	1.9	...	1.9	...	1.9
Risk-free interest rate	4.0	4.0	4.0	4.0	4.0	4.0	...	4.0	...	4.0
Brazil										
Inflation	4.8	4.1	4.2	4.3	4.4	4.5	...	4.5	...	4.5
Risk-free interest rate[1]	8.9	7.1	7.0	6.9	6.8	6.7	...	6.7	...	6.7
Relevered beta	0.80	0.80	0.80	0.80	0.80	0.80	...	0.80	...	0.80
Market risk premium	5.0	5.0	5.0	5.0	5.0	5.0	...	5.0	...	5.0
Cost of equity	13.1	11.2	11.1	11.0	10.9	10.8	...	10.8	...	10.8

[1] Brazilian risk-free rate estimated as: [(1 + U.S. risk-free rate)(1 + U.S. inflation)]/(1 + Brazilian inflation) − 1.

Source: IMF World Economic Outlook, Bloomberg.

risk premium. This holds even more so for emerging markets, given the lack of diversification in the local equity market. Furthermore, the quality and length of available data on equity and bond market returns usually make such data unsuitable for long-term estimates. To use a market risk premium that is consistent with the perspective of a global investor, use a global estimate (as discussed in Chapter 11) of 4.5 to 5.5 percent.

In Exhibit 33.10, we summarize the nominal cost of equity calculation for ConsuCo in the base case scenario. In this scenario, we have assumed a fairly stable inflation rate for the Brazilian economy. Due to the global slowdown, near-term inflation is expected to decrease somewhat and come back to about 4.5 percent in 2014, beyond which we have assumed it to be constant. For the downside scenario (not shown in the exhibit), inflation projections follow a different trajectory, and the cost of capital for this scenario is adjusted accordingly. (The resulting cost of equity is shown later, in the WACC estimate table, Exhibit 33.12.)

Estimating the After-Tax Cost of Debt

In most emerging economies, there are no liquid markets for corporate bonds, so little or no market information is available to estimate the cost of debt. However, from an international investor's perspective, the cost of debt in local currency should simply equal the sum of the dollar (or euro) risk-free rate, the systematic part of the credit spread (see Chapter 11 for details on the systematic part of credit spread), and the inflation differential between local currency and dollars (or euros). Most of the country risk can be diversified away in a global bond portfolio. Therefore, the systematic part of the default risk is probably no larger than that of companies in international markets, and the cost of debt should not include a separate country risk premium.

EXHIBIT 33.11 **ConsuCo: Cost of Debt Estimate**

percent

	2009	2010	2011	2012	2013	2014	...	2019	...	2024
Risk-free interest rate	8.9	7.1	7.0	6.9	6.8	6.7	...	6.7	...	6.7
A to BBB credit spread	1.0	1.0	1.0	1.0	1.0	1.0	...	1.0	...	1.0
Cost of debt	9.9	8.1	8.0	7.9	7.8	7.7	...	7.7	...	7.7
Tax rate	34	34	34	34	34	34	...	34	...	34
After-tax cost of debt	6.5	5.3	5.3	5.2	5.1	5.1	...	5.1	...	5.1

Source: Bloomberg.

This explains why the funding costs of multinationals with extensive emerging-market portfolios—companies including Coca-Cola and Colgate-Palmolive—have a cost of debt that is no higher than that of their mainly U.S.-focused competitors.

Returning to the ConsuCo example, we calculated the cost of debt in Brazilian reais. ConsuCo does not have its own credit rating, but based on comparison with peers, we estimate that ConsuCo would probably have a rating of BBB to A. ConsuCo's cost of debt can be estimated as the sum of the risk-free rate in Brazilian reais plus the systematic credit spread for U.S. and European corporate bonds rated BBB to A versus the government bond yield, as shown in Exhibit 33.11. Of course, the inflation assumptions underlying the estimates for cost of debt should be consistent with those for the base case and the downside scenario.

The marginal tax rate in emerging markets can be very different from the effective tax rate, which often includes investment tax credits, export tax credits, taxes, equity or dividend credits, and operating loss credits. Few of these arrangements provide a tax shield on interest expense, and only those few should be incorporated in the WACC estimate. Other taxes or credits should be modeled directly in the cash flows. For ConsuCo, we used the Brazilian corporate income tax rate of 25 percent plus social contribution tax of 9 percent.

Estimating WACC

Having estimated the cost of equity and after-tax cost of debt, we need debt and equity weights to derive an estimate of the weighted average cost of capital. In emerging markets, many companies have unusual capital structures compared with their international peers. One reason is, of course, the country risk: the possibility of macroeconomic distress makes companies more conservative in setting their leverage. Another reason could be anomalies in the local debt or equity markets. In the long run, when the anomalies are corrected, the companies should expect to develop a capital structure similar to that of their

EXHIBIT 33.12 **ConsuCo: WACC Estimate**

percent

	2009	2010	2011	2012	2013	2014	...	2019	...	2024
Base case										
After-tax cost of debt	6.5	5.3	5.3	5.2	5.1	5.1	...	5.1	...	5.1
Cost of equity	13.1	11.2	11.1	11.0	10.9	10.8	...	10.8	...	10.8
Debt/enterprise value	30	30	30	30	30	30	...	30	...	30
WACC	11.1	9.4	9.3	9.2	9.1	9.0	...	9.0	...	9.0
Downside scenario										
After-tax cost of debt	6.5	19.7	53.7	53.5	19.2	5.4	...	5.1	...	5.1
Cost of equity	13.1	33.5	86.6	86.2	32.7	11.3	...	10.8	...	10.8
Debt/enterprise value	30	30	30	30	30	30	...	30	...	30
WACC	11.1	29.4	76.7	76.4	28.7	9.5	...	9.0	...	9.0

global competitors. You could forecast explicitly how the company evolves to a capital structure that is more similar to global standards. In that case, you should consider using the adjusted present value (APV) approach discussed in Chapter 6.

For the ConsuCo case, we set the capital structure close to the peer group average at a ratio of debt to enterprise value of 0.3, which is also in line with its long-term historical levels. Exhibit 33.12 summarizes the WACC estimates for the base case and the downside scenario in nominal terms. Note how the extreme inflation assumption underlying the downside scenario leads to a radically higher cost of capital in the crisis years until 2014, when it starts to fall.

Estimating the Country Risk Premium

If you are discounting business-as-usual cash flows instead of expected cash flows, you should add a country risk premium to the WACC, as we saw earlier in this chapter in the section on incorporating emerging-market risks in the valuation. There is no agreed-upon approach to estimating this premium, but we have some advice.

Do not simply use the sovereign risk premium The long-term sovereign risk premium equals the difference between a long-term (e.g., 10-year) U.S. government bond yield and a dollar-denominated local bond's stripped yield[14] with the same maturity. This difference will reasonably approximate the country risk premium only if the cash flows of the corporation being valued move closely in line with the payments on government bonds. This is not necessarily

[14] Some emerging markets' country debt is partially guaranteed by international institutions or backed by U.S. Treasury bonds. For these bonds, you need to estimate the yield on the nonguaranteed part of the bond, the stripped yield. Stripped yields are available from bond data suppliers.

the case. In the consumer goods or raw-materials sector, for example, cash flows are only weakly correlated with local government bond payments and are less volatile.

Understand estimates from different sources   Estimates for country risk premiums from different sources usually fall into a very wide range, because analysts use different methods.[15] But they frequently compensate for high estimates of country risk premiums by making aggressive forecasts for growth and ROIC.

An example is the valuation we undertook of a large Brazilian chemicals company. Using a local WACC of 10 percent, we reached an enterprise value of 4.0 to 4.5 times EBITDA. A second adviser was asked to value the company and came to a similar valuation—an EBITDA multiple of around 4.5—in spite of using a very high country risk premium of 11 percent on top of the WACC. The result was similar because the second adviser made performance assumptions that were extremely aggressive: real sales growth of almost 10 percent per year and a ROIC increasing to 46 percent in the long term. Such long-term performance assumptions are unrealistic for a commodity-based, competitive industry such as chemicals.

Be careful to avoid setting the country risk premium too high   Make sure you understand the economic implications of a high country risk premium. We believe that a country risk premium for Brazil is far below the premiums of 5 percent and higher that analysts typically use.

One reason is that current valuations in the stock market do not support the discount rates implied by higher risk premiums. We estimated the trading multiples of enterprise value to the 2009 forecasted EBITA for the 50 industrial companies in the Bovespa, the Brazilian equity market index. The median value for the multiple was 7.8 in September 2009. We estimated the implied WACC by means of a DCF valuation. We set the future long-term return on invested capital at 12 percent, approximately equal to the median historical ROIC for these companies from 2004 to 2008. Assuming future long-term inflation at 4.5 percent and real growth at 3.5 percent for the Brazilian economy as a whole, the WACC for the Brazilian market implied by the EBITA multiple of 7.8 is around 10.8 percent. The WACC estimated with the CAPM previously described is around 10.0 percent.[16] This would imply a country risk premium for Brazil of around 0.8 percent. Of course, this is not a precise estimate; as the Brazilian market goes up and down, the implied WACC and country risk premium would change as well. But it does suggest a country risk premium that is far below the 5 percent that many analysts currently use.

[15] For an overview, see, for example, L. Pereiro, *Valuation of Companies in Emerging Markets: A Practical Approach* (New York: John Wiley & Sons, 2002), 118.
[16] Based on a real risk-free rate of 2 percent, long-term inflation of 4.5 percent, a market risk premium of 5.0 percent, cost of debt of 7.7 percent, and a debt-to-capital ratio of 0.25.

The other reason for such a low country risk premium is that historical returns in the Brazilian stock market do not support a high premium. The average real-terms return on the Brazilian stock market between December 1994 and December 2008 was approximately 5.5 percent per year, far below the level that would support a substantial country risk premium.

CALCULATING AND INTERPRETING RESULTS

Given the estimates for cash flow and the cost of capital, we can discount the free cash flows for ConsuCo under the base case and the downside scenario. The resulting present values of operations are shown in Exhibit 33.13. Under each scenario, the valuation results are exactly the same for the nominal and real projections. The next step is to weight the valuation results by the scenario probabilities and derive the present value of operations. Finally, add the market

EXHIBIT 33.13   **ConsuCo: Scenario DCF Valuation**

reais, million

		2009	2010	2011	2012	2013	2014	...	2019	...	2024
	Base case										
	Nominal projections										
	Free cash flow	(63)	(136)	(94)	(91)	(85)	113	...	301	...	516
	WACC (percent)	11.1	9.5	9.3	9.2	9.1	9.0	...	9.0	...	9.0
	Real projections										
	Free cash flow	(60)	(125)	(83)	(77)	(68)	87	...	187	...	257
	WACC (percent)	6.0	5.1	4.9	4.7	4.5	4.4	...	4.4	...	4.4
	DCF value	14,451									
	Nonoperating assets	1,139									
Probability	Debt and debt equivalents	(5,605)									
70%	Equity value	9,985									
	Value per share	42.4									
	Downside scenario										
	Nominal projections										
	Free cash flow	(149)	(777)	(2,533)	(4,504)	(2,677)	(558)	...	250	...	834
	WACC (percent)	11.1	29.4	76.7	76.4	28.7	9.5	...	9.0	...	9.0
	Real projections										
	Free cash flow	(142)	(593)	(1,105)	(1,123)	(534)	(106)	...	38	...	102
	WACC (percent)	6.0	3.5	1.0	0.8	2.9	4.3	...	4.4	...	4.4
	DCF value	6,313									
	Nonoperating assets	1,139									
Probability	Debt and debt equivalents	(5,605)									
30%	Equity value	1,847									
	Value per share	7.9									

Value per share 32

EXHIBIT 33.14   **ConsuCo: Historical Share Price Development**

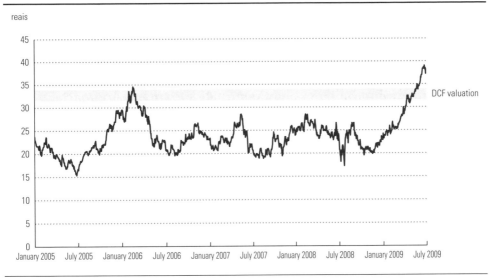

reais

Source: Datastream.

value of the nonoperating assets, and subtract the financial claims to get at the estimated equity value. The estimated equity value obtained for ConsuCo is about 32 reais per share, given a 30 percent probability of economic distress.

ConsuCo's share price, like the Brazilian stock market in general, has been quite volatile over recent years, as shown in Exhibit 33.14. Thus, you need to be careful in comparing the valuation outcome with the current (October 2009) share price. The share price development of ConsuCo clearly shows the rally since the beginning of 2009, following the first impact of the turnaround. Remember that the base case in our DCF model also assumes a recovery in sales productivity and growth performance. It is therefore not surprising that the DCF valuation comes out above the share price level of recent years. Obviously, any concerns around the continuation of results from the turnaround program would have significant implications for the DCF value.

In contrast to share prices in developed markets, share prices in emerging markets are not always reliable references for intrinsic value, for several reasons. First, free float is often limited, with large equity stakes in the hands of a small group of owners, leaving public shareholders with little or no influence. As a result, the share price in the market could well be below intrinsic value estimated using a DCF analysis. Also, liquidity in emerging-market stocks is often much lower than in developed markets. Share prices may not fully reflect intrinsic value, because not all information is incorporated in the market value. Finally, share prices in emerging markets are often much more volatile than in developed markets. The share price on any particular day could therefore be some way off intrinsic value.

ConsuCo has a primary listing on the Brazilian stock exchange. Turnover in the stock, as measured by the number of days to trade the free float, is not much different from typical levels in the United States and Europe. Still, because of the share price volatility, it is important to triangulate the DCF results with multiples and a country risk premium approach.

Triangulating with Multiples and Country Risk Premium Approach

To triangulate with multiples, we apply Chapter 14's guidance on how to do a best-practice multiples analysis to check valuation results. For the ConsuCo example, we compared the implied multiple of enterprise value over EBITDA with those of peer companies. All multiples are forward-looking multiples over EBITDA as expected for 2009. As Exhibit 33.15 illustrates, the implied multiple from our ConsuCo valuation is significantly higher than for U.S. and European peers but at the low end of the range for Latin American peers. Given the higher growth outlook for ConsuCo in the Brazilian market compared with that of large established chains in the United States and Europe (partly because of the relatively low penetration of durable goods in Brazil), the higher multiple is not surprising. Relative to regional peers, ConsuCo is already very well established and geographically widespread. It also has somewhat more exposure than listed peers have to the lower-growth food segment. Hence, a multiple at the low end of the range is not unreasonable.

EXHIBIT 33.15   **ConsuCo: Multiples Analysis vs. Peers**

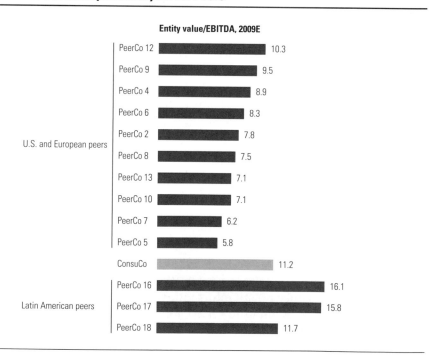

Entity value/EBITDA, 2009E

U.S. and European peers

PeerCo 12	10.3
PeerCo 9	9.5
PeerCo 4	8.9
PeerCo 6	8.3
PeerCo 2	7.8
PeerCo 8	7.5
PeerCo 13	7.1
PeerCo 10	7.1
PeerCo 7	6.2
PeerCo 5	5.8

ConsuCo	11.2

Latin American peers

PeerCo 16	16.1
PeerCo 17	15.8
PeerCo 18	11.7

The last part of the triangulation consists of a valuation of ConsuCo using a country risk premium approach. Earlier in this chapter, we estimated the country risk premium for Brazil at around 0.8 percent. Discounting the business-as-usual scenario at the cost of capital plus this country risk premium leads to a value per share of 20 reais, significantly below the 32-reais result obtained in the scenario DCF approach (more than 35 percent lower). The reason for this gap lies in ConsuCo's cash flow profile, and it highlights why a scenario approach is preferable to using a discount rate reflecting a country risk premium. Due to ConsuCo's high growth in the near term and corresponding investments, its free cash flows are negative for the first five years, pushing value creation forward in time. But the further ahead a company's positive cash flows, the more those cash flows are penalized by the country risk premium approach: a markup in WACC cumulates over time, making long-term risk adjustment exert more downward pressure on present value than near-term adjustment. This does not happen in a scenario approach, because the scenario probabilities affect all future cash flows equally. If ConsuCo were to have a lower-growth outlook, the country risk premium approach would produce a valuation much closer to the valuation from the scenario approach.

Note that irrespective of ConsuCo's cash flow profile, a risk premium of 5 percent (as is typically used in Brazil) would either result in unrealistically low valuations relative to current share price and peer group multiples, or require an unrealistically bullish forecast of future performance.

SUMMARY

To value companies in emerging markets, we use concepts similar to the ones applied to developed markets. However, the application of these concepts can be somewhat different. Inflation, which is often high in emerging markets, should be factored into the cash flow projections, using a combination of insights from both real and nominal financial analyses. Emerging-market risks such as macroeconomic or political crises can be incorporated by following the scenario DCF approach. This develops alternative scenarios for future cash flows, discounts the cash flows at the cost of capital without a country risk premium, and then weights the DCF values by the scenario probabilities. The cost of capital estimates for emerging markets build on the assumption of a global risk-free rate, market risk premium, and beta, following guidelines similar to those used for developed markets. Since the values of companies in emerging markets are often more volatile than values in developed markets, we recommend triangulating the scenario DCF results with two other valuations: one based on discounting cash flows developed in a business-as-usual projection but using a cost of capital that includes a country risk premium, and another valuation based on multiples.

REVIEW QUESTIONS

1. Define *purchasing power parity*. What is the importance of purchasing power parity when you are trying to establish value for a company located in an emerging market?

2. Identify four risks associated with emerging markets that affect enterprise discounted cash flow (DCF) valuation. How should these risks be treated within the enterprise DCF model?

3. Describe the benefits of a scenario DCF valuation model. What factors should be considered when constructing scenario parameters?

4. You are computing the value of a firm headquartered in an emerging market. Identify the factors unique to an emerging market that need to be evaluated when estimating the cost of equity using the Capital Asset Pricing Model (CAPM).

5. Volatilities for individual stock and market indexes in emerging economies are typically higher than those for U.S. stocks and indexes. Should that mean that the cost of capital for investments in emerging economies is higher, too? Explain your answer.

6. Discuss the relative merits of including risk adjustments in cash flow or in discount rates—especially for high-growth companies in emerging markets—and show how both approaches can be aligned.

7. To estimate the beta for a Brazilian telecommunications company, you have collected a sample of telecom peers in Latin America and Asia and peers in the United States and Europe. The median beta versus a world index is around 1.5 for the Latin American and Asian peers and around 0.9 for the U.S. and European peers (both subsamples are sufficiently large). What would you have to believe to choose either the Latin American/Asian peer beta or the U.S./European peer beta? What additional analyses would you undertake to test either choice?

8. Many emerging economies have restrictions on capital outflows to protect their growth and stability; for example, they may impose high taxes on repatriated profits by foreign companies. Where and how would you include such taxes in the DCF valuation of your company's subsidiary in a high-growth emerging economy, if the taxes are (1) levied in perpetuity or (2) gradually decreased to zero over the next 10 years as the economy starts to mature?

34

Valuing High-Growth Companies

Valuing high-growth, high-uncertainty companies is a challenge; some practitioners have even described it as hopeless. We find, however, that the valuation principles in this book work well even for high-growth companies. The best way to value high-growth companies (those whose organic revenue growth exceeds 15 percent annually) is with a discounted cash flow (DCF) valuation, buttressed by economic fundamentals and probability-weighted scenarios.

Although scenario-based DCF may sound suspiciously retro, it works where other methods fail, since the core principles of economics and finance apply even in uncharted territory. Alternatives, such as price-earnings multiples, generate imprecise results when earnings are highly volatile, cannot be used when earnings are negative, and provide little insight into what drives the company's valuation. More important, these shorthand methods cannot account for the unique characteristics of each company in a fast-changing environment. Another alternative, real options, still requires estimates of the long-term revenue growth rate, long-term volatility of revenue growth, and profit margins—the same requirements as for discounted cash flow.[1]

Since DCF remains our preferred method, why dedicate a chapter to valuing high-growth companies? Although the components of valuation are the same, their order and emphasis differ from the traditional process for established companies, and this chapter details the differences. Instead of analyzing historical performance, start by examining the expected long-term development of the company's markets and then work backward. In addition, since long-term projections are highly uncertain, always create multiple scenarios. Each scenario details how the market might develop under different condi-

---

[1] In Chapter 32, we demonstrate how real options can lead to a more theoretically robust valuation than scenario analysis. But unlike scenario analysis, real-options models are complex and obscure the competitive dynamics driving a company's value.

tions. Nevertheless, while scenario-based DCF techniques can help bound and quantify uncertainty, they will not make it disappear: high-growth companies have volatile stock prices for sound reasons.

VALUATION PROCESS FOR HIGH-GROWTH COMPANIES

When valuing an established company, the first step is to analyze historical performance. But in the case of a high-growth company, historical financial results provide limited clues about future prospects. Therefore, begin with the *future*, not with the past. Focus on sizing the potential market, predicting the level of sustainable profitability, and estimating the investments necessary to achieve scale. To make these estimates, choose a point well into the future, at a time when the company's financial performance is likely to stabilize, and begin forecasting.

Once you have developed a long-term future view, work backward to link the future to current performance. Accounting records of current performance are likely to mix together investments and expenses, so when possible, capitalize hidden investments, even those expensed under traditional accounting rules. This is challenging, as the distinction between investment and expense is often unobservable and subjective.

Given the uncertainty associated with high-growth companies, do not rely on a single long-term forecast. Describe the market's development in terms of multiple scenarios, including total size, ease of competitive entry, and so on. When you build a comprehensive scenario, be sure all forecasts, including revenue growth, profitability margins, and required investment, are consistent with the underlying assumptions of the particular scenario. Apply probabilistic weights to each scenario, using weights that are consistent with long-term historical evidence on corporate growth. As we saw during the Internet run-up, valuations that rely too heavily on unrealistic assessments can lead to overestimates of value and to strategic errors.

Start from the Future

When valuing high-growth companies, start by thinking about what the industry and company might look like as the company evolves from its current high-growth, uncertain condition to a sustainable, moderate-growth state in the future. Then interpolate back to current performance. The future state should be defined and bounded by measures of operating performance, such as penetration rates, average revenue per customer, and sustainable gross margins. Next, determine how long hyper growth will continue before growth stabilizes to normal levels. Since most high-growth companies are start-ups, stable economics probably lie at least 10 to 15 years in the future.

EXHIBIT 34.1 **OpenTable: Revenues**

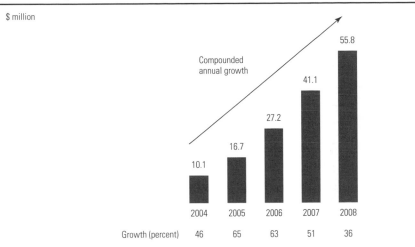

$ million

Compounded
annual growth

55.8

41.1

27.2

16.7

10.1

	2004	2005	2006	2007	2008
Growth (percent)	46	65	63	51	36

To demonstrate the specifics of the valuation process, let's examine OpenTable, an online provider of restaurant reservations. Between 2004 and 2008, revenues grew from $10 million to almost $56 million, representing a compounded annual growth rate of 53 percent per year (see Exhibit 34.1). As of 2008, approximately 34 million diners had used OpenTable to book reservations at 10,335 restaurants. More than 90 percent of the company's revenues are generated in the United States, but the company now handles reservations for restaurants in Germany, Japan, and the United Kingdom as well.

To estimate the size of a potential market, start by assessing how the company fulfills a customer need. Then determine how the company generates (or plans to generate) revenue. Understanding how a start-up makes money is critical. Many young companies build a product or service that meets the customer's need, but cannot identify how to monetize the value they provide. In the case of OpenTable, the company provides the end customer with an online up-to-date list of available restaurant seating near the customer's location. The list can be sorted by cuisine, price, and other features, and each restaurant provides a description of its establishment. With a single click, the user can select a restaurant, select a time for seating, and get directions. Although OpenTable provides a convenient service to the customer, it is not clear the customer will pay for this service. Most restaurant names appear on one site or another, so the customer can search for a restaurant and then dial the restaurant directly.

Instead of charging the end customer, OpenTable licenses a product called Electronic Reservation Book (ERB). Since many restaurants do not have computer technology, OpenTable installs a proprietary computer system that manages reservations, manages table seating, recognizes guests, and markets through e-mail. In return, the restaurant pays a one-time installation fee of $800, a monthly subscription fee averaging $250 per month, and seated-diner

EXHIBIT 34.2 **OpenTable: Business Model**

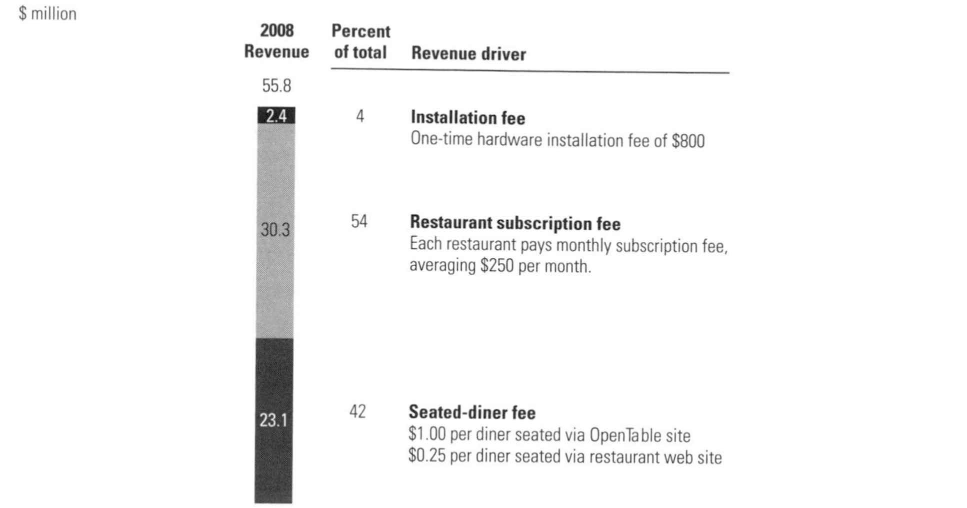

$ million

2008 Revenue	Percent of total	Revenue driver
55.8		
2.4	4	**Installation fee** One-time hardware installation fee of $800
30.3	54	**Restaurant subscription fee** Each restaurant pays monthly subscription fee, averaging $250 per month.
23.1	42	**Seated-diner fee** $1.00 per diner seated via OpenTable site $0.25 per diner seated via restaurant web site

fees of $1 per diner seated via OpenTable and 25 cents per diner seated via the restaurant's web site.[2] Exhibit 34.2 presents OpenTable's 2008 revenue breakdown by installation fees, subscription fees, and seated-diner fees.

Using these drivers as a guide, start by estimating the potential market for OpenTable, product by product. For the purpose of exposition, this chapter examines only one source of revenue in detail: restaurant subscription fees. We estimated the remaining two products (and future products) using a similar methodology, although the analysis is not presented here.

Sizing the market To forecast the potential market for subscription fees, first estimate the potential number of restaurants OpenTable can serve. According to management, OpenTable currently serves 30 percent of the 30,000 U.S.-based *reservation-taking* restaurants. The number of all U.S. restaurants is not a helpful anchor, since most U.S. restaurants serve fast food; the customer merely walks in and orders. All restaurants constitute the *total* market, whereas reservation-taking restaurants constitute the *addressable* market, a critical distinction in market sizing.

Since growth in restaurants matches that of the U.S. economy, the majority of OpenTable's subscription growth will come from higher penetration. To set an upper bound on the estimate of OpenTable's potential market share, consider San Francisco, the company's first market. As of 2008, the company served 60 percent of San Francisco reservation-taking restaurants—twice its

[2] To incentivize diners to use OpenTable and not book directly through the restaurant, OpenTable provides them with reward points for each booking.

EXHIBIT 34.3 **OpenTable: Market Share and Potential Market, 2008**

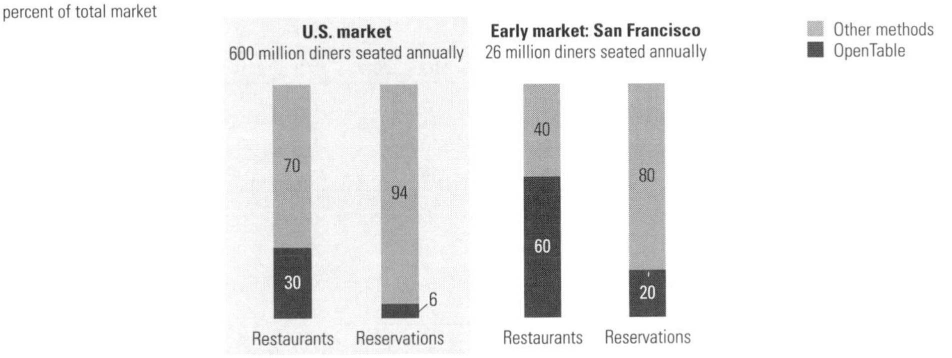

percent of total market

Source: Company reports.

share of the addressable U.S. market (see Exhibit 13.3). In our forecasts, we assume OpenTable can reach a 60 percent penetration nationwide by 2018.

For most start-ups, forecasting a 60 percent share is extremely aggressive, since additional competition is likely to enter the market. For this business, however, the largest company is likely to capture the entire online market. Restaurants desire a partner that generates the most traffic, and diners desire a web site with the most restaurants. This business is similar to other software businesses, such as Microsoft's Windows operating system and IBM's MVS mainframe software, both of which still retain more than 80 percent of their respective markets.

OpenTable estimates the number of reservation-taking restaurants in 2008 at 30,000. If the number of restaurants grows at 2 percent per year (twice the rate of population growth), this leads to an estimate of just over 36,500 restaurants by 2018. At a 60 percent share, OpenTable would serve 21,900 restaurants by 2018 in the United States. OpenTable has also entered international markets. For simplicity, we assume the growth in international restaurants will match that of U.S. restaurants, delayed by six years.[3] Therefore by year-end 2018 total restaurants served are projected at 37,930 restaurants.

Next, to convert restaurants served into total subscription revenues, multiply the number of restaurants by the estimated subscription revenue per restaurant. In 2018, OpenTable is projected to generate $431 per month, or $5,172 per year, in subscription revenue. Multiplying $5,172 per restaurant by average 2018 restaurants of 36,840 leads to a 2018 forecast of $190.7 million in restaurant subscription revenues. We present this calculation in Exhibit 34.4.

---

[3] If we were valuing OpenTable for the purpose of investment, we would build a detailed international forecast, country by country. Since we are examining OpenTable to demonstrate the process of valuation, we simplify the forecast methodology.

EXHIBIT 34.4 **OpenTable: Partial Revenue Model**

$ million

| | 2008 | | | | | Forecast | | | | | |
		2009	2010	2011	2012	2013	2014	2015	2016	2017	2018
Revenue											
Installation revenues	2.4	3.0	3.7	4.6	4.9	4.9	5.0	4.2	4.9	4.4	4.1
Restaurant subscription revenues	30.3	40.5	51.2	66.3	82.3	99.0	116.3	134.2	152.8	172.0	190.7
Seated diner revenues	23.1	28.4	35.7	43.7	54.1	63.9	73.8	83.5	93.0	103.0	112.0
Total revenues	55.8	72.0	90.7	114.6	141.2	167.9	195.0	221.8	250.7	279.4	306.8
Number of restaurants (year-end)											
U.S.	9,295	10,760	12,730	14,460	16,030	17,430	18,640	19,680	20,560	21,290	21,900
International	1,040	1,611	2,423	3,873	5,583	7,391	9,295	10,760	12,730	14,460	16,030
Number of restaurants	10,335	12,371	15,153	18,333	21,613	24,821	27,935	30,440	33,290	35,750	37,930
Restaurant subscription revenues											
Average restaurants during year	9,098	11,353	13,762	16,743	19,973	23,217	26,378	29,188	31,865	34,520	36,840
Subscription revenue per month (dollars)	277	297	310	330	343	355	367	383	400	415	431
Restaurant subscription revenues	30.3	40.5	51.2	66.3	82.3	99.0	116.3	134.2	152.8	172.0	190.7
Share of U.S. restaurants (percent)	31	35	41	45	49	53	55	57	58	59	60

Source: Morgan Stanley, Think Equity LLC, company reports.

Assessing reasonableness   Sizing the potential market for OpenTable requires numerous inputs, each of which is uncertain. Small miscalculations in individual forecast items can compound into large mistakes in aggregate. Therefore, search for clever checks to test your forecast. To put OpenTable's revenue growth in perspective, compare it with the first five years of revenue growth for Internet companies founded in the 1990s, once each company hit $10 million in revenue (see Exhibit 34.5). Between 2004 and 2008, OpenTable grew revenues from $10.1 million to $55.8 million, which matches the median Internet company passing the same threshold.[4] By 2012, research analysts project OpenTable to grow revenues to $141.2 million, slightly higher than the median Internet company but well within the bounds of the distribution.

Estimating operating margin, capital intensity, and ROIC   With a revenue forecast in hand, next forecast long-term operating margins, required capital investments, and return on invested capital (ROIC). To estimate operating margin, triangulate between internal cost projections (versus market prices) and operating margins for established players. For internal cost projections, we rely on company projections presented in Exhibit 34.6. Senior management recently discussed how economies of scale will lead to target margins between

---

[4] Median revenue provides a better comparison than average revenue. Average revenue is distorted upward by a handful of superstars, such as Amazon.com. The average is also affected by companies that fail, making any direct comparison awkward.

EXHIBIT 34.5 **Revenue Growth after Reaching $10 Million Threshold**[1]

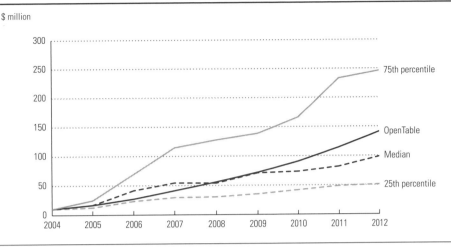

[1] Sample of 75 publicly traded Internet start-ups, normalized to OpenTable.

30 and 35 percent. Management forecast that every expense (operations, sales, technology, etc.) will drop as the company reaches scale.

OpenTable management projects eventual margins of 30 to 35 percent, but are these realistic? To address this question, examine other Internet companies that provide a similar conduit between consumers and businesses. For instance, online travel brokers (brokers that book reservations for air travel and hotels on behalf of consumers) have grown into a multibillion-dollar industry over the past 15 years. Exhibit 34.7 presents financial data for three public companies that dominate the online travel industry: Expedia, Priceline.com, and Orbitz Worldwide. For the three companies, there is a direct correlation

EXHIBIT 34.6 **OpenTable: Current and Target Margins**

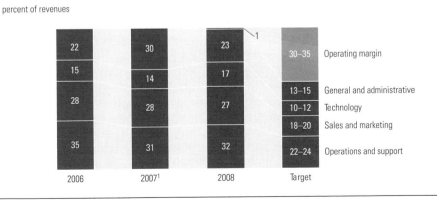

[1] Total sums to 103 percent of revenues because of operating losses.

Source: Company reports.

EXHIBIT 34.7 **Online Brokers: Key Value Drivers, 2007**

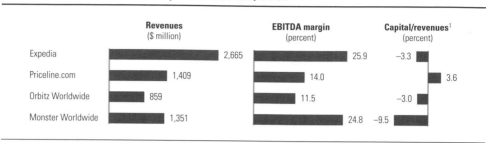

	Revenues ($ million)	EBITDA margin (percent)	Capital/revenues[1] (percent)
Expedia	2,665	25.9	−3.3
Priceline.com	1,409	14.0	3.6
Orbitz Worldwide	859	11.5	−3.0
Monster Worldwide	1,351	24.8	−9.5

[1] Capital turnover excludes goodwill and acquired intangibles and net merchant bookings.

between total revenues and margin. The largest company, Expedia, generates a 25.9 percent EBITDA margin, whereas the smallest player, Orbitz Worldwide, generates only 11.5 percent.[5] Given that OpenTable is a market leader with little competition, exceeding Expedia's EBITDA margin of 25.9 percent appears reasonable.

Perhaps a better comparison is Monster Worldwide. Monster provides online career services that match job seekers with potential employers. Unlike the highly competitive travel industry, Monster competes in a market where the largest player has a natural advantage. Similar to OpenTable's market, job seekers want to affiliate with a site that contains the most job postings, and employers want to post employment on a site with the most candidates. By 2007, Monster generated more than $1.3 billion in revenue and EBITDA margins of 24.8 percent. Based on this data, 30 to 35 percent appears somewhat aggressive. What prevents Monster Worldwide from reaching margins above 25 percent? Answering this question could provide a key insight concerning OpenTable's future.

To convert after-tax operating profit into cash flow, we next forecast capital requirements. Most businesses require significant capital to grow. This is not the case for OpenTable. In 2008, Open Table generated $5.5 million of capital on $55.8 million of revenues.[6] This is because operating liabilities, which include accounts payable and customer prepayments, exceed operating assets like property and equipment. Can OpenTable expect operations to continue providing capital? An analysis of other online companies says yes. Three of the four companies presented in Exhibit 34.7 have negative invested capital. Similar to OpenTable, Monster Worldwide generates 9.5 cents in capital for every $1 in revenue.

---

[5] In the online travel industry, most analysts analyze margin using earnings before interest, taxes, depreciation, and amortization (EBITDA). To remain consistent with their analysis, we do the same.

[6] Nearly every company invests capital to grow and consequently has positive invested capital. In a few cases, such as OpenTable, a company can have negative invested capital. This occurs when stakeholders such as customers, suppliers, and employees provide more capital than is needed for receivables, inventory, property, and equipment. To compute invested capital, we used the methodology outlined in Chapter 7.

With positive operating profits and negative invested capital, return on invested capital (ROIC) is no longer meaningful—mathematically, it is infinite. But what about the competition? If ROIC is infinite, shouldn't competitors enter and eventually force prices down? Perhaps, but the characteristics of OpenTable's market have created significant barriers. Second, because of rigid accounting rules, invested capital is probably understated, especially if early losses are reclassified as investments. We examine this issue in the next section.

Work Backward to Current Performance

Having completed a forecast for total market size, market share, operating margin, and capital intensity, reconnect the long-term forecast back to current performance. To do this, you have to assess the speed of transition from current performance to future long-term performance. Estimates must be consistent with economic principles and industry characteristics. For instance, from the perspective of operating margin, how long will fixed costs dominate variable costs, resulting in low margins? Concerning capital turnover, what scale is required before revenues rise faster than capital? As scale is reached, will competition drive down prices? Often, there are more questions than answers.

To determine the speed of transition from current performance to target performance, examine the historical progression for similar companies. Unfortunately, analyzing historical financial performance for high-growth companies is often misleading, because long-term investments for high-growth companies tend to be intangible. Under current accounting rules, these investments must be expensed. Therefore, both early accounting profits and invested capital will be understated. With so little formal capital, many companies have unreasonably high ROICs as soon as they become profitable.

Consider Internet retailer Amazon.com. In 2003, the company had an accumulated deficit (the opposite of retained earnings) of $3.0 billion, even though revenues and gross profits (revenues minus direct costs) had grown steadily. How could this occur? Marketing- and technology-related expenses significantly outweighed gross profits. In the years between 1999 and 2003, Amazon.com expensed $742 million in marketing and $1.1 billion in technology development. In 1999, Amazon's marketing expense was 10 percent of revenue. In contrast, Best Buy spends about 2 percent of revenue for advertising. One might argue that the 8 percent differential is more appropriately classified as a brand-building activity, not a short-term revenue driver. Consequently, ROIC overstates the potential return on capital for new entrants because it ignores historically expensed investment.

Develop Scenarios

A simple and straightforward way to deal with uncertainty associated with high-growth companies is to use probability-weighted scenarios. Even

EXHIBIT 34.8 **OpenTable: Key Drivers by Scenario, 2018 Forecast**

	Total revenues ($ million)	Total restaurants	Average subscription fee ($ per month)	Operating margin (percent)	Description
Scenario A					
Product extension	510	37,900	890	34	Installations grow as planned and subscription revenues double as new products are introduced.
Scenario B					
Base case	310	37,900	430	31	U.S. and international markets grow as planned. Margins stabilize at 31%.
Scenario C					
Slow international penetration	220	27,000	430	31	U.S. market continues to grow as planned, but international market fails to meet expectations.

developing just a few scenarios makes the critical assumptions and interactions more transparent than other modeling approaches, such as real options and Monte Carlo simulation.

To develop probability-weighted scenarios, estimate a future set of financials for a full range of outcomes, some optimistic, some pessimistic. For OpenTable, we have developed three potential scenarios for 2018, summarized in Exhibit 34.8.

In scenario A, we assume OpenTable progresses better than expected. The company parlays reservation management into general restaurant management, including food and beverage management, staffing, and accounting systems. By replacing competitors, OpenTable is able to more than double expected subscription fees for 2018, from $430 per restaurant to $890 per restaurant. This assessment leads to an estimated equity valuation of $1,140 million.

In scenario B, our base scenario, revenues grow to $310 million, restaurants served grow to 37,900, subscription fees average $430 per restaurant, and operating margins rise to 31 percent. In this scenario, OpenTable has an estimated equity value equal to $719 million.

Scenario C assumes that OpenTable generates only $220 million in revenue by 2018 because the international expansion goes poorly. Although the company has grown in the United Kingdom, Germany, and Japan, the company withdrew from France and Spain in 2008. If international growth is sluggish, the company will capture fewer restaurants. Over the short term, margins will stumble, only to rebound as OpenTable focuses on successful markets. In this scenario, OpenTable has an equity value of $545 million.[7]

---

[7] In pessimistic scenarios, the value of debt can exceed operating value. In these cases, set debt equal to operating value and value equity at zero. For more on scenario analysis and its impact on financial claims, see Chapter 13.

EXHIBIT 34.9 **OpenTable: Probability-Weighted Expected Value**

Scenario	Intrinsic equity valuation ($ million)	×	Probability (percent)	=	Contribution to equity valuation ($ million)
Product extension	1,140		20		228
Base case	719		50		360
International expansion fails	545		30		164
			100		751
			Millions of shares		22.0
			Value per share		34.2

Weight Scenarios Consistently with Historical Evidence

To derive current equity value for OpenTable, weight the potential equity value from each scenario by its estimated likelihood of occurrence. Exhibit 34.9 lists the potential equity value and the probability of occurrence for each scenario. To estimate the company's current equity value, find the sum of each scenario's contribution. Based on our probability assessments, we estimate OpenTable's equity value at $751 million and value per share at $34. In May 2009, OpenTable went public. Shares closed at $31.89 on the first day of trading.

Scenario probabilities are unobservable and highly subjective. As a result, the final valuation will be quite sensitive to probability weightings. Thus, any set of forecasts built on fundamental economic analysis—such as market size, market share, and competitor margins—should be calibrated against the historical performance of other high-growth companies. Otherwise, assigning too high a weight to an implausible scenario could make the valuation too high (or it will be too low if you are overly conservative).

UNCERTAINTY IS HERE TO STAY

By adapting the DCF approach, we can generate reasonable valuations for dramatically changing businesses. But investors and companies entering fast-growth markets like those related to the Internet should expect to face huge uncertainties. To see this, look at what could happen under our three scenarios to an investor who holds a share of OpenTable stock for five years after buying it in 2009 for $31.89. To facilitate the calculation, we assume the investor gradually learns about the most likely scenario.

If scenario A plays out, the investor will earn a 19 percent annual return, and as of 2009 the market will seem to have undervalued OpenTable. An annual return of 19 percent may not seem very high, but recall that much of OpenTable's potential success is already incorporated into the company's stock price. If scenario C plays out, the investment will generate only 3 percent a year,

EXHIBIT 34.10 **OpenTable and S&P 500: Share Price Volatility**

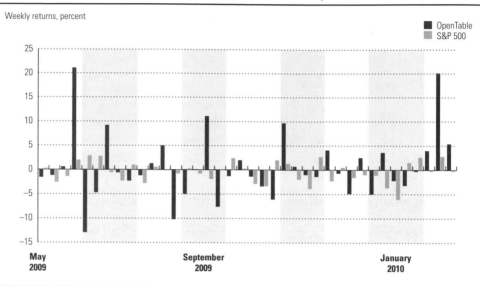

and it will appear that the company was overvalued in 2009. Going forward, these high or low potential returns should not be interpreted as implying that the current share price was irrational; they merely reflect uncertainty about the future.

Accurately predicting which scenario will occur is a laudable goal, but achieving it is unlikely. Investors struggle to incorporate new information every day, and this leads to high volatility in the share prices of young companies. OpenTable, for instance, had three times the volatility of the S&P 500 during its first year of trading (see Exhibit 34.10). As OpenTable's prospects begin to stabilize, however, it should be possible to tighten the range of potential outcomes. These gains in precision should be reflected in a decrease in the stock's volatility.

A great deal of uncertainty is associated with the problem of identifying the eventual winner in a competitive field. History shows that a few players will win big, while the vast majority will toil away in obscurity. It is difficult to predict which companies will prosper and which will not. Neither investors nor companies can eliminate this uncertainty: that is why advisers tell investors to diversify their portfolios, and why companies do not pay cash when acquiring young, high-growth firms.

SUMMARY

The emergence of the Internet and related technologies created impressive value for some high-growth enterprises at the end of the twentieth century. It also raised questions about the sanity of a stock market that appeared to assign higher value to companies, the more their losses mounted. But as this chapter demonstrates, the DCF approach remains an essential tool for understanding the value of high-growth companies. You must make some adaptations when valuing these companies: starting from the future rather than the present when making your forecast, thinking in terms of probabilities, and understanding the economics of the business model compared with peers. Though you cannot reduce the volatility of these companies, at least you can understand it.

REVIEW QUESTIONS

1. Explain how the process of valuing a high-growth company differs from valuing an established company.

2. How does the total market for a new product differ from a company's addressable market? Which market is more relevant for forecasting a company's revenues?

3. For a company with a new product, how can you estimate its potential market share?

4. How do you estimate the potential margin and capital turnover for a young, high-growth company? Are the company's current margin and capital turnover relevant?

5. Why do most young, high-growth companies have negative earnings?

6. Last year, GrowthCo traded at $20 per share. Over the past 12 months, the company's share price rocketed to $60 per share. Does this mean the share price was misvalued last year?

35

Valuing Cyclical
Companies

A cyclical company is one whose earnings demonstrate a repeating pattern of significant increases and decreases. The earnings of such companies, including those in the steel, airline, paper, and chemical industries, fluctuate because of large changes in the prices of their products. In the airline industry, earnings cyclicality is linked to broader macroeconomic trends. In the paper industry, cyclicality is largely driven by industry factors, typically related to capacity. Volatile earnings within the cycle introduce additional complexity into the valuation of these cyclical companies. For example, historical performance must be assessed in the context of the cycle, and a decline in recent performance does not necessarily indicate a long-term negative trend, but rather a shift to a different part of the cycle.

In this chapter, we explore the valuation issues particular to cyclical companies. We start with an examination of how the share prices of cyclical companies behave. This leads to a suggested approach to valuing these companies, as well as possible implications for managers.

SHARE PRICE BEHAVIOR

The share prices of companies with cyclical earnings tend to be more volatile than those of less cyclical companies. But their discounted cash flow (DCF) valuations are much more stable. So are cyclical companies exceptions to the rule that market values generally track return on invested capital (ROIC) and growth (see Chapter 15)?

When Market and DCF Valuations Diverge

Suppose you were using the DCF approach to value a cyclical company and had perfect foresight about the industry cycle. Would the company's value and earnings behave similarly? No, a succession of DCF values would exhibit much lower volatility than the earnings or cash flows. DCF reduces future expected cash flows to a single value. As a result, any single year is unimportant. For a cyclical company, the high cash flows cancel out the low cash flows. Only the long-term trend really matters.

To illustrate, the business cycle of Company A is 10 years. Exhibit 35.1, Part 1, shows the company's hypothetical cash flow pattern. It is highly volatile, containing both positive and negative cash flows. Discounting the future free cash flows at 10 percent produces the succession of DCF values in Exhibit 35.1, Part 2.

Exhibit 35.1, Part 3, compares the cash flows and the "perfect foresight" DCF values (the values are indexed for comparability). It shows that the DCF value is far less volatile than the underlying cash flow. In fact, the DCF value displays almost no volatility, because no single year's performance has a significant impact on the value of the company.

EXHIBIT 35.1 **The Long-Term View: Free Cash Flow and DCF Volatility**

Free cash flow pattern, Company A ($ million)

		Period (years)										
❶		0	1	2	3	4	5	6	7	8	9	10
	After-tax operating profit	10	9	6	3	–	(2)	3	18	7	6	10
	Net investment	3	3	2	2	1	3	5	3	3	3	3
	Free cash flow	7	6	4	1	(1)	(5)	(3)	15	4	3	7
				Cash flows valued from any one year forward								
❷	DCF value	34	33	27	28	30	35	40	33	33	34	31

❸ Free cash flow and DCF value patterns

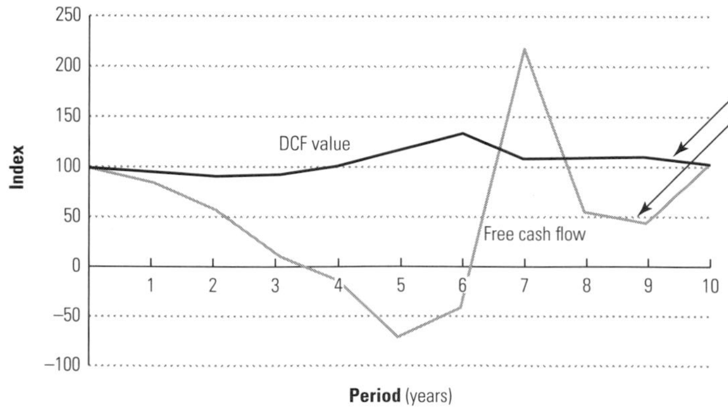

EXHIBIT 35.2 **Share Prices and EPS: 15 Cyclical Companies**

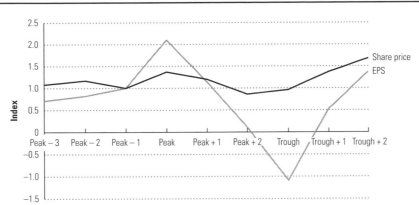

In the real world, the share prices of cyclical companies are less stable. Exhibit 35.2 shows the earnings per share (EPS) and share prices (indexed) for 15 companies with a four-year cycle. The share prices are more volatile than the DCF approach would predict—suggesting that market prices exhibit the bias of anchoring on current earnings described in Chapter 17.

Are Earnings Forecasts the Culprit?

How can we explain this apparent anomaly? We examined equity analysts' consensus earnings forecasts for cyclical companies to see if they provided any clues to the volatile stock prices of these companies.

What we found surprised us. Consensus earnings forecasts for cyclical companies appeared to ignore cyclicality entirely. The forecasts invariably showed an upward-sloping trend, whether the companies were at the peak or trough of the cycle. What appeared was not that the DCF model was inconsistent with the facts, but that the earnings and cash flow projections of the market (assuming the market followed the analysts' consensus) were to blame.

The conclusion was based on an analysis of 36 U.S. cyclical companies during 1985 to 1997. We divided them into groups with similar cycles (e.g., three, four, or five years from peak to trough) and calculated scaled average earnings and earnings forecasts. We then compared actual earnings with consensus earnings forecasts over the cycle.[1]

Exhibit 35.3 plots the actual earnings and consensus earnings forecasts for the set of 15 companies with four-year cycles in primary metals and manufacturing transportation equipment. The consensus forecasts do not predict

---

[1] Note that we have already adjusted downward the normal positive bias of analyst forecasts to focus on just the cyclicality issue. V. K. Chopra, "Why So Much Error in Analysts' Earnings Forecasts?" *Financial Analysts Journal* (November/December 1998): 35–42.

EXHIBIT 35.3 **Actual EPS and Consensus EPS Forecasts: 15 Cyclical Companies**

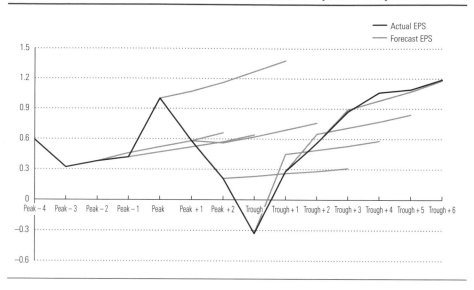

the earnings cycle at all. In fact, except for the next-year forecasts in the years following the trough, the earnings per share are forecast to follow an upward-sloping path with no future variation. You might say that the forecast does not even acknowledge the existence of a cycle.[2]

One explanation could be that equity analysts have incentives to avoid predicting the earnings cycle, particularly the down part. Academic research has shown that earnings forecasts have a positive bias that is sometimes attributed to the incentives facing equity analysts at investment banks.[3] Pessimistic earnings forecasts may damage relations between an analyst's employer—an investment bank—and a particular company. In addition, companies that are the target of negative commentary might cut off an analyst's access to management. From this evidence, we could conclude that analysts as a group are unable or unwilling to predict the cycles for these companies. If the market followed analyst forecasts, that behavior could account for the high volatility of cyclical companies' share prices.

The Market Appears Smarter than the Consensus Forecast

We know that it is difficult to predict cycles, particularly their inflection points. So it is not surprising that the market does not get it exactly right. However,

---

[2] Similar results were found for companies with three- and five-year cycles.
[3] The following articles discuss this hypothesis: M. R. Clayman and R. A. Schwartz, "Falling in Love Again—Analysts' Estimates and Reality," *Financial Analysts Journal* (September/October 1994): 66–68; J. Francis, and D. Philbrick, "Analysts' Decisions as Products of a Multi-Task Environment," *Journal of Accounting Research* 31, no. 2 (Autumn 1993): 216–230; K. Schipper, "Commentary on Analysts' Forecasts," *Accounting Horizons* (December 1991): 105–121; B. Trueman, "On the Incentives for Security Analysts to Revise Their Earnings Forecasts," *Contemporary Accounting Research* 7, no. 1 (1990): 203–222.

EXHIBIT 35.4 **When the Cycle Changes**

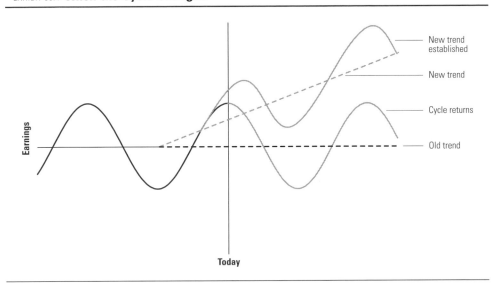

we would be disappointed if the stock market entirely missed the cycle, as the consensus earnings analysis suggests. To address this issue, we returned to the question of how the market should behave. Should it be able to predict the cycle and therefore exhibit little share price volatility? That would probably be asking too much. At any point, the company or industry could break out of its cycle and move to one that is higher or lower, as illustrated in Exhibit 35.4.

Suppose you are valuing a company that seems to be at a peak in its earnings cycle. In reality, you will never have perfect foresight of the market cycle. Based on past cycles, you expect the industry to turn down soon. However, there are signs that the industry is about to break out of the old cycle. A reasonable valuation approach, therefore, would be to build two scenarios and weight their values. Suppose you assumed, with a 50 percent probability, that the cycle will follow the past and that the industry will turn down in the next year or so. The second scenario, also with 50 percent probability, would be that the industry will break out of the cycle and follow a new long-term trend based on current improved performance. The value of the company would then be the weighted average of these two values.

We found evidence that this is, in fact, the way the market behaves. We valued the four-year cyclical companies three ways:

1. With perfect foresight about the upcoming cycle
2. With zero foresight, assuming that current performance represents a point on a new long-term trend (essentially the consensus earnings forecast)
3. With a 50/50 forecast: 50 percent perfect foresight and 50 percent zero foresight

EXHIBIT 35.5 **Market Values of Cyclical Companies: Forecasts with Three Levels of Foresight**

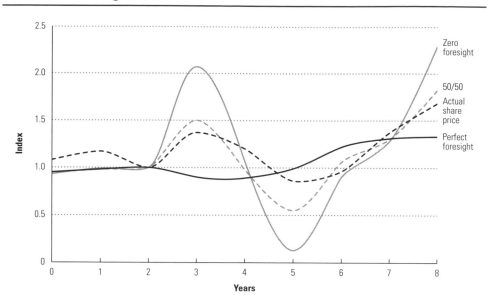

Exhibit 35.5 summarizes the results, comparing them with actual share prices. As shown, the market does not follow either the perfect-foresight or the zero-foresight path; it follows a blended path, much closer to the 50/50 path. So the market has neither perfect foresight nor zero foresight. One could argue that this 50/50 valuation is the right place for the market to be.

APPROACH TO VALUING CYCLICAL COMPANIES

No one can precisely predict the earnings cycle for an industry, and any single forecast of performance must be wrong. Managers and investors can benefit from following explicitly the multiple-scenario probabilistic approach to valuing cyclical companies, similar to the approach we used in Chapter 13 and the high-growth-company valuation in Chapter 34. The probabilistic approach avoids the traps of a single forecast and allows exploration of a wider range of outcomes and their implications.

Here is a two-scenario approach (in four steps) for valuing cyclical companies (of course, you could always have more than two scenarios):

1. Construct and value the normal cycle scenario, using information about past cycles. Pay particular attention to the long-term trend lines of operating profits, cash flow, and ROIC, because they will have the largest impact on the valuation. Make sure the continuing value is based on

a normalized level of profits (i.e., a point on the company's long-term cash flow trend line), not a peak or trough.

2. Construct and value a new trend line scenario based on the recent performance of the company. Once again, focus primarily on the long-term trend line, because it will have the largest impact on value. Do not worry too much about modeling future cyclicality (although future cyclicality will be important for financial solvency).

3. Develop the economic rationale for each of the two scenarios, considering factors such as demand growth, companies entering or exiting the industry, and technology changes that will affect the balance of supply and demand.

4. Assign probabilities to the scenarios, and calculate their weighted value. Use the economic rationale and its likelihood to estimate the weights assigned to each scenario.

This approach provides an estimate of the value as well as scenarios that put boundaries on the valuation. Managers can use these boundaries to improve their strategy and respond to signals about which scenario is likely to occur.

IMPLICATIONS FOR MANAGING CYCLICAL COMPANIES

Is there anything managers can do to reduce or take advantage of the cyclicality of their industry? Evidence suggests that, in many cyclical industries, the companies themselves are what drives cyclicality. Exhibit 35.6 shows the

EXHIBIT 35.6 **ROIC and Investment Rate: Commodity Chemicals, 1980–2001**

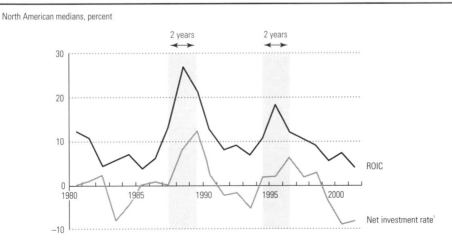

¹ Change in property, plant, and equipment (PP&E) adjusted for inflation.
Source: McKinsey chemicals database (CLTPD).

ROIC and net investment in commodity chemicals from 1980 to 2001. The chart shows that, collectively, commodity chemical companies invest large amounts when prices and returns are high. Since capacity comes on line in very large chunks, however, utilization plunges, and this places downward pressure on price and ROIC. The cyclical investment in capacity is the driver of the cyclical profitability. Fluctuations in demand from customers do not cause cyclicality in profits. Producer supply does.

Managers who have detailed information about their product markets should be able to do a better job than the financial market in figuring out the cycle and then take appropriate actions. We can only speculate why they do not do so. Still, based on conversations with these executives, we believe that the herding behavior is caused by three factors: First, it is easier to invest when prices are high, because that is when cash is available. Second, it is easier to get approval from boards of directors to invest when profits are high. Finally, executives are concerned about their rivals growing faster than themselves (investments are a way to maintain market share).

This behavior also sends confusing signals to the stock market. Expanding when prices are high tells the financial market that the future looks great (often just before the cycle turns down). Signaling pessimism just before an upturn also confuses the market. Perhaps it should be no surprise that the stock market has difficulty valuing cyclical companies.

How could managers exploit their superior knowledge of the cycle? The most obvious action would be to time capital spending better. Companies could also pursue financial strategies, such as issuing shares at the peak of the cycle or repurchasing shares at the cycle's trough. The most aggressive managers could take this one step further by adopting a trading approach, making acquisitions at the bottom of the cycle and selling assets at the top. Exhibit 35.7 shows the results of a simulation of optimal cycle timing. The typical company's returns on investment could increase substantially.

Can companies really behave this way and invest against the cycle? It is actually very difficult for a company to take the contrarian view. The CEO must convince the board and the company's bankers to expand when the industry outlook is gloomy and competitors are retrenching. In addition, the CEO has

EXHIBIT 35.7 **Relative Returns from Capital Expenditure Timing**

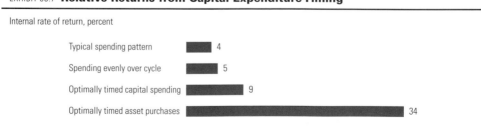

to hold back while competitors build at the top of the cycle. Breaking out of the cycle may be possible, but it is the rare CEO who can do it.

SUMMARY

At first glance, the share prices of cyclical companies appear too volatile to be consistent with the DCF valuation approach. This chapter shows, however, that share price volatility can be explained by the uncertainty surrounding the industry cycle. Using scenarios and probabilities, managers and investors can take a systematic DCF approach to valuing and analyzing cyclical companies.

REVIEW QUESTIONS

1. Assuming investors had perfect foresight, how would the volatility of a cyclical company's share price compare to the volatility of its profits?
2. Describe how analyst projections of cyclical company profits compare to actual performance. What are the possible reasons for the deviation?
3. Why should a scenario approach to valuation be used to value cyclical companies?
4. What are the potential reasons cyclical companies invest cyclically rather than countercyclically?

36

Valuing Banks

Banks are among the most complex businesses to value, especially from the outside in. Published accounts give an overview of a bank's performance, but the clarity of the picture they present depends largely on accounting decisions made by management. External analysts must therefore make a judgment about the appropriateness of those decisions. Even if that judgment is favorable, analysts are still bound to lack vital information about the bank's economics, such as the extent of its credit losses or any mismatch between its assets and liabilities, forcing them to fall back on rough estimates for their valuation. Moreover, banks are highly levered, making bank valuations even more contingent on changing economic circumstances than valuations in other sectors. Finally, most banks are in fact multibusiness companies, requiring separate analysis and valuation of their key business segments. So-called universal banks today engage in a wide range of businesses, including retail and wholesale banking, investment banking, and asset management. Yet separate accounts for the different businesses are rarely available.

When you are valuing banks, the basic approach to valuing industrial companies, set out in Part Two, is the right way to start. However, if you want your valuation to reflect the complexities of today's banking businesses and to yield insights into where and how a bank is creating value, then the process of valuation becomes more complicated, as there are significant analytical challenges to overcome. This chapter provides a general overview of how to value banks and highlights some of the most common valuation challenges peculiar to banks. First we discuss the economic fundamentals of banking and trends in performance and growth. Then we describe how to use the equity cash flow approach for valuing banks, using a hypothetical, simplified example. We conclude by offering some practical recommendations for valuing universal banks in all their real-world complexity.

The authors would like to thank Bas Deelder for his contribution to this chapter.

ECONOMICS OF BANKING

After years of strong profitability and growth in the U.S. and European banking sectors, the crisis in the mortgage-backed securities market in 2007 sent many large banks spiraling into financial distress in 2008. Many large institutions on either side of the Atlantic went into bankruptcy or had to be bailed out by governments. The fallout in the real economy from what was originally a crisis in the banking sector ultimately curtailed growth in almost all sectors around the globe, bringing economic growth to a halt worldwide in 2008.

The credit crisis demonstrates the extent to which the banking industry is both a critical and a vulnerable component of modern economies. Banks are vulnerable because they are highly leveraged and their funding depends on investor and customer confidence. This can disappear overnight, sending a bank into failure at great speed. As a result, more uncertainty surrounds the valuation of banks than the valuation of most industrial companies. Therefore, it is all the more important for anyone valuing a bank to understand the business activities undertaken by banks, the ways in which banks create value, and the drivers of that value creation.

Modern universal banks engage in any or all of a wide variety of business activities, including lending and borrowing, underwriting and placement of securities, payment services, asset management, proprietary trading, and brokerage. For the purpose of financial analysis and valuation, we group these activities according to the three types of income they generate for a bank: net interest income, fee and commission income, and trading income. "Other income" forms a fourth and generally smaller residual category of income from activities unrelated to the main banking businesses.

Net Interest Income

In their traditional role, banks act as intermediaries between parties with funding surpluses and those with deficits. They attract funds in the form of customer deposits and debt to provide funds to customers in the form of loans such as mortgages, credit card loans, and corporate loans. The difference between the interest income a bank earns from lending and the interest expense it pays to borrow funds is its net interest income. For the regional retail banks in the United States and retail-focused universal banks such as Standard Chartered, Banco Santander, and Unicredit, net interest income typically forms around half of total net revenues.

As we discuss later in the chapter, it is important to understand that not all of a bank's net interest income creates value. Most banks have a maturity mismatch as a result of using short-term deposits as funding to back long-term loans and mortgages. In this case, the bank earns income from being on different parts of the yield curve: typically, borrowing for the short term costs less than what the bank can earn from long-term lending. But not all of the income banks earn this way represents value, because it involves risks to shareholders.

Fee and Commission Income

For services including transaction advisory, underwriting and placement of securities, managing investment assets, securities brokerage, and many others, banks typically charge their customers a fee or commission. For investment banks (such as Morgan Stanley and Merrill Lynch) and for universal banks with large investment banking activities (UBS, Credit Suisse, Deutsche Bank), commission and fee income makes up around half of total net revenues. Fee income is usually easier to understand than net interest income, as it is independent of financing. However, some forms of fee income are highly cyclical; examples include fees from underwriting and transaction advisory services.

Trading Income

Over the past decade, proprietary trading has emerged as a third main category of income for the banking sector as a whole. This can involve not only a wide variety of instruments traded on exchanges and over the counter, such as equity stocks, bonds, and foreign exchange, but also more exotic products, such as credit default swaps and asset-backed debt obligations, traded mostly over the counter. Trading profits tend to be highly volatile: gains made over several years may be wiped out by large losses in a single year, as the credit crisis has painfully illustrated. For some investment banks, including Goldman Sachs and the former Lehman Brothers, trading contributed the largest component of total net revenues in the five years before 2008.

Other Income

In addition, some banks generate income from a range of nonbanking activities, including real estate development, minority investments in industrial companies, and distribution of investment, insurance, and pension products and services for third parties. Typically, these activities make only small contributions to overall income and are unrelated to the banks' main banking activities.

As Exhibit 36.1 shows for the European banking sector, the relative importance of these four income sources has changed radically over the past two decades. European banks have steadily shifted away from interest income toward commission and trading income.

As the banks have shifted their sources of income, the cyclicality of their profitability and market valuations has increased. This is measured by their return on equity and their market-to-book ratios (see Exhibit 36.2). The return on equity and market-to-book ratios for the sector as a whole rose sharply after

EXHIBIT 36.1 **Income Sources for European Banks,**[1] **1988–2007**

Income streams/total net revenues, percent

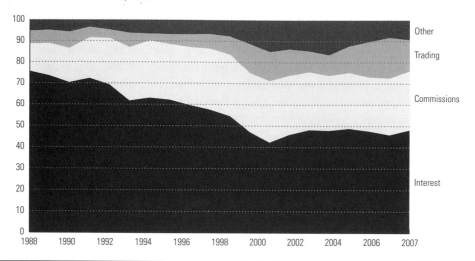

[1] Based on aggregate financials and valuation of 113 European banks, of which 109 were active in 2007.

Source: Compustat, Datastream, Bloomberg.

EXHIBIT 36.2 **Increased Cyclicality in Banking**

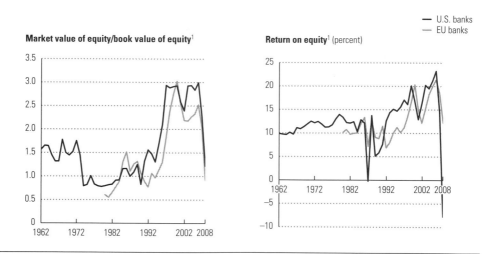

[1] Based on aggregate financials and valuation of 113 EU banks, of which 109 were active in 2007 and 957 US banks, of which 346 were active in 2007; book value of equity excludes goodwill.

Source: Compustat, Datastream, Bloomberg.

1995 to reach historic peaks in 2006. But they declined sharply during the credit crisis and by early 2010 were still far below their peak levels.

PRINCIPLES OF BANK VALUATION

Throughout most of this book, we apply the enterprise discounted cash flow (DCF) approach to valuation. Discounting free cash flows is the appropriate approach for nonfinancial companies where operating decisions and financing decisions are separate. For banks, however, we cannot value operations separately from interest income and expense, since these are the main categories of a bank's core operations. We need to value the cash flow to equity, which includes both the operational and financial cash flows. For valuation of banks, we therefore recommend the equity DCF method.[1] Whenever possible, you should triangulate your results by using a multiples-based valuation.

We will explain the principles of the equity DCF method using a stylized example of a retail bank. ABC Bank attracts customer deposits to provide funds for loans and mortgages to other customers. ABC's historical balance sheet, income statement, and key financial indicators are shown in Exhibit 36.3.

At of the start of 2009, the bank has $1,134 million of loans outstanding with customers, generating 6.5 percent interest income. To meet regulatory requirements, ABC must maintain an 8 percent ratio of Tier 1 equity capital to loan assets, which we define for this example as the ratio of equity divided by total assets. This means that 8 percent, or $91 million, of its loans are funded by equity capital, and the rest of the loans are funded by $1,043 million of deposits. The deposits carry 4.3 percent interest, generating total interest expenses of $45 million.

Net interest income for ABC amounts to $29 million in 2009, thanks to the higher rates received on loans than paid on deposits. All capital gains or losses on loans and deposits are included in interest income and expenses. Operating expenses such as labor and rental costs are $13 million, which brings ABC's cost-to-income ratio to 45 percent of net interest income. After we subtract taxes at 30 percent, net income equals $11 million, which translates into a return on equity of 12.2 percent.

As discussed in Chapter 6, the equity value of a company equals the present value of its future cash flow to equity (CFE), discounted at the cost of equity, k_e:

$$V_e = \sum_{t=1}^{\infty} \frac{\text{CFE}_t}{(1 + k_e)^t}$$

We can derive equity cash flow from two starting points. First, equity cash flow equals net income minus the earnings retained in the business:

$$\text{CFE}_t = \text{NI}_t - \Delta E_t + \text{OCI}_t$$

[1] See Chapter 6 for a comparison of the enterprise and equity DCF methods.

EXHIBIT 36.3 **ABC Bank: Historical Financial Statements**

$ million

	2005	2006	2007	2008	2009
Balance sheet[1]					
Loans	1,030.0	1,063.5	1,097.5	1,133.7	1,173.4
Total assets	1,030.0	1,063.5	1,097.5	1,133.7	1,173.4
Deposits	988.8	999.7	1,009.7	1,043.0	1,079.5
Equity	41.2	63.8	87.8	90.7	93.9
Total liabilities	1,030.0	1,063.5	1,097.5	1,133.7	1,173.4
Income statement					
Interest income	70.0	72.1	74.4	71.3	73.7
Interest expense	(48.0)	(47.5)	(47.0)	(45.4)	(44.9)
Net interest income	22.0	24.6	27.5	25.9	28.8
Operating expenses	(11.2)	(13.1)	(14.3)	(12.2)	(13.0)
Operating profit before taxes	10.8	11.6	13.2	13.7	15.9
Income taxes	(3.2)	(3.5)	(4.0)	(4.1)	(4.8)
Net income	7.5	8.1	9.2	9.6	11.1
Key ratios (percent)					
Loan growth	3.0	3.3	3.2	3.3	3.5
Loan interest rate	7.0	7.0	7.0	6.5	6.5
Deposit growth	3.0	1.1	1.0	3.3	3.5
Deposit interest rate	5.0	4.8	4.7	4.5	4.3
Cost/income	51.0	53.0	52.0	47.0	45.0
Tax rate	30.0	30.0	30.0	30.0	30.0
Equity/total assets	4.0	6.0	8.0	8.0	8.0
Return on equity[2]	18.9	19.7	14.5	10.9	12.2

[1] Book value per end of year.
[2] Return on beginning of year equity.

where CFE is equity cash flow, NI is net income, ΔE is the increase in the book value of equity, and OCI is other comprehensive income.

Net income represents the earnings theoretically available to shareholders after payment of all expenses, including those to depositors and debt holders. However, net income by itself is not cash flow. As a bank grows, it will need to increase its equity; otherwise, its ratio of debt plus deposits over equity would rise, which might cause regulators and customers to worry about the bank's solvency. Increases in equity reduce equity cash flow, because they mean the bank is issuing more shares or setting aside earnings that could otherwise be paid out to shareholders. The last step in calculating equity cash flow is to add other comprehensive income, such as net unrealized gains and losses on certain equity and debt investments, hedging activities, adjustments to the minimum

EXHIBIT 36.4 **ABC Bank: Historical Cash Flow to Equity**

$ million

	2005	2006	2007	2008	2009
Cash flow statement					
Net income	7.5	8.1	9.2	9.6	11.1
(Increase) decrease in equity	(1.2)	(22.6)	(24.0)	(2.9)	(3.2)
Other comprehensive income (loss)	0.2	–	–	–	–
Cash flow to equity	6.5	(14.5)	(14.8)	6.7	7.9

pension liability, and foreign-currency translation items. This cancels out any noncash adjustment to equity.[2]

Exhibit 36.4 shows the equity cash flow calculation for ABC Bank. Note that in 2005, ABC's other comprehensive income includes a translation gain on its overseas loan business, which was discontinued in the same year. ABC's cash flow to equity was negative in 2006 and 2007 because it raised new equity to lift its Tier 1 ratio from 4 to 8 percent.

Another way to calculate equity cash flow is to sum all cash paid to or received from shareholders, including cash changing hands as dividends, through share repurchases, and through new share issuances. Both calculations arrive at the same result. Note that equity cash flow is not the same as dividends paid out to shareholders, because share buybacks and issuance can also form a significant part of cash flow to and from equity.

Analyzing and Forecasting Equity Cash Flows

Exhibit 36.5 shows the generic value driver tree for a retail bank, which is conceptually the same as one for an industrial company. Following the tree's branches, we analyze ABC's historical performance.

Over the past five years, ABC's loan portfolio has grown by around 3.0 to 3.5 percent annually. Since 2005, ABC's interest rates on loans have been declining from 7.0 percent to 6.5 percent in 2009, but this was offset by an even stronger decrease in rates on deposits from 5.0 percent to 4.3 percent over the same period. Combined with the growth in its loan portfolio, this lifted ABC's net interest income from $22 million in 2005 to $29 million in 2009. The bank also managed to improve its cost-to-income ratio significantly from a peak level of 53 percent in 2006 to 45 percent in 2009.

Higher regulatory requirements for equity risk capital forced ABC to double its Tier 1 ratio (equity to total assets) from 4 to 8 percent over the period. The combination of loan portfolio growth and stricter regulatory requirements has required ABC to increase its equity capital by some $50 million since 2004.

[2] Of course, you can also calculate equity cash flow from the changes in all the balance sheet accounts. For example, equity cash flow for a bank equals net income plus the increase in deposits and reserves, less the increase in loans and investments, and so on.

EXHIBIT 36.5 **Generic Value Driver Tree for Retail Banking: Equity DCF Version**

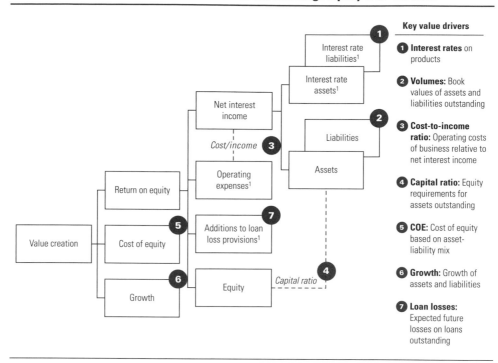

[1] After taxes.

As a result, ABC's return on equity declined significantly to 12 percent in 2009 from nearly 20 percent in 2006.

Exhibit 36.6 shows the financial projections for ABC Bank, assuming its loan portfolio growth rate increases to 4.5 percent in the short term and settles at 3.5 percent in perpetuity. Interest rates on loans and deposits are expected to decrease to 6.1 and 3.9 percent, respectively. Operating expenses will decline to 43 percent of net interest income. As a result, ABC's return on equity increases somewhat to 12.8 percent in 2011 and stays at that level in perpetuity. Note that a mere one percentage point increase in interest rates on loans would translate into a change in return on equity of around 12 percentage points, a function of ABC's high leverage (equity capital at 8 percent of total assets).

Discounting Equity Cash Flows

To estimate the cost of equity, k_e, for ABC Bank, we use a beta of 1.27 (based on the average beta for its retail banking peers), a long-term risk-free interest rate of 4.5 percent, and a market risk premium of 5 percent:[3]

$$k_e = r_f + \beta \times \text{MRP} = 4.5\% + 1.27 \times 5.0\% = 10.85\%$$

[3] See Chapter 11 for more details on estimating the cost of capital.

EXHIBIT 36.6 **ABC Bank: Financial Forecasts**

$ million

	2010	2011	2012	2013	2014	2015
Balance sheet[1]						
Loans	1,226.2	1,281.4	1,332.6	1,379.3	1,427.6	1,477.5
Total assets	1,226.2	1,281.4	1,332.6	1,379.3	1,427.6	1,477.5
Deposits	1,128.1	1,178.9	1,226.0	1,268.9	1,313.4	1,359.3
Equity	98.1	102.5	106.6	110.3	114.2	118.2
Total liabilities	1,226.2	1,281.4	1,332.6	1,379.3	1,427.6	1,477.5
Income statement						
Interest income	71.6	74.8	78.2	81.3	84.1	87.1
Interest expense	(41.6)	(43.4)	(45.4)	(47.2)	(48.9)	(50.6)
Net interest income	30.0	31.4	32.8	34.1	35.3	36.5
Operating expense	(13.5)	(13.5)	(14.1)	(14.7)	(15.2)	(15.7)
Operating profit before tax	16.5	17.9	18.7	19.4	20.1	20.8
Income taxes	(5.0)	(5.4)	(5.6)	(5.8)	(6.0)	(6.2)
Net income	11.6	12.5	13.1	13.6	14.1	14.6
Cash flow statement						
Net income	11.6	12.5	13.1	13.6	14.1	14.6
(Increase) decrease in equity	(4.2)	(4.4)	(4.1)	(3.7)	(3.9)	(4.0)
Other comprehensive (income) loss	–	–	–	–	–	–
Cash flow to equity	7.3	8.1	9.0	9.9	10.2	10.6
Key ratios (percent)						
Loan growth	1.5	1.5	1.0	3.5	3.5	3.5
Loan interest rate	6.1	6.1	6.1	6.1	6.1	6.1
Deposit growth	4.5	4.5	4.0	3.5	3.5	3.5
Deposit interest rate	3.9	3.9	3.9	3.9	3.9	3.9
Cost/income	45.0	43.0	43.0	43.0	43.0	43.0
Tax rate	30.0	30.0	30.0	30.0	30.0	30.0
Equity/total assets	8.0	8.0	8.0	8.0	8.0	8.0
Return on equity[2]	12.3	12.8	12.8	12.8	12.8	12.8

[1] Book value per end of year.
[2] Return on beginning of year equity.

where r_f is the risk-free rate, β is the equity beta, and MRP is the market risk premium. (Because we discount at the cost of equity, there is no need to adjust any estimates of equity betas of banking peers for leverage when deriving ABC's equity beta.)

In the equity DCF approach, we use an adapted version of the value driver formula presented in Chapter 2, replacing return on invested capital (ROIC) and return on new invested capital (RONIC) with return on equity (ROE) and return on new equity investments (RONE), and replacing net operating profit less adjusted taxes (NOPLAT) with net income:

$$CV = \frac{NI\left(1 - \frac{g}{RONE}\right)}{k_e - g}$$

where CV is the continuing value as of year t, NI is the net income in year $t +$ 1, g equals growth, and k_e is the cost of equity.

Assuming that ABC Bank continues to generate a 12.8 percent ROE on its new business investments in perpetuity while growing at 3.5 percent per year,[4] its continuing value as of 2015 is as follows:

$$CV = \frac{15.1\left(1 - \frac{3.5\%}{12.8\%}\right)}{10.85\% - 3.5\%} = 148.9$$

The calculation of the discounted value of ABC's cash flow to equity is presented in Exhibit 36.7. The present value of ABC's equity amounts to $118 million, which implies a market-to-book ratio for its equity of 1.3 and a price-to-earnings ratio of 10.2. As for industrial companies, whenever possible you should triangulate your results with an analysis based on multiples (see Chapter 14). Note that the market-to-book ratio indicates that ABC is creating value over its book value of equity, which is consistent with a long-term return on equity of 12.8 percent, which is above the cost of equity of 10.85 percent.

Pitfalls of Equity DCF Valuation

The equity DCF approach as illustrated here is straightforward and theoretically correct. However, the approach involves some potential pitfalls. These concern the sources of value creation, the impact of leverage and business risk on the cost of equity, and the cost of holding equity risk capital.

Sources of value creation   The equity DCF approach does not tell us how and where ABC Bank creates value in its operations. Is ABC creating or destroying value when receiving 6.5 percent interest on its loans or when paying

---

[4] If the return on new equity investments (RONE) equals the return on equity (ROE), the formula can be simplified as follows:

$$CV = \frac{NI(1 - \frac{g}{ROE})}{k_e - g} = E\left(\frac{ROE - g}{k_e - g}\right)$$

where E is the book value of equity.

EXHIBIT 36.7 **ABC Bank: Valuation**

$ million

	Cash flow to equity (CFE)	Discount factor	Present value of CFE
2010	7.3	0.902	6.6
2011	8.1	0.814	6.6
2012	9.0	0.734	6.6
2013	9.9	0.662	6.5
2014	10.2	0.597	6.1
2015	10.6	0.539	5.7
Continuing value	148.9	0.539	80.2
Value of equity			118.4
Market-to-book ratio			1.3
P/E[1]			10.2

[1] Forward price-to-earnings ratio on 2010 net income.

4.3 percent on deposits? To what extent does ABC's net income reflect intrinsic value creation?

You can overcome this pitfall by undertaking economic-spread analysis, described in the next section. As that section will show, ABC is creating value in its lending business but much less so in deposits, which were not creating any value before 2009. A significant part of ABC's net interest income in 2009 is, in fact, driven by the mismatch in maturities of its short-term borrowing and long-term lending. This does not create any value.

Impact of leverage and business risk on cost of equity As for industrial companies, the cost of equity for a bank such as ABC should reflect its business risk and leverage. Its equity beta is a weighted average of the betas of all its loan and deposit businesses. So when you project significant changes in a bank's asset or liability composition or equity capital ratios, you cannot leave the cost of equity unchanged.

For instance, if ABC were to decrease its equity capital ratio, its expected return on equity would go up. But in the absence of taxes, this should not increase the intrinsic equity value, because ABC's cost of equity would also rise, as its cash flows would now be more risky. The same line of reasoning holds for changes in the asset or liability mix. Assume ABC raises an additional $50 million in equity and invests this in government bonds at the risk-free rate of 4.5 percent, reducing future returns on equity. If you left ABC's cost of equity unchanged at 10.85 percent, the estimated equity value per share would decline. But in the absence of taxation, the risk-free investment cannot be value-destroying, because its expected return exactly equals the cost of capital for risk-free assets. In fact, if you accounted properly for the impact of the change in its asset mix on the cost of equity and the resulting reduction in the beta of its business, ABC's equity value would remain unchanged.

Cost of holding equity risk capital   Holding equity risk capital represents a key cost for banks, and it is important to understand what drives this cost. Consider again the example of ABC Bank issuing new equity and investing in risk-free assets, thereby increasing its equity risk capital. In the absence of taxation, this extra layer of risk capital would have no impact on value, and there would be no cost to holding it. But interest income *is* taxed, and that is what makes holding equity risk capital costly; equity, unlike debt or deposits, provides no tax shield. In this example, ABC will pay taxes on the risk-free interest income from the $50 million of risk-free bonds that cannot be offset by tax shields on interest charges on deposits or debt, because the investment was funded with equity, for which there are no tax-deductible interest charges.

The true cost of holding equity capital is this so-called tax penalty, whose present value equals the equity capital times the tax rate. If ABC Bank were to increase its equity capital by $50 million to invest in riskfree bonds, everything else held constant, this would entail destroying $15 million of present value (30 percent times $50 million) because of the tax penalty. As long as the cost of equity reflects the bank's leverage and business risk, the tax penalty is implicitly included in the equity DCF. However, in the economic-spread analysis discussed next, we explicitly include the tax penalty as a cost of the bank's lending business.

Economic-Spread Analysis

Because the equity DCF approach does not reveal the sources of value creation in a bank, some further analysis is required. To understand how much value ABC Bank is creating in its different product lines, we can analyze them by their economic spread.[5] We define the pretax economic spread on ABC's loan business in 2009 as the interest rate on loans minus the matched-opportunity rate (MOR) for loans, times the amount of loans outstanding at the beginning of the year:

$$S_{BT} = L\,(r_L - k_L) = \$1{,}133.7\,\text{million}\;(6.5\% - 5.1\%) = \$15.9\,\text{million}$$

where S_{BT} is the pretax spread, L is the amount of the loans, r_L is the interest rate on the loans, and k_L is the MOR for the loans.

---

[5] The approach is similar to those described by, for example, T. Copeland, T. Koller, and J. Murrin, *Valuation: Measuring and Managing the Value of Companies*, 4th ed. (New York: John Wiley & Sons, 2000); J. Dermine, *Bank Valuation and Value-Based Management* (New York: McGraw-Hill, 2009).

The matched-opportunity rate is the cost of capital for the loans—that is, the return the bank could have captured for investments in the financial market with similar duration and risk as the loans. Note that the actual interest rate that a bank is paying for deposit or debt funding is not necessarily relevant, because the maturity and risk of its loans and mortgages often do not match those of its deposits and debt. For example, the MOR for high-quality, four-year loans should be close to the yield on investment-grade corporate bonds with four years to maturity that are traded in the market. Banks create value on their loan business if the loan interest rate is above the matched-opportunity rate.

To obtain the economic spread after taxes (S_{AT}), we need to deduct the taxes on the spread itself and a tax penalty on the equity required for the loan business:

$$S_{AT} = L \, (r_L - k_L)(1 - T) - \text{TP}$$

where TP is the value of the tax penalty on equity.

The tax penalty on equity represents one of the most significant costs of running a bank. As noted already in this chapter, in contrast to deposit and debt funding, equity provides no tax shield because dividend payments are not tax deductible.[6] Thus, the more a bank relies on equity funding, the less value it creates, everything else being equal. Of course, banks have to fund their operations at least partly with equity. One reason is that regulators in most countries have established solvency restrictions that require banks to hold on to certain minimum equity levels relative to their asset bases. In addition, banks with little or no equity funding would not be able to attract deposits from customers or debt, because their default risk would be too high. As a result, banks typically have to incur a tax penalty on equity funding. For ABC's loan business,[7] the tax penalty in 2009 is calculated as follows:[8]

$$\begin{aligned}\text{TP} &= T \times L \, [k_L - (1 - e_L) k_D] \\ &= 30\% \; (\$1,133.7 \text{ million}) \, [5.1\% - (1 - 8.0\%) \, 4.6\%] = \$3.0 \text{ million}\end{aligned}$$

where e_L is the required equity capital divided by the amount of loans outstanding and k_D is the MOR for deposits.

The after-tax economic spread on loans is then derived as:

$$S_{AT} = \$15.9 \text{ million} \; (1 - 30\%) - \$3.0 \text{ million} = \$8.2 \text{ million}$$

[6] Following the Modigliani-Miller theorem on the value of the levered firm, debt funding provides a tax shield, and equity funding generates a tax penalty. See also Dermine, *Bank Valuation*, 77.

[7] In case of multiple loan products, you can allocate the tax penalty to the individual product lines according to their equity capital requirements.

[8] The tax penalty corrects for the fact that the loans are partly funded with equity, for which there is no tax deductibility, and the remaining funding is not at the MOR for loans but at the MOR for deposits.

EXHIBIT 36.8 **ABC Bank: Historical Economic Spread by Product Line**

$ million

	2005	2006	2007	2008	2009
Loans interest rate (percent)	7.0	7.0	7.0	6.5	6.5
Matched-opportunity rate (MOR) (percent)	5.5	5.5	5.5	5.5	5.1
Loans relative economic spread (percent)	1.5	1.5	1.5	1.0	1.4
Loans book value[1]	1,000.0	1,030.0	1,063.5	1,097.5	1,133.7
Loans economic spread before taxes	15.0	15.5	16.0	11.0	15.9
Taxes on economic spread	(4.5)	(4.6)	(4.8)	(3.3)	(4.8)
Tax penalty on loans	(2.1)	(3.1)	(3.8)	(4.5)	(3.0)
Loans economic spread[2]	8.4	7.8	7.4	3.2	8.2
Deposits interest rate (percent)	5.0	4.8	4.7	4.5	4.3
Matched-opportunity rate (MOR) (percent)	5.0	4.7	4.6	4.5	4.6
Deposits spread (percent)	–	−0.1	−0.1	–	0.3
Deposits book value[1]	960.0	988.8	999.7	1,009.7	1,043.0
Deposits economic spread[2]	–	(0.7)	(0.7)	–	2.2

[1] Beginning of year.
[2] After taxes.

This number represents the dollar amount of value created by ABC's loan business. Along the same lines, we can define the economic spread for ABC Bank's deposit products as well (see Exhibit 36.8). Note that our analysis explicitly includes the spread on deposits because banks (in contrast to industrial companies) aim to create value in their funding operations. For example, ABC Bank is creating value for its shareholders in its deposit business in 2009 because it attracted deposits at a 4.3 percent interest rate, below the 4.6 percent rate for traded bonds with the same high credit rating as ABC.

When comparing the spread across ABC product lines over the past few years, we can immediately see that most of the value created comes from its lending business. In fact, ABC was not making any money on its deposit funding from 2004 to 2008, as shown by the zero or negative spreads in those years.

From our calculations of the economic spreads of the two businesses, we can rearrange the value driver tree from the equity DCF approach shown previously (see Exhibit 36.9). The key drivers are virtually identical but highlight some important messages about value creation for banks:

- Interest income on assets creates value only if the interest rate exceeds the cost of capital for those assets (i.e., the matched-opportunity rate).
- Changes in the capital ratio affect value creation only through the tax penalty.

EXHIBIT 36.9 Generic Value Driver Tree for Retail Banking: Economic Spread

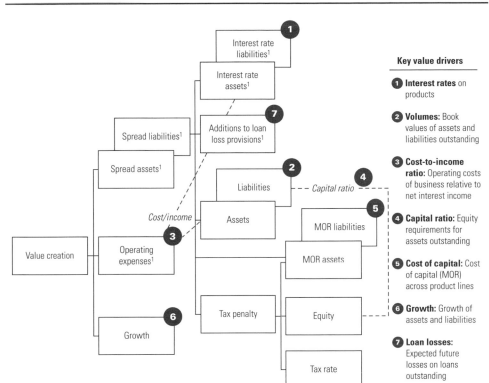

[1] After taxes.

- Growth adds value only if the economic spread from the additional product sold is positive (and sufficient to cover any operating expenses).

Note that we could further refine the tree by allocating the operating expenses to the product lines, represented by the different asset and liability categories. This is worth doing if there is enough information on the operating costs incurred by each product line and the equity capital required for each.

Economic Spread versus Net Interest Income

The spread analysis helps to show why a bank's reported net interest income does not reveal the value created by the bank and should be interpreted with care. For example, out of ABC Bank's 2009 net interest income after taxes of $20.2 million, only $10.3 million represents true value created (the economic spread on loans and deposits, as shown in Exhibit 36.10). The remaining

EXHIBIT 36.10 **ABC Bank: Net Interest Income and Value Creation**

$ million, 2009

	Net interest income[1]	Economic spread[1]	Mismatched-maturity charge	Matched-maturity charge
Loans	51.6	8.2	5.7	52.2
	$(L \times r_L)(1-T)$	$(1-T)L(r_L-k_L)-T(Lk_L-Dk_D)$	$L \times (k_L-k_D)$	$(L \times k_D)$
Deposits	(31.4)	2.2		(48.0)
	$-(D \times r_D)(1-T)$	$-(1-T)D(r_D-k_D)$		$-(D \times k_D)$
Total	20.2 =	10.3 +	5.7 +	4.2

[1] After taxes.

$9.9 million is income, but not value, because this amount is offset by the two types of charges shown in the exhibit.

The mismatched-maturity charge, amounting to $5.7 million of ABC's net interest income, arises from the difference in the duration of ABC's assets and deposits. To illustrate, when a bank borrows at short maturity and invests at long maturity, that creates income. The income does not represent value when the real risks of taking positions on the yield curve are taken into account. The maturity-mismatch charge represents the component of net interest income required to compensate shareholders for that risk.

The matched-maturity charge, amounting to $4.2 million for ABC in 2009, is the income that would be required on assets and liabilities if there were no maturity mismatch and no economic spread. In that case, all assets and liabilities would have identical duration (and risk) to deposits, so that their return would equal k_D (the MOR on deposits) and net interest income would equal equity times k_D. This component of net interest income also does not represent value: it only provides shareholders the required return on their equity investment in a perfectly matched bank.[9]

Because it provides such insights into value creation across a bank's individual product lines, we recommend using economic-spread analysis to understand a bank's performance and using the DCF model to do the valuation of the bank.

COMPLICATIONS IN BANK VALUATIONS

When you value banks, significant challenges arise in addition to those discussed in the hypothetical ABC Bank example. In reality, banks have many interest-generating business lines, including credit card loans, mortgage loans, and corporate loans, all involving loans of varying maturities. On the liability side, banks could carry a variety of customer deposits as well as different

[9] The cost of capital for the bank's equity would then also equal k_D because it is the value-weighted average of the cost of capital of all assets and liabilities.

forms of straight and hybrid debt. Banks need to invest in working capital and in property, plant, and equipment, although the amounts are typically small fractions of total assets. Obviously, this variety makes the analysis of real-world banks more complex, but the principles laid out in the ABC example remain generally applicable. In this section, we discuss some practical challenges in the analysis and valuation of banks.

Convergence of Forward Interest Rates

For ABC Bank, we assumed a perpetual difference in short-term and long-term interest rates. As a result, ABC generates a permanent, positive net interest income from a maturity mismatch: using short-term customer deposits as funding for investments in long-term loans. However, following the expectations theory of interest rates, long-term rates move higher when short-term rates are expected to increase, and vice versa. Following this theory, we need to ensure that our expectations for interest rates in future years are consistent with the current yield curve.

Exhibit 36.11 shows an example of a set of future one-, three-, five-, and ten-year interest rates that are consistent with the current yield curve as of 2010. The forecasts for a bank's interest income and expenses should be based on these forward rates, which constitute the matched-opportunity rates for the different product lines. For example, if the bank's deposits have a three-year maturity on average, you should use the interest rates from the forward

EXHIBIT 36.11 **Yield Curve and Future Interest Rates**

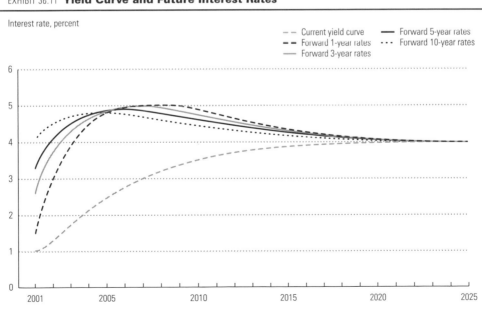

three-year interest rate curve minus an expected spread for the bank to forecast the expected interest rates on deposits in your DCF model. The rates are all derived from the current yield curve. To illustrate, the expected three-year interest rate in 2013 follows from the current three- and six-year yield:

$$r_{2013-2016} = \left[\frac{(1 + Y_{2016})^6}{(1 + Y_{2013})^3} - 1 \right]^{1/3} = \left[\frac{(1 + 2.82\%)^6}{(1 + 1.66\%)^3} - 1 \right]^{1/3} = 4.0\%$$

where $r_{2013-2016}$ is the expected three-year interest rate as of 2013 and Y_{2013} is the current three-year interest rate and Y_{2016} is the current six-year interest rate.

In practice, forward rate curves derived from the yield curve will rarely follow the smooth patterns of Exhibit 36.11. Small irregularities in the current yield curve can lead to large spikes and dents in the forward rate curves, which would produce large fluctuations in net interest income forecasts. As a practical solution, use the following procedure. First, obtain the forward one-year interest rates from the current yield curve. Then smooth these forward one-year rates to even out the spikes and dents arising from irregularities in the yield curve. Finally, derive the two-year and longer-maturity forward rates from the smoothed forward one-year interest rates. As the exhibit shows, all interest rates should converge toward the current yield curve in the long term. As a result, the bank's income contribution from any maturity difference in deposits and loans disappears in the long term as well.

Loan Loss Provisions

For our ABC Bank valuation, we did not model any losses from defaults on loans outstanding to customers. In real life, your analysis and valuation have to include loan loss forecasts, because loan losses are among the most important value drivers in retail and wholesale banking. For estimating expected loan losses from defaults across different loan categories, a useful first indicator would be a bank's historical additions to loan loss provisions or sector-wide estimates of loan losses (see Exhibit 36.12). Credit cards typically have the highest losses, and mortgages the lowest, with business loans somewhere in between. All default losses are strongly correlated with overall economic growth, so use through-the-economic-cycle estimates of additions to arrive at future annual loan loss rates to apply to your forecasts of equity cash flows.

To project the future interest income from a bank's loans, deduct the estimated future loan loss rates from the future interest rates on loans for each year. You should also review the quality of the bank's current loan portfolio to assess whether it has under- or overprovisioned for loan losses. Any required

EXHIBIT 36.12 **Annual Losses for U.S. Banks by Loan Category**

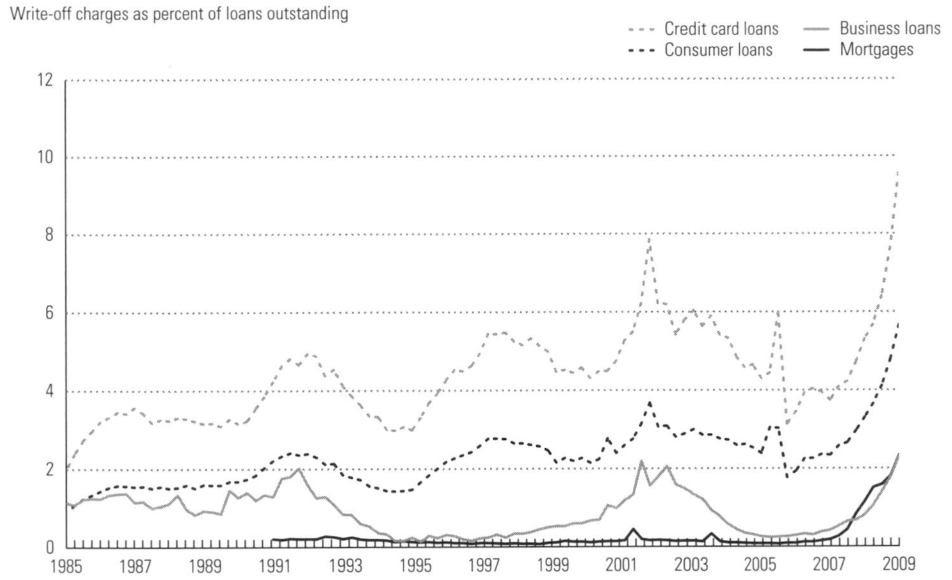

Write-off charges as percent of loans outstanding

- - - Credit card loans   —— Business loans
- - - Consumer loans   —— Mortgages

Source: Federal Reserve, "Charge-Off and Delinquency Rates on Loans and Leases at Commercial Banks," www.federalreserve.gov.

increase in the loan loss provision translates into less equity value. Many banks may need to make such an increase in the wake of the credit crisis.

Risk-Weighted Assets and Equity Risk Capital

Following the Basel II accords[10] implemented in 2007, banks have some flexibility to choose either internal risk models or standardized Basel approaches to assess their capital needs. All such models rest on the general principle that the amount of equity capital should be related to risk, so different types of products may require different rates of capital provision. However, banks do not publish the risk capital models that they use. Therefore, if you are doing an outside-in valuation, you need an approximation of a bank's equity risk capital needs.

To estimate a bank's equity risk capital requirements, use a percentage of risk-weighted assets (RWA). Risk-weighted assets are defined as a bank's asset portfolio weighted by the riskiness of different classes of borrowers or investments. Because banks typically provide information on total RWA but not on the risk weighting per asset category, you have to make an approximation of the key asset and investment categories' contribution to total RWA for the bank in order to project RWA and risk capital for future years.

[10] The Basel accords are recommendations on laws and regulations for banking and are issued by the Basel Committee on Banking Supervision.

EXHIBIT 36.13 **Estimating Risk-Weighted Assets (RWA) for a Large U.K. Bank**

£ billion

			Reported RWA		Estimated RWA parameters (percent)
	Year	Asset category	Loans outstanding	RWA	Estimated RWA/loans
Credit risk	2008	Loans to countries	29		20
		Loans to banks	41		35
		Loans to corporations	106		50
		Residential mortgages	115		50
		Other consumer loans	25		75
		Overall	316	150	47

	Year	VaR trading book	RWA	Estimated RWA/ VaR
Market risk	2007	6.32	5.3	
	2008	9.77	8.5	85

	Year	Average revenues[1]	RWA	Estimated RWA/ average revenues[1]
Operational risk	2007	10.8	10.1	
	2008	10.6	12.3	105

[1] Average over past 3 years.

Exhibit 36.13 shows such an outside-in approximation of RWA for a large U.K.-based bank. The bank separately reports the total RWA for credit risk, market risk, and operational risk.

- To approximate the RWA for *credit risk,* you can use the risk weights from the Basel II Standardized Approach (see Exhibit 36.14) and information on the credit quality of the bank's loans. Estimate the risk weighting and RWA for each of the loan categories in such a way that your estimate fits the reported RWA for all loans (£150 billion, in this example).

- *Market risk* is a bank's exposure to changes in interest rates, stock prices, currency rates, and commodity prices and is typically related to its value at risk (VaR), which is the maximum loss for the bank under a worst-case

EXHIBIT 36.14 **Risk Weights in Basel II Standardized Approach**

percent

	Asset category						
Credit risk	AAA to AA–	A+ to A–	BBB+ to BBB–	BB+ to BB–	B+ to B–	Below B–	Unrated
Loans to countries	–	20	50	100	100	150	100
Loans to banks	20	50	50	100	100	150	50
Loans to corporations	20	50	100	100	150	150	100

Residential mortgages	Local regulator flexibility: Mortgages with low loan-to-value ratio, 35%; otherwise, 100%.[1]
Other consumer loans	Risk weighting of 75%

[1] E.g., in the United Kingdom, the Financial Services Authority (FSA) sets cutoff point for 35% weighting at 80% loan-to-value ratio.

scenario of a given probability for these market prices. Use the reported VaR over several years to estimate the bank's RWA as a percentage of VaR (85 percent in the example).

- *Operational risk* is all risk that is neither market nor credit risk. It is usually related to a bank's net revenues (net interest income plus net other income). Use the bank's average revenues over the previous years to estimate RWA per unit of revenue (105 percent in the example).

Based on your forecasts for growth across different loan categories, VaR requirements for trading activities, and a bank's net revenues, you can estimate the total risk-weighted assets in each future year.

The 1988 Basel I accord established rules for banks regarding how much capital they must hold based on their level of risk-weighted assets. Basel I set the required ratio of Tier 1 capital to RWA at 4 percent, but many banks nowadays target around 10 percent of RWA, anticipating new regulations and increased investor requirements, as risks in the sector have increased since the credit crisis. Using your RWA forecasts and the targeted Tier 1 capital ratio, you can estimate the required Tier 1 capital. From the projected Tier 1 capital requirements, you can estimate the implied shareholders' equity requirements by applying an average historical ratio of Tier 1 capital to shareholders' equity excluding goodwill. Historical Tier 1 capital is reported separately in the notes to the bank's financial statements and is typically close to straightforward shareholders' equity excluding goodwill.

Currently, discussions are under way on new Basel III rules that build on lessons learned since the onset of the 2007 credit crisis. Although the precise outcomes of these discussions are still not clear, they are expected to include increased requirements for Tier 1 capital ratios and increased risk weightings for products and activities such as proprietary trading.

Multibusiness Banks

Given that many banks have portfolios of different business activities, sometimes as distinct as consumer credit card loans and proprietary trading, their businesses can have very distinct risks and returns, making the bank's consolidated financial results difficult to interpret, let alone forecast. The businesses are best valued separately, as in the case of multibusiness companies, discussed in Chapter 13. Unfortunately, financial statements for multibusiness banks often lack separately reported income statements and balance sheets for different business activities. In that case, you have to construct separate statements following the guidelines described in Chapter 13.

Interest-generating activities   Retail banking, credit card services, and wholesale lending generate interest income from large asset positions and risk capital.

EXHIBIT 36.15 **Value Drivers: Trading Activities (Simplified)**

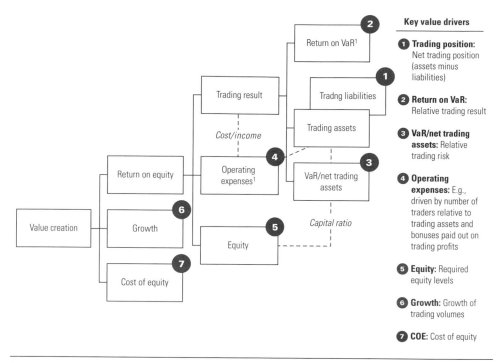

¹ After taxes.

These interest-generating activities can be analyzed using the economic-spread approach and valued using the equity DCF model, as discussed for ABC Bank in the previous section.

Trading activities   Like a bank's interest-generating activities, its trading activities also generate income from large asset positions and significant risk capital. However, trading incomes tend to be far more volatile than interest incomes. Although peak income can be very high, the average trading income across the cycle generally turns out to be limited. The key value drivers are shown in Exhibit 36.15, a simplified value driver tree for trading activities.

You can think of a bank's trading results as driven by the size of its trading positions, the risk taken in trading (as measured by the total value at risk or VaR), and the trading result per unit of risk (measured by return on VaR). The ratio of VaR to net trading position is an indication of the relative risk taking in trading. The more risk a bank takes in trading, the higher the expected trading return should be, as well as the required risk capital. The required equity risk capital for the trading activities follows from the VaR (and RWA), as discussed

EXHIBIT 36.16 **Value Drivers: Asset Management (Simplified)**

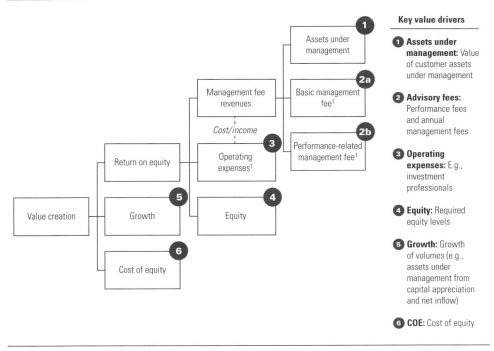

^{1} After taxes.

earlier in the chapter. Operating expenses, which include IT infrastructure, back-office costs, and employee compensation, are partly related to the size of positions (or number of transactions) and partly related to trading results (e.g., employee bonuses).

Fee- and commission-generating activities   A bank's fee- and commission-generating activities, such as brokerage, transaction advisory, and asset management services, have different economics, being based on limited asset positions and minimal risk capital. The value drivers in asset management, for example, are very different from those in the interest-generating businesses, as the generic example in Exhibit 36.16 shows. Key drivers are the growth of assets under management and the fees earned on those assets, such as management fees related to the amount of assets under management and performance fees related to the returns achieved on those assets. Along with these variables in activities, remember that banks are highly leveraged and that many of their businesses are cyclical. When performing a bank valuation, you should not rely on point estimates but should use scenarios for future financial performance to understand the range of possible outcomes and the key underlying value drivers.

SUMMARY

The fundamentals of the discounted cash flow (DCF) approach laid out in this book apply equally to banks. The equity cash flow version of the DCF approach is most appropriate for valuing banks, because the operational and financial cash flows of these organizations cannot be separated, given that banks are expected to create value from funding as well as lending operations.

Valuing banks remains a delicate task because of the diversity of the business portfolio, the cyclicality of many bank businesses (especially trading and fee-based business), and high leverage. Because of the difference in underlying value drivers, it is best to value a bank by its key parts according to the source of income: interest-generating business, fee and commission business, and trading. To understand the sources of value creation in a bank's interest-generating business, supplement the equity DCF approach with an economic-spread analysis. This analysis reveals which part of a bank's net interest income represents true value creation and which reflects not value but any maturity mismatch and capital charge. When forecasting a bank's financials, handle the uncertainty surrounding the bank's future performance and growth by using scenarios that capture the cyclicality of its key businesses.

REVIEW QUESTIONS

1. Why should you estimate the value of a bank by employing the equity cash flow method when throughout the text the enterprise DCF models have been stressed?

2. Identify the value drivers embedded in the equity cash flow model. How do the equity cash flow drivers differ from the drivers of the enterprise DCF models?

3. Define *maturity mismatch*. Why is maturity mismatch important for understanding a bank's risk and analyzing its performance?

4. If a bank increases its maturity mismatch, what happens to its economic spread before taxes and its economic spread after taxes (i.e., including the tax penalty)?

5. If a bank attracts new equity to increase its Tier 1 capital ratio, what happens to its cost of equity and its intrinsic value if it invests the new equity capital in (1) deposits with the central bank, or (2) a broad equity market index?

6. Consider a large banking group with businesses in retail banking, equity trading, and mergers and acquisitions (M&A) advisory. Discuss its potential for creating value based on the possible underlying sources of competitive advantage for each of these three business areas.

7. In a bank valuation, the amount of current loan loss provision is not deducted from the DCF result. Why is it then important to analyze the adequacy of the bank's current loan loss provisions?

8. In the economic spread analysis, a tax penalty is allocated to a bank's interest spread on loans but no tax credit is allocated to the interest spread on deposits. Why does that not violate the Modigliani and Miller theorem?

Economic Profit and the Key Value Driver Formula

In Chapter 2, we converted the growing cash flow perpetuity:

$$V = \frac{\text{FCF}_{t=1}}{\text{WACC} - g}$$

where V = value of operations
$\text{FCF}_{t=1}$ = free cash flow in year 1
g = growth in NOPLAT and free cash flow
WACC = weighted average cost of capital

into the key value driver formula:

$$V = \frac{\text{NOPLAT}_{t=1}\left(1 - \dfrac{g}{\text{RONIC}}\right)}{\text{WACC} - g}$$

where NOPLAT$_{t=1}$ = net operating profit less adjusted taxes in year 1
RONIC = return on new invested capital

The key value driver formula can be rearranged further into a formula based on economic profit. We do this to demonstrate that discounted cash flow is equivalent to the current book value of invested capital plus the present value of economic profit. A more general (and more technical) proof of their equivalence is provided in Appendix B. The economic-profit key value driver formula is necessary for estimating continuing value in economic-profit models.

By definition, invested capital times return on invested capital (ROIC) equals NOPLAT at time 1. Thus, we replace NOPLAT with invested capital times ROIC:

$$V = \frac{\text{Invested Capital}_0 \times \text{ROIC} \times \left(1 - \dfrac{g}{\text{RONIC}}\right)}{\text{WACC} - g}$$

If we assume that the return on new invested capital (RONIC) equals the return on existing invested capital (ROIC), we can simplify the preceding equation by distributing ROIC in the numerator:

$$V = \text{Invested Capital}_0 \left(\frac{\text{ROIC} - g}{\text{WACC} - g}\right)$$

This equation shows two requirements for using the key value driver formula: both WACC and ROIC must be greater than the rate of growth in cash flow. If WACC is less than the cash flow growth rate, cash flows grow faster than they can be discounted, and value approaches infinity. (Perpetuity-based formulas should never be used to value cash flows whose growth rates exceed WACC.) If ROIC is lower than the growth rate, cash flows are negative, producing a negative value. In actuality, this situation is unlikely; investors would not finance a company that is never expected to return positive cash flow.

To complete the transformation to economic profit, we next add and subtract WACC in the numerator:

$$V = \text{Invested Capital}_0 \left(\frac{\text{ROIC} - \text{WACC} + \text{WACC} - g}{\text{WACC} - g}\right)$$

We separate the fraction into two components and then simplify:

$$V = \text{Invested Capital}_0 \left(\frac{\text{ROIC} - \text{WACC}}{\text{WACC} - g}\right) + \text{Invested Capital}_0 \left(\frac{\text{WACC} - g}{\text{WACC} - g}\right)$$

$$= \text{Invested Capital}_0 + \frac{\text{Invested Capital}_0 (\text{ROIC} - \text{WACC})}{\text{WACC} - g}$$

Economic profit is defined as invested capital times the difference of ROIC minus WACC. Substituting this definition into the previous equation leads to our final equation:

$$V = \text{Invested Capital}_0 + \frac{\text{Economic Profit}_1}{\text{WACC} - g}$$

According to this formula, a company's operating value equals the book value of its invested capital plus the present value of all future economic profits. (The final term is a growing perpetuity of economic profits.) If future economic profits are expected to be zero, the intrinsic value of a company equals its book value. In addition, if future economic profits are expected to be less than zero, then enterprise value should trade at less than the book value of invested capital—an occurrence observed in practice.

Discounted Economic Profit Equals Discounted Free Cash Flow

In this appendix, we provide a generalized proof of the equivalence between discounted cash flow and discounted economic profit. A less technical but specialized proof of equivalence is demonstrated using the key value driver formula in Appendix A.

To prove equivalence, start by computing the present value of a periodic stream of cash flow:

$$V = \sum_{t=1}^{\infty} \frac{FCF_t}{(1 + WACC)^t}$$

where V = value of operations
FCF_t = free cash flow in year t
$WACC$ = weighted average cost of capital

To this value, add and subtract the cumulative sum of all current and future amounts of invested capital (IC):

$$V = \sum_{t=0}^{\infty} \frac{IC_t}{(1 + WACC)^t} - \sum_{t=0}^{\infty} \frac{IC_t}{(1 + WACC)^t} + \sum_{t=1}^{\infty} \frac{FCF_t}{(1 + WACC)^t}$$

where IC_t = invested capital for year t

Next, adjust the preceding equation slightly to restate the same value using terms that can be canceled later. First, strip invested capital at time zero from the first cumulative sum. Then modify the second cumulative sum to $t = 1$ to infinity, changing each t inside the second cumulative sum to $t - 1$. This new representation is identical to the original representation but will allow us to cancel terms later. The new representation is as follows:

$$V = IC_0 + \sum_{t=1}^{\infty} \frac{IC_t}{(1 + WACC)^t} - \sum_{t=1}^{\infty} \frac{IC_{t-1}}{(1 + WACC)^{t-1}} + \sum_{t=1}^{\infty} \frac{FCF_t}{(1 + WACC)^t}$$

Multiply the second cumulative sum by $(1 + WACC)/(1 + WACC)$. This action converts the exponent $t - 1$ in the denominator of the cumulative sum to t. Also substitute for free cash flow in the third cumulative sum, using its definition, NOPLAT less the increase of invested capital:

$$V = IC_0 + \sum_{t=1}^{\infty} \frac{IC_t}{(1 + WACC)^t} - \sum_{t=1}^{\infty} \frac{(1 + WACC)IC_{t-1}}{(1 + WACC)^t}$$
$$+ \sum_{t=1}^{\infty} \frac{NOPLAT_t - (IC_t - IC_{t-1})}{(1 + WACC)^t}$$

Because there is now a consistent denominator across all three cumulative sums, combine them into a single cumulative sum:

$$V = IC_0 + \sum_{t=1}^{\infty} \frac{IC_t - (1 + WACC)IC_{t-1} + NOPLAT_t - IC_t + IC_{t-1}}{(1 + WACC)^t}$$

In the second term of the numerator, distribute $(1 + WACC)IC_{t-1}$ into its two components, IC_{t-1} and $WACC(IC_{t-1})$:

$$V = IC_0 + \sum_{t=1}^{\infty} \frac{IC_t - IC_{t-1} - WACC(IC_{t-1}) + NOPLAT_t - IC_t + IC_{t-1}}{(1 + WACC)^t}$$

Simplify by collecting terms:

$$V = IC_0 + \sum_{t=1}^{\infty} \frac{NOPLAT_t - WACC(IC_{t-1})}{(1 + WACC)^t}$$

The numerator is the definition of economic profit, so the result is a valuation based on economic profit:

$$V = IC_0 + \sum_{t=1}^{\infty} \frac{Economic\ Profit_t}{(1 + WACC)^t}$$

The enterprise value of a company equals the book value of its invested capital plus the present value of all future economic profits. To calculate the value correctly, you must calculate economic profit using last year's (i.e., the beginning-of-year) invested capital—a subtle but important distinction.

The interdependence of invested capital, economic profit, and free cash flow is not surprising. Think of discounted cash flow this way: A portion of future cash flows is required to cover the required return for the investor's capital. The remaining cash flow is either used to grow invested capital (to generate additional future cash flows) or returned to investors as an extra bonus. This bonus is valuable, so investors desire (and are willing to pay a premium for) cash flows above the amount required. Subsequently, companies with positive economic profits will trade at a premium to the book value of invested capital.

Derivation of Free Cash Flow, Weighted Average Cost of Capital, and Adjusted Present Value

In Chapter 6, we numerically demonstrate the equivalence of enterprise discounted cash flow (DCF), adjusted present value (APV), and the cash-flow-to-equity valuation when leverage (as measured by the market-based debt-to-equity ratio) is constant. In this appendix, we derive the key terms in each model—namely, free cash flow (FCF) and the weighted average cost of capital (WACC)—and demonstrate their equivalence algebraically.

To simplify the analysis, we assume cash flows to equity are growing at a constant rate, g. This way we can use growth perpetuities to analyze the relationship between methods.[1]

ENTERPRISE DISCOUNTED CASH FLOW

By definition, enterprise value equals the market value of debt plus the market value of equity:

$$V = D + E$$

---

[1] For an analysis that applies to more complex situations (i.e., when cash flows can follow any pattern), see J. A. Miles and J. R. Ezzell, "The Weighted Average Cost of Capital, Perfect Capital Markets, and Project Life: A Clarification," *Journal of Financial and Quantitative Analysis* 15 (1980): 719–730 (for a discussion of enterprise DCF and WACC); and S. C. Myers, "Interactions of Corporate Financing and Investment Decisions: Implications for Capital Budgeting," *Journal of Finance* 29 (1974): 1–25 (for a discussion of adjusted present value).

To examine the components of enterprise value, multiply the right side of the equation by a complex fraction equivalent to 1 (the numerator equals the denominator, an algebraic trick we will use many times):

$$V = (D + E)\left(\frac{D(1 - T_m)k_d + CF_e - D(g)}{D(1 - T_m)k_d + CF_e - D(g)}\right) \qquad \text{(C.1)}$$

where T_m = marginal tax rate
k_d = cost of debt
CF_e = cash flow to equity holders
g = growth in cash flow to equity holders

Over the next few steps, the fraction's numerator will be converted to free cash flow (FCF). We will show later that the denominator equals the weighted average cost of capital. Start by defining FCF:

$$FCF = D(1 - T_m)k_d + CF_e - D(g)$$

If the market value of debt equals the face value of debt, the cost of debt will equal the coupon rate, and D times k_d will equal the company's interest expense. Therefore,

$$FCF = \text{Interest}(1 - T_m) + CF_e - D(g)$$

By definition, cash flow to equity (CF_e) equals earnings before interest and taxes (EBIT) minus interest minus taxes minus net investment plus the increase in debt. Assuming the ratio of debt to equity is constant, the annual increase in debt will equal $D(g)$. Why? Since cash flows to equity are growing at g, the value of equity also grows at g. Since the ratio of debt to equity remains constant (a key assumption), the value of debt must also grow at g. Substitute the definition of cash flow to equity into the preceding equation:

$$FCF = \text{Interest}(1 - T_m) + EBIT - \text{Interest} - \text{Taxes} - \text{Net Investment} + D(g) - D(g)$$

Next, distribute the after-tax interest expression into its two components, and cancel $D(g)$:

$$FCF = \text{Interest} - T_m(\text{Interest}) + EBIT - \text{Interest} - \text{Taxes} - \text{Net Investment}$$

Simplify by canceling the interest terms and rearranging the remaining terms:

$$FCF = EBIT - [Taxes + T_m (Interest)] - Net\ Investment$$

In Chapter 6, we define operating taxes as the taxes a company would pay if the company were financed entirely with equity. Operating taxes therefore equal reported taxes plus the interest tax shield (as interest is eliminated, taxes would rise by the interest tax shield). This leads to the definition of free cash flow we use throughout the book:

$$FCF = EBIT - Operating\ Taxes - Net\ Investment$$

Next, we focus on the denominator. To derive the weighted average cost of capital (WACC), start with equation C.1, and multiply CF_e by $k_e - g$ divided by $k_e - g$ (which equals 1):

$$V = (D + E) \left(\frac{FCF}{D(1 - T_m)k_d + \dfrac{CF_e}{k_e - g}(k_e - g) - D(g)} \right)$$

where k_e = cost of equity

If equity cash flows are growing at a constant rate, the value of equity equals CF_e divided by $(k_e - g)$. Therefore, the growing perpetuity in the denominator can be replaced by the value of equity (E) and distributed:

$$V = (D + E) \left(\frac{FCF}{D(1 - T_m)k_d + E(k_e) - E(g) - D(g)} \right)$$

In the denominator, collapse $E(g)$ and $D(g)$ into a single term:

$$V = (D + E) \left(\frac{FCF}{D(1 - T_m)k_d + E(k_e) - (D + E)g} \right)$$

To complete the derivation of WACC in the denominator, divide the numerator and denominator by $(D + E)$. This will eliminate the $(D + E)$ expression on the left and place it in the denominator as a divisor. Distributing the term across the denominator, the result is the following equation:

$$V = \frac{FCF}{\dfrac{D}{D + E}(k_d)(1 - T_m) + \dfrac{E}{D + E}(k_e) - \dfrac{D + E}{D + E}(g)}$$

The expression in the denominator is the weighted average cost of capital (WACC) minus the growth in cash flow (g). Therefore, equation C.1 can be rewritten as

$$V = \frac{FCF}{WACC - g}$$

such that

$$WACC = \frac{D}{D+E}(k_d)(1 - T_m) + \frac{E}{D+E}(k_e)$$

Note how the after-tax cost of debt and the cost of equity are weighted by each security's *market* weight to enterprise value. This is why market-based values, and not book values, should be used to build the cost of capital. This is also why free cash flow should be discounted at the weighted average cost of capital to determine enterprise value. Remember, however, that you can use a constant WACC over time only when leverage is expected to remain constant (i.e., debt grows as the business grows).[2]

ADJUSTED PRESENT VALUE

To determine enterprise value using adjusted present value, once again start with $V = D + E$ and multiply by a fraction equal to 1. This time, however, do not include the marginal tax rate in the fraction:

$$V = (D + E) \left(\frac{D(k_d) + CF_e - D(g)}{D(k_d) + CF_e - D(g)} \right)$$

Following the same process as before, convert each cash flow in the denominator to its present value times its expected return, and divide the fraction by $(D + E)/(D + E)$:

$$V = \frac{D(k_d) + CF_e - D(g)}{\frac{D}{D+E}(k_d) + \frac{E}{D+E}(k_e) - g}$$

In Appendix D, we show that if the company's interest tax shields have the same risk as the company's operating assets (as we would expect when the company maintains a constant capital structure), the fraction's denominator

---

[2] To see this restriction applied in a more general setting, see Miles and Ezzell, "Weighted Average Cost of Capital."

equals k_u, the unlevered cost of equity, minus the growth in cash flow (g). Make this substitution into the previous equation:

$$V = \frac{D\,(k_d) + CF_e - D(g)}{k_u - g}$$

Next, we focus on the numerator. Substitute the definitions of cash flow to debt and cash flow to equity as we did earlier in this appendix:

$$V = \frac{\text{Interest} + \text{EBIT} - \text{Interest} - \text{Taxes} - \text{Net Investment} + D(g) - D(g)}{k_u - g}$$

In this equation, the two interest terms cancel and the two $D(g)$ terms cancel, so simplify by canceling these terms. Also insert $T_m(\text{Interest}) - T_m(\text{Interest})$ into the numerator of the expression:

$$V = \frac{\text{EBIT} - \text{Taxes} + T_m(\text{Interest}) - T_m(\text{Interest}) - \text{Net Investment}}{k_u - g}$$

Aggregate reported taxes and the negative expression for $T_m(\text{Interest})$ into all-equity taxes. Move the positive expression for $T_m(\text{Interest})$ into a separate fraction:

$$V = \frac{\text{EBIT} - [\text{Taxes} + T_m\,(\text{Interest})] - \text{Net Investment}}{k_u - g} + \frac{T_m(\text{Interest})}{k_u - g}$$

At this point, we once again have free cash flow in the numerator of the first fraction. The second fraction equals the present value of the interest tax shield. Thus, enterprise value equals free cash flow discounted by the unlevered cost of equity plus the present value of the interest tax shield:

$$V = \frac{\text{FCF}}{k_u - g} + \text{PV(Interest Tax Shield)}$$

This expression is commonly referred to as adjusted present value.

In this simple proof, we assumed tax shields should be discounted at the unlevered cost of equity. This need not be the case. Some financial analysts discount expected interest tax shields at the cost of debt. If you do this, however, free cash flow discounted at the traditional WACC (defined earlier) and adjusted present value will lead to different valuations. In this case, WACC must be adjusted to reflect the alternative assumption concerning the risk of tax shields.

Levering and Unlevering the Cost of Equity

In Chapter 6, we value a company using adjusted present value (APV). One key input for APV is the unlevered cost of equity. In this appendix, we derive various formulas that can be used to compute the unlevered cost of equity under different assumptions.

Chapter 10 details a second application for the unlevered cost of equity. To determine the cost of equity for use in a company's cost of capital, we do not use raw regression results (because of estimation error). Instead, we rely on an unlevered *industry* beta that is relevered to the company's target capital structure. To build an unlevered industry beta, we use techniques identical to those used for building the unlevered cost of equity. We discuss both in this appendix.

UNLEVERED COST OF EQUITY

Franco Modigliani and Merton Miller postulated that the market value of a company's economic assets, such as operating assets (V_u) and tax shields (V_{txa}), should equal the market value of its financial claims, such as debt (D) and equity (E):

$$V_u + V_{txa} = \text{Enterprise Value} = D + E \tag{D.1}$$

A second result of Modigliani and Miller's work is that the total risk of the company's economic assets, operating and financial, must equal the total risk of the financial claims against those assets:

$$\frac{V_u}{V_u + V_{txa}}(k_u) + \frac{V_{txa}}{V_u + V_{txa}}(k_{txa}) = \frac{D}{D + E}(k_d) + \frac{E}{D + E}(k_e) \tag{D.2}$$

805

where k_u = unlevered cost of equity
$\quad\quad k_{txa}$ = cost of capital for the company's interest tax shields
$\quad\quad k_d$ = cost of debt
$\quad\quad k_e$ = cost of equity

The four terms in this equation represent the proportional risk of operating assets, tax assets, debt, and equity, respectively.

Since the cost of operating assets (k_u) is unobservable, we must solve for it, using the equation's other inputs. The required return on tax shields (k_{txa}) also is unobservable. With two unknowns and only one equation, we must therefore impose additional restrictions to solve for k_u. If debt is a constant proportion of enterprise value (i.e., debt grows as the business grows), k_{txa} equals k_u. Imposing this restriction leads to the following equation:

$$\frac{V_u}{V_u + V_{txa}}(k_u) + \frac{V_{txa}}{V_u + V_{txa}}(k_u) = \frac{D}{D+E}(k_d) + \frac{E}{D+E}(k_e)$$

Combining terms on the left side generates an equation for the unlevered cost of equity when debt is a constant proportion of enterprise value:

$$k_u = \frac{D}{D+E}(k_d) + \frac{E}{D+E}(k_e) \tag{D.3}$$

Since most companies manage their debt to value to stay within a particular range, we believe this formula and its resulting derivations are the most appropriate for standard valuation.

Unlevered Cost of Equity When k_{txa} Equals k_d

Some financial analysts set the required return on interest tax shields equal to the cost of debt. In this case, equation D.2 can be expressed as follows:

$$\frac{V_u}{V_u + V_{txa}}(k_u) + \frac{V_{txa}}{V_u + V_{txa}}(k_d) = \frac{D}{D+E}(k_d) + \frac{E}{D+E}(k_e)$$

To solve for k_u, multiply both sides by enterprise value:

$$V_u(k_u) + V_{txa}(k_d) = D(k_d) + E(k_e)$$

and move $V_{txa}(k_d)$ to the right side of the equation:

$$V_u(k_u) = (D - V_{txa})k_d + E(k_e)$$

EXHIBIT D.1 **Unlevered Cost of Equity**

	Dollar level of debt fluctuates	Dollar level of debt is constant
Tax shields have same risk as operating assets $k_{txa} = k_u$	$k_u = \dfrac{D}{D+E}\, k_d + \dfrac{E}{D+E}\, k_e$	$k_u = \dfrac{D}{D+E}\, k_d + \dfrac{E}{D+E}\, k_e$
Tax shields have same risk as debt $k_{txa} = k_d$	$k_u = \dfrac{D - V_{txa}}{D - V_{txa} + E}\, k_d + \dfrac{E}{D - V_{txa} + E}\, k_e$	$k_u = \dfrac{D\left(1 - T_m\right)}{D\left(1 - T_m\right) + E}\, k_d + \dfrac{E}{D\left(1 - T_m\right) + E}\, k_e$

Note: k_e = cost of equity
   k_d = cost of debt
   k_u = unlevered cost of equity
   k_{txa} = cost of capital for tax shields
   T_m = marginal tax rate
   D = debt
   E = equity
   V_{txa} = present value of tax shields

To eliminate V_u from the left side of the equation, rearrange equation D.1 to $V_u = D - V_{txa} + E$, and divide both sides by this value:

$$k_u = \frac{D - V_{txa}}{D - V_{txu} + E}(k_d) + \frac{E}{D - V_{txu} + E}(k_e) \tag{D.4}$$

Equation D.4 mirrors equation D.2 closely. It differs from equation D.2 only in that the market value of debt is reduced by the present value of expected tax shields.

Exhibit D.1 summarizes four methods to estimate the unlevered cost of equity. The two formulas in the top row assume that the risk associated with interest tax shields (k_{txa}) equals the risk of operations (k_u). When this is true, whether debt is constant or expected to change, the formula remains the same.

The bottom-row formulas assume that the risk of interest tax shields equals the risk of debt. On the left, future debt can take on any value. On the right, an additional restriction is imposed that debt remains constant (in absolute terms, not as a percentage of enterprise value). In this case, the annual interest payment equals $D(k_d)$ and the annual tax shield equals $D(k_d)(T_m)$. Since tax shields are constant, they can be valued using a constant perpetuity:

$$PV\,(\text{Tax Shields}) = \frac{D\,(k_d)\,(T_m)}{k_d} = D\,(T_m)$$

Consequently, V_{txa} in the general formula (in the bottom left corner) is replaced with $D(T_m)$. The equation is simplified by combining D within the parentheses.

LEVERED COST OF EQUITY

In certain situations, you will have already estimated the unlevered cost of equity and need to relever the cost of equity to a new target structure. In this case, use equation D.2 to solve for the levered cost of equity, k_e:

$$\frac{V_u}{V_u + V_{txa}}(k_u) + \frac{V_{txa}}{V_u + V_{txa}}(k_{txa}) = \frac{D}{D + E}(k_d) + \frac{E}{D + E}(k_e)$$

Multiply both sides by enterprise value:

$$V_u(k_u) + V_{txa}(k_{txa}) = D(k_d) + E(k_e)$$

Next, subtract $D(k_d)$ from both sides of the equation:

$$V_u(k_u) - D(k_d) + V_{txa}(k_{txa}) = E(k_e)$$

and divide the entire equation by the market value of equity, E:

$$k_e = \frac{V_u}{E}(k_u) - \frac{D}{E}(k_d) + \frac{V_{txa}}{E}(k_{txa})$$

To eliminate V_u from the right side of the equation, rearrange equation D.1 to $V_u = D - V_{txa} + E$, and use this identity to replace V_u:

$$k_e = \frac{D - V_{txa} + E}{E}(k_u) - \frac{D}{E}(k_d) + \frac{V_{txa}}{E}(k_{txa})$$

Distribute the first fraction into its component parts:

$$k_e = \frac{D}{E}(k_u) - \frac{V_{txa}}{E}(k_u) + k_u - \frac{D}{E}(k_d) + \frac{V_{txa}}{E}(k_{txa}) \tag{D.5}$$

Consolidating terms and rearranging leads to the *general equation* for the cost of equity:

$$k_e = k_u + \frac{D}{E}(k_u - k_d) - \frac{V_{txa}}{E}(k_u - k_{txa}) \tag{D.6}$$

If debt is a constant proportion of enterprise value (i.e., debt grows as the business grows), k_u will equal k_{txa}. Consequently, the final term drops out:

$$k_e = k_u + \frac{D}{E}(k_u - k_d)$$

We believe this equation best represents the relationship between the levered cost of equity and the unlevered cost of equity.

Levered Cost of Equity When k_{txa} Equals k_d

The same analysis can be repeated under the assumption that the risk of interest tax shields equals the risk of debt. Rather than repeat the first few steps, we start with equation D.5:

$$k_e = \frac{D}{E}(k_u) - \frac{V_{txa}}{E}(k_u) + k_u - \frac{D}{E}(k_d) + \frac{V_{txa}}{E}(k_{txa})$$

To solve for k_e, we replace k_{txa} with k_d:

$$k_e = \frac{D}{E}(k_u) - \frac{V_{txa}}{E}(k_u) + k_u - \frac{D}{E}(k_d) + \frac{V_{txa}}{E}(k_d)$$

Consolidate like terms and reorder:

$$k_e = k_u + \frac{D - V_{txa}}{E}(k_u) - \frac{D - V_{txa}}{E}(k_d)$$

Finally, further simplify the equation by once again, combining like terms:

$$k_e = k_u + \frac{D - V_{txa}}{E}(k_u - k_d)$$

The resulting equation is the levered cost of equity for a company whose debt can take any value but whose interest tax shields have the same risk as the company's debt.

Exhibit D.2 summarizes the formulas that can be used to estimate the levered cost of equity. The top row in the exhibit contains formulas that assume k_{txa} equals k_u. The bottom row contains formulas that assume k_{txa} equals k_d. The formulas on the left side are flexible enough to handle any future capital structure but require valuing the tax shields separately. The formulas on the right side assume the dollar level of debt is fixed over time.

EXHIBIT D.2 **Levered Cost of Equity**

	Dollar level of debt fluctuates	Dollar level of debt is constant
Tax shields have same risk as operating assets $k_{txa} = k_u$	$k_e = k_u + \dfrac{D}{E}\left(k_u - k_d\right)$	$k_e = k_u + \dfrac{D}{E}\left(k_u - k_d\right)$
Tax shields have same risk as debt $k_{txa} = k_d$	$k_e = k_u + \dfrac{D - V_{txa}}{E}\left(k_u - k_d\right)$	$k_e = k_u + \left(1 - T_m\right)\dfrac{D}{E}\left(k_u - k_d\right)$

Note: k_e = cost of equity
k_d = cost of debt
k_u = unlevered cost of equity
k_{txa} = cost of capital for tax shields
T_m = marginal tax rate
D = debt
E = equity
V_{txa} = present value of tax shields

LEVERED BETA

Similar to the cost of capital, the weighted average beta of a company's assets, both operating and financial, must equal the weighted average beta of its financial claims:

$$\frac{V_u}{V_u + V_{txa}}(\beta_u) + \frac{V_{txa}}{V_u + V_{txa}}(\beta_{txa}) = \frac{D}{D + E}(\beta_d) + \frac{E}{D + E}(\beta_e)$$

Since the form of this equation is identical to the cost of capital, we can rearrange the formula using the same process as previously described. Rather than repeat the analysis, we provide a summary of levered beta in Exhibit D.3. As expected, the first two columns are identical in form to Exhibit D.2, except that the beta (β) replaces the cost of capital (k).

By using beta, we can make one additional simplification. If debt is risk free, the beta of debt is 0, and β_d drops out. This allows us to convert the following general equation (when β_{txa} equals β_u):

$$\beta_e = \beta_u + \frac{D}{E}(\beta_u - \beta_d)$$

into the following:

$$\beta_e = \left(1 + \frac{D}{E}\right)\beta_u$$

EXHIBIT D.3 **Levered Beta**

	Dollar level of debt fluctuates	Dollar level of debt is constant and debt is risky	Debt is risk free[1]
Tax shields have same risk as operating assets $\beta_{txa} = \beta_u$	$\beta_e = \beta_u + \dfrac{D}{E}\left(\beta_u - \beta_d\right)$	$\beta_e = \beta_u + \dfrac{D}{E}\left(\beta_u - \beta_d\right)$	$\beta_e = \left(1 + \dfrac{D}{E}\right)\beta_u$
Tax shields have same risk as debt $\beta_{txa} = \beta_d$	$\beta_e = \beta_u + \dfrac{D - V_{txa}}{E}\left(\beta_u - \beta_d\right)$	$\beta_e = \beta_u + \left(1 - T_m\right)\dfrac{D}{E}\left(\beta_u - \beta_d\right)$	$\beta_e = \left[1 + \left(1 - T_m\right)\dfrac{D}{E}\right]\beta_u$

Note: β_e = beta of equity
β_d = beta of debt
β_u = unlevered beta of equity
β_{txa} = beta of capital for tax shields
T_m = marginal tax rate
D = debt
E = equity
V_{txa} = present value of tax shields

[1] When $\beta_{txa} = \beta_u$, the resulting formula holds for all debt patterns, not just constant debt.

This last equation is an often-applied formula for levering (and unlevering) beta when the risk of interest tax shields (β_{txa}) equals the risk of operating assets (β_u) *and* the company's debt is risk free. For investment-grade companies, debt is near risk free, so any errors using this formula will be small. If the company is highly leveraged, however, errors can be large. In this situation, estimate the beta of debt, and use the more general version of the formula.

Leverage and the Price-to-Earnings Multiple

This appendix demonstrates that the price-to-earnings (P/E) ratio of a levered company depends on its unlevered (all-equity) P/E, its cost of debt, and its debt-to-value ratio. When the unlevered P/E is less than $1/k_d$ (where k_d equals the cost of debt), the P/E falls as leverage rises. Conversely, when the unlevered P/E is greater than $1/k_d$, the P/E ratio rises with increased leverage.

In this proof, we assume the company faces no taxes and no distress costs. We do this to avoid modeling the complex relationship between capital structure and enterprise value. Instead, our goal is to show that there is a systematic relationship between the debt-to-value ratio and the P/E.

STEP 1

To determine the relationship between P/E and leverage, we start by defining the unlevered P/E (PE_u). When a company is entirely financed with equity, its enterprise value equals its equity value, and its net operating profit less adjusted taxes (NOPLAT) equals its net income:

$$PE_u = \frac{V_{ENT}}{NOPLAT_{t+1}}$$

where V_{ENT} = enterprise value
$NOPLAT_{t+1}$ = net operating profit less adjusted taxes in year $t+1$

This equation can be rearranged to solve for the enterprise value, which we will use in the next step:

$$V_{ENT} = NOPLAT_{t+1} (PE_u) \tag{E.1}$$

STEP 2

For a company partially financed with debt, net income (NI) equals NOPLAT less after-tax interest payments. Assuming the value of debt equals its face value, the company's interest expense will equal the cost of debt times the value of debt, which can be defined by multiplying enterprise value by the debt-to-value ratio:

$$NI_{t+1} = NOPLAT_{t+1} - V_{ENT} \left(\frac{D}{V}\right) k_d$$

Substitute equation E.1 for the enterprise value:

$$NI_{t+1} = NOPLAT_{t+1} - NOPLAT_{t+1}(PE_u) \left(\frac{D}{V}\right) k_d$$

Factor NOPLAT into a single term:

$$NI_{t+1} = NOPLAT_{t+1} \left[1 - PE_u \left(\frac{D}{V}\right) k_d\right] \tag{E.2}$$

STEP 3

At this point, we are ready to solve for the company's price-to-earnings ratio. Since P/E is based on equity values, first convert enterprise value to equity value. To do this, once again start with equation E.1:

$$V_{ENT} = NOPLAT_{t+1} (PE_u)$$

To convert enterprise value into equity value, multiply both sides by 1 minus the debt-to-value ratio:

$$V_{ENT} \left(1 - \frac{D}{V_{ENT}}\right) = NOPLAT_{t+1} (PE_u) \left(1 - \frac{D}{V_{ENT}}\right)$$

Distribute V_{ENT} into the parentheses:

$$V_{ENT} - D = NOPLAT_{t+1} (PE_u) \left(1 - \frac{D}{V_{ENT}}\right)$$

and replace enterprise value (V_{ENT}) minus debt (D) with equity value (E):

$$E = NOPLAT_{t+1} (PE_u) \left(1 - \frac{D}{V_{ENT}}\right)$$

Next, use equation E.2 to eliminate $NOPLAT_{t+1}$:

$$E = \frac{NI_{t+1} (PE_u) \left(1 - \frac{D}{V}\right)}{1 - PE_u \left(\frac{D}{V}\right) k_d}$$

Divide both sides by net income to find the levered P/E:

$$\frac{E}{NI_{t+1}} = \frac{PE_u - PE_u \left(\frac{D}{V}\right)}{1 - PE_u \left(\frac{D}{V}\right) k_d}$$

At this point, we have a relationship between equity value and net income, which depends on the unlevered P/E, the debt-to-value ratio, and the cost of debt. Debt to value, however, is in both the numerator and the denominator, so it is difficult to distinguish how leverage affects the levered P/E. To eliminate the debt-to-value ratio in the numerator, use a few algebraic tricks. First, multiply both the numerator and denominator by k_d:

$$\frac{E}{NI_{t+1}} = \frac{PE_u (k_d) - PE_u \left(\frac{D}{V}\right) (k_d)}{k_d \left[1 - PE_u \left(\frac{D}{V}\right) (k_d)\right]}$$

Next, subtract and add 1 (a net difference of 0) in the numerator:

$$\frac{E}{NI_{t+1}} = \frac{[PE_u (k_d) - 1] + \left[1 - PE_u \left(\frac{D}{V}\right) (k_d)\right]}{k_d \left[1 - PE_u \left(\frac{D}{V}\right) (k_d)\right]}$$

After separating the numerator into two distinct terms, you can eliminate the components of the right-hand term by canceling them with the denominator. This allows you to remove debt to value from the numerator:

$$\frac{E}{NI_{t+1}} = \frac{PE_u (k_d) - 1}{k_d \left[1 - PE_u \left(\frac{D}{V}\right) (k_d)\right]} + \frac{1}{k_d}$$

To simplify the expression further, divide both the numerator and denominator of the complex fraction by k_d:

$$\frac{E}{NI_{t+1}} = \frac{1}{k_d} + \frac{PE_u - \dfrac{1}{k_d}}{1 - PE_u \left(\dfrac{D}{V}\right)(k_d)}$$

Finally, multiply the numerator and denominator of the second term by -1:

$$\frac{E}{NI_{t+1}} = \frac{1}{k_d} + \frac{\dfrac{1}{k_d} - PE_u}{\left(\dfrac{D}{V}\right)k_d(PE_u) - 1}$$

As this final equation shows, a company's P/E is a function of its unlevered P/E, its cost of debt, and its debt-to-value ratio. When the unlevered P/E equals the reciprocal of the cost of debt, the numerator of the second fraction equals zero, and leverage has no effect on the P/E. For companies with large unlevered P/Es, P/E systematically increases with leverage. Conversely, companies with small unlevered P/Es would exhibit a drop in P/E as leverage rises.

Index

Q

R

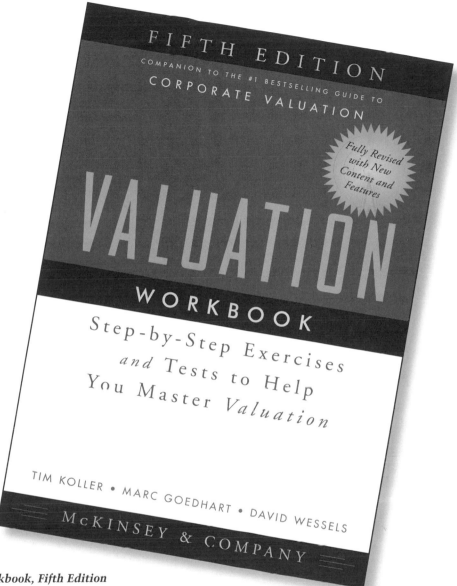

Valuation Workbook, Fifth Edition
978-0-470-42464-3 • Paper • 224 pages • $39.95

- The ideal companion to McKinsey's *Valuation, Fifth Edition*, the *Valuation Workbook, Fifth Edition* provides chapter-by-chapter review of the key concepts in the core text.
- Tests your comprehension of valuation issues and techniques with multiple-choice questions and problems.
- Aids the self-directed learning process through detailed solutions and explanations for each question and concept.
- Offers complete coverage of forecasting short, medium, and continuing value; calculating and interpreting results; real-option pricing methods; and much more.

Order your copy today!
Available at www.wileyvaluation.com and wherever books are sold.

Now you know.